INSTITUTIONS, MACROECONOMICS, AND THE GLOBAL ECONOMY

C a s e b o o k

Rafael Di Tella
Harvard University, USA

Huw Pill & Ingrid Vogel

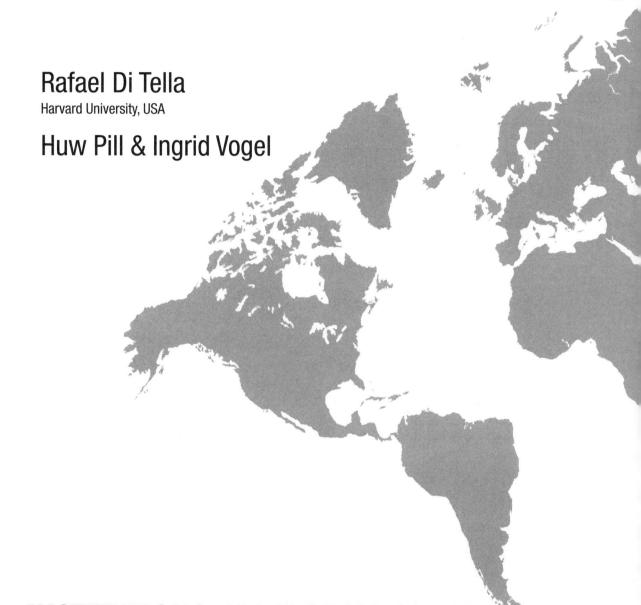

INSTITUTIONS, MACROECONOMICS, AND THE GLOBAL ECONOMY
C a s e b o o k

 **World Scientific**

NEW JERSEY • LONDON • SINGAPORE • BEIJING • SHANGHAI • HONG KONG • TAIPEI • CHENNAI

Published by

World Scientific Publishing Co. Pte. Ltd.

5 Toh Tuck Link, Singapore 596224

USA office: 27 Warren Street, Suite 401-402, Hackensack, NJ 07601

UK office: 57 Shelton Street, Covent Garden, London WC2H 9HE

Library of Congress Cataloging-in-Publication Data
Di Tella, Rafael.
  Institutions, macroeconomics, and the global economy (casebook) / Rafael Di Tella, Huw
Pill, Ingrid Vogel.
    p. cm.
  Includes bibliographical references.
  ISBN 981-256-336-9 (alk. paper) -- ISBN 981-256-337-7 (pbk. : alk. paper)
    1. Macroeconomics--Case studies. 2. Economic policy--Case studies. 3. Institutional
economics--Case studies. 4. Globalization--Economic aspects--Case studies. I. Pill, Huw.
II. Vogel, Ingrid. III. Title.

  HB172.5.D52 2005
  337--dc22

                                                                              2005047292

British Library Cataloguing-in-Publication Data
A catalogue record for this book is available from the British Library.

Printed in Singapore by B & JO Enterprise

Table of Contents

OVERVIEW

Institutions, Macroeconomics, and the Global Economy

Introduction

All managers face a business environment where international and macroeconomic phenomena matter. Understanding the genesis of financial and currency crises, stock market booms and busts, and social and labor unrest is a crucial aspect in making informed managerial decisions. Adverse macroeconomic phenomena can have a catastrophic impact on firm performance: witness the strong companies destroyed by the Mexican tequila crisis. Yet at the same time, such episodes also create business opportunities—and not just for the hedge funds and speculators that profit from them. Managers that have and use a coherent framework for analyzing these phenomena will enjoy a competitive advantage.

This book presents a series of case studies taught in the Harvard Business School course "Institutions, Macroeconomics, and the Global Economy." The course addresses the opportunities created by the emergence of a global economy and proposes strategies for managing the risks that globalization entails.

Objectives

The cases in *Institutions, Macroeconomics, and the Global Economy* have three objectives. First, they expose readers to important macroeconomic events that have shaped the way professional international macroeconomists think about their subject. Most of these events in the international economy are quite recent, such as the financial crises in Mexico, East Asia, and Argentina and the evolution of the New Economy in the United States. The case studies emphasize the role of confidence, expectations, and crowd psychology in creating aggregate macroeconomic behavior that is distinct from the sum of individual behavior. In so doing, the material bridges a gap between firm and household level behavior—which is typically well understood by a managerial audience—and aggregate phenomena—which are often not well understood by this audience.

Second, the material in the book explores the often vague question of what are the important institutions from the point of view of macroeconomic performance and how good institutions are built. In doing so it presents examples of how institutions can be developed that focus the uncoordinated actions of individual households and firms on good, rather than bad, overall outcomes. In some countries, legal, political, economic, and social institutions are able to coordinate private decisions on stable and productive paths. Where institutional development is weak—as seems to be the case in much of the developing world—private actions are poorly coordinated and the result is greater macroeconomic volatility and slower growth. Understanding what constitute good institutions and how they can be designed to influence economic and business behavior in desirable directions is therefore crucial.

Finally, the cases presented in the book are designed to teach simple macroeconomics. The basic framework is one where rational expectations play a key role and where there is the possibility of market failure in the form of disorganization of individual players and coordination failures. The simple framework is developed linking institutional design and macroeconomic performance. The framework can be used to evaluate a number of standard macroeconomic events, ranging from a simple recession in a closed economy to a speculative attack in a market for foreign exchange, including more broadly how globalization is likely to change the performance of specific markets.

Outline

The book is divided into four modules. The first module, "**Introduction and Conceptual Framework**," uses the experiences of two famous economic policy makers (Alan Greenspan and John Maynard Keynes) and two countries that suffered through tremendous economic dislocation in the 1980s and 1990s (Uganda and Mexico) to identify themes of communication, confidence, coordination, and institutional development that play a central role in the remaining cases.

The second module, "**Institutions: The Latin American Experience**," uses frameworks developed in the introductory cases to address macroeconomic and financial dynamics in Latin America. It emphasizes the view that macroeconomic problems typically have deeply rooted institutional causes. Hence, rather than blaming the macroeconomic instability that has plagued Latin America during the 20th century on poor policies, a more complete understanding requires an explanation of why policies have been so poorly designed and thus exploration of the institutional structure of Latin American countries.

The third module, "**Macroeconomics: The Dynamics of European Union**," uses the European experience to illustrate how different countries have developed institutions that permit coordination of individual business decisions on good aggregate economic outcomes. It introduces the idea—familiar from the literature on comparative international political economy—that labor market institutions (such as the structure of trade unions and employer associations, the legal framework for wage bargaining, etc.) will have important effects on inflation and employment dynamics. Moreover, it demonstrates how changes in the environment can render previously successful institutional structures outmoded, thereby creating both opportunities and risks for firms and households. A key insight is that alternative institutional structures exist to the Anglo-Saxon model of "free markets" and "weak unions" that can be successful over time and may, in the face of certain types of macroeconomic shock, even dominate the benchmark American framework. Ultimately, the module asks whether scope exists for a "third way" between the market-oriented approach characteristic of contemporary Anglo-Saxon economies and the social market economic model more prevalent in continental Europe.

The final module, "**The Global Economy: Globalization Meets National Institutions**," discusses how the increasing integration of global capital markets can affect the economic performance of previously successful nations by acting to undermine the internal coherence of the institutional structures on which their economic performance rested. It addresses the question of whether convergence on a single "American-style" form of capitalism is likely in an increasingly integrated world, and what the positive and negative implications of such a convergence would be.

Introduction and Conceptual Framework

Alan Greenspan

During the late 1990s, Federal Reserve Chairman Alan Greenspan achieved cult status in the United States and abroad. He was widely seen as the guarantor of America's unprecedented prosperity and the creator of a decade-long economic boom.

Greenspan's rise to the head of America's central bank had been long and, at times, convoluted. After working as a professional musician and leaving graduate school without his doctorate, Greenspan became a millionaire by the age of 40 on the back of his economic forecasting consultancy. A Republican, he served as President Ford's Chairman of the Council of Economic Advisors, but turned down an official position in the Reagan administration.

His biannual congressional testimony as Chairman of the Federal Reserve was notoriously obscure and became part of the cultural zeitgeist at the end of the millennium. On his words—most famously, his comments about "irrational exuberance" on Wall Street in 1996—financial markets throughout the world gyrated wildly.

Study Questions

1. Should so much power be given to unelected central bankers like Alan Greenspan?
2. Has Greenspan been a success at the Fed? What prepared him for the role of Chairman?
3. Should Greenspan speak more clearly and straightforwardly to Congress, the public, or financial markets? Why or why not?
4. Should economists be celebrities?

HUW PILL

Alan Greenspan

How many central bankers does it take to screw in a light bulb?
One. Greenspan—and the world revolves around him.

—Justin Martin, *Greenspan: The Man Behind the Money*[1]

For most people, mention of Alan Greenspan conjures up the image of a dour, bespectacled genius—an economist *par excellence*. Yet public perceptions of Greenspan are strangely schizophrenic.

On the one hand—on the basis of his apparently successful handling of U.S. monetary policy in the face of various internal and external crises during the economic boom of the late 1990s (see **Exhibits 1–4**)—Greenspan has been dubbed the "King of the Economy" or "Saint Alan the Savior." Winner of the 1999 A&E "Most Fascinating Person of the Year Award," Greenspan was depicted in cartoons as a buff lifeguard swooping in to rescue the world economy, a Jedi master battling overheated markets, and a Zen philosopher resisting the temptation of the dot-com goddesses.

On the other hand, some have accused Greenspan of excessive or inappropriate political maneuvering, social awkwardness, inattention to the growth of an unsustainable and dangerous economic bubble in the late 1990s, and tardiness in easing monetary policy in the face of the dot-com meltdown in 2000–2001.

Regardless of where on this spectrum observers found themselves, one thing was clear: Alan Greenspan had grown into a pop icon, an international celebrity unlike any Federal Reserve chairman before him.

Despite Greenspan's status as part of the cultural zeitgeist of the late twentieth century, many people did not fully understand his role or that of the institution he led—the Federal Reserve—in the U.S. and global economy. Moreover, while Greenspan stood out amongst his peers, central bankers across the globe seemed to be growing in importance and prominence at the turn of the century.

A number of explanations for their growing role have been offered. After the collapse of the Bretton Woods system of fixed exchange rates in the early 1970s, countries could pursue independent monetary policies. The consequent currency fluctuations highlighted the effects of monetary policy and attracted greater public attention. The growing influence of highly mobile, stateless capital necessitated stricter regulation, often administered by central banks. The psychological component

Allison Morhaim (MBA '02) prepared this case with assistance from Research Associate Ingrid Vogel under the supervision of Professor Huw Pill. This case was developed from published sources. HBS cases are developed solely as the basis for class discussion. Cases are not intended to serve as endorsements, sources of primary data, or illustrations of effective or ineffective management.

of inflation post-1970s demanded a credible institution with the mandate to fight inflation, while the increasing incidence of international financial crises necessitated central bank responses.[2]

Against this background, a "secret society" of central bankers emerged who were nominated not elected, operated largely behind closed doors, often kept decisions sealed from public viewing for great lengths of time, and spoke in veiled terms beyond the comprehension of the vast majority of the populations they served. According to Steven Solomon, author of *The Confidence Game: How Unelected Central Bankers are Governing the Changed World Economy*, central bankers functioned somewhere between markets and governments. In the industrialized world, they were bastions of integrity, transcending political firestorms with stubborn independence that led to their being celebrated as heroes in high times and demonized as punch bowl chaperones in bad times.[a] Greenspan was by far the most prominent of this sacred brotherhood.

Less commonly known was Greenspan's unconventional career prior to his assuming the chairmanship of the Federal Reserve. Before taking the helm at the Fed, Greenspan had been a professional musician, married a painter, and become a core member of a group of intellectuals called the Objectivists. He also became a millionaire by the age of 40. In examining his life, various themes recur: intellectual rigor supported by stark rationality; faith in free markets; an obsession with data and numbers; and an aloof independence. These qualities, built up over the first five decades of his life, served him well in his role as chairman of the Federal Reserve.

Though Greenspan's fourth term as Fed chairman would last only until August 2004, as of early 2002 no successor had been identified. Journalists, the financial markets, and the public alike speculated: "What happens when King Alan goes?"[3]

The Early Years: Washington Heights, Baseball, and Music

Alan Greenspan was born in 1926 to Rose and Herbert Greenspan, a lower-middle-class Jewish couple who lived in New York City. After a difficult marriage, Alan's parents divorced when he was only five years old. His father—said to be aloof and an abstract dreamer—played only a minor role in Greenspan's upbringing. During the course of Herbert's career as a businessman and economic consultant, he wrote a book entitled *Recovery Ahead!* which presented Keynesian arguments in support of Roosevelt's New Deal. Ironically, despite the lack of a close relationship between father and son, Herbert, through his book, had an important effect on his son's outlook. Herbert scrawled on the inside cover of the copy of the book he gave to Alan:

> *May this—my initial effort with a constant thought of you—branch into an endless chain of similar effort so that at your maturity you may look back and endeavor to interpret the reasoning behind these logical forecasts and begin a like work of your own.—Dad.*

Greenspan's mother, described as humorous and optimistic, moved Alan to her parents' home in Washington Heights, New York shortly after her divorce. According to his schoolteachers, Alan was a gifted child who could add three-digit numbers in his head by the age of five. An avid fan of the Dodgers baseball team, Greenspan loved nothing more than tracking statistical records of his favorite team.

---

[a] Former Federal Reserve Chairman William McChesney Martin, Jr. famously said the central banker's role was: "To take away the punch bowl just when the party gets going."

As a young adolescent, Greenspan revealed a deep commitment to moral rectitude. With a childhood friend, Alan founded a secret club called the Detective Scouts of Washington Heights, with the goal to "ferret out evil."[4] Despite a few close friendships, particularly with a set of cousins, Greenspan was viewed as rather aloof—even snobbish—by his classmates.

Greenspan attended George Washington High School just three years behind Henry Kissinger. While a good student, Greenspan was by no means an academic overachiever. He was involved in various high school activities, such as acting as president of his homeroom and participating in the lunch squad. His home life afforded him exposure to music. His mother sang and played the clarinet, while his grandfather served as a cantor at a Bronx synagogue. Their influence rubbed off on Alan: He learned to play the clarinet and the saxophone during his high school career and even played in a student band called "Lee Hilton and His Orchestra." His yearbook inscription read: "Smart as a whip and talented. He'll play the sax and clarinet too."

During his late teens, Greenspan grew increasingly passionate about pursuing a musical career. He was accepted at the acclaimed Julliard School of Art in Manhattan as a clarinet major. Frustrated by the theory of music fostered by the academic setting and hungry for a career performing music, Greenspan dropped out of Julliard to join a band called "Henry Jerome and His Orchestra" in 1944. A true swing band of the times, "Henry Jerome" played at casinos and hotel lobbies across the East Coast. Eventually, as the band's leadership lost interest in swing, "Henry Jerome" experimented with the new sound of bebop. Instead of joining in on the post-performance partying, Greenspan kept a low profile and in his spare time kept track of the band's expenses and taxes. It is said that between sets he also feverishly absorbed economics textbooks. Greenspan eventually left the band remarking: "I was a pretty good amateur musician, but I was average as a professional, and I was aware of that because you learn pretty quickly how good some professional musicians are. I realized it's innate. You either have it or you don't. . . . So I decided that, if that was as far as I could go, I was in the wrong profession."[5]

Early Adulthood: Economics, Marriage, and Objectivism

After giving up playing with the band, Greenspan found a new outlet in his second love, mathematics. He enrolled in New York University's School of Commerce where he focused on economics. At NYU, he studied under prominent professors who helped set the foundation of his economic views. Just as in high school, Greenspan joined in on campus activities, playing clarinet with the band, singing in the glee club, and presiding over the Symphonic Society and the Economics Society. In 1948, Greenspan graduated *summa cum laude* and received his Masters in economics in 1950.

Greenspan continued his study of economics at the graduate level at Columbia University, known best for its empirical approach to economics. As a Ph.D. student, Greenspan studied under Arthur Burns, a true anti-Keynesian thinker. In those days, Burns was a lonely voice because many saw the growth of the economy post-World War II as evidence of the strength of Keynesian theory. Yet Burns was a convincing voice—one that caused Greenspan to reverse his prior faith in Keynesian benevolent government toward a belief in the power of markets. Burns emblazoned on his students' minds that the primary cause of inflation was excessive government spending. Such teachings, as well as the relationship between Greenspan and Burns, would be of great importance: Burns served as chairman of the Council of Economic Affairs (CEA) and later as chairman of the Federal Reserve, a path subsequently followed by Greenspan.

While studying at Columbia, Greenspan was set up on a blind date with painter Joan Mitchell. After a courtship involving trips to cultural and artistic venues in New York City, the two were married just 10 months later in 1952. Running out of tuition for Columbia and losing his favorite professor when Burns moved to Washington, D.C., to act as chairman of the CEA, Greenspan left NYU to take a job at the National Industrial Conference Board (later known as the Conference Board). He spent tireless days at his job analyzing heavy industry and poring over economic statistics. On the weekends, he played golf instead of spending time with Mitchell. Although Greenspan and Mitchell did not fight a great deal, their differences were too great. They had their marriage annulled 10 months after their nuptials, but remained close friends thereafter.

Mitchell had been deeply involved with a group of intellectuals who called themselves the Objectivists. The Objectivists, dubbing their meetings the "Collective," built their circle around Ayn Rand, author of *The Fountainhead* and *Atlas Shrugged*. The Collective met on Saturday nights at Rand's Manhattan apartment to discuss art, literature, and economics. It had a unique culture, which Rand relentlessly dominated with her philosophy of freethinking, individualism, and rationality. Rand had spent her early years in Soviet Russia. Her ideology was rabidly anti-communist and vehemently pro-capitalist. Her admirers fiercely defended her, despite some peculiarities such as her belief that smoking cigarettes was a symbol of life. At first, Greenspan was disparaging of the Collective—a feeling that was mutual: apparently, upon first seeing Greenspan, Rand said he looked like an undertaker.[6]

Ironically, the Collective would eventually have a profound influence on Greenspan. As he grew familiar with the teachings of Objectivism, Greenspan was convinced. Not only did he become a permanent fixture in the Collective, he also formed a deep bond with Rand. It was at Collective meetings that Greenspan further honed his skills in arguing his perspective with utterly dispassionate rationality. As readers of *The Fountainhead* grew more and more interested in learning about Objectivism, one of Rand's disciples opened a training school to disseminate her ideas. Greenspan lectured at the school on "The Economics of Free Society," in which he supported the notion of a gold standard and blamed the depression on government interference.[7] Years later, Greenspan reflected: "When I met Ayn Rand, I was a free enterpriser in the Adam Smith sense, impressed with the theoretical structure and efficiency of the markets. What she did was to make me see that capitalism was not only efficient and practical, but also moral."[8]

Adulthood: Greenspan-Townsend and a Taste of D.C.

In 1953, while employed at the Conference Board, Greenspan worked closely with an economic consulting firm called Townsend-Skinner. Impressed by Greenspan's knowledge of heavy industry and his instincts about economic trends, Mr. Townsend eventually asked him to join as partner. According to a colleague, "He was the ultimate anatomist. He knew how the whole thing fitted together. He knew the bones, muscles, blood. By the late 1950s, nobody knew the numbers better than he did."[9] Due to his love of math, Greenspan had the ability to see through data where no one else could. He once told a reporter: "I get the same kind of joy from solving a hard mathematical problem as I do from hearing a Haydn quartet."[10] After his elder partner passed away, Greenspan bought out the firm and continued to run it successfully, becoming a millionaire by the age of 40.

In the late 1960s, while still working at Townsend-Greenspan, Alan was coincidentally reacquainted with Lenny Garment, an old band mate from "Henry Jerome and His Orchestra." Garment was working for Richard Nixon's presidential campaign and arranged for Greenspan and Nixon to meet. The president-to-be was impressed. Greenspan, who had previously been doubtful of government involvement, joined the campaign as a volunteer, heading the domestic policy area. After Nixon's election, Greenspan stayed on as budget liaison but refused offers to become an official in the administration. In 1970, he did, however, sit on the Gates Commission, which was created to consider ending the draft. True to form, Greenspan came out against conscription, which he believed to be immoral and against economic principles. Greenspan also acted as constructive critic of other Nixon policies. His harshest criticism was of Nixon's wage and price controls, put in place to control inflation in 1971. Greenspan felt these were the height of government intervention and were anathema to the ideals of free-market capitalism. He also feared the rampant inflation that would result when the controls on bottled-up prices were eventually lifted.

In 1974, Nixon offered Greenspan the post of chairman of the CEA. Convinced only by a patriotic calling to help end inflation—which at the time stood at 12%—Greenspan accepted the invitation. Yet on the eve of Greenspan's swearing-in, Nixon resigned and Gerald Ford became president. During his early days in the Oval Office, Ford felt compelled to hire new staff untainted by relationships with Nixon. Even though Nixon had originally selected Greenspan, he was viewed as above the fray and sworn in nevertheless.

In his new role as CEA chairman—a seat traditionally held by an academic—Greenspan grew close to Ford as the administration battled stagflation. While Greenspan was a proponent of minimal government intervention, he did believe in giving the economy a one-time "shot in the arm" via a tax decrease. Greenspan's role as advisor grew in prominence as he helped navigate Ford through the traumatic events of the mid-1970s, such as the near-bankruptcy of New York City.

During this period, Greenspan began to attend the Washington circuit of parties and social gatherings—which would have been a surprise for acquaintances from his earlier days. He even dated prominent members of the press, including Barbara Walters. However, this chapter of his life ended the day Jimmy Carter was sworn into office in 1977.

Greenspan symbolically flew out of Washington on Carter's inauguration day. He returned to his consulting firm in New York where he was able to keep abreast of developments in the U.S. economy. During this period, he continued to address audiences on economic issues and even appeared in an Apple IIc computer advertisement. In 1977, he finally received his Ph.D. from NYU for works previously published. In addition, Greenspan and his old high school classmate Henry Kissinger allegedly contemplated starting a foreign policy consulting firm together. But this time outside of Washington did not last forever. In 1981, President Ronald Reagan met with Greenspan and immediately invited him to act as an economic advisor, albeit formally outside the new administration. Greenspan accepted. For two years, while continuing his work at Townsend-Greenspan, he served on a commission on social security.

The Return to D.C.: Federal Reserve Chairmanship

"How are you, Alan?" asked SEC Chairman Arthur Levitt at a Kennedy Center performing arts affair in Washington, D.C. "I'm not allowed to say," Greenspan joked.

—Larry Kahaner, *The Quotations of Chairman Greenspan*[11]

The legendary cigar-smoking six-foot-seven-inch Paul Volcker, appointed by Democratic President Jimmy Carter in 1979, served as chairman of the Federal Reserve Board prior to Greenspan. While the chairmen prior to Volcker—Arthur Burns (1970–1978) and William Miller (1978–1979)—had failed to curb the inflation plaguing the United States during their tenures, Volcker became famous for his fight against rising prices in the early 1980s and, to that end, for his fearless tightening of monetary policy. His was a tough act to follow.

In 1987, frustrated by the political maneuvering around him, Volcker declined reappointment to a third term. Reagan nominated Greenspan instead. Skeptics hinted that Reagan was pleased to have rid the Fed of the hulking Democratic figure of Volcker and felt that he could exert greater influence over fellow-Republican Greenspan. The 1988 elections were on the horizon, and the Republican Party, with Vice President George Bush as its candidate, hoped to avoid additional interest rate hikes.

While lacking experience at the Federal Reserve Bank or Treasury Department, Greenspan was viewed as a known entity—someone with a fat Rolodex and a deep understanding of the economy. Greenspan apparently accepted the nomination "within milliseconds."[12] After undergoing confirmation hearings and disclosing his assets totaling $2.9 million, he was sworn in as chairman on August 11, 1987, becoming the nation's thirteenth central bank governor. His independence from political pressure was made clear almost immediately. One of his earliest actions as newly minted Fed chairman was to raise interest rates. In doing so, he signaled to the market that he was as serious about inflation as Volcker and that he was under no one's thumb.

Black Monday

Barely two months into his tenure as Fed chairman, Greenspan's mettle as central banker was tested. On October 19, 1987—"Black Monday"—stock markets across the world plunged, causing a systemic panic that nearly led to a total disruption of the financial system. Upon assuming office in August, Greenspan had established a task force to examine potential crises, including a stock market crash, facing the U.S. economy. The findings of this group were written in the so-called "Pink Book." Interestingly, the authors of the Pink Book imagined a worst-case scenario of a 150-point drop in the market, much lower than the eventual 500-plus drop that characterized Black Monday.[13]

In the aftermath of the stock market correction, observers cited many possible reasons for the crash. Due to a bond market meltdown in the spring of 1987, investors shifted their assets from bonds to equities, leading to an overvaluation of stocks relative to fixed income assets. Foreign investors, particularly the Japanese, shifted their money out of bonds into U.S. equities as well. At the same time, corporate debt levels were skyrocketing due to leveraged-buy-out activity.

A series of events occurred during the period just prior to October 19 to make matters worse. First, the German Bundesbank raised interest rates on October 14, leading investors searching for higher returns to sell off U.S. equities. Second, on October 15, the U.S. trade deficit was announced at $15.7 billion, well above expectations, while the U.S. government budget deficit stood at $150 billion. Between October 14 and 16, the Dow plunged by 250 points. The situation was made even worse by American Savings and Loan Association of California's announcement (on October 17) that it would default on certain loan obligations.

On Black Monday, markets plunged in Tokyo and London. "Portfolio insurance"—computerized mechanisms used by U.S. pension funds to sell stock automatically when values decreased beyond a certain floor—caused a flood of sale orders in stock index futures even before the 9:30 a.m. opening bell in New York. Trouble was clearly on its way.

Greenspan had been scheduled to travel to Dallas, Texas, to deliver his first public address of his Chairmanship at the American Bankers Association on Black Monday. As the market collapsed in morning trading, he boarded the plane to Texas, determined not to send a negative psychological message to the public; he was in control, and it was business as usual. Legend has it that Greenspan, upon landing in Dallas at 5:45 p.m., asked where the market had closed and received the following reply: "down five-o-eight." Breathing a sigh of relief, Greenspan thought the market had recovered during his flight to close down by 5.08. The truth—a collapse of 508 points—seemed unfathomable. In one day, the market had dropped by 22.6%, twice as much on a percentage basis as the crash of 1929. It was a meltdown of unprecedented proportions.

Over $500 billion in paper money was lost on the stock market. What threatened the overall economy most, however, was the potential impact on the credit markets. If banks got caught in the panic and stopped lending to both good and bad companies, the system could become stagnant and seized by illiquidity. If there was no liquidity in the market, businesses could not gain access to cash and could fall into default. In addition, the tidal wave of trading volume had strained the payments and settlements systems. Gerald Corrigan, then president of the New York Federal Reserve Bank, called these arrangements the "system's plumbing;" if the pipes got clogged, the entire system was in jeopardy of logjam. With the weight of the world falling on the shoulders of the Fed, Greenspan was aware of the importance of his and his colleagues' stance in the face of the crash. After getting a sound night's sleep on Monday, Greenspan ultimately cancelled his speech in Texas and flew back to Washington early Tuesday afternoon. Those around him were awed by his steely nerves and apparent calm during the crisis. They noted: "Greenspan didn't get rattled in these situations. He was in watchful mode."[14] Yet Greenspan knew the Fed had to react.

Similar circumstances faced the Federal Reserve during the 1929 stock market crash. Many observers blamed the Fed for having raised interest rates in the face of a slump, thus adding to illiquidity in the markets. Greenspan and his team knew this story well and would certainly not repeat that mistake. Some senior officials felt the Fed should remain quiet and calm in the face of the crash so as to avoid being perceived as bailing out the markets. Others presented the option of releasing a lengthy technical document to calm fears. Finally, Corrigan said to Greenspan via telephone, "Alan, you're it. Goddammit, it's up to you. This whole thing is on your shoulders."[15]

Corrigan helped refine the message that was released to the markets at 8:41 a.m. Tuesday morning:

> *The Federal Reserve, consistent with its responsibilities as the Nation's central bank, affirmed today its readiness to serve as a source of liquidity to support the economic and financial system.*

When Greenspan landed in Washington that afternoon to make his way to the Oval Office and meet with Treasury officials and President Reagan, White House Chief of Staff Howard Baker told him, "Those are the best lines I've read since Shakespeare."[16] The Fed had successfully walked the delicate line between instilling confidence in the system by declaring it would act as lender of last resort and creating potential moral hazard by directly addressing the stock market crash. To make sure the Fed statement had the intended effect, Corrigan spent countless hours on the phones with bankers on Wall Street, convincing them to lend as normal. Many refer to these tactics as "nods and winks"—the code-talk of the central banker.

Back in Washington, Greenspan met with President Reagan at the White House. Greenspan felt that Reagan should make an announcement that he would meet with Congress to consider ways to help achieve balance in the federal government budget. A bloated government deficit had led to concerns of inflation. The yield on the 30-year Treasury bill was over 10%, which lured investors to pull out of the stock market in search of higher returns. Such a statement from the president would strengthen the markets. Also, Reagan announced the establishment of a commission to examine the events of the crash, which ultimately produced the Brady Report.

Greenspan had taken charge and handled the crisis well. Within weeks, markets were subdued and a major catastrophe had been averted. Against the backdrop of headlines reading, "Passing a Test: Fed's New Chairman Wins a Lot of Praise for Handling the Crash,"[17] a colleague at the Fed said, "I think this was his real swearing in."[18]

The Greenspan Years

Who Needs Gold When We Have Greenspan?

—March 4, 1999 *The New York Times* Editorial[19]

Though established to function outside the political realm, the Fed often came under political pressure to stimulate the economy, especially near election time. By 1988, Greenspan smelled inflation on the rise and was looking to increase interest rates despite upcoming elections. A letter written by Treasury official Michael Darby suggested the Fed should desist, allowing the economy to grow. This elicited a strong response from Greenspan, who said: "We'll have to do the opposite." Interest rates were raised just before the Republican Convention in 1988.[20]

Even so, George Bush won the presidency in 1988. Not surprisingly, his relationship with Greenspan was initially chilly. After multiple bank closures in 1988–1992 (the savings and loan crisis) and tightening credit conditions, Greenspan eased monetary policy—but to no avail. The economy slipped into recession in 1990–1991. The recession was exacerbated by a credit crunch arising from the poor state of bank balance sheets after catastrophic losses in real estate in New England and California. But the recession was short lived, ending in spring 1991 at the time of the successful Desert Storm operation in the Gulf War. Bush nominated Greenspan for a second term in summer 1991, just one month before the end of his first term. While Greenspan started loosening interest rates, the economy grew only slowly since the banks, burdened with bad debt, remained reluctant to lend. In this context, Bill Clinton defeated George Bush in the 1992 elections. Bush always blamed Greenspan for his election loss.

Greenspan met with Clinton early on in the new president's tenure and convinced him that the economy needed the deficit to fall. A falling deficit would fight inflation and enable interest rate policy to have more impact. These early meetings proved to Greenspan that Clinton respected the independence of the central bank and took seriously the notion of fighting the deficit. The two men respected each other's intellect. But political maneuvering had not completely disappeared: To Greenspan's frustration, he was seated between Hillary Clinton and Tipper Gore during Clinton's first state of the union address, leading some to wonder about the independence of the Fed. Greenspan was caught unprepared by this political maneuvering and was angry with Clinton.

Despite protests from the White House, Greenspan hiked interest rates on seven occasions between 1994 and 1995, stating, "If you wait to see the eyes of inflation, then it's too late." Public opinion showed that there was concern that Greenspan was fighting inflation out of sheer paranoia. Nonetheless, Clinton renominated Greenspan in 1996. It was clear that despite the initial unpopularity of his policies, the preemptive strike against inflation proved a success. By the second half of the 1990s, the economy was growing and inflation was contained. Trouble would come later, when the world economic system was threatened by the fallout of the Asian Financial Crisis, the Long Term Capital Management debacle, and later, the slowdown of the U.S. economy after the dot-com crash and terrorist attacks of September 11, 2002.

Fed Speak: Constructive Ambiguity

Once in his new position as Fed chairman, Greenspan jokingly said at an early press conference: "Since I've become a central banker, I've learned to mumble with great coherence. If I seem unduly clear to you, you must have misunderstood what I said."[21]

Over the course of his time at the Fed, Greenspan perfected an already well-developed language of obfuscation. In the spirit of all central bankers, Greenspan's biannual Humphrey-Hawkins testimony before Congress was replete with Byzantine data that was often well over the heads of members of Congress. He once said, "I know you believe you understand what I said, but I am not sure you realize that what you heard is not what I meant."[22] According to noted economist Milton Friedman, "He is a genius for being able to blur the issues. I listen to his testimony before Congress and I am rapt with admiration for his ability to take all that crap and turn back around and deliver sentences that sound like he's saying something he's really not."[23] Greenspan said once, "I spend a substantial amount of my time endeavoring to fend off questions and worry terribly that I might end up being too clear."[24] Despite his attempts to hide his meaning, Greenspan could literally move markets with his words.

On December 5, 1996—at a dinner held in his honor by the American Enterprise Institute, where he was to receive the Francis Boyer Award—Greenspan made his fateful "irrational exuberance" remark that moved markets across the world. When discussing the asset bubble in Japan in 1989, he asked: "How do we know when irrational exuberance has unduly escalated asset values, which then become subject to unexpected and prolonged contractions as they have in Japan over the past decade?" As soon as the words left his mouth, reporters jotted down the quotation and word spread that Greenspan felt the U.S. stock market was overvalued. The Dow fell 145 points in the first half hour of trading the next day, but rebounded before the closing bell, down only 55 points for the day.[a]

Greenspan's ability to hold secret the moves of the Fed was legendary. Television station CNBC even had a "briefcase indicator" on days the Federal Open Market Committee met. A fat briefcase tucked under the chairman's arm meant a change in rates and a thin briefcase meant no change. Astonishingly, the indicator was correct the first 19 out of 20 times. One Web site, thestreet.com, translated Greenspan's "Fed Speak." For example, they translated the introduction to his congressional testimony as: "Thank you for this opportunity to answer my critics, who claim I am making up every word of the Federal Reserve's semiannual report on how I used to beat the living snot out of Bob Rubin at tetherball."[25]

President Clinton renominated Greenspan to his fourth term as Fed chairman in January 2000. The economy was growing rapidly, and people felt confident and were spending at record levels. However, signs pointed toward the potential for inflation, and the Fed hiked interest rates six times between June 1999 and May 2000. The year 2001 proved to be a challenging one for the U.S. economy, and just as Greenspan received great applause for his handling of the economy in the heyday, some criticized his actions. His legacy is undeniably interlinked with the performance of the nation's economy, yet as of 2002, it remained to be seen what he would be remembered for most.

---

[a] Greenspan's use of confusing language seemed to have had an impact on his personal life as well. Soon after the "irrational exuberance" incident, Greenspan proposed to longtime girlfriend Andrea Mitchell (NBC news correspondent, 20 years younger than Greenspan). As they opened Christmas gifts, he asked her if she would prefer a small or a large wedding. Apparently, he had attempted to ask her to marry him several times before, but due to his method of obfuscation in language, she had not caught on.

Glossary of Useful Terms

Discount Rate: The only interest rate set directly by the Federal Reserve Board, it is the rate at which banks can borrow from the Fed. It is considered to be a symbolic rate in that banks infrequently borrow from the Fed due to their reluctance to raise concern that they are shaky.

Fed Funds Rate: The rate at which banks can lend to each other, this is the rate that is set by the Federal Open Market Committee. The New York Federal Reserve Bank engages in open market operations (the buying and selling of U.S. government securities) in order to set this rate. For example, if the Fed purchases Treasuries, it releases money into the system and, as a result, the interest rate decreases.

Federal Reserve System: Founded in 1913 by an Act of Congress, the Federal Reserve System comprises a seven-person Board of Governors. Each is appointed by the president and sworn in by the Senate and 12 regional bank presidents. Its goal is to run the country's monetary policy. According to the 1977 Federal Reserve Act, monetary policy has two goals: to promote maximum output and employment and to promote stable prices.[26] The system is designed to be accountable to the Congress, but is independent from political pressure. The Federal Reserve's duties fall into four general areas: (1) conducting the nation's monetary policy; (2) supervising and regulating banking institutions and protecting the credit rights of consumers; (3) maintaining the stability of the financial system; and (4) providing certain financial services to the U.S. government, the public, financial institutions, and foreign official institutions.[27]

FOMC: The Federal Open Market Committee includes as voting members the seven members of the Board of Governors, the president of the New York Federal Reserve Bank, and four rotating members of the regional bank presidents. Only the president of the New York Federal Reserve Bank has a permanent seat on the committee. The committee meets eight times a year in Washington. Until 1994, the minutes of the FOMC meetings were not released before six weeks had passed, while by 2002, the minutes were released by 2:15 p.m. the same day.

Humphrey-Hawkins Testimony: Mandated by law in 1978, it is the biannual testimony of the Federal Reserve Chairman before Congress.

Reserve Requirements: Reserve requirements are one of the tools used by the Federal Reserve Bank to control the amount of money in circulation. Banks must hold a certain portion of deposits on reserve. If the Fed wants to slow money supply, it would increase the level of the reserve requirement.

Exhibit 1   Selected Macroeconomic Data

U.S. Real GDP 1960–2001 (% change per annum)

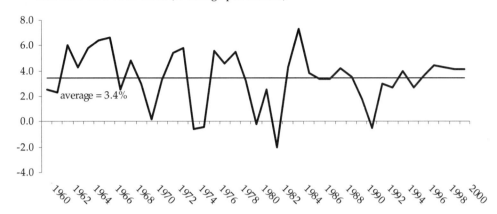

U.S. CPI Rate of Inflation 1960–2001 (% per annum)

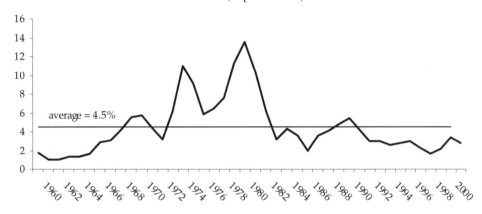

U.S. Federal Funds Rate 1960–2001 (%)

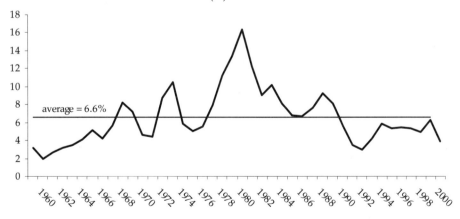

Source: Created by casewriter based on data from the Economic Report of the President, February 2002 <http://w3.access.gpo.gov/usbudget/fy2003/erp.html)>.

Exhibit 2   U.S. National Income Accounts 1987–2001 *(billions of "chained"[a] 1996 U.S. dollars)*

	GDP[b]	Consumption	Fixed Investment	Changes in Inventories	Government	Exports	Imports
1987	6,113	4,113	856	30	1,293	408	564
1988	6,368	4,280	887	18	1,308	474	586
1989	6,592	4,394	911	30	1,344	529	609
1990	6,708	4,475	895	17	1,387	576	632
1991	6,676	4,467	833	-1	1,403	613	629
1992	6,880	4,595	887	17	1,410	651	671
1993	7,063	4,749	958	20	1,399	673	732
1994	7,348	4,928	1,046	67	1,400	733	819
1995	7,544	5,076	1,109	30	1,406	808	887
1996	7,813	5,238	1,213	30	1,422	874	963
1997	8,160	5,424	1,329	64	1,455	982	1,095
1998	8,509	5,684	1,480	77	1,483	1,002	1,224
1999	8,857	5,968	1,595	62	1,532	1,035	1,352
2000	9,224	6,258	1,716	51	1,573	1,133	1,532
2001	9,334	6,450	1,683	62	1,629	1,082	1,490

Source: Created by casewriter based on data from the Economic Report of the President, February 2002 <http://w3.access.gpo.gov/usbudget/fy2003/erp.html)> June 2002.

Notes: [a]The "chained" U.S. dollar price deflator index allows for the change in the composition of GDP over time, thereby giving a more accurate reflection of price trends than a series based on a fixed year.

[b]Due to the use of chained dollars, the sum of components of GDP will not exactly equal GDP.

Exhibit 3   U.S. Unemployment, Inflation, and Interest Rates

	Unemployment Rate	CPI	Federal Funds Rate	10-year U.S. Bond	Moody's Corporate Bond Aaa Yield
	%	annual % change	annual % yield	annual % yield	annual % yield
1987	6.20	3.60	6.66	8.39	9.38
1988	5.50	4.10	7.57	8.85	9.71
1989	5.30	4.80	9.21	8.49	9.26
1990	5.60	5.40	8.10	8.55	9.32
1991	6.80	4.20	5.69	7.86	8.77
1992	7.50	3.00	3.52	7.01	8.14
1993	6.90	3.00	3.02	5.87	7.22
1994	6.10	2.60	4.21	7.09	7.96
1995	5.60	2.80	5.83	6.57	7.59
1996	5.40	3.00	5.30	6.44	7.37
1997	4.90	2.30	5.46	6.35	7.26
1998	4.50	1.60	5.35	5.26	6.53
1999	4.20	2.20	4.97	5.65	7.04
2000	4.00	3.40	6.24	6.03	7.62
2001	4.80	2.80	3.88	5.02	7.08

Source: Created by casewriter based on data from the Economic Report of the President, February 2002 <http://w3.access.gpo.gov/usbudget/fy2003/erp.html)> June 2002.

Exhibit 4   Exchange Rates, U.S. Money and Credit, and U.S. Stock Market

	Exchange Rates			Money and Credit		Stock Market	
	DM per U.S. Dollar	Dollar per Euro	Yen per U.S. Dollar	M2	Debt[a]	S&P 500 Index	Nasdaq Composite Index
				December, % growth over prior year	December, % growth over prior year	Average 1941–43=10	Feb. 5, 1971=100
1987	1.80	--	144.60	3.6	9.4	287	403
1988	1.76	--	128.17	5.8	9.1	266	374
1989	1.88	--	138.07	5.5	7.3	323	438
1990	1.62	--	145.00	3.8	6.5	335	409
1991	1.66	--	134.59	3.0	4.4	376	492
1992	1.56	--	126.78	1.6	4.6	416	599
1993	1.65	--	111.08	1.5	4.9	451	715
1994	1.62	--	102.18	0.4	4.7	460	752
1995	1.43	--	93.96	4.1	5.4	542	925
1996	1.50	--	108.78	4.8	5.4	671	1,165
1997	1.73	--	121.06	5.7	5.5	873	1,469
1998	1.76	--	130.99	8.8	6.9	1,086	1,795
1999	1.84	1.07	113.73	6.1	6.7	1,327	2,728
2000	2.12	0.92	107.80	6.1	5.3	1,427	3,784
2001	2.18	0.90	121.57	10.4	--	1,194	2,035

Source: Created by casewriter based on data from the Economic Report of the President, February 2002 <http://w3.access.gpo.gov/usbudget/fy2003/erp.html)> June 2002.

Note: [a]Consists of outstanding credit market debt of the U.S. government, state and local governments, and the private non-financial sectors.

Endnotes

1   Justin Martin, *Greenspan: The Man Behind the Money* (Cambridge: Persus Publishing, 2000), p. 221.

2   Steven Solomon, *The Confidence Game: How Unelected Central Bankers are Governing the Changed World Economy* (New York: Simon and Schuster, 1995), introduction.

3   "What Happens when King Alan Goes?" *The Wall Street Journal*, August 2, 2001.

4   Martin, p. 5.

5   Martin, p. 22.

6   Martin, p. 39.

7   Martin, p. 48.

8   Steven K. Beckner, *Back from the Brink: The Greenspan Years* (New York: John Wiley & Sons, 1996), p. 12.

9   Martin, p. 56.

10   Martin, p. 57.

11   Larry Kahaner, *The Quotations of Chairman Greenspan: Words from the Man who can Shake the World*, (Holbrook, Massachusetts: Adams Media Corporation, 2000), introduction.

12   Martin, p. 154.

13   Solomon, p. 47.

14   Martin, p. 176.

15   Bob Woodward, *Maestro: Greenspan's Fed and the American Boom* (New York: Simon and Schuster, 2000), p. 39.

16   Solomon, p. 61.

17   Woodward, p. 48.

18   Martin, p. 179.

19   Woodward, p. 214.

20   Martin, p. 186.

21   Beckner, p. 18.

22   Martin, p. 207.

23   Martin, p. 222.

24   Martin, p. 222.

25   Martin, p. 224.

26   Q&A, U.S. Monetary Policy: Federal Reserve Bank of San Francisco, September 1999.

27   Federal Reserve Web site <www.federalreserve.gov> December 2001.

Other Background Materials

Martin Mayer, *The Fed: The Inside Story of how the World's Most Powerful Financial Institution Drives the Market* (New York: The Free Press, 2001).

"Greenspan to the Rescue," *The Economist*, April 21, 2001.

"The Federal Reserve: A Fragile Superpower," *The Economist*, August 4, 2001.

John Maynard Keynes: His Life, Times, and Writings

John Maynard Keynes is one of the most famous and influential economists of all time and among the most important figures of the 20th century.

Keynes' contributions spanned an enormous range. He developed a novel set of theories, which created the new discipline of macroeconomics. Yet at the same time, Keynes was closely involved in the practical world of economic policymaking. He proposed a variety of responses to the Great Depression of the 1930s and was one of the chief architects of the Bretton Woods system of international finance and trade that emerged after the Second World War.

At the same time, Keynes managed an investment fund and made large sums of money for himself and his Cambridge College in the financial markets of the City of London. Keynes was also actively involved in the arts, marrying a Russian ballerina and creating and financing the Arts Theatre in Cambridge, England.

Keynes was particularly interested in how businesses and individuals made decisions in the face of uncertainty. Many of his policy proposals revolved around this issue.

Supplementary Material

Fiscal Policy and the Case of Expansionary Fiscal Contraction in Ireland in the 1980s

Study Questions

1. Keynesian economics is often viewed as justifying increases in deficit spending by the government to stimulate real economic activity. How does this proposal relate to Keynes' own writing reproduced in the case?
2. What role do confidence and psychology play in Keynes' understanding of the economy and the role of government?
3. Why is Keynes so concerned with uncertainty?
4. Does Ireland's experience in the late 1980s support or contradict Keynes' ideas?

HUW PILL

John Maynard Keynes:
His Life, Times, and Writings

John Maynard Keynes is widely regarded as one of the most influential economists in history and one of the most significant figures of the 20th century. This case consists of three parts. First, to summarize Keynes's fascinating life, his 1946 obituary from *The Times of London* is reproduced. Second, to recall the dramatic economic events of the times in which he lived, U.S. macroeconomic data from 1920–1940 are presented. Finally to provide some insight into Keynes's intriguing views of economic behavior, a number of excerpts from his key writings are reproduced.

Keynes's Life

Obituary
Lord Keynes A Great Economist[1]

Lord Keynes, the great economist, died at Tilton, Firle, Sussex, yesterday from a heart attack.

By his death the country has lost a very great Englishman. He was a man of genius, who as a political economist had a world-wide influence on the thinking both of specialists and of the general public, and he was also master of a variety of other subjects which he pursued through life. He was a man of action as well as of thought, who intervened on occasion with critical effect in the great affairs of state, and carried on efficiently a number of practical business activities which would have filled the life of an ordinary man. And he was not merely a prodigy of intellect; he had civic virtues—courage, steadfastness, and a humane outlook; he had private virtues—he was a good son, a devoted member of his college, a loyal and affectionate friend, and a lavish and unwearying helper of young men of promise.

The Right Hon. John Maynard Keynes, C.B. Baron Keynes, of Tilton, Sussex, in the Peerage of the United Kingdom, was born on June 5, 1883, son of Dr. John Nevile Keynes, for many years Registrary [sic] of Cambridge University. His mother was Mayor of Cambridge as lately as 1932. He was brought up in the most intellectual society of Cambridge. He was in college at Eton, which he dearly loved, and he was proud of being nominated by the masters to be their representative governor later in life. He won a scholarship to King's College, Cambridge, in mathematics and classics, writing his

Research Associate Ingrid Vogel prepared this case under the supervision of Professor Huw Pill. This case was developed from published sources. HBS cases are developed solely as the basis for class discussion. Cases are not intended to serve as endorsements, sources of primary data, or illustrations of effective or ineffective management.

essay on Héloïse and Abélard.   He was President of the Cambridge Union, won the Members' English Essay Prize for an essay on the political opinions of Burke, and was twelfth wrangler in the mathematical tripos.   Although he did not take another tripos, he studied deeply in philosophy and economics and was influenced by such men as Sidgwick, Whitehead, W.E. Johnson, GE Moore, and, of course, Alfred Marshall.

In 1906 he passed second into the Civil Service, getting his worst mark in economics—"the examiners presumably knew less than I did"—and chose the India Office, partly out of regard for John Morley and partly because in those days of a smooth working gold standard, the Indian currency was the livest monetary issue and had been the subject of Royal Commissions and classic controversies.   During his two years there he was working on his fellowship dissertation on "Probability," which gained him a prize fellowship at King's.   This did not oblige him to resign from the Civil Service, but Marshall was anxious to get him to Cambridge, and, as a token, paid him £100 a year out of his private pocket to supplement the exiguous fellowship dividend – those were before the days of his bursarship of the college. Anyhow, his real heart lay in Cambridge.   He lectured on money.   He was a member of the Royal Commission on Indian Currency and Finance (1913–14).   He served in the Treasury 1915–19, went with the first Lord Reading's mission to the United States, and was principal representative of the Treasury at the Paris Peace Conference and deputy for the Chancellor of the Exchequer on the Supreme Economic Council.   After his resignation he returned to teaching and to his bursar's duties at King's, but he always spent part of his time in London.   He was a member of the Macmillan Committee on Finance and Industry, and parts of its classic report bear the stamp of his mind.

In 1940 he was made a member of the Chancellor of the Exchequer's Consultative Council and played an important part in Treasury business.   He was appointed a director of the Bank of England. In 1942 he was created Lord Keynes, of Tilton, and made some valuable contributions to debate in the Upper House.   He became High Steward of Cambridge (Borough) in 1943.   His continued interest in the arts was marked by his trusteeship of the National Gallery and chair-manship of the Council for the Encouragement of Music and the Arts.   In 1925 he married Lydia Lopokova, renowned star of the Russian Imperial Ballet – "the best thing Maynard ever did," according to the aged Mrs. Alfred Marshall.   She made a delightful home for him, and in the years after his serious heart attack in 1937 was a tireless nurse and vigilant guardian against the pressures of the outside world.

Lord Keynes's genius was expressed in his important contributions to the fundamentals of economic science; in his power of winning public inerest in the practical application of economics on critical occasions; in his English prose style – his description of the protagonists at the Versailles Conference, first fully published in his Essays in Biography (1933), is likely long to remain a classic— and, perhaps it should be added, in the brilliant wit, the wisdom, and the range of his private conversation, which would have made him a valued member of any intellectual salon or coterie in the great ages of polished discussion.

In practical affairs his activities in addition to his important public services were legion.   As bursar of King's he administered the college finances with unflagging attention to detail.   By segregating a fund which could be invested outside trustee securities he greatly enlarged the resources of the college, and, unlike most college bursars, he was continually urging the college to spend more money on current needs.   From 1912 he was editor of the *Economic Journal*, which grew and flourished under his guidance, and from 1921 to 1938 he was chairman of the National Mutual Life Assurance Society. He ran an investment company.   He organized the Camargo Ballet.   He built and opened the Arts Theatre at Cambridge and, having himself supervised and financed it during its period of teething troubles, he handed it over, when it was established as a paying concern, as a gift to *ex-officio* trustees drawn from the university and city. He became chairman of C.E.M.A. in 1942 and of the Arts Council in 1945. He was chairman of the *Nation,* and later, when the merger took place, of the *New Statesman*; but he had too scrupulous a regard for editorial freedom for that paper to be in any sense a reflection of his own opinions. He also did duty as a teacher of undergraduates at King's College and played an important and inspiring part in the development of the Economics faculty at Cambridge. The better students saw him at his most brilliant in his Political Economy Club. He was interested in university business and his evidence before the Royal Commission (1919–22) was an important influence in causing it to recommend that the financial powers of the university should give it greater influence over the colleges.

To find an economist of comparable influence one would have to go back to Adam Smith. His early interest was primarily in money and foreign exchange, and there is an austere school of thought which regards his "Indian Currency and Finance" (1912) as his best book. After the 1914–18 war his interest in the relation between monetary deflation and trade depression led him on to reconsider the traditional theory about the broad economic forces which govern the total level of employment and activity in a society. He concluded that, to make a free system work at optimum capacity—and so provide "full employment"—it would be necessary to have deliberate central control of the rate of interest and also, in certain cases, to stimulate capital development. These conclusions rest on a very subtle and intricate analysis of the working of the whole system, which is still being debated wherever economics is seriously studied.

Popularly he was supposed to have the vice of inconsistency. Serious students of his work are not inclined to endorse this estimate. His views changed in the sense that they developed. He would perceive that some particular theory had a wider application. He was always feeling his way to the larger synthesis. The new generalization grew out of the old. But he regarded words as private property which he would define and redefine. Unlike most professional theorists, he was very quick to adapt the application of theory to changes in the circumstances. Speed of thought was his characteristic in all things. In general conversation he loved to disturb complacency, and when, as so often, there were two sides to a question he would emphasize the one more disturbing to the company present.

His "Treatise on Probability" is a notable work of philosophy. Although using mathematical symbols freely, it does not seek to add to the mathematical theory of probability, but rather to explore the philosophical foundations on which that theory rests. Written clearly and without pedantry, it displays a vast erudition in the history of the subject which was reinforced by and reinforced his activities as a bibliophile.

Keynes had on certain occasions an appreciable influence on the course of history. His resignation from the British delegation to the Paris Peace Conference and his publication a few months later of "The Economic Consequences of the Peace" had immediate and lasting effects on world opinion about the peace treaty. The propriety of his action became a matter of controversy. Opinions still differ on the merits of the treaty, but about the point with which he was particularly concerned, reparations, there is now general agreement with his view that the settlement—or lack of settlement—was ill-conceived and likely to do injury to the fabric of the world economy. His subsequent polemic against the gold standard did not prevent a return to it in 1925, but largely added to the ill repute of that system in wide circles since. It was mainly through his personal influence some years later that the Liberal Party adopted as their platform in the election of 1929 the proposal to conquer unemployment by a policy of public works and monetary expansion.

In two wars he had a footing in the British Treasury. The idea of deferred credits was contained in the pamphlet entitled, "How to Pay for the War," which he published in 1940. From 1943 he played a principal part in the discussions and negotiations with the United States to effect a transition from war to peace conditions of trade and finance which avoided the errors of the last peace, and to establish international organization which would avoid both the disastrous fluctuations and the restrictions which characterized the inter-war period. He was the leader of the British experts in the preparatory discussions of 1943 and gave his name to the first British contribution—"the Keynes Plan"—to the proposals for establishing an international monetary authority. In July, 1944, he led the British delegation at the Monetary Conference of the United and Associated Nations at Bretton Woods, where an agreed plan was worked out. He was the dominant figure in the British delegation which for three months, from September to December, 1945, hammered out the terms of the American Loan Agreement, which he defended brilliantly in the House of Lords. He was appointed in February Governor of the International Monetary Fund and the International Bank for Reconstruction and Development, and in these capacities had just paid a further visit to the United States, whence he returned only two weeks ago. These continuous exertions to advance the cause of liberality and freedom in commercial and financial policies as a means to expand world trade and employment imposed an exceptionally heavy and prolonged strain which, in view of is severe illness just before the war, Lord Keynes was physically ill-fitted to bear.

His life-long activities as a book-collector were not interrupted even by war. His great haul of unpublished Newton manuscripts on alchemy calls for mention. He identified an anonymous pamphlet entitled "An Abstract of a Treatise of Human Nature," acquired by his brother, Mr. Geoffrey Keynes, as being the authentic work of David Hume himself. He had it reprinted in 1938, and it will no doubt hereafter be eagerly studied by generations of philosophers. During the second war his hobby was to buy and then, unlike many bibliophiles, to read rare Elizabethan works. His interest in and encouragement of the arts meant much to him. From undergraduate days he had great friendships with writers and painters and, while his activities brought him in touch with many distinguished people of the academic world and public life, he was probably happiest with artistic people. At one period he was at the center of the literary circle which used to be known as "Bloomsbury" – Lytton Strachey, Virginia Woolf, and their intimate friends. More than fame and worldly honours he valued the good esteem of this very cultivated and fastidious society.

And finally there was the man himself—radiant, brilliant, effervescent, gay, full of impish jokes. His entry into the room invariably raised the spirits of the company. He always seemed cheerful; his interests and projects were so many and his knowledge so deep that he gave the feeling that the world could not get seriously out of joint in the end while he was busy in it. He did not suffer fools gladly: he often put eminent persons to shame by making a devastating retort which left no loophole for face-saving. He could be rude. He did not expect others to bear malice and bore none himself in the little or great affairs of life. He had many rebuffs but did not recriminate. When his projects were rejected, often by mere obstructionists, he went straight ahead and produced some more projects. He was a shrewd judge of men and often plumbed the depths in his psychology. He was a humane man genuinely devoted to the cause of the common good.

Keynes's Times

United States Macroeconomic Data, 1920–1940

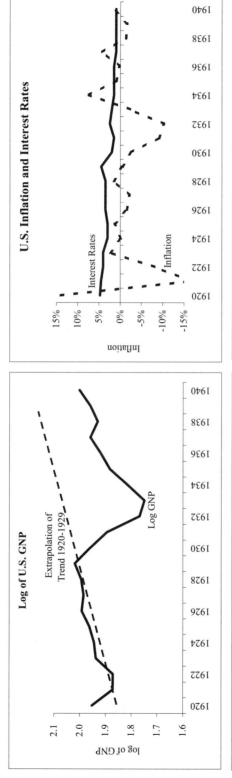

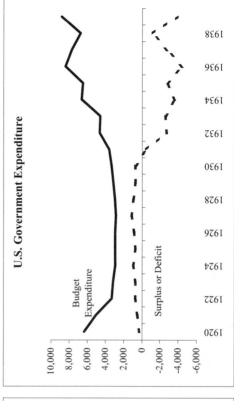

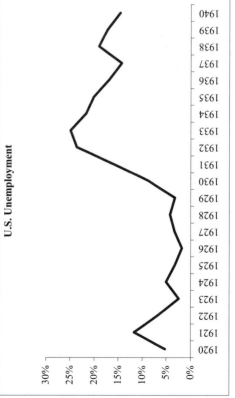

Sources: Adapted from Joseph Swanson and Samuel Williamson, "Estimates of National Product and Income for the United States Economy, 1919-1941" in *Explorations in Economic History* Vol. 10 (1), Fall 1972, p 53-73; and *Historical Statistics of the United States: Colonial Times to 1970* (New York: Cambridge University Press, 1997).

U.S. Macroeconomic Data, 1920–1940, Continued

Year	Nominal Gross National Product (billions dollars)	Inflation	Unemployment (% civilian labor force unemployed)	Government Finances Budget Expenditure (millions dollars)	Surplus / Deficit (millions dollars)	M1 Growth (annual % change)	Short-term Interest Rates (FRBNY discount rate)	S&P Index of Common Stocks (average 1941–1943=100)
1920	89.7	13.9%	5.2%	6,357	291	8.9%	4.8%	79.8
1921	74.5	-16.7%	11.7%	5,061	509	-9.4%	4.5%	68.6
1922	74.4	-8.1%	6.7%	3,289	736	0.7%	4.0%	84.1
1923	86.6	2.4%	2.4%	3,140	713	5.8%	4.0%	85.7
1924	88.0	-0.2%	5.0%	2,907	963	3.2%	3.0%	90.5
1925	91.9	1.4%	3.2%	2,923	717	8.4%	3.0%	111.5
1926	98.3	-1.5%	1.8%	2,929	865	2.0%	3.5%	125.9
1927	96.7	-2.2%	3.3%	2,857	1,155	-0.3%	3.5%	153.4
1928	98.7	1.6%	4.2%	2,961	939	1.1%	3.5%	199.5
1929	104.6	-0.4%	3.2%	3,127	734	1.0%	4.5%	260.2
1930	91.2	-2.6%	8.7%	3,320	738	-3.3%	2.0%	210.3
1931	78.5	-9.1%	15.9%	3,577	-462	-6.3%	1.5%	136.6
1932	58.6	-10.3%	23.6%	4,659	-2,735	-12.6%	2.5%	69.3
1933	56.1	-2.2%	24.9%	4,598	-2,602	-5.7%	2.0%	89.6
1934	65.5	7.4%	21.7%	6,644	-3,630	9.8%	1.5%	98.4
1935	76.5	0.9%	20.1%	6,497	-2,791	18.4%	1.5%	106.0
1936	83.1	0.2%	16.9%	8,421	-4,425	14.2%	1.5%	154.7
1937	91.2	4.2%	14.3%	7,733	-2,777	4.6%	1.0%	154.1
1938	85.4	-1.3%	19.0%	6,764	-1,177	-1.3%	1.0%	114.9
1939	91.2	-1.6%	17.2%	8,841	-3,862	11.9%	1.0%	120.6
1940	100.5	1.6%	14.6%	na	na	16.1%	1.0%	110.2

Sources: Adapted from Joseph Swanson and Samuel Williamson, "Estimates of National Product and Income for the United States Economy, 1919–1941" in *Explorations in Economic History* Vol. 10 (1), Fall 1972, p 53–73; and *Historical Statistics of the United States: Colonial Times to 1970* (New York: Cambridge University Press, 1997).

Keynes's Writings

Keynes on capitalism

The General Theory of Employment, Interest and Money was Keynes's seminal work. He wrote it against the backdrop of the collapse of the world economy and the potential collapse of democracy with the Great Depression. He is widely credited with "inventing macroeconomics" and revolutionizing economic thinking with the book's publication in 1936. The book outlined Keynes's view that governments should actively manage economies using government spending as the foremost policy tool. From the Chapter "Concluding Notes:"[2]

> The authoritarian state systems of to-day seem to solve the problem of unemployment at the expense of efficiency and of freedom. It is certain that the world will not much longer tolerate the unemployment which, apart from brief intervals of excitement, is associated – and, in my opinion, inevitably associated – with present-day capitalistic individualism. But it may be possible by a right analysis of the problem to cure the disease whilst preserving efficiency and freedom...

Keynes on the Great Depression

The Means to Prosperity was first published as a series of articles in *The Times of London* in 1933. Keynes used the mimeograph, later published as a pamphlet, to argue that the government should "spend its way out of the Depression" given the failure of other policies to halt or reverse the decline in economic activity after 1929.[3]

> If our poverty were due to famine or earthquake or war or if we lacked material things and the resources to produce them, we could not expect to find the means to prosperity except in hard work, abstinence, and invention. In fact, our predicament is notoriously of another kind. It comes from some failure in the immaterial devices of the mind, in the working of the motives which should lead to the decisions and acts of will, necessary to put in movement the resources and technical means we already have. It is as though two motor-drivers, meeting in the middle of a highway, were unable to pass one another because neither knows the rule of the road. Their own muscles are no use; a motor engineer cannot help them; a better road would not serve. Nothing is required and nothing will avail, except a little clear thinking.
>
> So, too, our problem is not a human problem of muscles and endurance. It is not an engineering problem or an agricultural problem. It is not even a business problem, if we mean by business those calculations and dispositions and organising acts by which individual entrepreneurs can better themselves. Nor is it a banking problem.... On the contrary, it is, in the strictest sense, an economic problem or, to express it better, as suggesting a blend of economic theory with the art of statesmanship, a problem of political economy.
>
> I call attention to the nature of the problem, because it points us to the nature of the remedy. It is appropriate to the case that the remedy should be found in something which can fairly be called a *device*. Yet there are many who are suspicious of devices, and instinctively doubt their efficacy. There are still people who believe that the way out can only be found by hard work, endurance, frugality, improved business methods, more cautious banking and, above all, the avoidance of devices. But the worries of these people will never, I fear, get by.

They may stay up all night, engage more sober chauffeurs, install new engines, and widen the road; yet they will never get by, unless they stop to think and work out with the driver opposite a small device by which each moves simultaneously a little to his left.

It is the existing situation which we should find paradoxical. There is nothing paradoxical in the suggestion that some immaterial adjustment, some change, so to speak, "on paper" should be capable of working wonders. The paradox is to be found in 250,000 building operatives out of work in Great Britain, when more houses are our greatest material need. It is the man who tells us that there is no means, consistent with sound finance and political wisdom, of getting the one to work at the other, whose judgment we should instinctively doubt. ...

When, on the contrary, I show ... that to create wealth will increase the national income and that a large proportion of any increase in the national income will accrue to an Exchequer, amongst whose largest outgoings is the payment of incomes to those who are unemployed and whose receipts are a proportion of the incomes of those who are occupied, I hope the reader will feel, whether or not he thinks himself competent to criticise the argument in detail, that the answer is just what he would expect – that it agrees with the instinctive promptings of his common sense.

Nor should the argument seem strange that taxation may be so high as to defeat its object, and that, given sufficient time to gather the fruits, a reduction of taxation will run a better chance than an increase of balancing the budget. For to take the opposite view today is to resemble a manufacturer who, running at a loss, decides to raise his price, and when his declining sales increase the loss, wrapping himself in the rectitude of plain arithmetic, decides that prudence requires him to raise the price still more....

Keynes on speculation

From *The General Theory of Employment, Interest and Money*; Chapter "Long-term Expectation:"[4]

[P]rofessional investment may be likened to those newspaper competitions in which the competitors have to pick out the six prettiest faces from a hundred photographs, the prize being awarded to the competitor whose choice most nearly corresponds to the average preferences of the competitors as a whole; so that each competitor has to pick, not those faces which he himself finds the prettiest, but those which he thinks likeliest to catch the fancy of the other competitors, all of whom are looking at the problem from the same point of view. It is not a case of choosing those which, to the best of one's judgment, are really the prettiest, nor even those which average opinion genuinely thinks the prettiest. We have reached the third degree where we devote our intelligences to anticipating what average opinion expects the average opinion to be. And there are some, I believe, who practise the fourth, fifth, and higher degrees...

Speculators may do no harm as bubbles on a steady stream of enterprise. But the position is serious when enterprise becomes the bubble on a whirlpool of speculation. When the capital development of a country becomes a by-product of the activities of a casino, the job is likely to be ill-done. The measure of success attained by Wall Street, regarded as an institution of which the proper social purpose is to direct new investment into the most profitable channels in terms of future yield, cannot be claimed as one of the outstanding triumphs of *laissez-faire* capitalism – which is not surprising, if I am right in thinking that the best brains of Wall Street have been in fact directed towards a different object.

These tendencies are a scarcely avoidable outcome of our having successfully organised 'liquid' investment markets. It is usually agreed that casinos should, in the public interest, be inaccessible and expensive. And perhaps the same is true of stock exchanges.

Keynes on uncertainty

"The General Theory of Employment"[5] was an article published in the *Quarterly Journal of Economics* in 1937. Keynes wrote it to clarify many of the ideas outlined in his prior book, *The General Theory of Employment, Interest and Money*, which had met with much criticism on publication and was the subject of vigorous debate (which continues to this day). The article developed reasoning Keynes had first outlined in his *Treatise on Probability*, published in 1921, which was the book that earned him his fellowship at Kings College, Cambridge.

We have, as a rule, only the vaguest idea of any but the most direct consequences of our acts. Now the whole object of the accumulation of wealth is to produce results, or potential results, at a comparatively distant, and sometimes at an *indefinitely* distant, date. Thus the fact that our knowledge of the future is vague and uncertain, renders wealth a peculiarly unsuitable subject for the methods of the classical economic theory.

By 'uncertain' knowledge, let me explain, I do not mean merely to distinguish what is known for certain from what is merely probable. The game of roulette is not subject, in this sense, to uncertainty. Or, again, the expectation of life is only slightly uncertain. The sense in which I am using the term is that in which the price of copper and the rate of interest twenty years hence, or the obsolescence of a new invention are uncertain. About these matters there is no scientific basis on which to form any calculable probability whatever. We simply do not know. Nevertheless, the necessity for action and for decision compels us as practical men to overlook this awkward fact and to behave exactly as we should if we had behind us a good Benthamite[6] calculation of a series of prospective advantages and disadvantages, each multiplied by its appropriate probability, waiting to be summed.

How do we manage in such circumstances to behave in a manner which saves our faces as rational economic men? We have devised for the purpose a variety of techniques, of which much the most important are the three following:

- We assume that the present is a much more serviceable guide to future than a candid examination of past experience would show to have been hitherto. In other words we largely ignore the prospect of future changes about the actual character of which we know nothing.

- We assume that the *existing* state of opinion as expressed in prices and the character of existing output is based on a *correct* summing up of future prospects, so that we can accept it as such unless and until something new and relevant comes into the picture.

- Knowing that our own individual judgement is worthless, we endeavour to fall back on the judgement of the rest of the world, which is perhaps better informed. That is, we endeavour to conform with the behaviour of the majority or the average. The psychology of' individuals each of whom is endeavouring to copy the others to what we may strictly term a *conventional* judgement.

Now a practical theory of the future based on these three principles has certain marked characteristics. In particular, being based on so flimsy a foundation, it is subject to sudden and violent changes. The practice of calmness and immobility, of certainty and security, suddenly breaks down. New fears and hopes will, without warning, take charge of human conduct. The forces of disillusion may suddenly impose a new conventional basis of valuation. All these pretty, polite techniques, made for a well-panelled board room and a nicely regulated market, are liable to collapse. At all times the vague panic fears and equally vague and unreasoned hopes are not really lulled and lie but a little way below the surface.

Keynes on the New Deal

Keynes wrote the following *letter to an American news correspondent* on July 4, 1933. In it, he discussed his reactions to U.S. President Roosevelt's plans to stimulate the economy after the Great Depression with the New Deal.

One fears your President is depending far too much on psychological as distinct from real factors. The operation of the psychological factors is… being flattered by the fact that it began at a point when you were entitled to a strong upward reaction, even without adventitious aids. On the other hand, real factors, such as open-market operations and public works, are being tackled much too timidly. There is a risk of a hiatus when the psychological stimulus will have exhausted itself before the real factors, which are slow moving, will have come into effective operation.

At any rate that is the risk. On the other hand, one must not underestimate – and I am always quarrelling with Kahn[7] about this – the cumulative effect of a recovery in working capital due to an upward movement, however engendered…What I call the Multiplier…may in the United States to-day be very large indeed. Thus it is not impossible that the programme may carry through successfully.

At any rate your country is making so much better an effort than any other to mend things, that in spite of my grave hesitations I am more disposed to sympathise than to criticise.[8]

Keynes on economists

From *The General Theory of Employment, Interest and Money;* Chapter "Concluding Notes:"[9]

Practical men, who believe themselves to be quite exempt from any intellectual influences, are usually the slaves of some defunct economist. Madmen in authority, who hear voices in the air, are distilling their frenzy from some academic scribbler of a few years back. I am sure that the power of vested interests is vastly exaggerated compared with the gradual encroachment of ideas…

Endnotes

1   *The Times of London*, Monday April 22, 1946.

2   John Maynard Keynes, *The General Theory of Employment, Interest and Money* (Cambridge, U.K.: The Macmillan Press Ltd., [1936] 1973) pp. 381–383 (last pages of book).

3   *The Collected Works of John Maynard Keynes*, Vol. 9 (London: Macmillan St. Martin's Press for the Royal Economic Society, 1972).

4   Keynes, *The General Theory of Employment, Interest and Money*, pp. 156–159.

5   John Maynard Keynes, "The General Theory of Employment," *Quarterly Journal of Economics,* Vol. 51, 2, 1937, pp. 209–223.

6   Benthamite refers to the Jeremy Bentham's theories regarding expected utility. Its fundamental tenant is that utility, or pleasure and pain, are innate in the individual and can therefore serve as the fundamental building block of economic theory.

7   Economist Richard F. Kahn is credited with providing Keynes with the foundations for the theory of the income-expenditure multiplier.

8   As quoted in Robert Skidelsky, *John Maynard Keynes: The Economist as Savior, 1920–1937* (New York: Penguin Books, 1992) p. 491.

9   Keynes, *The General Theory of Employment, Interest and Money*, pp. 381–383 (last pages of book).

TECHNICAL NOTE

Fiscal Policy and the Case of Expansionary Fiscal Contraction in Ireland in the 1980s

Prior to the Great Depression of the 1930s, governments accepted large fluctuations in the growth of output and income as inevitable. Rather than requiring policy actions to stabilize the economy, fluctuations in economic activity were seen as natural and self-correcting. In his seminal work "The Means to Prosperity" published in 1933, economist John Maynard Keynes challenged classical economic thinking by outlining his belief that problems of mass unemployment and idle capital were not always best left to market forces. Instead, Keynes proposed direct government intervention to stimulate aggregate demand and thereby restore full employment and economic growth.

After World War II, governments around the world began to use Keynesian economic management to shape economic cycles. For the first time, deficit spending was considered a valid tool to combat economic downturns. In the United States, President John F. Kennedy cited demand-side economic theory to argue for a substantial tax cut that was eventually passed in 1964. Although the cut was projected to lead to a fiscal deficit, national income indeed rose and an economic boom ensued. His economic advisers enthusiastically concluded that "economics has come of age in the 1960s."

Enthusiasm for Keynes' economic theory soured, however, with its perceived failure to combat worldwide recession following the abolishment of the Bretton Woods system of fixed exchange rates in 1971 and the oil crisis of 1973. Governments sought a new strategy for economic stabilization. Many settled on "Chicago-school" free-market economist Milton Friedman's prescription to focus on eliminating inflation through control of the money supply while empowering markets and minimizing state planning. Monetarists, led by Friedman, firmly rejected fiscal policy based on deficit spending to counteract recessions because they believed it led to "crowding out" of the private sector.

By 2000, most economists agreed that Keynesianism could not be used to fine tune the economy. However, in the face of a worldwide slowdown in economic growth, many countries—including the United States through President George W. Bush's tax cuts in 2001 and 2003—continued to try to use fiscal policy to orchestrate increased aggregate demand and, thereby, economic recovery.

Professor Huw Pill wrote the original version of this case [Ireland in the 1980s: A Case of Expansionary Fiscal Contraction, HBS No. 703-052] which is being replaced by this note prepared by Professor Rafael Di Tella and Research Associate Ingrid Vogel. HBS cases are developed solely as the basis for class discussion. Cases are not intended to serve as endorsements, sources of primary data, or illustrations of effective or ineffective management.

Fiscal Policy

Toward the common goal of economic stabilization, the monetarist approach stressed monetary policy whereas the Keynesian approach stressed fiscal policy.

Monetary policy is directed at controlling the money supply, often through the mechanism of influencing interest rates. In most countries, monetary policy is delegated to a partially or fully independent central bank that often relies on inflation as an indicator of economic stability. In an overheated economy with signs of rising inflation, a central bank might choose to dampen economic activity by decreasing the money supply through the sale of government bonds to the public in open-market operations. The central bank encourages the sale of bonds by lowering their price, equivalent to increasing their yield. Increasing interest rates also dampens investment directly by raising the cost of capital.

Fiscal policy centers on government decisions about taxation and spending. In Keynes' view, expansionary fiscal policy—increasing government purchases, increasing transfer payments, or decreasing taxes—could be used to increase aggregate demand, thereby stimulating GDP growth in a recessionary economy. Similarly, contractionary fiscal policy—decreasing government purchases, decreasing transfer payments, or increasing taxes—could be used to cool down an overheated economy through decreasing aggregate demand and national income. Some of these adjustments in government spending occur automatically. For example, government transfer payments such as unemployment insurance increase automatically during a recession, which helps to stimulate national income. Likewise, tax collection automatically increases during a boom, which reduces aggregate demand.

An important component of expansionary fiscal policy is the hypothesis of a multiplier effect, which predicts that an increase in government spending or an increase in income due to lower taxes will increase national income and GDP by an even greater amount. This happens because the initial additional income will lead to successive rounds of additional consumption and income. As a very simple example, suppose a tax cut leaves someone with $100 in extra income. Suppose everybody has a marginal propensity to consume (MPC) 40% of each additional dollar they receive on domestic products. The recipient of the initial $100 will then consume $40 on domestic products, such that national income is increased by $140 in total. The recipient of the secondary $40 will then consume 40% of that, or $16, on domestic products such that national income is increased by $156 in total. The effect continues indefinitely. In total, national income increases by $167, equivalent to the initial $100 times the income multiplier of 1 / (1-MPC), or 1/(1-.4), which equals 1.67.[a] The portion of the increase in income that is not consumed on domestic products goes to taxes, imports, and savings. Several studies have pointed to a multiplier of approximately 1.5 for the United States.

While Keynes focused on the demand-side effects of a tax cut, other economists focus on the supply side. Supply-side economists, whose thinking became popular in the 1980s, argue that cutting tax rates serves to encourage more work and production, leading to increased tax revenues and a growing GDP.

Either from a demand- or supply-side perspective, fiscal policy suffers from a number of disadvantages. Economists point out that it lacks flexibility and is subject to political manipulation. They also point out that the long time lag between proposal of a tax cut or an additional government spending program and implementation means that policies may be implemented counter-cyclically.

---

[a] Simple algebra shows that $1+x+x^2+x^3+x^4+\ldots = 1/(1-x)$.

While monetarists argue that expansionary fiscal policy crowds out private investment, classical economists believe that government intervention is unnecessary since prices and wages adjust quickly and automatically to restore general equilibrium in the economy. Other models of the economy assume that intelligent consumers recognize that any government spending increase or tax cut will be followed in the future by reduced spending or tax increases, so adjust their spending accordingly. Therefore, any attempt at expansionary or contractionary fiscal policy results in no change in national income.

The Case of Expansionary Fiscal Contraction in Ireland in the 1980s

While conventional economic theory suggests that fiscal contractions—higher taxes, reduced government spending, and lower public deficits—will lead to slower economic growth, in several cases, fiscal contraction may have actually boosted growth. For example, the Keynesian model of economic management appeared to be reversed in the case of Ireland in the 1980s. The key mechanism which reverses the view expressed by traditional Keynesian logic is the longer-term sustainability of the public finances. When this is in question, fiscal stimulus is likely to undermine private confidence and create expectations of higher future taxes, thereby reducing current consumption as expected lifetime income declines.

Expansionary Fiscal Contraction

Ireland experienced significant growth from 1987 to 1990 (see **Exhibit 1**). An "expansionary fiscal contraction" (EFC) has been suggested by several economists as the underlying cause of this performance.

In the standard Keynesian analysis, increases in government expenditure are passed on through a fiscal multiplier to increases in aggregate demand. The opposite also holds true: A decrease in government expenditure should lead to a decrease in aggregate demand and to fiscal contraction. However, this may not be true for countries that have very large budgetary deficits in addition to high debt ratios. In this case, fiscal contraction may actually lead to *increased* economic activity. This is because the role of "expectations" needs to be taken into account.

Suppose a government with a high debt ratio and budget deficit makes a firm and credible commitment to reduce its budget deficit extensively. If financial market players perceive this policy to be credible and to signal a commitment to price stability and financial integrity, the risk premium on long-term interest rates will decline. This decrease in long-term interest rates will have expansionary effects on both demand and supply as consumption and investment are stimulated. A wealth effect is created as a result of the lower cost of capital and lower debt servicing of households, firms, and the public sector.

Furthermore, higher taxes associated with tackling the current budget deficit lead to an expectation that future tax liabilities will be lower than the private sector had previously assumed. This increase in expected future wealth can further stimulate consumer spending. Investment can rise due to the expectation of a more vibrant private sector in the future and by an anticipation of lower interest rates. Business will respond positively to the increased stimulus on domestic demand.

In this example, EFC implies more than 100% crowding out. In other words, private sector spending due to the more optimistic assessment of the future is actually *greater* than the contraction in government spending. This results in an increase in aggregate demand, employment, and output.

It is important that governments exploit these market sentiments correctly. The credibility of a fiscal adjustment would be enhanced by up-front action to achieve the medium-term desired fiscal results. Furthermore, fiscal contraction through a decrease in spending seems to be more effective than through an increase in taxation, which raises an economy's cost structure and can worsen its competitiveness.

Ireland's experience in the late 1980s

In the mid-1980s, Ireland was plagued by persistent inflation, high costs of depressed industry, and long-term unemployment. A decade of severe budget deficits, financed largely by borrowing from abroad (see **Exhibit 2**), combined with a lack of concrete proposals for future surpluses raised doubts about the ability of any fiscal plan to address the country's deepening recession successfully.

A new government elected in 1987 aimed to turn Ireland's economic situation around (see **Exhibit 3**). The Fianna Fail party succeeded in ousting a fractious coalition led by the Fine Gael party from power, following the Irish pound's devaluation in August 1986 against the German Deutsch Mark in the European Exchange Rate Mechanism. Ireland had been forced to devalue in order to restore competitiveness against its major trading partner, the United Kingdom, whose pound had depreciated markedly in the first half of 1986 (see **Exhibit 4**).

Because it did not obtain an absolute majority in the election, Fianna Fail was forced to rely on the support of independents. The new government's first task was producing the 1987 budget. The tone of the budget was harsh as it attempted to tackle Ireland's public spending and borrowing problems. Much of the plan was based on the earlier failed proposals of the Fine Gael government. Fine Gael's conciliatory endorsement of the Fianna Fail party's new budget allowed it to proceed.

The three fundamental principles of the budget were:

- Public finance targets had to be consistent with good management of the economy.
- Borrowing and the servicing of national debt were to be significantly reduced.
- Particular focus was to be placed on productive economic activity and employment growth.

Ultimately, the budget was driven by the first two of these principles. The 1987 Exchequer (finance ministry) borrowing requirement was targeted at 1.85 billion Irish pounds (IEP), or 10.7% of GNP. This was a significant reduction from the 1986 borrowing requirement target of IEP 2.15 billion, or 13% of GNP. The current budget deficit target was reduced from 8.5% of GNP to 6.9% of GNP, representing IEP 1.2 billion.

The actual outcome was better than targeted. The current budget deficit came in IEP 20 million below target due to increased savings on expenditure. The borrowing requirement came in IEP 72 million below target due to lower than expected spending. This trend was continued in the following two years with the borrowing requirement decreasing to 2% of GNP by 1989. The current budget deficit achieved similar positive results over the same period (see **Exhibit 2**).

Wage growth was another key issue the government planned to tackle (see **Exhibits 5** and **6**). The Programme for National Recovery initiated in 1988 indexed social welfare and public sector pay to inflation. In the manufacturing sector, increases in weekly earnings fell from 4.9% in 1987 to 4.3% in 1988. Even more importantly, wages in Ireland's main trading partners were rising much more steeply. Moderate wage growth combined with Ireland's favorable exchange rate was estimated to have translated into a cost competitiveness gain of 3% against the United Kingdom.

Monetary policy targeted preserving the strength of the Irish pound as well as maintaining its stability. Following the stringent 1987 budget, markets began to trust that the Fianna Fail government did not intend to release an expansionary inflationary episode in the future. This expectation led to increased confidence and a 5 percentage point drop in interest rates between March and December 1987. Consumer price inflation dropped to 3.2%, the lowest rate since the 1960s. In 1988, even in the face of a less favorable international climate, interest rates dropped another percentage point. By the second half of 1988, Irish retail rates, a full 6 percentage points lower than in the United Kingdom, were at their lowest level for over a decade. In 1989, the weakness of the U.K. pound and net capital outflows from portfolio adjustments linked to a relaxation of exchange controls led to a slight increase in interest rates. However, by the end of 1989, the prime commercial rate was still 4 percentage points lower than in the United Kingdom (see **Exhibit 7**). Inflation on various measures remained low into 1990 (see **Exhibit 8**).

Economic effects

The policies followed by the government in the late 1980s had several noticeable effects on the Irish economy. Through a combination of price competitiveness and increased confidence, there was strong impetus for growth. In 1987, growth was focused outward. Both industrial production and export earnings enjoyed double-digit expansion. From 1988 onwards, growth was linked more closely to domestic demand.

Liquidity in the domestic banking system improved greatly as a result of a significant increase in official external reserves during 1987 and 1988 (see **Exhibit 9**). Private-sector credit growth increased from 4.7% in 1987 to 13.5% in 1988.

The stabilization and accompanying sharp fall in real interest rates subjected households to two policy shocks:

1) Income effect—a cut in current disposable income due to fiscal contraction.

2) Wealth effect—due to the unanticipated fall in nominal and real interest rates.

Nonetheless, private consumption increased by more than 3% in 1988 as households decreased their savings ratio. Similarly, investment began to pick up during the second half of 1988 and grew 10% in 1989. Growth was fuelled in particular by a boom in the property sector, with planning permission for development projects increasing by 20% in 1989. In contrast, public consumption dropped cumulatively by 10% between 1986 and 1989 (see **Exhibit 10**). The drop in public consumption and investment was more than compensated for by domestic demand and investment that increased the need for private sector employment (see **Exhibit 11**). In other words, the traditional Keynesian effects were more than offset by a combination of two factors: (a) the impact of other policies (e.g. devaluation); and (b) non-conventional effects of fiscal policy (e.g. improved confidence and lower expected future taxes).

This optimistic economic climate not only had a positive effect on GDP, but also facilitated the government's success in hitting its aggressive national debt and public finance targets. From the cost side, debt servicing was reduced due to the decrease in the interest rate. Similarly, social welfare payments were reduced as the private sector demanded more labor to deal with higher domestic demand and investment. From the revenue side, indirect taxes also benefited from the stronger economy. For example, VAT (value-added tax) was boosted by a widening of the tax base and growth in high-priced items. Tax revenues increased by 8% in 1988 over the previous year, spurred by a 9% increase in the value of consumer spending over the same period, as well as by a 25% increase in new car sales. Therefore, the fiscal consolidation started by the initial spending cuts were quickly augmented by higher tax revenues.

Exhibit 1   Gross National Product and Gross Domestic Product at Current Market Prices and Changes in GNP and GDP at Constant (1985) Prices

	GNP at Current Market Prices (£m)	Change in GNP at Constant (1985) Prices		
		Expenditure Basis	Output Basis	Average
1983	13,595.3	- 1.6	- 0.8	- 1.2
1984	14,767.8	2.3	1.0	1.6
1985	15,725.3	1.0	- 0.4	0.3
1986	16,779.8	- 1.2	- 0.7	- 0.9
1987	18,084.2	5.0	4.6	4.8
1988	18,940.0	1.4	3.3	2.4
1989	20,879.0	5.0	4.4	4.7

	GDP at Current Market Prices (£m)	Change in GDP at Constant (1985) Prices		
		Expenditure Basis	Output Basis	Average
1983	14,779.2	-0.2	0.5	0.1
1984	16,406.6	4.4	3.1	3.7
1985	17,690.9	2.5	1.2	1.8
1986	18,736.8	-0.4	0.1	-0.1
1987	20,041.3	4.4	4.6	4.2
1988	21.482.0	3.9	5.5	4.7
1989	23,919.0	5.9	5.3	5.6

Source: Adapted from EIU, *Ireland Economic Review* 1991, p. 35.

Exhibit 2   Public Sector Borrowing Requirement

	1982	1983	1984	1985	1986	1987	1988[1]	1989	1990	1991[2]
	£m	£m	£m	£m	£m	£m	£m	£m	£m	£m
Current Budget										
1. Expenditure	**5,896**	**6,671**	**6,991**	**7,615**	**8,105**	**8,331**	**8,007**	**8,019**	**8,421**	**9,019**
—Central Fund Services	1,400	1,658	1,928	2,214	2,253	2,403	2,431	2,453	2,604	2,797
—Supply Services	4,496	5,013	5,063	5,401	5,852	5,928	5,576	5,566	5,817	6,222
2. Revenue	**4,908**	**5,711**	**5,952**	**6,331**	**6,710**	**7,151**	**7,690**	**7,756**	**8,269**	**8,775**
—Tax	4,053	4,681	5,304	5,581	6,096	6,493	7,322	7,443	7,903	8,358
—Non-Tax	855	1,030	648	750	614	658	368	313	366	417
3. Current Budget Deficit	**988**	**960**	**1,039**	**1,284**	**1,395**	**1,180**	**317**	**263**	**152**	**244**
as % of GNP	*7.9*	*7.1*	*7.0*	*8.2*	*8.3*	*6.5*	*1.7*	*1.3*	*0.7*	*1.0*
Capital Budget										
4. Expenditure	2,000	1,872	1,916	1,761	1,744	1,619	1,362	1,433	1,684	1,869
5. Resources	1,043	1,076	1,130	1,030	994	1,013	1,060	1,217	1,374	1,653
6. Exchequer Borrowing Requirement for Capital purposes	957	796	786	731	750	606	302	216	310	216
as % of GNP	*7.7*	*5.9*	*5.3*	*4.6*	*4.5*	*3.4*	*1.6*	*1.0*	*1.4*	*0.9*
7. Exchequer Borrowing Requirement	1,945	1,756	1,825	2,015	2,145	1,786	619	479	462	460
as % of GNP	*15.6*	*12.9*	*12.4*	*12.8*	*12.8*	*9.9*	*3.3*	*2.3*	*2.0*	*1.9*
8. Public Sector Borrowing Requirement	2,466	2,277	2,375	2,444	2,506	2,056	751	667	681	803
as % of GNP	*19.8*	*16.7*	*16.1*	*15.5*	*14.9*	*11.4*	*4.0*	*3.2*	*3.0*	*3.4*

Source: Adapted from EIU, *Ireland Economic Review* 1991 p. 41.
Notes: [1]Inclusive of once-off tax amnesty receipts.
          [2]The nominal figures are the 1991 Budget targets. The percentages shown are based on the most recent GNP estimate.

Exhibit 2 (continued) Money Supply Formation (£ million)

	1985	1986	1987	1988	1989	1990
Budgetary component:						
Exchequer borrowing requirement	2,015	2,145	1,786	619	479	462
less:						
Small savings	371	254	186	339	161	86
Sales of securities to domestic non-bank public	680	916	727	170	-556	176
Monetary Financing	964	975	873	110	874	200
less:						
Official foreign borrowing	806	812	592	-443	-29	-44
Sales of securities to non-residents	83	240	460	867	1,320	64
(1) Domestic budget component	**75**	**-77**	**-179**	**-314**	**-417**	**180**
Foreign component:						
Current account balance	-650	-509	239	437	371	864
Government foreign borrowing	806	812	592	-443	-29	-44
Government sales of securities to non-residents	83	240	460	867	1,320	64
Other known capital transactions	293	298	-612	-374	-2,384	-1,191
Residual	-361	-908	-63	-147	-82	678
Change in official external reserves	171	-67	616	340	-640	371
Change in net external position of licensed banks	213	555	-419	495	-311	473
(2) Foreign component	**-42**	**-622**	**1,035**	**-155**	**-329**	**-102**
Banking sector:						
Advances to non-Government	294	642	443	1,302	1,628	1,358
Other	124	-31	-336	-211	-358	254
(3) Domestic banking component	**418**	**611**	**107**	**1,091**	**1,270**	**1,612**
Increase in money supply, M3 (=1+2+3)	**451**	**-88**	**963**	**622**	**524**	**1,690**

Source: Adapted from EIU, *Ireland Economic Review* 1991, p. 55.

Exhibit 3 General Election, Results

| | First Preference Votes | | | |
	Nov. 1982 (% share)	Feb. 1987 (% share)	Dail Seats (no) Outgoing Dail[c]	Incoming Dail
Fianna Fail	45.2	44.1	71	81
Fine Gael	39.2	27.1	68	51
Progressive Democrats[a]	-	11.8	5	14
Labour	9.4	6.4	14	12
Workers' Party	3.3	3.8	2	4
Sinn Fein	_[b]	1.9	_[b]	-
Others	2.8	4.8	6	4
Total	100.0	100.0	166	166

Source: Adapted from EIU, *Ireland Country Report* No. 1, 1987, p. 8.

Notes: [a]Established in 1985.

[b]Did not stand in 1982.

[c]Position at dissolution, excluding one vacant seat and the speaker.

Exhibit 4 Exchange Rates: Units per Irish Pound (Period Averages)

	U.S. Dollar	Sterling	DM	ECU	Effective Index
1980	2.06	0.89	3.73	1.48	74.0
1981	1.62	0.80	3.64	1.45	67.8
1982	1.42	0.81	3.45	1.45	67.4
1983	1.25	0.82	3.18	1.40	65.1
1984	1.09	0.81	3.08	1.38	62.3
1985	1.07	0.82	3.11	1.40	62.4
1986	1.34	0.91	2.91	1.37	66.7
1987	1.49	0.91	2.67	1.29	66.2
1988	1.52	0.86	2.67	1.29	65.1
1989	1.42	0.87	2.67	1.29	64.4
1990	1.66	0.93	2.67	1.30	68.3

Source: Adapted from EIU, *Ireland Economic Review* 1991, p. 56.

Exhibit 5 Consumer Price Inflation (%)

	Ireland	US	UK	Germany
1981	20.3	10.4	11.4	6.3
1982	17.2	6.2	8.1	5.3
1983	10.4	3.2	4.8	3.3
1984	8.6	4.4	4.1	2.4
1985	5.5	3.5	4.7	2.1
1986	3.8	1.9	2.9	-0.2
1987	3.1	3.6	3.1	0.3
1988	2.1	4.1	3.9	1.2
1989	4.1	4.8	5.2	2.8
1990	3.3	5.4	7.0	2.7

Source: Adapted from EIU Country Data, October 8, 2004.

Exhibit 6   Real Wages (annual % increase)

	Ireland	US	UK	Germany
1981	-3.2	-1.5	n.a.	0.7
1982	-2.3	-0.2	n.a.	0.4
1983	1.0	1.2	n.a.	0.7
1984	1.7	0.0	n.a.	0.7
1985	3.0	-0.5	n.a.	1.9
1986	3.6	0.5	n.a.	5.2
1987	2.6	-1.1	n.a.	4.9
1988	3.1	-0.7	4.7	3.0
1989	0.6	-0.9	3.8	1.3
1990	2.0	-1.2	2.5	2.6

Source: Adapted from EIU Country Data, October 8, 2004.

Exhibit 7   Interest Rates (%): End Period

	One Month Interbank Rate	Prime Overdraft Rate	Mortgage Rate[1]
1982	16.1	14.0	13.00
1983	12.2	12.8	11.75
1984	15.0	14.8	11.75
1985	10.4	10.5	9.75
1986	13.7	13.5 — 14.0	12.50
1987	8.2	9.0	9.75
1988	7.9	8.0	8.25
1989	12.4	11.0	11.25 — 11.95
1990 Q1	11.9	12.0	12.25 — 12.95
Q2	10.6	11.0 — 11.5	12 :00 — 12.70
Q3	10.7	11.0	11.50 — 12.20
Q4	11.1	10.5	11.00 — 11.70
1991 Q1	10.9	11.2	11.75 — 12.45
Q2	10.2	10.8	11.25 — 11.95

Source: Adapted from EIU, *Ireland Economic Review* 1991, p. 54.

Note: [1]Representative annuity mortgage rates. The basis of compilation of this table has been changed and the figures given for the years up to 1988 may not be directly comparable with later years.

Exhibit 8   Price Index Numbers and Percentage Changes, 1985 = 100

Period	Consumer Prices (all items)	Wholesale Prices (General Index)	Agricultural Output Prices	Agro Input Prices	Export Unit Value	Import Unit Value	Terms of Trade
1983	87.3	88.3	99.9	91.5	89.8	89.1	100.8
1984	94.8	97.1	102.8	98.6	97.3	97.7	99.6
1985	100.0	100.0	100.0	100.0	100.0	100.0	100.0
1986	103.8	97.8	99.5	96.2	92.7	88.9	104.3
1987	107.1	98.4	103.5	91.7	92.7	88.8	104.4
1988	109.4	102.4	114.4	94.2	99.3	94.6	105.0
1989	113.8	108.1	120.1	99.3	105.9	100.7	105.1
1990	117.7	105.1	106.5	99.5	95.9	95.7	100.2
Percentage Changes							
1983	10.4	6.5	6.3	7.9	8.8	4.7	3.9
1984	8.6	10.0	2.9	7.8	8.4	9.7	-1.2
1985	5.4	3.0	-2.7	1.4	2.8	2.4	0.4
1986	3.9	-2.2	-0.5	-3.8	-7.3	-11.2	4.3
1987	3.2	0.6	4.0	-4.7	0.0	-0.1	0.1
1988	2.1	4.1	10.5	2.7	7.1	6.6	0.6
1989	4.0	5.6	5.0	5.4	6.7	6.5	0.2
1990	3.4	-2.8	-11.3	0.2	-9.4	-5.0	-4.7

Source: Adapted from EIU, *Ireland Economic Review 1991*, p. 46.

Exhibit 9   Balance of International Payments

	1982	1983	1984	1985	1986	1987	1988	1989	1990
Current Account:									
Merchandise Trade[1]	-1,120.4	-521.5	-196.6	136.6	435	1,310	2,025	2,244	1,814
Services:	139.2	109.0	151.5	205.2	56	7	-58	59	264
—Tourism[2]	128.9	157.3	213.0	283.3	138	175	212	285	430
—Other Services	-10.3	-48.3	-61.5	-78.1	-82	-168	-270	-227	-166
Net Factor Income	-927.7	-1,183.9	-1,638.8	-1,965.7	-1,957	-1,957	-2,542	-3,039	-2,728
International Transfers	593.2	671.2	738.5	973.8	957	879	1,011	1,108	1,567
Balance on Current Account	**-1,315.7**	**-925.2**	**-945.4**	**-650.1**	**-509**	**239**	**437**	**371**	**864**
as % of GNP	-10.6	-6.8	-6.4	-4.1	-3.0	1.3	2.3	1.8	3.8
Capital Account:									
Private Capital	285.3	87.2	-137.6	-108.0	-407	-723	-826	-1,870	-1,814
Official Capital	1,220.7	712.7	854.3	1,028.9	1,198	1,231	523	964	59
Banking Transactions	132.3	605.6	368.2	285.7	554	-79	365	-186	727
Official External Reserves	-90.7	-227.1	32.7	-195.7	72	-606	-352	640	-513
Balance on Capital Account	**1,547.5**	**1,178.4**	**1,117.6**	**1,010.9**	**1,418**	**-176**	**-290**	**-453**	**-1,541**
Net Residual	231.8	-253.2	-172.2	-360.8	-908	-63	-147	82	678

Source: Adapted from EIU, *Ireland Economic Review 1991*, p. 53.

Notes: [1]Adjusted for balance of payments purposes.

       [2]Including passenger fare receipts.

Exhibit 10   Ireland National Income Accounts

as % GDP	1980	1981	1982	1983	1984	1985	1986	1987	1988	1989	1990	1991
GDP (mm current Irish pounds)	9,361	11,359	13,382	14,916	16,556	17,969	19,703	21,075	22,718	25,418	28,598	29,675
Private Consumption	66%	66%	60%	60%	59%	60%	62%	61%	61%	61%	60%	61%
Government Spending	20%	20%	20%	19%	19%	18%	18%	17%	16%	14%	15%	16%
Fixed Investment	29%	29%	26%	23%	21%	19%	18%	16%	16%	17%	18%	17%
Changes in Inventories	-1%	-1%	1%	1%	1%	1%	1%	0%	0%	1%	3%	2%
Exports	50%	48%	48%	52%	59%	60%	53%	56%	60%	63%	57%	58%
Imports	63%	63%	55%	55%	59%	58%	50%	51%	52%	56%	52%	53%
Total	100%	100%	100%	100%	100%	100%	100%	100%	100%	100%	101%	101%

Source: Compiled from International Monetary Fund, *International Financial Statistics CD-ROM,* May 2004.

Exhibit 11   Unemployment

	Thousands	As % of Labor Force[1]
1980	101.5	8.1
1981	127.9	10.1
1982	156.6	12.1
1983	192.7	14.7
1984	214.2	16.4
1985	230.6	17.7
1986	236.4	18.1
1987	247.3	18.8
1988	241.4	18.4
1989	231.6	17.9
1990 Q1	223.9[2]	17.2
Q2	222.5[2]	17.1
Q3	225.6[2]	17.3
Q4	226.9[2]	17.4
1990 Average	224.7[2]	17.2
1991 Q1	237.5[2]	18.2
Q2	251.5[2]	19.3

Source: Adapted form EIU, *Ireland Economic Review* 1991, pg. 45.

Notes: [1]Percentage of estimated labor force in mid-April each year and for 1991 as a percentage of 1990 labor force.
          [2]Seasonally adjusted.

Exhibit 11 (continued)   Population, Natural Increase and Net Migration, 1980–1991 (000's)

Year	Population at mid-April	Total Change (%)	Natural Increase (%)	Net Migration (%)
		Since mid-April of previous year		
1980	3,401	33	41	-8
1981	3,443	42	40	2
1982	3,480	37	38	-1
1983	3,504	24	38	-14
1984	3,529	25	34	-9
1985	3,540	11	31	-20
1986	3,541	1	28	-28
1987	3,543	2	29	-27
1988	3,538	-5	26	-32
1989	3,515	-23	23	-46
1990	3,503	-12	19	-31
1991[1]	3,523	20	22	-1

Source: Adapted from EIU, *Ireland Economic Review* 1991, p. 45.
Note: [1]Preliminary.

References

Alan Sutherland, "Fiscal crises and aggregate demand: Can high public debt reverse the effects of public policy?" *Journal of Public Economics*, 65 (1997).

Frank Barry and Michael Deveraux, "The macroeconomics of government budget cuts: can fiscal contractions be expansionary?" in Willman Robson and William Scarth, *Deficit Reduction: What Pain, What Gain*? pp. 202–204.

A. Chrystal & S. Price, *Controversies in Macroeconomics* (Hemel Hempstead: Harvester Wheatsheaf, 3rd edition 1994).

EIU, Ireland Economic Country Report No. 2, 1987 p. 4.

EIU, Ireland Economic Country Report No. 2, 1987 p. 11.

EIU, Ireland Economic Report 1988, p. 10.

EIU, Ireland Economic Report 1988, pp. 29–30.

EIU, Ireland Country Report No. 1, 1998, p. 17.

EIU, Ireland Country Report No. 1, 1988, p. 16.

EIU, Ireland Economic Review & Outlook 1988, p. 18.

EIU, Ireland Economic Review & Outlook 1989, p. 10.

EIU, Ireland Economic Review & Outlook 1989, p. 18.

EIU, Ireland Economic Review & Outlook 1989, p. 22.

EIU, Ireland Economic Review & Outlook 1989, p. 24.

EIU, Ireland Economic Review & Outlook 1990, pp. 17–18.

Uganda and the Washington Consensus

During the early 1990s, economic growth in Uganda—while not at the dizzying pace of the Asian tigers during their heyday—reached respectable annual rates of 6–7%. This performance stood in stark contrast both to Uganda's economic collapse in the 1970s and early 1980s and to growth rates observed in many neighboring sub-Saharan countries.

After prolonged civil war and violence, Yoweri Museveni took power in Uganda in 1987. At the behest of the international financial institutions and bilateral donors (European and American governments), Museveni embarked on a conventional macroeconomic stabilization and structural reform program. Born at the home of the IMF and World Bank in Washington, D.C., this policy package had been labeled the Washington consensus.

Ten years later, in 1997, U.S. President Clinton launched an Africa initiative to promote the interests of economic development in the continent. He toured Africa—including a stop in Kampala, the capital of Uganda. The American press followed President Clinton. At that time, an article assessing the policies of President Museveni appeared in *The New York Times,* with the headline "Uganda: An African Success Story?" The question mark was a telling comment on the country in the late 1990s.

Study Questions

1. Is Uganda "an African success story"? Why or why not?
2. To the extent that Uganda has enjoyed economic success, how much of the success is attributable to the Washington consensus policies advocated by the International Monetary Fund?
3. What is the Washington consensus missing? Can President Museveni provide the missing elements?
4. Is Joseph Stiglitz correct to lambaste the IMF and Washington consensus?

HUW PILL

Uganda and the Washington Consensus

In the ten years since Mr. Museveni came to power, Uganda has been transformed.

—*The Economist*, 13 April 1996

To hear some diplomats and African experts tell it, President Yoweri K. Museveni has started an ideological movement that is reshaping much of Africa, spelling the end of the corrupt, strong-man governments that characterized the cold-war era.... Political pundits across the continent are calling Mr. Museveni an 'African Bismarck.' Some people refer to him as Africa's 'Other Statesman,' second only to the venerated South African President, Nelson Mandela.

— *The New York Times*, 15 June 1997

A former Marxist and guerrilla commander, Yoweri Museveni came to power in Uganda following the blood-letting regimes of Milton Obote and Idi Amin. After Obote won a disputed presidential election in 1981, Museveni went into the bush to organize a guerrilla offensive. After a four-year war, he seized power in 1986. Subsequently, Museveni consolidated his power, introduced a series of institutional reforms and wedded his administration to textbook IMF-style economic stabilization and structural change. Under Museveni's rule between 1987 and 1994, Uganda's real GDP grew at an average rate of 7% per year. Real per capita GDP growth averaged 4% over the same period, and was forecast to accelerate to 6% for the years 1997-1999.

Although Museveni received considerable aid from the donor community, he consistently dodged their demands to establish full-fledged Western-style democracy. He countered the demands of some Ugandans and the West for multi-party elections by claiming that political parties divide society by race, ethnic group and religion, create more instability, and ultimately thwart the economic progress viewed as a prerequisite for political reform along Western lines. In Museveni's view, African countries like Uganda need a thriving economy and a middle class that can mobilize party activity around issues other than ethnicity before they can attempt democracy on the Western model. In response to cries for democracy, Museveni said Ugandans shall have it. But not all at once.

At the end of 1997, the government of Uganda stood at a crossroads. Flushed with the success of achieving East Asian rates of growth since 1987, the Museveni administration faced several economic challenges. Foremost was the massive overhang of external debt, the inheritance of a decade of IMF and World Bank stabilization and restructuring programs financed by foreign borrowing. This debt imposed a colossal burden on the Ugandan economy. While negotiating with foreign creditors for debt reduction, Museveni's government also pondered whether Uganda could grow its way out of

Research Associate Courtenay Sprague prepared this case under the supervision of Professor Huw Pill. HBS cases are developed solely as the basis for class discussion. Cases are not intended to serve as endorsements, sources of primary data, or illustrations of effective or ineffective management.

the debt problem. One group of ministers advocated the introduction of an activist national development strategy along Malaysian lines, while others preferred continued adherence to "Washington Consensus" structural reform, relying on market mechanisms rather than greater government intervention to stimulate growth.

Profile of Uganda

...for magnificence, for variety and color, for profusion of brilliant life—plant, bird, insect, reptile, beast—for the vast scale...Uganda is truly the pearl of Africa.

—Winston Churchill, 1908[1]

Nestled in the heart of the continent, Uganda is a landlocked country situated on the northern shore of Lake Victoria in East Central Africa (**Exhibit 1**). A lush green country replete with exotic wildlife and majestic mountains, it is slightly smaller in size than the U.S. state of Oregon. Lake Victoria is the major source of the Nile and is the largest lake on the continent. It is shared by Kenya to the east and Tanzania in the south. Uganda's other neighbors are the Democratic Republic of Congo (formerly Zaire) to the west, Sudan to the north and Rwanda to the southwest.

Uganda is bisected by the equator. Its climate is thus tropical and generally rainy. Each year there are two dry seasons, making possible two harvests. The country possesses some of the most fertile agricultural land in Africa, as well as a vast store of mineral resources including bismuth, cobalt, copper, gold, tin and deposits of salt, limestone and iron. Uganda's elevation ranges from 3,000 to 5,000 feet, and this variation in altitude is responsible for a wide range of flora and fauna species, including half the world's mountain gorilla population.

In 1996, Uganda's inhabitants totaled just over 19 million people, with an annual population growth rate of 3.2%. Between 1980 and 1994, life expectancy declined from 52 years to 42. Fifty percent of adult deaths were AIDS related. By 1997, it was estimated that 930,000 people were HIV positive, including 67,000 children under the age of 15. Access to medical services was poor. In 1996, there was one physician per 22,399 people. Illiteracy was also an enduring problem: 38% of men and 65% of women could not read and write (**Exhibit 2**).

Pre-Colonial Era

Following a series of disputes in the late nineteenth century among European nations over northern and eastern Africa, Britain gained control over Egypt, Kenya, Zanzibar and Uganda. There were more than 20 ethnic groups in what was to become Uganda. Conflicts were common among these groups, especially between the Nilotics[2] in the north and the Bantu in the south. There was also tension within the north between the Acholi and the Langi even though these Nilotic groups had similar languages and social organizations. Economic and social disparities were often the root causes of ethnic strife.

When the first Europeans arrived in Uganda, the area was controlled by four autonomous political kingdoms: Ankole, Toro, Bunyoro and Buganda. Buganda was the powerful kingdom of the southeast that had begun to dominate her neighbors prior to the establishment of British colonial rule in the late 19th century. Situated on the northwest corner of Lake Victoria, Buganda was well positioned to take advantage of trans-east African trading initiatives. Buganda had developed a strong infrastructure before the British arrived, including an extensive network of roads and causeways, maintained by an elaborate hierarchy of chiefs. The chiefs were ruled by their king, the

Kabaka. Baganda society (the inhabitants of Buganda Kingdom) was well organized internally, providing a solid base for expansion.

By the late 1840s, the first Muslim traders had arrived in Buganda from the Swahili coast, and Islam began to exert a strong influence on the culture. The language spoken by the Baganda, Luganda, was first written in Arabic characters. Buganda's status as an ancient kingdom held a mythic allure for the British. Early European explorers were astonished and impressed by the standard of Baganda civilization. In 1874, the famed Welsh-American correspondent, Henry Stanley, gained an audience with the Kabaka. While Kabaka Mutesa expressed some interest in Christianity, it was really an interest in acquiring the technology Stanley carried with him that led Mutesa to accept a European and Christian presence in his kingdom.

The British government granted a charter to the Imperial British East Africa Company (IBEAC) in 1890. The IBEAC was entrusted with the administration of Uganda and Frederick Lugard was dispatched as its emissary. As Stanley had promised, Buganda gained firearms and Christian missionaries. The missions began to establish schools in Buganda—offering the Baganda an early educational advantage over other Ugandans. With the introduction of Christianity, the influence of Islam[3] declined. An intense rivalry between Protestants and Catholics ensued, as each competed for converts. Religious denomination thus became a new fissure in Ugandan society.

Religious tensions culminated in the Catholic-Protestant War of 1892, in which Lugard played a pivotal role. Lugard was ordered to remain neutral except that, if battle broke out, he was to support the Protestant converts of the British missions, rather than the Catholic converts of the French missions. The Protestants then won a decisive victory.

Colonial Era

By the mid-1890s, the IBEAC had overextended itself.[4] On the verge of bankruptcy, it could no longer continue to look after Britain's interests in Uganda. As a result, Uganda was officially declared a British protectorate in August 1894. Uganda became a showcase for Britain's policy of indirect rule. Unlike Kenya (perhaps because of the kingdom states admired by British administrators), Uganda was never meant to be settled by Europeans. Chiefs retained power, although their role was dictated by the British. Traditional elements of Baganda rule were transplanted to all kingdoms, where the deployment of Baganda representatives was received with deep resentment by the non-Baganda. Land was held communally in a variety of forms. They included: customary, mailo, leasehold and freehold. In exchange for their assistance to the British, the Baganda were rewarded with large tracts of land (from other kingships).

Compounding matters, the British sought recruits into the army solely from the north. They believed the peoples of Acholi, Lango and West Nile to be more "martial" and "warlike" than other Ugandans. As a consequence, the "ethnically biased" army assembled by the British was composed of a group traditionally hostile to the ethnically biased administration.

The tension between Buganda and the rest of the country was further exacerbated under the 1900 Buganda Agreement, whereby Buganda gained the special status of "province," while the other kingships remained simply districts. Buganda enjoyed social and educational services earlier, and also grew cash crops before her compatriots. When farms were established by the Baganda, they employed a labor force from other parts of the country.

While Africans participated in the fringes of Uganda's commercial and government activities, the direction and control of national economic strategy were solely in the hands of Europeans. Society was divided along racial lines. From the late nineteenth century to the end of World War II, the British encouraged the entry of Asians (largely from India and Pakistan) into the commercial sector. The Asians were by no means a unified group, varying by origin and religion; they sought to maintain their own cultures while forming a successful and distinct immigrant community. Asians were granted exclusive rights to buy and market local produce. They were encouraged to buy land and given ready access to export licenses and credit facilities. Africans were mostly peasant farmers, while the Europeans were involved in large-scale crop marketing or administration. Asians came to dominate the commercial sector alongside the British. Despite these ethnic-economic separations, social mobility was never entirely restricted by race, and (in sharp contrast to Kenya), social relations between Europeans and Africans were not bound by strict notions of "master-servant" relationships.[5] Indeed, indigenous Ugandans entered into official tasks by 1920. Nonetheless, the Asian population achieved economic success unmatched by the Africans.

During the 1950s, the country's chief sources of foreign exchange were coffee and cotton. These two crops accounted for 85% of the total value of Uganda's exports. All cotton and 90% of coffee were grown by peasant farmers.

By 1960, the political climate was changing. Uganda's independence from Britain was imminent. British Prime Minister Harold Macmillan delivered his sweeping "Wind of Change" address, capturing the spirit of British policy towards all of Africa: "The wind of change is blowing through the continent. Whether we like it or not, this growth of national consciousness is a political fact."[6] Kabaka Mutesa, on the eve of Uganda's independence, expressed Buganda's concern over the coming changes: "We had struggled long and hard to retain our integrity during the life of the Protectorate Government. Now the situation was different.... Where would we stand in an independent Uganda?"[7] While the Kabaka was apprehensive, other Ugandans looked to political independence as the key to breaking economic dependence and stimulating growth.

Independence

Uganda as a nation must make the following choice: either the... autocracy will accede to the needs of a modern state with an all-embracing representative government, or else the prognosis for the future will be one of increasing ethnic and parochial strife.[8]

Upon receiving independence in 1962, Uganda's future appeared promising. The country's economy was one of the strongest on the continent. Her school system and health care were among the best. Farmers were growing coffee, tea, cotton and tobacco. Small-scale copper mining had started and the manufacturing sector had begun to expand.

At independence, the Asian segment of the population was given a choice: they could maintain their Indian or Pakistani citizenship, or they could become British or Ugandan citizens. Many hesitated, considering their options. Africans saw this as demonstrating a lack of confidence in the country, increasing the level of racial tension.

From the political groups vying for power at independence, two leading parties emerged and struggled to gain political control in a political environment modeled on Britain's parliamentary system. The Democratic Party (DP) and the Uganda people's Congress (UPC) shaped their identities along ethnic and religious lines. The DP was a primarily Catholic party which captured the support of the Bantu south. The UPC was Protestant based, with a strong constituency in the north. The UPC leader, Milton Obote (a northerner from Lango and an outspoken proponent of African independence), recognized the necessity of Baganda support for winning the first post-independence elections. A political party to represent the interests of the Buganda and the Kabaka was assembled, the Kabaka Yekka (KY, meaning Kabaka Only). Obote negotiated an alliance with the KY, which led to the UPC victory in the 1962 elections. Dividing the spoils of electoral success with the KY, the Kabaka of Buganda, Mutesa II, was named Uganda's first president and Obote, its prime minister.

Initially the transition to independence was peaceful, but it quickly disintegrated owing to cleavage politics and ethnic power struggles. Obote's UPC and the KY formed an odd-ball coalition. The marriage of north and south was one of convenience, rather than a manifestation of genuine national unity. With a weak coalition government bound by self-interest and no clear national strategy by which to advance the political and economic development of the country, Uganda seemed ill prepared for the challenges of independence. In addition to the differences with the KY, deep fissures began to appear within the UPC, first between ideological left and right, then along ethnic lines between Nilotics and Bantus.

Meanwhile, civil war was breaking out next door in the Congo (Zaire). Members of the KY accused Obote and a general in his army, Idi Amin, of misappropriating funds received from Congo rebels. In response to these allegations, Obote suspended the constitution, declared himself president for life and deported the Kabaka. He put the military on double pay in order to win their favor. The traditional kingdoms were dismantled just four years after independence. By 1969, Obote announced the "Move to the Left," a national plan to establish Socialism[9] on the Ghanaian model. The objectives of this plan were twofold: to cultivate national unity under UPC leadership, and to consolidate and expand Obote's political power.

Amin's Regime (1971–1979)

Over time, the relationship between Obote and Amin became strained. When Obote left the country to attend a conference in Singapore in January 1971, Amin mounted a military coup. Amin supplanted Obote's dictatorship with an even more authoritarian one of his own.

Amin was initially well received by the Ugandan population. Moreover, Britain welcomed the news of his accession; the Conservative government had been alarmed by Obote's leftist leanings, and, in particular, his intent to nationalize banks and other commercial enterprises. As a general, Amin was well aware of the power of the dominant faction in the army, composed of Acholis and Langis (Obote's ethnic affiliation). Although also from the north of the country, Amin was a Nubian and Muslim. Fearing army loyalty to Obote, Amin massacred the Langi and Acholi soldiers, replacing them with soldiers of his own ethnicity. By 1972, Uganda had become a military state in which politics was forbidden, with Amin as its autocratic leader.[10]

In 1972 in an attempt to curry popular favor, Amin announced his intent to "Africanize" the economy. On August 4 he ordered all Asians who held foreign passports to return to their country of citizenship within 90 days (estimates of the 1972 Asian population ranged from 50,000 to 70,000). He simultaneously expropriated their assets. At the time, many Africans lauded Amin's decision. The fact that East African Asians owned the bulk of assets in Uganda was greatly resented by many Africans. Some Africans held up the 1972 expulsions as "one of the few positive legacies of his [Amin's] regime."[11] For the first time, they argued, Africans had access to commercial markets. But grave economic dislocation followed. Recalling the events of the 1970s, a Ugandan citizen said:

Firms quickly collapsed due to a lack of capital, dwindling inventories and a lack of business experience on the part of the new owners.... Shops were given to people who didn't even know where to order the new inventories from. Everyone just thought the money was coming from heaven. Within three years, the government was faced with...an economy in shambles. [12]

Properties confiscated from the Asians were doled out to Amin's cronies. For instance, Amin promoted an army sergeant to the rank of colonel and appointed him manager of one of Uganda's largest companies: the previously Asian-owned Kakira sugar factory. Godfrey Lule, Amin's attorney general, recalled that the colonel: "knew nothing about management, but these people were above the law. They were untouchable. They were the government."[13]

Civil War (1972–1986)

Obote, having trained a Ugandan guerrilla group while exiled in Tanzania, launched an invasion from Tanzania in 1972. Civil war ensued. In reprisal for guerrilla attacks, Amin's soldiers terrorized civilians and prisoners of war were executed publicly. War and anarchy ravaged the country. Many commercial and industrial sectors were devastated, while institutions such as the renowned Makerere University, collapsed. The economy's market infrastructure was destroyed, forcing farmers to return to subsistence cultivation. Refugees fled the country, including a large fraction of Uganda's intellectuals, such as Makerere-trained doctors and engineers.

In 1976, Amin's international reputation plummeted further when an Air France jet with 103 Israeli and Jewish passengers was hijacked by members of the Popular Front for the Liberation of Palestine and forced to land at Entebbe Airport (Uganda's only international airport). When it became clear that Amin was assisting the hijackers, the international community was aghast. Israel launched a dramatic rescue, destroying most of Uganda's air force.

In 1978, Amin invaded Tanzania, claiming that Uganda was under attack by Tanzanian forces. Exiled guerrilla forces were based in Tanzania, as was the future president, Museveni.[14] In the resulting war, Tanzania—with the assistance of 1,000 Ugandans—defeated Amin's troops in January 1979. Finally, Amin's rule of terror came to an end.

Immediately afterward, several interim governments attempted to establish order in Uganda, but without success. Following the devastation under Amin, Milton Obote returned to power in 1980. He gained favor from Western governments by abandoning Socialist policies in favor of World Bank aid. Under Obote, Uganda began to receive external assistance in order to finance domestic reforms.

But Obote's legitimacy was weak. He had gained power in disputed elections while bringing back memories of corruption and ethnic division. The killing continued and the death toll during the Obote regime was subsequently estimated to exceed 300,000. Museveni formed the National Resistance Movement (NRM) in 1981 to oppose Obote. Begun in the bush with just 34 guerrillas, the NRM later grew to thousands, and its victory in the resistance war of 1981-1986 placed Museveni in power.

The economy Museveni inherited in 1986 was in a disastrous state. Between 1970 and 1980, Uganda's GDP had declined by 25%, import volumes by almost 50%, and exports by 60%. Massive increases in military expenditures had inflated the government budget deficit. Annual inflation exceeded 70%.

The Washington Consensus

Clearly we needed some outside help.... I think where the IMF helped us was in making us realise the importance of macro-economic tools, such as letting prices find their own level. This was something many of our people did not understand at first. They wanted to concentrate on producing goods rather than spending time working on macro-economic stimuli.

—President Museveni, 1997[15]

Although it managed to consolidate political and military control, the new Museveni government was overwhelmed by the economic woes of the country. Unilateral attempts at stabilization failed miserably. After one year, Museveni asked the World Bank and the International Monetary Fund to assist him in re-introducing economic stability. Following negotiations, President Museveni committed Uganda to a program of economic reform that was a textbook application of the Washington Consensus—the recipe for economic stability and growth prescribed by the IMF, World Bank and U.S. Treasury Department, all based in Washington, DC.

The program adopted a two-pronged approach. Macroeconomic stabilization aimed to eliminate inflation and bring Uganda's external accounts into a sustainable position. The IMF viewed fiscal imbalances as the root cause of macroeconomic instability. According to this view, government deficits were being financed by "printing money" in various guises. Specifically, the government was forcing the commercial banks to finance the deficit at artificially low nominal interest rates. The resulting loss of monetary control and the excessive demand arising from deficit spending was then responsible for inflation, trade deficits and external financing problems.

If fiscal rectitude was the key to macroeconomic stabilization, structural reform was the route to economic growth. The Washington Consensus was based on the belief that the market would efficiently allocate and distribute resources. Uganda's declining growth was attributable to excessive intervention in the market. Only by liberalizing the commodity, product, labor and financial markets—and exposing them to the competitive pressures of international competition—could efficiency in production and allocation be achieved and economic growth reignited.

Fiscal Policy

A restrictive fiscal policy was required to eliminate the government deficit and achieve financial and macroeconomic stability. In accordance with these objectives, government officials, under IMF supervision, concentrated on cutting government spending and raising revenue (**Exhibit 5**). Revenue was increased in part by privatizing public assets. Tax reform raised tax rates and enlarged the income tax base while the strengthening of the Uganda Revenue Authority (URA) increased the amount of tax collected. Nevertheless, Uganda was heavily reliant on donor support to finance domestic reforms. By 1996, her total stock of outstanding public external debt had grown to $3.4 billion.[16] This combination of fiscal tightening and increased aid allowed Uganda to arrest the previous pattern of bank borrowing to cover the fiscal deficit. As a consequence, Uganda was able to repay 17 billion Ugandan shillings[17] to the banking system—equivalent to 8% of initial money stock. By 1993, the government was a net creditor to the domestic banking system for the first time. Monetary policy could be directed towards price and exchange rate stability.

Exchange Rate Policy

In May 1987, at the outset of the IMF program, there was an initial 77% devaluation of the Ugandan shilling against the U.S. dollar (**Exhibit 6b**). Through October 1989, the official exchange rate was devalued several times to maintain and promote the competitiveness of Ugandan exports. Subsequently, the Ugandan authorities pursued a more flexible exchange rate policy, moving towards a market-determined exchange rate. Following the introduction of the more flexible exchange rate system, more realistic pricing by the market relieved the chronic shortage of foreign exchange that had previously constrained economic activity.

In 1987, the government established an open general licensing (OGL) system for foreign exchange, which was expanded in 1988. Under this system, rationing of foreign exchange and restrictions on the use of overseas earnings were removed for selected industrial firms and certain commodities. Progressively, entry to this foreign exchange market was liberalized. The IMF-sponsored structural adjustment policies implemented by Uganda sought to establish convertibility of the Ugandan shilling (that is, to create a unified free market in which shillings could be converted into foreign exchange). Convertibility for current account transactions was achieved in 1992, while capital account transactions became unrestricted in 1997.

Monetary Policy and Financial Sector Reform

Prior to reform, the IMF believed Uganda's under-developed financial sector was a severe constraint on growth. Only 70% of the economy was monetized (**Exhibit 3b**). The barter system was still a significant means of trade in goods and services. The ratio of broad money[18] to GDP was only 9% in 1995 (the ratio for Kenya was 45% and Tanzania, 35%). The government owned and controlled a large fraction of Uganda's banking sector and competition was lacking. Until 1992, interest rates were set by the Bank of Uganda (BOU), usually at levels well below inflation rates. The resultant negative real interest rates discouraged domestic private saving. Moreover, as discussed above, the banks were forced to finance the government and public corporations at artificially low interest rates, weakening their balance sheets and crowding out lending for productive private sector activity.

In pursuit of financial liberalization,[19] government officials sought to establish a market-based system of monetary control. From 1992, interest rates were liberalized significantly, and a unified treasury bill market was established. The Bank of Uganda relaxed reserve requirements and introduced open market operations in treasury bills as an instrument of monetary policy. At the same time, the Bank of Uganda ceased to be wholly subservient to the government and its fiscal needs. It was given some autonomy in both the setting of monetary policy and the management of foreign exchange reserves (**Exhibit 6a**). In response to Uganda's "bad loan saga"—the massive overhang of bad loans resulting from the politically directed lending of the pre-reform era—the Financial Institutions Act was introduced to strengthen both the BOU's supervisory capacity and the banking sector at large. A Non-Performing Assets Recovery Trust (NPART) was established in order to salvage 70 billion Uganda shillings in bad loans acquired by the Uganda Commercial Bank (UCB). The UCB, which had become mired in a morass of non-performing loans (due to poor lending practices), was privatized in October 1997.

Following the end of the civil war in 1987, gross domestic savings were estimated to be -12.6% of GDP. The macroeconomic stabilization efforts, particularly the reduction of inflation rates and the establishment of positive real interest rates, led to an increase in the domestic savings rate to 2.2% in 1993-1994. Low domestic savings rates forced Uganda to rely on foreign savings to finance domestic investment and growth. This came largely in the form of unilateral grants or concessional official loans, although the abolition of capital controls and the introduction of capital account convertibility were intended to attract private capital inflows.

Market, Trade & Foreign Investment Liberalization

Beginning in 1990, Uganda made the privatization[20] and restructuring of public enterprises a central part of government policy, instituting the Public Enterprise Reform and Divestiture Program in collaboration with the World Bank. Public flotation of companies and auction of public enterprises (about 20 major enterprises) took place. The Uganda Electricity Board was privatized in 1997. Uganda sold most of her state industries which encouraged significant levels of foreign investment (although some went to returning Asians at zero cost), and boosted domestic production and investment; 27 of 43 government enterprises privatized were bought by Ugandans.[21]

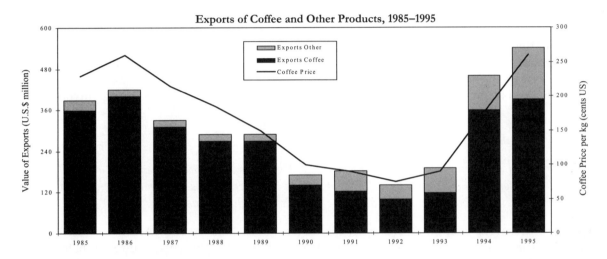

Exports of Coffee and Other Products, 1985–1995

Traditional agricultural exports were believed to be a key determinant of Uganda's growth performance. Therefore, Uganda liberalized domestic food and agricultural commodity prices and abolished marketing boards. "Surrender requirements" on export proceeds from traditional crops were abolished. After the liberalization of coffee prices, profits declined for the oligopolistic "middle men" (largely foreign-owned), and greater returns were reaped by Ugandan farmers.

Unfortunately, Uganda's terms of trade deteriorated as world coffee prices declined by 50% with the collapse of the International Coffee Agreement in 1987. Uganda abolished the tax on coffee exports in 1992, and broke up the processing, marketing and export cartels. From 1992–1994, coffee prices—boosted by the freeze damage to Brazil's crop in mid-1994—nearly tripled. Subsequently, exports of coffee grew significantly. Nonetheless, coffee exports of approximately 2.2 million bags in 1993–1994 were less than the 3.5 million bags exported in 1972–1973.

Uganda reduced most tariffs and abolished quotas. In 1993, Uganda lowered her highest import duty from 80% to 30%, and reduced her lowest import duty from 50% to 10%. The average tariff rate ranged from 14% to 19% in 1996. Foreign direct investment rules were also dramatically liberalized. The Uganda Investment Authority, established in 1991, licensed over 2,000 projects to foreign investors. Moreover, the Uganda Securities Exchange was launched in 1997 to attract inward portfolio investment.

Museveni's National Programs

Uganda needs two things. We need infrastructure and we need foreign investment.... The rest we shall do by ourselves.

—President Museveni, 1996[22]

Infrastructure & Regional Trade

While heeding the IMF's requests, Museveni's government spent resources on infrastructure, including the restoration of transportation and communications systems destroyed during the civil war. Sixty-five percent of the country's total network of roads was rehabilitated by 1995 (**Exhibit 2**).

Museveni spearheaded efforts to re-establish a regional trading bloc in East Africa in order to increase trade flows and encourage investment in the region.[23] This led to verbal agreements for a free trade regime among the countries of eastern and southern Africa. Existing trade links were weak, but the potential for improved trade flows, efficiency and integration appeared vast, especially for landlocked Uganda. In 1997, Kenya, Tanzania and Uganda conducted a comprehensive study to harmonize customs tariffs, and the three countries signed a tripartite double taxation agreement. The regionalization of the stock exchanges of Kenya, Tanzania and Uganda was also being pursued.

Social Programs

The effects of AIDS on village life are devastating.... Ugandans are buried in their traditional villages and it is customary for all the dead person's colleagues to attend the funeral. This can mean that entire government departments are absent for days at a time, attending funerals in far-flung parts.[24]

Before Museveni took office, the open discussion of sex (and even of AIDS) was off limits in Uganda as in much of the rest of Africa. AIDS spread rapidly, particularly through heterosexual intercourse. Museveni responded by personally leading a massive educational campaign of unsettling frankness. Meanwhile, international donors reacted to the epidemic by providing large amounts of assistance. The Aids Education Center, supported in part by grants from the U.S. government, offered anonymous same-day tests at low cost in several locations. According to health workers, these efforts led to a vast change in sexual behavior. At the same time, UNAIDS/WHO estimates of the fraction of adults infected with HIV in Uganda declined from 13% in 1994 to 9.5% in 1997. Elsewhere in southern Africa, the infection rate was rising rapidly. In 1997, it reached 25% in Botswana and Zimbabwe.

The government also sought to rebuild educational institutions. Museveni set a goal of 100% attendance for children in primary school (the number stood at 70% in 1997). To encourage enrollment, the Universal Primary Education initiative increased access to free education. The government set aside $28.6 million for the program and additional funding was to be provided by the World Bank.

The government also launched a poverty eradication plan (PEP) to improve infrastructure by opening up rural areas via upgrading existing truck roads and constructing feeder roads. This modernized agriculture through the control of agricultural pests, parasites and diseases and by strengthening links between farmers and extension workers. To improve Uganda's water supply, 45 water supply projects were underway in 1997, with 34 others under construction. [25]

Institution Building

Measures to curb corruption were introduced into law. For example, the position of Inspector General of Government was created to seek disclosure of assets by members of the government. Measures to ensure greater transparency and accountability within the government were gradually being adopted. Swift legal action was taken against leaders suspected of scandal. For example, five top commanders of the army were suspended and arrested on charges of embezzlement in 1997, and the former Cabinet Minister of Justice/Attorney General was charged with theft. An increasingly independent media was instrumental in exposing and reporting corruption to the public. Even so, corruption was one of the most insidious challenges faced by the country.

Museveni believed a smaller, more efficient administration was a prerequisite for economic success. The civil service was promptly reformed. Improved personnel management systems were introduced and government functions decentralized. From 1990 to 1995, the civil service was reduced in size, from 320,000 positions to 145,000. In addition, the government carried out an army demobilization program, reducing the size of the army by half, from 90,000 to 45,000 over the same period. As a result, Uganda cut military expenditure by a total of $87.4 million between 1993 and 1995. Discharged soldiers were re-integrated into other sectors of the economy. But by 1996, this trend was being reversed, as military spending increased due to recurring instability in northern Uganda as well as to the west, in the former Zaire (**Exhibit 6c).**

National Resistance Councils and Consultative Democracy

The African man must control his destiny by democratic means.

—President Museveni, 1997[26]

Museveni was doubtful of the benefits of Western multi-party democracy, fearing its impact on a society torn by economic, ethnic and religious divisions. Resistance Councils, tested in the bush during the Resistance War, were his preferred method of establishing legitimacy. In effect, the adults in a village (the electorate) would first form a Resistance Council (RC). The RC would then elect a committee of nine members to run the local affairs of the village on a daily basis. The range of responsibilities of the committee was wide, encompassing judicial powers, security as well as building schools and medical facilities. The villages thus gained a great deal of autonomy over their local affairs. Previously, the governance of the villages fell under the umbrella of the districts so funding went to the district rather than to the localities themselves.

The structure of the system as a whole would place the districts and central government at the top of a pyramid of local authorities. The RCs (renamed LCs by the Local Government Act of 1996) would elect representatives to higher tiers of councils, up to the level of parliament. The aim, according to Museveni's construct, was for Uganda to "develop from below while strengthening, not weakening or bypassing, the center."[27]

A Constituent Assembly (CA) was elected by universal suffrage in 1994. In 1995, after the National Resistance Council (the legislature) surrendered jurisdiction over the preparation of a new constitution to the CA, the CA produced this constitution.[28]

Land Tenure

Prior to 1987, considerable land was held under several forms of communal ownership. By 1998, a Land Bill finally passed, following a series of heated debates by Ugandan citizens. The Bill's intent was to establish a uniform system of land tenure throughout the country, based more closely on individual property rights. This undertaking called for extensive legal reform, a challenge compounded by the multiplicity of languages spoken by Ugandans and the adherence to varying customary laws, depending on ethnicity and religion. The bill was controversial, setting off a series of tense discussions among participants. For instance, the Baganda worried that all of their land was to be given away. Many others worried that Ugandans would be unable to afford the cost of registering their certificates of land ownership. In addition, the question of how the land in the north was to be surveyed, given the activity of the Lord's Resistance Army, was raised.[29] While progress was made, these dilemmas continued to frustrate the land reform process.

Rural Poverty

Eighty-three percent of the Ugandan population lived in rural areas in 1993 and were engaged almost entirely in agriculture. Of the 2.5 million farm households, 80% cultivated less than 2.5 hectares of land each.[30] Nearly 55% of food crop production was for subsistence. Crop yields were low and rural poverty persisted. The World Bank attributed low yields to "lack [of] access to improved technologies and inputs." Even so, Uganda remained self-sufficient in food production.

Key Outcomes

Uganda achieved stabilization with strong economic growth.... Inflation has remained low, with an annual rate of 6.0%.... Savings and investment have risen, and the export sector has performed very well.... This continues the remarkable trend in Uganda's economic performance... the economy has grown by 35% in real terms.

—The IMF, 1996[31]

The economy began to recover rapidly. On the local level, small markets sprang up, a consequence of local improvisation and individual initiative. The country's physical infrastructure, particularly in and around the capital city, was restored. The commercial sector—comprised, in large part, of the tea estates and business enterprises formerly owned by the Asian population—was being revived. In an attempt both to redress past wrongs and to boost economic performance, President Museveni encouraged the East African Asians to return and resume ownership of their seized properties.[32] About 4,000 of the 7,500 properties seized were returned to their original owners. By 1995, 2,000 Asians had returned, but many only to sell their assets.[33]

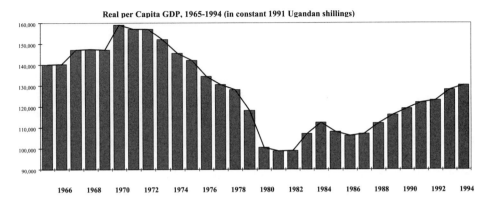

Real per Capita GDP, 1965-1994 (in constant 1991 Ugandan shillings)

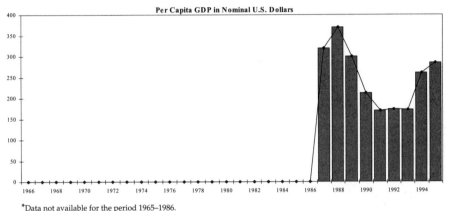

Per Capita GDP in Nominal U.S. Dollars

*Data not available for the period 1965–1986.

During the eight years of stabilization, growth averaged approximately 7% per year (1987–1994). By 1993, total recurrent government revenue had climbed to 9% of GDP. Inflation was curbed and stood at 10% in April 1997. On the other hand, the external current account deficit (excluding grants), worsened significantly as a percentage of GDP: from 8.5% in 1988-1989, to 16.9% in 1993–1994. Moreover, Uganda remained one of the world's poorest nations: its per capita GDP was only $240 in 1996.

While macroeconomic discipline, driven by the Washington Consensus, steered Uganda toward a more stable economic environment, illiteracy remained high and infant mortality rates increased. The World Bank did not attribute these problems to the reforms themselves. After a battery of poverty studies conducted until 1993, the World Bank concluded: "Most Ugandans appear not to have been adversely affected by the social costs of adjustment."[34]

At the same time, inequality increased. Much of the economic growth was concentrated in the south while the population in the north remained impoverished. Poverty was concentrated in the rural areas of the north, where 81% of the population had a real per capita monthly expenditure of less than 6,000 Ugandan shillings, equivalent to approximately $5.00.

Museveni's invitation to Asians prompted much speculation about a revival of the enmity among Africans and Asians. Although an underlying current of racial tension may have persisted, some Africans welcomed the Asians back, acknowledging the leading role the Asians traditionally played in the economic life of the country. The return of Asian capital to Uganda boosted foreign direct investment, from $113 million in 1995–1996 to $160 million in 1996–1997.[35]

Museveni made it a practice to invite individuals from a wide range of ethnic groups, including former enemies, into his cabinet to achieve stability and to gain representation from most districts. He had the Kabaka crowned as cultural head of Buganda. He also sought to ensure greater representation from African women in the political sphere. During the resistance war, Museveni invited women to take to the bush. Since then, he appointed a woman as his vice president and established a quota system by which women would be encouraged to hold political office. The army was effectively disciplined, and the abuses characteristic of preceding administrations were curbed.

Museveni was criticized for excessive spending on defense, particularly by the United States. Meanwhile, violence continued in the north, particularly at the hands of the Lord's Resistance Army. Two game parks in northern and western Uganda were closed to tourists in November 1997, due to security threats posed by LRA guerrilla activities. At root, the economic and political dominance of the south still provoked resistance from the north, impeding Museveni's progress towards peace.

Political upheaval in the region was one of the principal concerns of investors. Uganda's neighbors included such unstable countries as the Democratic Republic of Congo, Kenya, Rwanda and the Sudan. Museveni had an active foreign policy and was allegedly a principal player in attempts to depose rulers of neighboring states.

Since 1986, Museveni had imposed a ban on opposition political party activity and refused multi-party elections, repeatedly citing the ills of "tribalism"[36] to defend his government against demands for Western-style democracy. Museveni declared: "Western democracies criticise our system of government, but we ignore them.... They do not even research the Ugandan situation properly, but would just have their own system imposed on Uganda."[37] After postponing elections three times (the postponements were granted by the CA; Museveni effectively argued that his administration hadn't sufficient time to carry out reforms), Museveni finally capitulated to democratic pressures in 1996. He won the majority of votes. There were conflicting views as to the effect the ban on multi-party activity had on the development of the country's political culture. For instance, those who supported the ban claimed that Museveni managed to put this small East African economy in a different league. They contended that this could occur only after ethnic differences moved from the center of African life to the periphery.

Those who supported a multi-party system argued that Museveni's monopoly on power encouraged the type of one-party rule which had been abused by previous regimes. Critics warned that the existing system placed too much authority at the top without building the institutions to perpetuate economic success beyond Museveni's political tenure. Opponents claimed that, because they could not hold public rallies or sell membership cards, they were deprived of funds to run their national campaign offices.[38] A referendum was scheduled to be held by the Constituent Assembly in the year 2000, to determine whether a multi-party system should be re-introduced. Emmanuel Kirenga, Minister of State for Justice and Constitutional Affairs declared: "If the people decide in favour of the political parties, then the ban will be lifted."[39]

New Initiatives

External Debt

The size of Uganda's external debt remained troubling. During a debt crisis conference in 1997, it was noted:

> We continue to be concerned that the magnitudes of debt are unsustainable.... African countries devote a large proportion of their resources to servicing external debt when their social sectors and infrastructures are in dire need of rehabilitation and reform.[40]

The Museveni Administration regarded Uganda's total debt as unsustainable and negotiated the flow of required debt payments at regular intervals with bilateral and multilateral donors (**Exhibit 9**). In 1997, Uganda was selected as the first country to qualify for aid under the Heavily Indebted Poor Country (HIPC) initiative. Before this initiative, the World Bank and the IMF had not taken any steps to deal explicitly with the possibility that some of their loans might not be paid in full. Under this initiative, the two organizations gave joint assistance to countries whose debt burden they saw as unsustainable as long as these countries were deemed to be successfully implementing reforms. This assistance mostly took the form of grants that could be used to cover debt service obligations. In addition, the World Bank offered a new grant to fund free primary education. In total, the net present value of these grants was about $350 million, or about 20% of Uganda's foreign debt.

To receive this relief, Uganda had to continue its adherence to the IMF stabilization program for three years. Moreover, under World Bank stipulations, Uganda had to spend a specified amount of its budget on social and educational programs. Under the HIPC initiative, further grants would be considered if, after three years, the debt was still viewed as unsustainable.

Vision 2025

By the end of 1997, the IMF's program had achieved the macroeconomic stability that most observers regarded as necessary for Uganda's future development. However, many doubted that the structural reforms introduced by the Fund, which relied largely on market mechanisms, would prove sufficient to sustain growth and raise per capita incomes above the levels achieved in the early 1970s.

An influential group of ministers, led by Richard Kaijuka, the Minister for Economic Planning and Development, argued that the development model embodied in the IMF's program was inadequate. Minister Kaijuka advocated the introduction of a national development plan along Malaysian lines. During the second half of 1997, the Minister, in consultation with the academic, business and political communities, began to formulate Vision 2025 for Uganda, a development plan that drew its inspiration and title from Malaysia's[41] Vision 2020.

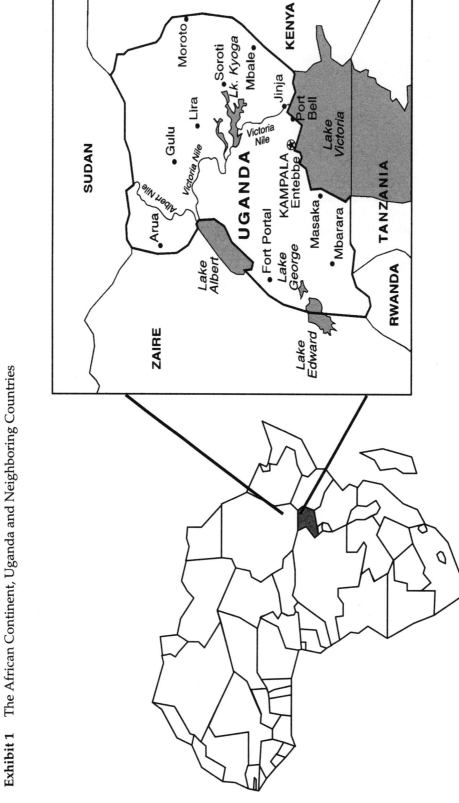

Exhibit 1   The African Continent, Uganda and Neighboring Countries

Exhibit 2   Social Indicators

	Uganda	Kenya	Sudan	Tanzania	Dem. Republic of Congo[a]
Infrastructure					
Telephone lines (per 1,000 people)	2	9	3	3	1
Number of roads, km, 1985	7,782	..	3,899	..	..
roads, km, 1995	10,000	25,838	5,200	18,100	..
Demographics					
Population (millions), 1996	19.6	26.7	28.1	29.7	43.9
Population growth rate,1995–2010					
(% per year)	2.6	2.2	2.2	2.6	..
Urban population, 1995 (%)	13%	28%	25%	24%	29%
Life expectancy at birth, 1995	M[d]-44	M-57	M- 52	M-50	..
	F[e]-44	F-60	F- 55	F-52	..
International poverty line[b], 1990					
(% population below poverty line)	50%	50%	..	16.4%	..
Urban poverty rate[c]	16%	29%	..	20%	..
Illiteracy rate, 1990	52%	31%	73%	..	28%
Population per physician, 1989–1991	22,399	21, 970	..	..	15,150
Health expenditures, 1990–1995					
(% of GDP)	3.9%	..	0.3%	..	..
Access to health services, 1993					
(% population)	71%	..	70%	93%	59%
Access to safe water, 1995					
(% population)	42%	28%	77%	49%	25%
Access to sanitation facilities, 1995					
(% population)	60%	49%	55%	86%	9%

Source: African Development Indicators; World Development Indicators, (Washington, DC: IBRD/World Bank, 1997).

Notes: [a]Formerly Zaire.

[b]The poverty line is set for all countries at one U.S. dollar per person per day, in 1985 international prices, and adjusted to local currency using exchange rates aimed at assuring purchasing power parity for consumption.

[c]Defined as the percentage of the population below 2/3 of the national mean per capita income.

[d]M=Male.

[e]F=Female.

Exhibit 3a   GDP at Constant (1991) Market Prices: Calendar Years 1986–1995 *(million shillings)*

	1986	1987	1988	1989	1990	1991	1992	1993	1994	1995
GDP @ factor cost	1,548,739	1,652,079	1,768,777	1,881,452	1,985,183	2,087,726	2,182,096	2,320,100	2,554,799	2,777,669
Indirect taxes	69,353	69,533	87,333	102,707	121,679	135,134	143,685	169,838	198,566	250,789
GDP @ market prices	1,618,092	1,721,612	1,856,110	1,984,159	2,106,862	2,222,860	2,325,781	2,489,937	2,753,365	3,028,459

Expenditure on GDP at Constant (1991) Market Prices: Calendar Years 1986–1995 *(million shillings)*

	1986	1987	1988	1989	1990	1991	1992	1993	1994	1995
Private consumption	1,476,278	1,561,779	1,701,427	1,814,710	1,905,276	1,995,117	2,062,076	2,170,531	2,455,296	2,687,547
Government consumption	178,202	186,499	163,088	177,419	196,529	206,111	216,001	235,768	255,172	277,298
Fixed capital formation	232,832	357,851	346,425	345,345	356,900	362,871	352,642	378,352	477,714	619,114
of which: Private	*111,473*	*137,111*	*134,059*	*148,645*	*172,711*	*193,379*	*200,752*	*228,580*	*307,006*	*391,314*
Public	*121,359*	*220,740*	*212,366*	*196,700*	*184,188*	*169,492*	*151,890*	*149,772*	*170,708*	*227,799*
Net change in stocks	0	0	0	0	0	1,099	-4,138	2,239	-5,424	-2,083
Exports	149,203	153,162	158,644	178,185	172,441	186,540	183,690	204,089	308,987	336,012
Imports	437,313	582,469	538,190	559,191	522,744	511,646	498,125	486,477	735,047	896,775
Expenditure measure of GDP	**1,599,203**	**1,676,822**	**1,831,394**	**1,956,468**	**2,108,402**	**2,240,091**	**2,312,147**	**2,504,503**	**2,756,697**	**3,021,114**
Statistical discrepancy	18,889	44,791	24,716	26,961	-1,541	-17,231	13,634	-14,566	-3,332	7,345
GDP at market prices	1,618,092	1,721,612	1,856,110	1,984,159	2,106,862	2,222,860	2,325,781	2,489,937	2,753,365	3,028,459

Exhibit 3b   GDP at Factor Cost at Current Prices: Calender Years 1986–1995 (*million shillings*)

Industry Group	1986	1987	1988	1989	1990	1991	1992	1993	1994	1995
Monetary										
Agriculture	14,899	54,350	153,669	281,855	365,487	510,765	850,905	868,544	1,260,706	1,366,845
Mining & quarrying	82	204	572	1,065	3,296	6,420	10,617	13,118	12,203	16,811
Manufacturing	3,382	10,660	35,428	59,711	87,485	122,487	193,812	237,589	289,108	354,480
Electricity/water	290	966	3,521	6,380	10,988	17,586	29,465	35,078	55,087	59,348
Construction	1,569	6,427	18,520	35,574	63,930	106,172	172,361	210,858	241,939	326,744
Wholesale & retail trade	9,305	31,251	85,760	148,787	183,526	237,290	386,134	408,943	506,726	578,923
Hotels & restaurants	576	2,053	6,470	11,803	17,545	26,786	43,188	56,406	75,490	94,079
Transport/ communication	1,757	6,437	18,361	38,905	58,599	87,968	133,017	157,573	178,143	221,021
Community services	7,060	20,717	68,793	119,197	200,456	317,577	510,459	654,911	751,024	895,152
Of which: Education	*1,580*	*4,704*	*16,523*	*30,640*	*51,933*	*75,863*	*117,877*	*167,693*	*182,272*	*207,319*
Health	*608*	*1,791*	*5,319*	*9,357*	*18,099*	*30,411*	*49,389*	*58,079*	*60,794*	*66,511*
Total monetary	38,920	133,065	391,096	703,277	991,311	1,433,053	2,329,958	2,643,020	3,370,426	3,913,403
Nonmonetary										
Agriculture	21,125	75,864	198,652	386,615	451,151	575,334	1,045,284	955,373	1,232,599	1,197,785
Construction	528	1,676	5,123	8,584	11,842	15,883	23,559	27,310	26,939	28,638
Owner-occupied dwellings	1,620	4,990	15,198	25,240	47,102	63,457	91,743	106,720	122,863	164,617
Total nonmonetary	23,273	82,530	218,974	420,438	510,095	654,674	1,160,586	1,089,404	1,382,401	1,391,039
Total GDP	62,193	215,595	610,070	1,123,715	1,501,406	2,087,726	3,490,544	3,732,424	4,752,827	5,304,443
Per capita GDP	4,234	14,283	39,306	70,373	91,399	123,534	199,471	206,634	255,158	276,388
GDP cost deflator (1991=100)	4.0	13.0	34.5	59.8	75.6	100	160.1	160.9	179.1	191.1

Source: The Republic of Uganda (Kampala: *Key Economic Indicators*, 1996), pp. 2 & 9. Prepared by the Ministry of Planning & Economic Development.

Exhibit 4 Balance of Payments (*million U.S. dollars*)

	1987–88	1988–89	1989–90	1990–91	1991–92	1992–93	1993–94	1994–95	1995–96	1996–97
Current Account	**-201**	**-230**	**-278**	**-187**	**-132**	**-96**	**-87**	**-164**	**-229**	**-221**
Trade Balance	-246	-281	-375	-370	-279	-416	-465	-508	-627	-607
Exports, fob	*298*	*282*	*210*	*176*	*172*	*157*	*237*	*577*	*590*	*622*
Imports, cif	*545*	*562*	*584*	*545*	*451*	*573*	*703*	*1085*	*1217*	*1229*
Non-factor services	-111	-128	-56	-102	-108	-131	-90	-210	-247	-268
Net factor payments	-57	-67	77	-58	-87	-49	-42	-63	-48	-18
Private unilateral transfers	120	114	78	81	136	241	270	355	421	371
Official unilateral transfers	92	131	153	262	206	259	258	261	273	301
Capital Account	**128**	**133**	**233**	**86**	**10**	**88**	**157**	**305**	**248**	**331**
Official	56	56	48	122	38	127	178	284	152	124
of which: Disbursements	186	211	292	214	163	231	294	377	235	230
Import support	*45*	*68*	*167*	*99*	*69*	*84*	*119*	*..*	*..*	*..*
Project support	*141*	*143*	*125*	*115*	*94*	*148*	*175*	*..*	*..*	*..*
Amortization due[1]	*..*	*..*	*..*	*-92*	*-125*	*-104*	*-115*	*-93*	*-83*	*-106*
Private[2]	72	77	185	-36	-28	-39	-22	21	96	207
Overall Balance	-74	-96	-45	-101	-121	-8	70	141	20	110
Financing	..	..	22	-15	-24	-38	-107	-169	-92	-134
Change in Reserves	..	..	-19	65	98	-330	-55	0	0	0
Change in Arrears[3]	..	..	42	51	47	376	92	28	72	24

Sources: The Republic of Uganda (Kampala: *Background to the Budget 1997–98*, 1997), Prepared by the Ministry of Planning & Economic Development; IMF staff estimates (Washington, DC: *Uganda Background Paper/IMF Staff Country Report No. 95/44*, 1995), p. 59.

Notes: [1] Amortization is principal payment due on outstanding debt.
[2] Includes commercial banks, private direct investment, and errors and omissions.
[3] Arrears are unpaid interest and principal payments owed to foreigners.

Exhibit 5 Summary of Government Budget and Financial Operations, Fiscal Years (*million shillings*)

Budget[1]	1994–1995 Out-Turn	1995–1996 Out-Turn	1996-1997 Out-Turn
Revenue and Grants	**785,070**	**947,813**	**1,095,435**
Revenue	531,194	622,790	744,344
Of which: *Income Taxes*	77,170	82,918	101,097
Trade Related: Indirect Taxes	205,154	250,353	301,194
Non-Trade Rel.: Indirect Taxes	188,404	246,201	319,467
Other	60,466	43,318	22,586
Grants	253,876	325,023	351,091
Total Expenditure	**916,624**	**1,060,685**	**1,215,626**
Recurrent expenditure	501,263	568,230	647,383
Of which: *Salaries & Wages*	128,721	170,335	233,902
Interest	53,362	47,662	55,954
Other recurrent	319,180	350,233	360,527
Development expenditure	404,014	489,655	566,243
Net lending	11,347	2,800	2,000
Overall deficit	**-131,554**	**-112,872**	**-120,193**
Excluding grants	-385,430	-437,895	-471,283
Change in arrears[2]	-22,182	-34,200	-30,000
Adjusted to cash	28,718	-2,098	-29,218
Overall deficit	-125,018	-149,170	-179,410
Financing	125,018	149,170	179,410
Foreign	211,719	209,432	231,400
Domestic	-86,701	-60,262	-51,990
Banking system[3]	-95,400	-29,300	-93,500
Non-bank	8,699	-30,962	41,510

Sources: The Republic of Uganda (Kampala: *Background to the Budget 1997–98, 1997*), Prepared by the Ministry of Planning & Economic Development, p. A17.

Notes: [1]For financial years ending in March.

[2]Both foreign and domestic.

[3]Bank of Uganda and commercial banks.

Exhibit 6a   Money and Credit, Fiscal Years[1] (*billion shillings*)

	1987–1988	1988–1989	1989–1990	1990–1991	1991–1992	1992–93	1993–94
Net foreign assets	-11.9	-43.1	-87.3	-151.5	-271.0	-207.2	-76.7
Bank of Uganda	-12.9	-45.2	-91.6	-165.8	-313.1	-277.4	-163.5
Commercial banks	1.0	2.1	4.3	14.3	42.1	70.2	86.8
Net domestic assets	40.3	103.4	181.8	290.1	507.8	545.2	505.5
Domestic credit	19.0	52.8	84.7	120.7	190.4	208.7	200.9
Claims on Government, net	6.7	10.2	14.0	12.9	57.2	40.0	-12.6
Claims on the private sector	12.3	42.6	70.7	107.8	133.2	168.7	213.5
Crop finance	*4.5*	*19.5*	*24.4*	*40.5*	*38.4*	*48.0*	*53.6*
Other private sector	*7.8*	*23.1*	*46.3*	*67.3*	*94.8*	*120.7*	*159.9*
Other items, net	21.3	50.6	97.1	169.4	317.4	336.5	304.6
Broad money-M2	27.2	60.5	94.4	138.6	212.7	301.9	402.6
Currency and demand deposits	*24.6*	*54.5*	*81.4*	*116.1*	*166.5*	*221.9*	*292.6*
Time and savings deposits	*2.6*	*6.0*	*13.0*	*22.5*	*46.2*	*80.0*	*110.0*
Foreign exchange deposits of residents	..	..	..	..	24.3	36.1	51.5
Monetization rates			*(In percent)*				
Monetary GDP/total GDP	65.1	65.2	65.7	68.4	69.4	68.1	68.7
M2/GDP	6.9	6.7	6.8	7.6	7.8	7.8	8.7
M2/monetary GDP	10.7	10.3	10.3	11.1	11.3	11.4	12.7
Cash/M2	53.7	48.4	40.9	40.6	39.7	33.1	33.7
Total deposits/GDP	3.2	3.5	4.0	4.5	4.7	5.2	5.8

Source: Statistics Department, Ministry of Finance and Economic Planning, *Key Economic Indicators*, 25th Issue, April 1996.

Note: [1]Stocks at end-March of each fiscal year.

Exhibit 6b Interest Rates, Inflation, and Exchange Rates, Fiscal Years (percent *per annum*)

	1987–88	1988–89	1989–90	1990–91	1991–92	1992–93	1993–94	1994–95	1995–96	1996–97
Interest rates										
91-day treasury bill rate	38.0	43.0	39.0	37.0	32.0	24.0	11.0	12.6	8.7	11.7
Paid by commercial banks on savings deposits	28.0	33.0	30.0	32.0	21.0	15.0	12.3	5.9	2.8	3.2
Inflation rate										
CPI	..	130.6	45.4	24.6	42.2	30.0	6.5	6.1	7.0	
GDP Deflator	..	116.3	43.0	25.6	46.5	29.5	6.6	9.2	6.1	6.6
Exchange rate										
Ugandan shillings per U.S. dollar[1]	44.67	106.25	234.17	430.42	724.58	1,145.43	1,195.02	979.45	968.65	1,045.28

Source: Statistics Department, Ministry of Finance and Economic Planning, *Key Economic Indicators*, 25th Issue, April 1996.
Note: [1] Official middle rate, end of calendar year.

Exhibit 6c Uganda Civil Service

Year	Grand Total of Civil Service Officers
End-1993	175,127
End-1994	160,903
End-1995	145,392
End-1996	150,379

Source: *The Republic of Uganda 1997 Statistical Abstract*, prepared by the Ministry of Planning and Economic Development, June 1997, p. 55.

Exhibit 7   Saving and Investment Ratios in Developing Countries (percent)

	1982–86	1987–93
Uganda		
Investment/GDP[1]	8.5	13.9
Savings/GDP[2]	-4.1	-3.8
All developing countries		
Investment/GDP	24.2	26.1
Savings/GDP	21.9	24.8
Africa		
Investment/GDP	22.4	19.6
Savings/GDP	19.3	17.7
Asia		
Investment/GDP	28.1	31.1
Savings/GDP	26.6	30.5
Middle East and Europe		
Investment/GDP	22.8	22.2
Savings/GDP	19.0	19.2
Western Hemisphere		
Investment/GDP	19.4	20.6
Savings/GDP	17.2	18.9

Source: *World Economic Outlook*, October 1994: IMF Occasional Paper 121, *Uganda Adjustment with Growth, 1987–1994* (Washington, DC: IMF, 1995), p. 12.

Notes: [1]Fiscal years 1983–1984–1986–1987.
[2]Fiscal years 1987–1988–1992–1993.

Exhibit 8a Annual Exports, 1990–1995 (*thousand U.S. dollars*)

Commodity	1990	1991	1992	1993	1994	1995
Traditional crops						
Coffee	140,384	117,641	95,372	106,775	343,289	384,122
Cotton	5,795	11,731	8,218	5,504	3,485	9,696
Tea	3,566	6,780	7,721	11,141	11,804	8,698
Tobacco	2,821	4,540	4,333	7,016	8,269	7,397
Non-traditional exports						
Livestock and producte	6,136	4,406	4,039	5,846	10,896	8,924
Fish	1,386	5,313	6,498	8,942	14,768	17,541
Manufactures[1]	1	46	303	1,302	1,740	2,631
Electricity[2]	1,218	923	1,537	738	2,245	2,414
Gold	..	..	..	..	224	23,197
Crops	12,720	19,447	13,424	42,031	43,873	36,355
Other	3,511	13,443	6,541	13,249	22,742	59,688

Source: *Key Economic Indicators*, 25th Issue, prepared by the Statistics Department, Ministry of Finance and Economic Planning, (Entebbe: April 1996), p. 22.
Notes: [1] Soap, hoes, and hand tools.
　　　　 [2] Sold to Kenya.

Exhibit 8b System of Government

Official name:	Republic of Uganda
Form of state:	Unitary republic
Legal system:	Based on English common, customary law and the 1995 constitution
National elections:	Next elections due by 2001 (presidential and legislative); referendum in 2000 to decide whether multi-party system to be reintroduced
Executive branch:	Head of state, President Yoweri K Museveni. Vice President, Dr. Specioza Wandera Kazibwe
Legislative branch:	Unicameral National Assembly (276 members; 214 directly elected by universal suffrage. The remainder selected by electoral colleges. All serve five year terms)
Judicial branch	Court of Appeals; High Court

Exhibit 9   Uganda's External Debt

Calendar Years	1987	1988	1989	1990	1991	1992	1993	1994
					(In millions of U.S. dollars)			
External payments arrears	30.0	77.0	106.0	95.0	377.7	609.2	279.7	249
Total outstanding public external debt	1,656	1,688	1,967	2,300	..	2,647.5	2,637	2,999
Total multilateral debt	834	896	1,008	1,290	..	1,756	1,816	2,156
Total bilateral debt	529	509	687	730	..	652	697	730
Foreign exchange reserves	31.0	35.0	36.0	25.0	49.8	73.6	111.9	208

Fiscal Years	1986–87	1987–88	1988–89	1989–90	1990–91	1991–92	1992–93	1993–94
			(In percent of exports of goods and nonfactor services)					
External debt (including arrears) including Fund obligations	309.0	563.0	626.0	895.0	1,246.2	1,357.8	1,300.7	909.5
Servicing cost of external debt:								
Including Fund obligations	54.0	62.0	74.0	81.0	95.9	127.7	85.1	56.5
Excluding Fund obligations	27.0	34.0	40.0	57.0	77.2	110.8	75.4	52.8
			(In months of imports of goods and nonfactor services)					
Foreign exchange reserves	0.7	0.7	0.8	0.5	1.3	2.2	1.8	2.9

Sources: *Uganda–Background Paper; IMF Staff Country Report No. 95/44* (Washington DC: IMF, May 1995) p. 7; *World Debt Tables*, p. 418; and Statistics Department, Ministry of Finance and Economic Planning, *Key Economic Indicators*, 25th Issue April 1996, p. 12.

Endnotes

1   Quote from Uganda's web page @ http://www.uganda.co.ug/.

2   Nilotic referred to civilizations along the Nile River. In Uganda an imaginary "Bantu Line" cut across the country, running along the Nile from Lake Albert to Lake Kyoga and southeast to Tororo. North of the line were speakers of Nilotic and Sudanic languages—comprising one-third of the population. The remainder of the population spoke a Bantu language, or a combination of English and Swahili. While Swahili was the language of commerce in East Africa and English the official language of Uganda in 1998, Luganda (the language of the Baganda) was the first language of the majority of the population. From M. Louise Pirouet, *Historical Dictionary of Uganda*, (Metuchen, NJ: The Scarecrow Press, Inc., 1995).

3   Muslim communities were concentrated in the south and west of the country.

4   By 1893, the Company was forced to withdraw from Uganda because it had made no profits, in part because of the expense incurred in wars and protecting peace and security. From *British East Africa, A History of the Formation and Work of The Imperial British East Africa Company* (London: Chapman and Hall, Ltd., 1895).

5   David E. Apter, *The Political Kingdom in Uganda*, (Princeton, NJ: Princeton University Press, 1961).

6   Anthony Sampson, *Macmillan: A Study in Ambiguity*, (New York: Simon and Schuster, 1967), 174–175.

7   P. Godfrey Okoth, Manuel Muranga and Ernesto Okello Ogwang, eds. *Uganda: A Century of Existence*, (Kampala: Fountain Publishers), p. 62.

8   David E. Apter, op cit.

9   Many African countries experimented with Socialism after receiving their independence from Britain. Capitalist ideology was strongly associated with British rule and therefore viewed as an unattractive option.

10 Amin's regime was infamous for murder, "disappearances" of high-ranking officials and systematic killings planned by employees of the State Research Bureau, whose members spied on the alleged enemies of the government and used torture to extract confessions. According to the *Historical Dictionary of Uganda*, op cit.: "The eight years of Amin's rule did incalculable damage to Ugandan society, sowing distrust through an army of informers, creating chaos in law—Amin ruled by decree—destroying the modern sector of the economy, and brutalizing a generation….Violence became a way of life."

11 *The Los Angeles Times*, 17 August 1993.

12 Ibid.

13 From the archives of *The Christian Science Monitor*: http://www.csmonitor.com/archive/archive.html.

14 Museveni's ethnic affiliation was Banyankore and he came from southwestern Uganda. He had worked in the president's office as a research assistant during Obote's first term and was Minister of State for Defense from April-November 1979.

15 From Yoweri K. Museveni, *Sowing the Mustard Seed: The Struggle for Freedom and Democracy in Uganda* (London: Macmillan Publishers Ltd., 1997), p. 180.

16 All figures are in U.S. dollars unless otherwise noted.

17 *Uganda-Background Paper-/IMF Staff Country Report*, no. 95/44, (Washington, DC: IMF, 1995), p. 33.

18 "Broad money" is M2, i.e., currency plus bank demand, savings and time deposits held by Ugandan private residents.

19 "Financial liberalization" can be defined as the abolition of explicit controls and direct government intervention in the pricing and allocation of credit. Liberalization may also involve the abolition of controls on international capital movements. Definition from Pill and Pradhan, "Financial Liberalization in Africa and Asia," *Finance and Development*, June 1997: 7–10.

20 Privatization was the subject of much debate within Uganda. A number of lecturers at Makerere University accused the government of "selling out to Western ideology." They were "pro-nationalization" and worried that foreign companies were taking out more revenues than they were bringing in. Museveni, a former Marxist, responded: "Privatizing is a method which will tap the energies of people to cause economic growth, while keeping the economy in public hands will cause its decline." He gave the example of a factory, which if not operational, adds nothing to the economy. Yoweri K. Museveni, *op cit.*, pp. 180–182.

21 *Recent Magazine,* vol. II, no. 6, p. 13 (October-November 1997).

22 Jeffrey Goldberg, "Our Africa Problem." *The New York Times,* 2 March 1997.

23 In the late 1960s, the East African Community (EAC), a trade regime comprised of Kenya, Tanzania and Uganda, established a joint airline, postal and telephone services; and a framework for regional trade and commerce was in the works. Economic and ideological differences, as well as Uganda's civil war, led to the collapse of this union.

24 The first AIDS cases were discovered in 1982 near the Tanzanian border.

25 By the year 2000, 800,000 Ugandans were expected to benefit if all the water supply projects were completed.

26 Yoweri K. Museveni, *op cit.,* p. 196.

27 Quote from David E. Apter, *Daedalus,* 22 June 1995.

28 The constitution was prepared following consultations with representatives from each of the 39 districts, together with representatives of the army, workers, youth and disabled groups.

29 The Lord's Resistance Army (LRA), a Christian fundamentalist group many experts saw as being only a minor problem, had maintained an active presence in the north for over a decade. Its leader, Joseph Kony, assembled an army comprised of children abducted from schools, trained in warfare and sent to coerce other children into their ranks by violent means.

30 Uganda's total land area =19.4 million hectares (ha). Land is distributed in the following manner: 4 million ha for annual crops; 1.5 million for permanent crops; 5 million for pastures and grazing land; 6.5 million for forests; and 2.4 million for very marginal use. From: *Uganda, Growing out of Poverty* (Washington, DC: World Bank/IBRD, 1993), pp. 68–70.

31 *Uganda-Background Paper-/IMF Staff Country Report,* op cit.

32 The first Ugandan to invite the Asians to return was actually Obote. In 1980 he received a great deal of his campaign financing from the Asian community. Upon returning to office, Obote appointed two Asians to top diplomatic posts, believing that the Asians' power and prestige were keys to future prosperity. From the archives of *The Christian Science Monitor,* op cit.

33 Of the estimated 5,000 Asians living in Uganda in 1995, approximately 1,000 were victims of the purge. From the *Los Angeles Times,* op cit.

34 Quote from *Uganda: Growing out of Poverty,* (Washington, DC: IBRD/The World Bank, 1993), pp. 55–56.

35 The *Financial Times* (London), 24 February 1998.

36 Edward Wamala of Makerere University notes: "It is not the case that African societies…had to be taught democracy as if they were completely ignorant about it. In the 'tribal' set-up, people had developed their own democratic procedures of discussions until they reached a consensus…. The political concept of opposition was, therefore, not alien to 'tribal' society, only that it was not the formal opposition as we know it today." From Okoth, Muranga and Ogwang, eds., op cit., pp. 64–65.

37 Yoweri K. Museveni, op cit., p. 195.

38   *Deutsche Presse-Agentur*, 26 January 1998.

39   *Africa News*, 4 February 1998.

40   *Reuter European Business Report*, 2 April 1997.

41   For more on Malaysia's Vision 2020, see HBS case no. 792-099, pp. 5–9, prepared by Professor Forest Reinhardt.

Mexico: The Tequila Crisis 1994–1995

After 1987, Mexican authorities—under the leadership of Presidents De la Madrid and Salinas—implemented a far-reaching program of macroeconomic stabilization and structural economic reform, modeled on the dictates of the Washington consensus advocated by the International Monetary Fund, World Bank, and U.S. Treasury Department.

The results of this reform program were initially extremely impressive. But in 1993 and 1994 a variety of cracks in the new Mexican system appeared: the current account deficit grew rapidly; the quality of bank loan portfolios deteriorated considerably; national savings rates fell dramatically; and political and social stability collapsed with the advent of the Chiapas uprising in the southern part of the country and numerous political assassinations.

Incoming President Zedillo's attempt to address these rising problems in December 1994 ended in chaos. The Mexican currency collapsed, plunging the country into a recession and financial crisis, with inflation rising rapidly, the currency in free fall, and economic activity collapsing.

Supplementary Material

The Choice of Exchange Rate Regime

Study Questions

1. What is your answer to the question posed by the Banco de Mexico officials on page 1 of the case: *'How could extensive and well-executed fiscal, supply-side and trade reforms end up in such a dismal situation?'*
2. What best explains the collapse of the Mexican currency: psychological factors (expectations and confidence) or fundamental factors (economic phenomena such as current account and fiscal deficits)?
3. Should Mexico be "bailed out" by the international community? How does your answer to this question relate to your position on questions 1 and 2 above?
4. Is Paul Krugman's analogy between the Mexican crisis and the "irrational exuberance" usually associated with the tulipmania a good one?

HUW PILL

Mexico: The Tequila Crisis 1994–1995

After 1987, an extensive program of macroeconomic stabilization and structural economic reform was pursued with increasing vigor in Mexico. Trade was liberalized, the financial system and other sectors were deregulated, restrictions on foreign direct investment were curtailed, and state enterprises were privatized. Mexico, the Latin American basket case of the debt crisis years (1982–86), suddenly became the darling of the international financial community and was lauded as a model reformer by the economic technocrats of the International Monetary Fund (IMF) and the World Bank in Washington, DC. To managers of "emerging market" investment funds in London and New York, Mexico was a new country. From 1990, financial capital flooded into Mexico on an unprecedented scale as foreign investors scrambled to obtain a stake in Mexico's embryonic economic miracle. Prospects seemed unbounded. The creation of a North American Free Trade Agreement (NAFTA) in January 1994 appeared to sustain Mexico's movement toward the ranks of developed nations.

But by the end of 1995, the situation was viewed quite differently by the international financial community. An attempt to devalue the *peso* (the Mexican currency) in December 1994 had ended in chaos. Capital fled the country as confidence evaporated. The exchange rate collapsed. Starved of foreign capital, Mexican output fell more than 6% in 1995, while inflation was reignited by the devaluation and its aftermath, peaking at 52% per annum. Mexico's banking system teetered on the verge of collapse. The country was forced to accept the humiliation of an American-led international "bail out." The dissatisfaction of the populace was evident: every day, the streets of Mexico City were brought to a halt by the demonstrations of various disaffected groups who loudly expressed their dissatisfaction with the chaotic state of the Mexican economy.

The exasperation of senior officials at the *Banco de Mexico* (the Mexican central bank) was understandable: "What went wrong? How could extensive and well-executed fiscal, supply-side, and trade reforms end up in such a dismal situation?"[1]

Mexico in 1987

Following the debt crisis of 1982, Mexico had been forced into a period of economic austerity.[2] The implementation of an "orthodox" stabilization program to contain inflation implied tight control of public finances, since fiscal deficits were believed to drive the inflation process. Starved of fiscal stimulus and lacking in confidence, the economy stagnated. The 1980s were to become known as Mexico's "lost decade." Any income generated by the Mexican economy was transferred abroad to

Professor Huw Pill prepared this case. This case was developed from published sources. HBS cases are developed solely as the basis for class discussion. Cases are not intended to serve as endorsements, sources of primary data, or illustrations of effective or ineffective management.

service the enormous burden of external debt accumulated during the misguided fiscal expansion of the late 1970s.

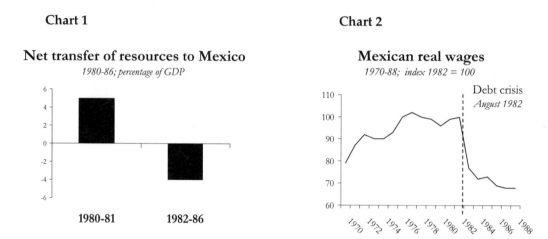

Chart 1

Net transfer of resources to Mexico
1980-86; percentage of GDP

Chart 2

Mexican real wages
1970-88; index 1982 = 100

Source: Created by casewriter based on Huw Pill and Helen Shapiro, "Mexico (B): Escaping from the Debt Crisis?" HBS Case No. 797-105.

Despite the program of economic austerity pursued by Mexico, in 1987 the Mexican stock market crashed. Once again, confidence ebbed and capital fled the country. Another deep devaluation of the *peso* was required, stoking an already unacceptably high rate of inflation. Following devaluation, the Mexican authorities attempted to peg the *peso* at the new lower rate in an attempt to reestablish monetary stability while maintaining the benefits of devaluation for competitiveness and exports. In spite of these measures, capital flight continued at an alarming rate and efforts to rein in inflation proved futile.

A new policy direction was required. The de la Madrid administration, which had taken office in the aftermath of the original 1982 crisis, introduced a new "heterodox" program of stabilization and reform.

Macroeconomic stabilization was implemented through the introduction of the *Pacto*—an agreement between government and representatives of business, the unions, and agriculture to cooperate and coordinate wage bargaining and price setting in support of the overall macroeconomic strategy. Proponents of the "heterodox" approach argued that fiscal deficits were as much a result of inflation as they were a cause. Inflation had achieved a momentum all of its own; expectations of inflation encouraged unions to demand higher money wages to protect their members' standard of living, but this only succeeded in raising labor costs and prices, thereby validating the original expectations of inflation. This vicious cycle was driving prices ever higher. Coordination in wage and price setting was required to break the inflationary wage-price spiral.

If the *Pacto* addressed macroeconomic stability, problems with the real economy were to be attacked by **far reaching structural reform** (see **Exhibit 2**). One legacy of previous economic policies in Mexico was government intervention in the economy. President de la Madrid vowed to open Mexico to the ventilating effects of market forces, precisely the prescription of the "Washington consensus" advocated by the IMF and World Bank.

Structural reform was pursued with even greater vigor by the Salinas administration that took office in December 1988. Mexico had joined the General Agreement on Tariffs and Trade (GATT) in 1986. The trade liberalization that membership implied was accelerated by Salinas as tariffs were slashed and free trade arrangements were introduced with Central American neighbors.   The crowning achievement was free trade with Mexico's northern neighbors, the United States and Canada. Negotiations were started that would ultimately lead to the creation of the North American Free Trade Agreement (NAFTA) in 1994.

Yet liberalization of the domestic economy was at least as great. State enterprises were privatized on a massive scale. The rules governing foreign direct investment were relaxed by the introduction of new legislation in 1991. The taxation and social security systems were overhauled to reduce evasion and improve economic incentives. Vast swathes of the economy were deregulated: road haulage, civil aviation, retailing—the list is impressively long. The market-oriented zeal of the reformers exceeded that seen in the industrialized countries, as privately operated toll roads became the mainstay of the new program of infrastructure investment.

These reforms were conducted in an environment of apparently growing fiscal and monetary stability (see **Exhibits 3** and **4**). As part of the *Pacto*, the exchange rate had been placed on a slow downward crawl,[3] in part to promote business cooperation and disinflation. The public sector finances moved into surplus as privatization proceeds rolled in and tax revenue increased in response to demand growth and improved collection. Inflation abated slowly as the *Pacto* successfully reduced inflation expectations (**Exhibit 5a**).

Financial Liberalization

Nowhere was this change of policy direction more apparent than in the financial sector. At the height of the 1982 crisis, then-President Lopez Portillo had nationalized the banking system in a vain attempt to stem the flood of capital fleeing Mexico. Throughout the 1980s, Mexican banks acted as an extension of government. Credit was primarily directed to Mexican companies by the whim of politicians rather than allocated on market criteria.

Under the new policy regime, this was set to change. Guillermo Ortiz, later *Secretario de Hacienda* (Mexican Finance Minister), laid out the goals of financial liberalization:

> In the context of structural economic reform, financial liberalization has two objectives. First, the Mexican financial system, whatever its institutional arrangements, must increase the generation of national savings.... Second, our financial system has to be capable of promoting the economy's productivity and competitiveness so that its integration into global markets is smooth and efficient, not vulnerable to changes in external circumstances.[4]

Towards these ends, the banking sector was deregulated from 1988, when interest rate controls were largely eliminated. Restrictions on the convertibility of the *peso* into foreign exchange—on both the current and capital account—were progressively relaxed, and eventually abolished. In 1989, the requirements for banks to finance the government and to lend to politically favored sectors were abolished. In April of that year, the interest rate ceiling on bank deposits was eliminated, and commercial banks were allowed to set their own rates according to the demand and supply of loanable funds. Reserve requirements—a punitive implicit tax on financial intermediation—were greatly reduced. This process culminated in a 13-month period from June 1991 to July 1992 during which 18 banks were privatized in a series of auctions.[5]

In tune with the market orientation of the time, banks were sold to the highest bidder. Foreign participation was restricted (although NAFTA would allow subsidiaries of American and Canadian banks to enter, on a phased basis, after 1994).[6] Diversified ownership was encouraged by preventing individuals from obtaining equity stakes greater than 5%; institutions were limited to 10%. Yet

Mexican banks were encouraged to coagulate into large financial conglomerates, incorporating insurance companies and stock brokers, in an attempt to exploit the economies of scale and scope associated with financial services.

Debt Restructuring

The only brake on Mexico's economic revival appeared to be the burden of enormous debt inherited from the fiscal profligacy of the late 1970s and early 1980s. The need to service this vast debt overhang starved the domestic private sector of financial resources. Several initiatives set out to address the problem. The Baker Plan of 1985 aimed to address the issue through debt restructuring alone. This proved insufficient.

It was only with the advent of an initiative led by U.S. Treasury Secretary Nicholas Brady in 1988 that the debt burden became tolerable. Although the final agreement between Mexico and her creditors involved some debt forgiveness and injections of new lending, its main feature was the conversion of bank debt into so-called "Brady bonds." These were guaranteed by the U.S. Treasury on the collateral of Mexican oil reserves. They permitted a change in the time profile of debt servicing. The burden of servicing Mexico's vast external debt was considerably reduced in the early years, freeing resources for development of the domestic economy with the hope that in the medium term it would be strong enough to pay off the burden in its entirety. With the signing of an agreement between Mexico and her creditors under the auspices of the Brady Plan in February 1990, the prerequisites for Mexican revival were thought to be in place.[7]

Mexico Rediscovered

As the reforms took effect, Mexico enjoyed a surge of confidence. The pain of the 1980s was to be replaced by an economic revitalization in the 1990s. Consumption rose in anticipation of future higher incomes, the fruits of economic reform and improved growth performance. Investment increased as indigenous entrepreneurs exploited the new opportunities offered by liberalization (see **Exhibit 6**). A private sector previously shackled by the red tape of regulation and an all-embracing bureaucracy was suddenly free to embark on new profitable endeavors.

But liberalization had also facilitated new access to two goods: credit, extended by the recently privatized and deregulated banking sector, and foreign goods, available as trade barriers came down. The Mexican domestic private sector was unable to resist the temptation of these commodities, denied to them for so long under the previous regime. Rapid growth of bank lending, much of it financed by borrowing from abroad, and a vast trade deficit were the results. The central issue became the following: had the attraction of newly available credit and foreign goods prompted Mexican consumers and firms to over-imbibe?

Purchases of imports created a vast current account deficit (see **Exhibit 7**). This deficit needed to be financed. Moreover, funds had to be raised to finance the rapid growth of bank lending (**Exhibit 4**). Mexico's financing requirements were enormous—but the international capital markets were all too pleased to meet them.

The structure of the global capital market had changed considerably since Mexico's previous flirtation with international borrowing in the late 1970s. International banks were no longer the only, or even main, source of funds. Institutional investment in the form of portfolio capital flows had become the norm. The number of "emerging market" funds ballooned in the early 1990s. These were institutionally managed funds (some mutual funds, some pension funds, some insurance company funds) that focused on investing in liberalizing developing countries. Raising money in the United States and elsewhere in the industrialized world, they purchased securities in developing country financial markets, increasingly those issued by the private rather than the public sector. Although the instruments purchased were ostensibly long term, they were marketable; impersonal securities markets did not offer the same symbiotic relationship between lender and borrower that bank lending provided,[8] nor were they "locked in" in physical form like much foreign direct investment.

As U.S. interest rates fell during the early 1990s in response to recession, investors seeking high yields increasingly looked to the emerging markets. Mexico—"so far from God, so close to the United States," as a Mexican proverb has it—was in prime position to receive a disproportionate share of these funds (see **Exhibit 10**). Moreover, the investment community shared Mexican confidence in the prospects for economic reform. The mistakes of previous years were being aggressively reversed. New York fund managers scrambled to send money south of the border to gain an early stake in Mexico's embryonic economic miracle. A series of quotes suggest the flavor of the time (note in particular the dates these quotations were made):

'At the moment, we are pretty unambiguously optimistic about investment in Mexico,' declared A. Peter Monaco, portfolio manager of the Scudder Latin American Fund, which has $500 million invested in Mexico. (*The New York Times*, 12 April 1993).

'There is no other country in the world where I can buy government securities that yield so much and are safe,' said Robert Beckwith, a mutual fund manager at Fidelity Investments, which maintains large holdings of Mexican government stock. (*The New York Times*, 22 April 1993).

'The time to be invested in Mexico is now,' recommended Maria-Elena Carrion, a portfolio manager who oversees $200 million in Latin American investments. (*Bloomberg Business News*, 23 August 1994).

Mexico was caught in a virtuous circle of reform, growing confidence, greater capital inflows, and accelerating expenditure growth. As capital flooded into Mexico, bank lending grew further, stimulating domestic consumption and investment. Greater activity swelled tax revenues and further improved the public finances. The apparent success of reform and stabilization made further liberalization and continued wage and price restraint under the *Pacto* more palatable to the parties concerned. Success in reducing inflation and raising the fiscal surplus only served to bolster foreign confidence and encourage a yet greater inflow of capital.

Some argued that the successes were more apparent than real. Fiscal surpluses were a product of creative accounting rather than actual improvements in financial control. Spending was moved off-balance sheet to nongovernmental organizations like the development banks.[9] To the extent that Mexican banks and firms enjoyed (possibly implicit) government guarantees, the government was accumulating large contingent liabilities as credit grew rapidly. The reduction in inflation appeared to be an artifact of administrative *diktat* rather than improved monetary control. The parties to the

Pacto were responsible for setting a large proportion of the prices that entered the statistical definition of inflation. The government alone controlled the prices of goods (such as gasoline and *tortillas*, a staple of the Mexican diet) accounting for more than 10% of the inflation index.

Yet these warnings were ignored in the clamor of the times. As Paul Krugman, a leading international economist, was later to write:

> It seems fairly clear that some of the enthusiasm for investing in developing countries in the first half of the 1990s was a classic speculative bubble. A modest recovery from the dismal 1980s led to large capital gains for those few investors who had been willing to put money into Third World stock markets. Their success led other investors to jump in, driving up prices still further. By 1993 or so, 'emerging market funds' were being advertised on television and in the pages of popular magazines.[10]

In fact, the inflow of capital was not merely sufficient to sustain the pace of Mexican bank lending and finance the growing current account deficit. Capital inflows actually exceeded the demands of the Mexican economy. The *Banco de Mexico* built up its stock of foreign exchange reserves. The exchange rate appreciated. The fluctuations of the *peso*/dollar rate had been confined to a band since 1991. The lower boundary of the band declined a small amount each day, allowing scope for a gradual depreciation (see **Exhibit 13**). But the magnitude of the capital inflows kept the actual rate at the top of the fluctuation band. There were incipient pressures for appreciation, rather than depreciation. From late 1992, the *peso*'s exchange rate against the dollar demonstrated remarkable stability, evidence in the authorities' eyes of the success of reform and foreign confidence in the future of Mexico.

Overvaluation?

Not everyone viewed the strength of the *peso* as a sign of success. Rather, from early 1993, a clique of increasingly vocal critics argued it was evidence of macroeconomic mismanagement. The *Pacto* had reduced inflation, but not to the low levels seen in the United States. A stable *nominal* exchange rate had resulted in an appreciating *real* exchange rate (see **Exhibit 9**). The prices of Mexican goods, when converted into dollars at the market rate, were rising more rapidly than those of equivalent American goods. Those warning of overvaluation argued that Mexico was pricing herself out of world markets.   The current account deficit was evidence of rapidly declining international competitiveness. In their view, slumping exports were causing domestic economic stagnation.

The leading exponent of this view was Professor Rudiger Dornbusch. He argued Mexico should tolerate the inflationary consequences of a devaluation in order to promote growth:

> A large over-valuation will not go away of its own accord.... Growth is sluggish and bad debts are accumulating.... Unless the exchange rate is devalued, either recession will be needed to eliminate the external problem and reduce inflation, or expansion will be needed to alleviate the lack of growth. Neither option is realistic. It is politically difficult to squeeze inflation through recession, especially in an election year, and fiscal stimulus, although more tempting, is not a feasible long-run solution for Mexico.... [I]nstead, a significant departure from the present exchange rate is needed.[11]

The Mexican authorities were unconvinced. They viewed the current account deficit as merely an accounting counterpart to the capital inflow, itself evidence of foreign expectations of the success of reform. Exports were growing, not stagnating (especially in 1994). Imports consisted of capital goods, necessary to reequip Mexican industry to face the blast of international competition as trade was liberalized (**Exhibits 7** and **8**). Other measures of the real exchange rate—notably the *Banco de Mexico*'s favored measure based on labor costs—showed less evidence of real appreciation. Such appreciation could be an equilibrium phenomenon as Mexican productivity improved rather than a sign of mismanagement. The very success of reform had rendered many of the public statistics misleading (see **Exhibit 6**).

Social Polarization?

The benefits of reform that were becoming apparent by 1994 were far from evenly distributed. Mexico was becoming divided into two nations: on the one hand, an increasingly sophisticated, modernizing elite oriented towards the global economy and the United States; and, on the other hand, a still predominantly agrarian remainder. The former had gained from reform. It was they who had obtained access to credit and imported consumer goods, while the latter had remained untouched. Nowhere was this polarization more pronounced than linguistically. Many of the peasants from the south could not speak Spanish, let alone the English ubiquitous in business circles.

Questions were raised about the sustainability of such a situation. One group had little stake in economic reform, the other little stake in social and political change. Jorge Castañeda, a political science professor at the National Autonomous University of Mexico, suggested: "Mexican society is split between those plugged into the U.S. economy and those that are not.... The Mexicans tied to the United States are retreating into a world of their own.... Because they have a way out of Mexico's misery, they are different from their countrymen."[12]

Focused on market reform, the Mexican authorities were convinced that the benefits of liberalization would eventually "trickle down" to every strata of the social scale. Moreover, social reform required resources that only economic reform could generate. Political democratization would naturally follow economic growth.

Financial Fragility?

The boom induced by the capital inflows of 1990-92 was nowhere more apparent than in the banking sector. Previously dormant, Mexican banks suddenly became international market leaders: among the 1,000 largest banks in the world, three of the 25 most profitable in 1992 were Mexican; in 1993, the corresponding figure was seven.[13] Yet this apparent success masked an underlying weakness.

During the years of nationalization, the institutional infrastructure of the banking system had withered away. With banks doing little more than channeling deposits to the government, expertise in risk assessment and credit control had atrophied. The new owners of the banks had little or no experience in the supposedly conservative business of retail commercial banking.

The newly privatized banks were ill prepared to cope with the enormous volume of lending that, as we have seen, resulted from the private sector's reaction to reform. For example, there was no credit bureau where the credit records of individual borrowers could be checked. It was possible to extend one's credit limit to its maximum, and then obtain a new credit line from another bank to service the accumulated debt. Banks were unable or unwilling to control the enormous implied credit risks, which in consequence multiplied rapidly (see **Exhibit 11**).

The poor institutional infrastructure within the banking sector was mirrored by the authorities' supervisory and regulatory bodies. A deposit insurance scheme was in place, but it was poorly designed. All bank deposits were insured, regardless of their size or the holder of the account. Banks were charged a flat rate to participate in the deposit insurance fund. The charge was unconnected to riskiness of the bank's underlying asset portfolio.[14] Banks were therefore being subsidized to take excessive risk. Public supervision to mitigate such behavior was under-staffed and poorly funded. Consistent with their belief in the market, the authorities were content to adopt a largely *laissez-faire* approach to banking regulation.

From 1992, bad loans in the banking system began to mount, although, because Mexican accounting standards failed to meet international standards, the magnitude of the problem was not immediately apparent abroad.[15] Perversely, the lack of regulation allowed the emergence of non-performing loans to encourage more destabilizing bank behavior, rather than conservatism. As equity capital held in banks declined, owners had an incentive to "gamble on their own resurrection" since the costs of bank failure to them would be negligible.

Undoubtedly these problems were exacerbated by illegal activities and fraud. The close relationship between banks and industrial companies—often cemented by family ties which were opaque to the minimal official regulation—allowed banks to extend credit to affiliated companies or bank insiders, never expecting to be repaid. The absence of legal and regulatory infrastructure allowed such problems to multiply.

Falling National Savings?

At the macroeconomic level, the spending boom initiated by reform and facilitated by financial liberalization had caused a dramatic collapse in private saving (see **Exhibit 12**). Consumption rose much more quickly than income; individuals denied access to foreign goods for so long were determined to obtain them while they had the chance and believed that the higher future incomes promised by reform justified more spending. Even though public saving rose as the fiscal accounts moved into surplus, the precipitous decline of saving by the private sector implied a collapse in overall national saving. Mexican national saving had never been high by the standards of the East Asian "tiger" economies. By 1994, private gross domestic saving had fallen to 12%, a low figure by historical standards.

The implications of this fall for Mexico's development strategy were profound. If she could not generate the financial resources to fund investment and development herself, Mexico had to rely on financing from the rest of the world. In accounting terms, the current account deficit was simply the shortfall of domestic saving relative to domestic investment, now reaching new heights as the latter was boosted by reform. Low national saving meant Mexican economic growth was dependent on continued inflows of foreign capital—the mechanism for transferring foreign savings into the Mexican economy. But this meant that Mexico's macroeconomic strategy was vulnerable to a reversal of international sentiment.

Mexico at the End of 1993

At the end of 1993, it appeared that Mexico had been transformed over the previous six years. The stabilization and reform instituted by de la Madrid and Salinas—two Harvard-educated economists apparently well prepared to transform Mexico into a market-oriented, modern developed state—seemed to have been successful. Certainly, problems remained. But these were minor irritations on an otherwise unblemished record of achievement.

Mexico's accession to the Organization for Economic Cooperation and Development (OECD) conferred on her membership of what had traditionally been regarded as the "rich countries' club." More significantly, the imminent creation of NAFTA appeared to guarantee the accumulated reforms while allowing Mexican industry enhanced access to the crucial American market. The capital markets were impressed and responded with renewed vigor. Capital inflows peaked in late November 1993 as the U.S. Congress, following doubts earlier in the month, passed legislation implementing the NAFTA program (see **Exhibit 15**).

At the same time, the United States began to emerge from recession. In February 1994, the Federal Reserve dramatically altered the stance of American monetary policy. Interest rates were raised to preempt possible inflationary pressures as the economy recovered (see **Exhibit 1**). The attraction of Mexico as a destination for capital seeking high returns was at once diminished. For the first time during the Salinas administration, external events took an adverse turn.

Mexican Politics Intervene

New Year's Day 1994 was supposed to mark the beginning of a new modern era for Mexico, as NAFTA took effect and the world's largest single free trade area was created. Instead, it was memorable for another reason: the peasant uprising in the southern Mexican state of Chiapas. Disaffected and disenfranchised, the poor agrarian economy of the south stood to gain little from the introduction of free trade with the United States. Although the violence was rapidly contained by government forces, it served as a salutary reminder to foreign investors. For all the claims of the technocratic elite, Mexico was a far-from-modern democratic society. Behind a thin veneer of sophistication in the financial and industrial circles of Mexico City, Monterrey, and Guadalajara, the country lacked the social, political, economic, and institutional infrastructure of a developed country.

The uprising was the first of several political events that were to have an important impact on economic prospects. It was election year, and Mexican elections and their aftermath were often associated with economic turbulence. Mexican economic history is punctuated with economic crises that match the electoral rhythm of the six-year presidential term. The economic landmarks of 1976, 1982 and 1987 illustrate precisely this regular beat. Would 1994 end the pattern?

On March 23, 1994, Luis Colosio, the presidential candidate of the ruling Institutional Revolutionary Party (PRI) and, as such, President Salinas' hand-picked successor and virtually president-elect,[16] was assassinated while on the campaign trail. Suddenly, economic reform seemed in jeopardy. Foreign confidence was severely jolted. The inflow of foreign capital dried up and began to reverse. To protect themselves from the financial consequences of possible devaluation, investors – foreign and domestic – began to move their savings to safe dollar accounts in Miami and elsewhere offshore.

Rather than accumulating foreign reserves, the *Banco de Mexico* was suddenly faced with reserve losses. The exchange rate, which had remained resolutely glued to the top of the fluctuation band for most of the preceding period, suddenly dropped to the bottom (see **Exhibits 13** and **15**). The economic consequences of the political shock were readily apparent.

Policy Response

Policy remained focused on the maintenance of a credible macroeconomic strategy. Some argued the currency depreciation brought on by Colosio's assassination was a blessing in disguise. Although the circumstances were unfortunate, Dornbusch had been arguing for a devaluation of similar magnitude for some time. Export growth picked up.

The *peso* exchange rate had become the centerpiece of anti-inflation policy, the coordinating mechanism on which the *Pacto* was based. The fluctuation band had to be defended at all costs. One response to the assassination could have been a sharp rise in Mexican short-term interest rates, more than offsetting the ongoing rises in U.S. rates. But the *Banco de Mexico*'s flexibility was severely constrained by the fragility of the financial system, especially the banks laden with non-performing loans. Higher rates might have been the final straw, pushing borrowers to default and banks to the wall. Since the integrity of the payments and financial systems—necessary for the smooth functioning of a market economy—had to be maintained, higher interest rates seemed not to be a viable response.

Similarly, the Mexican authorities rejected the option of reintroducing restrictions on the convertibility of the *peso* into foreign exchange. Imposition of exchange and capital controls might have been construed by the domestic and foreign private sectors as signaling the abandonment of economic liberalism. This, in turn, could have further undermined foreign investor confidence and precipitated the crisis that the controls were designed to prevent. Moreover, with Mexico's long and porous border with the United States and increasingly sophisticated financial markets, exchange restrictions would be difficult to implement.

Consequently, the authorities decided to absorb the effect of the political shock on the balance of payments by using foreign exchange reserves held at the central bank as a buffer to capital outflows. To maintain the gross level of reserves at levels sufficient to protect the exchange rate fluctuation band, the Mexican government borrowed dollars from abroad (compare **Exhibits 14** and **15**). In so doing, the Mexican authorities assumed the exchange rate risk on capital inflows that had previously been borne by foreign, particularly American, investors.

Issues of *tesobonos* were the vehicle for this borrowing. *Tesobonos* were short-term Mexican government debt instruments indexed to the dollar. The government shifted its borrowing from *cetes*—domestic currency-denominated Mexican Treasury bills—and longer-term *peso* debt into *tesobonos* through the summer and fall of 1994 in order to prevent the central bank's stock of dollar reserves from declining. As a result, the currency denomination of public debt became increasingly biased towards dollars (see **Exhibit 16).** The Mexican government was making itself vulnerable to a liquidity crisis. If the *tesobono* debt could not be rolled over—as it had to be every three months, given its short maturity—the central bank would simply not have enough dollars on hand to satisfy foreign creditors and finance the still vast current account deficit.

A New Administration

Election day was August 21, 1994. In what was by Mexican standards a remarkably clean and fair poll, the replacement PRI candidate, Ernesto Zedillo, won handsomely as expected. Despite the resolution of electoral uncertainties, foreign confidence did not recover to the levels of the previous year. As a result, the renewed capital inflows anticipated by policy-makers did not materialize. Indeed, rather than a reduction of uncertainty, new political shocks caused even greater concern. Yet another political assassination occurred[17]—Mexico was apparently fast disappearing into the abyss of political anarchy (see **Exhibit 1**).

The new Zedillo administration took office on December 1 in the midst of this growing political and economic uncertainty. Its new economic plan failed to demonstrate how the current account and banking problems could be corrected. At first it appeared the Zedillo government would resolutely maintain the exchange rate fluctuation band at existing levels. Indeed, the new Finance Minister undertook a "charm offensive" among the fund managers in New York to convince them of his commitment. But the hemorrhaging stock of reserves was too great a strain (see **Exhibit 15**). The central bank's policy of issuing *tesobonos* to replenish reserves could not last forever.

On December 20, the government changed course. The fluctuation band for the *peso*/dollar exchange rate was widened, allowing an effective devaluation of approximately 15%.

Crisis

This decision provoked chaos. New York fund managers felt betrayed and began to withdraw funds on a vast scale. Hedge funds gambled on further devaluation, undertaking highly geared operations against the prevailing *peso* rate. The virtuous circle described above was suddenly replaced with a vicious downward spiral of much greater pace. Fear of further *peso* devaluation prompted sales of the *peso* and therefore further actual depreciation, all at a continuously accelerating rate. With selling pressure on the *peso* so strong, the *Banco de Mexico* had insufficient foreign exchange reserves to maintain the fluctuation band. On December 22, the Mexican authorities were forced to float the *peso*, which immediately dropped like a stone.

The exchange rate collapse and consequent withdrawal of foreign capital imposed a massive liquidity squeeze on Mexican borrowers. The supply of loanable funds suddenly dried up. Interest rates rocketed as demand for credit exceeded supply, making it impossible for firms and households to service their large stocks of outstanding floating rate debt. The underlying banking crisis suddenly became all too real. Output plunged and inflation surged. The unhappy days of 1982–1987 appeared to have returned. The promise of reform had proved ephemeral once again.

Exhibit 1   Chronology of Major Events During the Mexican Crisis, 1994–1995

1994:

January 1	NAFTA comes into effect. Chiapas rebels seize six towns.
February 4	U.S. Federal Reserve raises federal funds rate 25 basis points, having left the rate unchanged at 3% since September 1992.
March 22	U.S. Federal Reserve raises rates another 25 basis points.
March 23	Mexican presidential candidate Luís Donáldo Colosio is assassinated.
April 18	U.S. Federal Reserve raises rates another 25 basis points.
May 17	U.S. Federal Reserve raises rates by 50 basis points.
August 16	U.S. Federal Reserve raises rates another 50 basis points.
August 21	Victory for PRI candidate Ernesto Zedillo in the election for president of Mexico.
September 28	José Francisco Ruíz Massieu, Secretary General of Mexico's ruling PRI party, is assassinated.
November 15	U.S. Federal Reserve raises rates by 75 basis points.
November 23	Mexican Deputy Attorney General resigns, alleging a cover-up of the murder of his brother, PRI Secretary General Massieu.
December 1	New Mexican government under Zedillo takes office.
December 19	Further violence in Chiapas.
December 20	Banco de Mexico announces 15% shift in the intervention limits for the *peso*, an effective devaluation of the Mexican currency.
December 22	Banco de Mexico withdraws from the foreign exchange market, allowing the *peso* to float against all other currencies.

1995:

January 11	U.S. President Clinton announces support for Mexico.
January 15	Direct talks begin between Mexican government and Zapatista rebels (who led the uprising in Chiapas).
January 26	Mexico signs letter of intent accepting IMF conditionality in return for a loan of $7.8 billion.
January 31	United States announces a $50 billion loan package for Mexico, consisting of $20 billion from the U.S., $18 billion from the IMF (including the $7.8 billion mentioned above), $10 billion from the Bank for International Settlements, and $3 billion from private commercial banks.
February 21	Mexico and United States sign loan agreement.
March 3	Mexican authorities take over a private bank (*Banpaís*) as crisis grips the domestic financial system.
March 9	Mexican government announces a new reform and stabilization plan.

Source: Adapted from International Monetary Fund, "Evolution of the Mexican Peso Crisis," *Capital Markets: Developments, Prospects, and Policy Issues*, August 1995, pp. 54–55.

Exhibit 2   Microeconomic and Structural Reforms after 1988

Domestic Deregulation and Privatization

1. Deregulation of more than 3,000 sectors of the Mexican economy, including foreign investment (through the foreign direct investment legislation of 1991), truck and bus transportation, and the financial system.

2. Privatization of around 1,000 public corporations, generating $25 billion of revenues used to reduce the outstanding government debt.

3. Reform of the land tenure system, opening the possibility of converting the *Ejído*, an outmoded communal organization, into a modern, efficient, and fair system of land tenure.

Trade Liberalization

4. Unilateral adoption of free trade policies, starting in 1985 and leading to the North American Free Trade Agreement (NAFTA) and trade agreements with Chile, Colombia, Venezuela, and Costa Rica.

5. Mexico joined the General Agreement on Tariffs and Trade (GATT) in 1986, and, in 1994, became the first new member of the OECD in 25 years.

Fiscal Reforms

6. Thorough attempt to achieve fiscal balance (see **Exhibit 3**).

7. Tax reform, including the introduction of lower rates, the consolidation of taxes into a simpler and more uniform system, and measures to increase compliance with the tax code.

8. Pension and housing fund reforms within the social security system.

9. Authorization of private sector investment in infrastructure projects such as the 4,000 miles of toll roads that were constructed during 1988-1994, seaports, electricity generation facilities, and municipal water distribution systems.

Institutional Reform

10. Independence granted to the Banco de Mexico, the Mexican Central Bank.

Source: Adapted from Francísco Gil-Díaz and Augustín Carstens, "Some Hypotheses Related to the Mexican 1994–95 Crisis," paper presented to the Annual AEA meetings in San Francisco, January 5–7, 1996, p. 4.

Exhibit 3   Mexican Government Finance, 1981–1994

	1981	1983	1985	1987	1989	1991	1992	1993	1994
Millions of Pesos									
Total Revenue and Grants	911	3,014	7,559	31,476	86,939	140,636	174,278	186,644	211,434
Exp.& Lending Less Repay	1,312	4,467	11,118	58,898	112,021	112,942	127,357	180,193	211,820
Expenditure	*1,302*	*4,437*	*11,086*	*58,705*	*111,503*	*144,023*	*158,189*	*183,876*	*217,249*
Lending Less Repay	*10*	*30*	*32*	*193*	*518*	*-31,081*	*-30,832*	*-3,683*	*-5,429*
Deficit (-) or Surplus	-401	-1,453	-3,559	-27,422	-25,082	27,694	46,921	6,451	-386
As % GDP	*-6.5%*	*-8.1%*	*-7.5%*	*-14.2%*	*-4.9%*	*3.2%*	*4.5%*	*0.5%*	*0.0%*
Total Financing	401	1,453	3,559	27,422	25,082	-27,694	-46,921	-6,451	386
Domestic	610	828	3,463	23,580	24,436	-28,934	-42,888	-1,397	4,934
Foreign	-209	625	96	3,842	646	1,240	-4,033	-5,054	-4,548
Billions of Pesos									
Gross Domestic Product	6.14	17.88	47.17	193.16	512.60	876.93	1034.73	1256.20	1423.36
Pesos per U.S. Dollar	0.03	0.14	0.37	2.21	2.64	3.07	3.12	3.11	5.33

Source: Created by casewriter based on data from International Monetary Fund, *International Financial Statistics Yearbook*, 2002.

Exhibit 4   Monetary and Credit Growth, 1989–1994 (% growth *per annum* in *peso* terms)

	1989	1990	1991	1992	1993
Money:					
Base money[a]	10.2	35.3	27.8	14.4	10.4
M1[b]	41.8	60.3	118.3	15.1	17.7
M4[c]	50.8	46.3	30.9	19.9	27.3
Credit to private sector:					
Total	52.1	53.9	45.4	45.9	27.8
For agriculture	34.6	28.4	19.1	27.1	15.4
Manufacturing	47.9	39.9	32.1	25.5	16.2
Construction	124.7	164.3	107.1	88.9	na
Housing	39.1	46.1	24.3	19.9	na
Consumption	49.9	120.1	93.6	57.8	na

Source: Created by casewriter based on data from Economic Research Department, Banco de Mexico.
Notes: [a]Base money consists of currency held outside the central bank plus commercial bank reserves held at the central bank.

[b]M1 consists of currency and demand bank deposits held by the domestic non-bank private sector.

[c]M4 consists of M1 plus time and saving bank accounts and other liquid assets held by the domestic non-bank private sector.

Exhibit 5a   Mexican Inflation and Interest Rates (% per annum, December to December)

	Consumer Price Inflation	Wholesale Price Inflation	Short-term Interest Rates
1986	105.7	91.4	150.7
1987	159.2	135.6	171.8
1988	51.7	107.8	56.3
1989	19.7	16.1	40.3
1990	29.9	23.3	29.2
1991	18.8	20.5	19.9
1992	11.9	13.4	21.7
1993	8.0	9.8	14.6
1994	7.0	7.2	16.9

Source: Adapted from Sergio Raimond-Kedilhac et al., *'Sintesis y Expectativas Economicas de Mexico,'* IPADE (May 1996), pp. 40–47.

Exhibit 5b   Mexican and U.S. Short-term Interest Rates, December 1994–July 1995 (weekly data, *% per annum*)

	Rate on:			
Date	Mexican 91-day *Cetes*[a]	U.S. 3-month Treasury Bills	Spread i^{MEX}-i^{US}	Nominal Exchange Rate (*peso*/US$)
2 December 1994	14.76	5.79	8.97	3.4340
9	14.76	5.82	8.94	3.4475
16	14.76	5.72	9.04	3.4535
23	16.75	5.70	11.05	4.6500
30	31.13	5.70	25.43	4.9400
1 January 1995	34.99	5.91	29.08	5.3000
13	34.99	5.73	29.26	5.2800
20	39.00	5.90	33.10	5.6700
27	38.00	5.92	32.08	5.7000
3 February 1995	33.49	5.96	27.53	5.3600
10	35.10	5.99	29.11	5.5400
17	40.99	5.87	35.12	5.7250
24	57.00	5.89	51.11	5.8750
3 March 1995	51.23	5.91	45.32	6.3050
10	59.00	5.95	53.05	6.3000
17	82.38	5.92	76.46	6.9700
24	82.65	5.83	76.82	6.8050
31	75.00	5.88	69.12	6.7850

Source: Created by casewriter based on data from Datastream, Inc. and International Monetary Fund, *International Financial Statistics Yearbook*, 1996.

Note: [a]*Cetes* are Mexican Treasury securities of less than one-year maturity, denominated in pesos.

Exhibit 6a   Mexican National Income Accounts, 1988–1995 *(millions of constant 1990 new pesos)*

Year	Private Consumption	Fixed Capital Formation	Change in Stocks	Government Consumption	Exports	Imports	GDP
1988	444.25	123.28	7.38	55.31	107.49	97.62	635.91
1989	462.90	119.61	27.85	55.67	105.25	106.41	664.85
1990	486.35	127.73	31.01	57.80	108.30	116.32	694.87
1991	510.15	138.37	30.46	64.03	98.17	121.01	720.15
1992	526.30	151.57	29.20	73.49	91.78	132.29	740.04
1993	524.17	149.34	23.48	79.34	91.05	122.20	745.17
1994	540.02	156.84	24.09	89.26	97.93	136.90	771.25
1995	483.34	117.06	22.25	74.61	172.57	151.91	717.92

Source: Created by casewriter based on data from International Monetary Fund, *International Financial Statistics Yearbook*, 1996.

Exhibit 6b   Mexican GDP (% growth *per annum*)

Year	1993 Weights	1980 Weights
1980	1.2	1.2
1989	3.7	3.3
1990	4.7	4.4
1991	4.1	3.6
1992	3.5	2.8
1993	1.2	0.6
1994	3.9	3.5

Source: Adapted from National Accounts System, *Instituto Nacional de Estadistica, Geografía e Informática*, and Banco de México, Economic Research Department, reproduced in Francisco Gil-Diaz and Augustin Carstens, p. 166.

Note: The massive restructuring of the Mexican economy brought about by extensive structural economic reform may have distorted the official statistics. As the importance of different sectors varies, statistics based on earlier sectoral weightings may be misleading: The Banco de México has argued the GDP series based on 1980 weights understates the economic growth in the early 1990s.

Exhibit 7 Mexican Balance of Payments, 1988–1995 (*millions of U.S. dollars*)

	1988	1989	1990	1991	1992	1993	1994	1995
Merchandise exports	30,692	35,171	40,711	42,687	46,196	51,885	60,879	79,543
Merchandise imports	-28,081	-34,766	-41,592	-49,966	-62,130	-65,366	-79,346	-72,454
Trade Balance	**2,611**	**405**	**-881**	**-7,279**	**-15,934**	**-13,481**	**-18,467**	**7,089**
Services: Credit	6,084	7,208	8,094	8,869	9,275	9,517	10,323	10,281
Services: Debit	-6,281	-7,880	-10,323	-10,959	-11,959	-12,046	-12,925	-9,407
Balance on Goods and Services	**2,414**	**-267**	**-3,110**	**-9,369**	**-18,618**	**-16,010**	**-21,069**	**7,963**
Income: Credit	3,049	3,160	3,273	3,523	2,789	2,694	3,348	3,705
Income: Debit	-10,092	-11,261	-11,589	-11,788	-11,998	-13,724	-15,709	-16,284
Balance on Goods, Services, & Income	**-4,629**	**-8,368**	**-11,426**	**-17,634**	**-27,827**	**-27,040**	**-33,430**	**-4,616**
Current transfers: Credit	2,270	2,559	3,990	2,765	3,404	3,656	4,042	3,993
Current transfers: Debit	-15	-16	-15	NA	-19	-16	-30	-31
Current Account	**-2,374**	**-5,825**	**-7,451**	**-14,888**	**-24,442**	**-23,400**	**-29,418**	**-654**
Direct investment	2,011	2,785	2,549	4,742	4,393	4,389	10,972	6,963
Portfolio investment: Assets	-880	-56	-7,354	-603	1,165	-564	-615	-663
Portfolio investment: Liabilities	1,001	354	3,369	12,741	18,041	28,919	8,185	-10,140
Other investment: Assets	-874	-1,114	-1,345	-395	4,387	-3,038	-5,057	-5,296
Other investment: Liabilities	-5,753	-859	11,222	8,654	-947	4,054	2,302	-2,645
Financial Account	**-4,495**	**1,110**	**8,441**	**25,139**	**27,039**	**33,760**	**15,787**	**-11,781**
Net errors and omissions	-3,192	4,503	1,229	-2,278	-851	-3,128	-4,035	-2,871
Change in Official Reserves	**10,061**	**212**	**-2,219**	**-7,973**	**-1,746**	**-7,232**	**17,667**	**15,306**

Source: Created by casewriter based on data from International Monetary Fund, *International Financial Statistics Yearbook*, 1996.

Exhibit 8a   Comparative Export Performance, 1985–1995

Volumes, 1985 = 100

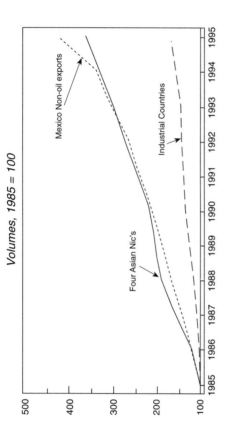

Source: Created by casewriter based on data from Economic Research Department, Banco de Mexico.

Exhibit 8b   Mexican Trade Performance, 1988–1995 *(millions of U.S. dollars)*

	Exports		of which:		Imports		of which:		
Year	Excluding Maquiladoras	Including Maquiladoras	Petroleum	Non-petroleum	Excluding Maquiladoras	Including Maquiladoras	Consumption Goods	Capital Goods	Intermediate Goods
1987	20.5	..	8.6	..	13.3	..	0.8	2.6	..
1988	20.5	..	6.7	..	20.3	..	1.9	4.0	..
1989	22.8	..	7.9	..	25.4	..	3.5	4.8	..
1990	26.8	..	10.1	..	31.3	..	5.1	6.8	..
1991	26.9	42.7	8.2	34.5	38.2	50.0	5.8	8.6	35.5
1992	27.5	46.2	8.3	37.9	48.2	62.1	7.7	11.6	42.8
1993	30.0	51.9	7.4	44.5	48.9	65.4	7.8	11.0	46.5
1994	34.6	60.9	7.4	53.4	58.9	79.3	9.5	13.3	56.5
1995	48.4	79.5	8.4	71.1	46.3	72.5	5.3	8.7	58.4

Source: Created by casewriter based on data from Datastream, Inc and Economic Research Department, Banco de Mexico.

Note: *Maquiladoras* are essentially assembly operations, permitted only along the Mexican border with the United States. Even prior to Mexico's 1991 liberalization of foreign direct investment, 100% foreign ownership of *maquiladoras* was permitted. Under sections 806-30 and 807 of the U.S. Tariff schedule, goods assembled in Mexican *maquiladoras* and re-exported to the United States are taxed only on the value-added in Mexico, rather than on the gross value of the export.

Exhibit 9   Real Exchange Indices (1999 = 100)

	Relative to the United States			Relative to the World[a]	
	CPI[b] Based	WPI[c] Based	Nominal Wage Based	CPI-Based	ULC[d]-Based
1988	106.3	101.9	126.9	102.3	121.2
1989	107.5	106.6	113.1	102.3	104.8
1990	100.0	100.0	100.0	100.0	100.0
1991	88.4	86.5	83.3	90.3	91.9
1992	80.2	78.0	73.8	83.0	84.8
1993	75.0	72.5	69.5	79.3	83.8
1994[e]	78.6	75.1	73.5	88.0	90.4
1995	134.1	1,131.5	167.4	--	--

Source: Adapted from Rudiger Dornbusch and Alejandro Werner, "Mexico: Stabilization, Reform and No Growth," *Brookings Papers on Economic Activity,* vol. 1 (1994), p. 261; Francisco Gil-Diaz and Augustin Carstens (op cit.), p. 165; Sergio Raimond-Kedihac et al., "*Sintesis y Expectativas Economicas de Mexico,*" IPADE (May 1996), pp. 45–48; International Monetary Fund, *International Financial Statistics* (February 1996).[f]

Notes: The real exchange rate is defined as the ratio of the domestic currency price of foreign goods to domestic goods. Thus, a *fall* in the real exchange rate index indicates an *appreciation*.

[a]The world is defined as a GDP-weighted group of 133 countries for the CPI-based measure and as a trade-weighted group of Mexico's six largest trading partners (the United States, Germany, Japan, Canada, the United Kingdom, and France, accounting for approximately 85% of total Mexican trade in manufactures) for the ULC-based measure.

[b]Consumer price index, measuring the price of a broadly based consumption basket, including manufactured goods and services.

[c]Wholesale price index, measuring the "factory gate" prices of manufactured and intermediate goods.

[d]Unit labor costs, measuring nominal wage growth net of gains in labor productivity.

[e]The exchange rate used for 1994 is an average of January through November. It therefore excludes the devaluation of 20 December and the consequences of the subsequent float on 22 December.

[f]Sources vary in their data for real exchange rates. The table embodies some averaging of the various sources.

Exhibit 10a   Mexican and U.S. Stock Market Indices (January 1990=100)

Source: Created by casewriter based on data from Datastream, Inc.

Note: The New York Stock Exchange index is based on the S&P 500. The Mexican Stock Market index is shown in *peso* terms (simply rebasing the stock market index) and in dollar terms (where the official stock market index is adjusted using the monthly average of spot *peso*-dollar exchange rates).

Exhibit 10b   Mexican and U.S. Short-term Interest Rates (% *per annum*)

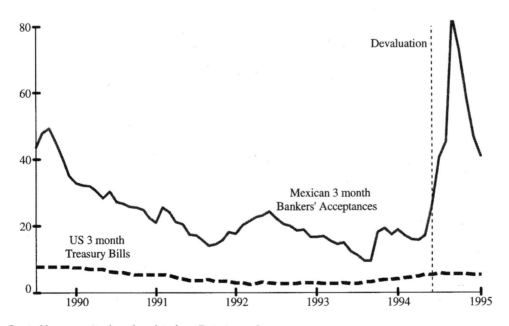

Source: Created by casewriter based on data from Datastream, Inc.

Exhibit 11   Nonperforming Consumer Loans, 1989–1994 (% of total consumer loans made by the commercial banking system)

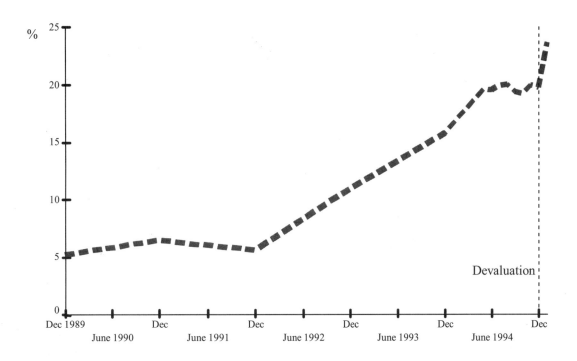

Source: Created by casewriter based on data from Klaus Desmet and Thomas Mann, "Lessons from the Mexican Banking Crisis," mimeo, Banco de Mexico (August 1996).

Exhibit 12   Mexican Domestic Saving (% of GDP)

	1983	1989	1994
Gross national saving	30.3	21.2	18.4
Private sector	26.9	19.5	18.5
Public sector	3.5	1.7	-0.1
Gross domestic saving	26.7	20.9	16.8
Private	21.8	15.7	12.1

Source: Adapted from Francisco Gil-Diaz and Augustin Carstens, "One Year of Solitude: Some Pilgrim Tales About Mexico's 1994–95 Crisis," *American Economic Association Papers and Proceedings*, vol. 86 (May 1996), p. 168.

Note: Gross national saving (GNS) is a GNP-based measure and therefore includes factor payments to overseas residents. Because of Mexico's large external debt, such factor payments were considerable. Hence the large discrepancy between GNS and the GDP-based measure, gross domestic savings.

Exhibit 13   *Peso*-Dollar Exchange Rate in Banco de Mexico's Fluctuation Band, 1992–1994 *(new pesos per dollar)*

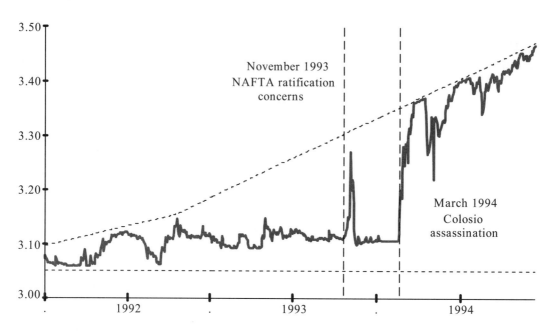

Source: Created by casewriter based on data from Economic Research Department, Banco de Mexico.

Exhibit 14   Mexican Foreign Exchange Reserves, 1994 *(billions of U.S. dollars, excluding gold)*

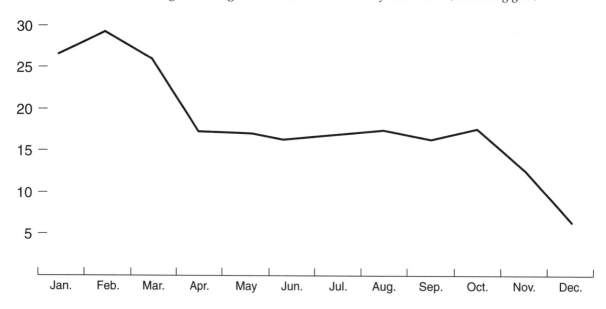

Source: Created by casewriter based on data from International Monetary Fund, *Capital Markets Report*, August 1995.

Exhibit 15   Foreign Exchange Intervention by the Banco de Mexico, 1993–1994 (daily data, *millions of U.S. dollars*)

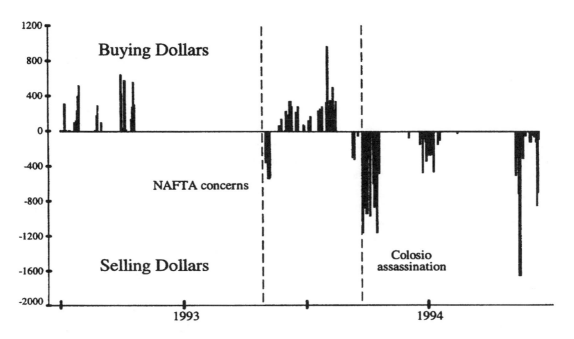

Source: Created by casewriter based on data from Economic Research Department, Banco de Mexico.

Exhibit 16   Composition of Mexican Public Debt *(billions of new pesos)*

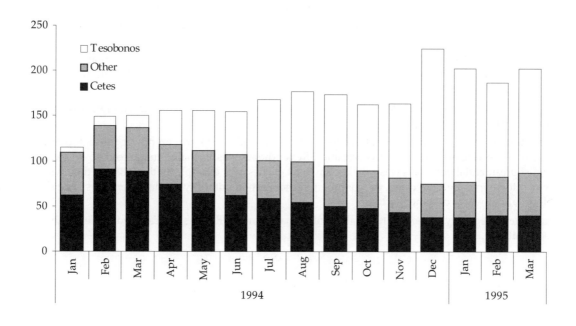

Source: Created by casewriter based on data from International Monetary Fund, *Capital Markets Report*, August 1995.

Endnotes

1   Excerpt from Francísco Gil-Díaz and Augustín Carstens, "Some Hypotheses Related to the Mexican 1994–95 Crisis," paper presented to the Annual AEA meetings in San Francisco, January 5–7, 1996.

2   Refer to Huw Pill and Helen Shapiro, "Mexico (B): Escaping from the Debt Crisis?" HBS Case No. 797-105.

3   Throughout this paper, I use the colloquial "downward" movement of a nominal exchange rate (say towards the "bottom" of a fluctuation band) to indicate a depreciation of the currency. Note that this is numerically the opposite of movements in the *peso*/dollar exchange rate as normally quoted (and as shown in **Exhibit 16**), where rises in the numerical value indicate a depreciation.

4   Guillermo Ortíz, *La Reforma Financiera y la Desincorporación Bancaría* (Mexico City: *Fondo de Cultura Económica*) (1994); translated in Mauricio Naranjo, "The Mexican Financial Market: Liberalization and New Regulation," mimeo, Banco de Mexico, pp. 80–81 (June 1995).

5   Much of this information is drawn from Mauricio Naranjo (op cit.), pp. 80–84, Abraham E. Vela, "Implementation of Monetary Policy through Open Market Operations: A Short Essay," mimeo, Banco de Mexico (March 1996) and from interviews conducted by the author at the Banco de Mexico and Hacienda (Ministry of Finance) in August 1996.

6   Under a special arrangement, Citibank had long operated in Mexico.

7   See Courtenay Sprague/Huw Pill, "Debt Restructuring Under the Brady Plan" HBS Case No. 796-130 (April 1996).

8   See Huw Pill, "Portfolio Capital Flows to Emerging Markets," HBS Case No. 796-129 (April 1996).

9   See Jeffrey Sachs, Aaron Tornell and Andres Velasco, "Lessons from the Mexican Crisis," *Economic Policy*, vol. 21, no. 1, pp. 67–108 (April 1996).

10 From Paul Krugman, "Dutch Tulips and Emerging Markets," *Foreign Affairs*, vol. 74, no. 4 (August 1995).

11 From Rudiger Dornbusch and Alejandro Werner, "Mexico: Stabilization, Reform and No Growth," *Brookings Papers on Economic Activity*, vol. 1 (1994).

12 From Jorge G. Castañeda, "Mexico's Circle of Misery," *Foreign Affairs*, vol. 75, no. 4, pp. 92–105 (June 1996).

13 From the annual survey of international banks conducted by *The Banker* (1994, 1995); quoted in Mauricio Naranjo (op cit.), pp. 83–84.

14 From Alejandro Díaz de León and Moises J. Schwartz, "Crisis Management and Institutional Change Aimed at the Prevention of Future Crises," mimeo, Banco de Mexico, pp. 8–10 (June 1996) and interviews by the author at the Bank in August 1996.

15 See Klaus Desmet and Thomas Mann, "Lessons from the Mexican Banking Crisis," mimeo, Banco de Mexico (August 1996).

16 The PRI had never lost a presidential election and maintained a firm grip on power through patronage and control of the electoral system. As such, the PRI candidate was virtually guaranteed to be elected in the August presidential poll. This was well known to all parties. For example, in the 1988 election, when Salinas seemed to be in danger of losing, the computer at the election authority headquarters mysteriously crashed before Salinas was proclaimed victor.

17 The General Secretary of the Institutional Revolutionary Party (PRI) was assassinated on September 28, 1994 (see **Exhibit 1**).

The Choice of Exchange Rate Regime

An exchange rate is the price of one currency in terms of another currency. For example, the exchange rate most people follow in Argentina is the price in pesos of one dollar. As the case with any other good, the price of a currency is affected by supply and demand. As demand for a currency increases (or supply decreases), its price will rise (i.e., it will take more foreign currency to purchase domestic currency). This is referred to as an appreciation. Conversely, as demand for a currency decreases or supply increases, its value will depreciate. In the example of the exchange rate followed in Argentina, when the exchange rate (or "the dollar") is said to have gone up, people usually mean the peso has depreciated (lost value) since more pesos are required to buy a dollar (see **Chart 1**).[a]

Chart 1   Exchange Rate: Argentine Pesos per U.S. Dollars, November 2001 – December 2003 (monthly averages)

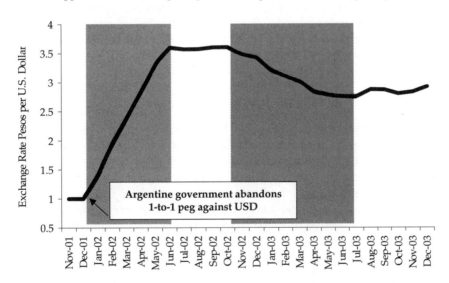

Source: Adapted from International Monetary Fund, *International Finance Statistics CD-ROM*, May 2004.

---

[a] Some countries quote the exchange rate the other way around (i.e., as the price in foreign currency of the local money).

Professor Rafael Di Tella and Research Associate Ingrid Vogel prepared this note as the basis for class discussion.

Supply and demand for currencies can shift rapidly and dramatically with thousands of participants in the foreign exchange market obtaining foreign currency to buy foreign goods and services, to invest in foreign assets, or simply to speculate.

The prospect of large and rapid swings in exchange rates introduces uncertainty into the business environment. For example, a company may rely on inputs from a foreign country (and hence priced in a foreign currency) in its production process. The company's profit, then, would be tied to the price it must pay for those inputs—which will depend to a large degree on the exchange rate. Some firms choose to mitigate this risk and better control their financial performance through hedging transactions in the forward exchange market. Such hedging, however, can be quite costly.

Exchange rate fluctuations can also have important macroeconomic implications. For example, when a country's currency depreciates, its goods abroad become cheaper while foreign goods become more expensive (holding price levels constant in the two countries). Since the basket of goods consumed in the country is composed of tradable goods with prices that may increase with the exchange rate, workers may demand higher wages to maintain their standard of living. Wage increases often lead to price increases and, depending on how expectations react and how monetary policy is constructed, could ultimately fuel a wage-price spiral. Foreign exchange traders speculating on further currency depreciation could compound this effect and force the country into a "vicious circle" of depreciation and inflation that would be difficult to escape.[1]

Countries can choose to mitigate their exposure to exchange rate risk. At one extreme, a group of countries can decide to form a monetary union and adopt a common currency—thereby eliminating all exchange rate differentials. At the other extreme, countries choose to allow the exchange rate to float, so that market forces determine the price of foreign currency with little government intervention. In fact, countries can choose from a spectrum of options for managing their exchange rates, each with its own benefits and drawbacks.

Floating Exchange Rate Regimes

Countries including the United States, the United Kingdom, and Japan have **independently floating (or flexible) currency arrangements** (see **Exhibit 1** for a list of exchange rate regimes and participating countries). Their exchange rates are therefore determined by market forces. These can be divided into long-run and short-run factors. The theory of **purchasing power parity** (PPP), which relates to arbitrage in the slow and imperfect goods market where transaction costs are high, helps explain exchange rate behavior in the long run. The **interest parity condition**, which relates to arbitrage in the rapid and effective financial markets where transaction costs are low, helps explain behavior in the short run.

PPP emerges from the **law of one price**, which states that in competitive markets, identical goods sold in different countries should sell for the same price. Any difference in price not justified by transportation or other transactions costs would disappear over time through the forces of supply and demand. For example, if steel cost less in Germany than in Japan, excess demand for German steel would push German prices higher while excess supply of Japanese steel would push Japanese prices lower. Eventually, prices will equalize and the market will be in equilibrium.

PPP extends this law of one price for commodities to overall national price levels. It states that exchange rates between any two currencies will adjust to reflect levels of inflation in the two countries. In other words, if one country experiences higher inflation than another country, its currency will depreciate an offsetting amount in terms of the other currency (see **Exhibit 3**). PPP thus predicts that changes in **nominal exchange rates** (the relative price of two currencies) will always offset inflation such that the **real exchange rate** (the relative price of two output baskets) remains constant.

The Economist produces a light-hearted interpretation of PPP with its McDonald's Big Mac and Starbuck's tall-Latte Indices (see **Exhibits 2a** and **2b**). The Latte Index compares the U.S. dollar cost of a Starbuck's tall Latte in countries around the world to the U.S. price to determine whether currencies are under or overvalued. For example, in January 2004, a latte cost 33% more in dollar terms in the euro area than in the United States. The index takes the latte price as indicative of a country's overall price level, and, relying on the theory of PPP, predicts that the euro should depreciate 33% against the U.S. dollar over time.[a]

PPP is considered to provide a useful framework for thinking about exchange rates in the longer term, but its predictive power in the short term is weak. This is due in large part to the importance of the interest parity condition. Under interest parity, expected rates of return (interest rates adjusted for any expected currency depreciation or appreciation) on deposits held in different currencies converge. If returns differ, investors operating in an environment of capital mobility will produce excess demand for the higher return asset and excess supply of the lower return asset and will force a currency's value to change in response. For example, if the dollar interest rate is 6%, the euro interest rate is 2%, and the dollar is expected to depreciate against the euro by 3% (from, say, $1.00 per euro to $1.03 per euro) over the year, then the expected return on euro deposits would be 2% versus an expected return of 3% (6% interest rate minus 3% depreciation) for dollar deposits. Investors will immediately create excess supply of euro deposits and excess demand for dollar deposits, and the dollar's value will increase against the euro in response, say to $0.99 per euro. Assuming the value for the future expected euro/dollar exchange rate remains $1.03 per euro, the newly more valuable dollar therefore has further to fall to reach this level. The increase in the expected depreciation of the dollar against the euro (in this case, closer to 4%) serves to decrease the expected return on dollar deposits, such that expected returns on euro and dollar deposits equalize (at 2%). More generally, an increase in dollar interest rates causes the dollar to appreciate against other currencies, while an increase in the interest rates of other currencies causes the dollar to depreciate against those other currencies.

Flexible exchange rates are subject to considerable oscillations over time. This is explained, in part, by the phenomenon labeled "overshooting."[2] Suppose a country increases its money supply. In the long term prices will rise, and, under PPP, the currency will depreciate. In the short term, though, interest rates will fall. Under the condition of interest parity, investors would only choose to hold dollar assets if the lower interest rate were offset by a currency appreciation. Clearly, this conflicts with predictions for long-term currency depreciation.[3] The overshooting phenomenon predicts that, to reconcile this conflict, the currency must fall well below its long-term value in the short term, so that it has room for the necessary appreciation that will persuade investors to hold dollar assets.

Currencies are rarely allowed to float strictly according to these rules. While central banks of countries classified as independently floating do not intervene in foreign exchange markets to establish a level for their currencies, they do regularly intervene to moderate the rate of change and prevent extreme fluctuations in the exchange rate. The central bank of a supposedly independently floating currency will occasionally intervene to affect the value of the country's currency—which is referred to as a "dirty float."

In contrast, a **managed float** is one in which the central bank openly influences the movement of the exchange rate through active intervention in the foreign exchange market without explicitly

---

[a] The validity of such an index is questionable, given that Starbuck's lattes are not traded across borders. Furthermore, prices are affected by differences in taxes and the cost of non-tradable items such as rents.

specifying a desired path for the exchange rate. Under a managed float, monetary policy is influenced by exchange rate changes but is not constrained by the requirements of a fixed rate. For example, a country that may keep its currency's value close to a particular level against the U.S. dollar may choose to react to unemployment with expansionary monetary policy and thereby let its currency depreciate. **Exhibit 1** lists countries with managed floats in 2001.

Fixed Exchange Rates

A **fixed (or pegged) exchange rate** simply requires the central bank to promise to exchange currency at a specified rate against another currency (or basket of currencies). For example Aruba pegs its florin to the U.S. dollar at a rate of 1.79 florin per dollar. The Aruban central bank must always be willing to buy florin with dollars or to buy dollars with florin in any amount at the fixed rate of 1.79 florin per dollar. Otherwise, there could be excess supply of or demand for florin and its value would depreciate or appreciate to restore equilibrium. For example, if there were excess demand for florin (because of, say, a cold winter in the United States that encourages a 50% increase in tourism), the florin would become more valuable relative to the dollar, and the number of florin to buy a dollar would decrease, implying appreciation of the florin. In order to prevent such a move in the exchange rate, the Aruban central bank intervenes in foreign exchange markets to meet the excess demand by increasing the supply of florin through buying dollars. Thus, while the exchange rate doesn't move, the dollar reserves of the central bank do change.

This situation can also be evaluated in terms of interest rates. In order for interest parity to hold, the florin interest rate must equal the dollar interest rate plus the expected depreciation of florin in terms of dollars. If the exchange rate is credibly fixed, there is no expected depreciation. This implies that the interest rate on florin deposits must equal the interest rate on dollar deposits.[a] The increase in demand for florin due to more tourism would increase the florin interest rate. If confidence in the fixed exchange rate holds, then a higher florin interest rate would attract investors who offer dollars and demand florins. Since the central bank wants to fix the exchange rate it must intervene by increasing the florin money supply, otherwise traders would push up the value of florin in terms of dollars.

If confidence in the fixed exchange rate falters, however, the interest rates will no longer be equal. Suppose tourism falls dramatically in Aruba after a hurricane hits, and demand for florin therefore decreases. Traders may anticipate that Aruba will be forced to devalue its exchange rate to, say, 2.5 florin per dollar in order to attract new tourists. Interest parity will then predict that the interest rate on florin deposits be equal to the interest rate on dollar deposits plus the expected depreciation from 1.79 to 2.5 florin per dollar. Unless the Aruban central bank increases the interest rate on florin deposits to compensate for the expected depreciation, traders will sell florin for dollars, depleting the Aruban Central Bank's foreign exchange reserves. Were these reserves to run out, the Aruban central bank would indeed have little choice but to float the florin.

In order to avoid the need to respond to all movements in the supply and demand for currency, a country may **fix its currency within a band** to allow some fluctuation in value. For example, from 1979 to 1998, a number of countries participated in the European Monetary System. Under this system, countries' exchange rates were fixed but allowed to fluctuate up or down by as much as 6% (widened to 15% in 1993) relative to an assigned par value. The bands allowed countries some latitude with choosing monetary policies and also were intended to reduce the risks of speculative attacks. In 2004, only one large economy—Denmark—used this type of exchange rate regime.

---

[a] In reality, there may be some other risks priced into the Aruban interest rate, such as sovereign or default risk or the risk that the peg will be abandoned. These risks will make the Aruban interest rate higher in equilibrium.

Another variation on a fixed exchange rate regime is the **crawling peg** or **crawling band**. Under a crawling peg, the central bank adjusts the value of its currency periodically in small amounts at a fixed, pre-announced rate or in response to changes in specific indicators. Crawling pegs became popular in Latin America in the late 1970s as a way to anchor expectations in the fight against inflation. Pre-announced schedules of domestic currency depreciation against the U.S. dollar that were below the ongoing rates of inflation were announced to reduce the rate of increase in the prices of internationally traded goods. In early 2004, only nine countries were classified as using crawling pegs or bands.

In any case, the ability of the central bank to defend its currency under a fixed exchange rate regime is limited by its stock of foreign exchange reserves and by its ability to raise interest rates. If there is persistent excess demand for dollars, the central bank must sell dollars and its reserves therefore fall. If the central bank's reserves run low and it is unable to secure financing from private markets, it may have to devalue the exchange rate. Likewise, countries may be unable to increase interest rates to the levels necessary to defend their national currency, maybe because unemployment is too high already or the public debt is becoming unsustainable.

The Debate between Fixed versus Floating Exchange Rate Regimes

There are advantages and disadvantages to fixed and floating exchange rate regimes. Debate centers on the impact of exchange rate regime on trade, the risk of destabilizing speculative attack, and institutional credibility versus monetary autonomy.

Trade Advocates of fixed exchange rate systems argue that they benefit economies around the world by providing stability in international prices and therefore encourage the conduct of trade. As evidence in favor they contrast the difficulty faced by firms engaged in international trade after the breakdown of the Bretton Woods System of fixed exchange rates in 1973. They also point out Japan's success as an export nation under relatively fixed exchange rates in the post-war period. (See the Annex for a discussion of the Bretton Woods System and the Gold Standard. See **Exhibit 4** for dollar-yen and dollar-mark exchange rates from 1948 to 2003.) Although exchange rate risk could be hedged under a floating exchange rate regime, such hedges could be expensive.

Risk of destabilizing speculative attack A significant weakness of fixed exchange rates regimes is that they are subject to destabilizing speculative attacks. For example, in 1992 Britain was forced to withdraw from the EMS after a prolonged speculative attack on the pound. German reunification in 1990 had resulted in high interest rates, which the United Kingdom was forced to adopt during a time of high unemployment. Currency traders speculated that Britain would be unable politically to increase rates high enough to support the sterling's peg to the DM. Expecting a devaluation, they sold sterling until, indeed, its value could no longer be supported. Such speculative attacks on fixed currencies have become more frequent under increasingly mobile international capital markets. While Britain emerged relatively unscathed from its experience, speculative attacks in emerging market economies, such as many east Asian countries (including Thailand, Malaysia, and South Korea) in 1997 and Argentina in 2001, have led to particularly destabilizing episodes, including meltdown of financial systems and devastating economic contractions.

Institutional credibility versus monetary autonomy A major benefit of fixed exchange rate regimes, particularly in developing countries, is that they can signal discipline and promote institutional credibility. Fixed exchange rates require countries to adopt restrictive monetary and fiscal policies, which foster an anti-inflationary environment. On the negatives side, fixed rates may be maintained at rates that are inconsistent with economic fundamentals, thereby exacerbating periods of recession. Unlike under a floating exchange rate regime, a central bank under a fixed regime would be unable to respond to unemployment through lowering the interest rate to stimulate investment because of concerns about the effect on the exchange rate.

Advocates of floating exchange rate regimes emphasize the greater importance of central bank autonomy over monetary policy in responding to negative shocks. Critics, however, claim that the greater autonomy supposedly afforded under flexible regimes is illusory. They argue that a "fear of floating"[4] prevents countries from ignoring movements in the exchange rate. This is particularly relevant in small emerging market economies where exports, imports, and international capital flows comprise a relatively large share of the economy, such that large swings in the exchange rate can cause substantial swings in the real economy. In addition, in a country where banks make significant loans in U.S. dollars, a depreciation of the domestic currency against the dollar disrupts the financial system as borrowers with domestic currency income would have difficulty repaying dollar loans. Finally, in countries with an inflationary past most economic actors are "looking" at the dollar, in that a depreciation has an immediate impact on prices. Because of such factors, countries adopting floating exchange rates would be reluctant to allow their exchange rates to fluctuate freely. In the words of several economists, these countries would, therefore, "forgo the benefits of predictable currency values on international trade and investment while still laboring under the constraint of avoiding excessive exchange rate fluctuations."[5]

Strengthening Commitment to Fixed Exchange Rates

A more credible guarantee of a country's commitment to a fixed exchange rate would arguably limit the ability of traders to launch speculative attacks against the local currency. A **currency board** would come closer to offering such a guarantee by bolstering the central bank's commitment to a fixed exchange rate and thereby helping to reduce chances of devaluation. It has three important components: the establishment of a fixed exchange rate, the requirement that central bank reserves cover 100% of the monetary base at that exchange rate, and the obligation that the central bank meet all demand for dollars. As such, a currency board imposes discipline on governments by prohibiting increases in money supply beyond the level of reserves. It also prohibits the central bank from extending credit to commercial banks and rules out a role as lender of last resort.

A currency board benefits from automatic adjustment mechanisms. Suppose a currency becomes overvalued because inflation is higher domestically than in the country of the reserve currency. In other words, the real exchange rate appreciates (while the nominal exchange rate remains fixed). In this case, imports become relatively less expensive than exports. Thus, foreign demand for a country's goods and services decreases while the country's demand for foreign goods and services increases. As a result, importers will sell more domestic currency than exporters will demand. The currency board automatically eliminates the excess supply of domestic currency by exchanging it for foreign currency at the fixed rate. The domestic money supply therefore shrinks and domestic interest rates are driven higher. The higher interest rates slow investment and create a recessionary environment. This drives down the overall price level and serves to correct the real exchange rate appreciation. In countries with highly flexible prices and wages and high labor mobility, this process is fast and painless. Likewise, if individuals become skeptical of the fixed exchange rate and choose to convert local currency into the reserve currency, money supply shrinks and interest rates rise sharply in response. Eventually, interest rates on local currency deposits become high enough to attract investors.

Clearly, a currency board does not make a country immune to speculative attack. Argentina adopted a currency board-like system in 1991 but was forced to abandon it in 2002 after soaring interest rates brought about a prolonged recession.[6] Some observers argued that Argentina should have adopted **dollarization**, under which the commitment to a fixed exchange rate is even stronger.[7]

Under dollarization, a country replaces its local currency with a foreign currency such as the U.S. dollar or the euro. As such, it eliminates currency volatility and the possibility of future currency crises. Without a domestic currency, it would become much more difficult for the government to regain control of monetary policy and devalue. Therefore, sudden capital outflows motivated by fears of devaluation would arguably not occur. As a result, international investors would have a higher level of confidence in the country, which would lead to lower interest rate spreads on international borrowing. It also would promote lower transactions costs and could arguably strengthen institutions, encouraging further investment.

On the negative side, countries that dollarize have to surrender (or export) a large amount of goods to obtain the dollars needed to replace the local currency. In addition, similar to under a currency board, their central banks lose the ability to serve as a lender of last resort in the event of a banking crisis. Only two sizable countries have adopted dollarization: Ecuador (since 2000) and Panama (since 1904). With limited historical experiences to evaluate, economists have been unable to make a conclusive case for or against dollarization.[8]

Annex: A Short History of Fixed Exchange Rates

An early system of fixed exchange rates existed under the **gold standard**, which was in effect from 1870 to 1914. Under the gold standard, all major countries set values for their currencies in terms of gold and agreed to buy and sell gold on demand with any other country at that rate. As such, all exchange rates were fixed against one another. For example, the United States agreed to buy and sell gold for $20.67 per ounce, while Britain set the rate at 4.2474 pounds per ounce. The dollar-pound exchange rate was therefore fixed at 4.8665 dollars per pound. If the exchange rate veered from this value to, say, 5 dollars per pound, gold traders could buy gold in the United States for $20.67 and sell it in London for $21.237. With excess demand for U.S. gold, the exchange rate would quickly be pushed back to 4.8665 dollars per pound.

In order to fix their exchange rates in this way, countries had to maintain adequate gold reserves. The gold standard was suspended with the outbreak of World War I, which interrupted trade flows, restricted the free movement of gold, and resulted in high inflation for many countries. Multiple attempts in the following years to revive the gold standard failed.

After World War II, a modified gold standard was successfully introduced. Between 1944 and 1973, most countries participated in the system of fixed exchange rates established under the **Bretton Woods** agreement (which also created the International Monetary Fund and the World Bank). Countries pegged their currencies to the U.S. dollar, while the United States pegged to gold and agreed to exchange gold for dollars with foreign central banks on demand at a price of $35 an ounce. Central banks were required to intervene in the foreign exchange market to support their pegs. For example, if the German mark were to fall in value, the German central bank would sell dollars and buy marks in order to reduce the supply of marks and thereby increase their value. The German central bank could sell gold to the United States to obtain dollars, if necessary. Under certain conditions, such as if a currency became too weak to defend, a country could devalue its currency (decrease its value to a new fixed rate).

In 1971, the United States suspended official convertibility of gold, and most major currencies chose to float against the dollar. By early 1973, the Bretton Woods system of fixed exchange rates was abandoned altogether.[9]

Exhibit 1 Exchange Rate Arrangements Worldwide (as of March 31, 2001)

Exchange Rate Regime		Anchor, etc.	Countries and Regions	Number	
Strong Fixed Rate	Exchange Arrangements with No Separate Legal Tender	Euro Area	Austria, Belgium, Finland, France, Germany, Greece, Ireland, Italy, Luxembourg, Netherlands, Portugal, Spain	12	40
		West African Economic and Monetary Union	Benin, Burkina Faso, Cote d'Ivoire, Guinea-Bissau, Mali, Niger, Senegal, and Togo	8	
		East Caribbean Currency Union	Antigua & Barbuda, Dominica, Grenada, St. Kitts & Nevis, St. Lucia, and St. Vincent & the Grenadines	6	
		Central African Economic and Monetary Community	Cameroon, C. African Rep., Chad, Congo, Rep. Of, Equatorial Guinea, and Gabon	6	
		Other Currencies	Argentina, Ecuador, Kiribati, Marshall Islands, Micronesia, Palau, Panama, and San Marino	8	
	Currency Board Arrangements		Bosnia and Herzegovina, Brunei Darussalam, Bulgaria, Hong Kong, Djibouti, Estonia, and Lithuania	7	
Fixed Rate	Conventional Fixed Peg Arrangements	Against a single currency	Aruba, The Bahamas, Bahrain, Barbados, Belize, Bhutan, Cape Verde, P.R. Mainland China, Comoros, Congo, Eritorea, El Salvador, Iran, Iraq, Jordan, Lebanon, Lesotho, Macedonia, Malaysia, Maldives, Namibia, Nepal, Netherlands Antilles, Oman, Qatar, Saudi Ar	31	44
		Against a composite	Bangladesh, Botswana, Fiji, Kuwait, Latvia, Malta, Morocco, Myanmar, Samoa, Seychelles, Solomon Islands, Tonga, and Vanuatu	13	
	Pegged Exchange Rates Within Horizontal Bands	Exchange Rate Mechanism II	Denmark (+/- 2.25%)	1	6
		Other Currencies	Cyprus (+/- 2.25%), Egypt (+/- 1%), Libyan A.J. (+/- 77.5%), Suriname (+/- 9.1%), and Vietnam (0.1% daily movement, one-sided)	5	
	Crawling Pegs		Bolivia, Costa Rica, Nicaragua, and Zimbabwe	4	
	Exchange Rates within Crawling Bands		Honduras (+/- 7%), Hungary (+/-2.25%), Israel (+/- 20%), Uruguay (+/- 3%), and Venezuela (+/- 7.5%)	5	
Floating Rate	Managed Floating with no Preannounced Path for Exchange Rate		Algeria, Azerbaijan, Belarus, Burundi, Cambodia, Croatia, Czech Republic, Dominican Rep., Ethiopia, Guatemala, India, Jamaica, Kazakhstan, Kenya, Kyrgyz Republic, Lao PDR, Mauritania, Nigeria, Norway, Pakistan, Paraguay, Romania, Russian Federation, Rwand	33	
	Independent Floating		Albania, Afghanistan, Angola, Armenia, Australia, Brazil, Canada, Chile, Colombia, Gambia, Georgia, Ghana, Guinea, Guyana, Haiti, Iceland, Indonesia, Japan, Korea, Liberia, Madagascar, Mauritius, Malawi, Mexico, Moldova, Mongolia, Mozambique, New Zealand	47	
			Total:	186	

Source: Adapted from International Monetary Fund, *International Financial Statistics,* August 2001.

Exhibit 2a   Economist Big Mac Index (April 26, 2003)

		Big Mac prices		Implied PPP of the dollar	Actual dollar exchange rate 4/22/03	Under (-) / over (+) valuation against dollar, %
		in local currency	in dollars			
United States	$	2.71	2.71			
Argentina	Peso	4.10	1.42	1.51	2.88	-47
Aruba	Florin	4.10	2.29	1.51	1.79	-15
Australia	A$	3.00	1.86	1.11	1.61	-31
Brazil	Real	4.55	1.48	1.68	3.07	-45
Britain	Sterling	1.99	3.14	0.73	0.63	16
Canada	C$	3.20	2.21	1.18	1.45	-19
Chile	Peso	1,400	1.96	517	716	-28
China	Yuan	9.90	1.20	3.65	8.28	-56
Denmark	DKr	27.75	4.09	10.24	6.78	51
Euro area	Euro	2.71	2.98	1.00	0.91	10
Hong Kong	HK$	11.50	1.47	4.24	7.80	-46
Japan	Yen	262	2.18	97	120	-19
Mexico	Peso	23.00	2.18	8.49	10.53	-19
New Zealand	NZ$	3.95	2.22	1.46	1.78	-18
Peru	New Sol	7.90	2.28	2.92	3.46	-16
Russia	Rouble	41.00	1.32	15.13	31.10	-51
Singapore	S$	3.30	1.85	1.22	1.78	-32
South Africa	Rand	13.95	1.85	5.15	7.56	-32
South Korea	Won	3,300	2.70	1,218	1,220	0
Switzerland	SFr	6.30	4.60	2.32	1.37	70
Thailand	Baht	59.00	1.38	21.77	42.70	-49
Venezuela	Bolivar	3,700	2.32	1,365	1,598	-15

Source: Adapted from "McCurrencies," *The Economist*, April 24, 2003.

Exhibit 2b   Economist Starbucks Tall-Latte versus McDonald's Big Mac Index (January 15, 2004) Local currency under (-) / over (+) valuation against the dollar, %, using:

	Starbucks Tall-Latte index	McDonald's Big Mac index
Australia	-4	-17
Britain	+17	+23
Canada	-16	-16
China	-1	-56
Euro area	+33	+24
Hong Kong	+15	-45
Japan	+13	-12
Malaysia	-25	-53
Mexico	-15	-21
New Zealand	-12	-4
Singapore	+2	-31
South Korea	+6	0
Switzerland	+62	+82
Taiwan	-5	-21
Thailand	-31	-46
Turkey	+6	+5

Source: Adapted from "Burgers or Beans?," *The Economist*, January 15, 2004

Exhibit 3 Purchasing Power Parity: Inflation versus Depreciation in Selected Countries (1974–2002)

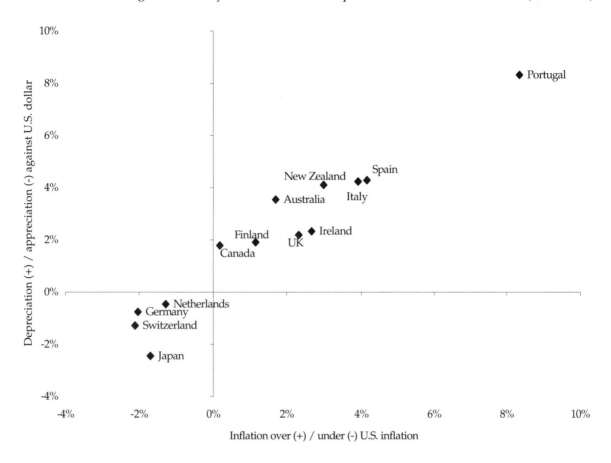

Source: International Monetary Fund, *International Finance Statistics CD-ROM,* August 2003.

Notes: The x-axis is the average of yearly inflation from 1974–2002 minus U.S. average inflation over the same period.
The y-axis is average of yearly annual percentage change in currency per U.S. dollar over same period.

Exhibit 4   The Bretton Woods System and Beyond: Mark/Dollar and Yen/Dollar Exchange Rates

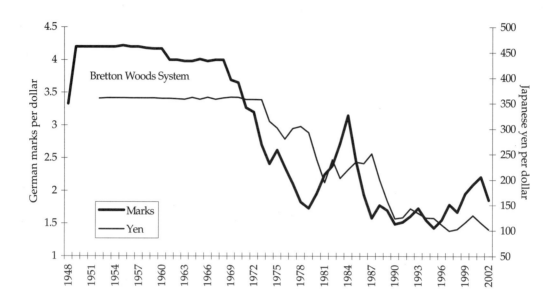

Source: International Monetary Fund, *International Finance Statistics CD-ROM*, August 2003.

Endnotes

1. For a more technical discussion, see Paul R. Krugman and Maurice Obstfeld, *International Economics: Theory and Policy, Sixth Edition* (Boston: Addison Wesley, 2003), where this example is discussed, in addition to John B. Taylor, *Economics* (Boston: Houghton Mifflin Company, 1995).

2. See the seminal paper Rudiger Dornbusch, "Expectations and Exchange Rate Dynamics," *Journal of Political Economy* 84 (6), August 1976, pp. 1161–76.

3. As described in "Rudiger Dornbusch (Obituary)," *The Economist,* August 10, 2002; and Paul Krugman, "Exchange Rates," The Concise Encyclopedia of Economics, available at <http://www.econlib.org/library/Enc/ExchangeRates.html> (accessed February 3, 2004).

4. Guillermo A. Calvo and Carmen Reinhart, "Fear of Floating," *The Quarterly Journal of Economics,* Vol. 117, Is. 2, 2002.

5. Guillermo A. Calvo and Frederic S. Mishkin, "The Mirage of Exchange Rate Regimes for Emerging Market Countries," *Journal of Economic Perspectives,* Vol. 17 No. 4, Fall 2003.

6. For more, see Rafael Di Tella and Ingrid Vogel, "Argentina 2001: Crisis, Default, and Beyond," HBS No. 704-004, January 2004.

7. Such as Guillermo A. Calvo and Carmen M. Reinhart in "Capital Flow Reversals, the Exchange Rate Debate, and Dollarization," *Finance & Development,* September 1999.

8. See Andrew Berg and Eduardo Borensztein, "The Pros and Cons of Full Dollarization," IMF Working Paper WP/00/50, March 2000.

9. See Daniel Pope and Michael G. Rukstad, "The Decline of the Dollar," HBS Case No. 384-116 for more on the Bretton Woods system of fixed exchange rates.

Institutions: The Latin American Experience

The Argentine Paradox: Economic Growth and the Populist Tradition

At the end of the 19th century, Argentina was among the richest countries in the world. Under the Gold Standard, international capital flooded into the country to exploit the apparently unbounded investment opportunities.

Yet one hundred years later, Argentina had been overtaken by many other countries in Europe and Asia. While still one of the more prosperous countries in Latin America, it no longer featured among the group of richest nations but rather languished towards the bottom of the middle-income group.

The political development of Argentina during this period had gone through several phases. Among the dominant figures were Juan Peron and his charismatic wife Evita. Their populist policies had fundamentally shaped Argentina's political, economic, and social evolution.

Study Questions

1. Why did Argentina fall from being one of the world's richest nations to an "also ran?"
2. What is populism? Was Peron a populist? In what ways?
3. Why was populism more influential in Argentina than in other countries?
4. What have been the positive aspects of populism for Argentina?

RAFAEL DI TELLA
INGRID VOGEL

The Argentine Paradox:
Economic Growth and the Populist Tradition

"A born leader of men, [Perón] had all the qualities needed to appeal to the masses—good looks, personal charm, eloquence, power of oratory, an extraordinary understanding of mass psychology and, what is rare in a dictator, a sense of humor. He created in Argentina a movement that bore his name, whose strength lay in the urbanized working class, which remains the strongest political force in the country."[1]

Argentina, endowed with abundant natural resources including oil and a vast area of productive agricultural land, appeared to be on its way to becoming a major world economic power through the first half of the 20th century. In 1890, it ranked sixth worldwide in per capita income and was the tenth largest trading nation. Argentina maintained an average annual inflation rate of only 1.5% for 50 years after 1890, during the days of the global gold standard. Low inflation accompanied a healthy growth rate; from 1900 to 1930, Argentina's economy grew at an average annual rate of 4%, more rapidly than the United States, Australia, or Canada. Attracted by the country's favorable prospects, almost three million European immigrants arrived from 1900 through 1920.[2] They were amply rewarded when Argentina survived both the Great Depression and World War II in better shape than many European countries. In 1950, Argentine per capita income was on a par with continental European nations, as it had been throughout the first half of the 20th century (see **Table 1**).

Table 1   GDP per Capita for Selected Countries as Percent of U.S.

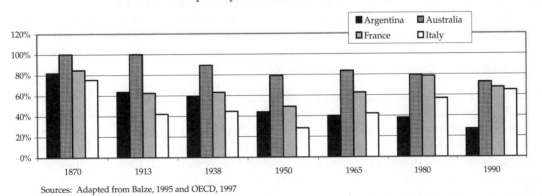

Sources: Adapted from Balze, 1995 and OECD, 1997

This case derives in part from an earlier case, "Menem and the Populist Tradition in Argentina," HBS No. 700-061, prepared by Research Associate Eliseo Neuman under the supervision of Professor Rafael Di Tella. This version was prepared by Research Associate Ingrid Vogel under the supervision of Professor Rafael Di Tella, and was developed based on published sources. HBS cases are developed solely as the basis for class discussion. Cases are not intended to serve as endorsements, sources of primary data, or illustrations of effective or ineffective management.

In 1946, Colonel Juan Domingo Perón became president of Argentina. He would dominate the political and economic evolution of the country until his death in 1974. Perón introduced significant labor reform and undertook considerable social investment. Between 1943 and 1948, his policies led to a 25% increase in the country's GDP. Over the same period, workers received wage increases of up to 37%.[3] But in the following decades, against a backdrop of substantial improvements in social indicators such as literacy and schooling rates, Argentina's macroeconomic performance deteriorated, culminating in a serious economic crisis in 1989 (see **Exhibits 1 and 11**).

The same year, Carlos Saúl Menem was elected president on a platform that included a massive wage hike and reclaiming the Falkland-Malvinas Islands through war. Initially, the flamboyant politician was unable to control Argentina's spiraling problems, including hyperinflation, stagflation, and mounting foreign debt. But observers knew that endemic economic hardship had not always been Argentina's fate. Instead, Argentina's political and economic misfortunes during the second half of the 20th century had long been considered an enigma. How did a country enjoying natural advantages and experiencing such promising beginnings encounter so many difficulties in fulfilling its great economic potential?

Historical Background

Argentina gained its independence in 1816 when the bourgeoisie of Buenos Aires freed itself from the onerous duties and taxes imposed by a feeble Spanish vice-royal administration. The Argentine union, however, took several decades to consolidate, as internal struggles among member provinces emerged. The provinces were ruled by warlords, known as *caudillos,* who resisted the hegemonic ambitions of Buenos Aires. In 1860, liberal elements from Buenos Aires established a federal republic under a common constitution. But Argentina was still an under-populated and oligarchic rural economy. The ruling conservative alliance, comprised of the Argentine "elite," set out to expand the agro-export economy, lure foreign capital to Argentina, and people the country by attracting immigrants. Increasing exports of wool and leather, and later, grain and meat fueled a wave of foreign, largely British, direct investment in railroads, meat packinghouses, and utilities. A massive influx of immigrants, mostly from Italy, Spain, and Eastern Europe, followed. In this period, economic growth matched and even exceeded demographic expansion, so that by the 1890s, Argentina had the sixth highest income per capita in the world.[4]

Land, the prized asset in the mainstream economy, was not openly distributed to the arriving immigrants. They remained in their arrival cities, principally Buenos Aires, confined to work as employees in light industry or as tradesmen. Even for their descendents, the right to vote was restricted. Deprived of what they saw as their economic and political entitlement, many immigrants joined ranks around labor organizers inspired by anarchist movements. In time, together with the local middle class, they formed the Radical party. Its initial focus was to broaden political representation. After a period of campaigning, electoral law reform eventually provided for universal and mandatory male suffrage and secret ballots. Under the new and more inclusive system, the Radicals beat the ruling Conservative Party in the 1916 election to take power. Under the Radical's democratic rule, from 1919 to 1929 Argentina's economy grew at an annual rate approaching 6% (see **Exhibit 4**).[5]

Strong economic growth emerged in spite of the constraints imposed by Argentina's export dependent economy. A succession of external shocks had exposed the risks of an economy so heavily dependent on trade. Argentina imported 60% of its industrial goods and almost all intermediate goods and capital equipment.[6] At the same time, it relied on revenues generated from exports of its agricultural products, mostly meat, wool, leather, cereals, and flax. Following World War I, many Western countries adopted protectionist measures, decreasing capital inflows to Argentina and reducing its exports (see **Exhibit 5**). As a result of its adherence to the gold standard,[7] pressure on the balance of payments followed. Imports fell even more dramatically, providing a stimulus to the domestic textile, chemical, and metal industries.[8] When, in 1929, Argentina abandoned the gold standard altogether, the peso depreciated rapidly and the price of imports increased, providing protection to the newly emerging Argentine manufacturing companies, but also pushing the country precariously close to defaulting on its debt.

Coalition Rule (1930–1943)

In 1930, the conservative "elites" were restored to power under the first of what, over the decades, would be a long series of military interventions. The 1930s brought developments with important long-term consequences. First, the appeal of nationalism spread from the exclusive domain of Conservatives to the middle and working classes. Second, competing nationalist and conservative factions emerged within the army. Third, a system was instituted whereby a coalition front remained in power through fraudulent elections.[a]

More significantly, the agro-export model was adjusted to allow for an industrial policy emphasizing more active import-substitution.[9] Initially, domestic industry received only limited support from the government: import duties were increased; a system of multiple exchange rates established prices more favorable to industrial than agricultural activities; and a public works program was initiated. The resulting industrial growth led to the migration of rural workers to urban centers. By implication, the composition of labor organizations and of the working class itself was drastically altered. Industrial labor demand increased drastically. Yet real wages remained stagnant, and concessions were made to foreign trading partners, principally Britain, at the expense of emerging local industrial interests.[10] By the end of the decade, workers felt disenfranchised and soon became idle political capital ready for the taking.[11] Years of fraudulent elections since 1930 had eroded the elected government's legitimacy, and the army, which included an ambitious young colonel named Perón, took over the Conservative government in 1943.

The Rise of Juan Domingo Perón

Historians have struggled to define Perón's ideology. He was no friend of the United States, but was often perceived to be perhaps the most reliable long-term safeguard against the spread of Marxism into Argentina. The image he projected was one of *caudillo*-like strength.

Perón's rise was dramatic. An undistinguished colonel in the ski troops in 1943, he became president less than three years later. Born in 1895, he began his military life at 16 when he left his family's small farm in Patagonia to enroll in the Military College. After graduating, he was posted to the remote interior where he experienced his first taste of labor unrest and the conditions of the rural poor. In 1926, he was promoted to captain and spent four years as a student at the Superior School of War before lecturing there for six additional years.[12]

---

[a] The coalition, known as the Concordancia and dominated by the "elites," consisted of Conservatives, dissenting Radicals, and technocrats.

A few months before the outbreak of World War II, Perón was sent to Italy to study mountain warfare. Mussolini and, in particular, some of his policies for reconciling the interests of capital and labor through cooperative planning greatly impressed Perón, who had until then been completely apolitical.[a] Upon his return to Buenos Aires in 1942, Perón helped establish the GOU (*Grupo de Oficiales Unidos*), a military group concerned with exploring possible post-war policies. The new president of Argentina, installed by the 1943 military coup, named Perón to the hitherto harmless post of secretary of labor and social welfare. Feeling threatened by Perón's growing popularity, he attempted to suppress his activism and oust his supporters in government. Perón thwarted those efforts and eventually forced the president's resignation in 1944.[13]

In the same year, Perón met the radio performer Eva Duarte, better known as the legendary Evita, who would become his second wife and most devoted political supporter. Perón claimed to have selected and trained Evita carefully to take in his ideas and "create in them a second I." He especially encouraged Evita's focus on the poor or "*descamizados*" (shirtless). Her charitable foundation and personal life eventually transformed her into the soul of the Peronist party, earning her the title "Spiritual Chief of the Nation."[14]

The sources of Evita's commitment to elevating the conditions of Argentina's poor and working class could be found in her personal background. Evita was an illegitimate child who grew up in relative poverty in the pampas, 150 miles from the capital. She longed for the life she saw portrayed in Hollywood films, and, at age 15, left her mother and four siblings to become an actress in Buenos Aires. Her ambition landed her roles first in radio, and later in theatre and film. In 1943, when the military came into power, she worked with the new regime to produce pro-military radio programs. At 23 years old, she was already one of the most highly paid radio performers in the country. After marrying Perón, Evita indulged even more in her passion for designer clothes and expensive jewelry. If anything, this brought her closer to Argentina's poor, who saw in her, perhaps, a symbol of upward mobility.[b]

Perón's Pre-Presidential Policies (1943–1946)

Perón's springboard to the presidency was his performance as secretary of labor and social welfare. From that post he enacted a comprehensive set of pro-labor laws that included the introduction of labor courts with exclusive jurisdiction over labor conflicts; a scheme to establish and periodically adjust minimum wages, often leading to increases in real terms; yearly paid vacations; retirement and health insurance benefits; and an annual mandatory bonus equal to an additional month's salary.[15] He also instituted the Agricultural Worker Statute (*Estatuto del Peon*) in late 1944. This statute outlined the specific rights and obligations of both worker and employer in the rural context and was perceived as a defiance of the landed elite. By the time Perón was forced to step down as Secretary, Argentina had advanced from a laggard to a world leader in labor legislation.[16]

Simultaneously, Perón took advantage of his position to promote labor activism. Mimicking the approach he had seen Mussolini adopt in Italy, Perón increased union membership and essentially took over the labor movement. In 1945, he enacted the Law on Professional Associations, which gave his Labor Secretariat veto power on the formation of new unions.[17] Between 1946 and 1950, union

---

[a] Mussolini implemented neo-corporatist policies under his strict authoritarian rule. He co-opted trade unions and employers' associations (together with representative groups for agriculture and the professions) into government sponsored programs and policy discussions, while at the same time outlawing independent trade unions.

[b] She died from cancer at age 33 in 1952 after having renounced the offer of the vice-presidency in a spectacular rally.

membership increased from 880,000 to 2 million. By 1954, more than 2.5 million workers belonged to unions, representing 42.5% of all workers.[18] In just two years, Perón became vice-president, minister of defense and, through the labor movement, had assumed a power base of his own.

Next, a series of political developments played into Perón's hands, helping to propel him into the presidency. Chief among these was the arrival of Spruille Braden as U.S. ambassador, a stereotypical figure that the liberal elite loved and that Argentine nationalists, irrespective of their class, hated. His high profile and aggressive approach helped polarize the political landscape in ways never foreseen by the traditional political class. Perón had distanced himself successfully from the losing pro-Axis faction of the army and the increasingly repressive nature of the military regime. Yet he maintained a nationalist discourse that earned him accusations of fascism from traditional quarters while helping him garner popular support.

In 1945, leaders of the conservative faction in the army, still threatened by Perón's growing popularity, forced his resignation and took him under arrest.[19] They called on the Radicals to participate in a transition government, but negotiations led nowhere. The army then turned to the reactionary Supreme Court. Perón's sympathizers suddenly united against a return to the ways of the "patriotic fraud" of the previous decade. The labor unions called for a general strike on October 17, 1945, but the workers instead marched *en masse* to the presidential palace. They would not leave until Perón was brought to address them. Overwhelmed by this show of support, the authorities complied. This occasion marked the birth of mass mobilized politics and of the Peronist labor movement. An election was called. Under the campaign slogan, "Braden or Perón," the charismatic new leader carried 55% of the vote against a coalition of all other parties in the first clean elections since 1928. [20]

The First Peronist Regime (1946–1955)

Perón rewrote the constitution to provide for his reelection and presided over the country for nine years before he was ousted in 1955.[21] During this period, he consolidated a power base that relied on a highly disciplined party bureaucracy composed of a virtually unquestioning union apparatus and legislature along with the police and the ultimately ambivalent army.

His political style has been described as populist, paternalistic, even fascist. As much as he relied on his political allies, Perón depended on the existence of various political enemies, whom he repeatedly antagonized to generate popular support in large, highly emotive rallies. These enemies included the landed elite (which he called the "oligarchy"), the liberal wing of the armed forces, the progressive opposition comprised of Radicals and Socialists, and intellectuals and the universities. Perhaps most significantly, the enemy included foreign "imperialistic" powers, against which he advocated a policy of neutrality or "third position;" *"ni yanquis ni marxistas, Peronistas."* In 1947, an isolationist Argentina, believing that both the Bretton Woods Agreement and GATT exclusively favored the interests of the United States and other advanced nations, chose not to participate in the new world economic order based on multilateral trade and finance.

Perón started his presidency with a bold five-year plan. Consistent with his creed of "economic independence," he opted for redistributive measures aimed at expanding the internal market as opposed to stressing traditional exports. During World War II, uncertainty regarding future exports had become a recession that tested the then-ruling coalition of Conservatives, Radicals, and technocrats to its limits. With the combined goals of reducing foreign dependence, raising productivity, improving the distribution of wealth, and broadening the domestic economic base, the government had accelerated its policy of industrialization through import-substitution. Although the landed elite, fearing the diversion of resources to the industrial sector, withdrew its support, industrialization gained a new champion in the army, which pressed for a local, state-led armaments industry in response to the withdrawal of U.S. military assistance in retaliation for Argentina's neutrality in the war. On March 27, 1945, Argentina formally declared war against Germany and Japan, but never actively participated in the struggle against either country.

In 1943, the policy was showing results, as non-agricultural industrial production exceeded farm production for the first time, and industrial products accounted for 20% of Argentine exports (see **Exhibit 6**).[22] Domestic production accounted for over 80% of Argentina's total consumption of manufactured products, versus 60% in the late 1930s and between 40% and 50% during the previous three decades.[23] The military regime created a Secretariat of Industry to centralize industrial policy and a state-owned bank to extend credit and foreign exchange to manufacturers. Nearly 25,000 new industrial enterprises sprang into existence between 1942 and 1946. [24]

Perón took industrialization even further. Although he set five-year plans, his government often improvised policies to react to short-term economic and political pressures. Such policies included defending existing post-war industries, regardless of their efficiency; subsidizing technologically complex and expensive activities, such as atomic energy; saving some private companies from bankruptcy; and enacting credit policies to favor certain branches of manufacturing.

The policies initially favored the low-income sectors of society. Between 1943 and 1948, real wages for skilled industrial workers rose by 27% and those for unskilled workers by 37%.[25] GDP for the same period grew by 25%.[26] At the same time, Perón called for price stability, lavish public spending, and full employment (see **Exhibit 7**).[27] The national external debt was paid down completely, enabling a "Declaration of Economic Independence."[28] Perón also widened the role of the state through purchasing a merchant fleet, developing commercial air transportation, and nationalizing the telephone company (ITT), the docks, and the British-owned railroads.

In contrast, the traditional agricultural sector was neglected. The government used the sector to generate resources to cross-subsidize welfare programs and the heavily protected industries. With diminished incentives, the area under agricultural use shrank and its infrastructure investment lagged.

Between 1949 and 1952, salary increases outpaced productivity gains as lax credit policies continued to expand the money supply. Inflation climbed to annual rates of over 30%, and industrial output and employment eventually suffered (see **Exhibit 8**).[29] Perón responded with a drastic austerity plan and brokered an agreement between the union leadership and employers under which wages were frozen for two years.

Despite these harsh measures, Perón's unusual charisma combined with Evita's extravagant acts of charity to the poor endeared the pair to the workers. By the early 1950s, Evita's charitable foundation was estimated to have over $200 million in assets and 14,000 workers on the payroll. With an objective of satisfying the "basic needs for a better life of the less privileged classes," the foundation distributed items such as shoes and sewing machines and built homes and hospitals.[30] During the first six months of 1951 alone, Evita's foundation is alleged to have distributed among the needy 25,000 houses and three million packages containing medicine, furniture, clothes, toys, and bicycles. Evita often interviewed the petitioners herself, dressed in expensive designer clothes. The foundation was funded through "donations" from companies (it was rumored that significant pressure was applied to ensure firms' involvement), as well as a day of annual wages from every Argentine worker.

The Downfall of Perón (1954–1955)

Over the years, Perón's regime turned increasingly totalitarian, controlling growing areas of civil society. The opposition was systematically terrorized, the press censored, independent unions and professional bodies subjugated, and the education system turned over to party propaganda. His enemies, however, remained formidable, and he used them as targets to generate popular support. For example, Perón incited his nationalist supporters to burn down the Jockey Club, a bastion of the elite.

But when, in late 1954, Perón turned against the Catholic Church, a deeply rooted and powerful institution hitherto aloof but tolerant of his rule, disparate opposition factions gathered mass as Perón's own supporters had in October 1945. A divorce law and other provocative anti-clerical legislation were met with peaceful demonstrations against the regime. When an army coup attempt failed, Perón called for retribution, and loyalist labor groups burned churches throughout Buenos Aires.[31]

Perón's remaining supporters turned against him when he reached a controversial agreement with Standard Oil of California in 1955 that allowed exploitation of oil resources in Patagonia. Not only was this considered a blow to their nationalist sentiments, but the army and the populace perceived it as a means of granting military air bases to the United States. In September 1955, army factions from garrisons in the province of Córdoba instigated yet another coup. Navy planes threatened to bomb Perón's recently built oil refineries. His regime was spent. He took flight in a Paraguayan gunboat and left the country, as he would later claim, to prevent a civil war.[32]

Ruling against the Ghost of Perón (1955–1973)

From Perón's removal in 1955 until his return in 1973, ten different presidents led Argentina. The first established the "Liberating Revolution" with the twin objectives of obliterating Peronism and liberalizing the economy by embarking on a program of rapid industrialization financed largely by foreign capital.[33] In the ten years following Perón's ouster, the economy recovered, growing at an annual average rate of 4%. But inflation again increased, this time to an average 33% per annum, requiring periodic massive currency devaluations.[34] Although smaller than under Perón, large public sector deficits, driven primarily by the inability of the government to collect taxes and by loss-making public enterprises, were to blame. Economic policy changed dramatically under the new regime. Controls on foreign exchange, pricing, and wages were eliminated in favor of reliance on market forces, leading to a major redistribution of income. Urban workers suffered most under the new policy. The poorest 60% of Argentines experienced an average 5% decrease in income; the middle 30% a 2% decline; while the top 10% achieved a 5% increase.[35]

As real wages dropped 26% in 1959 alone, the Peronist unions felt defrauded and responded with strikes.[36] The business sector interpreted the government's concessions as a sign of captivity to labor interests. In 1962, the military stepped in to provide for a transition to new elections. The traditional Radicals won, though by a margin only negligibly larger than the blank votes representing the proscribed Peronists. The unions mounted a hostile campaign of periodic strikes and even conspired tactically with elements of the army itself. Wages had declined from 48.2% of GDP in the second half of Perón's tenure to less than 40% by the early 1960s.[37]

In 1966, political and economic chaos led the business sector to call for military intervention, and an army coup soon followed. The army's interventionist economic plan initially controlled inflation through price and wage controls, as well as controls on public spending. Politically isolated, the army tried to co-opt a pragmatic faction of the union leadership under the notion of "Peronism without Perón."[38] This, however, radicalized the opposition. In 1969, a riot in the city of Córdoba left 14 casualties and created a crisis in the military leadership.

In the early 1970s, the military aimed to weaken the power of urban interests in the formation of policy by increasing the malapportionment of Argentina's already highly unrepresentative legislative branch.[39] Sparsely populated peripheral provinces gained political power at the expense of the more populated and productive provinces. The citizens of Buenos Aires and other major areas therefore became even more underrepresented in congress and the senate and had even less say in government.[a][40]

From his exile in Spain, Perón encouraged the increasingly combative Peronist youth movement, rapidly consolidated under the existing Montoneros urban guerilla organization, [41] which helped press for new elections by 1973.

The Return of Perón and the Collapse of Democracy (1973–1983)

In the 1973 elections, Perón's favored candidate won with support of both the Montoneros and the more traditional core of union bosses. The former drew new followers through their active and colorful militancy, and soon engaged the latter in a spiral of violence over the control of the party. Only Perón could be expected to restore order. Finally relenting to the demands of his supporters, the military allowed Perón to return to Argentina. But his return itself was an occasion for carnage as veterans of his security detail and the union bureaucracy shot at the Montoneros columns in an airport rally, leaving hundreds dead. A new election was called, which Perón won with his third wife on the ticket and an unprecedented 62% of the vote.[42]

The economy called for conservative measures, and Perón forged another "social pact" between labor and capital. But adverse external factors, chiefly the oil crisis, made the industrialists and the unions abandon their price and wage freezes. Inflation mounted and so did violence. Perón died only a few months later, and the least savory elements of his entourage took over the government from his unprepared wife. Political assassinations, kidnappings of businessmen, intimidation, and chaos became common as the "dirty war" began. In 1975, one political death took place every 19 hours.[43] The economic nadir occurred that June when a drastic stabilization plan devalued the currency by 50%. Inflation spiraled and the public deficit for 1975 reached 16% of GDP (see **Exhibit 9**). By March 1976, annualized inflation reached 3,000%,[44] and the armed forces took over the government yet again.

The military regime of 1976-83 earned the country an international reputation for endemic human rights' abuses. But its less famous record of economic mismanagement was no less notorious. Initial measures resulted in a remarkable 40% drop in real wages from the previous five-year average.[45] The regime blamed the country's problems on excessive government intervention and taxation of the agricultural sector to support an inefficient industry. Trade and exchange rate liberalization was

---

[a] Under a perfectly apportioned system, the votes of all citizens are balanced equally. In contrast, a malapportioned system allows the votes of some citizens to weigh more than the votes of other citizens. Malapportionment persists. Acemoglu, et al. (2002) write that the four provinces of Buenos Aires, Santa Fe, Cordoba, and Mendoza contain 78% of national industrial production and 70% of the total population, but control just 8 of the 48 seats in the senate and 48% of the seats in congress. According to Samuels and Snyder (2001), Argentina ranked as having the 1st most malapportioned upper chamber in the world and 12th most malapportioned lower chamber in the world.

followed by financial reform. In 1976, following foreign debt renegotiations with the International Monetary Fund (IMF), an oversupply of cheap foreign financing from U.S., European, and Japanese banks glutted with petrodollars greatly eroded the government's ability to restrict domestic credit, and financial speculation displaced productive investment (see **Exhibit 10** for information on Argentina's foreign debt burden).

In 1979, the government shifted to fixing the nominal exchange rate, but various fiscal policies and wage and price controls designed to contain inflation failed. The real exchange rate appreciated rapidly, becoming seriously overvalued. In consequence, imports climbed and local industries were left to fail. Eventually, the situation became unsustainable. In early 1981, capital flight soared, and foreign exchange reserves decreased by more than $2 billion. Pressure on the currency increased, and the first of a series of devaluations resulted. A cycle soon took root. In the following 18 months, the peso depreciated by 100%, while average monthly inflation reached 20%, industrial activity fell, real wages decreased, investment dropped, and the public deficit reached 20% of GDP.[46]

Further chaos ensued in 1982 when the Argentine military embarked upon a surprise invasion of the Falkland-Malvinas Islands. The U.K. quickly repelled the assault, but foreign investors lost even more confidence in the country and withdrew their funds. As foreign reserves plummeted, the government suspended payments on its external debt. Private foreign debt had soared in local currency terms, with no external sources of refinancing. Large parts of the private sector were on the brink of bankruptcy. The government eventually nationalized the foreign private debt while simultaneously restructuring the domestic private debt. The man behind this plan was the young and energetic president of the Central Bank, Domingo Cavallo. Constant change and growing uncertainty led to the withdrawal of economic agents from the formal market: skilled workers and capital fled the country, and off-the-books employment increased.

The Restoration of Democratic Rule (1983–1989)

In the aftermath of the debt crisis and military defeat in the Falkland-Malvinas Islands, the armed forces called elections in the end of 1982. For the first time, the Radicals won a free election against the Peronists. The new president, Raul Alfonsín, was greeted with euphoria and the expectation that he would restore order to the economy. Perhaps his most noteworthy decision was to prosecute the officers responsible for human rights' violations in the preceding military regime. Resulting military uprisings forced Alfonsín to limit the scope of such prosecutions drastically. With the Peronist opposition in disarray, Alfonsín strove to introduce labor legislation aimed at weakening the unions. But this initiative failed, only emboldening the union leadership. Angered by Alfonsín's anti-union actions and failure to improve severely deteriorating public services, the unions embarked on a course of systematic opposition that was to last throughout the Alfonsín administration and included thirteen general strikes between 1984 and 1989.[47]

The Plan Austral

In June 1985, the government announced the *Plan Austral* (see **Exhibit 12**), named after the new currency it instituted. It comprised comprehensive structural reforms, economic liberalization, and debt renegotiations. Structural reforms included cutting subsidies and deregulating and privatizing state industries. Economic liberalization took the form of a reduction in protectionist policies and comprehensive wage and price freezes to control inflationary expectations. The government also instituted a fixed exchange rate. The plan was initially successful and elicited strong support from the

U.S., leading to a refinancing of the foreign debt. By mid-1986, inflation had dropped from annual rates of 650% to 50%, the government deficit had decreased, and positive GDP growth had resumed. The Plan Austral was being hailed worldwide as "the new Argentine Miracle."[48]

In April 1986, in order to combat overvaluation of the currency, the price freeze and fixed exchange rate were abandoned in favor of price guidelines and a crawling-peg, under which the exchange rate would be adjusted periodically to inflation. This formally marked the end of the first phase of the Austral Plan. The government had cut public spending and tackled tax evasion. But it stopped short of successfully implementing the required structural reforms, and tax revenues declined throughout the rest of the Alfonsín administration. In a move that was criticized, the government courted a group of Peronist unions with selective wage increases—an apparent move to recreate Peronism. Inflation took off, and the overvalued currency compromised the trade surpluses required under the IMF stabilization plan. By the third quarter of 1986, the plan began to unravel as retail prices increased beyond levels projected by the price guidelines, and as many of the plan's proposed reforms failed in the face of political opposition and intra-government squabbles.[49] For example, a plan to privatize the state-owned airline was fiercely opposed by the Peronists and the trade unions. MIT economist Rudiger Dornbusch remarked that Argentina seemed like a country made up of Italian taxpayers and British trade unions.

In February 1987, the "Australito" plan re-imposed wage and price controls. But the *Plan Austral* was not saved. In September 1987, the Radical Party lost the Lower House to the Peronists, signaling the demise of the *Plan Austral*.

New Elections

In August 1988, in an effort to bridge the remaining months before the presidential election, Alfonsín's government devised the "Spring Plan" to contain inflationary expectations by fixing the exchange rate. The plan relied on an agreement with the Industrial Union and the Chamber of Commerce, which rallied against the prospect of a victory by the Peronist candidate, Carlos Saúl Menem.

Menem was calling for, among other things, a recovery of the Falkland-Malvinas Islands by force, a moratorium on the foreign debt, and massive across-the-board salary increases (the *salariazo*). As the campaign intensified and Menem's lead in the polls grew, expectations of increased pressure on wages led to inflation and a depletion of dollar reserves. When the Central Bank suspended foreign currency operations, the price of the dollar skyrocketed. As the whole country monitored the dollar, all bets on the new plan were off. In May 1989, prices rose by 78%, while the dollar tripled in value against the austral.[50]

With food riots raging in the country's supermarkets, Menem did not need to attack the record of the Radicals as much as stick to the traditional Peronist battle cries over the course of his campaign. For example, he passionately declared: "For the hunger of poor children, for the sadness of rich children, for the young and the old, with the flag of God, which is faith, and the flag of the people, which is the fatherland, for God, I ask you: follow me. I will not let you down."[51]

He carried 47% of the vote in May 1989 (see **Exhibit 13**).[52] For the first time in Argentine history, a constitutionally elected president handed over power to a member of the opposition. In fact, with prices rising 197% in July alone, the transfer was brought forward by six months to deal with the developing crisis.

Exhibit 1 Argentine General Economic Indicators (1900–1990) (*annual average % increase, unless otherwise noted*)

	Conservative 1900 – 1915	Radicals 1916 – 1929	Coalition 1930 – 1942	Military / Peron 1943 – 1955	Ten Presidents 1956 – 1972	Peron and 3rd Wife 1973 – 1976	Military "Dirty War" 1977 – 1982	Alfonsin 1983 – 1988	Menem 1989 – 1990
Real GDP Growth	5.00	5.00	1.75	3.71	3.85	2.14	0.46	1.16	-3.08
Per Capita Real GDP Growth	1.37	2.30	0.05	1.69	2.26	0.46	-1.08	-0.16	-4.30
Consumer Price Inflation	2.45	2.00	0.46	16.69	30.51	178	147	368	2697
Investment/GDP	24.52	16.13	14.37	16.67	22.70	24.98	26.48	19.96	16.17
M3/GDP	48.09	50.79	52.75	49.96	27.25	28.25	29.68	16.62	7.50
Public Expenditure/GDP	13.14	10.54	17.88	28.83	25.02	27.70	28.98	29.46	23.53
Public Deficit/GDP[a]	2.80	1.35	3.21	8.08	3.72	11.35	12.07	9.29	4.27
Average of exports and imports/GDP	21.57	20.05	13.80	7.51	6.42	6.03	9.06	8.46	9.79

Source: Adapted from IEERAL, 1986 and OECD, 1997.

Note: [a]Series from 1913–1990.

Exhibit 2 Argentine National Income Accounts (*millions constant 1985 U.S. dollars*)

	1916	1930	1943	1956	1973	1977	1983	1989[a]
Gross Domestic Product	**19,806**	**37,802**	**48,485**	**79,277**	**149,797**	**166,961**	**166,130**	**160,034**
Household Consumption	16,201	30,296	36,070	58,852	101,971	101,423	110,375	92,652
Government Consumption	1,252	2,036	3,945	7,082	9,479	11,354	15,150	29,423
Investment	1,904	7,984	5,645	13,894	37,598	49,850	35,016	27,200
Private	*1,686*	*7,205*	*4,562*	*12,001*	*30,144*	*37,101*	*25,843*	*na*
Public	*218*	*779*	*1,083*	*1,894*	*7,454*	*12,748*	*9,173*	*na*
Exports	4,261	4,763	5,205	4,596	9,671	14,672	16,472	20,093
Imports	3,812	7,277	2,380	5,147	8,921	10,338	10,885	9,335
Consumer Goods	*1,500*	*1,846*	*477*	*304*	*278*	*343*	*554*	*347*
Intermediate Goods	*1,915*	*4,231*	*1,817*	*4,038*	*6,913*	*6,926*	*8,464*	*7,727*
Capital Goods	*397*	*1,200*	*85*	*805*	*1,730*	*3,069*	*1,867*	*1,261*

Source: Adapted from IEERAL, 1986; OECD, 1997; and EIU Country Data.

Note: [a]Split between Household and Government Consumption in 1989 uses a different methodology.

Exhibit 3   Argentine Balance of Payments

	(millions current pesos)		(millions current U.S. dollars)				
	1938	1946	1955	1973	1977	1983	1989
Current Account	-505	1,416	-217	726	1,126	-2,436	-1,305
Trade Balance	-109	1,743	-244	1,308	1,852	3,716	5,709
Exports	1,371	3,918	928	3,315	5,651	7,835	9,573
Imports	1,480	2,175	1,173	2,007	3,799	4,119	3,864
Net Services	-63	171	21	-192	-16	-769	-600
Net Income	-366	-451	-21	-401	-741	-5,399	-6,422
Net Transfers	na	na	-3	11	31	16	8
Net Other	33	-47	30	0	0	0	0
Financial Account	53	-1,845	207	79	605	-2,391	-8,083
Net Direct Investment	na	na	1	10	145	183	1,028
Net Private Long Term Investment	-68	-329	9	6	-1	649	-1,098
Net Private Short Term Capital	0	0	0	40	481	-2,370	-7,527
Net Official	121	-1,516	197	23	-20	-853	-486
Net Errors and Omissions	-9	-75	11	53	134	-447	-249
Reserves and Related Items[a]	461	504	0	-858	-1,865	5,274	9,637

Source: Adapted from IMF, *International Financial Statistics*; and IMF, *Balance of Payments Yearbook*.

Note: [a]Because of data availability, 1938 includes all short-term official capital and monetary gold. Years 1946 and 1955 include only monetary gold.

Exhibit 4   Argentine GDP Growth

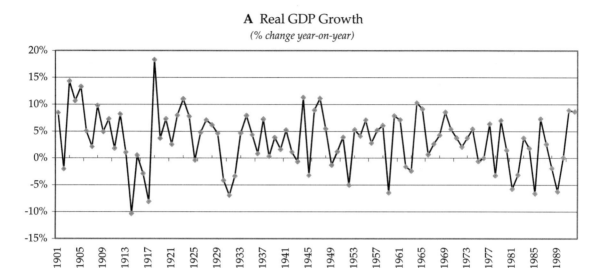

A Real GDP Growth
(% change year-on-year)

B Real GDP Index
(1900 = 100)

Source: Adapted from OECD, 1997.

Exhibit 5   Argentine Trade

A Exports and Imports as % GDP

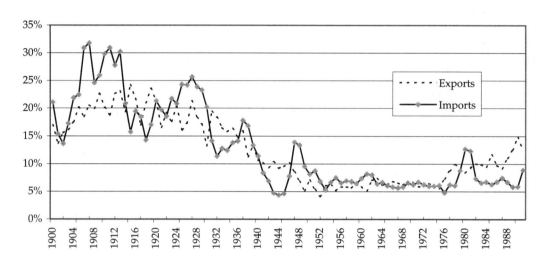

B Trade Balance as % GDP

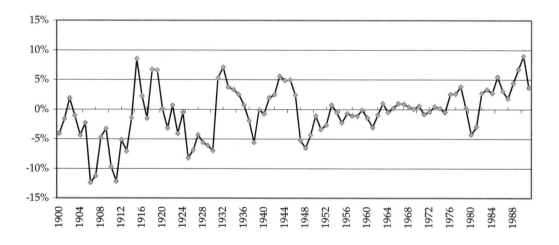

Source: Adapted from OECD, 1997.

Exhibit 6   Argentine Sector Composition

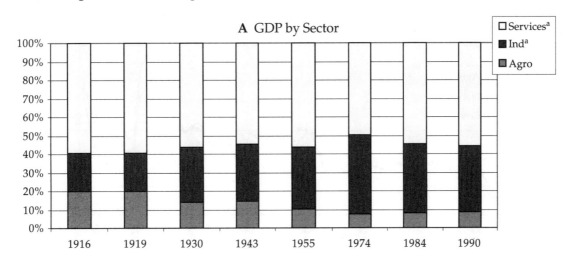

A GDP by Sector

Source: Adapted from OECD, 1997.

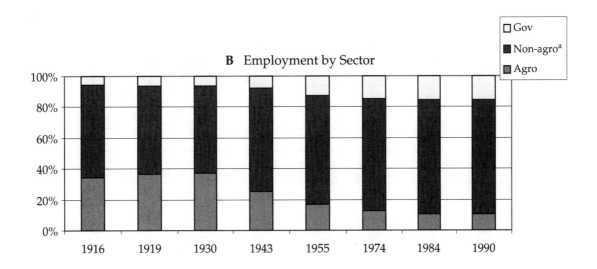

B Employment by Sector

Source: Adapted from IEERAL, 1986.

Note: [a]In **A**, both services and industry include some agricultural activities. For example, in the early 1910s, agriculture accounted for more than 50% of industrial production through processing and related equipment. Likewise, services included transportation and trade related to agriculture. The same is true for Non-agro in **B**.

Exhibit 7   Argentine Wages and Public Expenditure

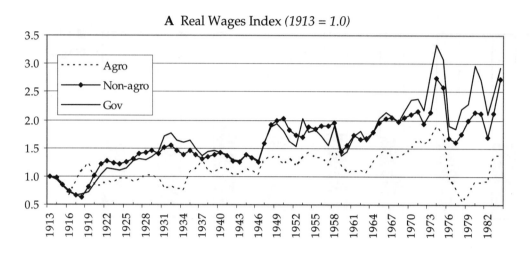

A Real Wages Index *(1913 = 1.0)*

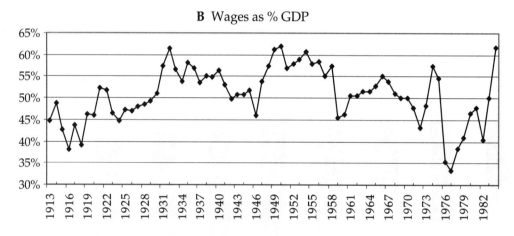

B Wages as % GDP

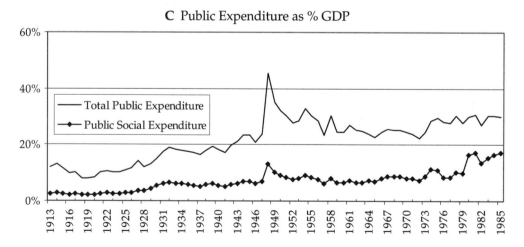

C Public Expenditure as % GDP

Source: Adapted from IEERAL, 1986 and OECD, 1997.

Exhibit 8   Argentine Inflation

A Yearly Rate of Inflation 1900–1955

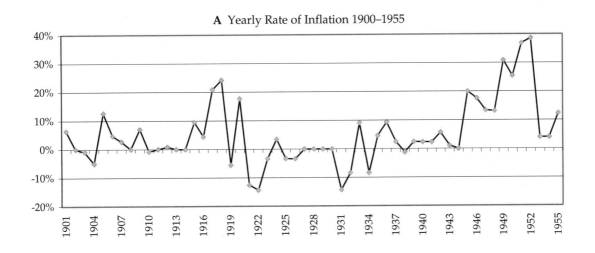

B Yearly Rate of Inflation 1945–1990
(Logarithmic Scale)

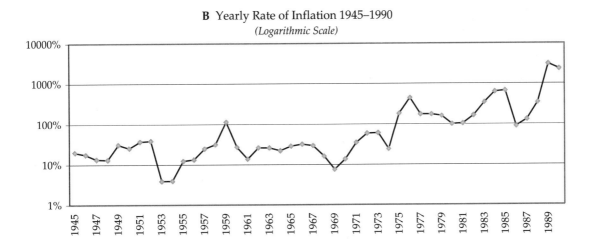

Source: Adapted from OECD, 1997.

Exhibit 9   Argentine Public Deficit *(% GDP)*

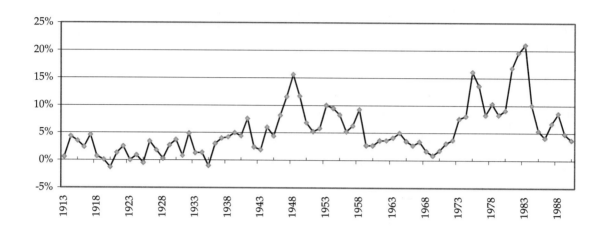

Source: Adapted from IEERAL, 1986 and OECD, 1997.

Exhibit 10   Argentine Foreign Debt

A Foreign debt indicators (1970–1986) *(millions current U.S. dollars except where noted)*

	Reserves	Gross foreign debt	Net foreign debt	Foreign debt service	Interest rate on foreign debt (%)
1970	725	3,259	2,534	289	11.4
1971	317	3,762	3,445	341	12.1
1972	529	4,694	4,165	387	10.8
1973	1,412	5,210	3,798	479	10.9
1974	1,341	6,274	4,933	421	9.6
1975	618	7,495	6,877	487	8.9
1976	1,772	7,899	6,128	492	6.9
1977	3,862	9,307	5,445	578	8.5
1978	5,829	12,496	6,667	681	9.6
1979	10,137	19,034	8,897	920	10.2
1980	7,288	27,162	19,874	1,531	11.8
1981	3,719	35,671	31,952	3,700	16.2
1982	3,013	43,243	40,230	4,718	14.1
1983	3,205	45,079	41,874	5,408	13.1
1984	3,499	46,171	42,672	5,712	13.2
1985	6,153	49,326	43,173	4,882	11.1
1986	5,580	51,704	46,124	3,970	8.7

B Gross foreign debt / exports ratio

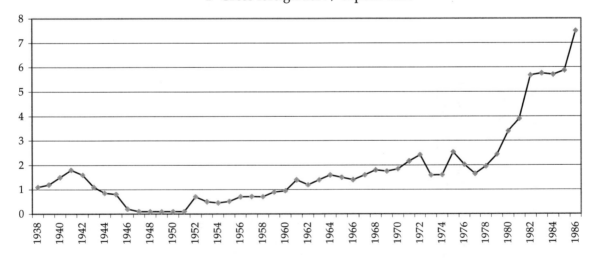

Source: Adapted from Carlos A Rodrigues, "Argentina's Foreign Debt: Origins and Alternatives," in *Debt, Adjustment and Recovery*, 1989.

Exhibit 11 Argentine Social Indicators

A Argentina % Population (15–64) by Education Level

	No Education	At least Primary	At least Secondary	Higher
1910	25	75	12	1
1930	22	78	9	1
1947	14	86	9	1
1960	10	91	20	4
1970	6	95	26	5
1980	3	97	32	7
1991	2	98	43	11

Source: Adapted from OECD, 1997.

B Average Number Years Schooling for Selected Countries

	Argentina	Brazil	Mexico	Chile	U.S.
1950	4.6	1.8	2.3	4.9	9.5
1960	6.2	2.4	na	na	9.5
1970	na	na	4.2	5.9	10.6
1980	7.2	3.9	4.9	7.6	12
1989	9.1	5.3	6.6	8.5	13

Source: Adapted from OECD, 1997.

C Income Distribution of Selected Countries

	Income share by quintile of population					
	1 poorest 20%	2	3 middle 20%	4	5 richest 20%	ratio 5:1
1980 Argentina	6.6	10.8	14.9	21.9	46.1	7.0
Brazil (1979)	3.2	6.7	10.2	17.5	62.5	19.5
Chile	2.7	6.4	10.6	18.3	62	23.0
Mexico (1984)	4.1	7.8	12.3	19.9	55.9	13.6
USA (1985)	4.7	11	17.4	25	41.9	8.9
1989 Argentina	4.8	9.4	13.5	20.2	52.1	10.9
Brazil	2.1	4.9	8.9	16.8	67.5	32.1
Chile	3.7	6.8	10.3	16.2	62.9	17.0
Mexico	3.6	8.1	13	20.4	54.9	15.3
USA (1985)	4.7	11	17.4	25	41.9	8.9

Source: Adapted from *World Development Report*, Volume 25; "Neoliberalism and Income Distribution in Latin America," 317.

Exhibit 12   Austral Plan

Argentine Monthly Inflation

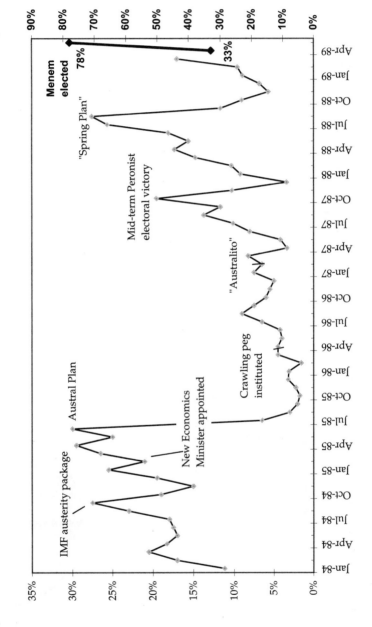

Source: Adapted from Smith, 1989 and IMF, *International Financial Statistics.*

Exhibit 13   Results of the Argentine May 1989 Election

A Presidential Elections

Candidate	Position during Campaign	Party	% Vote	Electoral Votes[a]	Platform
Carlos Saul Menem	Governor La Rioja	Peronist	47%	317	Populist platform, including significant wage increase, lower taxes, recovery of Falklands-Malvinas by force, repudiation of foreign debt or five-year moratorium.
Eduardo Angeloz	Governor Cordoba	Radical	37%	232	Distance self from current Radical regime. In summary: sell inefficient state industries, reduce the role of the state in the economy, maintain a free exchange rate, spur exports and revamp organized labor.
Nine other candidates	Various	Various	16%	51	Various

Source: Adapted from Associated Press, 15 May 1989.
Notes: Voter turnout: 85% (voting obligatory for Argentines between the ages of 18 and 70).
         [a]600 electoral votes in total. Winner requires more than 300 to avoid contest in electoral college.

B Legislative Elections

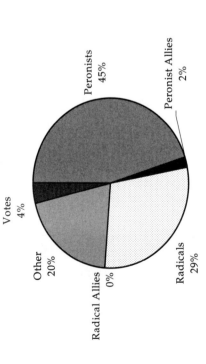

Peronists
45%

Peronist Allies
2%

Radicals
29%

Radical Allies
0%

Other
20%

Blank and Spoiled Votes
4%

Source: Adapted from Georgetown University Political Database of the Americas.

Endnotes

1   Eva Duarte Perón, *Evita by Evita: Eva Duarte Perón Tells Her Own Story* (London and New York: Proteus, 1978), from Appendix I newspaper obituary article "President Juan Peron: Flamboyant creator of modern Argentina."

2   Carlos F. Díaz Alejandro, *Essays on the Economic History of the Argentine Republic* (New Haven and London: Yale University Press, 1970), 424.

3   Joseph Page, *Perón: A Biography* (New York: Random House, 1983), 176 and William C. Smith, *Authoritarianism and the Crisis of the Argentine Political Economy* (Stanford, CA: Stanford University Press, 1991), 27.

4   "Back in the Saddle: A Survey of Argentina," *The Economist* (November 26, 1994): 3.

5   Felipe de la Balze, *Remaking the Argentine Economy* (New York: Council on Foreign Relations Press, 1995), 27.

6   Marie-Ange Véganzonès with Carlos Winograd, *Argentina in the 20th Century: An Account of Long-Awaited Growth* (Paris: OECD Development Centre Studies, 1997), 29.

7   Argentina left the gold standard temporarily in 1914, as did all major countries of the Northern Hemisphere. Until 1927, Argentina used a managed float aimed at preventing appreciation of the exchange rate and preserving the export sector's profitability. In 1929, Argentina moved away from the gold standard altogether.

8   de la Balze, *Remaking the Argentine Economy*, 26.

9   Smith, *Authoritarianism and the Crisis of the Argentine Political Economy*, 23.

10   Ibid., 25.

11   Ibid., 25.

12   Nicholas Fraser and Marysa Navarro, *Eva Perón* (London: Andre Deutsch, 1980), 36-45.

13   Ibid., 36-45.

14   For a general appraisal of Perón's ideology and political style during his first and second terms as president, see: Page, *Perón: A Biography*, Chapter 25 "The Conductor."

15   Juan Carlos D'Abate, "Trade Unions and Peronism," in *Juan Perón and the Reshaping of Argentina*, eds. Frederick C. Turner and Jose Enrique Miguens (Pittsburgh: University of Pittsburgh Press, 1983), 59–61.

16   Robert J Alexander, *Juan Domingo Perón: A History* (Boulder, CO: Westview Press, 1979), 37.

17   Ibid., 40.

18   Smith, *Authoritarianism and the Crisis of the Argentine Political Economy*, 31.

19   Fraser, *Eva Perón*, 49-68.

20   This was to be the worst electoral result in Perón's political career. *See* Luna, *El 45*, 469.

21   This reform of the constitution extended the vote to women.

22   Luna, *El 45*, 27-28.

23   Smith, *Authoritarianism and the Crisis of the Argentine Political Economy*, 23.

24   Luna, *El 45*, 27.

25   Page, *Perón: A Biography*, 176.

26   Smith, *Authoritarianism and the Crisis of the Argentine Political Economy*, 27.

27   Page, *Perón: A Biography*, 170.

28   For economic statistics on Argentina from 1913-1984, refer to Instituto de Estudios Económicos sobre la Realidad Argentina y Latinoamerica (IEERAL), "Estadisticas de la Evolución Económica de Argentina, 1913-1984," *Estudios* no. 39 (July/September 1986): 103–184.

29   Smith, *Authoritarianism and the Crisis of the Argentine Political Economy*, 28.

30   Fraser and Navarro, *Eva Perón*, 118.

[31] For an account of Perón's last days in office in the 1950s, *see* Page, *Perón: A Biography*, Chapters 34-36 (<u>At War with the Church</u>, <u>The Beginning of the End</u>, and <u>The Liberating Revolution</u>).

[32] Perón made this claim in an interview with Felix Luna. *See* Luna, *El 45*, 59.

[33] U.S. investment in Argentina tripled in less than a decade, from $427 million in 1960 to nearly $1.2 billion in 1968, and was mainly dedicated to the expanding sectors of the local industry: petroleum, chemicals and petrochemicals, transportation, metallurgy, and electrical equipment. *See* Smith, *Authoritarianism and the Crisis of the Argentine Political Economy*, 34.

[34] Smith, *Authoritarianism and the Crisis of the Argentine Political Economy*, 33.

[35] Alejandro, *Essays on the Economic History of the Argentine Republic*, 129 and Smith, *Authoritarianism and the Crisis of the Argentine Political Economy*, 34.

[36] Smith, *Authoritarianism and the Crisis of the Argentine Political Economy*, 40–41.

[37] Ibid., 35.

[38] Edwin Williamson, "Argentina: The Long Decline," in *The Penguin History of Latin America* (London: Penguin Books, 1992), 473.

[39] Daron Acemoglu, Simon Johnson, James Robinson, and Yunyong Thaicharoen, "Institutional Causes, Macroeconomic Symptoms: Volatility, Crises and Growth" National Bureau of Economics Working Paper W9124, September 2002.

[40] Sebastian M. Saiegh and Pablo T. Spiller, "A Parliamentary System for Argentina," NYU Working Paper, June, 2002, available at <http://homepages.nyu.edu/~sms267/parliam.pdf> (accessed February 26, 2004); Daron Acemoglu, Simon Johnson, James Robinson, and Yunyong Thaicharoen, "Institutional Causes, Macroeconomic Symptoms: Volatility, Crises and Growth" National Bureau of Economics Working Paper W9124, September 2002; and David Samuels and Richard Snyder, "The Value of a Vote: Malapportionment in Comparative Perspective," in *British Journal of Political Science* 31:3, 2001.

[41] For a comprehensive account of the emergence, development, and ultimate demise of the urban guerrilla movement in Argentina, including the resulting divisions within the Peronist movement, *see* Gillespie, Richard. *Soldiers of Perón, Argentina's Montoneros*. New York: Oxford University Press, 1982 *and* Moyano, Maria Jose. *Argentina's Lost Patrol: Armed Struggle 1969-1979*. New Haven: Yale University Press, 1995.

[42] Williamson, "Argentina: The Long Decline," 475.

[43] Jaime Malamud Goti, *Game without End: State Terror and the Politics of Justice* (Norman: University of Oklahoma Press, October 1996), 40.

[44] Smith, *Authoritarianism and the Crisis of the Argentine Political Economy*, 229–30.

[45] Ibid., 235.

[46] Adolfo Canitrot, "Crisis and Transformation of the Argentine State (1978–1992)" in *Democracy, Markets, and Structural Reform in Latin America*, eds. William C. Smith, Carlos H. Acuna, and Eduardo A. Gamarra (Coral Gables: North-South Center Press, 1993), 80.

[47] Carlos H. Acuna, "Politics and Economics in the Argentina of the Nineties (Or, Why the Future No longer is What it Used to Be)," in *Democracy, Markets, and Structural Reform in Latin America*, eds. William C. Smith, Carlos H. Acuna, and Eduardo A. Gamarra (Coral Gables: North-South Center Press, 1993), 33.

[48] "Three biggest borrowers: They may make their payments this year, but; Can Third World debtors climb out of the hole?" *U.S. News & World Report* (January 20, 1986): 40.

[49] Canitrot, "Crisis and Transformation of the Argentine State (1978–1992)," 82.

[50] Acuna, "Politics and Economics in the Argentina of the Nineties (Or, Why the Future No longer is What it Used to Be)," 37.

[51] "Survey of Argentina: Learning a New Dance," *The Economist*, 26 November 1994, 3.

[52] Ibid., 37.

Argentina's Convertibility Plan

In 1991, President Menem—a member of the Peronist party—introduced a dramatic new currency system under the guidance of technocratic, Harvard-educated Finance Minister Domingo Cavallo to address Argentina's seemingly intractable economic, political, and social problems.

Under Cavallo's convertibility plan, Argentine peso notes were backed 100% by dollar assets. Pesos were made freely convertible into dollars and a fixed exchange rate of one peso to one dollar was established.

Following the implementation of Cavallo's plan, inflation was eliminated, economic growth resumed, and capital inflows returned. Yet the new currency system exposed Argentina to international financial disturbances. When the financial and currency crises struck Mexico in 1994–1995, Argentina was immediately affected as capital inflows dried up and (because of the currency regime) domestic interest rates rose.

Study Questions

1. Why is a populist president introducing such an orthodox and rigid policy as the Argentine currency board? Why is the Peronist president in league with such a technocratic, market-oriented economist?

2. Did the convertibility plan work well for Argentina in the period discussed in the case?

3. In the context of the impact of the tequila crisis on Argentina in early 1995, what is the dilemma faced by President Menem? What tradeoffs does he face? Should he respond by abandoning the currency board?

RAFAEL DI TELLA
INGRID VOGEL

Argentina's Convertibility Plan

"For the hunger of poor children, for the sadness of rich children, for the young and the old, with the flag of God, which is faith, and the flag of the people, which is the fatherland, for God, I ask you: follow me. I will not let you down."[1]

– Presidential candidate Menem during his 1989 campaign

Presidential candidate Carlos Saúl Menem delivered emotionally charged campaign speeches amidst a severe economic crisis in 1989. Throughout the 1980s, Argentina had faced periods of hyperinflation, stagflation, and huge fiscal deficits. The government had attempted to bring order to the economy under a number of varying and promising programs over the years, but only succeeded in creating temporary solutions that escalated into spiraling economic problems. Choosing to believe in his broad-spectrum promises for a brighter future, the people elected Menem to the presidency in May 1989.

In March 1991, much to the surprise and satisfaction of international markets, Menem managed to bring about a quick and decisive success with the Convertibility Plan—brainchild of his freshly appointed economics minister, Harvard-trained Domingo Felipe Cavallo. Almost immediately, inflation converged to international levels. Even more remarkable, convertibility overcame inflation without causing an economic slowdown. Instead, an economy that contracted by 7% in 1989 and registered almost no growth in 1990 grew at an average annual rate of almost 8% in the following four years. In defiance of the conventional wisdom that stabilization programs had an adverse effect upon the countries implementing them, the Argentine government had stabilized its economy without sacrificing short-term growth.

But by late 1995, the viability of convertibility was being questioned in the wake of the Mexican economic crisis. Mexico's peso devaluation in December 1994 and the subsequent fear that it might default on its debt had brought turmoil to emerging markets and placed the Argentine economy under severe pressure. Inflation remained around 2% in 1995, but economic growth was faltering and capital flight was mounting. The economy contracted by more than 4% in the first three quarters of 1995.[2] In addition, unemployment reached a record 18.3%, as concern about the social costs of the new economic model dominated public debate (see **Exhibit 1**).

This case derives in part from an earlier case, "Menem and the Populist Tradition in Argentina," HBS No. 700-061, prepared by Research Associate Eliseo Neuman under the supervision of Professor Rafael Di Tella. This version was prepared by Research Associate Ingrid Vogel under the supervision of Professor Rafael Di Tella, and was developed based on published sources. HBS cases are developed solely as the basis for class discussion. Cases are not intended to serve as endorsements, sources of primary data, or illustrations of effective or ineffective management.

Despite the disruption in the Argentine economy, the people had nevertheless reelected incumbent President Carlos Saúl Menem in May of 1995. It seemed they trusted him *again* with the difficult task of leading the country out of its economic predicament and reviving the "Argentine Miracle." The third quarter of 1995 was just beginning, and President Menem had to determine how to avoid a reversion to the economic chaos of the prior decade.

Menem's Background

Carlos Menem, born in 1930 to Syrian immigrants, experienced a humble upbringing in the poor province of La Rioja. He was born into a Muslim family, but associated with the Catholic community as a child and later converted to Catholicism. As a law student at the University of Córdoba in 1951, he first met President Juan Domingo Perón, the controversial founder of the populist Peronist movement under which labor gained an influential voice in politics. President Perón and his charismatic wife Evita impressed the young Menem, who became politically active upon Perón's ousting in 1955.[a] The same year, Menem received his law degree and started legally representing labor and Peronists who were being harassed under the new military regime. Increasing his activism, in 1957 he became the president of the Peronist Youth of La Rioja.

His political aspirations ran deeper, but not until the proscription of Peronism was overturned in 1973 could they be fulfilled. In 1964, Menem visited Perón in his exile in Madrid. Perón recognized Menem's potential and his growing influence in the La Rioja Province, and allegedly encouraged him through introductions and mentoring. In return, Menem worked with other supporters during the early 1970s to help secure Perón's return to Argentina and the presidency. In 1973, Perón was reelected president, and Menem became governor of La Rioja. Menem's term ended prematurely in 1976 when the military took over the national government and imprisoned him during the "dirty war." Two years after his release, he again became governor of La Rioja before being elected president in 1989.[3] Despite his negative experience with the military, Menem portrayed himself during his first presidential campaign as an intense nationalist who ardently supported reclaiming the Falkland-Malvinas Islands even through a military invasion.

As governor and later president, Menem chose not to suppress the more colorful side of his personality. He had a reputation for enjoying dancing, socializing, fine clothes, and the company of attractive women. Throughout his campaigns and tenure as president, the media liked to draw attention to his idiosyncratic character. Various journals and papers joked about the presence of his hairdresser on official state visits. They emphasized his wild style of dress and enormous sideburns, which some claimed played homage to 19th-century *caudillo* Facundo Quiroga.[b] The press also copiously covered his dramatic personal life, including the 1990 eviction of his wife from the presidential residence and the following brawl over Menem's womanizing. He retaliated, stating "I'm a seducer, not a womanizer. Let's say I'm an ordinary man."[4] One journal wrote of him:

> " 'The man's a psychoanalyst's nightmare,' argues one Buenos Aires psychiatrist, who reckons that Mr. Menem, unlike most Argentines, is without either guilt or self-analysis. (Indeed, asked whether he has made any mistakes, Mr. Menem waffles charmingly and then

---

[a] Perón was president of Argentina from 1946-1955 and again from 1973 until his death in 1974. For more information about Perón and Peronism, see the HBS case 702-001 "The Argentine Paradox: Economic Growth and the Populist Tradition."

[b] Juan Facundo Quiroga, a 19th-century provincial warlord from La Rioja, reigned for decades over northwest Argentina with his gaucho army until he was waylaid and murdered by rivals from the larger Córdoba province.

eventually quotes Frank Sinatra: 'I did it my way.') Affection for Mr. Menem's idiosyncracies tends to divide along class lines. A lawyer will shudder as he tells you about how Mr. Menem rejigged his schedule to meet Claudia Schiffer, a supermodel; but taxi drivers admire him for it. The same goes for his taste in clothes."[5]

Menem Takes Office

Upon taking office, Menem surprised public opinion by calling on Bunge & Born, one of Argentina's oldest and most important multinational enterprises, to formulate economic policy. Perón had resorted to "social pacts" before. But never had so much been entrusted to a single group that, as an important participant in the agro-export sector and a leading representative of the traditional Argentine elite, symbolized Peronist opposition to free-market capitalism.[a]

Menem, enjoying less parliamentary support and party discipline than Perón, repeatedly resorted to rulings by presidential decree. During his first five years in office, Menem issued over 330 decrees that extended executive influence into areas traditionally under the authority of the legislature.[b] One of his initial measures expanded the reformist powers of the executive branch, preemptively further reducing eventual legislative interference from the Radical opposition.[6] At the same time, members of the Conservative Party were incorporated as advisors to the government.

Foreseeing strong labor opposition to structural reforms, Menem appointed loyal union leaders to the Ministry of Labor. These appointments split the union movement into a loyalist arm, recognized by the government, and a contentious arm, which was subsequently marginalized. His reforms were indeed carried out at the expense of the traditional union bureaucracy, which he was reputed to have neutralized through favors and "unorthodox" rewards. Indeed, critics singled out corruption as a pervasive feature of his rule.[c]

In a highly controversial move, he pardoned the heads of the military *juntas* convicted for crimes during the "dirty war" by the previous administration. At the same time, he abolished military service and reduced the military budget—both important steps in reducing government spending. The armed forces eventually acknowledged excesses during the "dirty war" of the mid-1970s, when political assassinations and intimidation were common, and issued an apology. The army also followed Menem's orders to suppress an uprising by recalcitrant elements of its own.

In foreign policy matters, Menem's years in power involved a radical departure from the isolationist stance of Perón's "third position." In fact, Menem's government was often criticized for excessive alignment with U.S. and NATO interests.

Close to the end of his first term, Menem, just as Perón had, reformed the constitution to provide for his own reelection and altered the composition of the judiciary. Perón had done so through the impeachment of Supreme Court Justices; Menem by packing the Court and through alleged persistent meddling with its independence.

---

[a] The head of the Bunge & Born Group at the time, Jorge Born, had been kidnapped by Montoneros, a Peronist guerrilla group, in 1974 and was liberated after payment of a $60 million ransom.

[b] By comparison, Raul Alfonsín, the preceding president, had issued only 10 executive decrees during his six years in office.

[c] In 1995 and 1996, Argentina ranked in the bottom half [i.e., more corrupt range] of most international corruption-perception rankings. Argentina's standing worsened during the Menem administration.

Off to a Shaky Start

The plan implemented under Bunge & Born attempted to stabilize the economy through heterodox measures including a fixed exchange rate combined with price and wage freezes. In its initial months, the plan succeeded in curbing hyperinflation. Consumer price increases fell from 197% in July 1989 to 6% in October (see **Exhibit 5**). But the fiscal deficit grew and was financed through a growing stock of short-term debt. Lingering inflation resulted in overvaluation of the local currency. Under speculative pressure, the government devalued the currency by 50%, while the fiscal deficit was addressed through extensions on maturing bonds and increases in export taxes and fuel prices.

But these measures were perceived as mere quick fixes, and the Bunge & Born team was replaced within months by Erman González, a veteran advisor from Menem's province. He decontrolled prices, unified the foreign exchange market under a floating rate, rescheduled the long-term domestic public debt, and reversed increases in export taxes. Anticipating a further hike in inflation, he also allowed a significant wage increase. The business sector responded with raised prices, and the dollar increased in value by 100% in December 1989. The country was once again in a hyperinflationary spiral. In 1989, consumer prices rose by 3,080% while GDP fell by almost 7%. In response, the government tightened the money supply, legalized bank deposits in U.S. dollars, and limited expenditure to fiscal revenue. In a controversial move, it exchanged, by force, the public's bank deposits for government long-term bonds.[7]

Hyperinflation was arrested within three months. Yet 1990 registered a 2,370% increase in prices, almost no increase in GDP, and a 3.5% drop in real wages. A normal year-end increase in the demand for U.S. dollars led to a 62% depreciation of the national currency. The fiscal deficit exceeded 10% of GDP, and public sector debt exceeded 100% of GDP. All business sectors remained skeptical of Menem's ability to stabilize Argentina's economy. In January 1991, after a run on the national currency led to a single day 20% plunge in its value, the economics minister and Central Bank governor both resigned.[8]

Economics Minister Domingo Cavallo

To fill the post of economics minister, Menem selected 44-year old then-Foreign Minister Domingo Felipe Cavallo who pledged to pursue Menem's unpopular free market policies. In a government that had been tarnished by allegations of corruption, Cavallo had a reputation of integrity and had enjoyed the near-universal endorsement of both local and foreign observers for some time.

In the 1970s, Cavallo earned a doctorate in economics from Harvard University, where classmates included former Mexican President Carlos Salinas de Gortari and Chilean Finance Minister Alejandro Foxley. On his return to Argentina, he founded the *Fundación Mediterránea,* a respected economics think tank, and held various positions in government, including president of the Central Bank from 1981 to 1982.[9] In conflict with the economics minister at the time, as president of the Central Bank during the military dictatorship, Cavallo was an active supporter of national industry and of large wage increases to counterbalance the effect of high inflation on workers. Shortly before resigning as president of the Central Bank over differences with the administration, he introduced policies favorable to financially strapped companies, essentially nationalizing the foreign debt of the private sector prior to the debt crisis of 1982.[10]

The Convertibility Plan

Cavallo devised a comprehensive plan—the so-called Convertibility Plan—upon his appointment as Economics Minister. The plan deepened several existing policies and started new ones, such as trade reforms, further privatization and deregulation, tax reforms, and generally tighter fiscal policies. But the key to his plan was the formation of a currency board.

Annex: A History of Currency Boards

Currency boards were introduced in the British colonies of Africa, Asia, the Caribbean, and the Middle East in the 19th century. At one point, over 70 currency boards were in operation, allowing ruling empires to run their monetary systems efficiently while devolving at least some responsibility and seigniorage to their colonies.* Currency boards consisted of three elements: a fixed exchange rate; guaranteed convertibility; and 100% backing. In other words, a pure currency board had the limited role of exchanging, upon demand, local currency for reserve currency at a fixed rate. To fulfill this requirement, the country had to hold reserves at least equal in value to the domestic currency outstanding. Unlike Central Banks, currency boards were prohibited from open market operations and could not act as lenders of last resort.

With the end of colonialism after World War II, most currency boards were abandoned. But currency boards were still favored by some small open economies with relatively limited expertise in monetary management. Countries establishing currency boards in the post-war period included Brunei Darussalam (1967), Djibouti (1949), and member countries of the Eastern Caribbean Central Bank (1965).

In the 1980s and 1990s, at least six other countries introduced currency boards, including Argentina, Hong Kong, and four former Communist countries. Hong Kong had abandoned its original currency board in 1974. It introduced a new currency board based on the U.S. dollar in 1983 after the early 1980s attack on the Hong Kong dollar that had resulted from the uncertainties created by the prospect of China's renewed rule of the island in 1997. Hong Kong succeeded in reinstating a stable exchange rate and confidence in the economy and therefore continued to thrive as an international financial and trading center. In 1994, almost every major bank had a branch or representative office in the country. Furthermore, the Hong Kong Stock Exchange provided a source of capital to local and mainland Chinese enterprises as well as a forum for international brokers to invest in Asian equity.

* Seigniorage here refers to the interest earned by colonies on their foreign reserves backing.

The Convertibility Plan pegged the local currency to the U.S. dollar at a fixed exchange rate of 1-to-1, at which the Central Bank was obliged to convert currency.[11] It also required that the gold and foreign currency reserves of the Central Bank at all times be equivalent to 100% of the monetary base, defined as all currency in circulation plus the banking system reserves required by the Central Bank[a] (see **Exhibit 6**). In addition, convertibility eliminated indexation of prices and wages and created a fully independent Central Bank under which the term of the Bank's president would be longer than the government's electoral cycle.[12]

The rationale behind convertibility was to send investors the most credible signal possible of the government's commitment to stability and monetary and fiscal discipline. Unlike under prior unsuccessful fixed exchange rate regimes, the Central Bank could no longer intervene in a slowdown by easing the money supply through open market operations. In the past, these interventions had avoided contractions in the monetary base (and thus avoided higher interest rates and recession) but sacrificed reserves in the process. The currency board, by contrast, imposed a rigid mechanism for monetary discipline. The Central Bank could ease the broader money supply (such as M1) only

---

[a] Unlike under a true currency board, the Central Bank of Argentina was allowed to use Argentine government bonds denominated in U.S. dollars to back up to 20% of the monetary base. After 1995, this was increased to one-third. In practice, foreign reserve coverage had always been maintained close to 100% —except during the Mexican crisis.

through measures that did not compromise the full backing of the monetary base, such as reducing reserve requirements of banks. The Central Bank was also prohibited from extending credit to commercial banks. Convertibility imposed fiscal discipline as well, because additional government spending could only be financed through increases in government tax revenues or market loans rather than forcing the Central Bank to "print money."

Moreover, such a mechanism would function automatically during an adverse shock, free of government discretion, through a natural adjustment in interest rates. In the case of an overvalued peso, imports would exceed exports. With the Central Bank simply converting the extra pesos into dollars, the money supply would shrink. Liquidity constraints would drive interest rates higher. A higher interest rate would dampen investment and economic activity, until imports dropped to the level that could be afforded with the new level of exports. A high interest rate would also attract capital inflows and thereby ease the adjustment process. In the most extreme example, the Central Bank was expected to allow a massive conversion of pesos for dollars (until the monetary base was zero), rather than break the peg.

A currency board of this kind was feasible at the time mainly because the Argentine economy was already heavily 'dollarized.' Even though the local currency remained legal tender, the U.S. dollar had effectively become the preferred store of value and unit of account. Most large transactions were denominated in dollars. Furthermore, the bulk of resident savings were held offshore in dollar accounts (as much as 100% of GDP against only 5% in local deposits).[13] In fact, by the end of 1989, about 80% of Argentines' total liquid assets were invested in foreign financial instruments. Recent hyperinflationary episodes had reduced the monetary base to manageable levels (by 1990, M3, a broader measure of money, had diminished to half its 1988 level as a percent of GDP, as shown in **Exhibit 1**), and net international reserves were sufficient to support the peg at the chosen rate.

In reflection, Cavallo said of the Plan:

"The most important aspect was the decision to legalize the use of the dollar as the currency not only for transactions but also for financial intermediation—something that people had been doing for some time to defend themselves from inflation but which was illegal. We decided to legalize the use of the dollar for commercial as well as financial transactions and introduce a local currency as strong as the dollar. From that came the idea of introducing a convertible peso and organizing a currency board to regulate it.

… The most important decision was not the introduction of the currency board but rather the decision to give people the freedom to elect either the dollar or the peso … and to allow the financial system to function with both currencies. That decision created the security for the people that the government would respect the commitment of the currency board. Why? Because as soon as the government would take a decision to devalue or place the value of the peso at risk, everyone would automatically switch to dollars. It was this freedom that people had that required the government to defend the value of the peso."[14]

Other Related Reforms

Convertibility amounted to a veritable coup. The reliable exchange rate became the most compelling 'story' to lure foreign investors. It also provided the stability needed to implement a number of structural reforms, including:

Debt Reduction. Menem set a target of reducing foreign debt by at least 30% in 1992 through the Brady Plan.[15] The Brady Plan in turn supported the privatization program, as bidders were given the option to pay for part of their purchases in Brady Bonds, then trading well below par. As a result, the government retired a considerable portion of its foreign debt. Foreign debt stood at 33% of GDP in 1994 versus 48% at the end of 1990.

Privatizations. Menem completed a comprehensive privatization program in record time. His plan called for the continued privatization of deficit-prone state-owned enterprises, a process that had been initiated early in his tenure as president with the passage of the Law of the Reform of the State that set up the regulatory framework for the transfer of assets and firms from the public to the private domain. About 90% of state companies were privatized between 1991 and 1994 alone, with proceeds of over $22 billion (including both cash and the retirement of public debt) that were used mostly to refinance or reduce public debt. The process cut employees of these companies from 302,000 to 138,000. The government relied on summary Supreme Court rulings to overcome constitutional challenges to certain privatizations, particularly by the unions, whose power was largely curtailed in the process. To attract high bid prices and high levels of investment in the often technologically outdated companies, the government introduced regulations that resulted in higher prices to consumers. The government typically retained a minority stake (around 39%) in the privatized companies, required a yet smaller stake to be distributed to employees (around 10%), and ceded control to proven operators. The key privatized sectors included oil, natural gas, petrochemicals, electricity, telecommunications, steel, and transportation[16] (see **Exhibit 7**).

Deregulation. Menem abolished all wage and price controls, and established a framework to deregulate the sugar, grain, and meat markets among others, dissolving the corresponding state regulatory entities. Wholesale and retail trades, as well as professional services, were also deregulated. The privatization of ports, oil and gas companies, public utilities, and transport entities also led to the deregulation of those sectors. Efficiencies, lower prices, and output quality improvements followed.

Tax and Administrative Reform. Argentina's tax structure and collection methodology was overhauled. Value Added Tax (a consumption tax) and income tax were eventually raised, deductions eliminated, tax forms greatly simplified, and enforcement stepped-up. A *"Pacto Fiscal"* distributed a minimum of the tax revenue to the provinces in exchange for the elimination of the more regressive taxes, such as the stamp tax. It also shifted the bulk of education and health expenditures to the provinces and called for downsizing the central administration. The tax reform, however, could not separate spending from tax collections, which typically increased during booms when spending was less needed.

Trade Reform. The plan sought to deepen trade reform and further integrate the country into the global economy. Export tariffs and non-tariff import barriers (except for those on shoes, some textiles, and automobiles) were abolished and import tariffs reduced. These changes benefited the agricultural sector but also reduced distortions in relative factor prices and greatly stimulated investment. The Mercosur customs union with Brazil, Paraguay, and Uruguay was also strengthened.

Pension Fund Reform. The pay-as-you-go pension system was actuarially broke. It paid out extremely low pensions and was a fiscal drain. Menem's plan called for the creation of a fully funded, private pension system. Business contributions were reduced while the minimum retirement age was increased. The reform transferred the management of pension assets from the government to consortiums of local banks, with a view to developing the local capital market. In doing so, the government gave up revenues from contributors while retaining the liability for pensions payable to existing retirees. This resulted in an ongoing yearly loss of fiscal revenue, which amounted to 1.4% of GDP in 1996.

Labor Reform. The plan called for increased labor flexibility, although of all the markets Menem sought to liberalize, the labor market remained the most resistant. A combination of presidential decrees and legislation attempted to lower labor costs, weaken union influence, and facilitate temporary labor arrangements. The new laws aimed to curtail workers' compensation and reduce severance payments to some degree. Unions were addressed through legislation allowing smaller scale alternative unions, diffusing management over collective bargaining processes, and making worker contributions to unions optional. Nevertheless, the IMF continued to pressure the Argentine government since progress in this area was so slow (see **Exhibit 8**).

Early Results of the Convertibility Plan

The Convertibility Plan yielded prompt results. Inflation fell from 3,080% in 1989 and 2,370% in 1990, to 25% in 1992, and to international levels by third quarter 1993. GDP, which had fallen by 7% in 1989 and registered almost no growth in 1990, grew by 8.9% in 1991, 8.7% in 1992, 6.0% in 1993, and 7.4% in 1994. This growth was accompanied by comparable increases in investment, total-factor productivity, and foreign direct investment.

The recovery in GDP growth, along with the reduced spending on deficit-ridden privatized companies, the overall downsizing of the central administration, and higher tax collections, helped improve Argentina's fiscal situation (see **Exhibit 4**). As opposed to a fiscal deficit in 1989 and 1990, the federal government achieved surpluses from 1991 through 1993. Menem boasted that, in contrast to most European economies at that time, Argentina satisfied the European Union's Maastricht convergence criteria for membership in the nascent single European currency.

The new economic environment, including the elimination of restrictions on foreign investment and on capital account transactions, proved auspicious for capital markets. Stability resulted in the repatriation of large amounts of flight capital. Total deposits grew from $14 billion at the end of 1991 to $45 billion at the end of 1994. In part aided by the growing popularity of Argentine government bonds in international capital markets, foreign investment flows into Argentina between 1992 and 1994 reached over $30 billion. Foreign direct investment jumped from under $2 billion in 1990 to more than $4 billion in 1995 (see **Exhibit 7b**). Bank lending to the non-financial private sector also experienced impressive growth, from $5 billion in April 1991 to $36 billion in October 1994. A consumption boom followed as home mortgages and purchases of consumer durables soared in a country unused to living on credit.[17] Reflecting Argentina's improved situation, the country risk premium came down significantly during the period, from 66% in 1991 to just 3% in 1993 (see **Exhibit 9**).

The balance of payments reflected the interest in lending to Argentina (see **Exhibit 3**). The trade balance, at a surplus of $8.6 billion in 1990, deteriorated to a deficit of $2.4 billion by 1993. Increased imports and spending on tourism outweighed increases in exports. The current account deficit increased from $2.8 billion in 1991, to $8.9 billion in 1993.

A significant downside of the Convertibility Plan was that unemployment was steadily increasing: from 6% and 7% in 1991 and 1992, to 9% by the end of 1993, and finally to 12% in 1994, probably reflecting the restructuring of industry implied by opening the economy to international competition. The problem worsened when U.S. interest rates rose in February 1994 and capital inflows into Argentina slowed, calling into question the sustainability of the current account deficit. The higher interest rates were passed on to Argentina through the currency board mechanism, irrespective of conditions in the Argentine economy. The budget ultimately moved back into deficit as the economy slowed and tax revenues decreased.

Vulnerability of the Currency Board: The Tequila Crisis as Test Case

Rising U.S. interest rates were also one of the triggers of Mexico's peso devaluation in December 1994. Investors feared that Mexico would be forced to default on its debt obligations. Financial markets lost confidence in Latin America as a whole, especially in Argentina which had a fixed exchange rate that could be attacked, and convertibility was severely tested. To worsen things, Argentina's current account deficit had deteriorated significantly in the last quarter of 1994. Foreign investors believed that Argentina's peso was overvalued, leading to a steep drop in capital inflows, a massive conversion of the currency into U.S. dollars, and a consequent rise in interest rates. Businesses were unable to obtain credit at these new rates. After increasing by 200% in the two years up to November 1994, total deposits in the banking system dropped almost 10% in March 1995 alone, and 18% by May 1995.[18] Banks faced liquidity constraints and difficulty in fulfilling their ordinary business of taking short-term deposits and giving long-term loans.

Under the currency board, the Central Bank was unable to increase the monetary base and issue credit unless it had backing in U.S. dollars. As base money shrank by 20% in the first four months of 1995, the Central Bank reacted by temporarily reducing reserve requirements.[19] GDP fell by 9.7% between the fourth quarter of 1994 and the third quarter of 1995.[20] Unemployment, which was already rising, reached the record level of 18.3% in May 1995. The recession combined with high interest rates made Argentina's debt even more difficult to service, pushing default rates higher.

Despite Argentina's precarious position, Menem succeeded in winning a second presidential term during the May 1995 elections. It was now October, and the Argentine people expected him to restore order to the economy. He faced a number of possible options, including abandoning convertibility, reinforcing commitment to convertibility by completely substituting the peso with the U.S. dollar through "dollarization," devaluing the currency, avoiding intervention, or taking some other action. In making his decision, he had to weigh carefully the economic, social, and political implications.

Exhibit 1a   Argentine General Economic Indicators

percentage	1988	1989	1990	1991	1992	1993	1994	Q3 1995
Real GDP Growth	-1.7	-6.9	0.1	8.9	8.7	6.0	7.4	-4.4
Real Per Capita GDP Growth	-3.0	-8.3	-1.3	7.5	7.3	4.7	6.1	-5.8
Consumer Price Inflation	343	3080	2370	172	24.9	10.7	4.1	2.7
Investment/GDP	18.6	15.5	14.0	14.6	16.7	19.1	19.9	18.1
M3/GDP[a]	11.5	9.0	5.7	11.1	14.4	19.0	20.0	18.1
Public Expenditure/GDP	29.3	25.9	26.6	27.0	27.2	27.6	na	na
Average of exports and imports as % GDP	7.9	9.8	7.5	6.9	7.5	8.1	9.1	10.0
units as described								
Unemployment *(%)*	6.9	7.1	6.3	6.0	7.0	9.3	12.2	15.5
International Reserves *(billions current U.S. $)*	4.8	2.9	6.0	7.4	11.4	15.5	16.0	16.0
Foreign Debt *(billions current U.S. dollars)*[a]	60.2	63.3	62.2	65.4	67.6	70.0	77.0	86.0

Source: Adapted from EIU Country Data; IMF, *International Financial Statistics*; OECD, 1997; Balze, 1995; and Smith, 1989.
Note: [a]1995 data for year-end.

Exhibit 1b   Argentine and U.S. Comparative Economic Indicators

1993=100	1989	1990	1991	1992	1993	1994	1995
Argentina							
GDP Deflator	1.8	38.9	90.9	102.4	100.0	102.8	106.1
Consumer Price Index	1.1	26.6	72.3	90.3	100.0	104.1	107.6
Producer Price Index	2.6	44.1	92.9	98.4	100.0	100.7	108.5
Nominal Wage Index	0.0	26.6	78.1	93.2	100.0	109.2	106.2
U.S.							
GDP Deflator	88.5	92.0	95.3	97.7	100.0	102.1	104.3
Consumer Price Index	85.8	90.4	94.3	97.1	100.0	102.6	105.5
Producer Price Index	94.4	97.8	98.0	98.5	100.0	101.3	104.9
Nominal Wage Index	89.1	92.4	95.2	97.6	100.0	102.6	105.5
Nominal Exchange Rate	na	na	1.0	1.0	1.0	1.0	1.0

Source: Adapted from IMF, *International Financial Statistics Yearbook*, 2000.

Exhibit 2   Argentine National Income Accounts *(billions constant 1996 U.S. dollars)*

	1988	1989	1990	1991	1992	1993	1994	Q1-Q3 1995
Gross Domestic Product	**208.4**	**194.1**	**188.2**	**211.2**	**235.1**	**250.9**	**265.5**	**193.2**
Household Consumption	128.2	115.0	119.3	143.0	166.1	173.6	185.7	132.5
Government Consumption	34.4	36.5	31.6	33.8	33.6	33.9	35.0	25.0
Gross Fixed Investment	38.8	30.1	26.3	30.9	39.3	47.8	52.9	34.9
Changes in Stocks	*na*	*na*	*na*	*na*	*na*	1.5	0.0	1.1
Exports *(goods and services)*	19.9	25.2	19.7	16.4	15.7	17.5	20.1	19.2
Imports *(goods and services)*	12.9	12.8	8.7	12.9	19.5	23.4	28.1	19.5
Domestic Demand	202	182	177	208	239	257	274	194

Source: Adapted from IMF, *International Financial Statistics Yearbook*, 2000.

Exhibit 3   Argentine Balance of Payments *(millions current U.S. dollars)*

	1988	1989	1990	1991	1992	1993	1994	Q3 1995
Current Account	**-1,572**	**-1,305**	**4,552**	**-647**	**-5,715**	**-8,158**	**-11,158**	**-1,048**
Trade Balance	4,242	5,709	8,628	4,419	-1,396	-2,364	-4,139	712
Exports	*9,134*	*9,573*	*12,354*	*11,978*	*12,399*	*13,269*	*16,023*	*5,319*
Imports	*4,892*	*3,864*	*3,726*	*7,559*	*13,795*	*15,633*	*20,162*	*4,606*
Net Services	-687	-600	-674	-1,599	-2,514	-3,218	-3,700	-697
Net Income	-5,127	-6,422	-4,400	-4,260	-2,455	-2,979	-3,679	-1,135
Net Transfers	0	8	998	793	650	403	359	72
Financial Account	**369**	**-8,083**	**-5,884**	**182**	**7,443**	**20,397**	**11,350**	**2,319**
Net Direct Investment	1,147	1,028	1,836	2,439	3,264	2,090	2,620	1,164
Net Portfolio Investment	-718	-1,098	-1,346	-34	4,513	33,731	8,389	1,218
Net Short Term Capital	-65	-7,527	-5,873	-2,303	1,009	-5,228	-629	-154
Net Government	5	-486	-501	80	-1,343	-10,196	969	90
Net Errors and Omissions	**-165**	**-249**	**715**	**-341**	**165**	**-1,117**	**-866**	**-1,242**
Reserves and Related Items	**1,368**	**9,637**	**617**	**806**	**-1,894**	**-11,122**	**675**	**-29**

Source: Adapted from IMF, *International Financial Statistics Yearbook*, 2000.

Exhibit 4   Argentine Government Finance (*millions current pesos*)

	1989	1990	1991	1992	1993	1994	1995
Total Revenue	319	7,208	34,042	48,600	56,686	61,537	57,852
Primary Expenditure	na	na	34,866	50,917	60,030	66,174	63,411
Primary Deficit (+) / Surplus (-)	na	na	824	2,317	3,344	4,637	5,559
Interest Payments	na	na	4,800	4,727	3,973	4,788	5,810
Other Payments	na	na	-5,835	3,050	4,018	-470	1,191
Overall Deficit (+) / Surplus (-)	-12	-245	-211	10,094	11,335	8,955	12,560
% of GDP			-0.1	4.8	4.8	3.5	4.9

Source: Adapted from (1989-1990) IMF, *Government Finance Statistics,* 2000 and (1991-1995) Mario Teijeiro, "Una Vez Mas, La Politica Fiscal...," Centro de Estudios Publicos, 2001, unpublished article. The data for 1991–1995 adopts a very strict, pessimistic approach, which is not strictly comparable to the earlier period.

Exhibit 5   Argentine Annualized Quarterly Inflation (*logarithmic scale*)

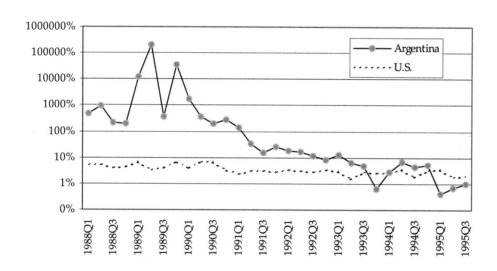

Source: Adapted from IMF, *International Financial Statistics Yearbook,* 2000.

Exhibit 6   Argentine Reserves and Monetary Base *(millions current U.S. dollars)*

Year	Reserves	Monetary Base	Backing	Year	Reserves	Monetary Base	Backing
1991	5,594	6,093	92%	Nov-94	13,972	14,978	93%
1992	8,809	9,256	95%	Dec-94	15,314	16,268	94%
1993	12,314	12,987	95%	Jan-95	13,572	14,310	95%
Jan-94	15,195	16,376	93%	Feb-95	12,818	14,142	91%
Feb-94	15,125	16,162	94%	Mar-95	10,114	12,383	82%
Mar-94	14,574	14,822	98%	Apr-95	11,155	13,639	82%
Apr-94	14,242	15,380	93%	May-95	10,768	13,287	81%
May-94	14,663	15,718	93%	Jun-95	11,804	13,185	90%
Jun-94	14,667	14,458	101%	Jul-95	12,403	14,671	85%
Jul-94	14,985	16,087	93%	Aug-95	11,252	13,520	83%
Aug-94	14,895	15,922	94%	Sep-95	11,565	13,824	84%
Sep-94	14,395	14,372	100%	Oct-95	12,135	14,207	85%
Oct-94	14,264	15,432	92%				

Source: Adapted from Carta Economica.

Exhibit 7   Argentine Privatization Program

A Sale Proceeds for Selected Privatizations (*millions current U.S. dollars*)

Enterprise	Cash	Debt[a]
YPF	3040	855
ENTel	2271[b]	5000
Aerolineas Argentinas	260	1610
Petrochemicals	53	0
Oil fields	1560	0
Power (SEGBA, AYE)	308	955
Real Estate	107	0
Steel companies	143	40
Natural gas	300	2651
Ports	14	0

Source: Adapted from "Argentina's Privatization Program," World Bank Publication, 1993.
Notes: [a]Face value.
          [b]Plus $380 in promissory notes.

B Privatization and FDI *(1990–1995)*

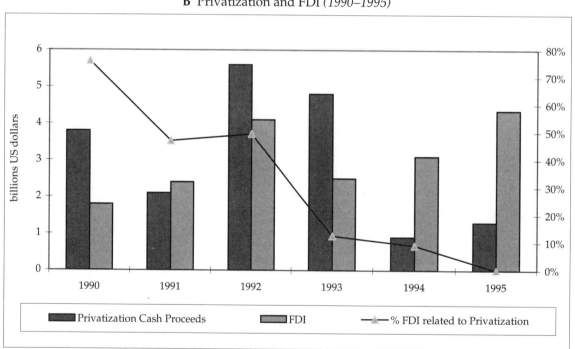

Source: Adapted from Japan External Trade Organization, "Privatization in Developing Countries," 1998.

Exhibit 8   Labor Market Institutions in Argentina and the OECD

	Payroll Tax Rate (%) 1989-94 [a]	Union Density (%) 1988-94 [b]	Union Coverage Index 1988-94 [c]	Ratio of Minimum to Average Wage 1990s [d]	Percent of Workers at or near Minimum 1990s [e]	Notice and Severance Pay for No-Fault Dismissals Rankings [f]	Difficulty of Dismissal Rankings [g]	Overall Employment Protection Ranking 1990 [h]	Duration of Parental Leave (weeks) 1995 [i]	Benefit Replacement Ratio (%) 1989-94 [j]	Benefit Duration (years) 1989-94 [k]	Active Labour Market Policies 1991 [l]	Regional Mobility (Percent Persons changing region of residence each year) 1980-87 [m]	Percent of Households who are Owner Occupiers 1990 [n]
Austria	22.6	46.2	3	0.62	4	10	11	16	104	50	2.0	8.3	-	54
Belgium	21.5	51.2	3	0.60	4	13	3	17	(260)	60	4.0	14.6	-	65
Denmark	0.6	71.4	3	0.54	6	11	5	5	28	90	2.5	10.3	-	55
Finland	25.5	72.0	3	0.52	-	9	4	10	156	63	2.0	16.4	1.5	78
France	38.8	9.8	3	0.50	11	7	6.5	14	156	57	3.0	8.8	1.3	56
Germany	23.0	32.9	3	0.55	-	2	12	15	156	63	4.0	25.7	1.1	42
Greece	-	-	-	-	-	12	10	-	-	-	-	-	-	-
Ireland	7.1	49.7	3	0.55	-	3	6.5	12	18	37	4.0	9.1	-	76
Italy	40.2	38.8	3	0.71	-	16	15	20	46	20	0.5	10.3	0.6	68
Netherlands	27.5	25.5	3	0.55	3.2	1	8	9	40	70	2.0	6.9	-	45
Norway	17.5	56.0	3	0.64	-	6	14	11	52	65	1.5	14.7	2.5	78
Portugal	14.5	31.8	3	0.45	8	15	16	18	40	65	0.8	18.8	-	58
Spain	33.2	11.0	3	0.32	6.5	14	13	19	52	70	3.5	4.7	0.4	75
Sweden	37.8	82.5	3	0.52	0	8	9	13	78	80	1.2	59.3	3.7	56
Switzerland	14.5	26.6	2	-	-	4	2	6	14	70	1.0	8.2	1.1	28
UK	13.8	39.1	2	0.40	-	5	1	7	40	38	4.0	6.4	1.1	65
Canada	13.0	35.8	2	0.35	-	-	-	3	38	59	1.0	5.9	1.6	63
US	20.9	15.6	1	0.39	4	-	-	1	12	50	0.5	3.0	2.9	64
Japan	16.5	25.4	2	-	-	-	-	8	52	60	0.5	4.3	2.7	59
Australia	2.5	40.4	3	-	-	-	-	4	52	36	4.0	3.2	1.7	70
New Zealand	-	44.8	2	0.46	-	-	-	2	52	30	4.0	6.8	-	71
Argentina	33 (pre 1996) / 23.9 (post 1996)	45.0	2	0.31	5	15.0	7.0	10	26	50	1.0	0.6	1.1	68 (1991) / 81 (1997)

Source: Adapted from Sebastian Galiani and Stephen Nickell "Unemployment in Argentina in the 1990s" ITDT Working Paper 219.

Notes: [a] Defined as the ratio of labor costs to wages (less unity). Note that this includes pension and other mandated payments by employers. Argentina: employer mandated payments as a percent over wages: Pension system 16, employees benefits: 7.5, Employment National Fund: 1.5, employees health system (obras sociales): 6 and National Institute of Pensioned Social Services (INSSJYP): 2. Since 1996, employee's health system contributions were reduced to 5 percent while the other mandated payments have been reduced between 30 and 80 percent depending on the geographical area. We compute the payroll tax applying a reduction of 30 percent. The figures pre-1996 are computed under the tax/wage legislation of 1995.

[b] Trade union members as a percentage of all wage/salary earners.

[c] An index, 3 = over 70% covered, 2 = 25-70%, 1= under 25%.

[d & e] For Argentina the data includes all the employees reporting wages for a 30 days period, over 18 years of age and exclude rural and domestic workers.

[f] The average of Notice of period and Severance pay. Notice of period: the lapse between issuance of a dismissal notice and the effective cessation of employment, in months, for workers who have been with the employer 9 months, 4 years, and 20 years. And Severance pay: a lump-sum payment to the dismissed employee at the time of cessation of employment.

[g] The average of Unfair Dismissal, Trial period, Compensation at 20y and Reinstatement. Unfair Dismissal: scored 0 when worker capability or redundancy of the job are adequate grounds for dismissal, and highest when worker capability can never be a basis for dismissal. Trial period: the maximum length of the period after hiring during which an appeal against dismissal on grounds of unfairness cannot be made. Compensation at 20y: the compensation payable to a worker who has been unfairly dismissed after 20 years with the employer. Reinstatement: scored 0 if, following a court judgment of unfair dismissal, reinstatement is never granted and highest if the employee always has the option of reinstatement.

[h] A ranking that increases with the strictness of employment protection. Unweighted average of regular procedural inconveniences and columns f and g.

[i] Argentina: 26 weeks is the maximum entitlement although 13 of these weeks is paid at full salary by the social security system.

[j & k] Argentina: the 50 percent rate only applies for the first four months. This decreases by 15 percent for the next four months and by 30 percent for the last four, the maximum entitlement being for one year. 4 years = indefinite.

[l] The variable is dated 1991 and measures current active labor market spending as % of GDP divided by current unemployment. Expenditure on the disabled is excluded.

[m] Percentage of persons changing region of residence each year. Excludes persons who have changed their country of residence.

[n] Source: Oswald (1996), "A Theory of Homes and Jobs" Working Paper Warwick University.

Exhibit 9   Argentine Interest Rates

A Argentine and U.S. Money Market Rates *(1988–1995)*

%	1988	1989	1990	1991	1992	1993	1994	1995
Argentina	524	1,387,180	9,695,420	71.3	15.1	6.3	7.7	9.5
U.S.	7.7	9.0	8.1	5.9	3.8	3.2	4.7	5.9

B Spread Argentine over U.S. Money Market Rate *(Q2 1991–Q3 1995)*

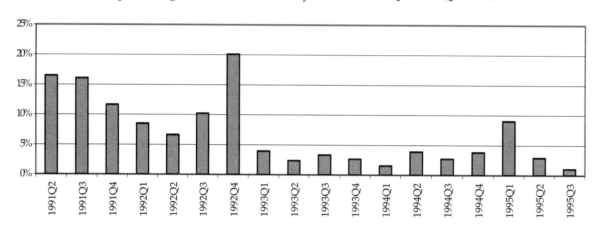

Source: Adapted from IMF, *International Financial Statistics Yearbook*, 2000.
Notes: **Argentine rate:** average rate on local currency loans up to 15 days between financial institutions in the country
U.S. rate: three-month commercial paper rate for firms with AA rating
Spread: (Argentine rate) - (U.S. rate)

Exhibit 10   Trade Partners

Argentine Trade by Country or Region *(millions current U.S. dollars)*

	1991	1992	1993	1994	1995
Total Exports To:	**11,976**	**12,235**	**13,118**	**15,839**	**20,963**
Latin America	3,369	2,327	3,684	4,804	6,770
Brazil	*1,489*	*1,671*	*2,814*	*3,655*	*5,484*
Other Latin America	*1,880*	*656*	*870*	*1,149*	*1,286*
US	1,245	1,349	1,278	1,737	1,804
European Union	3,956	3,732	2,646	3,891	4,466
Japan	454	375	467	445	457
Other	2,952	4,452	5,043	4,962	7,466
Total Imports From:	**8,284**	**14,872**	**16,784**	**21,590**	**20,122**
Latin America	2,748	3,755	4,214	3,784	4,511
Brazil	*1,532*	*3,339*	*3,570*	*4,286*	*4,175*
Other Latin America	*1,216*	*416*	*644*	*(502)*	*336*
US	1,871	3,226	3,859	4,373	4,207
European Union	2,033	3,633	4,139	6,140	6,025
Japan	393	697	669	986	711
Other	1,239	3,561	3,903	6,307	4,668

Source: Adapted from "Argentina Recent Economic Developments," IMF Staff Country Report No 98/38, April 1998.

Endnotes

[1]   "Survey of Argentina: Learning a New Dance," *The Economist*, 26 November 1994, 3.

[2]   "Winter Hits Argentina," *The Economist*, 6 July 1996.

[3]   For more information about Menem's background, refer to Carlos Menem, *Yo, Carlos Menem* (San Isidro, Argentina: Editorial CEYNE S.R.L., 1989).

[4]   Publications include: "Is El Presidente A 'Mufa,' a Bearer Of Very Bad Luck? --- Argentina's Leader Is Linked To Mayhem and Mishap - He Says He Isn't Cursed," *The Wall Street Journal*, 22 June 1990; "Presidential Tango," *Newsday*, 13 June 1990; "Argentine President's Popularity Sours - Once-flamboyant Menem Facing Economic, Personal Pressures," *The San Diego Union-Tribune*, 18 June 1990; "Peronist Candidate, Riding Anger over Economy, Heads for Victory in Argentina," *Los Angeles Times*, 15 May 1989.

[5]   "Survey of Argentina: The Meaning of Menemism," *The Economist*, 26 November 1994, 15.

[6]   The Law of Economic Emergency suspended subsidies to the private sector and most extraordinary public expenditure. It also allowed the executive branch to rule by decree for 180 days. The Law of Reform of the State set up the regulatory framework for the transfer of assets and firms from the public to the private domain.

[7]   Carlos H. Acuna, "Politics and Economics in the Argentina of the Nineties (Or, Why the Future No Longer is What it Used to Be)," in *Democracy, Markets, and Structural Reform in Latin America* eds. William C. Smith, Carlos H. Acuna, and Eduardo A. Gamarra (Coral Gables: North-South Center Press, 1993), 39–41. This is the BONEX Plan. The plan consisted of a forced conversion of government short-term debt into longer-term bonds (BONEX). Since local banks were long on such debt and a liquidity crunch ensued, the government allowed the banks to pay deposits by the public with BONEX.

[8]   Acuna, "Politics and Economics in the Argentina of the Nineties," 43.

[9]   "A Conversation with Domingo Cavallo," *Financial World* (New York), 1 February 1994.

[10]   For more on Cavallo's nationalization of the private sector debt and the 1982 debt crisis, see Carlos A. Rodriguez, "Argentina's Foreign Debt: Origins and Alternatives," in *Debt, Adjustment and Recovery: Latin America's Prospects for Growth and Development*, eds. Sebastian Edwards and Felipe Larraín (Oxford: Basil Blackwell, Ltd., 1989), 185; William C. Smith, *Authoritarianism and the Crisis of the Argentine Political Economy*, (Stanford, CA: Stanford University Press, 1989), 247; and news 1982 news articles, including "Economy Minister, Central Bank President Resign in Argentina," *The Globe and Mail*, 25 August 1982.

[11]   Originally, 10,000 australes, the local currency at the time, were pegged to 1 U.S. dollar. As of January 1992, 10,000 australes were converted into 1 peso.

[12]   For a concise and clear explanation of the rationale as well as mechanics underlying currency boards and Convertibility in particular, *see* Alberto Ades, "Currency Boards: Implications for Argentina," *Latin America Economic Research* (New York: Goldman, Sachs & Co., 21 February 1995).

[13]   Alberto Ades, "Argentina: In Transition," *Global Economics Paper*, no. 22 (New York: Goldman, Sachs & Co., 29 July 1999), 3.

[14]   "In Their Own Words," interview with Domingo Cavallo, *Latin Finance*, July 1998, 100.

[15]   The "Brady Plan" (called after U.S. President Bush's Treasury Secretary Nicholas Brady) allowed several Latin American countries to replace their costly bank debt with government bonds (Brady Bonds). In the process, creditor banks agreed to reduce the value of debt payments in exchange for more liquid bonds, with interest and some principal payments backed by collateral.

16 For a general description of the privatization process in Argentina, as well as the source for the data in this paragraph, see The World Bank, *Argentina's Privatization Program: Experiences, Issues, and Lessons*, (Washington, D.C.: The World Bank, 1993).

17 The World Bank, *Argentina's Privatization Program: Experiences, Issues, and Lessons* (Washington, D.C.: The World Bank, 1993), 4–5.

18 Charles Calomiris and Andrew Powell, "Can Emerging Market Bank Regulators Establish Credible Discipline? The Case of Argentina, 1992 – 1994," *National Bureau for Economic Research Working Paper No. 7715*, May 2000, 9–10.

19 Valeriano Garcia, "Black December: Banking Instability, the Mexican Crisis and its Effect on Argentina," *World Bank Latin American and Caribbean Studies, Viewpoints* (Washington, D.C.: The World Bank, 1997), 2. As a comparison, note that during the Great Depression, the U.S. money stock declined 35% over a period of four years.

20 Alberto Ades, "Argentina: Don't Cry for Convertibility," *Global Economics Paper*, no. 16 (New York: Goldman, Sachs & Co., 4 June 1999), 4.

Argentina's Financial System: The Case of Banco de Galicia

In the aftermath of the tequila crisis, the Argentine financial system was transformed in many respects. In particular, a large number of Argentina's large domestic banks were sold to foreigners (especially Spanish financial conglomerates).

Banco de Galicia emerged from this process as the only large, domestically owned, private bank in Argentina. Ownership was concentrated among a small number of Argentine families who had extensive additional interests in Argentine business.

In the mid-1990s, a dispute broke out between two members of the leading family over a change in ownership structure. This triggered prolonged litigation in the Argentine courts, as well as appeals to various U.S. institutions (such as Nasdaq).

Study Questions

1. Should the Argentine authorities encourage or discourage the sale of Argentine banks to foreigners? What are the pros and cons of foreign ownership of the domestic banking sector?
2. If you were a minority shareholder in Banco de Galicia, would you accept the tender offer described in the case? Why or why not?
3. As an adviser to the Argentine government, what legal framework for governing share trading would you recommend in the light of the case of Banco de Galicia? Is your recommendation feasible in Argentina?

RAFAEL DI TELLA
TARUN KHANNA
HUW PILL

Argentina's Financial System: The Case of Banco de Galicia

On May 22, 2000, Eduardo Escasany, Chairman and CEO of Banco de Galicia, left Buenos Aires on a 15-day road show through the United States and Europe to meet with international investors. A few days earlier, the management of the bank had announced a plan to reorganize Banco de Galicia into a new holding structure. Shareholders were being offered the opportunity to exchange their existing shares for shares in the newly created holding company, Grupo Financiero Galicia. Banco de Galicia shareholders had until the offer expired on July 21 to decide what to do. Their decision was not easy; a great deal of controversy surrounded the offer.

Since 1995, the Argentine banking sector had seen a wave of consolidations and foreign takeovers. The Convertibility Plan of 1991, which pegged the peso to the U.S. dollar and required that the entire money supply be backed by dollar reserves, created macroeconomic stability in the country for the first time in decades (see **Exhibits 1** to **4**). After the tequila crisis of 1995, bank regulation and supervision was dramatically improved. With investors eager to exploit the new opportunities created by the stable macroeconomic environment, deposits and credit, as well as foreign investment, flooded into the country.

By 2000, after strong foreign investment in the financial sector, Banco de Galicia was the only large domestically owned private bank left in the country. Many stakeholders wanted to see the bank stay under Argentine control and recognized that the exchange offer was an important step in that direction. But critics protested that the transaction required shareholders to sacrifice too much in pursuit of this objective. They argued that management was taking advantage of minority shareholders, and that by condoning such behavior, Argentina would drive away future potential equity investors, hindering further financial development. As Argentina entered its seventh quarter of negative or negligible GDP growth, critics worried that driving down equity investment would only exacerbate the looming recession and retard Argentina's growth potential.

Research Associates Ingrid Vogel and Alexandra Alquier, with assistance from the Harvard Business School Latin America Research Center, prepared this case under the supervision of Professors Rafael Di Tella, Tarun Khanna, and Huw Pill. This case was developed from published sources. HBS cases are developed solely as the basis for class discussion. Cases are not intended to serve as endorsements, sources of primary data, or illustrations of effective or ineffective management.

The Argentine Financial System

Prior to the 1990s, Argentina's financial system was underdeveloped relative to other countries of comparable per capita income levels.[1] Financial institutions had become government financing vehicles rather than channels of credit to productive sectors of the economy. As a result, large bank rescues were common, and quality banking services were virtually nonexistent. In 1990, Argentina's ratio of deposits to GDP was just 8%, a reflection of the high rates of inflation and poor protection of depositors in Argentina. The Central Bank of Argentina estimated that $100 worth of deposits placed in Argentine banks in 1944 would have been worth just one cent in 1990.[2]

In 1991, Argentina's financial system went through a profound transformation with the successful introduction of the Convertibility Plan. A currency board was established, complemented by trade liberalization, elimination of capital controls on foreign direct investment and repatriation, and privatization of a majority of state-owned entities, including some banks.[3] Inflation decelerated and intermediation of financial services began in earnest. Within four years, credit to the private sector almost doubled from 10% to 19% of GDP.[4]

But the tequila crisis, which resulted when the Mexican peso devaluation of late 1994 brought a general loss of confidence to Latin American markets, wreaked havoc on the recently strengthened Argentine financial system. Initially, the reaction in Argentina was contained; a flight to quality ensued as deposits were transferred from smaller institutions to large retail and public banks. However, over a two-week period in March 1995, in response to a rumor that the government would freeze bank deposits as it had in 1989, roughly $4 billion of deposits fled the country. By the end of May, $8 billion, representing 18% of total deposits, were withdrawn from the Argentine banking system. Over the same period, the Central Bank lost $5 billion, representing 30%, of international reserves.[5]

In the face of such withdrawals, all banks were confronted with liquidity crises, and many weaker banks failed. Argentina's currency board required that the Central Bank hold a dollar for each peso in circulation and thus prohibited the Central Bank from printing money to support the banks in the event of a run on deposits. In other words, a key feature of the currency board was that the Central Bank could not act as a lender of last resort. Depositors in liquidated institutions lost $477 million, equivalent to roughly 50% of their investments. Creditors lost an additional $249 million. Academics noted that these losses demonstrated unparalleled market discipline; banks were allowed to fail rather than being bailed out by the government.[6]

Addressing the Tequila Crisis

Since constraints of the currency board prevented the Central Bank from bailing out financial institutions, Argentina was forced to alternative domestic policies and international assistance to address the financial crisis. After a $5 billion multilateral aid package reintroduced a degree of stability to the country, Argentina accelerated the transformation of its financial system. Rules and regulations for accounting and reporting were strengthened, capital requirements were increased to reflect banks' trading risks, a database on the condition of bank borrowers was expanded and made publicly available, and credit rating requirements were introduced. Banks were also required to issue subordinated debt to encourage monitoring and discipline from investors and supervisors. In addition, a contingent liquidity facility was negotiated with international banks in order to be able to inject emergency liquidity in the case of a liquidity shock.[7] Many of the new standards actually exceeded requirements set by the Basle Committee on Banking Supervision, the international body that set prudential standards for the regulation of international banks.

Bank privatizations also were pursued more aggressively. While only three institutions were privatized between 1992 and 1994, 15 institutions were privatized between 1995 and 1999. Due to political resistance, however, the two largest public banks, Banco de la Nación Argentina and Banco de la Provincia de Buenos Aires, remained publicly owned. As a result, even in 1999, public banks had an influential role with 35% of total deposits. Along most measures, they demonstrated lower profitability than private banks (see **Exhibit 5**).

The number of private banks also declined significantly between 1995 and 1999—from 67 to 38 (see **Exhibit 6**). Overall, the number of banks in Argentina fell from 168 to 93 over the four-year period. Consolidation of the banking sector was also apparent through the distribution of deposits: Between January 1994 and January 2000, deposits held by the ten largest banks increased from 50% of total deposits to 71%.[8]

Ultimately, Argentina's financial system emerged stronger from the tequila crisis. By the late 1990s, the quality of Argentine bank regulation was ranked by the World Bank on a par with Hong Kong and second only to Singapore against all other developing countries.[9] From 1996 to 1998, deposits grew at a 30% annual rate. Most remarkably, Argentina survived the Asian crisis of 1997, the Russian crisis of 1998, and the Brazil devaluation of 1999 without a run on deposits or international reserves.[10]

Despite the strength of Argentina's financial system, however, the degree of bank penetration continued to be low by international standards. By the end of 1999, deposits were equivalent to just 27% of GDP, a huge increase over the early 1990s, but low in comparative terms (the ratio of deposits to GDP was 46% in Chile and 67% in Spain).[11] In addition, only 30% of the Argentine population was using banking services.[12]

Foreign Entry

A large part of the consolidation process in the Argentine banking sector was led by foreign banks. Argentina opened its banking sector to foreign competition in 1992 as part of the Convertibility Plan. In part, it hoped to strengthen its own financial system through importing bank supervision from foreign banks subject to regulation by their home countries. After the tequila crisis, foreign banks aggressively entered the market, predominantly through acquisition of larger private banks with extensive existing networks (see **Exhibit 7**). Between 1994 and 1999, the number of foreign banks in Argentina increased from 31 to 38.[13] Over the same period, deposits in banks under foreign control increased from 17% to 42% of total deposits (see **Exhibit 8**).[14] By 1999, approximately half of banking sector assets were under foreign control. Only one large private domestic bank, Banco de Galicia, remained.

As a result of the entry of foreign banks, Argentina's financial system was strengthened in several respects. Foreign banks were perceived as "safe havens" from which, during financial crises, depositors would be less likely to withdraw funds. In addition, because of their more diversified capital and funding bases, the banks themselves were expected to be less likely to shrink credit during such crises. In fact, data indicated that foreign banks in Argentina appeared to have provided loan growth during periods of economic distress and actually served as important stabilizers of credit.[15] At the same time, bank customers were expected to benefit from increased competition and improved banking services resulting from the importation of new management practices and information technologies.

The competitive environment became increasingly difficult for domestic banks. Most of the international banks, especially the Spanish ones including BBV (Banco Bilbao Vizcaya) and BSCH (Banco Santander Central Hispano), were present not only in Argentina, but also in other Latin American countries.[16] These banks benefited from their experiences in more liberal markets such as in Europe, where the lack of regulatory constraints allowed for the creation of "universal" banks. One of the most liberal countries in this respect was Spain, where the leading banks were also leading local brokerage houses, investment banks, pension companies, asset management entities, and insurance companies. As Argentina's banks migrated toward a more universal model, these foreign banks were thought to enjoy a competitive advantage.

Foreign banks in Argentina were clearly different from domestic banks (see **Exhibit 9**). They tended to be larger and to have better quality loan portfolios, higher net worth, and higher ratios of operating income to costs (see **Exhibits 5** and **10**).[17] Critics attributed this to the tendency of foreign banks to "cherry-pick" the most profitable segments of the market and suggested that foreign banks observed more restrictive lending practices than domestic ones, especially with regard to small and medium-sized businesses.[18] They also pointed out that despite the increased foreign presence and competition in the banking sector, the cost of banking services both to local companies and to consumers continued to be well above international standards. Furthermore, critics of foreign bank entry worried that domestic banks would be weakened, and, as a result, that Argentine regulatory and monetary authorities would have limited ability to alter bank behavior.

Capital Markets

Despite the progress Argentina made in developing its financial system, it still had low ratios of equity market capitalization to GDP and company bond and private debt to GDP[19] relative to other countries. By the end of 1999, stock market capitalization was 30% of GDP, compared with 67% in Spain and 113% in Chile.[20] Argentina also had a lower rate of IPO activity and fewer listed firms relative to its population. Academics argued that Argentina's less-developed capital markets could be attributed to institutional weaknesses in its financial system, following at least in part from its legal system, which was based on the French civil law tradition.[a]

The Theory

Legal systems divide into two types. On the one hand, the civil legal tradition, the oldest and most widely dispersed worldwide, originates in Roman law. Its principle is to provide all citizens with an accessible and written collection of the laws that apply to them and that judges must follow. Civil law can be divided into three families—French, German, and Scandinavian—and is practiced in most of Europe, Latin America, and in parts of Africa and Asia. Common law, on the other hand, is shaped by case law and precedents from judicial decisions. Judges have considerable leeway in interpreting the law. Common law countries include England and its former colonies (including the United States), among others.

Different legal traditions have been found to afford different degrees of protection to shareholders and creditors. In part, this could be explained by the fact that common law, unlike civil law, has greater flexibility and therefore allows for adaptation to changed circumstances. For example,

---

[a] The Capital Markets section derives predominantly from the research of economists Rafael La Porta, Florencia Lopez-de-Silanes, Andrei Shleifer, and Robert W. Vishny in papers cited in the endnotes.

common law allows for interpretation of torts or contracts with respect to company formation and bankruptcy.

The first aspect of investor protection comprised the specific laws of a country. On the whole, French civil law countries, like Argentina, had weaker bankruptcy and shareholder laws targeted at preventing interference by insiders (see **Exhibit 11a**). Shareholder laws included, among other rights, the voting rights attached to shares and the right to seek legal action against directors. Another set of important laws were creditor laws, which included whether secured creditors had the right to collateral ahead of government and employees and whether management could file for reorganization without creditor consent.

Enforcement and accounting standards were thought to be equally, if not more important aspects of investor protection, since they could reinforce or undermine a country's formal legal rules. Again, researchers found that French civil law countries performed, on average, more weakly along measures of enforcement and accounting, even after controlling for GDP per capita. According to the International Country Risk Guide, French civil law countries tended to have less efficient judicial systems, more corruption in government, and higher risk of expropriation and contract repudiation by government (see **Exhibit 11b**). However, the differences in the quality of enforcement along most measures between common law and civil law countries were found not to be statistically significant.

In summary, according to academic research, most countries with legal systems based on the French civil law tradition afforded less protection to both minority shareholders and creditors than countries with legal systems based on the English common law tradition. In other words, in French civil law countries minority shareholders were more likely to experience expropriation by managers or dominant shareholders, and creditors were less likely to get payments to which they were entitled.

Academics concluded that:

...law and the quality of its enforcement are potentially important determinants of what rights security holders have and how well these rights are protected. Since the protection investors receive determines their readiness to finance firms, corporate finance may critically turn on these legal rules and their enforcement.[21]

For example, in French civil law countries corporate finance is characterized by companies with a much higher degree of ownership concentration. Controlling shareholders often have control rights in excess of their cash flow rights. This is particularly true of family groups, who are also usually managers of the companies they own. Researchers described this phenomenon as an adaptive response to poor shareholder protection.

Most significantly, the theory implied that corporate finance in French civil law countries would be characterized by a reliance on retained earnings rather than external funds. Since poorly protected investors would be less willing to finance firms at attractive terms, capital markets would be less developed (see **Exhibit 12**). Many academics argued that well-established capital markets, particularly equity markets, were a foundation for economic growth through the creation of an open market for corporate control.[22] However, the empirical basis for this argument appeared questionable.

The Case of Shareholder Protection in Argentina

Surprisingly, unlike in other French civil law countries, Argentina's legal rules, at least in principle, provided minority shareholders with a fairly high degree of protection. For example, a shareholder needed just 5% ownership of a company in order to be able to demand an extraordinary shareholders' meeting. The world median for this measure was 10%. In addition, the Argentine Companies Law forced companies to offer to repurchase shares of minority shareholders who objected to certain decisions of management, such as mergers or asset sales. This rule protected shareholders from oppression and outright fraud by management. The Argentine Companies Law also granted shareholders the first opportunity to buy new issues of stock in order to protect current shareholders from dilution that would occur if shares were issued to favored investors at below market prices.

Despite Argentina's seemingly protective laws, there was, in the words of several economists: "widespread investor criticism about the quality of protection afforded to shareholders" in the country.[23] Argentina's weak legal enforcement could help explain this inconsistency. In a sample of 49 countries, Argentina was ranked 6th from the bottom in terms of accounting standards and the risks of government expropriation and repudiation of contracts (see **Exhibit 11b**).[24] According to Gallup polls, only 18% of the Argentine population trusted the country's judicial system in 2000. The U.S. Department of State described it as "subject to political influence…hampered by inordinate delays, procedural logjams, changes of judges, inadequate administrative support and incompetence."[25] In addition, Domingo Cavallo, Argentina's former Minister of Economics, claimed that one of the major issues he faced under President Carlos Menem was "organized corruption." He argued:

> Argentina will manage to defeat corruption when, from the President of the Nation downward, there is a strong commitment toward this objective, and when judges who protect the corrupt are removed by political trial.[26]

Ultimately, equity investors—especially minority investors—would demand to be compensated with higher returns for the risk of investing in companies located in countries, such as Argentina, with poor shareholder protection. Along these lines, some economists priced the control premium for Argentine firms as high as 26% of their equity values (as compared with 1% in the United States and United Kingdom and 65% in Brazil).[27] Companies and entrepreneurs would be reluctant to issue securities at the unattractive terms required, which could help explain Argentina's relatively less-developed equity markets.

Some academics argued, however, that the problem of low minority shareholder protection could be addressed by listing (through depository shares or directly) on foreign exchanges. By listing on U.S. exchanges, companies would commit to becoming subject to the enforcement powers of the Securities and Exchange Commission (SEC), to investor ability to exercise legal remedies such as class-action lawsuits, and to providing fuller financial disclosure, including reconciling financial statements to U.S. GAAP principles. In addition, they would be exposed to the scrutiny of "reputational intermediaries" such as U.S. underwriters (if the listing were part of an IPO), auditors, debt rating agencies, and securities analysts. As noted by one academic, "listing in the United States resembles a bonding instrument…which reduces the potential for the expropriation of minority investors."[28] The empirical support for this argument, however, was inconclusive, as other academics argued that "SEC action against any U.S.-listed foreign firm has been rare and mostly ineffective."[29]

The Banco de Galicia Exchange Offer

Both the minority shareholder and foreign bank ownership issues had important implications for the Banco de Galicia exchange offer. As the only remaining large private domestically owned bank in

Argentina, Galicia had a number of supporters who were keen to have future control of the bank remain within Argentina. At the same time, however, it was important for the country to show a commitment to protecting the interests of the minority shareholders of the bank.

Banco de Galicia Overview

Founded in 1905, Banco de Galicia provided a wide spectrum of financial products and services to two million customers, including the government, large corporations, individuals, and small and medium-sized companies. In 1999, with credit exposure to the latter of $1.7 billion, comprising 19.5% of its total loan portfolio, Galicia was the primary private institution serving companies with annual sales of less than $30 million. Many of these businesses were in the agricultural and livestock sector. Overall, Galicia was the largest private bank in Argentina in terms of assets, loans, and deposits. Galicia's commercial services included personal, mortgage, and corporate loans, fiduciary and custodial services, deposits, credit cards, and electronic banking. In addition, it offered securities brokerage facilities, mutual funds, insurance products, investment banking capabilities, and project finance services.

Galicia also played an important role in providing loans to Argentine provinces and acted as a market maker for certain federal government securities. Loans to the non-financial government sector were an increasing component of Galicia's total loan share: from 15% in 1997 and 1998 to 22% in 1999. For the fiscal year 1999, Galicia, with 11% market share, was third most significant among the 12 participants in the primary market for government debt issues.

Galicia operated one of Argentina's most extensive and diversified bank distribution networks. As a participant in a concession to provide postal services within the country, Galicia was establishing points-of-service in official postal outlets. It also had branches in Uruguay, New York, and the Cayman Islands. Galicia's comprehensive network allowed it to cater to a broad spectrum of Argentina's population—from the large "un-banked" segment to the most sophisticated customers.[30]

Since the introduction of the Convertibility Plan in 1991, Galicia had grown quickly. Between 1992 and 1999, its market share in total assets increased from 3.6% to 9.6%. Over the same period, Galicia's shares appreciated almost 440%, outperforming Argentina's Merval Index by a multiple of eight and shares of comparable Banco Frances by a factor of two. See **Exhibits 13** and **14** for summary financial information.

Ownership and Management of Banco de Galicia

Historically, three families—Escasany, Ayerza, and Braun—had controlled Banco de Galicia. In 1959, they took a 98% combined ownership stake in the bank. In 1992, their stake amounted to about 77% of the bank's equity. They held their shares through a complex structure of multiple holding companies to ensure that control would remain with the families. Multiple generations of the three families had been represented on Galicia's Board of Directors: the Escasanys since 1923, the Ayerzas since 1943, and the Brauns since 1947. In 2000, each of the three families had one representative on the five-person board.

Four out of the five directors were engaged on a full-time basis in the management of the bank. Board members received compensation representing up to 12% of pre-tax profits.[a31] In 1999, board members granted themselves the full 12% honorarium.

In 1993, Galicia embarked on a capital expansion program to support an aggressive acquisition strategy. First, the bank raised $65.3 million through a placement of American Depository Receipts traded on Nasdaq.[b] In 1996, Galicia raised an additional $143.3 million of equity through an international offering.[32] As a result, the ownership stake of the controlling families was diluted to 51.7%. When a family member withdrew her shares from the family holding structure in March 1999 (as described below), the Escasany, Ayerza, and Braun combined holding was reduced to 46.3% (see **Exhibit 15a** for a list of all shareholders), and the families lost their majority stake.

Grupo Financiero Galicia Overview

Grupo Financiero Galicia (GFG) was established in September 1999 as a holding company by the Escasany, Ayerza, and Braun families. Its only asset was the families' 46.3% stake in Banco de Galicia. GFG had two classes of shares: Class A shares, owned by the controlling families as a group, accounted for 51.8% of the company and were entitled to five votes each, while Class B shares, owned by individual members of the controlling families, accounted for 48.2% of GFG and were entitled to one vote each (see **Exhibit 15b**).

Terms of the Exchange Offer

In May 2000, the founding families announced a plan to reorganize Banco de Galicia into the GFG holding company structure through a share offering. They offered to exchange each Banco de Galicia share for 2.5 new GFG Class B shares. The GFG Class B shares would continue to be entitled to one vote each, while GFG Class A shares would have five votes each.

The offer was subject to a minimum tender of 70% of the Banco de Galicia shares, including the shares already owned by GFG. If between 70% and 89% of Galicia's shares were converted, GFG Class B shareholders would receive a preferred dividend equal to 130% of the usual dividend, which would be paid out before the dividend on GFG Class A shares. Under this scenario, the board of directors would still be entitled to the management fee of 12% of pre-tax profits. If more than 89% of Galicia's shares were converted, the 12% management fee would be changed to an incentive payment equivalent to no more than 6% of pre-tax profits, and all shares would receive the same dividend (see **Exhibit 16**).

GFG's exchange offer prospectus warned shareholders that, "If you do not exchange your Banco de Galicia securities, your shares may experience reduced liquidity," since a successful transaction would imply fewer shares outstanding. If enough shares were tendered, Banco de Galicia would no longer meet Nasdaq eligibility requirements[c] and would have to delist from the exchange.[33]

---

[a] The *Comisión Nacional de Valores* (the Argentine equivalent of the U.S. Securities and Exchange Commission) set a limit to board compensation of 25% of after-tax profits. A PricewaterhouseCoopers study found that Argentine executive and board compensation was among the highest in Latin America.

[b] American Depository Receipts (ADRs) are stocks of foreign corporations that a bank or brokerage in the U.S. has bought in large quantities and reissued on one of the U.S. exchanges.

[c] Eligibility requirements included, among other things, a minimum of 500,000 publicly held shares and 800 shareholders or one million publicly held shares and 400 shareholders.

Precedent to the Exchange Offer

Argentine law prevented existing listed companies from issuing preferential shares. However, a company previously created with a preferential share structure could apply for listing. This was the case with GFG, as it had been with PC Holding, an unrelated company that four months prior had executed a similar transaction.

Under the PC Holding transaction, the Perez family completed an exchange of shares of oil giant Perez Companc for PC Holding Class B shares. Like GFG, PC Holding had a dual share structure: Class A shares, owned by the Perez family, were entitled to five votes each, and Class B shares were entitled to one vote each.

The offer was conditional on conversion of 53% of Perez Companc shares. As an incentive to shareholders to tender their shares, a preferential dividend equivalent to 150% of the normal dividend was offered. Analysts agreed that the compensation was not adequate.[34] But according to a local financial journal, "shareholders had little choice but to accept the share swap or risk holding on to what could end up being illiquid shares."[35]

Despite the unattractiveness of the exchange offer, the larger institutional investors, mutual funds, and individual holders all went along with it. Fully 98% of Perez Companc shares were tendered. As a result of the swap, the Perez family increased its voting control of the company from 58% to 80%, while retaining the same economic rights.[36]

Eduardo José Escasany

Mr. Eduardo José Escasany had served as Chairman and CEO of Banco de Galicia since 1989—the third Escasany to lead the bank since 1920. He graduated with a degree in Economics from one of Argentina's top private universities and joined Galicia at age 21 after interning at Chase Manhattan in the U.S., Germany, and England.[37] In 2000, he also served as President of the Argentine Bankers Association, a trade association that represented the interests of Argentina's most powerful banks.[38] Eduardo personally owned approximately 7% of Banco de Galicia.

Eduardo liked to maintain a low profile and was described by the press as quiet but also "feared, hated, controversial, and tenacious." He was close to the most important political figures of Argentina's recent history, including former Presidents Raul Alfonsín and Carlos Menem, current President Fernando De la Rúa, and former Economics Minister Domingo Cavallo.[39]

As one of Argentina's most influential bankers, he met with President De la Rúa and Economics Minister José Luís Machinea in May 2000 to discuss the GFG exchange offer. According to the local press, the government was worried about the bank falling under foreign control.[40]

Eduardo's perspective: rationale behind the exchange offer

Eduardo and the rest of GFG management highlighted multiple reasons for the proposed restructuring.[41] First, management explained that a holding company structure would allow Galicia to pursue more aggressively other financial businesses, including asset management, insurance, and e-commerce, without being subject to the strict capital regulations of the Central Bank. Second, they claimed that the autonomy of the bank's individual units would be reinforced. This would allow the units to optimize their capital structure and would improve their growth potential. Lastly, management noted that the new structure would facilitate the formation of strategic alliances and new business development by the company. In sum, Eduardo remarked that with the restructuring, "we will have more flexibility amid market fluctuations, and we can improve our products and services, building a share of greater value for our shareholders."[42] Indeed, most analysts agreed that the move to a holding company structure made good long-term economic sense.[43]

Although not emphasized in the offer prospectus or filings with the U.S. SEC and the *Comisión Nacional de Valores* (CNV), another important consideration for the transaction was the issue of control. Galicia's controlling families wanted to keep the business growing, which would inevitably require significant amounts of additional capital. At the same time, they did not want to dilute their ownership stake and thereby subject Galicia to the threat of a hostile takeover by a foreign bank. Shortly before announcing the details of the exchange offer, Eduardo had stated: "we are facing the threat of a hostile takeover. We don't want to sell. We can compete with the large international financial groups. As Argentines, we have to give ourselves an opportunity."[44]

Their fears had some basis. As of 2000, Galicia was Argentina's only large private bank controlled by local shareholders. BSCH had a particularly aggressive expansion strategy in Latin America. In 1997, BSCH had acquired ownership control of Banco Rio de la Plata, one of Galicia's main competitors. In 1998, BSCH, claiming that its interest was strictly financial and not strategic, acquired a 9.8% stake in Galicia. When BSCH launched a takeover bid for 100% of Banco Rio de la Plata in 2000, observers worried about Galicia's fate.[45] The local press speculated that "the operation is part of BSCH's expansion strategy for Latin America, which consists of having control of those institutions in which it holds a stake, and is a step towards a possible merger of Banco Rio de la Plata with Banco de Galicia."[46]

Most analysts and bankers agreed that retaining an Argentine-owned bank was desirable. For example, Manuel Sacerdote, CEO of BankBoston Argentina since the late 1970s, stated: "I think Eduardo's aspiration to keep control of the bank in Argentina is perfectly legitimate. Personally, I feel that having a large local player contributes to the soundness of the system."[47]

Most analysts also agreed that Galicia had a strong management team. Salomon Smith Barney commented that "Galicia's management team has demonstrated that they are able to compete with more sophisticated institutions equally. The preservation of this company and this management should be sought for as long as they are able to remunerate shareholders adequately."[48] Goldman Sachs agreed:

> ...this control group and management team has an excellent track record with respect to execution and shareholder value creation. We have all the respect in the world for Banco Galicia's control group and give them great credit for what they have done with this bank. We have high esteem for Banco Galicia's management team and have long considered it the best in the Argentine banking sector and one of the best in the region. We sincerely wish that Banco Galicia's management team will remain where it is, because we are convinced that few are more qualified than them to grow the business and capitalize on all the opportunities that an expanding Argentine financial services sector can bring.[49]

María Isabel Escasany

After the death of Eduardo's father Eduardo Escasany senior in 1973, Eduardo had developed a strained relationship with younger sister María Isabel (known as Marisa to her friends and in the press), a successful architect and business woman. Throughout the 1990s, she had requested a restructuring of the family ownership of Banco de Galicia that would allow her to take control of her stake, worth 5.4% in 1996, and have a say in the management of the bank. At the time, her shares were part of the complex family holding structure that hindered individual control. In a 1998 interview, Marisa remarked:

> For more than ten years, I have been fighting for my rights as a shareholder. Eduardo is the one who calls all the shots and nobody can oppose him. I don't want my children to inherit the same limitations that I have today with my shares.[50]

In 1996, Eduardo is reported finally to have given Marisa an ultimatum, stating "I am tired of discussing these issues with you. If you don't like how things are done, look for a lawyer."[51] Other members of the Escasany family, including sister María Ofelia (with a 5% stake) and mother María Ofelia Hordeñana, aligned themselves behind Eduardo.

In 1997, Marisa did indeed seek legal advice and eventually filed 41 commercial cases that questioned the validity of the shareholder meetings and distribution of dividends within the family holding company structure. In one of the cases, she accused her brother, as part of the board of directors, of granting himself an honorarium much higher than market standards at the expense of the rest of the shareholder base.[52]

In November 1998, a judge invalidated the resolutions of the shareholder meetings of one of the holding companies. Marisa had been asked to sign the minutes of meetings that never took place. Compared to other charges, this was relatively minor. Even so, this first legal setback and the negative public exposure that might have followed apparently convinced Eduardo to negotiate with his sister.[53] Finally, in March 2000, Marisa obtained control of her Galicia stake.

Insisting that she did not intend to sell her shares, she refused her brother's purchase offers. The control group retained preferential rights to acquire Marisa's equity stake in the event she decided to sell, but lost the majority vote that they had previously enjoyed.

Marisa's perspective: criticism of the exchange offer

The strained relationship between Eduardo and Marisa flared up again with her vocal opposition to the GFG exchange offer. She appealed to the entire shareholder base with a harsh criticism of the deal in Argentine newspaper advertisements. She claimed the exchange implied "an obvious damage for the minority shareholders." She invited shareholders to join her in opposing the deal and asked them to contact her attorney, Luis Moreno Ocampo, one of Argentina's best-known litigators.[54] Ocampo was well known for previously having prosecuted multiple human rights violations by the military and had a very high profile in the media.

At the request of Ocampo, the U.S. law firm Morrison & Foerster evaluated the terms of the exchange to determine whether it would have been approved under U.S. law. In their final report, Morrison & Foerster concluded: "A U.S. court following Delaware law would have ample precedent for rejecting this transaction as inconsistent with established principles of corporate governance."[55] Many observers claimed that the key objection of U.S. courts to the GFG transaction would be that the members of management (who were also shareholders) of the bank would be acting in their own self-interest, and thus violating their fiduciary duty to other shareholders. By participating in the exchange and voting their shares, they would stand to benefit as owners of the bank (because of the increased voting power) from their actions as managers of the bank, to the detriment of other shareholders. At the same time, they would benefit as managers of the bank from their decisions as owners of the bank, since the transaction would help maintain management control by avoiding takeovers. The burden would rest with management to prove otherwise—which would give Marisa a tremendous amount of leverage.

Paradoxically, Argentina's laws were, in actuality, much stricter than U.S. laws in prohibiting the erection of takeover defenses by management.[a] Although U.S. courts, observing the common law tradition, had more discretion to rule on individual cases than Argentine courts, they were in general unlikely to rule against management actions—except in such instances of self-dealing.

Salomon Smith Barney went so far as to criticize the rationale behind the proposal. "A financial holding company makes sense in principle, but Galicia can be extremely competitive without the holding company, everyone else is venturing into new businesses at the banking level."[56] In response to the claim that the holding company structure would allow shareholders to circumvent strict Central Bank regulations, Salomon pointed out that it could identify only two such regulations: banks could only own up to 12.5% of insurance companies, and Internet ventures required more reserve capital at the banking level than under a holding structure. Other analysts noted that reserve requirements on credit cards would also be lower under a holding structure.

Marisa's involvement in the deal approval process

Because of Banco de Galicia's Nasdaq listing, the GFG exchange offer required approval from the SEC in the United States as well as the CNV in Argentina. Marisa worked with Ocampo to obstruct the approval process. First, she filed criminal charges against the directors of Banco de Galicia for "fraudulent administration." She argued that they had had no right to use the bank's name, trademark, offices, Internet site, and top management know-how to create a new company (GFG) and to organize the exchange offer. She also insisted that three CNV representatives, including its President, had a conflict of interest with the Galicia decision. Furthermore, Ocampo denounced the alleged illegal use of influence in the exchange approval process to the Argentine Anticorruption Office, the head of the Intelligence Agency, the Secretary of Human Rights, and the CNV.[57] President De la Rúa later denied those accusations personally.[58]

As Marisa's campaign against the offer gathered momentum, institutional investors and mutual funds were reported to be coordinating efforts to force changes to the terms of the exchange.[59] Some equity analysts began to question whether Grupo de Galicia would be able to convince the necessary 70% of Banco de Galicia shareholders to accept the offer to convert their shares.

---

[a] This is known as "strict neutrality." Under strict neutrality, company boards are forbidden from erecting any defense against hostile tender offers without explicit majority shareholder consent. In contrast, the United States uses the "modified business judgment rule." Under the modified business judgment approach, boards of management are allowed to act on the behalf of shareholders, without their explicit consent, in response to the threat of takeover, within reason. For more on this issue, refer to: "The EU's 13th Directive on Takeover Bids: Unlucky for Some?" HBS No. 703-014.

Exhibit 1   Argentine General Economic Indicators

%	1995	1996	1997	1998	1999	1st Half 2000[a]
Real GDP Growth	-2.8	5.5	8.1	3.9	-3.4	0.2
Real Per Capita GDP Growth	-4.2	4.2	6.8	2.6	-4.7	-1.8
Consumer Price Inflation	3.4	0.2	0.5	0.9	-1.2	-1.1
Investment/GDP	17.9	18.1	19.4	19.9	17.9	16.0
M3/GDP[b]	20.14	22.69	26.47	28.65	31.47	31.76
Public Expenditure/GDP	15.8	15.4	15.3	15.4	na	na
Average exports and imports/GDP	9.9	10.8	11.6	11.7	10.6	11.1
units as described						
Unemployment *(%)*[b]	15.5	15.5	13.9	11.8	13.0	14.6
International Reserves[b] *(billions current U.S. dollars)*	14.3	18.1	22.3	24.8	26.3	25.1
Foreign Debt[b] *(billions current U.S. dollars)*	98.8	111.4	128.4	141.5	147.9	148.6

Notes: [a]Annual basis, except where noted.
          [b]Year-end data for 2000.

Exhibit 2   Argentine National Accounts

(millions current pesos)	1995	1996	1997	1998	1999	1st Half 2000
Gross Domestic Product	258,032	272,150	292,859	298,948	283,260	141,353
Household Consumption	176,909	186,487	203,029	206,434	197,204	98,682
Government Consumption	34,446	34,023	35,325	37,353	38,918	18,420
Gross Fixed Investment	46,285	49,211	56,727	59,595	50,629	22,603
Changes in Stocks	1,361	4,035	4,080	3,012	1,307	2,422
Exports (goods and services)	25,017	28,470	30,939	31,122	27,759	15,323
Imports (goods and services)	25,985	30,077	37,240	38,568	32,558	16,097

Exhibit 3   Argentine Balance of Payments

(millions current U.S. dollars)	1995	1996	1997	1998	1999	1st Half 2000
Current Account	**-5,210**	**-6,877**	**-12,344**	**-14,626**	**-12,039**	**-4,688**
Trade Balance	2,358	1,760	-2,123	-3,099	-794	1,531
Exports	*21,162*	*24,043*	*26,431*	*26,433*	*23,309*	*13,040*
Imports	*18,804*	*22,283*	*28,554*	*29,532*	*24,103*	*11,509*
Net Services	-3,456	-3,582	-4,450	-4,509	-4,155	-2,404
Net Income	-4,662	-5,500	-6,224	-7,416	-7,472	-3,963
Net Transfers	550	445	453	398	382	148
Financial Account	**4,929**	**11,850**	**16,641**	**19,044**	**14,781**	**4,676**
Net Direct Investment	4,112	5,349	5,508	4,966	22,630	3,560
Net Portfolio Investment	1,851	9,720	10,097	8,788	-6,911	3,314
Net Short Term Capital	-2,250	-3,130	813	3,256	-548	-2,604
Net Government	1,216	-89	223	2,034	-390	406
Net Errors and Omissions	**-2,030**	**-1,715**	**-966**	**-328**	**-729**	**1,231**
Change in Reserves and Related Items	**-2,311**	**3,258**	**3,331**	**4,090**	**2,013**	**1,219**

Source (Exhibits 1–3):   Compiled from IMF, *International Financial Statistics,* October 2001 and EIU Country Data.

Exhibit 4   Argentine Government Finance (*millions current pesos*)

	1995	1996	1997	1998	1999
Total Revenue	57,852	57,950	67,427	70,235	66,858
Primary Expenditure	63,411	63,855	68,162	70,573	72,359
Primary Deficit (+) / Surplus (-)	5,559	5,905	735	338	5,501
Interest Payments	5,810	6,454	7,315	8,122	9,775
Other Payments	1,191	2,643	-1,973	2,426	3,309
Overall Deficit (+) / Surplus (-)	12,560	15,002	6,077	10,886	18,585
% of GDP	*4.9*	*5.5*	*2.1*	*3.7*	*6.6*

Source: Adapted from Mario Teijeiro, "Una Vez Mas, La Politica Fiscal…".

Exhibit 5   Average Size and Performance by Type of Bank

	Private Domestic			Foreign			Public		
	1995	1996	1997	1995	1996	1997	1995	1996	1997
Total deposits *(million current pesos)*	162.9	260.2	278.6	258.8	328.1	488.5	545.1	834.4	1,065.7
Net worth/liabilities	0.25	0.20	0.21	0.27	0.25	0.22	0.12	0.06	0.16
Operating income/costs	1.26	1.28	1.35	1.41	1.38	1.43	0.94	0.99	1.29
Past due/total loans	0.20	0.23	0.22	0.09	0.12	0.12	0.41	0.46	0.41

Source: Adapted from Clarke, Cull, D'Amato, and Molinari (World Bank), Table 2.

Exhibit 6 Consolidation in the Argentine Banking Sector

Number of Banks	1994	1995	1996	1997	1998	1999
National Public	3	3	3	3	3	2
Provincial Public	29	27	17	17	14	13
Private Domestic	67	57	64	50	44	38
Private Foreign	31	30	28	37	39	38
Private Cooperative	38	10	8	6	4	2
Total Number of Banks	**168**	**127**	**120**	**113**	**104**	**93**

Source: Compiled from EIU, *Argentina Country Profile 2000-2001.*

Exhibit 7 Entry of Foreign Capital into the Argentine Banking Sector after the Tequila Crisis

	Local Bank	Purchasing Institution	Origin	Share
Q2 1995	na	ABN Amro Bank	Netherlands	100%
Q4 1995	Banco Bansud	Banamex	Mexico	60%
Q3 1996	Banco Tornquist	BSCH	Chile - Spain	100%
Q4 1996	Banco Frances del Rio de la Plata	BBV	Spain	30%
Q2 1997	Liniers Sudamericano	BT LA Holdings LLC	U.S.	51%
Q3 1997	Trasandino	Abinsa	Chile	51%
Q3 1997	Credito de Cuyo	Abinsa	Chile	67%
Q3 1997	Banco Rio de la Plata	BSCH	Spain	50%
Q3 1997	HSBC Banco Roberts	Hong Kong Shanghai Banking Corp.	U.K.	100%
Q3 1997	Banco de Credito Argentino	BBV	Spain	28%
Q4 1997	Los Tilos	Caja de Ahorros Prov. San Fernando	Spain	40%
Q4 1997	Finvercon	Norwest-Finvercon	U.S.	100%
Q4 1997	Quilmes	Scotia International	Canada	70%
Q1 1998	B.I. Creditanstalt	Bank Austria	Austria	49%
Q3 1998	Compania Financiera Argentina	AIG Consumer Finance Group	U.S.	91%
Q4 1998	Del Buen Ayre	Banco Itau	Brazil	100%
Q4 1998	Banco de Galicia	BSCH	Spain	10%
Q1 1999	Bisel	Caisse Nationale de Credit Agricole	France	36%
Q2 1999	Entre Rios	Caisse Nationale de Credit Agricole	France	82%

Source: Adapted from Calomiris (NBER), Table 9; and Dages, Goldberg, and Kinney (N.Y. Federal Reserve Bank), Table 1.

Exhibit 8   Deposits Growth in Argentina

A   Distribution of Deposits by Type of Bank

B   Deposits as % GDP

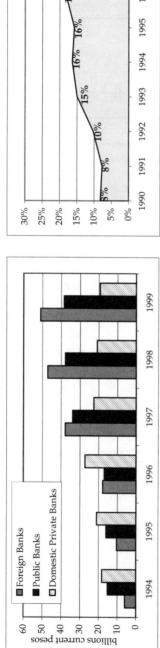

Sources: Based on Joe Peek and Eric S. Rosengren, Table 2; and IMF, *International Financial Statistics.*

Exhibit 9   Portfolio Distributions of Banks

Initial Status: *Action over Period:*	Private Domestic *Remained Private*		Foreign *Remained Foreign*		Private Domestic *Liquidated / Merged*		Private Domestic *Bought by For. Bank*		Public *Remained Public*	
	Q1 95	Q2 97	Q1 95	Q2 97	Q1 95	Q2 97	Q1 95	Q2 97	Q1 95	Q2 97
Portfolio Distribution (% of financing)										
Consumer Lending	16.3%	18.9%	3.3%	4.0%	19.4%	-	11.8%	10.7%	14.9%	12.9%
Property Lending and Mortgages	17.1%	13.0%	6.3%	13.33%	11.8%	-	13.0%	17.8%	22.1%	20.9%
Lending to Public Sector	1.0%	1.7%	10.0%	30.0%	40.0%	-	40.0%	3.9%	13.0%	19.9%
Lending in Federal Capital District	55.2%	58.7%	95.2%	94.1%	28.9%	-	77.3%	80.1%	19.6%	19.4%
Portfolio Distribution by Sector (% of financing)										
Lending to:										
Manufacturing	18.2%	16.7%	36.4%	34.1%	11.8%	-	28.3%	19.2%	10.6%	10.3%
Primary Production	6.7%	5.8%	6.0%	4.7%	10.3%	-	8.5%	5.6%	12.3%	11.2%
Electricity, Gas, and Water	0.0%	0.0%	2.8%	2.9%	0.0%	-	2.7%	2.9%	0.0%	0.0%
Construction	4.4%	5.4%	3.9%	4.4%	3.7%	-	3.5%	4.0%	5.0%	3.5%
Wholesale Trade	5.0%	4.9%	7.7%	4.9%	7.1%	-	5.6%	4.3%	2.9%	2.7%
Retail Trade	11.0%	9.6%	3.4%	3.0%	20.5%	-	9.7%	7.0%	16.9%	13.8%
Service (incl. Gov't and Finance)	17.9%	19.2%	14.4%	16.7%	13.5%	-	13.7%	17.4%	25.4%	28.4%
'Other'	3.2%	2.7%	6.8%	3.5%	3.9%	-	7.6%	6.5%	4.5%	3.1%
Families	32.3%	34.8%	16.2%	24.3%	27.3%	-	19.6%	29.5%	19.1%	23.7%

Source: Adapted from Clarke, Cull, D'Amato, and Molinari (World Bank), Tables 3 and 4.

Exhibit 10   Ranking of Argentine Banks

(%, as of December 1999)	Class[a]	Loan Mkt. Share	Dep. Mkt. Share	Asset Mkt. Share	ROA	ROE	Net Interest Margin	Over-head Ratio	Past Due/ Total Loans	Loans/ Deposits
Banco de la Nación Argentina	P	12.39	15.19	11.76	-0.20	-2.03	2.99	74.29	22.77	82.90
Banco de la Provincia de B.A.	P	11.36	10.89	9.30	0.12	1.27	2.36	95.43	12.05	106.10
Banco de Galicia	D	8.95	9.23	8.76	1.19	12.87	4.17	62.15	3.35	98.60
Banco Rio de la Plata	F	7.03	7.26	7.74	1.03	10.02	4.38	67.30	2.14	98.47
BankBoston	F	7.01	5.94	7.45	0.07	1.14	4.01	68.19	3.83	120.05
Banco Frances	F	7.63	8.43	6.37	1.07	9.78	7.31	76.53	5.09	92.11
Banco Hipotecario	P	4.74	0.40	3.42	3.01	6.30	5.10	41.71	13.37	1206.14
HSBC Banco Roberts	F	2.95	3.33	3.29	0.02	0.29	3.81	81.17	8.27	90.13
Banca Nazionale del Lavoro	F	2.66	2.61	2.33	1.10	12.37	6.00	56.23	7.8	103.68
Banco de la Ciudad de B.A.	P	1.74	2.83	2.21	0.80	10.41	4.87	62.58	9.04	62.50
Banco Quilmes	F	1.90	1.81	1.97	0.22	4.24	3.44	81.72	9.69	106.85
ABN Amro Bank	F	0.77	1.01	1.84	0.08	2.87	1.42	93.23	4.47	77.68
Banco Bansud	F	1.72	1.37	1.65	-2.68	-20.54	5.77	83.95	18.65	127.66
Banco Credicoop Coop. Lim.	D	1.60	1.84	1.44	0.91	8.29	7.53	81.88	5.49	102.26
Banco de la Prov. de Cordoba	P	1.15	2.02	1.41	-0.96	-57.44	3.05	113.11	17.95	57.65
Banco Suquia	D	1.31	1.48	1.29	1.77	18.87	5.71	67.16	4.78	89.99
Lloyds Bank	F	0.76	0.99	0.74	-1.73	-22.13	4.76	80.74	17.35	102.71
Banco Tornquist	F	0.76	0.63	0.64	-17.03	-195.10	4.73	151.84	14.99	122.45
Deutsche Bank	F	0.27	0.25	0.60	1.16	15.62	1.37	105.62	0.00	111.22

Source: Adapted from Salomon Smith Barney, "Argentine Bank Reference Guide," 22 March 2000, 36–37.

Notes: [a] **P**=public, **D**=domestic private, **F**=foreign private.

Net Interest Margin = net interest income / average total assets.

Overhead Ratio = operating expenses / total revenue.

This list, compiled by Salomon Smith Barney, excludes Citibank, which would be among the top 5 along most measures.

Exhibit 11a   Degree of Shareholder Legal Protection in Different Legal Traditions

Legal Tradition

		Common Law	Civil Law		
		English	French	German	Scandinavian
Degree of Shareholder Legal Protection	5 (Highest)	Canada Hong Kong India Pakistan South Africa U.K. U.S.	Chile		
	4	Australia Ireland Malaysia New Zealand Singapore	Argentina Spain	Japan	Norway
	3 (Medium)	Israel Kenya Nigeria Sri Lanka Zimbabwe	Brazil Colombia France Peru Philippines Portugal	Taiwan	Finland Sweden
	2	Thailand	Ecuador Egypt Greece Indonesia Netherlands Turkey Uruguay	Switzerland South Korea Austria	Denmark
	1		Italy Jordan Mexico Venezuela	Germany	
	0 (Lowest)		Belgium		

Source: Created by case writer based on data presented in La Porta and Lopez-de-Silanes, "Capital Markets and Legal Institutions," 1998.

Notes: "Degree of shareholder protection" measures the number of shareholder laws, out of a possible six, that countries have adopted. The six laws include:

(1) the country allows shareholders to mail their proxy vote;

(2) shares are not blocked prior to the General Shareholders' Meeting;

(3) cumulative voting or proportional representation of minorities on the board of directors is allowed;

(4) an oppressed minorities mechanism is in place allowing shareholders with <10% ownership to challenge management or force management to purchase their shares;

(5) the minimum percentage of share capital that entitles a shareholder to call for an Extraordinary Shareholders' Meeting is less than or equal to 10% (the sample median); and

(6) shareholders have preemptive rights (i.e., first opportunity to buy newly issued stock).

For more details, refer to source.

Exhibit 11b   Index of Enforcement and Accounting Standards

The indices (taken from La Porta, et al.) are based on:

Accounting: Evaluation of company financial statements for the inclusion of specific items;

For all other measures, ratings are provided by *International Country Risk Guide* and *Business International Corporation*. These measures are defined as:

Judicial System: "'Efficiency and integrity of the legal environment as it affects business, particularly foreign firms.'"

Rule of Law: "'Assessment of the law and order tradition in the country.'"

Corruption: "Whether 'high government officials are likely to demand special payments' and 'illegal payments are generally expected throughout lower levels of government.'"

Risk of Expropriation: "Risk of 'outright confiscation' or 'forced nationalization.'"

Repudiation of Contracts by Government: "'Risk of modification in a contract taking the form of a repudiation, postponement, or scaling down due to budget cutbacks, indigenization pressure, a change in government, or a change in government economic and social priorities.'"

For more details, refer to source.

Source: Created by case writer based on data in La Porta, et al., "Law and Finance," 1998.

Note: [a]Accounting data not available.

Exhibit 12   Relationship between Degree of Investor Protection and Capital Market Development

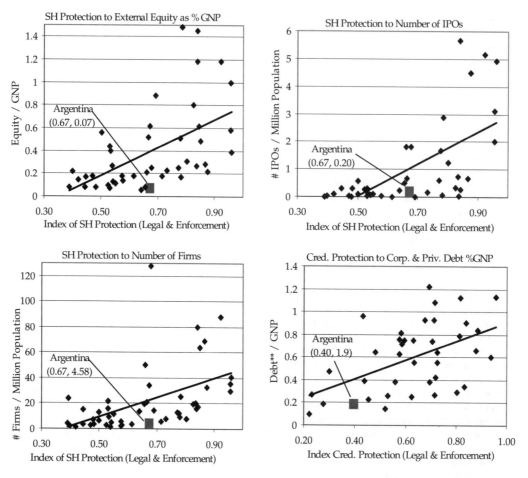

Source: Created by case writer based on La Porta and Lopez-de-Silanes, "Capital Markets and Legal Institutions," 1998.

Notes: **External equity** refers to a country's total stock market capitalization multiplied by % of equity held by minority shareholders of top 10 companies in the country.

   Debt refers to corporate and private sector debt.

   Index of shareholder protection refers to average of legal and enforcement country data presented in exhibits 11a and 11b.

   Index of creditor protection refers to average of enforcement data presented in exhibit 11b with data on creditor legal protection from the source.

Exhibit 13   Banco de Galicia Performance Against Peers

	Mkt Cap May 31, 2000	EPS			P/E			Book Value / Share		Price / Book Value	
		1998	1999	2000E	1998	1999	2000E	1999	2000E	1999	2000E
Banco de Galicia	$1.8 bn	0.98	1.11	1.25	15.40	13.50	12.00	10.33	11.28	1.5	1.3
Banco Frances	$1.4 bn	1.64	1.43	2.14	11.80	13.60	9.10	13.46	14.96	1.4	1.3
Banco Rio de la Plata	$2.2 bn	0.60	0.71	1.03	22.10	18.70	12.90	7.19	8.01	1.9	1.7
Bansud	$93 mm	(0.86)	(0.94)	(0.46)	(1.70)	(1.50)	(3.10)	5.10	4.64	0.3	0.3

Source: Adapted from Deutsche Bank, "Banco Galicia: Successful Exchange Likely, Estimates and Rating Reduced," June 2000.

Exhibit 14a   Banco de Galicia Summary Financial Statements

(millions pesos, except as noted, according to Argentine GAAP)	1999	1998	1997	1996	1995
Consolidated Income Statement					
Interest income	1,280.6	1,096.3	899.7	718.4	616.5
Interest expenditures	708.1	662.8	462.7	375.0	304.9
Adjustment	-	-	-	1.4	33.1
Net interest income	**572.6**	**433.4**	**437.1**	**342.0**	**278.5**
Allowance for losses on loans & receivables	216.0	84.8	112.4	100.7	79.7
Net income from services	294.2	230.5	183.4	168.6	183.2
Administrative expenses	561.8	474.2	368.0	303.5	301.5
Net operating income	**88.9**	**104.9**	**140.0**	**106.4**	**80.5**
Other	134.2	29.3	25.8	5.3	10.0
Income before taxes	**223.1**	**134.1**	**165.8**	**111.7**	**90.5**
Income tax	72.5	19.9	49.1	35.2	23.0
Net income	**150.6**	**114.3**	**116.7**	**76.5**	**67.5**
Consolidated Balance Sheet					
Total assets	**13,721**	**13,002**	**10,915**	**7,771**	**5,551**
Cash	792	982	452	337	488
Government securities	676	1,009	1,582	634	152
Loans, net	8,446	7,618	6,010	5,000	4,057
Consumer	*20.3%*				
Large corporations	*18.6%*				
Non-financial government	*22.1%*				
Small and medium-sized companies	*19.5%*				
Of which: agribusiness	*7.4%*				
Other	*19.5%*				
Other	3,806	3,393	2,870	1,800	854
Total Liabilities	**12,510**	**11,913**	**10,013**	**7,149**	**4,994**
Deposits	7,850	7,142	5,977	4,599	3,354
Other funds	4,660	4,771	4,036	2,550	1,640
Total shareholders' equity	**1,211**	**1,089**	**902**	**622**	**557**

Source: Based on Offer Prospectus, 22 June 2000, 33.

Exhibit 14b   Banco de Galicia Share Performance against Merval Index *(November 1, 1994 = 1)*

Source: Based on Datastream.

Exhibit 15a   Banco de Galicia Ownership *(May 2000)*

Shareholder:	Stake:
Grupo Financiero Galicia	46.3%
Argentine Pension Fund Companies (AFJPs)	12.0%
- Major investors in AFJPs included BSCH, BBV, HSBC, and Citigroup. As of March 2000, AFJPs had seven million enrollees and over $18.2 billion in assets under management	
Banco Santander Central Hispano	9.8%
- Spanish universal bank with strong Latin American presence	
Capital Research and Capital International	6.8%
- Subs of Capital Group, CA-based asset mgmt group, a top mutual fund firm noted for being a long-term, fundamental investor (manages Fidelity Investments, Vanguard Group, and The American Funds Group)	
Maria Isabel Escasany	5.4%
- Dissident member of controlling family group	
Schroder Investment Management Group	2.4%
- Sub of UK-based Schroders, worldwide asset management firm	
Fleming (Robert) Holding Limited	1.1%
- UK-based private investment bank involved primarily in underwriting, M&A, and asset-management for wealthy individuals	
Others (Goldman Sachs, HSBC, Putnam, Amex, individuals, and others)	16.2%

Sources: Based on BBV Securities, "Banco Galicia (Buy)" 25 May 2000, 5; Yahoo!Finance, 19 May 2000; and Consulate of Argentina Newsletter, April 2000.

Exhibit 15b   Grupo Financiero Galicia Ownership *(May 2000)*

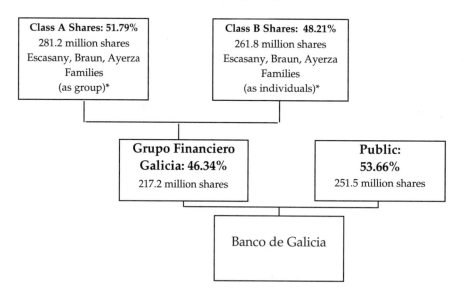

Source: Based on Offer Prospectus, 22 June 2000.

Note: Individual family members did not have access to their Class A shares, whereas they could trade their Class B shares freely.

Exhibit 16   Effect of Exchange Offer on Ownership and Voting

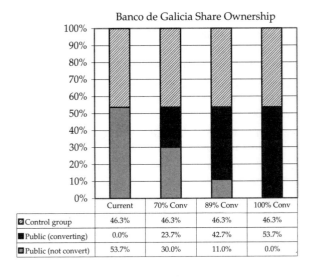

Banco de Galicia Share Ownership

	Current	70% Conv	89% Conv	100% Conv
Control group	46.3%	46.3%	46.3%	46.3%
Public (converting)	0.0%	23.7%	42.7%	53.7%
Public (not convert)	53.7%	30.0%	11.0%	0.0%

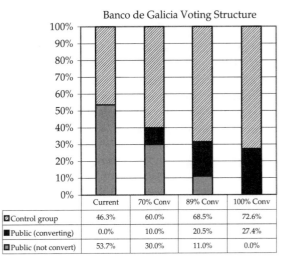

Banco de Galicia Voting Structure

	Current	70% Conv	89% Conv	100% Conv
Control group	46.3%	60.0%	68.5%	72.6%
Public (converting)	0.0%	10.0%	20.5%	27.4%
Public (not convert)	53.7%	30.0%	11.0%	0.0%

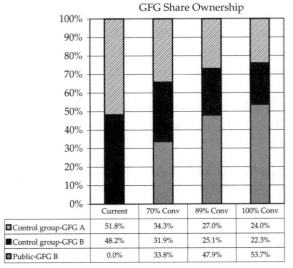

GFG Share Ownership

	Current	70% Conv	89% Conv	100% Conv
Control group-GFG A	51.8%	34.3%	27.0%	24.0%
Control group-GFG B	48.2%	31.9%	25.1%	22.3%
Public-GFG B	0.0%	33.8%	47.9%	53.7%

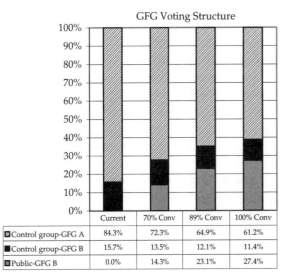

GFG Voting Structure

	Current	70% Conv	89% Conv	100% Conv
Control group-GFG A	84.3%	72.3%	64.9%	61.2%
Control group-GFG B	15.7%	13.5%	12.1%	11.4%
Public-GFG B	0.0%	14.3%	23.1%	27.4%

Source: Adapted from Offer Prospectus, 22 June 2000, 7–8.

Notes: **Public (converting)** refers to non-control group shareholders who accept the offer to tender their shares
Public (not convert) refers to non-control group shareholders who choose not to accept the offer.
Control group-GFG A refers to the shares owned by family members as a group that are not accessible to individuals.
Control group-GFG B refers to the shares owned by family members that can be traded freely by individuals.

Endnotes

1   George R.G. Clarke, Robert Cull, Laura D'Amato, and Andrea Molinari, "The Effect of Foreign Entry on Argentina's Domestic Banking Sector," Policy Research Working Paper (Washington, D.C.: The World Bank Development Research Group, Regulation and Competition Policy, and Finance, August 1999), 6.

2   Charles W. Calomiris and Andrew Powell, "Can Emerging Market Bank Regulators Establish Credible Discipline? The Case of Argentina, 1992–1999," NBER Working Paper Number w7715, (Cambridge, Massachusetts: National Bureau of Economic Research, May 2000), 1.

3   For more information about Argentina's Convertibility Plan, refer to Rafael Di Tella and Ingrid Vogel, "Argentina's Convertibility Plan," HBS No. 702-002 (Boston: Harvard Business School Publishing, 2001).

4   B. Gerard Dages, Linda Goldberg, and Daniel Kinney, "Foreign and Domestic Bank Participation in Emerging Markets: Lessons from Mexico and Argentina," Economic Policy Review (New York Federal Reserve Bank), Vol. 6 (3), September 2000), 8.

5   Calomiris and Powell, "Can Emerging Market Bank Regulators Establish Credible Discipline?" 9–10.

6   Cited in Calomiris and Powell, "Can Emerging Market Bank Regulators Establish Credible Discipline?" 9.

7   Calomiris and Powell, "Can Emerging Market Bank Regulators Establish Credible Discipline?" 2.

8   BBV Securities, "Banco Galicia (Buy): Good Time to Bank on the Stock," 21 June 2000, 8.

9   Calomiris and Powell, "Can Emerging Market Bank Regulators Establish Credible Discipline?" 2.

10 Calomiris and Powell, "Can Emerging Market Bank Regulators Establish Credible Discipline?" 28.

11 International Monetary Fund, International Financial Statistics, October 2001.

12 Economist Intelligence Unit, EIU Country Profile 2000-2001, (London: EIU, 2001) and Economist Intelligence Unit, EIU Country Profile 1999–2000, (London: EIU, 2000).

13 Economist Intelligence Unit, EIU Country Profile 2000-2001, and EIU, EIU Country Profile 1999–2000.

14 Joe Peek and Eric S. Rosengren, "Implications of the Globalization of the Banking Sector: The Latin American Experience," New England Economic Review (New England Federal Reserve Bank), September/October 2000, 55.

15 Dages, Goldberg, and Kinney, "Foreign and Domestic Bank Participation in Emerging Markets: Lessons from Mexico and Argentina," 14 and Peek and Rosengren, "Implications of the Globalization of the Banking Sector: The Latin American Experience," 53.

16 Salomon Smith Barney, "Argentine Bank Reference Guide," March 22, 2000.

17 Clarke, Cull, D'Amato, and Molinari, "The Effect of Foreign Entry on Argentina's Domestic Banking Sector," 9.

18 Calomiris and Powell, "Can Emerging Market Bank Regulators Establish Credible Discipline?" 4.

19 The authors of the study justify their decision to evaluate private debt as well as corporate bonds by noting that many entrepreneurs raise money on their personal accounts to finance their firms. They also note that availability of exclusively corporate bond data per country is limited.

20 Economist Intelligence Unit, EIU Country Profile 2000–2001.

21 Rafael La Porta and Florencio Lopez-de-Silanes, "Law and Finance," Journal of Political Economy, Vol. 106 (6), December 1998, 1113–55.

22 Rafael La Porta, Florencio Lopez-de-Silanes, Andrei Shleifer, and Robert W. Vishny, "Investor Protection and Corporate Governance," Journal of Financial Economics, Vol. 58 (1–2), Oct/Nov 2000, 19, citing Robert King and Ross Levine "Finance and Growth: Schumpeter Might be Right," Quarterly Journal of Economics, Vol. 108, 1993, 717–738.

23 Rafael La Porta and Florencio Lopez-de-Silanes, "Capital Markets and Legal Institutions," Annual World Bank Conference on Development in Latin America and the Caribbean, 1998: Banks and capital markets: Sound financial systems for the 21st century: Proceedings of a conference held in San Salvador, El Salvador. Burki, Shahid Javed Perry, Guillermo E., eds., With Augusto de la Torre, Mila Freire and Marcela Huertas. Latin American and Caribbean Studies: Proceedings series (Washington, D.C.: World Bank, 1999), 81.

24 Refer to data tables in Rafael La Porta, et al., "Law and Finance," *Journal of Political Economy*, Vol. 106 (6), December 1998, 1113–55.

25 U.S. Department of State, "Argentina Country Report on Human Rights Practices for 1998" (Washington, DC: Bureau of Democracy, Human Rights, and Labor, 26 February 1999), 4. Available at <http://www.state.gov/www/global/human_rights/1998_hrp_report/argentin.html> (as of 12 January 2002).

26 Domingo Cavallo, *"El Peso de la Verdad: Un Impulso a la Transparencia en la Argentina de Los 90,"* Planeta - Espejo de la Argentina, 268.

27 Alexander Dyck and Luigi Zingales, in "Private Benefits of Control: An International Comparison," *Journal of Finance* (forthcoming).

28 John C. Coffee, Jr., "Racing Toward the Top?: The Impact of Cross-Listing and Stock Market Competition on International Corporate Governance," Columbia Law School Working Paper No. 205, May 2002, 28-30.

29 Jordan Siegel, "Can Foreign Firms Bond Themselves Effectively by Renting U.S. Securities Laws," unpublished version, 20 January 2003 (an earlier version of this paper is available at http://www.afajof.org/Pdf/ 2003program/articles/siegel.pdf).

30 Banco de Galicia, Annual Report, 30 June 2000.

31 The 12% honorarium and the 25% limit set by the CNV are outlined in Banco de Galicia's 1993 Prospectus: Banco de Galicia, The First Boston Corporation, Baring Securities Inc., and Goldman, Sachs & Co., "Prospectus: 3,000,000 American Depository Shares," 11 June 1993, 20.

32 Salomon Smith Barney, "Banco de Galicia: Well Positioned for Growth," 16 June 1997.

33 Offer Prospectus: Grupo Financiero Galicia S.A. and J.P. Morgan, "Offer to Exchange American Depository Shares and Class B Shares of Grupo Financiero Galicia S.A. for American Depository shares and Class B Shares of Banco de Galicia y Buenos Aires S.A.," 10.

34 AFX Europe, "Perez Companc Share Swap Proposal Bad Deal for Investors," 18 November 1999.

35 Financial Times Information - Global News Wire, "PC Holdings gains control of 98.21% of Perez Companc," 27 January 2000.

36 Dow Jones International News, "Argentina's Perez Companc: Share Swap To Go Forward," 26 January 2000.

37 Noticias (Editorial Perfil), *"Eduardo Escasany: El Nuevo Jefe del Establishment,"* 8 November 2001.

38 Offer Prospectus: Grupo Financiero Galicia S.A. and J.P. Morgan, "Offer to Exchange American Depository Shares and Class B Shares of Grupo Financiero Galicia S.A. for American Depository shares and Class B Shares of Banco de Galicia y Buenos Aires S.A.," 22 June 2000, 124.

39 Noticias (Editorial Perfil), *"Eduardo Escasany: El Nuevo Jefe del Establishment,"* 8 November 2001 (author translation).

40 Buenos Aires Economico (BAE), *"Los Controlantes del Galicia se Blindan Para Resistir un Takeover,"* 18 May 2000.

41 These are outlined in detail in the Offer Prospectus: Grupo Financiero Galicia S.A. and J.P. Morgan, "Offer to Exchange American Depository Shares and Class B Shares of Grupo Financiero Galicia S.A. for American Depository shares and Class B Shares of Banco de Galicia y Buenos Aires S.A.," 15.

42 Dow Jones Newswires, "Argentina's Galicia Makes Swap Offer for All Its Shares," 17 May 2000.

43 Refer to Raymond James Argentina Sociedad de Bolsa S.A., "Galicia: Turning into a Different Animal," 18 May 2000; Merrill Lynch, "Banco de Galicia y Buenos Aires, S.A.: New Holding Company Structure Should Boost Long-term Economic Growth," 8 June 2000; Goldman Sachs Latin American Financial Services, "Banco Galicia," 19 May 2000; and others.

44   Pagina/12, *"El Galicia Mueve Fichas Para no Bajar la Bandera,"* (author translation) 18 May 2000, 14.

45   Dow Jones International, "BSCH Banco Rio Bid May Start Latin American Consolidation," 10 February 2000.

46   El Pais, "BSCH makes a takeover bid for 100% of Banco Rio in order to consolidate itself in Argentina (*El BSCH lanza una OPA por el 100% del Banco Rio para consolidarse en Argentina*)," (translation provided by World Reporter), 11 February 2000.

47   Interview with Gustavo Herrero.

48   Salomon Smith Barney, "Banco de Galicia y Buenos Aires," 19 July 2000, 2.

49   Goldman Sachs Latin American Financial Services, "Banco Galicia," 19 May 2000, 5.

50   Noticias (Editorial Perfil), *"La Guerra del Galicia,"* 21 November 1998 (author translation).

51   As sources close to the family reported in Mercado, *"Banco Galicia: Como la Familia Dejo de Estar Unita,"* June 1999.

52   Noticias (Editorial Perfil), *"La Guerra del Galicia,"* 21 November 1998.

53   For more details on the ruling, refer to Mercado, *"Como la Familia Dejo de Estar Unita,"* June 1999.

54   The Wall Street Journal Europe, "Global Finance: Banco de Galicia Shareholder Assails Revamp," 23 May 2000.

55   Busca AAAFlash, "Argentina: Accusation of Pressure in Stock Swap Investigation Dropped by Anti-Corruption Unit," 12 July 2000.

56   Dow Jones Newswires, "Shareholders May Lose in Argentina's Galicia Swap Offer," 17 May 2000.

57   Noticias (Editorial Perfil), *"Escasany vs. Escasany: Presiones Cruzadas,"* 15 July 2000.

58   Diario La Nacion, *"Case Galicia: Niegan Trafico de Influencias: De la Rua Dijo que no Hubo Presiones,"* 13 July 2000.

59   Refer to La Nacion Line, *"Los Accionistas Minoritarios del Galicia Daran Pelea,"* 25 May 2000; and Merrill Lynch, "Banco de Galicia y Buenos Aires, S.A.: Negative Investor Sentiment to Share Exchange Proposal is Mounting," 22 May 2000.

The 2001 Crisis in Argentina: An IMF-Sponsored Default? (A)

In early 2002, Argentina's economy and society both appeared on the verge of collapse. The one-to-one peg between the Argentine peso and the U.S. dollar implied by the currency board had been broken in the context of massive capital flight. To prevent the collapse of the domestic financial system, the Argentine authorities had imposed controls on the convertibility of bank deposits into cash (the "corralito").

In protest to this perceived expropriation—as well as to the general economic crisis—the Argentine middle class took to the streets of Buenos Aires and other cities. A succession of increasingly ineffectual presidents shuffled through the presidential palace, each seemingly more powerless to confront the crisis than the last.

Increasingly blamed for their role in Argentina's collapse, the International Monetary Fund and the international financial community debated whether to provide further emergency support to the Argentine government or withdraw assistance altogether.

Supplementary Material

The 2001 Crisis in Argentina: An IMF-Sponsored Default (B)

Study Questions

1. What caused the breakdown of Argentina's economy and society?
2. What was the IMF's role?
3. What should the Argentine authorities do in response?
4. Should the International Monetary Fund "bail out" Argentina? On what terms?

RAFAEL DI TELLA
INGRID VOGEL

The 2001 Crisis in Argentina:
An IMF-Sponsored Default? (A)

In Argentina, and in general in all emerging countries, there is a need for a deeper understanding of the events of the last 10 years. We need to admit that what has happened was not the fault of a small group of economists. The real cause of Argentin
a's problems for more than a century has been the expectation to find fantastic solutions to fix real problems. Argentines are taught when they are 10 that they belong and were born in a rich country. If you believe that you are born in a rich country, you don't accept the step-by-step way that Chile has had to adapt, or even Brazil. Brazil defines itself as a large country, but never as a rich country. So they adopt step-by-step policies based on exports; on production; on austerity. But Argentina is always looking for shortcuts to the first world.

—Javier Gonzalez Fraga, former Argentine Central Bank president[1]

At the end of 2001, Argentina's economy and society both appeared on the verge of collapse. Between 1998 and 2001, Argentina had endured an increasingly severe recession and multiple failed attempts to restore growth and control government spending. Interest rates soared and foreign investment dried up. On December 1, 2001, in the face of increasing capital flight, the government resorted to drastic measures in the form of deposit freezes—the "*corralito*"—which limited cash withdrawals from all bank accounts. Just four days later, the IMF declared that Argentina had not done enough to control its public deficit and stopped disbursing funds to the country. The stage was set for Argentina to default on its $141 billion in foreign debt outstanding, in what would become the largest sovereign default in history.

On December 20, Argentines, already frustrated by worsening social conditions and by what they perceived as confiscation of their private property through the *corralito*, responded with outrage to the government's IMF-appeasing announcement of future dramatic spending cuts. In violent rioting, stores were looted, buildings burned, and more than 22 people died. Argentine President Fernando De La Rua and his entire cabinet resigned.

On January 2, 2002, Eduardo Duhalde was selected interim president by Argentina's Congress and would serve as Argentina's fifth president in two weeks. At the helm of Argentina's flailing economy, he had a number of decisions to make. Among these were what to do with Argentina's decade-long peg to the dollar under the Convertibility Plan.

Professor Rafael Di Tella and Research Associate Ingrid Vogel prepared this case. This case was developed from published sources. HBS cases are developed solely as the basis for class discussion. Cases are not intended to serve as endorsements, sources of primary data, or illustrations of effective or ineffective management.

Chronology of the Crisis

After a long history of economic and political instability marked by periods of hyperinflation, banking collapse, bailouts to the private sector, and military coups, Argentina finally achieved the consensus necessary to implement substantial economic reform in the early 1990s. In 1991, under President Carlos Saul Menem and Economics Minister Domingo Felipe Cavallo, Argentina adopted the Convertibility Plan, which resulted in macroeconomic stability and allowed the introduction of free-market reforms such as financial and trade liberalization, deregulation, and privatization. Most significantly, the plan called for a currency-board-like arrangement, called convertibility, which pegged the peso at par to the U.S. dollar, at which the Central Bank was obligated to convert currency on demand. Convertibility also restricted the money supply to the level of hard-currency reserves.[a]

Under this arrangement, the Argentine economy appeared to be doing well, and, in a complete reversal of fortune, the country even came to be seen as a model of economic stabilization and reform. By 1997, inflation had fallen from 5,000% per year to international levels, GDP was growing by an annual average 6%, foreign investment was pouring in, the country risk premium (sovereign bond spread over U.S. Treasuries) ranged from 3%–5%, and exports and productivity were increasing. Academics lauded the country for introducing a set of reforms in the banking industry in response to the "tequila crisis" of 1995[b] that allowed it to weather the Asian crisis of 1997 and the Russian default of 1998 in a strong position[2] (see **Exhibits 1** through **4** for basic macroeconomic data). Although the Argentine economy had begun to show some signs of weakness in late 1998, most observers expected a full recovery after the 1999 elections.

The De La Rua Presidency

In December 1999, Fernando De La Rua, leader of the opposition center-left coalition of parties called *La Alianza*, won the presidential election against Peronist anti-market candidate Eduardo Duhalde. De La Rua won on a platform of revitalizing the sluggish economy within the pro-market economic model of the 1990s and ending corruption after the 10-year rule of Menem. *La Alianza* represented a merger between *FREPASO* (a splinter group of left-wing former Peronists—the populist party named after its founder, Peron[c]) and the Radical party (a traditional party founded in the late 19th century), which included a vocal left-leaning faction led by former Argentine president Raul Alfonsin. De La Rua represented the Radical party, while his Vice President Carlos Alvarez represented *FREPASO*.

With a fragmented political base, President De La Rua's task was challenging. Along with his Economics Minister Jose Luis Machinea, De La Rua believed fiscal mismanagement to be the source of Argentina's economic problems and, therefore, implemented a number of policies meant to address the public sector deficit. First, in January 2000, after emphasizing that the situation was much worse than they had anticipated, De La Rua and Machinea raised taxes in what became known as the *Impuestazo*. Instead of lowering the deficit, however, the *Impuestazo* was followed by weakened

---

[a] The Central Bank was required to hold dollar reserves against its domestic monetary liabilities, which included currency outstanding and commercial bank reserves. The government could, in certain emergency situations, hold up to 20% of its assets in government debt. For more details and background, see "Argentina's Convertibility Plan," HBS Case No. 702-002.

[b] The Tequila crisis (Mexico's devaluation in December 1994) brought fears of debt default throughout Latin America.

[c] For more on Peron and Peronism, see "The Argentine Paradox: Economic Growth and the Populist Tradition," HBS Case No. 702-001.

consumption indicators and a deepening of the recession. Four months later, in May 2000, the government announced $1 billion in spending cuts. These cuts were met with wide-scale protest.

A corruption scandal erupted when it was discovered that bribes had been paid to senators in exchange for support of the government's initiative to bring flexibility to the labor market. The government denied being involved. But in October, as the investigation progressed, De La Rua's vice president resigned, citing the government's lack of commitment in fighting corruption. This dramatically weakened the coalition, making the government dependent on Peronist support to pass legislation.

Machinea and De La Rua had more success in December 2000 with the negotiation of a $40 billion loan package (known as the *Blindaje*) with international and domestic financial institutions. The package was granted based on promises that economic reforms would be deepened and public expenditure reduced. Initially, markets reacted favorably and Argentina's country risk premium fell to 800 basis points, from 1000 in November.

It soon became apparent, however, that the government lacked the political stamina to implement the required reforms. The economy continued to deteriorate: The fiscal deficit during the first two months of 2001 exceeded agreed-upon targets, consumer confidence faltered, and tax revenues fell.

Against this backdrop, Machinea resigned in March 2001. He was replaced by Ricardo Lopez Murphy, who proposed a tough $4.5 billion austerity plan with severe cuts in education.[3] Two weeks later, after six government officials resigned in protest to the cuts, Lopez Murphy also resigned.

Cavallo's Return as Economics Minister

Despite concern from members of his cabinet, De La Rua appointed Cavallo, architect of the 1991 Convertibility Plan, once again as economics minister. Aware of his predecessors' failures to reduce spending and increase tax revenues, Cavallo focused instead on promoting economic growth. He immediately unveiled his "Competitiveness Plans," which aimed to reduce costs in productive sectors of the economy by eliminating distortionary taxes. Affected businesses were expected to agree to reduce prices and maintain employment levels. Cavallo's reputation was important in getting support from international markets. In this context, Cavallo famously told financial analysts in a conference call, "I am a legend."

Overall, however, these measures did little to solve Argentina's immediate problem of a public deficit in excess of IMF targets. As confidence in the country flagged, rating agencies began downgrading its public and private securities. In March 2001, depositors withdrew $5.5 billion from Argentina's banking system—the most severe bank run in Argentina's history (see **Exhibit 5**). Most capital flight occurred in domestic banks (see **Exhibit 6**).[4]

In April 2001, in another effort to improve Argentina's competitiveness, Cavallo sent a bill to Congress that would tie the peso to an average of the euro and dollar once the euro appreciated to parity with the dollar. Although Cavallo emphasized the continuation of convertibility and presented this measure as an attempt to align the peso with Argentina's trading patterns, markets interpreted it as a *de facto* devaluation and a threat to the foundation of Argentina's Convertibility Plan.

To make matters worse, President of the Central Bank Pedro Pou came under investigation for his alleged participation in a money-laundering scheme. A congressional committee was put together to study the charges levied against Pou. He eventually resigned, citing pressure from Cavallo and other government officials to improve banking sector liquidity through reducing reserve requirements. Deposits again fell in response to the apparent lack of independence of the Central Bank.

Shortly after, with interest and principal payments still looming, Cavallo began planning a voluntary debt swap—the *Megacanje*. In early June 2001, Argentina announced that it successfully swapped almost $30 billion of debt. Although the rates paid to borrow at longer maturities were high (around 15% per annum), the swap would defer debt service costs of around $8 billion through 2002 and a total of $16 billion through 2005. While investors initially welcomed the program, Cavallo and members of his economic team were accused of bribe-taking in the *Megacanje* (although the judicial investigation could not proceed while they were in office).

In mid-June, again trying to promote growth, Cavallo announced new measures targeted at reactivating the demand for exports. These included a modified exchange rate for exports of 1.08 pesos to 1 dollar. Markets became uneasy about Argentina's commitment to its currency-board-like arrangement.

In July 2001, the government finally accepted that the fiscal deficit could no longer be financed. As a result, a "zero-deficit" policy was introduced that aimed to end deficit spending through measures including a reduction in pensions and state salaries of up to 13%. With these reforms underway, the government was able to negotiate an $8 billion increase in Argentina's standby loan agreement with the IMF (see **Exhibit 7** for IMF disbursements and repayments).

In November, facing heavy capital and interest payments, Argentina attempted to execute another debt swap, guaranteed by fiscal revenue. In contrast to the *Megacanje*, the swap was not well received. Instead, capital flight escalated and country risk climbed to 1,700 basis points (see **Exhibits 8** and **9** for interest rate and bond spread data).

At the end of 2001, Argentina's economic problems escalated into a full-blown crisis. On December 1, in order to stem the outflow of bank deposits, a set of capital controls known as the "*corralito*" were instituted. The *corralito* limited monthly withdrawals of cash from checking and savings accounts to $1000,[a] but did not restrict the use of credit cards, debit cards, checks, and bank transfers within Argentina. It also limited foreign money transactions to operations related to exports and imports.

On December 5, the IMF announced that it would suspend disbursement of funds since the country had failed to achieve the (relatively small) adjustment necessary to meet austerity measures. It was widely expected that Argentina would soon be forced to default on its debt obligations. On December 17, the government presented its new budget, which included plans to reduce spending by nearly 20%. The Argentine people, already suffering from high unemployment and worsening public services, reacted with looting and violence.[b] De La Rua and the rest of his cabinet were forced to resign.

Duhalde's Challenge

De La Rua's immediate successor, Adolfo Rodriguez Saa, officially announced that Argentina would default on its debt. He also promised to maintain convertibility of the peso and started issuing

---

[a] The $1,000 limit was set based on research that 99% of Argentines cashed less than that amount per month.

[b] It is unclear how spontaneous the protests were. Some observers claimed that elements of the government of the Province of Buenos Aires were involved.

a third, non-convertible, floating currency to pay most public expenses and to bail out the banks. The default and some controversial appointments in his administration were seriously criticized by the media. After a confusing episode in which he was approached by elements of the Buenos Aires Peronist party, Rodriguez Saa, too, was forced to resign.[a]

On January 2, 2002, the former governor of the province of Buenos Aires, Eduardo Duhalde, was sworn into office, where he would remain until the next election. Economic chaos continued through the beginning of his presidency. On January 3, Argentina formally went into default as expected on a portion of its $141 billion in foreign debt, missing a payment of $28 million on an Italian lira bond, in what became the largest government default in history.

Possible Explanations for the Crisis

Explanations for Argentina's economic crisis abounded. Some observers blamed the country's restrictive currency arrangement, while others cited fiscal mismanagement. Other observers felt that problems of overvaluation and deficits could have been solved and attributed Argentina's final collapse instead to the policies adopted to try to address the oncoming crisis.

Fixed Exchange Rate under Convertibility

In the popular press, Argentina's economic failure was often attributed to its currency-board-like arrangement. By restricting the money supply to the level of foreign reserves, convertibility implied that the government could no longer print money to affect interest rates or act as a lender of last resort to the banking system. The fixed exchange rate to the U.S. dollar forced Argentina to align monetary policy with the United States, despite cyclical differences and the low level of trade between the two countries. It also left the country vulnerable to movements in the multilateral exchange rate.

The argument went as follows: In the late 1990s, the peso became overvalued as the dollar strengthened relative to most other currencies. As a result, Argentina's competitiveness suffered. The country's current account deficit persisted, requiring growing foreign debt levels. The devaluation of the Brazilian real in 1999 further exacerbated the situation.

In theory, competitiveness could have been restored through a decrease in the overall price level. But, as several economists pointed out, "the deflation required to adjust to the shocks would have been politically hard or impossible to achieve."[5] Rigid labor laws and strong union pressure in Argentina kept what should have been an automatic adjustment mechanism from functioning; public sector wages in particular remained high. It was argued that this prevented the fall in production costs that could have reignited growth.[6] (See **Exhibit 10** for comparative inflation indicators for Argentina and the United States.)

---

[a] After Saa's resignation, power passed to Senate leader Ramon Puerta, who refused the job and passed it on to Chamber of Deputies leader Eduardo Camano from the Province of Buenos Aires. Camano held the post until Duhalde was chosen by Congress.

Fiscal Management

In the management of its fiscal affairs, Argentina is like a chronic alcoholic—once it starts to imbibe the political pressures of deficit spending, it keeps on going until it reaches the economic equivalent of falling-down drunk.[7]

—Michael Mussa, former chief economist of the IMF, 2002.

A related view gave more weight to what was considered Argentina's loose fiscal policy. Argentina had a long history of political pressures leading to government spending well in excess of revenues. With its Convertibility Plan, Argentina appeared to have quelled this tendency, even recording a small fiscal surplus in 1993. Critics—such as former chief economist of the IMF Michael Mussa—argued, however, that Argentina should have taken the opportunity to tighten fiscal policy during its boom years.[8] They pointed out that deficits were in fact larger than they appeared. First, from 1993 to 1998, Argentina realized $3.1 billion in non-recurring privatization proceeds. Second, the Brady bond restructuring acted as an implicit loan by substantially back-loading interest payments. Furthermore, continued borrowing took Argentina's public debt as a percentage of GDP from 29% in 1993 to 51% in 2000 (see **Exhibit 11**). *The Economist* noted: "Instead of printing money, as in the bad old days, [Argentina] printed bonds to finance its fiscal deficit."[9]

Although low by international standards, a 50% debt-to-GDP ratio was worrisome in the case of Argentina. First, most of Argentina's debt was denominated in foreign currency, and much was held externally. With a debt-to-export ratio of 400%—much higher than in most other countries—Argentina's ability to pay off its debt in hard currency was questionable. Second, Argentina was vulnerable to external shocks as well as to shifts in market sentiment.[10] Indeed, starting in 1998 Argentina could no longer service all of its external debt after the "sudden stop" in global capital flows to emerging market economies.[11] Third, there seemed to be a structural tendency for deficits. The high debt servicing costs were added to a generous informal welfare state, prompted by high unemployment, particularly in the provinces. In addition, the country's tax system was inefficient and suffered from high levels of tax evasion. The government collected only 20% of GDP in taxes, versus 30% in Brazil and in excess of 50% in Europe.

Fiscal indiscipline at the provincial level was seen as another structural weakness. Under Argentina's Constitution of 1853, the collection of taxes and payment of debt were maintained at the national level. The federal government was charged with distributing a portion of the taxes collected to the provinces. In the early 1990s, percentage-based revenue-sharing between the national government and the provinces was replaced with a rigid system of minimum revenue guarantees. But provincial authorities used these guarantees as collateral that enabled them to run up significant private-sector debts for which the central government was ultimately responsible.[12]

Political economists argued that "federal transfers emboldened provincial officials to flout the preferences of national politicians and dramatically expand provincial payrolls."[13] As a result, the provinces ran significant, persistent deficits.

"An Institutional Coup"[14]

It was argued that the rigidity of the currency board and the mismanagement of fiscal affairs alone were not enough to have pushed Argentina to collapse. For example, Harvard economists Ricardo Hausmann and Andres Velasco took a different stance on the fiscal management issue: "We do not share this view. The fiscal imbalance was not large. . . . The fiscal balance that emerged was related to the recession and hence is best understood as a consequence rather than a cause of the crisis. It is hard to make the case that a more forceful fiscal adjustment would have made a very significant difference."[15]

They argued that much of the overall deficit was attributable to the social security system, which had begun reform from a state pay-as-you-go system to individual private accounts in 1994. They pointed out that the savings of the newly privatized pension system backed up a full two-thirds of the social security deficit of 2.4% of GDP in 2000.

Furthermore, they argued that, in fact, excluding social security, the national government had generated enough of a primary surplus to cover the increased cost of debt service of the national debt. They concluded, "the numbers here are not those of a profligate country, and [are] hard to square with the catastrophe that followed"[16] (see **Exhibit 4**).

Instead, some observers claimed that the manner in which the Argentine government handled the oncoming crisis was the problem. Former Economics Minister Cavallo argued that an institutional coup at the end of December 2001 organized by indebted industrial and media interest groups with the help of members of the Buenos Aires Peronist party promoted detrimental economic policies, including default and devaluation. Cavallo argued that devaluation would represent an assault on property rights and irreparably damage the trust of Argentines in their government, creating, in Cavallo's words, "real economic and social chaos requiring considerable time from which to recover."[17] As Cavallo wrote in a widely read article:

> Those who pressed for this institutional breakdown thought that by defaulting on the debts and moving away from convertibility, the heavily indebted private sector would eventually have its financial problems solved: if Argentina "pesofied" its economy—that is, forcing the conversion of all dollar contracts into peso contracts and then devaluing the peso—a huge amount of resources would be automatically transferred from creditors to debtors.[18]

Cavallo went on to claim that the media played a significant role in this coup. As heavily indebted corporations of the private sector, media firms stood to gain significantly if their debts were transformed from dollars into pesos that would then be devalued. According to Cavallo, to promote change in "the rules of the game," the media exaggerated problems associated with the *corralito* in order to discredit the government and create the climate for riots. The media then chose to publicize suggestions by academics, notably Ricardo Hausmann, that Argentina de-dollarize. (Hausmann was calling for combining de-dollarization with a floating exchange rate anchored by strict inflation targets, which would prevent Argentina from "inflating the debt away."[19]) Other academics, whom Cavallo came to call "mad intellectuals," were getting attention in the press with their demands for the government to default on its debt.[20] According to Cavallo: "The politicians that had been advocating these measures began to get media support, which facilitated their creation of a new government in early 2002."[21] Members of the opposition party were ultimately able to appoint Duhalde, well known for his anti-convertibility stance, as president without elections.

The International Monetary Fund

Another target of intense blame was the IMF. First, critics questioned why IMF staff had allowed Argentina to maintain its currency-board-like arrangement when the IMF, as well as most other economists, began to publicly favor floating over fixed exchange rate regimes through the 1990s.[22] Even as some signs of the exchange rate overvaluation became visible and the current account deficit increased,[23] the IMF still chose to support Argentina's restrictive currency arrangement.

Second, some economists argued that the IMF exacerbated Argentina's recession through contractionary policy requirements. Joseph Stiglitz, Nobel Prize winner and former chief economist at the World Bank, wrote:

> The world had hardly recovered from the 1997–1998 financial crisis when the 2000–2001 global slowdown started, worsening Argentina's situation. Here the IMF made its fatal mistake: It encouraged a contractionary fiscal policy, the same mistake it had made in East Asia. Fiscal austerity was supposed to restore confidence. But the numbers in the IMF programme were fiction; any economist would have predicted that contractionary policies would incite slow-down, and that budget targets would not be met. Needless to say, the IMF programme did not fulfill its commitments. Confidence is seldom restored as an economy goes into a deep recession and double-digit unemployment.[24]

Still others argued that the Fund failed to push the *right* contractionary policies. For example, the Fund failed to have Argentina modify its constitutionally defined provincial spending rules.

Third, some critics alleged that the IMF provided *too much* financing without requiring sufficient policy adjustment. Michael Mussa (former IMF chief economist) pointed out that between 1995 and 1998, "more than half of the time, waivers were granted for missed fiscal performance criteria, or these criteria were met but only after they had been revised upward, or the violations (at the ends of some years) were simply ignored by the Fund and effectively swept under the rug."[25] Seemingly endless waivers allowed Argentina to survive without addressing fundamental economic and political problems. Mussa noted that when the economy was growing, the IMF should have made use of its conditionality to press the Argentines to enact more prudent fiscal policy.

Observers were left to wonder why the IMF continued to support the country despite its weaknesses. Some economists posited that, through the *Blindaje* and subsequent bailouts, the IMF was trying to generate self-fulfilling optimism as a way to promote recovery.[26] In another possible explanation, Mussa pointed out: "A star pupil that the Fund had praised and supported as model of economic stabilization and reform was in danger of turning into a basket case."[27] The Fund, already under scrutiny for its involvement in Asia prior to that region's collapse, was particularly eager for Argentina to succeed in order to be able to point to a program country in which it was supporting successful pro-market economic policies.

Martin Feldstein, former chairman of President Reagan's Council of Economic Advisers, viewed things differently:

> One reason is that Argentina has interest and principal payments of $4.9 billion that are due to the IMF this year. By withholding that amount from any gross loan that it now makes, the IMF could maintain the fiction that its borrowers do not default on their loans. That claim is important to the IMF's ability to get funds from the U.S. and other industrial governments. Since lending just $5 billion to Argentina would make this slight of hand obvious, the IMF wants to lend more.[28]

In its own defense, the IMF pointed out that the ultimate responsibility for a member country's economic policy lay with its own national authorities. In fact, under its own terms of operation, the IMF was required to support the basic policy strategies chosen by program countries, given at least a reasonable chance of success.[29]

Proposals

To most people, mad scientists are either harmless eccentrics toiling away in a basement or malevolent individuals bent on world domination. Which category do economics professors fall into?

A handful of leading economists in the United States take a particular interest in Latin America, particularly Argentina. The likes of Rudiger Dornbusch, Ricardo Hausmann, Adam Lerrick and Jeffrey Sachs have showered the authorities in Buenos Aires with advice in private consultations or through the columns of the Financial Times and the Wall Street Journal. Their ideas, which run the gamut from useful to pedestrian to bizarre, are some of the more colorful features of Argentina's financial collapse.[30]

—LatinFinance, May 2002

The biggest decision facing Duhalde was whether or not to devalue the peso and break its decade-long peg to the dollar. He encountered a flurry of policy suggestions, both to address these issues as well as others.

Some economists were pressing for moving beyond convertibility to dollarization. With net foreign reserves as a percentage of the monetary base ranging from 109% to 193% over 2001, dollarization would indeed have been feasible.[a][31] Other economists, such as former Argentine Central Bank President Javier Gonzalez Fraga, were strictly opposed to maintaining any fixed exchange rate regime—let alone one as extreme as dollarization. Along with other supporters of Duhalde, Fraga firmly believed that devaluation was an important mechanism through which the Argentine economy could again become productive and competitive.

Some observers characterized the reliance on devaluation coupled with distortionary taxes as "productivism," as opposed to the "neoliberalism" of the 1990s. They reacted bitterly to the idea that devaluation represented a step toward a productivity-based development strategy. Besides its effect on income distribution, the increase in "productivity" was perceived as minimal and brought about by devaluation in sectors related to tradable goods, import substitution, and tourism only. Cavallo, for example, argued that allowing the peso to float would serve only to boost exports "at the expense of extremely low salaries in terms of U.S. dollars. Such type of benefit induces exporters to exploit their installed capacity intensively, but it does not foster investment or the development of additional capacity, because there is no certainty that salaries in dollars will continue to be so low in the medium term."[32]

Argentina's other immediate challenges were resolving the *corralito* and addressing the defaulted debt. Political economists Allan Meltzer and Adam Lerrick suggested ending the *corralito* by allowing banks to issue government-guaranteed deposit receipts as money. On the issue of the defaulted debt, J.P. Morgan proposed a market-based framework for a two-step bond exchange. It was designed to address free-riding problems during sovereign debt restructuring. In the first step, investors would give up their long-term bonds in exchange for short-term securities and, if necessary as an additional incentive, cash. The second step would implement the exact terms of an agreed restructuring. After debt sustainability was established, investors would exchange their short-term securities for newly restructured long-term bonds.[33]

More longer-term proposals emphasized returning to the "neoliberal" policies of the prior decade through strengthening market-based reform. Sebastian Edwards, former chief economist for Latin America at the World Bank, suggested that Argentina adopt a plan similar to that of Chile in 1985,

---

[a] Net foreign reserves exclude Central Bank holdings of Argentine government bonds denominated in foreign currencies. Monetary base includes currency outstanding and commercial bank reserves.

three years after its own economic collapse.[34] The first part of Chile's plan was encouraging investment through reducing taxes on corporate earnings and lowering government expenditures. Another important component was the adoption of sound monetary policy. To this end, Edwards recommended reinstating Argentine Central Bank President Pou, whose dismissal in 2001 had, according to Edwards, sacrificed the country's monetary credibility. Edwards also referred to Chile's example in recapitalizing banks. After making cash infusions into the banks, the Chilean government became their owners. It then sold the banks to dispersed shareholders (more than 100,000) and ensured that the new banking environment was competitive. The fourth part of the plan involved trade liberalization, which could be achieved in Argentina through reducing import tariffs and halting relations with, what Edwards called, "the protectionist customs union known as Mercosur."[35]

Other prescriptions were more drastic and controversial. MIT economists Rudiger Dornbusch and Ricardo Caballero went so far as to suggest that Argentina surrender its financial and economic sovereignty for an extended period. They compared Argentina in 2002 to Austria at the end of World War I and recommended a similar arrangement in which resident foreign commissioners would take on important responsibilities:

> Specifically, a board of experienced foreign central bankers should take control of Argentina's monetary policy.... The new pesos should not be printed on Argentine soil. Another foreign agent would be required to verify fiscal performance and sign the cheques from the nation to the provinces.... Another experienced foreign agent should control these processes [of privatization and regulation], as well as make sure that the proceeds end up somewhere safe for all present and future Argentines to share.[36]

As Argentines pondered the implicit assumption that they themselves were the problem, newly appointed President Duhalde reflected on the tough choices he was facing.

Appendix

Timeline of Key Events in Argentina, December 1999–January 2002

December 10, 1999	Fernando De La Rua, leader of a center-left coalition, becomes Argentina's president on a platform of ending corruption and maintaining free-market reforms and convertibility.
January 2000	Taxes are raised in what becomes known as the *Impuestazo*.
May 29, 2000	Argentina announces $1 billion in spending cuts. Two days later, 20,000 protesters take to the streets against the cuts.
October, 2000	De La Rua's vice president resigns after a corruption scandal, significantly weakening the coalition.
December 18, 2000	Government announces $40 billion aid package (the *Blindaje*), largely secured by the IMF. Markets react with a strong rally.
March 2, 2001	Machinea resigns as economy minister. Ricardo Lopez Murphy succeeds him and two weeks later unveils a tough $4.5 billion two-year austerity program with severe cuts in education. Six officials from the left-leaning faction of the coalition resign in protest to the cuts.
March 20, 2001	De La Rua appoints Cavallo to replace Lopez Murphy.
March 21, 2001	Cavallo unveils his Competitiveness Plans.
April 17, 2001	Cavallo sends a bill to Congress that would eventually tie the peso to a 50-50 average of euro and dollar, once the euro reached parity with the dollar.
April 25, 2001	Argentine Central Bank President Pou is charged in a money-laundering scheme. He resigns, citing pressure from government officials to improve banking sector liquidity.
June 3, 2001	Argentina swaps $30 billion of debt (the *Megacanje*), which defers debt service costs of around $8 billion through 2002 and by a total of $16 billion by the end of 2005.
June 15, 2001	Argentina announces a new exchange rate system for exports at 1.08 pesos to one dollar.
July 3, 2001	Argentine stocks fall to 28-month low after rumors of the resignation of De La Rua.
July 30, 2001	The government's key austerity bill is passed. The "zero deficit" law aims to end deficit spending and slash state salaries and some pensions by up to 13%.
August 21, 2001	IMF Managing Director Horst Koehler agrees to recommend an $8 billion increase in Argentina's stand-by loan agreement with the IMF.
November, 2001	A new debt swap is poorly received by markets.
December 1, 2001	Cavallo announces restrictions on bank account withdrawals. Known as the *corralito*, the measures include a monthly limit of $1000 on cash withdrawals and caps on offshore transfers.
December 5, 2001	IMF announces it will suspend disbursements to Argentina.
December 6, 2001	Cavallo says fixed-term deposits held in banks by private pension funds will be transformed into treasury bonds or government-guaranteed loans.
December 13, 2001	Government says jobless rate rose to 18.3% in October, the highest since the start of the recession in mid-1998. Major unions call nationwide strike.
December 17, 2001	Government presents 2002 budget, which includes spending cuts of nearly 20%.
December 18, 2001	IMF says Argentina can delay payment on loan of about $1 billion due in January, but also says Argentina's economic policy is unsustainable.
December 19, 2001	Government declares state of siege giving it special powers to stop the worst looting and riots in a decade. The lower house of Congress repeals special powers granted to Cavallo.
December 20, 2001	Cavallo resigns and the rest of the cabinet tender their resignations.
December 21, 2001	De La Rua resigns after thousands take to the streets of the capital to protest the government's handling of the country's worsening economic crisis. At least 22 people are killed in riots and looting around the country.
December 23, 2001	Adolfo Rodriguez Saa becomes president of Argentina. Announces default of debt. Resigns on December 28, citing pressure from elements of the Buenos Aires Peronist party.
January 2, 2002	Eduardo Duhalde, strongman of the Buenos Aires Peronist party, sworn into office.

Exhibit 1a   Argentine General Economic Indicators

Units as shown	1990	1991	1992	1993	1994	1995	1996	1997	1998	1999	2000	2001	2002
Real GDP Growth (% change pa)	-3.0	12.2	11.3	6.7	5.8	-2.8	5.5	8.1	3.9	-3.4	-0.8	-4.5	-10.9
Real Per Capita GDP Growth (% change pa)	-4.3	10.7	9.9	5.4	4.4	-4.0	4.3	6.8	2.6	-4.5	-1.9	-5.5	-11.9
Consumer Price Inflation (% change to year-end)	1343.9	84.0	17.5	7.4	3.9	1.6	0.1	0.3	0.7	-1.8	-0.7	-1.5	41.0
Stockmarket Index (% change pa, $ value)	n/a	n/a	-46.0	35.3	-21.0	12.8	25.2	5.9	-37.4	28.0	-24.3	-29.1	-46.5
Average Nominal Wages (% change pa)	n/a	n/a	32.2	13.4	6.0	5.3	6.1	1.4	1.2	-0.5	0.8	-4.1	2.0
M1 Growth (% change pa)	n/a	148.6	49.0	33.0	8.2	1.6	14.6	12.8	0.0	1.6	-9.2	-20.1	78.6
Units as shown													
Nominal Ex. Rate (pesos per dollar period end)	0.6	1.0	1.0	1.0	1.0	1.0	1.0	1.0	1.0	1.0	1.0	1.0	3.3
Real Ex. Rate (increase = appreciation, 1997=100)	59.8	82.7	95.2	104.2	104.2	98.6	97.3	100.0	103.5	108.7	109.3	113.3	46.8
Unemployment (%)	7.5	7.5	7.5	8.8	10.5	15.5	15.5	13.9	11.8	13.0	14.6	16.4	18.8
International Reserves (current $ bns, year-end)	6.0	7.4	11.4	15.5	16.0	16.0	19.7	22.4	24.9	26.4	25.2	14.6	10.5
Foreign Debt (current $ bns, year-end)	62.2	65.4	68.3	64.7	75.1	98.8	111.4	128.4	141.5	145.3	145.9	136.7	127.4

Source: Casewriter, based on data from EIU Country Data, August 2003.

Exhibit 1b   Real GDP Growth and Unemployment

Source: Casewriter, based on data from EIU Country Data, August 2003.

Exhibit 1c   Argentine Monthly Industrial Production Index (seasonally adjusted)

Source: Casewriter, based on data from National Institute of Statistics and Census Data, <http://www.indec.gov.ar>, accessed October 2003.

Exhibit 2 Argentine National Income Accounts (billions of constant 1996 U.S. dollars)

	1990	1991	1992	1993	1994	1995	1996	1997	1998	1999	2000	2001	2002
Gross Domestic Product	**188.1**	**211.1**	**235.0**	**250.9**	**265.5**	**258.0**	**272.2**	**294.3**	**305.7**	**295.3**	**293.0**	**280.1**	**249.6**
Household Consumption	121.8	142.4	164.8	174.3	184.9	176.8	186.6	203.3	210.4	206.2	204.8	193.0	165.3
Government Consumption	31.2	32.6	32.2	32.9	33.1	33.3	34.0	35.1	36.3	37.3	37.5	36.7	34.8
Gross Fixed Investment	23.4	30.4	40.3	48.0	54.1	47.2	53.4	62.3	65.3	54.3	52.2	46.0	28.7
Exports	18.7	18.0	17.8	18.7	21.5	26.4	28.4	31.8	35.2	34.8	35.7	36.7	37.8
Imports	6.9	12.3	20.4	23.5	28.5	25.7	30.2	38.3	41.5	36.8	36.8	31.6	15.8
Nominal GDP (current $ bns)	141.4	189.7	229.0	236.8	257.7	258.1	272.2	293.0	299.1	283.7	284.3	268.8	102.0

Source: Casewriter, based on data from EIU Country Data, August 2003.
Note: GDP does not equal sum of components because of rebasing to 1996, which alters the relative importance of individual components.

Exhibit 3 Argentine Balance of Payments (millions of current U.S. dollars)

	1990	1991	1992	1993	1994	1995	1996	1997	1998	1999	2000	2001
Current Account	4,552	-647	-5,660	-8,169	-11,171	-5,175	-6,825	-12,243	-14,532	-11,902	-8,879	-4,554
Trade Balance	8,628	4,419	-1,396	-2,364	-4,160	2,357	1,760	-2,123	-3,097	-795	2,558	7,451
Exports	12,354	11,978	12,399	13,269	16,043	21,162	24,043	26,431	26,434	23,309	26,410	26,610
Imports	3,726	7,559	13,795	15,633	20,202	18,804	22,283	28,554	29,531	24,103	23,852	19,159
Net Services	-674	-1,599	-2,560	-3,329	-3,777	-3,417	-3,528	-4,365	-4,435	-4,106	-4,307	-4,094
Net Income	-4,400	-4,260	-2,473	-2,997	-3,697	-4,669	-5,502	-6,218	-7,406	-7,398	-7,372	-8,095
Net Transfers	998	793	769	521	463	553	446	463	406	397	241	183
Capital Account	n/a	n/a	16	16	18	14	51	94	73	86	87	101
Financial Account	-5,884	182	7,630	20,388	11,360	4,990	11,713	16,755	18,996	14,926	8,770	-13,590
Net Direct Investment	1,836	2,439	3,265	2,088	2,622	4,112	5,348	5,507	4,965	22,812	10,639	3,337
Net Portfolio Investment	-1,346	-34	4,767	33,706	8,357	1,852	9,717	10,096	8,788	-6,908	-2,392	-7,496
Net Government	-501	80	-1,396	-10,193	977	1,217	-89	222	2,035	-391	1,362	1,551
Net Other	-5,873	-2,303	994	-5,213	-596	-2,191	-3,263	930	3,209	-588	-839	-10,981
Net Errors and Omissions	715	-341	299	-10,282	-881	-2,140	-1,682	-1,276	-447	-1,098	-1,154	-3,361
Balance/Change in Official Reserves	-617	-806	2,286	1,954	-675	-2,311	3,258	3,331	4,090	2,013	-1,176	-21,405

Source: Casewriter, based on data from IMF, *International Financial Statistics CD-ROM*, July 2003 (data for 2002 not available).

Exhibit 4   Argentina's Fiscal Accounts, as a % of GDP

	1993	1994	1995	1996	1997	1998	1999	2000	2001
Primary Spending									
Provinces	11.3	11.3	11.3	10.8	10.8	11.3	12.3	11.9	12.0
Social Security	5.3	5.9	6.1	5.7	5.9	5.8	6.1	6.1	6.1
Rest of National Government (excluding transfers to provinces)	8.0	7.1	6.8	6.2	6.5	6.1	7.0	6.4	6.3
Total Primary Spending	24.6	24.3	24.2	22.7	23.2	23.2	25.4	24.4	24.4
Ordinary Revenues									
Provinces (excluding transfers from national government)	4.9	4.8	4.6	4.6	4.7	4.8	4.9	5.1	5.1
Social Security	5.6	5.5	5.3	3.8	4.2	4.0	3.8	3.8	3.5
Rest of National Government	15.5	14.1	13.7	13.5	14.5	14.8	15.8	16.0	15.2
Total Ordinary Revenues	26.0	24.4	23.6	21.9	23.4	23.6	24.5	24.9	23.8
Primary Balance									
Provinces (including transfers from national government)	-0.6	-0.8	-1.1	-0.4	-0.1	-0.4	-1.1	-0.5	-1.1
Social Security	0.3	-0.4	-0.8	-1.9	-1.7	-1.8	-2.3	-2.3	-2.6
Rest of National Government (including transfers to provinces)	1.7	1.3	1.3	1.5	2.0	2.6	2.5	3.3	3.1
Total Primary Balance	1.4	0.1	-0.6	-0.8	0.2	0.4	-0.9	0.5	-0.6
Debt Service	0.8	1.3	1.4	2.7	2.3	2.6	3.4	4.1	4.6
Overall Balance	**0.6**	**-1.2**	**-2.0**	**-3.5**	**-2.1**	**-2.2**	**-4.3**	**-3.6**	**-5.2**
Memo Item: Transfers to Provinces from National Government	*5.8*	*5.7*	*5.6*	*5.8*	*6.0*	*6.1*	*6.3*	*6.3*	*5.8*

Source: Adapted from Richard Hausmann and Andres Velasco, "Hard Money's Soft Underbelly: Understanding the Argentine Crisis," Kennedy School of Government, Harvard University, unpublished paper prepared for *Brookings Trade Forum*, July 2002, p. viii.

Exhibit 5   Argentina's Bank Deposit Flow

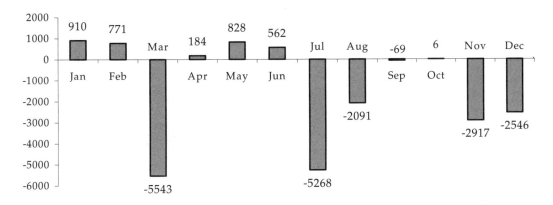

Bank Deposit Flow, 2001
(variation US$ millions)

Source: Created by casewriter based on data from Banco Central de la Republica de Argentina.

Exhibit 6   Deposit Flight by Type of Bank

	2001 Crisis			Tequila Crisis		
	Deposit outflows (millions)	Deposit outflows (as % total deposits)	Outflows as % Total Outflows	Deposit outflows (millions)	Deposit outflows (as % total deposits)	Outflows as % Total Outflows
National private	-5,665	-40%	29%	-3,415	-21%	52%
Foreign	-5,085	-17%	26%	111	1%	-2%
National public	-2,430	-18%	13%	-216	-3%	3%
Provincial public	-4,084	-31%	21%	-937	-8%	14%
Others	-2,171	-19%	11%	-2,075	-38%	32%
Total	**-19,434**	**-23%**	**100%**	**-6,532**	**-14%**	**100%**

Source: Created by casewriter based on data from Banco Central de la Republica de Argentina.

Exhibit 7   Financial Transactions between Argentina and the IMF

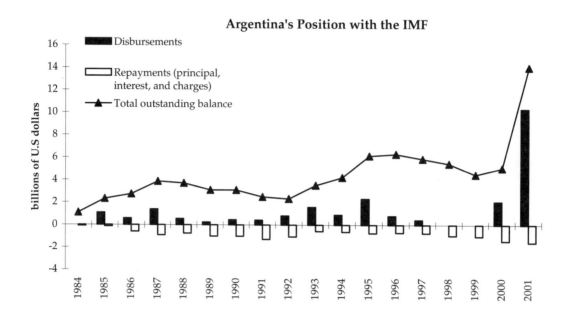

Source: Created by casewriter based on data from IMF, *International Financial Statistics CD-ROM*, July 2003.

Exhibit 8   Argentine Interest Rates on Loans to Prime Companies, 30-day Term, in Annual Nominal %

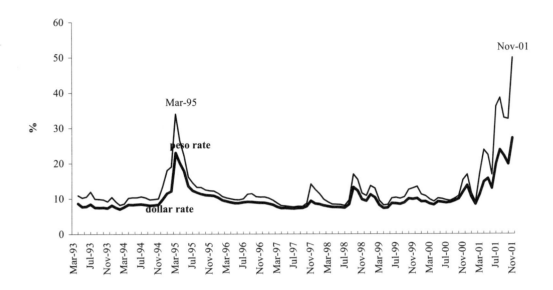

Source: Created by casewriter based on data from Banco Central de la Republica de Argentina, Monetary and Financial Department, August 2003.

Exhibit 9   J.P. Morgan Emerging Market Bond Indices (monthly average EMBI)

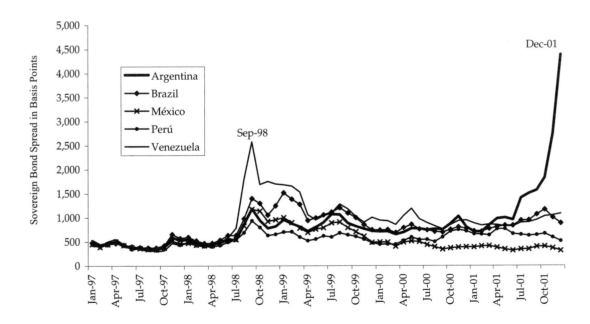

Source: Created by casewriter based on data from The Center for International Economics, <http://cei.mrecic.gov.ar/>, August 2003.

Note: The J.P. Morgan EMBI covers only Brady Bonds. One hundred basis points equals 1%.

Exhibit 10   Inflation Indicators in Argentina and the United States

	1990	1991	1992	1993	1994	1995	1996	1997	1998	1999	2000	2001
United States (1995=100)												
Producer Price Index	93.2	93.4	93.9	95.3	96.6	100.0	102.4	102.3	99.7	100.6	106.4	107.6
Consumer Price Index	85.7	89.4	92.1	94.8	97.3	100.0	102.9	105.3	107.0	109.3	113.0	116.2
Average Wage Index	87.5	90.2	92.5	94.9	97.3	100.0	103.3	107.3	111.7	115.7	120.3	124.8
Argentina (1995=100)												
Producer Price Index	40.7	85.6	90.7	92.2	92.8	100.0	103.7	102.6	99.2	95.2	98.7	96.7
Consumer Price Index	24.7	67.2	84.0	92.9	96.7	100.0	100.2	100.7	101.6	100.4	99.5	98.4
Average Wage Index	n.a.	59.8	79.0	89.6	95.0	100.0	106.1	107.6	108.9	108.3	109.2	104.7

Source: Created by casewriter based on data (for wages) from EIU Country Data, October 2003 and (for CPI and PPI) from International Monetary Fund, *International Financial Statistics CD-ROM*, August 2003.

Exhibit 11   Argentina's External Debt, as % of GDP

	Total External Debt	Consolidated Government Debt		
		Total	External	Domestic
1993	27.7	28.7	22.1	6.6
1994	29.6	30.9	23.5	7.4
1995	39.0	34.8	26.8	8.0
1996	41.8	36.6	27.3	9.3
1997	44.8	38.1	28.2	9.9
1998	48.6	41.3	30.5	10.8
1999	53.6	47.4	33.2	14.2
2000	54.0	51.0	33.9	17.1
2001	58.3	54.1	33.2	20.9

Source: Adapted from Perry and Serven, "The Anatomy of a Multiple Crisis," 2002, p. 47.

Endnotes

1   Based on interview with Fraga by casewriter and unpublished paper: Javier Gonzalez Fraga, "Convertibility and the Argentine Banking Crisis," November 2002.

2   Charles W. Calomiris and Andrew Powell, "Can Emerging Market Bank Regulators Establish Credible Discipline? The Case of Argentina 1992–1999," NBER Working Paper Number w7715, May 2000, p. 28.

3   Reuters, "Argentine EconMin Could Quit if Cuts Blocked," March 19, 2001.

4   See "Argentina's Financial System: The Case of Banco de Galicia," HBS No. 703-033.

5   Guillermo Perry and Luis Serven, "The Anatomy of a Multiple Crisis: Why Was Argentina Special and What Can We Learn From It," Latin America and Caribbean Regional Office, World Bank, May 10, 2002, p. 31. The same point is made in D. Rodrik, "Argentina: Globalization Gone Too Far or not Far Enough," Kennedy School of Government, Harvard University, January 2, 2002; and Independent Evaluation Office (IEO) of the IMF, "The Role of the IMF in Argentina, 1991–2002," July 2003, available at <http://www.inf.org/external/np/ieo/2003/org/>, accessed December 16, 2003.

6   Martin Feldstein, "Argentina's Fall: Lessons from the Latest Financial Crisis," *Foreign Affairs*, March/April 2002, p. 12.

7   Michael Mussa, *Argentina and the Fund: From Triumph to Tragedy* (Washington: Institute for International Economics, 2002), p. 10.

8   In addition to Mussa, *Argentina and the Fund*, see Miguel Braun and Luciano di Gresia, "Towards Effective Social Insurance in Latin America: The Importance of Countercyclical Fiscal Policy," Inter-American Development Bank, March 23, 2003, available at <http://www.iadb.org/res/publications/pubfiles/pubWP-487.pdf>, accessed December 16, 2003.

9   "A Decline Without Parallel," *The Economist*, February 28, 2002.

10 These arguments are from Mussa, *Argentina and the Fund*, pp. 16–17.

11 Guillermo Calvo and Carmen Reinart, "When Capital Inflows Come to a Sudden Stop: Consequences and Policy Options," in P. Kenen and A. Swoboda, *Key Issues in Reform of the International Monetary and Financial System* (Washington, DC: International Monetary Fund, 2000).

12 This relationship is described in Eaton, "Menem and the Governors," 2003. (For complete citation, see note 13.)

13 For more on this topic, see Mariano Tommasi and Pablo Spiller, *Las Fuentes Institucionales del Desarrollo Argentino* (Buenos Aires: Editorial Universidad de Buenos Aires, 2000). The quote comes from: Kent Eaton, "Menem and the Governors: Intergovernmental Relations in the 1990s," 2003, p. 2 of unpublished manuscript, forthcoming in Steve Levitsky and M. Victoria Murillo, eds., *Rethinking Dual Transitions: Argentine Politics in the 1990s in Comparative Perspective*, 2003, available at <http://www.wws.princeton.edu/keaton/> (accessed July 21, 2003) summarizing Karen Remmer and Eric Wibbels, "The Subnational Politics of Economic Adjustment: Provincial Politics and Fiscal Performance in Argentina," *Comparative Political Studies* 33 (4): 419–451.

14 The name of Cavallo's widely read article: Domingo Cavallo, "An Institutional Coup," April 19, 2002, presented at National Bureau of Economic Research conference *The Argentina Crisis*, July 17, 2002. The paper is available at <http://www.cavallo.com.ar/>, accessed July 21, 2003.

15 Ricardo Hausmann and Andres Velasco, "Hard Money's Soft Underbelly: Understanding the Argentine Crisis," Kennedy School of Government, Harvard University, unpublished paper prepared for *Brookings Trade Forum*, July 2002.

[16]   Hausmann and Velasco, "Hard Money's Soft Underbelly," 2002.

[17]   Domingo Cavallo, "The Fight to Avoid Default and Devaluation," unpublished paper, April 25, 2002, available at <http://www.cavallo.com.ar/>, accessed July 21, 2003.

[18]   Cavallo, "An Institutional Coup," 2002.

[19]   Ricardo Hausmann, "A Way Out for Argentina," *The Financial Times,* October 29, 2001.

[20]   John Barham, "Revenge of the Mad Intellectuals," *LatinFinance,* May 1, 2002.

[21]   Interview with Cavallo by casewriter.

[22]   Feldstein, "Argentina's Fall," 2002.

[23]   As described in Mussa, *Argentina and the Fund,* 2002.

[24]   Joseph Stiglitz, "Lessons From Argentina's Debacle," *Straits Times,* January 10, 2002.

[25]   Mussa, *Argentina and the Fund,* 2002, pp. 18–19.

[26]   Hausmann and Velasco, "Hard Money's Soft Underbelly," 2002, 9–12.

[27]   Mussa, *Argentina and the Fund,* 2002.

[28]   Martin Feldstein, "Argentina Doesn't Need the IMF," *The Wall Street Journal,* May 28, 2002.

[29]   Mussa, *Argentina and the Fund, 2002,* p. 24.

[30]   Barham, "Revenge of the Mad Intellectuals," 2002.

[31]   Jim Saxton (R-NJ), Vice Chairman of the Joint Economic Committee of the U.S. Congress, "Argentina's Economic Crisis: Causes and Cures," June 2003, p. 20.

[32]   Domingo Felipe Cavallo, "'Productivism' versus 'Neoliberalism,'" January 13, 2003, available at <http://www.cavallo.com.ar/Documentos/Productivism.PDF> (as of October 3, 2003).

[33]   Ed Bartholomew, "Two-Step Sovereign Debt Restructuring," J.P. Morgan document, April 24, 2002, available at <www.emta.org/keyper/barthol.pdf>, accessed July 21, 2003.

[34]   Sebastian Edwards, "A Simple Answer for Argentina: Follow Chile's Example," *The Wall Street Journal,* January 25, 2002.

[35]   Edwards, "A Simple Answer for Argentina," 2002.

[36]   Rudiger Dornbusch and Ricardo Caballero, "Argentina Cannot Be Trusted," *The Financial Times,* March 7, 2002.

RAFAEL DI TELLA
INGRID VOGEL

The 2001 Crisis in Argentina: An IMF-Sponsored Default? (B)

On January 2, 2002, Eduardo Duhalde was appointed president of Argentina amidst a severe economic, political, and social crisis. The country had endured more than two years of a worsening recession with no relief in sight: By the end of 2001, unemployment had risen beyond 20%, GDP had dropped substantially, bank deposits had fallen 20%, the Central Bank had lost almost half its foreign reserves, and the country was set to default on $141 billion in foreign debt outstanding in what would become the largest and most complicated sovereign default ever. In December 2001, to curb escalating capital flight, the government imposed controls on bank account deposits. These controls, known as the *"corralito,"*[a] combined with increasing social unrest and dire social conditions, infuriated Argentines who took to the streets in protest. After violent rioting in which more than 22 people died, a "state of siege" was declared. Days later, the entire government was forced to resign.

Duhalde, a Peronist who was serving as senator of Buenos Aires before his selection as interim president by Argentina's legislative assembly, faced the enormous challenge of reestablishing macroeconomic fundamentals and restoring confidence in Argentina's financial system. To this end, he faced a number of important decisions, including what to do with Argentina's decade-long peg to the U.S. dollar under the 1991 Convertibility Plan. While the Convertibility Plan had been credited with Argentina's impressive economic performance in the 1990s, the currency-board-like system it imposed was now a primary source of blame for Argentina's collapse.

With Duhalde well known for his anti-convertibility stance, it came as no surprise when he devalued and floated the peso within five days of taking office. His subsequent actions, however, were less expected. With 70% of bank deposits and 79% of loans denominated in dollars in Argentina, devaluation would mean bankruptcy for many debtors who were selling domestically. In February, Duhalde decreed, therefore, that dollars would be converted into pesos: Bank deposits at an exchange rate of 1.4 pesos per dollar, and bank loans at one peso per dollar. This asymmetric pesofication, combined with the freezing of bank term deposits (depositors had the option to convert their deposits into government bonds), became known as the *"corralon."*

---

[a] The *corralito* limited cash withdrawals from bank accounts to $1000 per month. It did not limit debit card and credit card payments and other transfers within Argentina.

Despite these extreme alterations to Argentina's economic model, however, recovery proved elusive. By April 2002, Argentina's financial system was near collapse as banking and foreign exchange activity was suspended, and Argentina's domestic banks required an expensive bailout. For example, Banco de Galicia, Argentina's largest domestically owned private bank, received 4 billion pesos from the Central Bank and an additional 600 million pesos in loans from other local and international banks and Argentina's deposit guarantee system.[1] As reported in *The Economist*, "When told by an economy ministry official that Duhalde would, as a last resort, lift restrictions on bank withdrawals and 'let happen whatever God wants,' one banker is said to have replied: 'the only problem is that even God wants dollars.'"[2]

Duhalde came to pin his hopes on an IMF rescue.[3] But the IMF was skeptical of his ability to implement needed reforms, and relations between Argentina and the Fund remained strained through a year of on-and-off negotiations. Finally, in January 2003, the Fund's board (against the advice of its senior staff) agreed to a transition loan that would cover payments due to the IMF through the next presidential elections in late April 2003.

During Duhalde's 16 months in office, Argentina had accumulated new domestic bonds totaling $28 billion. In reflecting on what else had happened in Argentina under his leadership, observers were left to question whether Duhalde had made the right decisions, especially during his first few weeks of office, or whether he had simply served to worsen Argentina's already damaged position.

Nestor Kirchner Takes Office

The election of May 2003 pitted former notorious Argentine Peronist President Carlos Saul Menem against another Peronist, Nestor Kirchner, previously the obscure governor of the sparsely populated province of Patagonia. Menem withdrew his candidacy after receiving only 24% of the vote, against Kirchner's 22%, in the first stage of the election. Polls showed that the runoff that should have taken place between the two would have led to a clear victory, with 70% of the votes for Kirchner, who had the backing of Duhalde. However, the official numbers would thereafter reflect Kirchner's poor performance, and it was worried that this would deny him the popular mandate necessary to effect change in the country.[4]

Kirchner took office amidst signs of growing poverty. In the middle of 2003, almost 60% of the population lived below the official poverty line, and the unemployment rate stood at 18% (excluding the almost two million participants in the Heads of Household program described below). Kirchner chose to maintain peaceful relations with the poorest sectors of society through welfare programs. A key aspect of these was a commitment to broad social subsidies, such as through continuation of Duhalde's Heads of Household program (*Plan Jefes y Jefas de Hogar*), which provided about US$45 per month to heads of households with dependents. In exchange, beneficiaries had to engage in a work or training activity, although charges of clientelism were often made.

In contrast, signs of economic recovery were promising (see **Exhibits 1** through **4**). After contracting 4% in 2001 and 11% in 2002, the Argentine economy was expected to grow 5% in 2003. Inflation was decreasing over the previous year, although there appeared to be a continued tendency for granting wage concessions (see **Exhibits 5** and **6**). The peso had appreciated over the first half of the year (see **Exhibit 7**), from a low of 3.8 pesos per U.S. dollar in June 2002, to 2.8 pesos per dollar at the end of April (see **Exhibit 8**). In addition, consumer confidence was rising, while the country risk premium was falling (see **Exhibit 9**).

Furthermore, Argentina's trade account was strengthening and the country was meeting IMF fiscal targets—thanks in part to a large tax on exports. As a result, Argentina was able to negotiate an interim loan agreement with the IMF that continued to roll over its multilateral debt despite failure to have met several qualitative economic commitments. The program also created a new loan installment of $320 million. A three-year package was expected to be agreed upon in August 2003.

Both the IMF and Argentina were under pressure to end the negotiations for the medium-term package successfully and speedily. With $77 billion in defaulted obligations (including arrears and interest) through the end of the year, Argentina required assistance to be able to offer its private creditors a credible restructuring plan.[5] The IMF needed to be sensitive to its reputation, as many outside observers were blaming the Fund at least in part for Argentina's economic collapse.

Kirchner's "Defeat" of the IMF

Worries of Kirchner serving as a weak and ineffectual leader quickly proved unfounded. Within weeks, he purged the army and police of 52 senior officers accused of human rights abuses during the country's 1976–1983 military dictatorship. He also planned to introduce stricter controls over the notoriously corrupt pension system. Furthermore, he campaigned to reform the Supreme Court, which was packed with judges loyal to Menem. Ultimately, this resulted in the resignation of the court's president.

With Argentina facing poverty rates in excess of 50% and high, albeit decreasing, unemployment levels, Kirchner promised in his inaugural address that his government would not make debt repayments "at the price of the hunger and exclusion of Argentines."[6] To that end, he took a hard line in his negotiations with the IMF. Building on popular sentiment, Kirchner blamed the 1999 IMF-backed austerity plan and 10 years of "very bad advice" for pushing the country into four years of recession. He told IMF Managing Director Horst Kohler outright: "You are greatly responsible for what happened in Argentina."[7]

The two sides argued for months, with Kirchner remaining firm in refusing to agree to any terms that he thought would weaken his country's incipient recovery. Finally, on September 9, 2003, Argentina, with seemingly little to lose, defaulted on a $2.9 billion payment due to the IMF—representing the largest non-payment of a loan in the Fund's history. The next day, the IMF was forced to concede to a three-year deal at favorable terms to Argentina. Under the terms of the agreement, $21 billion-worth of debt would be refinanced with multilateral lenders, of which $12.3 billion was with the IMF. In actuality, it was expected that the IMF would continue to roll over Argentina's debt through 2013.[8] At the same time, the IMF agreed to accept a 3% primary fiscal surplus (it had originally demanded 3.5%) and to drop demands for tariff increases at the country's utilities. The agreement left Argentina open to begin debt-restructuring negotiations with its private creditors.

The "Haircut"

Emboldened by his success with the IMF, Kirchner declared, to cheering crowds, that private bondholders "could not be paid back in full while half of his country's people live in abject poverty."[9] He remained true to this populist rhetoric as Argentina achieved yet another macroeconomic world record. On September 22, it announced a negotiating position with its private creditors that would involve at least a 75% reduction in the value of defaulted sovereign debt, plus likely reductions in interest rates on the new bonds. Facing the most severe "haircut" ever in the largest debt restructuring ever, bondholders were furious and threatened to reject the offer despite Argentina's firm stance. In contrast, the IMF ended up with just a small "haircut" as a result of extending the maturity on payments due.

Appendix

Timeline of Key Events in Argentina, December 1999–October 2003

December 10, 1999	Fernando De La Rua, leader of a center-left coalition, becomes Argentina's president on a platform of ending corruption and maintaining free-market reforms and convertibility.
January 2000	Taxes are raised in what becomes known as the *Impuestazo*.
May 29, 2000	Argentina announces $1 billion in spending cuts. Two days later, 20,000 protesters take to the streets against the cuts.
October, 2000	De La Rua's vice president resigns after a corruption scandal, significantly weakening the coalition.
December 18, 2000	Government announces $40 billion aid package (the *Blindaje*), largely secured by the IMF. Markets react with a strong rally.
March 2, 2001	Machinea resigns as economy minister. Ricardo Lopez Murphy succeeds him and two weeks later unveils a tough $4.5 billion two-year austerity program with severe cuts in education. Six officials from the left-leaning faction of the coalition resign in protest to the cuts.
March 20, 2001	De La Rua appoints Cavallo to replace Lopez Murphy.
March 21, 2001	Cavallo unveils his Competitiveness Plans.
April 17, 2001	Cavallo sends a bill to Congress that would eventually tie the peso to a 50-50 average of euro and dollar, once the euro reached parity with the dollar.
April 25, 2001	Argentine Central Bank President Pou is charged in a money-laundering scheme. He resigns, citing pressure from government officials to improve banking sector liquidity.
June 3, 2001	Argentina swaps $30 billion of debt (the *Megacanje*), which defers debt service costs of around $8 billion through 2002 and by a total of $16 billion by the end of 2005.
June 15, 2001	Argentina announces a new exchange rate system for exports at 1.08 pesos to one dollar.
July 3, 2001	Argentine stocks fall to 28-month low after rumors of the resignation of De La Rua.
July 30, 2001	The government's key austerity bill is passed. The "zero deficit" law aims to end deficit spending and slash state salaries and some pensions by up to 13%.
August 21, 2001	IMF Managing Director Horst Koehler agrees to recommend an $8 billion increase in Argentina's stand-by loan agreement with the IMF.
November, 2001	A new debt swap is poorly received by markets.
December 1, 2001	Cavallo announces restrictions on bank account withdrawals. Known as the *corralito*, the measures include a monthly limit of $1000 on cash withdrawals and caps on offshore transfers.
December 5, 2001	IMF announces it will suspend disbursements to Argentina.
December 6, 2001	Cavallo says fixed-term deposits held in banks by private pension funds will be transformed into treasury bonds or government-guaranteed loans.
December 13, 2001	Government says jobless rate rose to 18.3% in October, the highest since the start of the recession in mid-1998. Major unions call nationwide strike.
December 17, 2001	Government presents 2002 budget, which includes spending cuts of nearly 20%.
December 18, 2001	IMF says Argentina can delay payment on loan of about $1 billion due in January, but also says Argentina's economic policy is unsustainable.
December 19, 2001	Government declares state of siege giving it special powers to stop the worst looting and riots in a decade. The lower house of Congress repeals special powers granted to Cavallo.
December 20, 2001	Cavallo resigns and the rest of the cabinet tender their resignations.
December 21, 2001	De La Rua resigns after thousands take to the streets of the capital to protest the government's handling of the country's worsening economic crisis. At least 22 people are killed in riots and looting around the country.
December 23, 2001	Adolfo Rodriguez Saa becomes president of Argentina. Announces default of debt. Resigns on December 28, citing pressure from elements of the Buenos Aires Peronist party.
January 2, 2002	Eduardo Duhalde, strongman of the Buenos Aires Peronist party, sworn into office.
January 7, 2002	Peso devalued and convertibility to be suspended January 9, 2002.
February 3, 2002	*Corralon* announced: Dollar-denominated bank deposits and loans converted to pesos at asymmetric rate (1.4 pesos per dollar for deposits, 1.0 pesos per dollar for loans); bank term deposits frozen.
December 2, 2002	Some provisions of the *corralito* are rescinded.
May 25, 2003	Nestor Kirchner elected president. Economy shows some signs of improvement.
September 9, 2003	Argentina defaults on $2.9 billion payment to the IMF, in the largest non-repayment of an IMF loan ever.
September 10, 2003	IMF agrees to three-year loan package with Argentina, at favorable terms for the country.
September 22, 2003	Argentina announces 75% reduction in principal in starting position for debt restructuring.

Exhibit 1a　Argentine General Economic Indicators

Units as shown	1990	1991	1992	1993	1994	1995	1996	1997	1998	1999	2000	2001	2002
Real GDP Growth (% change pa)	-3.0	12.2	11.3	6.7	5.8	-2.8	5.5	8.1	3.9	-3.4	-0.8	-4.5	-10.9
Real Per Capita GDP Growth (% change pa)	-4.3	10.7	9.9	5.4	4.4	-4.0	4.3	6.8	2.6	-4.5	-1.9	-5.5	-11.9
Consumer Price Inflation (% change to year-end)	1343.9	84.0	17.5	7.4	3.9	1.6	0.1	0.3	0.7	-1.8	-0.7	-1.5	41.0
Stockmarket Index (% change pa, $ value)	n/a	n/a	-46.0	35.3	-21.0	12.8	25.2	5.9	-37.4	28.0	-24.3	-29.1	-46.5
Average Nominal Wages (% change pa)	n/a	n/a	32.2	13.4	6.0	5.3	6.1	1.4	1.2	-0.5	0.8	-4.1	2.0
M1 Growth (% change pa)	n/a	148.6	49.0	33.0	8.2	1.6	14.6	12.8	0.0	1.6	-9.2	-20.1	78.6

Units as shown	1990	1991	1992	1993	1994	1995	1996	1997	1998	1999	2000	2001	2002
Nominal Ex. Rate (pesos per dollar period end)	0.6	1.0	1.0	1.0	1.0	1.0	1.0	1.0	1.0	1.0	1.0	1.0	3.3
Real Ex. Rate (increase = appreciation, 1997=100)	59.8	82.7	95.2	104.2	104.2	98.6	97.3	100.0	103.5	108.7	109.3	113.3	46.8
Unemployment (%)	7.5	7.5	7.5	8.8	10.5	15.5	15.5	13.9	11.8	13.0	14.6	16.4	18.8
International Reserves (current $ bns, year-end)	6.0	7.4	11.4	15.5	16.0	16.0	19.7	22.4	24.9	26.4	25.2	14.6	10.5
Foreign Debt (current $ bns, year-end)	62.2	65.4	68.3	64.7	75.1	98.8	111.4	128.4	141.5	145.3	145.9	136.7	127.4

Source:　Casewriter, based on data from EIU Country Data, August 2003.

Exhibit 1c　Argentine Monthly Industrial Production Index (seasonally adjusted)

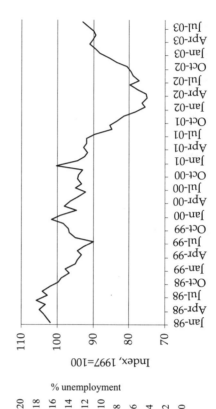

Source:　Casewriter, based on data from National Institute of Statistics and Census Data, <http://www.indec.gov.ar>, accessed October 2003.

Exhibit 1b　Real GDP Growth and Unemployment

Source:　Casewriter, based on data from EIU Country Data, August 2003.

Exhibit 2   Argentine National Income Accounts (billions of constant 1996 U.S. dollars)

	1990	1991	1992	1993	1994	1995	1996	1997	1998	1999	2000	2001	2002
Gross Domestic Product	**188.1**	**211.1**	**235.0**	**250.9**	**265.5**	**258.0**	**272.2**	**294.3**	**305.7**	**295.3**	**293.0**	**280.1**	**249.6**
Household Consumption	121.8	142.4	164.8	174.3	184.9	176.8	186.6	203.3	210.4	206.2	204.8	193.0	165.3
Government Consumption	31.2	32.6	32.2	32.9	33.1	33.3	34.0	35.1	36.3	37.3	37.5	36.7	34.8
Gross Fixed Investment	23.4	30.4	40.3	48.0	54.1	47.2	53.4	62.3	65.3	54.3	52.2	46.0	28.7
Exports	18.7	18.0	17.8	18.7	21.5	26.4	28.4	31.8	35.2	34.8	35.7	36.7	37.8
Imports	6.9	12.3	20.4	23.5	28.5	25.7	30.2	38.3	41.5	36.8	36.8	31.6	15.8
Nominal GDP (current $ bns)	141.4	189.7	229.0	236.8	257.7	258.1	272.2	293.0	299.1	283.7	284.3	268.8	102.0

Source: Casewriter, based on data from EIU Country Data, August 2003.

Note: GDP does not equal sum of components because of rebasing to 1996, which alters the relative importance of individual components.

Exhibit 3   Argentine Balance of Payments (millions of current U.S. dollars)

	1990	1991	1992	1993	1994	1995	1996	1997	1998	1999	2000	2001
Current Account	4,552	-647	-5,660	-8,169	-11,171	-5,175	-6,825	-12,243	-14,532	-11,902	-8,879	-4,554
Trade Balance	8,628	4,419	-1,396	-2,364	-4,160	2,357	1,760	-2,123	-3,097	-795	2,558	7,451
Exports	12,354	11,978	12,399	13,269	16,043	21,162	24,043	26,431	26,434	23,309	26,410	26,610
Imports	3,726	7,559	13,795	15,633	20,202	18,804	22,283	28,554	29,531	24,103	23,852	19,159
Net Services	-674	-1,599	-2,560	-3,329	-3,777	-3,417	-3,528	-4,365	-4,435	-4,106	-4,307	-4,094
Net Income	-4,400	-4,260	-2,473	-2,997	-3,697	-4,669	-5,502	-6,218	-7,406	-7,398	-7,372	-8,095
Net Transfers	998	793	769	521	463	553	446	463	406	397	241	183
Capital Account	n/a	n/a	n/a	16	16	18	14	51	94	73	86	101
Financial Account	-5,884	1,836	7,630	20,388	11,360	4,990	11,713	16,755	18,996	14,926	8,770	-13,590
Net Direct Investment	1,836	2,439	3,265	2,088	2,622	4,112	5,348	5,507	4,965	22,812	10,639	3,337
Net Portfolio Investment	-1,346	-34	4,767	33,706	8,357	1,852	9,717	10,096	8,788	-6,908	-2,392	-7,496
Net Government	-501	80	-1,396	-10,193	977	1,217	-89	222	2,035	-391	1,362	1,551
Net Other	-5,873	-2,303	994	-5,213	-596	-2,191	-3,263	930	3,209	-588	-839	-10,981
Net Errors and Omissions	715	-341	299	-10,282	-881	-2,140	-1,682	-1,276	-447	-1,098	-1,154	-3,361
Balance/Change in Official Reserves	-617	-806	2,286	1,954	-675	-2,311	3,258	3,331	4,090	2,013	-1,176	-21,405

Source: Casewriter, based on data from IMF, *International Financial Statistics CD-ROM*, July 2003 (data for 2002 not available).

Exhibit 4   Argentina's Fiscal Accounts, as a % of GDP

	1993	1994	1995	1996	1997	1998	1999	2000	2001
Primary Spending									
Provinces	11.3	11.3	11.3	10.8	10.8	11.3	12.3	11.9	12.0
Social Security	5.3	5.9	6.1	5.7	5.9	5.8	6.1	6.1	6.1
Rest of National Government (excluding transfers to provinces)	8.0	7.1	6.8	6.2	6.5	6.1	7.0	6.4	6.3
Total Primary Spending	24.6	24.3	24.2	22.7	23.2	23.2	25.4	24.4	24.4
Ordinary Revenues									
Provinces (excluding transfers from national government)	4.9	4.8	4.6	4.6	4.7	4.8	4.9	5.1	5.1
Social Security	5.6	5.5	5.3	3.8	4.2	4.0	3.8	3.8	3.5
Rest of National Government	15.5	14.1	13.7	13.5	14.5	14.8	15.8	16.0	15.2
Total Ordinary Revenues	26.0	24.4	23.6	21.9	23.4	23.6	24.5	24.9	23.8
Primary Balance									
Provinces (including transfers from national government)	-0.6	-0.8	-1.1	-0.4	-0.1	-0.4	-1.1	-0.5	-1.1
Social Security	0.3	-0.4	-0.8	-1.9	-1.7	-1.8	-2.3	-2.3	-2.6
Rest of National Government (including transfers to provinces)	1.7	1.3	1.3	1.5	2.0	2.6	2.5	3.3	3.1
Total Primary Balance	1.4	0.1	-0.6	-0.8	0.2	0.4	-0.9	0.5	-0.6
Debt Service	0.8	1.3	1.4	2.7	2.3	2.6	3.4	4.1	4.6
Overall Balance	**0.6**	**-1.2**	**-2.0**	**-3.5**	**-2.1**	**-2.2**	**-4.3**	**-3.6**	**-5.2**
Memo Item: Transfers to Provinces from National Government	*5.8*	*5.7*	*5.6*	*5.8*	*6.0*	*6.1*	*6.3*	*6.3*	*5.8*

Source: Adapted from Richard Hausmann and Andres Velasco, "Hard Money's Soft Underbelly: Understanding the Argentine Crisis," Kennedy School of Government, Harvard University, unpublished paper prepared for *Brookings Trade Forum*, July 2002, p. viii.

Exhibit 5 Argentine Monthly Inflation

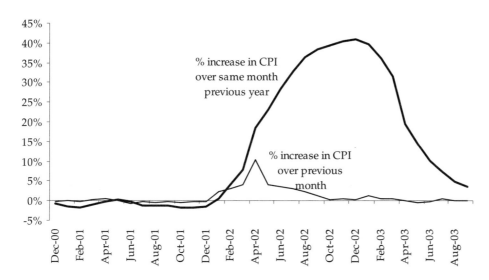

Source: Casewriter, based on data from National Institute of Statistics and Census Data, <http://www.indec.gov.ar>, accessed October 2003.

Exhibit 6 Argentine Nominal Monthly Wage Increases

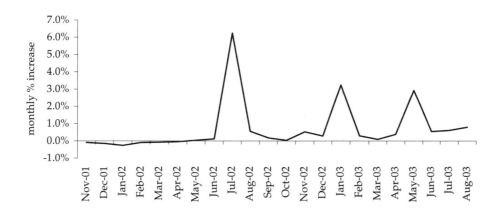

Source: Casewriter, based on data from National Institute of Statistics and Census Data, <http://www.indec.gov.ar>, accessed October 2003.

Exhibit 7   Argentine Monthly Multilateral Real Exchange Rate

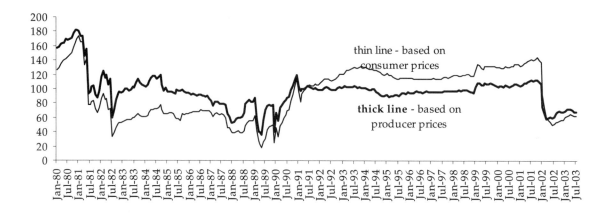

Multilateral Real Exchange Rate (1991=100)
(increase implies appreciation)

Source: Casewriter, based on data from The Center for International Economics, <http://cei.mrecic.gov.ar>, accessed August 2003.

Exhibit 8   Weekly Exchange Rate

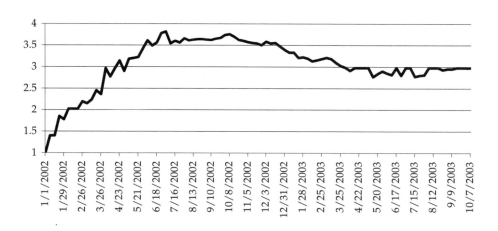

Argentine pesos per U.S. dollar, end of period

Source: Casewriter, based on data from Oanda.com.

Exhibit 9   J.P. Morgan Emerging Market Bond Indices (monthly average EMBI)

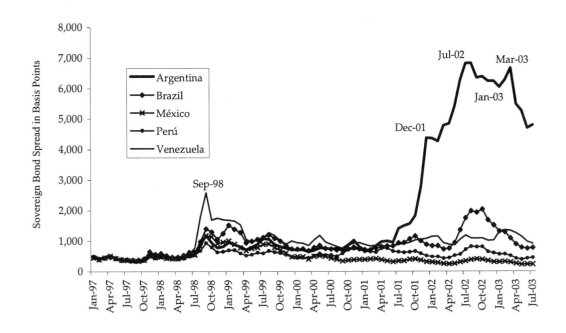

Source: Casewriter, based on data from The Center for International Economics, <http://cei.mrecic.gov.ar>, accessed
October 2003.

Note: The J.P. Morgan EMBI covers only Brady Bonds. One hundred basis points equals 1%.

Endnotes

1   Economist Intelligence Unit, "Country Finance, Argentina," August 31, 2002.

2   "Return to the Dark Ages," *The Economist*, April 25, 2002.

3   "Return to the Dark Ages," *The Economist*, April 25, 2002.

4   "Out of Patagonia," *The Economist*, May 24, 2003.

5   Adam Thomson, "IMF Deal 'Vital to Argentina's Future,'" *The Financial Times*, July 9, 2003.

6   "The Talking Begins," *The Economist*, August 9, 2003.

7   "First Blows," *The Economist*, July 5, 2003.

8   Alan Beattie, "Argentina Offer Dismays its Private Creditors," *The Financial Times*, September 23, 2003.

9   Tony Smith, "Holders of Argentine Bonds Reject 25% Redemption Offer," *The New York Times*, September 23, 2003.

Bolivia: Globalization, Sovereignty, or Democracy?

In the mid-1980s, Bolivia entered a hyperinflation as the institutional, economic, and social fabric of the country was placed under increasing strain by the burdens of the 1980s international debt crisis.

Finance Minister Gonzalo Sànchez de Lozada, in association with Harvard Professor Jeffrey Sachs, designed and implemented an "orthodox" stabilization plan in early 1986, which reduced inflation dramatically.

In the aftermath of the macroeconomic stabilization, Bolivia's growth resumed. But by the mid-1990s, some problems were beginning to reemerge. In particular, the largely disenfranchised, rural indigenous population clamored for greater influence and economic status.

Study Questions

1. How did the Lozada/Sachs plan work? Why was it successful while previous attempts to eliminate inflation had not been?
2. What role did political factors play in the stabilization? Were these unique to the time and place?
3. Can Bolivia be a participant in the global economy (and, in particular, the global financial market) and remain a full democracy? Do the political rights of the poor, rural, indigenous population have to be suppressed if Bolivia is to be able to access these international markets?

RAFAEL DI TELLA
HUW PILL

Bolivia: Globalization, Sovereignty, or Democracy?

Bolivia before we stabilized the economy was a poor country with hyperinflation; Bolivia after we stabilized the economy is a poor country with stability.

— Gonzalo Sánchez de Lozada, primary architect of Bolivia's
"shock therapy" program to end hyperinflation in 1985[1]

On June 30, 2002 Bolivia held elections for its 121st president. The race was incredibly close. After more than a week of tallying votes, it was determined that the top three candidates received 22.46%, 20.94%, and 20.91% of the popular vote, respectively. By law, it was up to Bolivia's congress to select the next president from the top two candidates, since there was no winner of the majority.

One of the candidates, Gonzalo Sánchez de Lozada, with a plurality of the popular vote, had a strong international reputation. He had served as president from 1993–1997 and was the owner of the country's largest mining company. Evo Morales, with second most votes, was a controversial figure. Of indigenous Quechua and Aymara descent, he was the leader of the powerful Bolivian coca-growers union fighting the U.S.-backed effort to eradicate coca crops, some of which were used to make cocaine. Morales campaigned on a platform to bring coca leaf production back to Bolivia and to roll back previously implemented market-based economic policies. As an ardent defender of farmers' human rights, he had been nominated for the Nobel Peace Prize in 1995. Retired Army Captain Manfred Reyes Villa missed the consideration of congress to become Bolivia's president by just 0.03% of the vote.

Sánchez de Lozada ultimately prevailed in congress by forming an alliance with a rival party. The government coalition faced the difficult task of addressing Bolivia's faltering economy. Sánchez de Lozada was no stranger to tough economic reform: The new president was well known in Bolivia as one of the chief architects of Bolivia's successful shock-therapy economic stabilization program of 1985 that had relied on aggressive pro-market reform. This plan had halted hyperinflation and brought about immediate improvement in Bolivia's GDP growth, inflation, and fiscal deficit.

The effects of the stabilization on Bolivia's poor, however, had been less favorable. Unemployment had risen and many felt that social services had suffered. Beginning in 1990, the country experienced constant labor protests, which escalated in the new millennium. Many segments of Bolivian society, including miners, teachers, pensioners, coca-growers, and members of the middle class, became active in displaying their dissatisfaction with government policy.

Cinthia Fernholz Violand (MBA '02), Miguel López de Silanes Gómez (MBA '02), and Research Associate Ingrid Vogel prepared this case under the supervision of Professors Rafael Di Tella and Huw Pill. This case was developed from published sources. HBS cases are developed solely as the basis for class discussion. Cases are not intended to serve as endorsements, sources of primary data, or illustrations of effective or ineffective management.

In early 2003, when President Sánchez de Lozada agreed to cut government spending and raise income taxes in return for IMF support, protests escalated into full-scale riots. Many Bolivians feared another wave of aggressive pro-market reform to the detriment of the needs of the poor and unemployed. On February 12, in what was considered to be the worst display of civil disorder for more than 50 years, protestors, including large numbers of armed police, faced the military in front of the presidential palace and burned down numerous public buildings. Sánchez de Lozada was smuggled out of his bullet-ridden residence in an ambulance. The confrontation left at least 27 dead and more than 100 injured. One week later, President Sánchez de Lozada's entire cabinet resigned.

The situation left many observers debating whether market-oriented policies could ever produce real improvements in living conditions for the region's average citizens. More generally, they questioned whether a stable, internationally integrated economy could ever coexist with democracy in a sovereign developing nation.

Country Profile

The Republic of Bolivia is located in the heart of South America. Surrounded by five nations, this landlocked country is characterized by a diversity of topography and climate. The arid and cold western part of the country, delineated by the Andes Mountains, is rich in minerals. The middle of the country is comprised of valley formations and offers fertile agricultural land. The eastern lowlands, formed by the Amazon basin, are semi-tropical with petroleum and natural gas reserves (see **Exhibit 1** for a map of Bolivia). Although exploitation of the country's ample mineral and hydrocarbon resources was traditionally dominated by public enterprises, by 2001 private sector participation was encouraged and rapidly increasing.[2]

Social Organization

By the turn of the millennium, Bolivia had an estimated population of 8.3 million (see **Exhibit 2**), including approximately 6 million indigenous people, 2 million people of mixed descent, and a remainder of European or other foreign origin.[3] The country's three official languages were Quechua, Aymara, and Spanish. While Quechua and Aymara were the first language of 34% and 24% of the population, respectively, Spanish was spoken by more than 80% of Bolivians.[4]

In 2001, social indicators such as infant mortality, life expectancy, and literacy identified Bolivia as one of the poorest and most unequal nations of Latin America (see **Exhibit 6**). Bolivia's income distribution also pointed to enormous inequality, with the upper 20% of the population in control of more than 60% of the country's total earnings, versus the bottom 20% with less than 2%.[a][5] Official estimations classified approximately 60% of the population as living in poverty, including 52% of the urban population and 82% of the rural population.[6] Other sources identified 90% of Bolivians as living near or below the poverty line.[7] As the rural poor moved to the cities in search of better conditions, the urban population was rising rapidly, from just over 30% of the total in the late 1960s to over 60% in the late 1990s.[8] Bolivia remained one of the most sparsely populated countries of Latin America.

---

[a] In 1997, the Gini coefficient for the country was 58.9. The Gini index measures inequality in the distribution of income. A value of zero represents perfect equality and a value of 100 perfect inequality. For Latin America and the Caribbean, the range is from 35 to 60. (Source: Human Development Index, United Nations Development Report, 2001.)

Bolivia's society seemed to be divided along clear class lines. The majority of the indigenous population belonged to the lower classes, a middle class living on modest means comprised less than 10% of the population, and a small number of European descendants formed a technocratic elite largely in control of Bolivia's business and government. Only one of Bolivia's 20 active political parties was headed by an indigenous leader at the turn of the millennium. Class mobility had always been difficult but was being addressed slowly through the expansion of government jobs, the opening of free universities, and the growth of the commercial sector.

Historical Overview

Bolivia was home to one of the first great Andean empires. The Tiahuanacan civilization emerged in 600 BC, spread across the southern end of Lake Titicaca, and developed advanced agricultural and architectural techniques before it collapsed around 1200 A.D. Subsequently, the northern highlands (or the *Altiplano*) came to be dominated by the Aymara tribes until the Quechuas established the Inca Empire in the early part of the 15th century. The Incas spread the Quechua language and culture across Bolivia until the Spanish conquest in 1532.

Colonial Rule and the Formation of a Modern State

The legacy of 300 years of Spanish rule left an imprint on the political, economic, and social spheres of the country. Bolivian silver mines produced much of the Spanish empire's wealth. Using forced indigenous labor, entrepreneurs extracted the minerals and shipped them to Spain in accordance with prevailing mercantilist practices. Potosi, site of the famed *Cerro Rico* (Rich Mountain), was the largest silver mine in the world and the largest city in the Western Hemisphere for many years.

Independence from Spain was finally proclaimed in 1809. But 16 years of struggle followed before the establishment of the republic, named after its Venezuelan liberator, Simón Bolívar, on August 6, 1825. The country's first 60 years encompassed a period of political instability, characterized by rivalries among *caudillos* (local war lords) that resulted in numerous coups and countercoups and short-lived constitutions.

Bolivia lost access to the sea during the War of the Pacific (1879–1880). The effect on the country was profound. United by their anger over the Chilean aggression, Bolivians developed a "national soul" for the first time in the country's history. They empowered the government to act as a guarantor of territorial integrity, and erratic *caudillo* rule was replaced with a relatively stable civilian government. At the same time, an increase in the world price of silver and the growth of commercial agriculture, rubber production, and tin extraction helped improve the economy. Both the Conservative and Liberal parties were primarily interested in further development of the mining sector as well as in political modernization. A succession of governments controlled by the economic and social elites followed laissez-faire capitalist policies. Bolivia experienced almost 50 years of political stability and relative economic prosperity.

Stability ended in 1920, however, with the collapse of the international tin market (see **Exhibit 7**) and, later, the onset of the Great Depression. Amid social unrest, the Republican Party rose to power, fragmenting the political system. In 1930, the first military junta took over (albeit for a short period) due to the popular belief that the civilian government would fail to bring the country out of its depression.

Although civilian rule was soon reestablished, Bolivia's situation deteriorated following its devastating defeat by Paraguay in the Chaco War (1932–1935). The loss discredited the traditional leadership and brought back military rule. From 1936–1939, military governments tried to reform the country with a program of "military socialism" that involved a blend of authoritarian and socially progressive measures. In 1937, the hydrocarbon industry was nationalized and the concessions of Standard Oil of New Jersey were taken over—the first of such steps taken in Latin America. The government also facilitated the formation of a number of new parties that agreed on the need to limit the power of the tin magnates.

In the 1940s, the middle class became increasingly frustrated with the government's inability to address economic stagnation and increasing inflation. In response, a number of new political parties with strikingly different ideological outlooks gained control of Congress. The most important of these was the radical leftist group called the Nationalist Revolutionary Movement (MNR). The MNR was remarkable in the country's history in that it was the first party with both blue- and white-collar workers as members. It emphasized social spending, which helped the party build ties with the country's large number of miners.

The Bolivian National Revolution, 1952–1964

In the late 1940s, Bolivia's economic situation deteriorated severely with high social spending and low tin and other export prices. The weak economy combined with low taxes for the upper class drove even ordinary people to revolt against the government. A bloodless transformation, dubbed the "Bolivian National Revolution," followed and was a turning point in the country's history. The MNR, which came to power with the support of the miners, *campesinos* (peasants), and other leftist groups, undertook a wide set of reforms under the leadership of Víctor Paz Estenssoro. These included the nationalization of the mining sector, the abolishment of forced labor, the distribution of land to the *campesinos* under far-reaching agrarian reform, and the adoption of universal suffrage without literacy or property requirements—an action that increased the electorate from some 200,000 to 1 million voters.[9]

One of the cornerstones of the Bolivian National Revolution was the inclusion of the middle and lower classes in the political system. Two notable changes occurred: first, the miners' organization, *Central Obrera Boliviana* (COB) was formed, which in the years to come would demand participation in the government and significant benefits for its members; and second, the Ministry of Peasant Affairs was created to support the rights of the *campesinos*. The *campesinos* would remain a powerful political force in Bolivia during subsequent governments.[10]

On the economic front, the Bolivian National Revolution marked the beginning of the state as the dominant force in the economy under a "statist system." From 1952–1964, the government was in the hands of populist parties that placed an emphasis on the role of labor unions and pushed for higher wages and a larger role for public sector workers. Similar to other Latin American countries during this period, this shift towards populism proved to be decisive in the transformation of the state.

Military Rule, 1964–1982

In the early 1960s, the Revolution lost momentum as conflicts and corruption emerged within the MNR and as Paz Estenssoro's policies lost their populist flavor. In 1964, a military coup led by his vice-presidential running mate, General René Barrientos Ortuño, ended civilian rule and further expanded the statist system. Through tariff protection and state investment, the military government encouraged the development of local industry, diversification into agriculture, and the continuation of mineral exports.[11]

By 1971, upheaval in the military leadership led reformists to support the more radical General Hugo Banzer Suarez. Ironically, Banzer's major support came from an alliance of the MNR under Paz Estenssoro with one of the most radical right-wing parties, the *Falange Socialista Boliviana* (FSB).[a] Under Banzer, Bolivia experienced an economic boom, fueling high government spending. Foreign inward investment increased, particularly in large infrastructure projects, as an abundance of international loans at attractive rates became available. In addition, exports tripled with increased production of petroleum, natural gas, tin, and cotton.

In 1976, however, the economic boom proved to be precariously built. Bolivia's economy faltered with the fall in the prices of oil and cotton. Banzer's regime came under attack and became increasingly repressive, especially toward the left. In 1978, growing national discontent combined with increased pressure from U.S. President Jimmy Carter forced Banzer to call for presidential elections. But the results were annulled due to widespread fraud, and Banzer's handpicked candidate General Juan Pereda Asbun carried out yet another coup.

Transition to Democracy, 1978–1982

Between 1978 and 1982, Bolivia endured five different military regimes and one interim civilian government, marking a period of increased unrest in the country.[12] The *campesinos* began to organize large-scale demonstrations for the first time since their rebellion in the late colonial period. At the same time, workers initiated general strikes. In 1980, national elections were finally held. After leftist party leader Hernán Siles-Suazo won 38% of the popular vote, Congress was expected to name him president. But only in late 1982, after a general strike brought the country close to civil war, did the military finally step down and allow Siles-Suazo to assume the presidency.

Hyperinflation and Economic Crisis, 1982–1985

Siles-Suazo was confronted with a difficult political environment and a turbulent economic situation. First, the value of Bolivia's exports decreased with another fall in international commodity prices and an overvalued exchange rate, reducing Bolivia's tax revenues. At the same time, the government faced pressure from various constituencies and was unable to reduce fiscal spending. Second, international interest rates soared in response to the Latin American debt crisis that began in 1982 when Mexico declared that it would no longer be able to service its debt. The capacity of the Siles-Suazo regime to repay its total external debt—which stood at 81% of GDP at the end of 1981[13]— came into question. International lending ceased and the government resorted to printing money to cover the expanding fiscal deficit.

---

[a] The MNR and the FSB had been enemies for almost three decades. FSB members were persecuted during the revolution of 1952 and later during Paz Estenssoro's second term in office. The chaotic regime of General Torres, who preceded Banzer, gave them a chance for political comeback in league with conservative elements in the armed forces.

Seignorage
(per quarter, as a percentange of annual GDP)

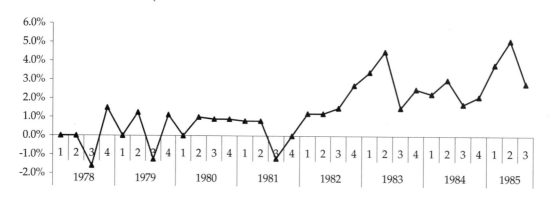

Source: Created by casewriter based on data from International Monetary Fund, *International Financial Statistics Yearbook*, 2002.

This monetary expansion led to accelerating inflation and peso depreciation (see **Exhibit 8**). Inflation was further fed by the increase in import prices and newly implemented wage indexation policies insisted on by the powerful labor unions.[14] In February 1985, inflation reached a record monthly level of 180%. For the 12 months prior to September 1985, inflation was an astonishing 27,000%.[a] Economic agents sought to protect the dollar value of their goods and assets by adjusting prices according to movements in the parallel black market exchange rate. Bolivia's hyperinflationary experience[b] during this period had no counterpart in the history of any other nation, as, for the first time, a hyperinflationary period did not occur as a result of a war or extended social conflict.

Spiraling inflation had a devastating impact. Real income in urban areas dropped by 60% between 1980 and 1985. The poor suffered most, while the wealthy were able to protect the value of their incomes and assets from inflation through speculative dealing, land ownership, and foreign bank accounts. In fact, the share of total urban income accounted for by the wealthiest five percent of the population doubled over the period.

---

[a] In August 1985, for example, a loaf of bread, which cost one peso a year before, was priced at approximately 500,000 pesos. In order to pay, people had to carry around carts with paper money. Necessities became scarce as shopkeepers hoarded their goods expecting higher and higher prices.

[b] A hyperinflationary period is defined as more than two consecutive months in which the inflation rate is higher than 50%, following the classic definition given by Columbia University economist Philip Cagan.

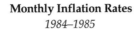

Monthly Inflation Rates
1984–1985

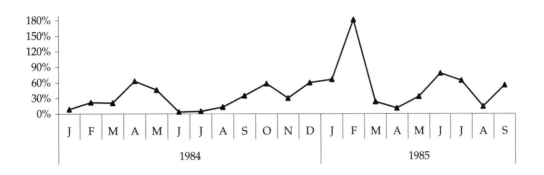

Source: Created by casewriter based on data from Institute of National Statistics, Bolivia.

The country's inadequate tax system contributed to the crisis. Taxes were denominated as fixed amounts and were not indexed. As a result, annual tax revenues collapsed with hyperinflation, worsening public sector accounts (see **Exhibit 5**). In addition, existing government price and exchange rate controls created distortions in the economy, leading to black markets in goods ranging from gasoline to U.S. dollars.[a] By 1984, more than half the labor force was employed in the informal sector.

Bolivia's problems mounted. Daily general strikes reflecting Bolivians' frustration with the scarcity of basic goods paralyzed the country. The few remaining foreign investors fled. In the spring of 1984, the government suspended debt service payments to commercial banks—in essence, declaring itself bankrupt. In August 1985, one year before his term ended, Siles-Suazo called for elections and resigned. He was replaced by Paz Estenssoro, still head of the MNR.

The New Economic Policy

Paz Estenssoro immediately embarked on developing a new economic plan. He appointed President of the Senate Gonzalo Sánchez de Lozada, raised and educated in exile in the United States, to coordinate a team of two ministers, two businessmen, two economists, and two lawyers. Harvard University economist Jeffrey Sachs eventually served as an advisor to the team.[b] A plan was developed that was record breaking in terms of both its magnitude and speed; Bolivia's history of short and unstable governments necessitated quick action. Sachs commented: "When you are at 24,000% inflation there is no gradual way out—you either stabilize or you don't."[15] Sánchez de Lozada added:

---

[a] For example, in August 1985 the official exchange rate of the Bolivian Peso was 67,000 per U.S. dollar, while the parallel market rate soared to 1,145,000 pesos per U.S. dollar.

[b] There had been some attempts to stabilize the economy before (November 1982 and April 1985), but they failed because the government had been too weak and did not resist pressure from the various political constituencies to continue deficit financing and money creation.

We had to do the job in one to three weeks because the world was collapsing around us. The secret was that we analyzed the whole process from a political perspective. This was not the way the IMF and the banks do things. They are much more rigid. Anyway, Bolivia was on their black list at the time, so we knew we would have to work alone.[16]

The New Economic Policy (NEP), approved just a few weeks after Paz Estenssoro's inauguration, included measures in a wide range of fields, including trade policy, monetary policy, labor and wage policy, and exchange rate policy. Specific policies included:[17]

- A stable and unified exchange rate backed by sound fiscal and monetary policies;[a]

- Increased public sector revenues, via tax reform and increases in public sector prices;

- Reduced public sector expenditures, through curtailment of employment in state enterprises and lower rates of real compensation;

- An effective elimination of debt servicing, through a combination of rescheduling with official creditors and an actual default on payments to private creditors until a more permanent settlement could be arranged; and,

- A resumption of foreign financial assistance from governments and multilateral institutions.

Many of the leading trade and labor organizations, including the COB, were against the new policies and called for a general strike. Such strikes had been the main cause of the failure of previous stabilization measures. With this in mind and with support from the majority of the population, the government declared a state of siege against the strikers. Bolivians wanted an end to instability and were willing to accept the harshness of the conditions imposed by the NEP. Lozada noted: "Things had gotten so bad that the population was ready for anything."[18]

Effects of the Reform

The first goal of the NEP was to achieve exchange rate stability and thereby lower inflation.[b] The government began by dramatically devaluing the peso, taking the official rate from 75,000 pesos per U.S. dollar to the black market rate of 1,000,000 pesos per U.S. dollar overnight (see **Exhibit 8**). The government then adopted what was in effect a "managed float" system under which most demand for dollars was met in order to prevent the reoccurrence of a parallel currency black market.

The architects of the plan argued that the cure for hyperinflation would require a change in short-term expectations only: the belief that the exchange rate would be stable for a brief period of time—up to one month—would be sufficient. Indeed, with inflation spectacularly eliminated in one week, their hypothesis appeared to be confirmed. Over the long term, widespread skepticism regarding sustainability of a stable exchange rate remained.

---

[a] A unified exchange rate requires that all agents have access to foreign exchange with no controls. Thus, there is no black market.

[b] In a highly dollarized economy like Bolivia's during the hyperinflation, most prices are quoted in dollars but paid for in the domestic currency. During the hyperinflation, the exchange rate loses value and depreciates at approximately the same rate that domestic prices increase. Economists argue that if the exchange rate can be stabilized, domestic prices can also be stabilized. (Source: "Chapter 23: Stopping High Inflation", in *Macroeconomics in the Global Economy*, by Jeffrey Sachs and Felipe Larrain [Prentice Hall 1993], which also studies the Bolivia case specifically.)

The NEP also required the adoption of tight monetary policy (effectively a stop to printing money), tight fiscal policy, and sufficient foreign exchange reserves. To close the fiscal deficit, nominal government spending was frozen and public enterprises were required to deposit revenues into custodial accounts with the Central Bank. The use of those funds was contingent on approval from the Ministry of Finance. The government immediately froze public sector salaries, spending, and investment. Social spending suffered major cuts, with the largest reductions in education and social security.

Another important factor was the government's decision to continue to suspend payments on its private international debt, which gave it much needed room to breathe. Defaulting on its debt implied economic, diplomatic, and political challenges for the country. Initially, the IMF demanded that Bolivia continue its debt servicing when the first signs of stabilization emerged. Sachs argued that doing so would have destabilized the exchange rate system.[19] After negotiations, the IMF finally endorsed the reforms and awarded Bolivia an assistance package. International creditors, faced with, on the one hand, accepting Bolivia's plans to postpone payment or, on the other hand, immediately losing their loans, also agreed to renegotiate the debt. In the end, most international creditors lost their money. Testament to its diplomatic skills, Bolivia managed to maintain close and friendly relations with creditor governments and institutions in spite of the default.

The main goal of the reform was to cut the budget deficit permanently in a sustainable way. This implied a major shift away from the statist system. According to Sachs, the NEP "was nothing less than a call to dismantle the system of state capitalism that had prevailed over the previous 30 years."[20] One of the most dramatic symbols of change was the firing of 20,000 miners working for the state-owned mining company Comibol (see **Exhibit 9**).

The NEP also liberalized prices and interest rates.[a] Gasoline subsidies were removed and prices quickly rose to international levels. This raised the profits of the state oil company which helped to shrink the budget deficit. Similarly, interest rates were set on the basis of the equilibrium exchange rate and international prices.

A series of subsequent reforms over the following years supported the immediate NEP measures (see **Exhibit 10**). These included reform of the tax system, opening the economy to foreign trade and capital flows, simplification of import tariffs to a single maximum rate, and reforms in the Central Bank and in private banks. In effect, the NEP aimed at, as Lozada put it, "reinventing a country that lived on coca, chaos, and foreign aid."[21] In 1986, a few months after the stabilization effort was launched, the government introduced a new currency, the *Boliviano*, at an exchange rate of 1 million old pesos for each new Boliviano.

Most economic indicators showed improvement in the Bolivian economy. The real growth of GDP rose from 2.1% in 1987 to 4% in 1991. The fiscal deficit fell from 29% of GDP in 1984 to 4% in 1986. Inflation fell from an annual average of 12,000% in 1985 to approximately 15% in 1987.[22]

Costs of Adjustment

The tight austerity measures of the NEP were hard on the poor and working classes—groups that already had carried a heavy burden during the preceding crisis. As Bolivia's social conditions deteriorated, daily strikes threatened the reforms of the Paz Estenssoro administration.

---

[a] This is contrary to heterodox stabilization programs characterized by wage and price controls.

Just as welfare benefits were being severely cut, unemployment was increasing. The combination of a policy of slow money supply growth and strong demand for currency (by people eager to spend in the improved economy) helped to push interest rates to high levels. On top of that, investors, still skeptical about the long-term prospects of the country, were requiring a hefty premium when lending to Bolivians. In 1987, the annualized real interest rate on savings reached 20% while the real lending rate stood at 45%. These high interest rates helped to push unemployment up from 16% in 1984 to 20% in 1986.

The NEP also led to growth in the informal sectors of the Bolivian economy. Contraband and cocaine production increased as displaced workers and miners were forced to find alternative means for subsistence.[23]

Finally, the plan hurt Bolivian industry. Companies were unprepared for the international competition brought about by lower import tariffs. Furthermore, the strategy of fighting inflation with a strong domestic currency resulted in its overvaluation and a worsening of the trade balance as Bolivia's goods were priced out of international markets (see **Exhibit 4**).

Despite the downsides of the NEP, Sachs argued that Bolivia's situation in the mid-1980s had demanded an immediate solution. Evaluating the trade-off between, on the one hand, ending hyperinflation and, on the other hand, the associated social costs had not been an option. He claimed hyperinflation had to be abolished before Bolivia could begin to address its underlying social and structural problems:

> Chaos does not help the poor. Instead, the government needs to begin gathering resources—through canceling foreign debt, starting a social fund, or obtaining help from the U.S. or multilateral organizations such as the World Bank. Raising energy prices ten fold to reach market prices is the socially responsible thing to do because it gets money to the government so it can start to address underlying problems. Ending hyperinflation is a positive social goal for the poorest of the poor.[24]

The Bolivian government took some steps along these lines to address the social costs of the plan. The most important was the establishment of the Emergency Social Fund, to which the World Bank and other international agencies contributed. The fund aimed to create jobs as well as build and improve infrastructure. During its four years of existence, the fund provided desperately needed income and infrastructure and, according to some historians, became an integral asset to the political sustainability of Bolivia's reforms.[25]

Bolivia after the NEP

Political Situation

The NEP had a profound impact on the country's political system as well as on its economic and social spheres. Driven by support from Bolivia's elite, a broad consensus emerged between the left-wing MNR, still led by Paz Estenssoro, and the conservative ADN, led by former-dictator Banzer. The two parties established the so-called "Pact for Democracy" in preparation for the 1985 elections. The Pact symbolized an entirely new approach to politics and a significant break from a tradition of intense conflict. It was, according to one economist, "one of the most significant attempts at institutionalizing a working arrangement between the government and the principal opposition party."[26] The consensus among most political parties proved critical in preventing the collapse of the NEP on several occasions after 1985.

In the 1989 elections, the ADN and the Movement of the Revolutionary Left (MIR), under the leadership of Paz Estenssoro's nephew Jaime Paz Zamora, formed a political coalition called the "Patriotic Accord." The union of Zamora's left-wing party with Banzer, his former oppressor, further illustrated how the ideological barriers among different parties had eroded. The new administration demonstrated a commitment to continued reform and lifted controls on foreign direct investment. They also implemented the Capitalization Program under which state-owned companies were privatized,[a] with 50% ownership offered to international investors and 50% reserved for Bolivian pension funds.

In 1993, Sánchez de Lozada was elected president through a coalition between the MNR and the MIR. Under him, Bolivia took a major step toward integrating more fully into the world economy by signing free-trade agreements with Mexico and Mercosur.[27] At the same time, he introduced social reform through the Popular Participation and Administrative Decentralization programs, representing a shift from a centralized to a decentralized public expenditure framework. Under these reforms, poverty decreased and access to services infrastructure increased. However, critics argued that the reforms failed to make sufficient improvements in social services delivery.[28]

As the gap between rich and poor continued to grow, Banzer, promising greater social equity, returned to the presidency in the 1997 election.[b]

Economic Situation

Beginning in the early 1990s, a campaign of protests arose from a population dissatisfied with the failure of the NEP to achieve medium- to long-term economic objectives. Protestors felt that the NEP, combined with Bolivia's new political paradigm, had led to mixed results in the country's economic situation.

On the one hand, Bolivia's hyperinflation had ended and the foundations of economic growth had been laid. Bolivia's GDP growth averaged 4% per year from 1990 to 1995, and 3.5% from 1995 to 2000 (see **Exhibit 3** for Bolivia's National Income Accounts). Inflation averaged 6.3% between 1986 and 2000.

On the other hand, many of Bolivia's economic problems remained. Budget deficits, financed with foreign debt, became structural as the government continually yielded to its constituencies. In addition, the overvaluation of the currency resulted in a worsening of the trade balance.

The situation escalated in the early 2000s. In the first six months of 2001, the police intervened in 102 protests. Many segments of Bolivian society, including miners, teachers, pensioners, coca growers, and members of the middle class, became active in displaying their dissatisfaction with government policy.[29] Moderately wealthy individuals with debts at banks and micro-lending institutions complained about what they saw as arbitrary decisions by the banks and preferential treatment of privileged debtors. The impoverished population protested the privatization of a local water company when the new owner raised prices to market levels, which was much higher than what many citizens could pay.

---

[a] This included privatization of railroads, the state airline, and electric power, telephone, and national oil companies.

[b] The government represented a coalition of ADN, MIR, and *Unidad Cívica de Solidaridad* (UCS).

President Sánchez de Lozada's Challenges

On the political front, the country had to face the growing disillusionment of Bolivians with the political system and established parties. A number of new parties emerged to represent disenfranchised groups, with the unfortunate consequence of exacerbating the fragmentation of the country's political system. The fact that Bolivia lacked parties with strong leadership and representation in congress was challenging the country's ability to implement much needed structural reforms.

The fragmentation was made tangible to all Bolivians by the close presidential race of 2002. Each of the top three candidates, with completely different platforms, received between 21% and 22.5% of the popular vote. As in 1993, an alliance emerged in congress between the MNR and the MIR, and Sánchez de Lozada assumed the presidency.

After announcing plans to reduce government spending and increase income taxes, Sánchez de Lozada faced violent riots that left many dead or injured and destroyed public buildings—including the congressional archive. Days later, on February 18, 2003, he faced the resignation of his entire cabinet in a gesture meant to indicate the government's willingness to back down on the IMF-imposed austerity measures. It remained an open question how Bolivia would address its fiscal deficit, which had grown to almost 9% in 2002.

The situation left many observers debating whether market-oriented policies could ever produce real improvements in living conditions for the region's average citizens. More generally, they questioned whether a stable, internationally integrated economy could ever coexist with democracy in a sovereign developing nation.

Appendix

Chronology of Events in Bolivia

1910–1920: Bolivia begins the decade in political stability and prosperity under a liberal president. When World War I leads to a decline in mineral exports, support for a new Republican Party increases. A bloodless coup in 1920 puts Republicans in power.

1921–1930: Tin prices decline, slowing economic growth. Labor and Indian uprisings are suppressed. A military junta overthrows President Siles Reyes, then allows elections that give reformist Daniel Salamanca the presidency.

1931–1935: Salamanca fails to suppress social unrest or solve the economic problems the Depression engenders. In 1932 he leads Bolivia into a three-year war with Paraguay. Loss of life and territory discredit the traditional ruling class and prompt a military coup.

1936–1939: Coup leader Colonel Toro attempts a program of "military socialism," but is overthrown by the more radical Colonel Busch. A new constitution favors government intervention in social and economic affairs. Busch replace him with General Enrique Peñaranda.

1940–1943: New socialist and leftist groups gain control of Congress, including the Nationalist Revolutionary Movement (MNR). With the help of reformist military officers, the MNR overthrows Peñaranda and replaces him with Major Villaroel.

1944–1946: Villaroel resumes reformist policies, but fails to gain the support of miners and peasants. Political terrorism and rivalry between the MNR and the military ensue. In 1946 students, teachers, and workers seize arms, kill Villaroel, and take over the presidential palace.

1947–1952: Social unrest and economic decline intensify under Conservatives. The tin industry falters and inflation and food imports rise. The MNR sides with workers and native-population Indians, overthrows the government, and makes Víctor Paz Estenssoro president.

1953–1956: The Bolivian National Revolution begins. President Paz Estenssoro establishes universal suffrage and nationalizes the 3 major tin companies. Influenced by peasants, the government enacts agrarian reform. Miners organize the Bolivian Labor Federation (COB).

1956–1960: Representing the MNR's right wing, new president Hernán Siles-Suazo continues the revolution. He turns toward the stagnant economy and, under advice from the IMF, freezes wages and implements a stabilization plan. Weakening relations between the MNR and the COB are further damaged when Siles-Suazo rebuilds the armed forces to quell unrest.

1961–1964: The revolution loses momentum. Paz Estenssoro returns as president, but conflicts within the MNR and corruption grow. Paz Estenssoro loses the support of the left when he restructures the tin industry, ends workers' control over Comibol, and reduces salaries. Vice President General René Barrientos receives military assistance in occupying the presidential palace and assumes the title of president.

1965–1969: Despite promises to the contrary, Barrientos continues his predecessor's policies. The economy improves, aided by rising tin prices. Barrientos encourages private and foreign investment. His attempts to control labor anger miners. Che Guevara's radical guerilla movement is set back when troops kill him in 1967. Barrientos dies in a helicopter crash, and General Ovando takes power in a coup.

1970–1971: In the spirit of "revolutionary nationalism," Ovando nationalizes the U.S.-owned Gulf Oil Company, but workers don't want to cooperate with a military government. The military itself is polarized, and reformists now support a more radical general who overthrows Ovando. Lacking authority, strategy, and political experience, he is quickly ousted in a military coup led by Colonel Hugo Banzer.

1972–1978: Growing exports and foreign borrowing fuel strong economic growth until 1976, when oil production declines and cotton prices fall. The governing alliance disintegrates. Banzer announces the formation of a "new Bolivia" under increasingly repressive military rule, especially brutal to the left. Elections in 1978 are annulled due to fraud, and Banzer's candidate carries out a coup.

1979–1981: A series of military governments rules briefly, each overthrown by the next. Political parties are fragmented, the armed forces divided, and austerity measures provoke social unrest. Arrests, torture, and disappearances destroy the opposition. The government takes part in cocaine trafficking. Under growing pressure, the military allows the 1980 Congress to choose Siles-Suazo as president again.

1982–1984: The political arena is characterized by infighting and corruption. The international recession and domestic fiscal mismanagement put the Bolivian economy in a state of crisis. The government prints money, fueling inflation. Per capita income falls below 1965 levels, with more than half the labor force employed in the informal sector. Paz Estenssoro is elected president again.

1985–1988: Shifting his focus away from the center left that elected him, Paz Estenssoro institutes a drastic New Economic Policy that liberalizes trade, deregulates the financial sector, privatizes some state enterprises, and implements tax-reform law. These "shock-therapy" measures succeed in reducing record inflation and bringing about slow but steady economic growth. Success comes at a high social cost.

1989–1993: Jaime Paz Zamora is elected president. He continues his uncle's neoliberal reforms, maintaining slow economic growth. Cocaine trafficking contributes to the economy. Social tensions explode in a series of forcefully suppressed strikes for higher wages and against privatization. Sánchez de Lozada, architect of the shock-therapy program, is elected president.

1994–1997: Lozada enacts political decentralization and implements a coca-eradication program. Capitalization of several state enterprises brings economic growth in capital-intensive sectors. Banzer returns as president after civil disturbances, promising greater social equity.

1998–1999: The Brazilian and Asian financial crises bring Bolivia's slow economic growth nearly to a halt. Income per capita falls as unemployment rises. Bolivia participates in a World Bank/IMF debt reduction initiative for heavily indebted countries.

2000–2002: Violence erupts as farmers, teachers, union members, and the poor protest privatization, low wages, the lack of public investment, and the U.S.-backed coca-eradication program. Banzer imposes a state of siege and deploys soldiers to control the crisis. Vice President Jorge Quiroga takes over amid political conflict when an ailing Banzer resigns. Sanchez de Lozada is elected president in 2002.

2003: February riots force Sanchez de Lozada to reevaluate his aggressive pro-market stance.

Source: Adapted from "Commanding Heights," PBS, 2002.

Exhibit 1   Map of Bolivia

Source: Library of Congress and CIA World Factbook,
        <http://www.cia.gov/cia/publications/factbook/geos/bl.htm> (accessed June 2002).

Exhibit 2   Bolivian General Economic Indicators

	1982	1984	1986	1988	1990	1992	1994	1996	1998	2000	2002
% change over prior year											
1. Real GDP Growth	-3.9	-0.2	-2.6	2.9	4.6	1.6	4.7	4.4	5.0	2.4	1.9
2. Real Per Capita GDP Growth	na	-2.2	-4.6	0.8	2.5	-0.4	1.8	1.5	2.1	-0.5	-0.9
3. Consumer Price Inflation	124	1281	276	16.0	17.1	12.1	8.8	12.4	7.7	4.6	0.9
% GDP											
4. Investment/GDP	9.7	9.5	12.0	13.9	12.8	16.2	13.3	16.2	23.8	18.4	14.4
5. Current Account/GDP[b]	-6	-7	-10	-7	-4	-9	-2	-5	-8	-6	-5
6. Fiscal Surplus (+) or Deficit (-)/GDP[a][b]	-1.7	-29.3	-0.1	-0.7	-1.7	-2.6	-3.3	-2.4	-2.3	-3.4	-8.6
7. M2/GDP	18	11	7	17	20	30	42	41	46	47	na
units as described											
8. Population (millions at mid-year)	5.2	5.4	5.7	5.9	6.2	6.4	6.8	7.2	7.6	8.0	8.5
9. Population in Urban Areas (%)	47	49	51	53	56	57	59	60	61	62	na
10. Urban Unemployment (%)[b][c]	7.1	5.8	na	na	7.3	5.5	3.1	4.2	6.1	7.6	8.5
11. Official Exchange Rate (bols. per dollar, year-end)	200	8,800	1.9	2.5	3.4	4.1	4.7	5.2	5.6	6.4	7.5
12. International Reserves (millions current U.S. dollars)	192	290	202	144	205	220	489	995	1,183	1,171	1,106
13. Foreign Debt (millions current U.S. dollars)	3,329	4,317	5,575	4,905	4,275	4,235	4,877	5,195	5616	5,762	5,868

Sources: Created by casewriter based on data (for 1, 2, 3, 8, 11, 12, 13) from EIU Country Data, February 2003; (for 4, 6) International Monetary Fund, *International Finance Statistics Yearbook CD-ROM*, 2002; (for 10) CEPAL / ECLAC, *Statistical Yearbook*, 2001; and (for 5, 7, 9) World Bank, *World Development Indicators CD-ROM*, 2001.

Notes: [a]1981 data instead of 1982 data.

[b]Data from 2002 from other sources, so not strictly comparable to prior years.

[c]Underemployment (employed people earning less than minimum wage) is much higher—some estimates show 50%–60% or more.

Exhibit 3   Bolivian National Income Accounts (*millions constant 1996 U.S. dollars*)

	1982	1984	1986	1988	1990	1992	1994	1996	1998	2000	2002
Gross Domestic Product	**5,520**	**5,286**	**5,064**	**5,339**	**5,798**	**6,204**	**6,771**	**7,397**	**8,154**	**8,382**	**8,647**
Household Consumption	4,047	3,845	4,197	4,366	4,594	4,915	5,227	5,557	6,167	6,491	6,714
Government Consumption	1,089	994	790	789	795	852	901	986	1,058	1,099	1,179
Gross Fixed Investment	536	502	607	741	740	1,008	900	1,201	2,010	1,467	1,249
Exports	812	774	749	808	1,119	1,214	1,471	1,670	1,741	1,738	1,786
Imports	836	713	1,182	1,271	1,406	1,740	1,716	2,017	2,802	2,382	2,243

Source: Created by casewriter based on data from EIU Country Data, February 2003.

Note: GDP does not equal sum of components because of rebasing to 1996, which alters the relative importance of individual components.

Exhibit 4   Bolivian Balance of Payments (*millions of current U.S. dollars*)

	1982	1984	1986	1988	1990	1992	1994	1996	1998	2000
Current Account	**-174**	**-179**	**-389**	**-304**	**-199**	**-534**	**-90**	**-404**	**-678**	**-464**
Trade Balance	332	312	-51	-48	55	-432	-30	-236	-655	-381
Exports	*828*	*725*	*546*	*543*	*831*	*608*	*985*	*1,132*	*1,104*	*1,230*
Imports	*496*	*412*	*597*	*591*	*776*	*1,041*	*1,015*	*1,368*	*1,759*	*1,610*
Net Services	-139	-160	-125	-127	-165	-146	-142	-183	-190	-244
Net Income	-411	-415	-309	-265	-249	-198	-183	-208	-162	-225
Net Transfers	44	84	95	135	159	243	264	222	330	385
Capital Account	**1**	**4**	**5**	**1**	**1**	**1**	**1**	**3**	**10**	**0**
Financial Account	**-49**	**29**	**-96**	**-37**	**48**	**367**	**315**	**701**	**1,083**	**508**
Net Direct Investment	61	13	20	-12	26	91	128	472	955	731
Net Portfolio Investment	-15	-1	0	0	0	0	0	0	-75	55
Net Other	-96	17	-116	-25	22	276	187	229	203	-278
Net Errors and Omissions	**4**	**-18**	**126**	**47**	**-11**	**34**	**-316**	**-32**	**-314**	**-84**
Change in Official Reserves	**-219**	**-164**	**-354**	**-294**	**-161**	**-132**	**-90**	**268**	**101**	**-40**

Source: Created by casewriter based on data from International Monetary Fund, *International Finance Statistics Yearbook CD-ROM, 2002.*

Exhibit 5   Bolivian Government Finance

	(billions current pesos)		(millions current bolivianos)							
	1981	1984	1986	1988	1990	1992	1994	1996	1998	2000
Total Revenue	**14**	**792**	**1,013**	**1,442**	**2,275**	**3,887**	**5,413**	**7,658**	**9,002**	**10,188**
% GDP	*4%*	*4%*	*13%*	*13%*	*15%*	*18%*	*20%*	*20%*	*19%*	*20%*
Tax Revenue	12	573	750	810	1,172	2,244	3,097	5,484	7,111	7,276
Nontax Revenue	2	172	250	540	939	1,096	1,432	960	1,117	1,741
Capital Revenue	0	0	0	3	1	38	84	121	72	262
Grants	0	47	13	88	163	509	800	1,093	701	909
Total Expenditure	**21**	**6,891**	**1,010**	**1,515**	**2,530**	**4,461**	**6,400**	**8,627**	**10,340**	**12,314**
% GDP	*5%*	*33%*	*13%*	*14%*	*16%*	*20%*	*23%*	*23%*	*22%*	*24%*
General Public Services			98	112	321	697	797	1,037	1,211	799
Defense			147	180	357	436	527	630	993	865
Public Order & Safety			61	86	167	268	393	651	746	939
Education			186	313	455	743	1,181	1,512	2,023	2,443
Health			19	116	59	365	454	347	352	1,287
Social Security & Welfare			250	173	449	560	935	1,580	2,682	2,588
Housing and Community Amenities			8	5	5	6	41	35	107	278
Economic Affairs and Services			173	432	483	718	1,158	1,828	1,341	1,855
Other			68	98	235	668	914	1,007	884	1,260
of which interest payments			*na*	*na*	*na*	*318*	*610*	*750*	*776*	*891*
Lending Minus Repayment	**0**	**16**	**9**	**6**	**7**	**-1**	**-81**	**-75**	**-246**	**-397**
Overall Deficit (-) /Surplus (+)	**-7**	**-6,115**	**-5**	**-79**	**-262**	**-573**	**-906**	**-895**	**-1,092**	**-1,730**
% GDP	*-2%*	*-29%*	*-0.1%*	*-0.7%*	*-1.7%*	*-2.6%*	*-3.3%*	*-2.4%*	*-2.3%*	*-3.4%*
Financing	**7**	**6,115**	**6**	**79**	**262**	**573**	**906**	**895**	**1,092**	**1,730**
Abroad	-1	-333	-63	50	107	506	1,242	1,388	872	644
Domestic	8	6,448	69	30	155	67	-336	-494	219	1,086
GDP	*400*	*20,900*	*7,610*	*10,806*	*15,443*	*22,014*	*27,636*	*37,537*	*46,471*	*51,261*

Source: Created by casewriter based on data from International Monetary Fund, *Government Finance Statistics Yearbook*, 1990 and 2001.

Exhibit 6a   Comparative Social Indicators, 1999

	Life Expectancy at Birth (yrs)	Adult Literacy Rate	School Enrollment (%)	GDP per Capita	Under-nourished People (%)	Under-five Mortality Rate	Human Development Rank
		(age 15 and up)	(prim., sec. + tert.)	(U.S. $)	(% total pop)	(per 1000)	(out of 150)
Bolivia	**62.0**	**85.0**	**70**	**2,355**	**23**	**83**	**104**
Argentina	73.2	96.7	83	12,277	-	22	34
Chile	75.2	95.6	78	8,652	4	12	39
Brazil	67.5	84.9	80	7,037	10	40	69
Ecuador	69.8	91.0	77	2,994	5	35	84
Mexico	72.4	91.1	81	8,297	5	33	51
Nicaragua	68.1	68.2	63	2,279	31	47	106
Peru	68.5	89.6	80	4,622	18	52	73
Averages:							
Latin America and Caribbean	69.6	87.8	74	6,880	12	39	-
OECD	76.6	-	87	22,020	-	6	-

Source: Adapted from UN, *Human Development Report, 2001*.
Note: The Human Development Rank ranks countries according to multiple factors, including those in the table.

Exhibit 6b   Comparative Social Indicators, 1960–1999

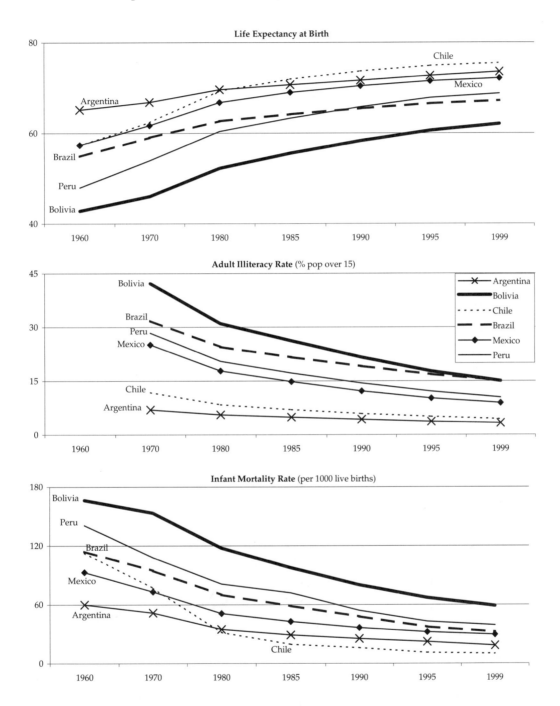

Source: Adapted from World Bank, *World Development Indicators CD-ROM*, 2001.

Exhibit 7   Tin Prices, Production, and Bolivian Exports

Tin Prices and World Production

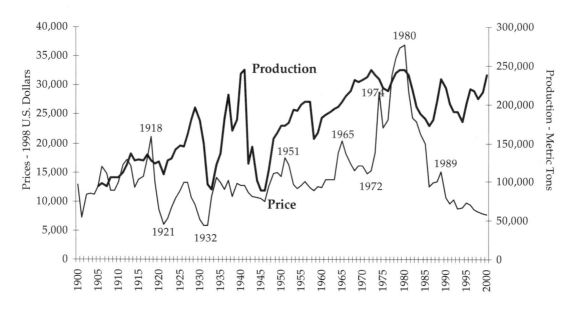

Source: Created by casewriter based on data from U.S Geological Survey, Open File Report 01-006
          <http://minerals.usgs.gov/minerals/pubs/of01-006/tin.html> June, 2002 .

Bolivia Tin Export Price and Volume Indices (1995=100)

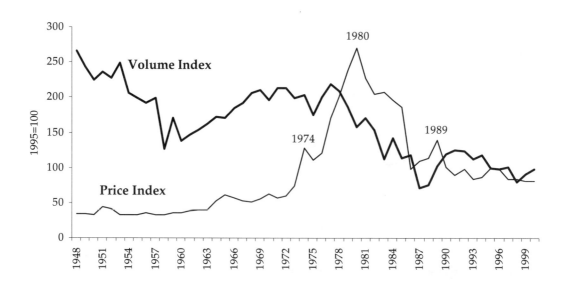

Source: Created by casewriter based on data from International Monetary Fund, *International Financial Statistics Yearbook
          CD-ROM*, 2002.

Exhibit 8   Official and Parallel Boliviano / U.S. Dollar Exchange Rates

	1983		1984		1985		1986		1987	
	Official	Parallel	Official	Parallel	Official	Parallel	Official	Parallel	Official	Parallel
Jan	196	376	500	1,875	8,571	65,776	2,062,839	2,272,445	1.93	1.94
Feb	196	475	500	2,050	45,000	126,249	1,836,571	1,883,750	1.94	1.94
Mar	196	488	500	2,615	45,000	123,871	1,888,194	1,572,710	1.98	1.98
Apr	196	408	2,000	3,490	45,000	159,734	1,904,600	1,554,252	2.01	2.02
May	196	363	2,000	3,435	67,000	240,645	1,904,323	1,954,758	2.03	2.04
Jun	196	375	2,000	3,305	67,000	458,080	1,904,933	1,937,817	2.06	2.08
Jul	196	575	2,000	3,460	67,000	824,355	1,904,161	1,927,371	2.07	2.08
Aug	196	765	2,000	7,110	67,000	1,121,612	1,909,355	1,928,162	2.09	2.09
Sept	196	770	2,000	13,303	1,044,567	1,048,000	1,915,133	1,919,617	2.11	2.12
Oct	196	998	2,000	15,065	1,102,839	1,112,983	1,921,129	1,927,500	2.12	2.13
Nov	500	1275	8,571	18,039	1,209,067	1,316,028	1,924,967	1,930,250	2.15	2.17
Dec	500	1190	8,571	22,852	1,589,567	1,707,424	1,932,767	1,945,807	2.19	2.21
Avg	247	671	2,720	8,050	446,468	692,063	1,917,414	1,896,203	2.06	2.07

Source: Adapted from Juan Cariaga, *Estabilización y Desarrollo*, 1997.

Exhibit 9   Bolivia Public Sector Employment and Spending

Public Sector Employment (1980–1989)
(Number of employees)

	Companies	Government	Total
1980	55,193	137,925	193,118
1981	56,643	143,319	199,962
1982	55,888	148,128	204,016
1983	59,718	164,717	224,435
1984	60,851	175,071	235,922
1985	61,514	184,065	245,579
1986	54,827	166,156	220,983
1987	41,327	171,115	212,442
1988	35,846	168,889	204,735
1989	34,731	174,351	209,082

Social Public Spending (1980–1988)
(Percent of GNP)

	Education	Ministry of Health	Social Security
1980	4.1	0.8	1.4
1981	2.9	0.5	1.2
1982	3.2	0.4	1.1
1983	3.4	0.4	0.8
1984	3.2	0.4	2.0
1985	3.3	0.4	1.0
1986	2.3	0.3	0.7
1987	2.6	0.5	na
1988	2.6	na	na

Source: Adapted from Unidad de Análisis de Polpíticas Económicas (UDAPE), Estadíticas Económicas de Bolivia 2, La Paz, 1991 and World Bank, *Public Sector Expenditures Review with a Special Emphasis on the Social Sectors*, 1989.

Exhibit 10   Phase One of Bolivia's New Economic Policy, August 1985

Fiscal Policy
    Public expenditures equal to revenues
    No public investment
    Tax reform
    Privatization (mining, banking, and development)
Monetary Policy
    Real interest rates
    Debt negotiation
Trade Policy
    Tariff reform - 20% uniform tariffs
    Import prohibitions abolished
    Swiss Societe Generale de Surveillance to manage customs
    Export incentives
Labor and Wage Policy
    Freely negotiated wages between labor and management
    Fondo de emergencia social
Exchange Rate Policy
    93% devaluation (auctioning system)
    Unified rates and established crawling peg

Source: Adapted from Marc Lindenberg, "Bolivia (A): Stabilization and Adjustment 1985-88: Did it Work?,"
        Harvard University Kennedy School of Government, Case C16-951.1.

Endnotes

1 Transcript of interview with Gonzalo de Lozada on "Commanding Heights" PBS television program, available at: http://www.pbs.org/wgbh/commandingheights/shared/pdf/int_gonzalodelozada.pdf.

2 World Bank Group, *Bolivia Country Report* (Washington, D.C.: 2001).

3 The Economist Intelligence Unit (EIU), *Bolivia Country Report* (London: EIU, September 2001), 3–14.

4 EIU, 3–14.

5 World Bank Group, *World Development Indicators 2001 CD-ROM*, (Washington, D.C.: 2001).

6 EIU, 3–14.

7 J. Torrontegui, "Wages of Misery in Bolivia, " *El Pais (English Edition)*, February 20, 2003.

8 EIU, 3–14.

9 Based on the United States Library of Congress Country Studies, available online at <http://memory.loc.gov/frd/cs/cshome.html> (accessed February 19, 2003).

10 The true inclusion of the peasantry in the political system is debatable. It has been argued, for example, that while the peasants did gain power after the revolution, the MNR bosses manipulated peasant masses to achieve a populist gain.

11 Robert E. Kennedy, "Banco Solidario: The Business of Microfinance," Harvard Business School Case 702-019 (Cambridge, MA: Harvard Business School Publishing, 2002).

12 These regimes included the following: General David Padilla Arancibia (1978–79), Colonel Alberto Natusch Busch (1979), General Luis García Meza (1980-81), General Celso Torrelio Villa (1981–82), General Guido Vildoso Calderón (1982).

13 Juan-Antonio Morales, "Inflation Stabilization in Bolivia," in eds. Michael Bruno, Guido Di Tella, Rudiger Dornbusch, and Stanley Fisher, *Inflation Stabilization: The Experience of Israel, Argentina, Brazil, Bolivia, and Mexico* (The MIT Press, Cambridge, MA: 1988), 310.

14 Cariaga, Juan, *Estabilizacíon y Desarrollo: Importantes Lecciones del Programa Económico en Bolivia* (Bolivia: Amigos del Libro, 1997).

15 Interview with Jeffrey Sachs by casewriters.

16 Lindenberg, Marc, "Bolivia (A): Stabilization and Adjustment 1985–1988: Did it work? (Sequel)," Harvard University Kennedy School of Government Case C16.90.951.1.

17 Sachs, Jeffrey and Juan Antonio Morales, *Bolivia 1952–1986* (International Center for Economic Growth, Institute for Contemporary Studies Press, 1988), 28.

18 Marc Lindenberg, "Bolivia (A): Stabilization and Adjustment 1985–88: Did it Work? (Sequel)."

19 Interview with Jeffrey Sachs by casewriters.

20 Sachs, Jeffrey and Juan Antonio Morales, *Bolivia 1952–1986* (International Center for Economic Growth, Institute for Contemporary Studies Press, 1988), 28.

21 Jeffrey Sachs quoting Gonzalo Sanchez de Lozada during interview with casewriters.

22 The numbers in the text do not match the numbers in the exhibits due to differences in sources.

23 By 1986, it was estimated that the informal activity in Bolivia represented approximately one half of the total economy, with the informal sector comprising roughly a third of Bolivia's working population. *The Economist*, June 15, 1985, 54.

24 Interview with Jeffrey Sachs by casewriters.

25 PBS, "Bolivia Country Report," *Commanding Heights*, available at: http://www.pbs.org/wgbh/commandingheights/lo/countries/bo/bo_full.html.

[26] Eduardo A. Gamarra, "Crafting Political Support for Stabilization: Political Pacts and the New Economic Policy in Bolivia," in William C. Smith, Carlos Acuña, and Eduardo Gamarra, *Democracy, Markets and Structural Reform in Latin America. Argentina, Brazil, Bolivia, Chile and México* (Miami: North South Center Press, University of Miami, 1996) 107.

[27] Mercosur was comprised of Argentina, Brazil, Chile, Uruguay, Paraguay, and Bolivia.

[28] George Gray Molina, "Popular Participation, Social Service Delivery, and Poverty Reduction, 1994–2000," a paper prepared for the "Citizen Participation in the Context of Fiscal Decentralization: Best Practices in Municipal Administration" project, sponsored by INDES and the Japan Program at the Inter-American Development Bank (IDB), Tokyo and Kobe, September 2–6, 2002.

[29] EIU, 3–14.

Fresh Start? Peru's Legacy of Debt and Default

Like many Latin American countries, Peru accumulated a large external debt during the late 1970s and early 1980s. Under attack from Shining Path guerillas, upon his election in 1985 populist President Alan Garcia unilaterally limited interest payments on external debt to 10% of export earnings.

In taking this step, Garcia followed a previous pattern. Peru had defaulted on external debt in the 1920s and 1930s as the country suffered through financial crises and the global Great Depression.

A new president, Alberto Fujimori, was elected in 1990. He faced the consequences of Garcia's decision and considered how to address Peru's broader economic problems.

Study Questions

1. What was the basis for Alan Garcia's decision? Does it make economic and / or political sense?
2. Why is Peru so prone to debt problems?
3. What should President Fujimori do?
4. In the light of Peru's experience, does the "sovereign debt restructuring mechanism" proposed by the IMF in 2003 make sense?

JULIO J. ROTEMBERG
LISA H. LEWIS

Fresh Start? Peru's Legacy of Debt and Default

In June of 1990 Alberto Fujimori had just won the presidential election without articulating a clear governmental program and many people wanted to know how he would conduct Peru's domestic and foreign affairs. He was slated to meet UN Secretary General and fellow Peruvian Javier Perez de Cuellar to discuss Peru's economic crisis and its relationship with the international financial community. They were to be joined by the heads of the World Bank, IMF and Inter-American Development Bank (IDB). It was the first time top multilateral organization officials had met with a president-elect. However Peru's situation was unique[1].

The country was facing a severe crisis. June's monthly inflation rate was 42.6%, GDP per capita was reduced to levels not seen since the early 1960s, and only 18.6% of the population considered themselves adequately employed. Malnutrition was rampant and income distribution continued to be extremely unequal with 52% of 1990 income going to the top 20% of the population while 4% went to the bottom 20%.[2] In addition, a guerrilla group called *Sendero Luminoso* (Shining Path) was in control of parts of the country and sought to terrorize Lima. While Peru had faced crises before, this one seemed unprecedented and required that Fujimori think about a broad set of decisions. His main opponent in the presidential campaign, the writer Mario Vargas Llosa, lost the election in part because he promised an "orthodox shock" involving a drastic devaluation, large cuts in government spending, and dramatic increases in interest rates. These were the kind of policies favored by the IMF and international creditors. Fujimori took a more moderate position and received support from people who would doubtless be hurt by such policies in the short run.

Vargas Llosa also promised he would start paying back Peru's debt. Fujimori's predecessor, Alan García, took the dramatic step of declaring that these payments would not exceed 10% of Peruvian export earnings. Now Fujimori needed to consider how much he wanted to repay and the extent to which he would rather use Peru's limited international reserves to buy back Peruvian debt on the secondary market, where it was trading at a sharp discount. There was also the question of how the war with leftist guerrillas, whose casualties already numbered over 20,000, should be conducted. If the military were given free reign to conduct this war, complaints against human rights abuses by the military were likely to increase. Amnesty International already criticized Peru's security forces for the death, disappearance and torture of civilians, and cited Peru for having the worst record on disappearances in the world. One suggestion involved the widespread arming of peasants, many of whom appeared to resent Sendero's bloody and ruthless government in those territories it controlled.

Research Associate Lisa Lewis prepared this case under the supervision of Professor Julio Rotemberg. This case was developed from published sources. HBS cases are developed solely as the basis for class discussion. Cases are not intended to serve as endorsements, sources of primary data, or illustrations of effective or ineffective management.

This could increase casualties, however. In 1983, a group of primitively armed peasants had apparently killed eight journalists when they tried to investigate the peasants' anti-Sendero actions.[3]

Geography and Historical Overview

Peru was the third largest country in South America in size, with an area of 1.28 million square kilometers, and had, in 1990, the third lowest per capita income (after Paraguay and Bolivia). It was a land of huge contrasts. The Andes ran the length of the country, dividing it into three main regions. The arid coastal region had the capacity to produce bountiful cash crops (sugar and cotton) under irrigation. It was both the most populous and the richest region in per capita terms. The *selva* (jungle), comprised both the tropical rain forest (which once exported rubber) and the eastern mountain slopes where coca was grown. Lastly, the *sierra* (mountains) was made up of the areas in the Andes above 2,000 meters. In some of the sierra's valleys, for example around Huancayo, farmers owning relatively small plots prospered supplying foodstuffs for consumption in the cities. Wool for export was produced in other valleys. In some parts of the sierra, however, Quechua-speaking Indians practiced subsistence farming, often under communal ownership, and found survival difficult.

Quechua was the language of the Inca Empire whose capital was Cusco and which, before Pizarro's arrival in 1532, covered a third of South America and had an estimated population of between 9 and 16 million.[4] Under the Incas, all land was controlled by the state, though it was cultivated communally. The Incas also had a tax called the *mita*, which required individuals to work for a specified time for the state, for example in mines or on public work projects. When the head Inca visited Pizarro in his Cajamarca encampment, he was captured after failing to accept Catholicism and the Spanish King. Pizarro, who was accompanied by 62 horsemen and 106 foot soldiers, followed this capture—and the killing of the head Inca after he paid a vast amount of gold as ransom—by allying himself with some Inca rulers against others. He thereby conquered all of Peru.

Individuals favored by Pizarro, and by the viceroys that succeeded him, were given *encomiendas*. This entitled them to collect tribute from a group of Indians in exchange for guaranteeing their spiritual welfare. Indians were in principle allowed to keep the land they cultivated, and use the produce to pay this tribute. However, idle land belonged to the Crown, which either granted or sold it to individuals. This allowed the Crown to take over land as Indians were relocated or as their numbers dwindled through disease. The result was the creation of relatively large landholdings called *haciendas*. In addition, the Spanish used a variant of the *mita* system to force Indians to devote some of their time to work in mines. This forced labor allowed Peru to be the principal American exporter of silver in 1600.[5]

Not surprisingly, there were several Indian revolts. In part because Indians remained at the bottom of the income distribution such revolts continued after independence. These revolts were met with a mixture of bloody repression and legislation protecting Indian rights. However, many Indians were not given the right to vote until July 1980, the first election in which individuals who were not literate in Spanish were allowed to vote.

In the war of independence from Spain, many creoles fought on the Spanish side while two foreigners, the Argentinean José de San Martín and the Venezuelan Simón Bolívar, led the armies that won Peruvian independence in 1824. While constitutions from then on specified that power belonged to elected representatives, it often went to those that staged military uprisings. Even in the twentieth century, the military took control in the coups of 1914, 1930, 1948, 1962, and 1968. Some of these coups, such as the 1948 Odría coup, favored liberalization; while others, particularly the 1968 junta of Velasco, massively increased the role of the state in the economy. The military also played a crucial role in Peru's border disputes with Bolivia, Chile, and Ecuador, whose boundaries were left unclear at independence. The biggest of these disputes was the War of the Pacific which lasted from 1879 to 1884 and which gave Chile control over valuable resources that Peru and Bolivia claimed as their own. Tensions over borders have continued since then and escalated as recently as 1975.[6]

Much of the economic development of Peru has been described as "export-led." This referred to the fact that, on several occasions, increases in the exports of commodities (sometimes due to increases in international demand, sometimes due to discoveries) have been associated with bursts of growth in income and GDP. The first boom of this type may have been the guano boom of the 1840s. A more recent example was the production of fishmeal, which took off in the 1950s in part as a result of technological innovation. This expansion allowed total exports to rise by a remarkable 21% per year from 1959 to 1962, and GDP grew by 9% per year during this period.[7]

While export booms centered on specific industries, Peru's exports became more diversified over time. One notable feature of most Peruvian export industries, however, was that they involved high concentrations of ownership. In some of these industries, a few large producers predominated from the beginning. In others, such as silver mining and fishmeal production, a large number of small producers competed initially but the industry consolidated over time. The resulting concentration of wealth was particularly dramatic at the beginning of the twentieth century, when it was said that just 30 or 40 families owned most of the Peruvian assets used for exports.

This concentrated wealth and power was, at first, almost exclusively in the hands of whites. Over time, however, *mestizos*—a group that included both those of mixed European and Indian heritage, as well as educated, white collar and urban Indians—were able to move into the middle and upper classes. At the same time, Peru has progressively become more urban. By 1990, about 69% of the Peruvian population of 21.5 million lived in cities, with around 25% concentrated around Lima, the capital founded by the Spanish near the coast.[8]

Debt and Default in the 1920s and 1930s

Cycles of international borrowing and default have recurred in Peruvian history (see **Exhibit 1**). In the 1920s, for example, the Peruvian government sought to modernize the country with vast public works programs financed by substantial loans arranged by U.S. bankers. At the time, these banks were aggressively marketing bonds issued by foreign national, provincial, and municipal authorities, and the terms of these bonds became increasingly favorable to borrowers. Indeed, the president of the Reserve Bank of Peru at one point attempted to reduce the size of a loan that was being negotiated, and instead wound up not only with the initial loan, but with additional loans following shortly thereafter. By the end of the 1920s Peru's outstanding government bonds of $94.5 million and £3.85 million were worth 2.7 times its merchandise exports. Other countries had similar experiences; Argentina had a debt of 2.8 times exports.[9]

The 1929 stock market crash and the Great Depression strained Peru's ability to meet its debt service and Peru responded with a unilateral moratorium on debt service payments. By early 1932, essentially all Peruvian debt was in default. President Sánchez Cerro was quoted as saying "Peru could not pay . . . one cent of her foreign debt. To ask her to do so would be like asking a starving man to give up food necessary for his life." Peru was the second country (after Bolivia) to default on its debt, but all Latin American countries except Argentina, Haiti, and the Dominican Republic suspended normal debt payments by 1934. By the end of 1936, 76% of Latin American bond issues were in partial or total default.[10]

The debt issue was not resolved until the end of the 1940s. An offer to repurchase some of the debt was extended publicly in 1937, when Peruvian bonds were trading at around 18 cents on the dollar. Although the U.S. Foreign Bondholders Protective Council[a] (FBPC) advised against the deal, calling it "entirely inadequate and unacceptable," two-thirds of bondholders accepted the offer. While negotiations continued to fail in the 1940s, Peru repurchased a substantial fraction of its debt by paying about 20% of its face value. In 1947, Peru extended another offer (**Exhibit 3b**), which the FBPC again recommended against because it called "for the complete cancellation of . . . arrears of interest in default." The deal involved the exchange of old bonds for a new 1947 series. The principal of the new bonds was the same as that for the old ones, but interest rates were slashed and the maturity dates extended for 50 years. Despite the FBPC's negative endorsement, some bondholders accepted the deal and the outstanding dollar debt was reduced to just over $64.5 million by the end of 1952.[11]

General Odría, the leader of the 1948 coup, was committed to reinserting Peru into the international financial system and negotiated a new deal. This deal was accepted by the FBPC and went into effect in January 1953. This deal led the secondary market price for Peruvian debt to equal about 39% of its face value in 1953, where it had been equal to about 15% in 1948. It involved the exchange of new bonds for old bonds where the principal of the new bonds was the same as that of the original issue or the 1947 bonds and the interest rate was 3%. In addition, bondholders received noninterest-bearing certificates equal to 10% of total arrears to be paid out in biyearly installments over 15 years (**Exhibit 3c**). By 1958, nearly 95% of bondholders accepted the 1953 deal.

Odría succeeded in obtaining both foreign loans and foreign direct investment. The latter surged in part because taxation on foreign-owned mines was reduced, the exchange rate was depreciated, and the foreign exchange market was freed so that anyone could transact at a single market-determined exchange rate. As *Fortune* put it in November 1956: "[Peru] has maintained a scrupulous respect for private property and for the principle of free markets and convertibility." At the same time, a Peruvian conservative pronounced in *Foreign Affairs:* "Peru has come to be looked upon as one of the most attractive countries for foreign investment in Latin America."[12]

It is interesting to compare Peru's experience with Argentina's. The difference in the two countries' repayment histories was dramatic. Jorgensen and Sachs computed that the present value as of 1920 of Argentina's repayments on the 1920's debt was 1.25 times larger than the present value of its borrowings, while the corresponding ratio for Peru was 0.52.[b] Despite this difference, neither country received new funds from the international capital markets from 1931 to the end of World War II. The only loans Argentina obtained in this period were for refinancing purposes. After 1950, both countries obtained significant inflows. However, in the period 1950-1964, Peru's government and private sectors each received net inflows that were a larger fraction of total exports than the corresponding figures for Argentina. Relative to exports, Peru also attracted more official transfers and more foreign direct investment.[13]

---

[a] The Foreign Bondholders Protective Council was organized in the United States in 1933 to represent the interests of holders of bonds issued by foreign sovereigns. The owners of the debt were individuals, and thus could not create a unified negotiating force without such an organization. A similar organization existed to protect British bondholders, the Corporation of Foreign Bondholders, founded in 1868. (Eichengreen, p. 15–16).

[b] These present values were computed using the yields to maturity on U.S. long-term bonds .

The Accumulation of International Debt in the Pre-García Period

Foreign investment and loans continued to flow into the country throughout the 1950s and 1960s. By the end of the 1960s the government's foreign debt had grown substantially while foreign ownership, mainly by U.S. companies, was widespread. In 1968, foreigners controlled one-third of the fishing industry, one-half of manufacturing, two-thirds of commercial banking and three-quarters of mining.[14] The 1968 military coup led by General Juan Velasco Alvarado drastically changed Peruvian institutions. This regime embraced the Inca past while seeking a "socialist revolution" to overcome Peru's foreign "dependency" while reducing the power of the domestic "oligarchy."

Upon taking office, the government expropriated the International Petroleum Company, a Standard Oil subsidiary that had been mired in controversy over its high profits and its low level of taxation for a very long time. While IPC was the junta's first nationalization, it was not the last. The number of public enterprises rose from fewer than 20 in 1968 to over 170 by 1975, in activities ranging from banking to fishing. The state held monopolies on oil refining and marketing; marketing of all agricultural products and most exports, the telecommunications, electrical, and water systems; and much of the transportation and tourism industry. The commercial banking sector, for example, went from two-thirds foreign owned to two-thirds government owned by 1975. An analyst summarized the government's role by saying, "In 1975, in round numbers, the public sector handled nine-tenths of exports and half of all imports on the one hand and [was] responsible for about two-fifths of employment and one-third of output in the modern sector."[15]

The compensation received by the original owners varied widely. Observers said that payments to Chase Manhattan, which later helped Peru obtain international loans, were generous. Other nationalizations were confiscatory. Owners of IPC and those of another symbolic oil facility as well as the owners of a money-losing railroad received nothing. However, the Nixon administration did not formally sanction Peru because it heeded the desires of other Latin American countries and of the North American business community in Peru. While the flow of aid and of loans from international organizations under U.S. influence did slow, the administration did not invoke the Hickenlooper Amendment, which required the United States to stop giving economic and military aid to countries that did not take "steps" towards "equitable and speedy compensation" for expropriated American assets. Instead, the U.S. government formally settled in 1974. As part of this settlement, a series of other nationalized U.S. companies who initially claimed to be due $250 million received $76 million in compensation. Although some companies received nothing, the United States signed an agreement stating: "The Government of the United States declares that the payment of the sum referred to in Article II cancels any liability or obligation of the Government of Peru to United States nationals, their subsidiaries, branches and affiliates."[16]

Owners of large agricultural properties also fared badly. Velasco expropriated all large *haciendas* and gave the land to "cooperatives" administered by government-appointed officials. The original owners were paid in long-term nominal Peruvian bonds, which later lost a large fraction of their value as a result of inflation. These expropriations gave large windfalls to the politically well-organized coastal peasants engaged in sugar and cotton production. However, they did less for subsistence farmers in the sierras. At the same time, Velasco tried to help industrial workers by raising average tariffs to 69% from his predecessor's already high level of 61% and by essentially forbidding firms from firing workers that had worked for at least three months.[17]

This revolution did not end capital inflows. The U.S. government even authorized a 1974 loan by the Export-Import bank. Interestingly, this loan helped finance an expansion of a U.S.-owned copper mine. This investment proceeded even though a law passed in 1970 gave the government a monopoly in the marketing of mineral exports.[18]

Between 1970 and 1975, the amount of debt owed in the form of syndicated commercial bank loans more than doubled, to reach 43% of total debt, up from just 13%. In the period 1971–1976, 167 foreign banks loaned funds to Peru. Citibank, Wells Fargo, and Manufacturers Hanover were each a "lead" bank in more than 20% of the loans Peru received, though each kept only about 10% of the syndicated loans it generated and parceled the rest to others. About half the funds came from U.S. banks with the rest coming from Canadian, Japanese, and European banks. Of the funds that went to the government, about half refinanced earlier debts, 15% financed specific projects (including oil exploration), and 28% were granted without a specific purpose.[19] The terms Peru obtained from banks were similar to those of other Latin American debtors. In the period 1968–1981, its average spread over LIBOR (the London Interbank Overnight Rate) was 1.43% while that of Argentina was 1.15%.[20]

In 1975, Velasco became ill and was replaced by General Francisco Morales Bermudez Cerrutti. Morales Bermudez was more moderate than his predecessor, and turned away from Velasco's radical reforms by, for example, allowing workers that had worked for less than three years to be fired. By late 1975, the external debt was over $3 billion, with an annual debt service of $500 million. Combined with a fall in the catch of fish and in the price of copper, the Peruvian balance of payments came under pressure. Morales Bermudes thus agreed to a 1976 stabilization package demanded by U.S. banks, which the president had approached to avoid the IMF. This package lowered real wages, as wage increases were limited while the sol was devalued by 44% and subsidies to basic consumer goods were cut.[21] This led to strikes and general unrest, thereby paving the way for a return to a civilian government, starting with elections to a Constitutional Assembly in June 1978.

In these elections, the *Alianza Popular Revolucionaria Americana* (American Popular Revolutionary Alliance—or APRA) won the largest block of seats, thus allowing its founder, Victor Raúl Haya de la Torre, to become the leader of this body. When it was founded in 1924, APRA favored nationalizations of land and industry, Latin American unity, actions against "Yanquee imperialism," and "solidarity of all oppressed people." While the party remained popular, particularly among peasants, it grew increasingly moderate in the decades it was kept from power. Haya de la Torre's popularity and his role in drafting the new Constitution suggested he would finally win the 1980 presidential election. However he died in 1979, leaving APRA without a well-known candidate and thus opening the door for Fernando Belaúnde Terry's election in 1980.

Belaúnde had already been president from 1963 to 1968 and had, at that time, inaugurated an era of high tariff barriers and increased government spending on highways, education, housing, and public health. Government spending rose from 11.5% of GDP to 16% during his first term. His 1980 campaign promised similar programs, including public works and economic expansion in the provinces.[22]

Belaúnde did keep his promise to build infrastructure projects, particularly those involving irrigation and roads. At the same time, Belaúnde decided to lower tariffs, have frequent mini-devaluations and keep interest rates high. These policies were advocated by several advisors who spent the period of military government in the United States. Initially, they bolstered international confidence and brought in foreign loans, particularly as the Velasco era investments in copper and petroleum were coming on line at a time when prices for minerals and oil were high. The export boom proved short lived, however, and the government found itself heavily reliant on foreign loans—by the end of 1981 the government had borrowed $734 million, of which 75% was from private banks.[23] At the same time, interest rates were on the rise, with LIBOR reaching above 16% that year.

International lending evaporated when Mexico found itself with insufficient reserves to meet its debt service in August 1982. By the end of 1982, the bank loans Peru obtained were on very poor terms—as much as 2.25% over LIBOR for five-year maturities. IMF-World Bank mandated structural adjustment programs were initiated in return for standby loans. The program was undermined by a number of factors, including Belaúnde's grandiose public works projects and the effects of El Niño weather patterns on exports. El Niño was a recurrent reversal of the Humboldt current that, in 1983, led to a devastating drought in southern Peru while torrential rains inundated the north. In addition to causing a great deal of suffering, it decimated the fishing industry and ravaged the textile industry, which lost its essential inputs. Broader indices of economic activity fell as well, with GDP down by 13% in 1983, official unemployment standing at 10.8% in 1984 and underemployment estimated at 60% of the labor force. One complication with interpreting these statistics is that their coverage of the informal sector is unclear. Relative to other Latin American countries, the informal sector was very large in Peru and it grew significantly in this period so that, by the mid-1980s, some analysts thought it employed a third of the workforce.[24]

Whether the loss in economic activity was exacerbated by Belaúnde's policies or not, Belaúnde was accused of handing over the nation's wealth to foreigners, and his popularity plummeted. Adding to his troubles was the rise of radical insurgent groups, Sendero Luminoso and *Movimiento Revolucionario Tupac Amaru* (MRTA). Sendero, the larger of the two groups, was started by Abimael Guzmán Reynoso, a philosophy professor in the education program at Ayacucho's University.

Guzmán believed that Peru's conditions paralleled those Mao had found in China and imbued his followers with his belief that Peru's semi-feudal condition was conducive to revolution through armed struggle. The poor prospects of his students, who could expect to become low-paid teachers at their village of origin, may have led many of them to join Sendero at its inception. Sendero started out by operating in the area surrounding Ayacucho where average income was the lowest in Peru and 54% of the population was illiterate. Sendero's first overt violent act was to burn ballot boxes in 1980. Later, it bombed economically valuable assets (such as electricity towers) while also killing government officials (who were labeled "enemies of the people"), uncooperative peasants (who were labeled "traitors"), and development workers. It gained some support by taking on abusive bureaucrats, creditors who were perceived to be exploitative, and cattle rustlers. Sendero's "revolutionary justice" also dealt harshly with adulterers and drunkards. By 1983, Sendero had expanded its operations a great deal and was bombing factories in Lima.[25]

While slow to react, Belaúnde eventually gave the armed forces both political and military responsibility in the affected areas. The initial repression of people deemed to be "Sendero sympathizers" was brutal. As the number of casualties mounted to 4,300 in 1984, thereby belying the government's claims that it had matters under control, the Lima press started carrying stories about atrocities committed by the military.[26]

Conditions worsened over the remainder of Belaúnde's term, as a global recession reduced export prices over 20% between 1983 and 1985. In 1984 the economic situation was so poor that the administration stopped servicing Peru's international debt, leaving the country largely isolated. This situation provided the backdrop for the first round of the presidential election of 1985, which Sendero sought to boycott but which had an 80% turnout.[27] It was a triumph of the left with the candidate of a Marxist party, Alfonso Barrantes, getting 23% of the votes and Alan García getting 47% of the votes.

The García Years

Alan García was a dashing 36-year-old when he won Peru's presidency. He had studied law in Lima and then continued his studies in Spain and France, where he claimed to have supported himself by playing the guitar in the streets of Paris. He was 6'4" tall and a spellbinding orator. While his political experience was limited to one term in congress, he had strong party credentials. He was the son of APRA militants, had been a member of the party since age 11, had served as Haya's personal assistant during his last years, and had support from high-ranking party members.

In his campaign, García maintained APRA's anti-imperialist rhetoric. However, unlike Barrantes who proposed a complete moratorium on debt payments, García said he would devote 20% of export earnings to these payments although he would negotiate directly with creditor banks and not through the IMF. García also promised to focus on issues of concern to modern peasants and the urban poor, particularly those who worked in the enormous informal sector. Combined, these groups accounted for 70% of the population, yet earned only 25% of the income. García dubbed them "the forgotten ones" and the "future of the nation." At the same time García emphasized APRA's commitment to all Peruvians and presented APRA as a moderately progressive social democratic party that, unlike Barrantes, did not seek mass nationalizations. [28]

The 1985 Limit on Debt Payments

The policies outlined in García's inauguration speech on July 28, 1985, and over the following few months initially raised his domestic popularity, but caused an international uproar. In his speech García reaffirmed his intention not to negotiate with the IMF, which he blamed for having encouraged Peru to borrow in the 1970s even though these funds were used for growing the government and for unproductive investments. But he also went beyond his campaign rhetoric by saying, "In the next 12 months, as long as the situation does not change, we will allot for the servicing of our foreign debt no more than 10% of the total value of our exports and not the 60% that has been required of us. I am thus reasserting Peruvian economic sovereignty and the right each people has to decide its future without the hated mediation of organizations that are only at the service of large international interests." [29]

In justifying his debt stance García recalled that, while in Roman times insolvent debtors could be quartered or sold as slaves, modern legislation prevented creditors from seizing either human rights or individual salaries. He thus argued that "Peru's national salary, which is the product of its exports" could not be seized either and went on to say, "They will not divide us in pieces nor convert us into slaves." He did not, however, suggest that Peru should stop all its payments. Instead he saw such payments as part of the government's "responsibility in the continuity of Peru." He went on to state, "We must accept this responsibility because, even if we must denounce the unjust origins of the debt, we must also accept that we did not have sufficient strength and courage as a people to change our history earlier." [30]

García made frequent public appearances and gave unannounced speeches from the balcony of the National Palace. He also maintained tight control over all policy and decision making. Many of his reforms were passed by decree, which was allowed by the 1980 Constitution in cases of national emergency and meant that the reforms did not involve legislative approval. Often, even his closest advisors did not know about major policy initiatives until they had been announced publicly (this was the case, for example, with the 10% debt policy in his inaugural speech).

After making his unilateral debt policy proclamation, García sought to convince other Latin American debtors to default as well. He did so by being very critical of the United States and the IMF. He called the latter a "viceroyal court" and labeled the IMF's letters of intent "letters of colonial submission" while saying, "The IMF calls for austerity only in poor countries, while favoring the most powerful nation on earth. Ever since the U.S. dollar was taken off the gold standard in 1971, the United States has been the only country that can issue currency indefinitely to cover its own deficit."[31]

Other major debtor countries did not follow García's lead, however, and continued negotiations with their creditors throughout the 1980s. This may have been due in part to U.S. Secretary of State James Baker. His October 1985 "Baker plan" called for fresh loans from both private and official creditors to countries that implemented suitable adjustment programs.

While failure to meet all scheduled payments had already begun under Belaúnde, García's made nonpayment of debt an official policy, unilaterally deciding to pay only what he regarded as reasonable and which creditors would receive payment first. García and his advisors understood that this would cut inflows of foreign capital but Peru's Central Bank president, Richard Webb, thought it would be possible to finance growth of 4% to 5% without having to rely on foreign funds. He said "We don't need fresh money, we're better off without it for the next five or ten years. Not only might it be badly used, but the effort that needs to be made won't be made if it's available."[32]

Domestic "Heterodox" Policies 1985–1987

Based on the existence of excess capacity, García and his advisors believed that cost pressures and inflationary expectations caused inflation in Peru. This stood in contrast to the orthodox view (as espoused by the IMF and other international organizations) that viewed inflation as being due mostly to an excessive demand for goods. Thus, while the currency was devalued and gasoline prices increased when García took office, his administration also took some heterodox steps. In particular, it sought to control cost pressures and inflationary expectations by freezing all prices as well as the exchange rate even as minimum wages were increased. While the price freeze was initially supposed to last six months, it was later extended through the end of 1986.

To encourage the expansion of domestic production the government banned certain imports, lowered interest rates and increased access to credit for small enterprises. The heterodox program counted on domestic investment to spur economic expansion, in keeping with the program's goal of creating a self-sufficient domestic economy. Tax cuts and other investment incentives were offered to businesses, and in July 1986, García began meeting regularly with the leaders of the largest industrial concerns in the country, which the press called the 12 apostles.

Policies geared toward increasing urban employment included micro-lending programs, a substantial easing of firing restrictions, and a temporary public works employment targeted at those in the informal sector. The government promised it would increase transfers to the poor areas in which Sendero was active. This was supposed to reduce Sendero's appeal and was suggested by García's inaugural speech when he said, "The 62% of the people who live in the Andean highlands make do with less help from central authority than their ancestors received in the days of the Incas."[33] However, these promises of help were largely unfulfilled.

García's administration also sought to save money in a variety of ways. For example, Alan García lowered his own salary and those of his ministers. A more important source of savings involved cuts in the military budget, where García cut an order for 26 Mirage aircraft in half.

This was not the only source of tension with the military. When, just after García took the reigns of power, evidence was presented that the military had been involved in killings at Accomarca, García dismissed three senior officers including the head of the Armed Forces Joint Command. The military saw this as an unprecedented reduction in their autonomy even though it was consistent with García's emphasis on human rights while pursuing the war with Sendero. García alienated the military further while losing credibility on the human rights front in June 1986, when he asked the armed forces to deal with a set of coordinated Sendero prison uprisings. This resulted in the killing of at least 249 prisoners. Many of these were killed after they surrendered and García and the military each sought to blame the other for this atrocity.[34]

Economic conditions at the beginning of García's administration improved. The monthly inflation rate fell to 2.7% in November 1985 (from 12.2% in April)[35] and the country posted a trade surplus of $1.2 billion, helping to build up new reserves. Growth continued to be strong in 1986, with a growth rate of over 9% that outshone the rest of Latin America. Real family income rose 25% between July 1985 and October 1986, thus spurring demand, consumption, and production. Unemployment rates were lowered—unemployment in greater Lima dropped to a low of 4.8% in 1987. Some positive income redistribution was achieved, as growth was concentrated in those industries affected by domestic demand, such as manufacturing, agriculture, and construction, rather than in traditional export industries. At the same time, renewed confidence led to a decline in dollar and dollar-linked accounts, which had become popular during the Belaúnde years.[36]

Relations with Creditors

Soon after García's inauguration, Peru's debt rating was downgraded. The debt was declared "value-impaired" in October—a move which made it nearly impossible for Peru to obtain any new commitments from commercial sources. At the same time, the secondary market value of Peru's debt fell. It traded at 20% of its face value by April 1986, even as the market rate of the debt of Argentina, Brazil, Chile, Ecuador, Mexico, and Venezuela stood at 60% or more of face value (see **Exhibit 14**).

García's stance on foreign debt eased after his initial announcement. García claimed that he was willing to negotiate with creditors, just not via the IMF as a middleman. However, several scheduled negotiations were cancelled and rescheduled. At the same time, creditors were receiving some payments. Payments followed an informal hierarchy within the 10% limitation. The idea was to pay first those who continued to lend more money than they were being repaid. Second in line for Peruvian funds were creditor governments, with priority for Latin American countries, then came commercial banks, and last of all the IMF.

Furthermore, García initially used a generous interpretation of the 10% limit, whose parameters had not been defined precisely in his inauguration speech. At first, the 10% limitation applied only to the public sector's medium- and long-term debt, and left private debts, barter deals and debt payments to Latin American countries out of the equation. Moreover, the percentage was applied to the exports of goods and services, not just of goods. Thus, the administration made payments of 13.6% of merchandise exports in 1985. When payments on all other debt—public, private, and central bank debt—was included, the corresponding payments equaled roughly 38.9% of merchandise exports. Claiming that private debt repayments were a channel for capital flight, García put all debt payments, including those on private debt, under the 10% ceiling in 1986. By 1987, rules were instituted which implied that commercial banks would receive no payments on Peru's "old debts".[37]

In early 1986 García narrowly avoided being declared ineligible for further IMF assistance by making a token $35 million payment to the fund. A similar token payment of $17.8 million was made to keep the commercial banks at bay, and the United States also received small payments. In August 1986 Peru was declared ineligible for further IMF funds, with outstanding arrears amounting to about $160 million. Although the World Bank provided no new loans, it continued making disbursements on previous commitments. These included, for example, programs of agricultural development that provided funds for farm credits and road improvements as well as education projects whose funds were earmarked for school construction, the purchase of textbooks and the training of both teachers and educational administrators. Disbursements in 1986 equaled $135 million against payments of $115 million. Disbursements continued until May 1987, when the flow of funds turned negative, and Peru stopped making payments.

While official aid from the United States declined, some western European countries actually increased overseas development assistance (ODA) during the period. European Community ODA to Peru jumped nearly threefold from 1986 to 1987, and continued to increase through 1990 (see **Exhibit 8**). By contrast, total financial inflows declined during García's term, from $1,021 million in 1984 to only $682 million in 1985, and down to $239 million in 1990, when financial flows turned negative.

On the other hand, Peru's foreign trade was not severely disrupted. No Peruvian goods were seized and trade credit continued to be extended. Trade credit allowed exporters to get paid when they shipped goods while importers paid only when they received them. Procedurally, an importer who opened a letter of credit and promised future payment could be sure that the exporter would only be paid if he complied with the conditions stipulated in the credit. Banks who operated in this market could guarantee this because they had a great deal of experience reading the relevant documents. Thus trade credit, which could only be partly collateralized by the goods in transit and which was simplified by offering credit lines to importers, facilitated international trade.[38]

Trade credit lines, particularly those from U.S. banks, did drop to about $300 million when Belaúnde stopped making payments, and Belaúnde responded by moving Peruvian reserves to European banks. However, trade credit did not drop significantly at the beginning of the García administration and García diligently repaid these debts. In 1986, Peru also obtained a trade credit line from the Panamian subsidiary of the Bank of Credit and Commerce International (BCCI) which held Peru's reserves on terms unfavorable to Peru. In a subsequent U.S. Senate hearing it was alleged that BCCI had paid bribes to obtain this desirable position vis-à-vis Peru.[39]

It was also rumored that that Peru had used intermediaries to buy back some of its debt on the secondary market at about 22 cents on the dollar. Some scholars thought such "buybacks" were not in Peru's interest because they benefited only the creditors. In particular Jeremy Bulow and Kenneth Rogoff (who would later become chief economist of the IMF) argued that the fact that Peruvian debt traded at a steep discount suggested both that this debt would not be repaid in its entirety and that the amount that Peru would repay was unlikely to depend very much on the nominal debt outstanding. They thought future repayments were more likely to depend on fears of sanctions for nonpayment, and that the cost to Peru of these sanctions would not fall significantly if its total debt were reduced somewhat. Thus, the only real gainers from buybacks of debt by Peru would be creditors, who would see the secondary market price rise.[40]

Difficulties after 1987

By the beginning of 1987, Peru's economy showed signs of strain. One set of difficulties concerned the collection of government revenue. Public sector income fell in 1986 and 1987, despite GDP growth. In 1987, public sector revenue accounted for only 26% of GDP, as compared to 43% in 1985. Tax proceeds also dropped, from 14% of GDP in 1985 to 8.8% in 1987. Several factors contributed to the decline. First, the VAT had been cut nearly in half because the government thought that reactivation would compensate for the loss of income (lower rates would spur increased consumption as well as reduce evasion). Second, the freeze of fuel prices reduced income from the gas tax, which accounted for about a quarter of tax revenues. Third, tariff income fell because the government banned imports that had previously been subject to high tariffs and because it gave tariff exemptions to some public enterprises. Fourth, the government increased tax exemptions to the private sector in its efforts to encourage investment. However, large companies—both public and private—had traditionally been the largest contributors to the tax base. Further, public sector companies were not performing well. Much of the burden of the heterodox program fell upon the public companies, as they were used for anti-inflationary and public welfare purposes through price controls and subsidies. [41]

There were also difficulties in the foreign exchange market. The 1985 exchange rate freeze created a secondary, or parallel, market for dollars in which value was based on supply and demand. For the first year the government was successful in its efforts to stabilize the currency, and the parallel price for dollars exceeded the official one by around 25%. However by October 1986 this began to change and the gap rose to over 40% in late 1986 then to 100% in the first half of 1987. García responded by devaluing the inti for certain transactions (particularly certain exports) while dollars continued to be exchanged for a smaller number of intis in the case of other transactions (particularly traditional exports and imports of goods that were deemed essential).

In his July 1987 annual speech, García announced that he intended to nationalize all banks, finance, and insurance companies. The administration publicly claimed the nationalization was a necessity, that only a "democratization of credit" would help overcome historic social and geographic inequalities, and force the business community to invest in Peru. García also said that the bankers were acting as a conduit for capital flight, and that nationalization of the banking system would allow him to ensure that capital remained within the country. Many insiders, however, considered the move to be an attempt to rally populist sentiment in order to regain standing in public opinion polls (which had been falling) and regain unity within the party. [42]

The proposed nationalization had the opposite effect. The cause failed to resonate with the public at large, and many people sided with the banks. A newspaper reported that 130,000 people attended a demonstration against this nationalization, which counted among its organizers the world-famous writer and political novice Mario Vargas Llosa. In the declaration that led to this demonstration, Vargas Llosa stated that "the concentration of political and economic power in the governing party could mean the end of free expression and ultimately of democracy." This attempted nationalization, which had to be abandoned, also ruined the relationship García had built with the 12 apostles and caused the private sector to lose whatever faith remained in the administration. Businesspeople began to disinvest. The move also increased the polarization between the left and right wings of APRA. [43]

The proposed nationalization, together with Peru's balance of payments problems, led Peru to lose lines of credit particularly among subsidiaries of foreign banks. While Peru still had $400 million in trade credit lines at the end of 1987, half of these involved collateral deposits. In mid-1988, Banque Louis Dreyfus extended a further $600 million in credit in exchange for Peru using silver exports as collateral.[44]

To cope with its economic difficulties, García had four different finance ministers in 1988 and each one introduced a dramatic "package" of policies. One common component of the March, July, September, and November 1988 packages was a substantial increase in controlled prices (by 300% in the September package) with the aim of bringing them back to their historical levels in real terms and thereby close the deficits of state-owned enterprises. At the same time, the exchange rate was depreciated, wages were increased and interest rate ceilings were raised. In September, the exchange rate was also "unified" so that the central bank would stop losing money by selling foreign exchange to importers for a lower price than it paid exporters. However, by December 1989, there were five exchange rates ranging from 4,963 to 12,221 intis to the dollar.[45]

While inflation rose dramatically, economic activity slowed. This reduced demand for imports, thus allowing the central bank to accumulate reserves in 1989. In November 1989, the government sold foreign exchange in futures markets while also letting exporters keep more of the foreign exchange they generated in an attempt to revive the economy before the upcoming presidential elections. The result was that, coming into the elections of April 1990, foreign exchange reserves were depleted once again.

Meanwhile, Sendero's strength appeared to grow. It was particularly successful in extending its reach into the coca-growing region where it simultaneously prevented drug-dealers from paying low prices and fought the government's antidrug efforts. García had taken a tough stance on the coca industry that led to the destruction of an estimated 80 tons of cocaine in his first two months in office. He also cooperated with the U.S. "war on drugs" and U.S. helicopters were used to destroy coca crops. However these efforts appeared to backfire. Sendero was able to essentially take control of the region and started collecting a 10% tax on the export of coca. Moreover, coca production grew rapidly with sales in the late 1980s being estimated at $800 million. García's exchange rate policy during this period as well as the drop in agriculture prices during the 1988-89 recession may both have encouraged farmers to grow coca instead of other crops.[46]

Sendero also increased its influence in the parts of the sierra that provided Lima's food and power as well as in Lima itself, where the newspaper *El Diario* became a Sendero organ in 1986. One of Sendero's effective tactics became the *paro armado*, or armed strike, in which compliance with strikes decreed by Sendero was ensured by the threat of violence against strikebreakers. Meanwhile, the military's ability to respond to the increased violence was stultified by the economic crisis, as morale was low, salaries of military officers had dropped, and both corruption and desertion rates increased. The judicial system, too, seemed unable to deal effectively with those arrested on terrorism charges. Bribes were paid to prison guards and judges, who were also routinely intimidated. Delays in the judicial process were long, and the combination of weak cases and legal loopholes led to low conviction rates. According to the estimates of the U.S. Department of State, the conviction rate for terrorists was 20% in 1988.[47]

In the meantime, García's relationship with the world financial community remained tense. The government did make attempts to return to the good graces of the IMF and World Bank during 1988 and 1989, going as far as to invite delegations of each to visit Peru. Indeed, the administration worked to create an adjustment plan under the auspices of the World Bank in December 1987, although the World Bank recommendations were only implemented piecemeal. In addition, some payments were made to the IMF in September 1989. However, the IMF kept Peru on its ineligible list on the grounds that its arrears were large. In 1988, several commercial banks including Chase Manhattan accepted in-kind payments, including some in the form of automobile shock absorbers. Nonetheless, in March 1990, 11 leading commercial creditors including Chase, Wells Fargo, Bank of America, Citibank, and Manufacturers Hanover Trust filed a lawsuit against the government of Peru. This was the largest lawsuit ever filed against a sovereign debtor.[48]

The 1990 Elections

The parties of the left entered the election with low support, in part because they failed to unite behind a single candidate. Moreover, the most popular and more moderate left wing candidate, Alfonso Barrantes, had difficulties separating himself from the failed policies of García since the latter had adopted many of Barrantes' 1985 campaign proposals. By contrast, the right had an eloquent candidate in Vargas Llosa. Vargas Llosa believed ardently in political and economic freedom. He wanted to reinsert Peru into the international financial community and proposed not only a tightening of monetary and fiscal policy to bring down inflation but also a long term program of privatization to reduce the role of the government in Peru. In February 1985, a few months before the election, Vargas Llosa had a solid lead in the polls and the main goal of his campaign was to obtain over 50% of the vote so he would gain a grip on Congress while avoiding a runoff election.

In a poll published on March 24, 1990, Alberto Fujimori was the preferred candidate of only 4.8% of the voters. The son of Japanese immigrants, Fujimori had been mathematics professor and dean of a college for agronomists. He lived in a modest neighborhood but had acquired a moderate fortune in real estate transactions. He had never held a political office and was affiliated with a party he had created called Cambio 90. His slogan was "honesty, technology and hard work." Declaring himself not to be a politician, he did not articulate a clear government program. Yet on April 8, 1990 Fujimori received 24% of the vote to Vargas Llosa's 29%.[49]

This incredible turnaround has been given a variety of explanations. Some have blamed García himself, who caused many stories about Fujimori to be published in APRA's newspaper, and thereby helped to deny APRA's own candidate a slot in the runoff. Others have blamed Vargas Llosa for making it clear that the shock treatment he intended to apply would entail large short run costs. Vargas Llosa's most serious problem, however, may have been that he came to be seen as an arrogant candidate of the white rich minority. This perception was fueled in part Vargas Llosa's alliance with two traditional right wing parties (including Belaúnde's) whose members engaged in massive advertising campaigns to improve their individual chances in the congressional elections. These campaigns were widely seen as extravagant.[50]

In the campaign for the runoff election Fujimori emphasized his independence from traditional parties. He accused Vargas Llosa of seeing Fujimori's campaign as that of one *"chino"* and four *"cholos"* where these widely used ethnic labels referred to people of Asian and Indian descent respectively. Another successful slogan for Fujimori was the simple "say no to the shock." With support from APRA and the left, Fujimori won the runoff election on June 8 with 60% of the vote.

Fujimori's Choices

Against this backdrop, Fujimori had to make key decisions about both domestic and foreign policy. One option was to seek support from international organizations, though this would probably require that Peru make a new deal with its creditors and that it follow the sort of program that Fujimori appeared to have campaigned against. He also had to decide the extent to which he wanted to seek tighter relations with the United States. This decision too, could have implications both for the war with Sendero and for Peru's development. Still, the lack of clear campaign commitments and the receptivity of the international community after five years of facing García might allow Fujimori to make a fresh start.

Exhibit 1 Debt and Default History

End of Colonial Era	Borrowing	Deficit spending.
Early 1820s	Borrowing	Loans contracted on the London market at high interest rates to pay for war debts and import financing.
1827	Default	By the late 1820s, the foreign debt was five times the government's annual revenues.[a]
1840s-1850s	Borrowing	Exports of guano boomed, but deficit spending continued. Consolidation of national debt began.
1856	Repayment	Repayment of consolidated debt began.
1860s-1870s	Borrowing	Guano boom continued, as did deficit spending, however repayment allowed Peru to obtain significant 'guano secured' loans. Guano reserves were declining, however, at the same time the government's reliance upon guano income was increasing—it accounted for roughly 80% of state income.
1876	Default	Unilateral moratorium on debt service.
1889	Repayment	Grace contract erased Peru's debt and restored the country's credit rating, but required significant concessions, including control of the railway system for 66 years.
WWI	Default	Short-lived default as a result of reduced trade from war.
1916	Repayment	Export boom allowed resumption of debt service.
1920s	Borrowing	Bonds issued in New York and London. U.S. bankers aggressively encouraged developing country debt.
1931-1932	Default	Peru stopped making payments on bonds.
1947-1949	Repayment	In 1947 Peru offered repayment deal to bondholders, but it was considered unsatisfactory by bondholders' councils.
1953	Repayment	New offer extended in 1951, went into effect and repayments began in 1953. Accepted by bondholders' councils.
1958-1959	IMF program	IMF standby packages.
1968-1969	IMF program	IMF standby packages. Debt rescheduled.
1970	IMF program	IMF standby package.
1970s	Borrowing	US bankers encouraged developing country borrowing.
1977-1978	IMF program	IMF standby packages. Debt rescheduled.
1982	IMF program	IMF standby package. Loans dried up post-Mexican default.
1984	Default	IMF standby package. Payments stopped on foreign debt.
1985	Default	Garcia elevated nonpayment of debt to plank of public policy by officially limiting debt service to 10% of export earnings.

Sources: Adapted from Peter Flindell Klarén, *Peru: Society and Nationhood in the Andes*, (New York: Oxford University Press, 2000); John Crabtree, *Peru Under Garcia* (London: MacMillan Academic and Professional Ltd., 1992); and Chandra S. Hardy, *Rescheduling Developing-Country Debts, 1956–1981: Lessons and Recommendations* (Washington, DC: Overseas Development Council, 1982), pp. 6–7, 36, 63–65.

Note: [a]Klarén, p. 144.

Exhibit 2   Map of Peru

Source: Courtesy of University of Texas at Austin, Perry-Castañeda Library Map Collection.

Exhibit 3 Interwar Bonds—Original Dollar Bond Issues

Loan	Issue Date	Maturity Date	Issue Amount	Interest Rate	Bond Denominations	Issue Price	Default Date
National 1	1927	1959	$15,000,000	7%	$500 / $1000	96.5	Sep-31
National 2	1927	1960	$50,000,000	6%	$500 / $1000	91.5	Jun-31
National 3	1928	1961	$25,000,000	6%	$500 / $1000	91	Apr-31
Callao	1927	1944	$1,500,000	7½%	$500 / $1000	99	Jan-32
Lima	1928	1958	$3,000,000	6½%	$1000	93	Mar-32

Source: Adapted from the *Foreign Bondholders Protective Council Annual Report 1934*.

Exhibit 3a   1947 Bond Offer

Original Loan	1947 Issue	Issue Date	Maturity Date	Interest Rates			
				1947–1948	1949–1950	1951–1952	1953 on
N1	Series A	1947	1997	1%	1½%	2%	2½%
N2	Series B	1947	1997	1%	1½%	2%	2½%
N3	Series C	1947	1997	1%	1½%	2%	2½%
Callao[a]	Series D	1947	1997	1%	1½%	2%	2½%
Lima[b]							

Source: Adapted from the Foreign Bondholders Protective Council Annual Report 1946 through 1949.
Notes: [a]The Callao issue was assumed by the Republic in 1947.
　　　　[b]There was no offer made on the Lima issue at this time.

Exhibit 3b   1953 Bond Offer

Original Issue	1947 Issue	1953 Issue	Issue Date	Maturity Date	Interest Rate as of January 1953	Scrip Certificate Value (total) per $1,000 Bond
N1	Series A	Series A	1952	1997	3%	$103.83
N2	Series B	Series B	1952	1997	3%	$90.50
N3	Series C	Series C	1952	1997	3%	$91.50
Callao	Series D	Series D	1952	1997	3%	$113.00
Lima[a]		Series L	1952	1997	3%	$135.42

Source: Adapted from the *Foreign Bondholders Protective Council Annual Report 1953 through 1954*.
Note: [a]The Lima issue was assumed by the Republic in January 1953.

Exhibit 4   Basic Indicators

	1980	1981	1982	1983	1984	1985	1986	1987	1988	1989	1990
Real GDP (1979 intis billions)	3,661.20	3,849.70	3,840.70	3,356.60	3,550.60	3,625.40	3,960.90	4,291.20	3,938.70	3,473.40	3,322.00
Inflation(%)	59.3	75.1	63.9	110.9	110.0	163.2	78.1	86.0	667.2	3,398.7	7,481.7
Real wages (% change)	3.8	-0.4	-0.9	-15.6	-4.3	-8.2	19.5	6.2	-27.7	-33.7	-17.1
Total population (millions)	17,295	17,720	18,144	18,568	18,992	19,417	19,840	20,261	20,684	21,112	21,550
Working population (thousands)	5,587	5,774	5,960	6,151	6,341	6,531	6,740	6,952	7,160	7,379	7,570
Public employment (thousands)	468	467	483	502	526	591	634	687	715	750	n/a
Level of international reserves (year end, US$ millions)	1,480	793	914	889	1,125	1,493	958	43	-352	357	531
Dollar index of traditional export prices[a]	189.5	160.4	133.0	146.0	134.6	118.2	101.4	112.5	133.3	131.7	138.1
Dollar index of import prices[a]	124.2	128.4	129.1	132.0	133.3	130.5	152.7	168.2	178.0	179.4	195.6
LIBOR rates[b]	14.19	16.87	13.29	9.72	10.94	8.40	6.86	7.18	7.98	9.28	8.31

Sources: Banco Central de Reserve del Peru, *Memoria*, 1992; Richard Webb, *Peru en Números*, (Lima, Peru: Cuanto S.A., 1992), pp. 483, 1047; IMF *International Financial Statistics Yearbook*, 1988, 2001.
Notes: [a]1978 = 100.
              [b]LIBOR rates offered on three-month U.S. dollar deposits.

Exhibit 5   Government Budget (% of GDP)

	1980	1981	1982	1983	1984	1985	1986	1987	1988	1989	1990
Central government											
Current revenue	17.0	14.4	14.3	12.0	13.9	14.8	12.5	9.0	9.2	7.1	10.2
Current expenditure	15.0	14.3	14.2	16.3	15.0	14.4	13.1	12.3	10.5	10.5	11.8
Defense	4.1	3.5	4.5	4.3	3.0	3.5	3.0	3.0	2.0	2.0	2.2
Internal security	1.6	1.5	1.6	1.9	1.8	1.6	1.9	2.1	1.5	1.3	1.3
Education	3.0	3.2	2.9	3.0	2.9	2.8	3.5	2.3	2.4	2.6	2.1
Health	1.1	1.1	0.9	1.1	1.1	1.0	1.0	0.9	0.8	0.7	0.6
Capital expenditure	4.3	4.1	3.4	3.2	3.4	2.7	3.1	2.4	1.5	2.3	1.4
Deficit	-2.3	-4.0	-3.2	-7.5	-4.4	-2.2	-3.7	-5.7	-2.8	-3.4	-2.3
External finance	.6	1.2	2.4	4.0	3.3	2.7	1.3	0.7	1.4	1.4	1.6
Domestic finance	1.7	2.8	0.8	3.5	1.1	-0.5	2.4	5.0	1.4	4.0	1.8
State owned enterprises[a]											
Revenue	26.5	22.3	24.5	31.3	25.3	28.1	18.9	15.2	15.3	13.9	13.7
Expenditure	28.3	25.1	28.7	33.7	27.4	28.7	20.7	16.4	19.7	15.1	14.1
Deficit	-1.8	-2.8	-4.2	-2.3	-2.1	-0.6	-1.8	-1.2	-4.4	-1.2	-0.7
External finance	1.1	0.4	3.6	1.6	1.3	1.4	1.1	0.6	0.7	0.7	0.6
Domestic finance	0.7	2.3	0.6	0.7	0.7	-0.8	0.7	0.6	3.6	0.5	0.2

Sources: Adapted from Banco Central de Reserva del Peru, *Memoria* 1989, 1992; and Richard Webb, *Peru en Números*, 1990, p. 854; 1992, p. 968.
Note: [a]Does not include financial enterprises.

Exhibit 6 Composition of GDP (% of nominal GDP)

	1980	1981	1982	1983	1984	1985	1986	1987	1988	1989	1990
By factor demand											
Personal consumption	57.8	59.1	58.4	64.3	65.7	65.6	70.3	70.2	71.1	71.5	77.3
Public expenditures	10.5	10.2	11.0	11.2	9.7	9.5	9.6	10.0	7.4	6.9	6.4
Investment	28.8	34.3	33.6	24.3	20.6	18.4	21.4	21.5	24.2	19.2	16.8
Public	6.1	7.3	8.5	8.7	8.1	6.2	5.4	4.4	4.3	3.5	2.6
Private	18.8	21.5	21.3	15.0	12.8	12.0	15.1	15.4	18.2	15.5	14.1
Change in inventory	4.0	5.5	3.8	0.6	-0.3	0.2	0.9	1.6	1.7	0.1	0.2
Exports of goods and services	22.3	16.1	16.5	19.7	19.3	23.0	13.9	11.0	13.5	14.7	13.1
Imports of goods and services	19.3	19.7	19.5	19.5	15.4	16.5	15.3	12.7	16.2	12.3	13.7
By productive sector											
Agriculture	9.8	10.3	10.6	10.9	11.5	11.4	10.9	10.6	12.2	13.3	12.7
Fishing	0.5	0.5	0.5	0.4	0.6	0.7	0.8	0.7	0.9	1.1	1.1
Mining	12.3	11.5	12.3	13.2	13.1	13.6	12.0	10.7	9.7	11.6	11.8
Manufacturing	24.1	23.6	22.4	20.7	21.1	21.9	23.7	24.9	23.6	21.6	21.5
Construction	5.7	6.5	6.6	6.0	5.6	4.9	5.6	6.0	6.3	5.9	6.5
Government	6.4	6.2	6.3	7.7	7.8	7.7	7.6	7.3	8.2	8.4	8.5
Other	39.6	40.5	41.8	41.2	40.4	39.8	39.4	39.9	39.1	38.0	37.9
Total compensation of employees	30	31	33	34	32	29	32	34	32	27	

Source: Adapted from Banco Central de Reserva del Peru, *Memoria*, 1988, 1992; Richard Webb, *Peru en Números*, 1991, p. 373.

Exhibit 7 External Debt (US$ millions)

	1970	1980	1981	1982	1983	1984	1985	1986	1987	1988	1989	1990
Long-term debt	2,655	7,480	7,453	8,629	9,849	10,671	11,677	12,645	14,166	13,928	14,258	14,987
Public and publicly guaranteed	856	6,218	6,048	6,965	8,270	9,206	10,335	11,308	12,733	12,505	12,669	13,343
Official creditors	373	3,110	3,057	3,079	3,547	3,904	4,776	5,540	6,613	6,531	6,664	7,123
Multilateral	148	513	648	834	981	1,047	1,339	1,660	2,137	2,052	2,031	2,192
Bilateral	225	2,596	2,409	2,245	2,566	2,857	3,436	3,880	4,476	4,479	4,632	4,930
Private creditors	483	3,108	2,990	3,885	4,723	5,302	5,559	5,768	6,119	5,975	6,006	6,221
Commercial banks	148	1,706	1,564	2,244	2,946	3,607	3,765	3,836	3,958	3,914	3,914	3,967
Private nonguaranteed	1,799	1,262	1,405	1,664	1,579	1,465	1,342	1,337	1,433	1,423	1,589	1,554
Interest arrears	--	0	0	0	0	374	703	1,319	2,243	2,878	3,426	5,453
Short-term	--	2,084	2,479	3,016	1,440	1,704	1,795	2,612	3,634	4,269	4,904	5,453
Total	--	10,038	10,319	12,294	11,987	13,050	14,174	15,986	18,644	18,999	19,921	21,105

Source: Adapted from World Bank, *World Debt Tables*, (Washington, D.C.: World Bank, 1989), vol. 2, p. 306; 1991, vol. 2, p. 314.

Exhibit 8   Overseas Development Assistance (*in U.S.$ millions, from selected OECD countries*)

	1980	1983	1984	1985	1986	1987	1988	1989	1990
Belgium	4.6	3.4	1.7	1.8	3	3.5	4.1	2.2	3.8
Canada	2	6.8	14.5	13.1	17.1	15.4	22.5	22.4	23.2
Denmark	0.9	0.1	0.4	0	0.1	0	0.1	0.6	1.9
Finland	-0.1	3.1	2.3	3.2	1.4	3.6	6.4	3.5	2.8
France	5.2	7	9	3.5	3.9	3.7	3.8	4.7	6.5
Germany	58.6	41.3	35.3	35.6	62.8	71.4	48.6	55.3	60.4
Italy	0.5	6.5	4.2	8.9	8.5	19.2	35.8	77.9	80.6
Japan	11.1	45.1	24.9	21.4	32.3	37.5	28.4	27.9	39.8
Netherlands	34.3	21.1	29.4	15.2	18.2	31.5	22.5	23.5	30
Spain	--	--	--	--	--	2.2	3.9	4.8	6.3
Sweden	0.8	0.6	0.5	0.1	0.7	0.6	0.7	0.8	1
Switzerland	2.9	4.5	4.1	3.8	3.8	8.2	6	6.3	10.7
United Kingdom	1.7	6.5	0.6	1.2	1.8	1.7	2.4	1.8	2.1
United States	53	89	114	177	95	63	61	36	79
Multilateral EC	1.2	7.8	3.1	4.7	4.2	12.8	15.1	19.7	21.9
Total donors[a]	203.2	297.1	310.1	316.4	271.5	294.4	276.1	309.8	400.2

Source: Adapted from OECD.

Note: [a]Includes mulitlateral donor aid.

Exhibit 9   Nominal GDP, Money Supply, and Exchange Rates (intis)

	1980	1981	1982	1983	1984	1985	1986	1987	1988	1989	1990
Nominal GDP (millions)	6,005	10,544	17,312	31,155	68,804	188,384	359,550	717,158	4,306,000	105,197,000	6,280,418,000
Money supply (millions)											
Currency in circulation	273	433	625	1,104	2,488	8,089	16,175	41,768	256,878	5,308,000	271,168,000
Demand deposits	251	331	424	888	2,049	6,847	14,775	33,729	189,515	2,431,000	111,988,000
Quasi-money—dom. cur. deposits	450	970	1,697	2,833	5,232	14,620	31,128	58,835	250,170	10,124,000	222,384,000
Quasi-money—for. cur. deposits	380	654	1,481	3,265	9,392	12,926	7,986	14,877	325,786	4,800,000	533,215,000
Exchange rates (intis per US$)											
Bank rate	.34	.51	.99	2.35	5.82	17.4	20.0	62.8	500.0	12,473.0	495,000.0
Official rate (MUC)	.34	.51	.99	2.27	5.70	14.0	14.0	33.0	500.0	5,261.0	516,923.0
Parallel market rate	.34	.51	.99	2.35	5.82	17.4	20.0	92.0	1,700.0	12,940.0	547,500.0

Sources: Banco Central de Reserva del Peru, *Memoria* 1985, 1992; and Richard Webb, *Peru en Números,* 1991, pp. 982–3.

Exhibit 10 Balance of Payments (*U.S.$ millions*)

	1980	1981	1982	1983	1984	1985	1986	1987	1988	1989	1990
Current account balance	-102	-1,729	-1,609	-806	-149	161	-1,095	-1,597	-1,282	94	-1,092
Trade balance	1,722	826	-523	293	1,007	1,172	-65	-521	-99	1,197	340
Exports, fob	3,916	3,249	3,293	3,015	3,147	2,978	2,531	2,661	2,691	3,488	3,231
Imports, fob	-3,090	-3,802	-3,722	-2,722	-2,140	-1,806	-2,596	-3,182	-2,790	-2,291	-2,891
Investment income	-909	-1,019	-1,033	-1,039	-1,088	-983	-855	-862	-981	-924	-1,014
Public sector	-437	-456	-548	-636	-818	-752	-700	-697	-810	-770	-883
Private sector	-472	-563	-485	-403	-270	-231	-155	-165	-171	-154	-131
Other services	-166	-318	-314	-279	-226	-162	-325	-394	-413	-414	-665
Transfers	147	161	167	219	158	134	150	180	211	235	247
Long term capital	463	565	1,194	1,372	1,139	721	691	882	959	913	783
Public sector	371	305	989	1,431	1,404	859	701	838	934	856	796
New inflows	1,208	1,620	1,934	1,530	1,026	693	495	585	350	380	245
Official creditors	256	149	137	156	161	229	129	148	153	174	118
Socialist countries	137	118	71	108	25	56	22	92	5	62	12
International organizations	177	186	238	200	260	206	205	220	94	17	40
Commercial banks	331	853	838	436	181	5	0	0	0	18	4
Suppliers	307	314	650	630	399	197	139	125	98	109	71
Refinancing	372	80	109	1,024	499	201	0	0	0	699	0
Amortization	-1,203	-1,394	-1,054	-1,145	-1,441	-1,329	-1,453	-1,591	-1,492	-1,251	-1,143
Arrears	-6	-1	--	22	1,320	1,294	1,659	1,844	2,076	1,028	1,694
Private sector	92	260	205	-59	-265	-138	-10	44	25	57	-13
Short-term capital & errors and omissions	361	660	539	-606	-743	-602	-113	-70	-75	-144	445
Change in reserves	-722	504	-124	40	-247	-280	517	785	398	-863	-136

Source: Banco Central de Reserva del Peru, *Memoria*, 1988, 1990, 1992.

Exhibit 11   Peru's Exports *(U.S.$ millions)*

Exports	1976	1977	1978	1979	1980	1981	1982	1983	1984	1985	1986	1987	1988	1989	1990
Traditional exports	1,204	1,502	1,619	2,866	3,071	2,548	2,531	2,460	2,421	2,264	1,886	1,952	1,944	2,509	2,265
Fishmeal	168	184	196	256	195	141	202	79	137	118	206	223	357	410	336
US$/TM	*284.2*	*421.8*	*405.3*	*389.7*	*469.4*	*448.0*	*328.5*	*386.7*	*342.4*	*232.6*	*287.7*	*305.7*	*438.7*	*374.1*	*310.3*
Cotton	71	48	38	49	72	64	85	44	23	51	39	19	30	65	42
US$/qq	*91.4*	*103.3*	*96.5*	*113.7*	*101.8*	*92.8*	*66.1*	*66.4*	*92.5*	*82.5*	*81.6*	*103.5*	*136.8*	*90.1*	*97.2*
Sugar	85	78	47	34	13	--	20	35	49	23	2	15	16	20	36
US$/qq	*13.8*	*8.7*	*8.1*	*8.7*	*11.4*	*--*	*15.2*	*17.9*	*19.4*	*16.8*	*18.5*	*20.4*	*20.4*	*21.1*	*21.2*
Coffee	106	198	168	245	141	106	113	117	126	151	275	143	121	153	98
US$/qq	*104.0*	*204.8*	*144.6*	*162.1*	*146.9*	*107.4*	*119.4*	*96.8*	*112.7*	*115.9*	*169.1*	*94.2*	*114.3*	*82.5*	*68.0*
Copper	236	385	425	693	751	529	460	443	442	476	449	559	613	759	700
US¢/lb	*58.8*	*54.4*	*55.3*	*83.5*	*97.4*	*74.1*	*62.3*	*68.8*	*59.5*	*59.3*	*58.7*	*72.2*	*104.5*	*116.8*	*111.1*
Iron	63	91	74	85	95	93	108	75	58	76	60	61	60	56	58
US$/TLN	*14.1*	*14.9*	*15.5*	*14.8*	*16.5*	*17.7*	*19.1*	*17.5*	*13.9*	*14.6*	*14.4*	*14.0*	*13.4*	*14.8*	*15.8*
Gold	8	19	17	13	40	74	56	69	67	43	7	1	0	2	9
US$/Oz.Tr.	*123.0*	*143.4*	*191.6*	*265.2*	*616.5*	*472.7*	*375.6*	*420.8*	*366.7*	*320.6*	*353.1*	*353.8*	*0*	*356.3*	*371.7*
Silver	90	116	119	222	315	312	205	391	227	140	107	92	60	98	79
US$/Oz.Tr.	*4.3*	*4.6*	*5.3*	*9.3*	*19.7*	*11.1*	*7.9*	*11.9*	*8.5*	*6.3*	*5.6*	*6.8*	*6.7*	*5.7*	*4.9*
Lead	107	140	164	330	383	219	216	293	234	202	172	256	191	204	185
US¢/lb	*28.2*	*38.3*	*45.1*	*96.2*	*114.4*	*68.0*	*55.2*	*69.6*	*58.7*	*52.7*	*57.4*	*78.5*	*81.1*	*54.2*	*53.1*
Zinc	180	155	137	174	210	267	268	307	340	268	246	250	281	429	416
US¢/lb	*19.7*	*16.7*	*14.0*	*18.6*	*20.4*	*25.4*	*24.8*	*26.7*	*30.2*	*26.4*	*23.4*	*25.5*	*31.7*	*42.4*	*36.0*
Petroleum[a]	50	52	186	652	792	689	719	544	618	645	232	274	166	217	258
US$/B.	*10.5*	*12.6*	*13.6*	*27.1*	*35.2*	*34.6*	*31.6*	*26.6*	*26.3*	*23.9*	*10.8*	*15.4*	*10.7*	*14.2*	*16.6*
Others	40	36	8	113	64	54	79	63	100	71	71	59	49	95	49
Nontraditional	137	224	353	810	845	701	762	555	726	714	645	709	747	979	966
Total	1,341	1,726	1,972	3,676	3,916	3,249	3,293	3,015	3,147	2,978	2,531	2,661	2,691	3,488	3,231

Source: Banco Central de Reserva del Peru, *Memoria* 1985, 1992.

Note: [a]Includes crude petroleum and derivatives.

Exhibit 12 Nominal Exchange Rates for International Trade (intis per US$)

	Traditional Exports	Nontraditional Exports		Export Average	Priority Imports (MUC)	Import Average
		Nonpriority	Priority			
Dec 1985	14.02	14.59	14.59	14.15	13.98	13.98
Dec 1986	15.00	19.14	20.88	16.09	13.98	16.17
Dec 1987	34.98	38.19	38.19	35.88	28.05	34.43
Dec 1988	543.89	543.89	543.89	543.89	500.00	710.69
Dec 1989	9,545.43	11,993.47	12,221.27	10,238.96	4,963.35	7,504.11

Source: Banco Central de Reserva del Peru, *Memoria* 1989.

Exhibit 13 Maximum Allowable Nominal Domestic Interest Rates

Date of Regulation	Bank Loan Rates	Savings Account Rates
02/01/79	32.5	29.0
01/05/81	49.5	30.5
05/15/81	47.5	50.5
01/14/82	47.5	50.5
09/01/83	60.0	55.0
12/15/84	66.0	60.0
02/01/85	72.0	66.0
07/01/85	90.0	68.0
08/05/85	110.0	83.0
08/26/85	75.0	46.0
10/01/85	45.0	30.0
02/16/86	40.0	19.0
05/16/86	40.0	19.0
04/16/87	40.0	22.0
07/16/87	32.0	22.0
03/16/88	55.0	35.5
06/16/88	12.0	72.0
09/01/88	255.0	120.0
12/01/88	791.6	204.0
03/01/89	1,355.2	252.0
10/01/89	1,158.9	252.0
11/16/89	934.9	288.0
01/16/90	1,221.5	252.0
03/16/90	229.0	300.0
06/01/90	5,102.1	384.0
07/01/90	6,911.0	420.0

Source: Adapted from Richard Webb, *Peru en Números*, 1991, p. 904.

Exhibit 14   Latin American Comparison—Peru, Argentina, Brazil and Mexico

	1980	1985	1986	1987	1988	1989	1990
Peru							
Secondary market bond prices[a]	--	n/a	21.00	8.00	5.00	6.25	4.75
Balance of goods and services							
(US$ millions)	661	980	-405	-871	-466	939	33
GDP (US$ billions)	20.8	17.2	25.9	42.7	33.7	39.4	29.0
Argentina							
Secondary market bond prices	--	66.00	64.00	36.00	22.00	12.62	13.64
Balance of goods and services							
(US$ millions)	-3,285	4,342	1,543	245	3,555	5,109	7,954
GDP (US$ billions)	209.0	88.2	105.9	108.8	126.9	76.6	141.4
Brazil							
Secondary market bond prices	--	78.00	74.00	46.00	40.00	23.50	23.92
Balance of goods and services						13,32	
(US$ millions)	-5,957	10,762	5,731	8,794	16,145	7	6,986
GDP (US$ billions)	236.3	223.8	269.2	295.2	330.5	388.0	465.0
Mexico							
Secondary market bond prices	--	70.00	56.00	50.00	43.00	36.00	44.71
Balance of goods and services							
(US$ millions)	-4,979	7,683	4,416	8,913	2,414	-267	-3,110
GDP (US$ billions)	195.8	183.6	128.8	140.2	183.1	223.0	262.7

Sources: Adapted from James Wilkie, et al., eds, *Statistical Abstract of Latin America*, vol. 31, (Los Angeles: UCLA Latin American
          Center Publications, University of California, 1995), p. 941; and IMF *International Financial Statistics Yearbook*, 2001.

Note: [a]Prices 1985–1989 for December, 1990 for June.

Exhibit 15   García's Popularity Ratings (Greater Lima area)

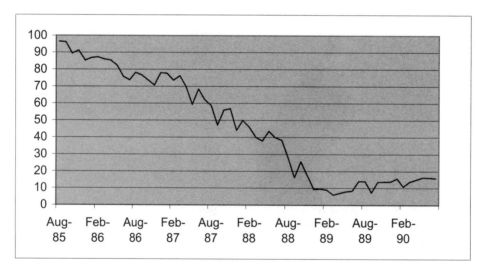

Source: Adapted from Datum International.

Endnotes

1   Robert Graham, "Financial leaders to meet on Peru," *The Financial Times*, June 28, 1990.

2   The World Bank, *World Development Indicators, 2001.* CD-ROM, (Washington, DC: World Bank, 2001).

3   Sandra Woy-Hazleton and William Hazleton, "Shining Path and the Marxist Left," in *The Shining Path of Peru*, ed. David Scott Palmer (New York: St. Martin's Press, 1992), p. 217; Mario Vargas Llosa, "The Story of a Massacre," *Granta*, 9: 1983, pp. 62–83.

4   Peter Flindell Klarén, *Peru: Society and Nationhood in the Andes*, (New York: Oxford University Press, 2000), p. 35.

5   Klarén, *Peru: Society and Nationhood in the Andes*, p. 68.

6   David P. Werlich, *Peru, A Short History*, (Carbondale, IL: Southern Illinois University Press, 1978), pp. 106–19, 224–25, 360.

7   Klarén, *Peru: Society and Nationhood in the Andes*, p. 305.

8   Richard F. Nyrop, ed., *Peru: A Country Study*, 3rd ed. (Washington, DC: Government Printing Office, 1981) p. 72; The World Bank, *World Development Indicators, 2001*.

9   Raul L. Madrid, *Over-exposed: U.S. Banks Confront the Third World Debt Crisis*, (Washington, DC: Investor Responsibility Research Center, 1990), p. 9; Foreign Bondholders Protective Council, Inc., *Annual Report 1936*, (New York: Lenz & Reicker, Inc., 1937), 665; Erika Jorgensen and Jeffrey Sachs, "Default and Renegotiation of Latin American Foreign Bonds in the Interwar Period," in *The International Debt Crisis in Historical Perspective*, eds. Barry Eichengreen and Peter H. Lindert, (Cambridge, MA: The MIT Press, 1989), p. 53.

10 Klarén, *Peru: Society and Nationhood in the Andes*, p. 271; Pedro Aspe Armella, et al, eds., *Financial policies and the World Capital Market: The Problem of Latin American Countries*, (Chicago: University of Chicago Press, 1983), p. 7; Foreign Bondholders Protective Council, Inc., *Annual Report 1936*, p. 12.

11 Foreign Bondholders Protective Council, Inc., *Annual Report 1937*, (New York: Lenz & Reicker, Inc, 1938), p. 564; Foreign Bondholders Protective Council, Inc., *Annual Report 1941 through 1944*, (New York: Lenz & Reicker, Inc., 1945), p. 749; Jorgensen and Sachs, "Default and Renegotiation of Latin American Foreign Bonds in the Interwar Period," p. 68; Foreign Bondholders Protective Council, Inc., *Annual Report 1951 through 1952*, (New York: Lenz & Reicker, Inc., 1953), pp. 195, 200.

12 Shane Hunt, "Direct Foreign Investment in Peru: New Rules for an Old Game," in *The Peruvian Experiment*, ed. Abraham F. Lowenthal (Princeton, NJ: Princeton University Press, 1975), pp. 303, 305.

13 Jorgensen and Sachs, "Default and Renegotiation of Latin American Foreign Bonds in the Interwar Period," pp. 74–77.

14 Klarén, *Peru: Society and Nationhood in the Andes*, p. 343.

15 James D. Rudolph, *Peru: The Evolution of a Crisis*, (Westport, CT: Praeger Publishers, 1992), p. 61; Klarén, *Peru: Society and Nationhood in the Andes*, p. 343.

16 Hunt, "Direct Foreign Investment in Peru: New Rules for an Old Game," pp. 316–317, 351; Werlich, *Peru, A Short History*, p. 331.

17 Carlos Boloña Behr, *Politicas Arancelarias en el Peru, 1880-1980*, (Lima, Peru: Instituto de Economía de Libre Mercado, 1981), p. 71.

18 Hunt, "Direct Foreign Investment in Peru: New Rules for an Old Game," pp. 329, 331.

19 Robert Devlin, *Transnational Banks and the External Finance of Latin America: The Experience of Peru*, (Santiago, Chile: The United Nations, 1985), pp. 88–89, 110, 303.

20 Sule Ozler "Have Commercial Banks Ignored History?" *American Economic Review*, June 1993, pp. 608–620. Ozler shows that these spreads are somewhat related to a country's earlier default history. According to her calculations, this spread averaged 1.33 for countries that defaulted in the 1930s while it averaged 1.08 for those that did not.

[21] Rudolph, *Peru: The Evolution of a Crisis,* pp. 66, 68.

[22] Klarén, *Peru: Society and Nationhood in the Andes,* p. 332.

[23] Robert Devlin and Enrique d la Piedra, "Peru and Its Private Bankers: Scenes from an Unhappy Marriage," in *Politics and Economics of External Debt Crisis: The Latin American Experience,* ed. Miguel S. Wionczek, (Boulder, CO: Westview Press, 1985), p. 408.

[24] Devlin and Piedra, "Peru and Its Private Bankers: Scenes from an Unhappy Marriage," p. 408; Rudolph, *Peru: The Evolution of a Crisis,* pp. 82-83; John Crabtree, *Peru under Garcia: An Opportunity Lost,* (London: MacMillan Academic and Professional, Ltd., 1992), p. 8.

[25] Ton de Wit and Vera Gianotten "The Center's Multiple Failures," in *The Shining Path of Peru,* ed. David Scott Palmer (New York: St. Martin's Press, 1992), p. 51; Rudolph, *Peru: The Evolution of a Crisis,* p. 86; Crabtree, *Peru under Garcia: An Opportunity Lost,* p. 103.

[26] Rudolph, *Peru: The Evolution of a Crisis,* p. 89.

[27] Cynthia McClintock, "Thories of Revolution and the Case of Peru" in *The Shining Path of Peru,* ed. David Scott Palmer (New York: St. Martin's Press, 1992), p. 232.

[28] Klarén, *Peru: Society and Nationhood in the Andes,* p. 383.

[29] Alan García Perez, *A la Immensa Mayoría,* (Lima, Peru: DESA S.A., 1988) p. 510.

[30] Ibid., pp. 95, 507.

[31] Ibid., p. 52.

[32] James Rowe Jr., "Peru creditors wary of García strategy of confrontation," *The Washington Post,* November 3, 1985.

[33] William D. Montalbano, "Peru's Garcia: Appealing Master of Mixed Signals," *Los Angeles Times,* August, 9, 1985.

[34] Enrique Obando "Civil-Military Relations in Peru 1980-1996' in *Shining and Other Paths,* ed. Steven Stern (Durham, NC: Duke University Press, 1998), p. 391.

[35] Crabtree, *Peru under Garcia: An Opportunity Lost,* p. 34.

[36] Ibid., pp. 34, 48.

[37] Ibid., pp. 40–44.

[38] Harry Venedikian and Gerald Warfield, *Global Trade Financing,* (New York: John Wiley & Sons, Inc., 2000), pp. 43, 354–62.

[39] Hugh O'Shaughnessy, "Peru Moves International Reserves from U.S. Banks," *The Financial Times,* February 13, 1985 and Peter Montagnon, "Peru Loans Downgraded by U.S. Banking Agencies,"*The Financial Times,* October 31, 1985; Senator John Kerry and Senator Hank Brown, "The BCCI Affair: A Report to the Committee on Foreign Relations, United States Senate," December 1992, 102 Congress, 2d Session, Senate Print 102–140, section 5.

[40] Jeremy Bulow and Kenneth Rogoff, "The Buyback Boondoggle," Brookings Papers on Economic Activity, (Washington, DC: The Brookings Institution, 1998), no. 2, pp. 675–698.

[41] World Bank, "World Bank Report, Peru," in *The Peru Report,* December 1988, vol. 2, no. 12, v, vi.

[42] Crabtree, *Peru under Garcia: An Opportunity Lost,* p. 123.

[43] Rudolph, *Peru: The Evolution of a Crisis,* p. 139; Vargas Llosa, "The Story of a Massacre," pp. 40, 44.

[44] Barbara Durr, "Peru's Banker Plans for Crisis," *The Financial Times,* November 11, 1987; "Peru plans to withhold silver to fund imports," *International Trade Finance,* July 28, 1988; Barbara Durr, "State Bank Plan Hits Peru's Credit Lines," *The Financial Times,* August 22, 1987.

[45] Armando Caceres and Carlos E. Parades, "The Management of Economic Policy, 1985-1989," in *Peru's Path to Recovery,* eds. Carlos E. Parades and Jeffrey D. Sachs, (Washington, DC: The Brookings Institution, 1991), pp. 89–97.

46 Riordan Roett, "The Message From García," *Foreign Affairs*, Winter 1985/1986, p. 274; Rudolph, *Peru: The Evolution of a Crisis*, p. 121; Woy-Hazleton and Hazleton, "Shining Path and the Marxist Left," p. 215; José Gonzalez, "Guerrillas and Coca in the Upper Huallaga Valley," in *The Shining Path of Peru*, ed. David Scott Palmer (New York: St. Martin's Press, 1992), p. 113; and Klarén, *Peru: Society and Nationhood in the Andes*, p. 396.

47 Crabtree, *Peru under Garcia: An Opportunity Lost*, pp. 188, 190; Klarén, *Peru: Society and Nationhood in the Andes*, p. 407; Rudolph, *Peru: The Evolution of a Crisis*, p. 122.

48 Crabtree, *Peru under Garcia: An Opportunity Lost*, p. 131.

49 Rudolph, *Peru: The Evolution of a Crisis*, p. 143.

50 Mario Vargas Llosa, *El Pez en el Agua*, (Barcelona, Spain: Seix-Barral, 1993), p. 410.

Macroeconomics: The Dynamics of European Union

The Blair Wealth Project: Antecedents and Prospects

Britain's economy after the Second World War is often seen as having evolved according to a "stop–go" pattern, with spurts of economic growth alternating with contractions required to dampen inflation and correct balance of payment imbalances.

Prime Minister Margaret Thatcher (1979–1990) attributed this pattern to the weakness of the supply-side of Britain's economy and lack of discipline among macroeconomic policy makers. She set out to address the former problem with a series of structural reforms, notably of the trade unions and labor market. Rule-based macroeconomic policies (starting with monetarism) dealt with the latter issues.

Britain boomed briefly in the mid-1980s following Mrs. Thatcher's revolution, but the boom culminated in a recession in the early 1990s. This ultimately led to Tony Blair's New Labour government coming to power in 1997, charged with a mandate to address what were seen as shortcomings in the Thatcherite reforms.

Supplementary Material

Europe: Data Supplement 1950–2003

Study Questions

1. What were the causes of Britain's "stop–go" economy?
2. Did Prime Minister Margaret Thatcher address these problems successfully?
3. What is the difference, if any, between "stop–go" in the 1950s and 1960s and what Gordon Brown, New Labour's Chancellor of the Exchequer (i.e., Finance Minister) has called "twenty years of Tory boom and bust" under Mrs. Thatcher and her Conservative successor?
4. Do you believe that the policies implemented by Blair's New Labour government will finally abolish the macroeconomic instability that has plagued the United Kingdom through the second half of the 20th century?

HUW PILL
INGRID VOGEL

The Blair Wealth Project:
Antecedents and Prospects

Never Mind the Euro, it's the Hospitals.

> – posters placed throughout London on the eve of the introduction of euro
> notes and coins in January 2002, hinting at lyrics to a *Sex Pistols* song from 1977

Britain's June 2001 general election pitted incumbent Labour Prime Minister Tony Blair against William Hague, leader of the opposition Conservative Party. A vociferous euro skeptic, Hague focused on one issue during the election campaign: whether the United Kingdom—like 12 of its partners in the European Union (EU)—should abandon the pound sterling in favor of the nascent euro, the new single European currency. In response, Blair equivocated. Rather than committing one way or the other, he simply proposed holding a referendum on adoption of the euro within two years of reelection.

Hague's political antenna seemed astute. His doubts about the euro appeared vindicated by the new currency's weakness against the dollar and the slow economic growth and high unemployment endured by many euro area countries. With the British public skeptical about further European integration—opinion polls showed 70% against joining the euro, with 50% in favor of leaving the EU altogether[1]—Hague's anti-euro campaign strategy seemed to make sense.

Yet Hague's campaign faltered, with the electorate having other priorities. The Labour Party was reelected with a large parliamentary majority (see **Exhibit 5**), albeit with the lowest voter turnout in more than 80 years.[2] Perhaps the public doubted whether the Labour administration would ever actually push Britain into the euro area. Indeed, many outside observers claimed that continental Europe had much to learn from the United Kingdom, rather than vice versa. Britain had emerged from a history of industrial conflict and relatively poor economic performance after World War II with a strong record of growth throughout the 1990s and into the new millennium.

As the inheritor of both this complex history and a relatively attractive economic conjuncture, Blair sought to establish his new priorities. He was the first-ever Labour Prime Minister to be reelected for a full second term with a working Parliamentary majority. In addition to addressing issues of European integration, Blair planned to focus on pressing domestic issues, which the electorate apparently saw as more important. Blair wanted to ensure that Britain's recent

Research Associate Ingrid Vogel prepared this case under the supervision of Professor Huw Pill. This case was developed from published sources. HBS cases are developed solely as the basis for class discussion. Cases are not intended to serve as endorsements, sources of primary data, or illustrations of effective or ineffective management.

improvement in economic growth and wealth was sustainable into the medium term, and did not come at the expense of social cohesion. (See **Exhibits 1-4** for summary macroeconomic information.)

The British Economy after World War II

The Attlee Labour Government (1945–1951)

Once the most prominent worldwide imperial power and industrial leader,[3] Britain emerged from World War II in a weakened position. Not only had its share of world manufacturing exports decreased by one quarter (from 35% at the turn of the century to 26% in 1950), but it had also lost its colonies and was forced in 1949 to devalue the pound. The United States had become the predominant global economic and political force. Other European nations (and, eventually, even Japan) outpaced Britain in terms of productivity and output growth during the post-war period.

Yet the first signs of Britain's relative economic decline had appeared decades earlier, when, at the end of the 19th century, its steel production began to lag behind foreign production. Explanations of Britain's continued relative decline abounded. Some blamed ineffective economic policies and institutions. Others blamed the failure of British firms to react to the challenges of mass production and mass marketing created by the Second Industrial Revolution with appropriate new technologies and management practices.

In an effort to turn around Britain's relative decline, the Labour government elected in 1945 under the leadership of Clement Attlee implemented a highly coordinated, tightly managed economy. This involved continuing the high level of government economic intervention that had characterized the wartime period.

State involvement extended into the area of welfare. The famous Beveridge Report, written during World War II and shaped by the British experience of the Great Depression, recommended sweeping reform. Newly implemented programs included universal and free education, the provision of health care regardless of ability to pay (through the National Health Service), employment insurance, benefits for mothers with dependent children, and housing subsidies.

Attlee employed macroeconomic policies directed toward achieving full employment. The experience of mass unemployment during the Great Depression of the 1930s had created a lasting political and economic legacy. At the same time, monetary and financial discipline was enforced by the maintenance of a fixed exchange rate with the United States dollar under the Bretton Woods system.[a] The Treasury was charged with not only guarding public finances, but also managing aggregate demand using Keynesian tools of monetary and fiscal policy. In 1946, its position was strengthened with the nationalization of the Bank of England, Britain's central bank, which thereby subjected monetary policy to the Treasury's control.

Further nationalizations affected one fifth of the British economy and more than two million employees.[4] Based on the strong performance of the French and Italian economies with significant public ownership, the move toward nationalization was seen as a modernizing force. Britain's "commanding heights," including the coal, steel, airline, railway, gas, and electricity sectors, were transferred into public ownership.

---

[a] Bretton Woods is the international financial system consisting of fixed exchange rates and limited cross-border capital movements that prevailed after the World War II.

The Post-war Consensus (1951–1971)

In the years after the Attlee administration up to 1971, Labour and Conservative administrations broadly agreed on economic management at both the macro and micro levels. In 1951, the British post-war consensus was coined "Butskellism," derived from the combination of the names of outgoing Labour Chancellor of the Exchequer Hugh Gaitskell and incoming Conservative Chancellor "Rab" Butler.[a] Under Butskellism, both major political parties continued to pursue full employment through a Keynesian demand management framework and to maintain a fixed exchange rate with the United States. They also maintained the welfare state and continued to follow interventionist industrial policies.

The twin goals of full employment and a fixed exchange rate were not always complementary. This was often viewed as having led to so-called stop-and-go cycles. As one economist put it, under "stop-go," the British government "behaved like simple Pavlovian dogs responding to two main stimuli: one was '500,000 unemployed' and the other was a 'run on reserves.'"[5] In other words, as unemployment rose, the government would implement expansionary policies such as tax cuts, higher public expenditures, and lower interest rates. This would lead to inflation and a deterioration in the balance of payments. Given a finite stock of dollar reserves and limited capital mobility, devaluation of the pound could be avoided only through a reversal of expansionary policies. Predictably, unemployment would follow such a reversal, and the United Kingdom would find itself back where it started. Between 1951 and 1971, Britain underwent four such cycles (see **Exhibit 6**).

Industrial Relations

Many observers saw Britain's system of industrial relations as being at the heart of the "stop-go" problem. The adversarial nature of the relationship between workers and employers prevented the wage moderation required for full employment to be consistent with price stability. Unions enjoyed an attractive legal environment in which no vote was required to strike, secondary picketing was allowed (i.e. disrupting the operations of parties not directly involved in a dispute), and "closed shops" were common (i.e. companies that were required to hire union workers).

Unions   Britain's trade unions were a highly fragmented and internally contentious group. Demarcation disputes over membership domain were commonplace and uncoordinated wage bargaining the rule. In part, this was a reflection of the origins of the trade union movement. Unions had emerged in the nineteenth century as disparate craft organizations representing workers with particular skills across companies and industries. Craft-based unions were followed by other small unions representing unskilled and semi-skilled workers, and later, white-collar workers.

The Trades Union Congress (TUC) was an umbrella organization first formed in 1868. It represented the collective interests of the many unions. In the early 1900s, the TUC founded the Labour Party - which it continued to finance for the next 100 years - and unions were co-opted into Britain's system of governance. Because of their involvement in the war and in newly nationalized entities, unions became a powerful force after World War II. By 1950, unions comprised 45% of British workers, three-quarters of whom were organized by the TUC. By the mid-1970s, the TUC organized 90% of the more than 50% of workers who were unionized. But affiliated unions jealously guarded their financial and decision-making independence. The TUC therefore remained an outwardly formidable but ultimately weak organization of fragmented affiliates with no control over members' operations or funds.[6]

---

[a] The Chancellor of the Exchequer is Britain's Finance, Economics, and Budget minister.

The power of shop stewards, elected by workers at the firm level, added to the contentious nature of Britain's industrial relations. Shop stewards were responsible for negotiating directly with management on issues including wages and working conditions. They were subject to little control from union officials and frequently threatened or instigated "wildcat strikes" to gain negotiating leverage. By the 1960s, with uncoordinated wage bargaining at a national level and the growing influence of shop stewards at the firm level, labor was gaining an increasing share of proceeds from Britain's economic growth. At the same time, labor productivity was continuing to lag behind that of comparable countries.[7]

Employers In 1965, the Confederation of British Industry (CBI) was created to unite Britain's various employers' associations. Approximately 75% of all British businesses (including nationalized firms) were members of employer associations. Originally, these associations had helped their members work jointly on labor relations and represented their interests before the government. As the centralized nature of bargaining broke down on the union side, British firms grew more accustomed to acting individually in collective bargaining and in relations with the government. As a result, both the CBI and British employers' associations were weaker than their counterparts in Germany and Japan.

Government Intervention in Markets

Like the previous Attlee government, subsequent administrations tried to address Britain's problematic industrial relations through market intervention. In 1962, drawing on the apparently successful French experience with "indicative" economic planning, the Conservative Macmillan government established the National Economic Development Council (NEDC). The NEDC consisted of representatives from government, unions, and business. One of its objectives was the revitalization of British manufacturing through national planning. Another objective was to control inflation by providing businesses and unions a forum to cooperate in the control of wage growth.

During this period, tight controls on bank lending, credit, and cross border flows of capital were maintained. But unlike other European governments, the U.K. permitted the unregulated Euro markets to develop.[a] In addition, it allowed the equity market to create a competitive market for corporate control. After the successful 1953 hostile takeover by Charles Clore of footwear retailer Sears,[b] takeovers were regarded, in the words of one economist, as a "catalyst for change in both the complacent attitude of company directors towards their shareholders, and in the passive and undemanding attitude of shareholders towards their investment."[8]

In the late 1950s, rising inflation forced many firms to seek alternatives to expensive debt financing and investors to find sources of higher returns. As a result, demand for corporate equities increased. New issues, including some from companies long committed to family ownership but facing unfavorable taxation,[c] met the increased demand. As the number of listed firms increased, the

---

[a] The Euro markets, based in London but denominated in currencies other than the pound sterling, were not subject to the controls of the domestic banking sector.

[b] In 1953, Charles Clore, a leader in takeover bidding, recognized that the share price of Sears, the country's largest chain of footwear shops, did not reflect the value of the store's properties. He offered the shareholders a higher price for their shares.

[c] For example, in 1970 Pilkington, a glass making company run by members of the fourth generation of the founding family, sold 10% of its equity to the public. By 1979, the family holdings had been reduced to less than 20%. The primary reason for going public, according to Chairman Lord Pilkington, was the effect of taxation on the financial position of family members. He remarked "Modern taxation makes it very difficult to either pass on the wealth you have accumulated or keep it in the company. And without a public market for the stock, death duties could place large individual shareholders in an impossible cash bind."

discipline imposed by the competitive market for corporate control extended across a broader range of the British economy.

The Breakdown of Consensus (1971–1979)

By the late 1960s, economic growth had slowed markedly, and inflation and the balance of payments deficit were approaching worrying levels (see **Exhibits 2** and **4a**), leading to yet more "stop-go" policy decisions. In 1966, Labour Prime Minister Harold Wilson, himself a trained economist, initiated an austerity program including a wage freeze. Strikes ensued, which were met by sizable wage concessions. In 1967, Britain was forced to devalue the pound. Wilson attempted to introduce union reform, but met with rebellion from within the Labour Party, which was still financed largely by the unions. In 1970, dissatisfied voters replaced the Wilson administration with the Conservatives led by Edward Heath, a grocer's son who had worked his way into Britain's "establishment."

Prime Minister Heath embarked on a program of tighter monetary and fiscal policy and reduced government intervention in the economy. He liberalized financial markets by abolishing credit controls, allowing the market to establish interest rates and to direct credit. He introduced a new Industrial Relations Act to address Britain's endemic strikes and inflationary pressures. The Industrial Relations Act established a more coordinated union structure, based on the German model, by allowing for constructive dialogue among unions, government, and business. He also reined back government expenditure.

But Heath was soon forced into a policy U-turn. His tight macroeconomic policies placed strain on British firms as domestic demand fell, and many companies failed. As workers lost jobs, officials warned Heath that social disintegration would follow if unemployment levels were permitted to rise above one million. Consequently, when Rolls Royce went bankrupt in 1971, Heath chose to back down on his policy of reduced state intervention and bailed the company out.

Britain's precarious economic situation during this period was exacerbated by external shocks. After 1971, the Bretton Woods system was abolished and Britain adopted a floating exchange rate. In 1973-1974, oil prices skyrocketed, followed by a 25% rate of inflation—untempered by Heath's Industrial Relations Act. Unions perceived this legislature to be an effort to curb their autonomy and resented its imposition by a Conservative government. Living up to its tradition as Britain's most militant union, the National Union of Mineworkers (NUM), with its roots in the coal industry, went on strike for twelve weeks during 1974. After energy shortages and widespread elective power cuts, Heath was forced to declare a state of emergency and impose a three-day work week. Three months later, Heath held elections with a challenge to Labour's dependence on the unions. He adopted the campaign slogan, "Who governs Britain?" The end result—he himself did not, because his party lost the election.

The new Labour administration, again under the leadership of Harold Wilson, introduced a so-called Social Contract to address Britain's growing economic problems. This was an explicit agreement between the Labour government and the unions, exchanging increased social benefits and greater equality for wage restraint. Negotiated with the unions at a national level, the Social Contract collapsed when shop stewards threatened employers with "wildcat strikes" and obtained local wage increases at the factory level.

In 1976, the government failed once again to obtain agreement to reduce public expenditure. Wilson resigned and Labour Chancellor James Callaghan became the new Prime Minister. But he too was unable to cure Britain's economic woes. The British pound plummeted on international exchanges as speculators lost confidence in Britain's ability to curb inflation and control fiscal deficits. Callaghan was forced to turn to the International Monetary Fund (IMF) for a large loan and to accept its strict austerity plan, including the imposition of monetary targets and lower government spending. Predictably, these controls did succeed in taming inflation, but at the expense of employment.

When introducing the IMF-imposed reforms at the 1976 Labour Party conference, Callaghan's statement renounced Keynesianism:

> We used to think that you could spend your way out of a recession, and increase employment by cutting taxes and boosting Government spending. I tell you in all candor that that option no longer exists, and that in so far as it ever did exist, it only worked by injecting a bigger dose of inflation into the economy, followed by a higher level of unemployment as the next step. Higher inflation followed by higher unemployment. We have just escaped from the highest rate of inflation this country has known; we have not yet escaped from the consequences: high unemployment. That is the history of the last 20 years.[9]

With wage increases below the rate of inflation and public employees working near or below the poverty level, conflict between unions and government came to a head. In the winter of 1978-1979, successive public sector unions went on strike in support of wage demands greater than the prevailing rate of inflation. Chaos ensued in what became known as the Winter of Discontent. The specter of "rubbish on the streets" and "the dead left unburied" as a consequence of local government worker strikes was to haunt the electoral chances of the Labour party and the public image of the trade unions for the next 18 years.

Margaret Thatcher and Eighteen Years of Conservative Rule

Mrs. Thatcher's Revolution (1979–1987)

Britain was now ripe for sweeping change. The Conservatives, led by Margaret Thatcher, were victorious in the 1979 election, called after Callaghan suffered a vote of no confidence in Parliament. The new administration was committed to encouraging economic growth and restoring Britain to its former position as a global political and economic leader. Thatcher's remedy was liberalizing the economy, allowing full rein to market forces, and adopting monetarist policies to contain inflation.

Thatcher wanted to distance herself from her party's earlier failures. First, she emphasized her intention to abandon the post-war consensus when she declared "I am not a consensus politician. I am a conviction politician."[10] Next, alluding to the famous Heath U-turn, Thatcher firmly stated, "The lady is not for turning."[11] In addition, after witnessing the political failure of Britain's three prior Prime Ministers due to labor conflict, Thatcher made it no secret that she intended to change the industrial relations environment so that her administration would not suffer the same fate. Chancellor of the Exchequer Nigel Lawson summarized the major policy shift:

> Instead of seeking to use macroeconomic (i.e. fiscal and monetary) policy to promote growth and microeconomic policy (of which incomes policy, such as wage and price controls, was a key component) to suppress inflation, the Government should direct macroeconomic policy to the suppression of inflation and rely on microeconomic (or supply-side) policy, such

as tax and labour market reform, to provide the conditions favorable to improved performance in terms of growth and employment.[12]

The End of Keynesianism

According to government officials in the early 1980s, "the Conservative Party decided that the elimination of inflation should take precedence over all other economic objectives."[13] Thatcher saw the adoption of monetarist policies as the solution to inflation. Monetarism implied that inflation could be controlled through managing the money supply. But monetarism was still largely untested, prompting Harvard Economist John Kenneth Galbraith to ask "what better people to try it on than the British, whose famous phlegm will put up with anything."[14]

Thatcher's economic plan also relied on tight fiscal policy through reduced government spending and an overall increase in taxes. The tax adjustment included a decrease in income taxes more than offset by a doubling of Value Added Tax (sales tax) (see **Exhibit 11**).

By 1980, it was clear that Thatcher's new macroeconomic policies were not working. Inflation climbed close to 20% in response to the "Second Oil Shock" (a worldwide phenomenon) and the sales tax increase. As the Bank of England attempted to meet its money supply growth targets, short-term interest rates reached an unprecedented 18%, crippling domestic investment. As a consequence of the tight monetary policy and the discovery of North Sea oil, the pound sterling appreciated rapidly, damaging the British export market. At the same time, the burden of recession-related benefits payments grew. The administration found it impossible to adhere to fiscal targets. Thatcher's monetary policy, which was meant to be gradual, had now become draconian, and the British economy entered its deepest recession since the Great Depression (see **Exhibits 4a-c**).

In 1981, Thatcher refused to reflate the economy through traditional measures such as increased government spending. Instead, fiscal policy was tightened. This prompted outrage from members of her Cabinet as well as from 364 leading British economists who published a letter in *The Times* newspaper arguing "there is no justification in economic theory or supporting evidence" for the tightening[15] (see **Annex**). The public confirmed its dissatisfaction with Thatcher's plans with a low 25% approval rating. But Mrs. Thatcher's role in resolutely defending Britain's interests raised her popularity. In 1982, following an Argentine invasion, Britain retook the Falkland/Malvinas Islands, which some felt renewed a sense of national pride.

Thatcher's 1983 reelection prospects were further improved by the 1982 recovery in the British economy. High unemployment and weak demand brought inflation down to 5%, and economic growth resumed. With inflationary expectations broken, interest rates were lowered and the pound depreciated (especially against the rising U.S. dollar), despite continued rapid monetary growth above the announced monetary targets. By the mid-1980s, recovery had turned into a full-fledged consumption boom. In 1987, the Conservatives, still led by Thatcher, won an unprecedented third term in office.

Transforming Industrial Relations

While Thatcher claimed that fighting inflation was her top priority, many believed the most singular achievement of her first two terms was the curbing of trade union power. Unions had depended on Keynesian demand management, under which the government afforded high priority to full employment, for tight labor markets and negotiating leverage. In the United Kingdom, where the reversal of Keynesianism and the move to monetarism had been particularly sharp, the decline in the power of centralized unions was pronounced. The Thatcher government further curtailed the power of the trade unions through a number of direct measures, including legislation making it more difficult for unions to initiate industrial action (especially strikes) and to secure collective bargaining rights. Specific legislation included requiring secret ballots to strike, outlawing secondary picketing, outlawing "closed shops," and introducing enforced liability for the economic consequences of strikes at the firm level. Thatcher also abolished the NEDC, effectively severing the trade union voice within government. Union membership had by now dropped from about 60% of the workforce to just over 30%[16] (see **Exhibit 9**).

Early in her first term, Thatcher successfully suppressed unions in key nationalized companies, including British Steel, British Leyland Motor Corporation, and Upper Clyde Shipbuilders. But the miners, as they had under Heath, proved much more resistant to change. Only in 1984, at the beginning of her second term, had Thatcher established enough credibility and enough of a power base to confront the NUM. She made plans to rationalize the state-owned mining industry. To this end, she appointed her admirer, Scottish-born and U.S.-educated Ian MacGregor – a former Chairman of British Steel – to be Chairman of British Coal. MacGregor wanted to save Britain from what he saw as its fate as "a country sinking slowly into the sea under the weight of bloody-minded trade unions and namby-pamby managements."[17] The government prepared months in advance for strikes it anticipated would result from future announcements of coalmine closures. Coal stocks were discreetly moved from pithead to power station, facilities were retrofitted to produce power from oil, and plans were drawn up to handle possible civil emergencies. The government's preparations proved critical when the announcement of 21 pit closures brought on a NUM strike lasting one year. The Labour Party largely supported the strikes. The NUM's militancy under leader Arthur Scargill who called strikes without authorization and refused to negotiate with the government, however, prevented full Labour endorsement.

Describing the pit closures, one journalist reported: "The majority of the miners saw it as a challenge to their birthright. Intuitively, they recognized the move to close pits—*their* pits—as an attack on *their* estate. That is what made the entire dispute unique. . . . It was not about the pay packet . . . [or] a traditional conflict with management. . . . It was a fight against the remote accountants who were trying to destroy '*our*' way of life."[18] After spending an estimated five billion pounds and conceding to no NUM demands, the Conservative administration succeeded in suppressing the miners' power. The mining crisis proved to be a major turning point in Thatcher's administration, as she won a resounding – and to many – a surprising victory.

Scholars noted that through its success, Thatcher's government "wholly secured the right to make the coal industry – and thus any other industry, since that was the strongest bastion of non-market production – profitable and market oriented."[19] Thatcher's administration continued to face up to union strikes. They provided support to employers, for example, in the form of police protection in cases such as when Rupert Murdoch confronted the print unions. Ultimately, Britain's unions were transformed, losing much of the power to which that had been accustomed.

Subsequently, it has been argued whether Thatcher did too much or too little in the area of union reform. Many critics blame her for widespread unemployment and social problems in the traditional industrial areas. But others credited Thatcher's industrial relations policies with the creation of a more flexible labor environment. An incentive-oriented system, with performance pay and recruitment at market price allowed, led to more mobility in the market and, some argued, better firm performance. New social legislation—namely Thatcher's decision to index unemployment benefits to prices rather than earnings—meant workers were better off in work than unemployed. However, the tradeoff to the more flexible labor environment was higher income inequality (see **Exhibit 4d**). In terms of income distribution, Britain began to resemble the United States much more than it resembled the rest of Europe.[20]

Promoting Private Enterprise

Thatcher also implemented major reform in reducing the role of the state in the economy. She promoted private enterprise through deregulating financial markets and implementing a massive privatization program.

Financial markets One of her first actions in office had been to remove foreign exchange and capital controls. The resulting stimulation of dramatic transformation in U.K. financial markets became known as the "Big Bang." Reduced controls permitted freer flows of capital into and out of the country. This implied wider access to funding for British companies, but only under the condition that they could provide internationally competitive returns. In response, the share of equities owned by foreigners rose from less than 4% in the early 1980s to nearly 30% by the end of the 1990s[21] (see **Exhibit 10b**). Among the new shareowners were U.S. fund managers, who tended to take a much more aggressive stance than their British counterparts at pressing for management changes. For example, in 1995 a Chicago-based fund intervened in the management of the advertising firm Saatchi & Saatchi, forcing the removal of chairman and co-founder Maurice Saatchi.

In addition, the Big Bang led to the restructuring of the financial services industry. The London Stock Exchange could no longer impose anti-competitive rules, including fixed commissions, which allowed certain firms to earn monopoly profits. Financial institutions reacted by expanding their offerings and becoming more competitive. The entry of large, aggressive U.S. banks into the London financial markets further stimulated competition and led to the reduction of the costs of doing business.

Thatcher also liberalized the retail financial sector. For the first time, building societies[a] were permitted to expand their deposit base beyond personal savings. They were allowed to borrow from the wholesale markets, gain access to the inflow of foreign capital, and aggressively expand lending. As a result, lending grew by more than 25%.

Privatization program Thatcher's privatization program marked an even sharper break from previous post-war government policies. In 1979, nationalized industries accounted for 10% of GDP, 15% of national investment, and 8% of employment. By 1997, employment in nationalized industry had fallen to just under 1.5%, and more people were employed in Britain's Indian restaurants than in coal mining, steel, and iron combined.[22]

The privatization program was implemented in three phases. Under the first, the more obviously competitive sectors and companies, such as Amersham International (a nuclear products company), Cable and Wireless, and British Aerospace, were addressed. The next phase involved segments of Britain's "commanding heights," including steel, coal, and shipbuilding. Third, utilities, including electricity, were privatized. As part of the overall privatization program, Thatcher also transferred a large proportion of the local-owned public housing stock to private hands.

The program's first objective was to improve the performance of loss-making nationalized industries. Proponents argued that privatization would reduce excess employment, modernize production processes, and streamline management of formerly publicly owned British companies.

---

[a] A British building society is a mutually owned financial institution specializing in retail savings and mortgages, similar to an American savings & loan institution.

Studies through the late 1990s attempting to establish whether productivity and performance were indeed better under private ownership yielded vastly differing, often conflicting, results. In general, they pointed out the greater significance of introducing competition into markets. In the case of British utilities, competition came 10 years after privatization.[23]

The program's second and third objectives, raising funds for the cash-strapped government and drawing out the public's entrepreneurial spirit through promoting share ownership, were more clearly met. The Conservatives felt that "the widespread ownership of private property is crucial to the survival of freedom and democracy."[24] The 1984 sale of British Telecom (BT) through a public offering proved particularly successful in fulfilling the Conservatives' third objective. Approximately 2.3 million people bought shares in the company. Starting in 1984, most privatizations occurred as public offerings. From 1979 to 1989, the proportion of shareholders among the adult population increased from 7% to 25%. See **Exhibit 7** for details on the privatization program.

Reorganizing the Welfare State

Since the end of World War II, the cost of welfare benefits had increased at a rate five times faster than prices. Like many of her Conservative colleagues, Thatcher believed that Britain's welfare state placed too heavy a financial burden on the government and stifled individual initiative. At the same time, she recognized that any reduction in social spending would have to be weighed against political consequences threatening her tenure as Prime Minister. Ultimately, her administration avoided imposing truly major changes. Social service deteriorated, most notably in education, where Britain was seen already to be lagging far behind the rest of Europe. Even so, due to recession-related benefits, social spending increased significantly during Thatcher's terms.

The Decline of Conservative Power (1987–1997)

By 1987, Britain had the highest economic growth rate in Europe. Many attributed this to Thatcher's success in promoting private enterprise and ultimately bringing down inflation. Critics, however, noted the economy's dependence on North Sea oil. Regardless of its origins, Chancellor of the Exchequer Nigel Lawson recognized that the consumption boom, which had helped Thatcher win her third term in office, was unsustainable. He was worried that the economy was becoming overheated.

Lawson believed that increasing the credibility of Britain's commitment to fighting inflation was critical to stabilizing Britain's precarious economic situation. To that end, he proposed joining the European Monetary System (EMS). Under the EMS, the pound would be fixed against the Deutsche Mark, and interest rate decisions would largely be devolved to the Bundesbank, Germany's central bank.[25] When Thatcher resisted, Lawson chose instead to shadow the DM. This allowed him to maintain a stable exchange rate against the DM without taking on all the institutional commitments implied by membership in the EMS.

However, the DM shadowing had the unintended effect of further accelerating the economic boom. Huge capital inflows resulted as investors recognized that they could get higher returns in Britain relative to Germany because of higher British interest rates combined with minimal short-term risk of sterling depreciation. Additional capital flowed into Britain in the form of foreign direct investment. Foreign firms including Nissan, Honda, and Sony established footholds into the rest of Europe through U.K. factories, taking advantage of the tariff-free Common Market (later the European Union).

Britain's economic boom was further fed by a lowering of the income tax rate and a speculative bubble in the housing market. People previously unable to raise funds to buy a house were able to borrow to do so. By 1988, house prices were increasing at very high rates.

Lawson sought a means to provide a soft landing for the now overheated economy and increased short-term interest rates. But a soft landing proved elusive as the speculative housing bubble and consumption boom both burst. A recession rivaling that of the early 1980s ensued.

Not surprisingly, Thatcher's popularity plummeted. The deepening recession and her stubborn insistence on the poll tax (a flat tax levied on all residents by local authorities) turned the public against her. Her anti-European stance polarized her party. As a result, her authority diminished, and she was finally forced into joining the EMS. But Britain's timing proved unfortunate. German reunification in 1990 had resulted in high interest rates, which recessionary United Kingdom was forced to adopt at a time when it needed the opposite. Currency traders speculated that Britain would be unable politically to increase rates high enough to support the sterling's peg to the DM. They sold sterling in anticipation of a devaluation. Pressure increased until on September 16, 1992, Britain was forced to withdraw from the EMS (see **Exhibit 8**).

Despite the humiliating EMS failure, the Conservatives (since 1990 under the leadership of John Major, who had replaced Thatcher) were successful in winning a fourth consecutive election. The new administration emphasized long-term economic performance and policy credibility. The Treasury was assigned the task of maintaining a stable economic environment through low inflation, sound public finance, and an effective tax policy. The Treasury was also expected to strengthen the outlook for jobs with supply-side policies including further privatization and the effective management of public expenditure. In order to increase the credibility of Britain's commitment to inflation targeting, the independence of the Bank of England was increased. The Treasury set interest rates, while the Bank was made responsible for the implementation, including timing, of interest rate changes and was given greater leeway to make its policy assessment and advice public. The administration was successful in meeting inflation targets for its entire term.

Meanwhile, takeovers continued to function as a way to improve firm performance, although with increasing controversy. Critics claimed the threat of takeovers encouraged a "short-termist" attitude among firms by making them reluctant to invest in projects with longer-term payback, thereby jeopardizing Britain's future prospects. But by the early 1990s, takeover activity had tapered off (see **Exhibit 10a**); the recession reduced funding sources, few easy targets were left, and management theory encouraged focus rather than diversification. The government hoped large institutional investors would take an increasing role in monitoring company performance.

Despite Britain's strong economic performance, the Conservative Party began to become unpopular. John Major's administration was hamstrung by divisions over Europe and opted out of both the single currency and, to protect Thatcher's union reforms, the Social Chapter of the European Union's Maastricht Treaty. The Party's credibility was further hurt by its reputation for "sleaze", brought on by corruption and a series of sex scandals.

Recognizing its political opportunity, the Labour Party prepared for the 1997 elections with growing optimism. In 1995, Labour leadership succeeded in disassociating itself from nationalization by amending the infamous Clause 4 of the party's constitution, which committed Labour to public ownership of Britain's means of production.[a] As a first step in overhauling its relationship with the unions, Labour reduced the TUC's block vote at the annual TUC conference from 70% to 50%.

---

[a] Former Labour Chancellor Gaitskell had tried in 1960 to make the same change but was unsuccessful.

Furthermore, Labour Party leader Tony Blair announced at the TUC conference that the unions would have no more influence than employers over the policy agenda. He promised to "govern for the whole nation, not any vested interest within it."[26] These measures proved convincing. Labour, coining itself "New Labour," finally was elected back to office.

Tony Blair and "New Labour"

For the first time in postwar history, Labour was assuming office without facing the immediate challenge of an economic crisis. The Blair administration could focus on maintaining an already stable economy and improving the social conditions of the worst-off. As part of the stability focus, Blair undertook measures to make the U.K. economy conform to Maastricht convergence criteria, a precondition for adoption of the euro. Welfare reform presented more of a challenge; namely, how to balance commitment to free market ideology with the realization of social change.

Maintaining Macroeconomic Stability

Chancellor of the Exchequer Gordon Brown demonstrated commitment to stability when he promised "no more return to Tory [Conservative] boom-and-bust."[27] Prime Minister Blair's first major policy move in this direction was to introduce increasing central bank independence. He fully transferred the responsibility of establishing interest rates from the Treasury to the Bank of England. Government officials claimed that as a result of the increased autonomy of the Bank and consequent greater credibility of British monetary policy, bond spreads between Germany and the United Kingdom decreased from 2% in 1997 to 0.5% in 1999. Interest rates were actually set by a Monetary Policy Committee (MPC) consisting of nine members, with Bank of England officials in the majority and other members appointed by the Chancellor of the Exchequer. The MPC convened once a month and had the strict mandate of meeting the government's inflation target of 2.5%.

In order to increase the accountability of the Bank of England, the Governor of the Bank reported to the Treasury Select Committee of the House of Commons. In addition, the Governor was expected to explain any incidences of missed inflation targets and to outline an action plan for returning to target in an open letter to the Chancellor.

During its first four years with increased independence, the Bank was successful at reducing the volatility of inflation and meeting its target. Inflation averaged just 2.1% for 2000. Low inflation was matched by low unemployment and strong economic growth. By 2001, for the first time since 1975, fewer than one million people were collecting unemployment benefits. The unemployment rate stood at 5.1%. Blair built upon Major's success in encouraging economic growth. By the middle of 2001, output had increased each quarter since 1992.[28]

Blair also emphasized a coordinated fiscal policy in his first term as Prime Minister. The administration matched the Conservative Party's spending and deficit targets, agreeing to fund current spending exclusively with revenues from taxation. On average over the economic cycle, it would borrow money only to invest. In addition, the administration made a goal of reducing net debt to 40% of GDP by 2004.

Improving Industrial Relations

Blair adhered to his pre-election commitment not to defer to the vested interests of the unions. Prior to the 1997 election, he had promised the unions that he would introduce a minimum wage and obligate firms to recognize and negotiate with unions where they were supported by a majority of employees. In 1998, Labour introduced the minimum wage, but at a lower rate than the unions demanded. Labour also obligated union recognition by firms, but tightened the definition of "majority of employees" to a majority of those voting and at least 40% of those eligible to vote.

Blair was much more active in the area of individual worker rights. The Employment Relations Act, establishing family-friendly benefits for parents, regulation against unfair dismissal and discrimination based on union membership, and the provision of public funds to train union representatives was greeted with enthusiastic support from the unions. Blair also signed on to the Social Chapter of the Maastricht Treaty. Under this agreement, British companies with at least 1000 employees had to establish consultative structures with the workforce, similar to the German model. In addition, British companies could not force employees to work more than 48 hours per week.

While doing much for the individual worker, the Employment Relations Act and the Social Chapter did little to support trade unions. For example, even though the Employment Relations Act provided mandatory union recognition and bargaining, it did nothing to force employers to bargain in good faith. In addition, there was no stipulation that an individual employee could not agree on terms with an employer different from those established with the recognized trade union. Without a government dedicated to supporting the rights of the trade unions, Britain experienced further decline in the adoption of collective bargaining. Successive British governments had basically eliminated national bargaining structures altogether. By 1998, only 41% of employees were working under wages set by collective bargaining with unions, down from 70% in 1984.[29]

At the same time, shop stewards remained a dominant force. As one historian argued, "for many employers, despite the adoption of 'union free' approaches, no thoroughgoing alternative to steward based collective bargaining has been pursued. The basic infrastructure for wage and conditions bargaining remains intact in many areas."[30] Others agreed: "the Confederation of British Industry sees a continued role for shop stewards, but . . . a very limited role for trade unions external to the firm. This implies a preference, where unions do exist, for something akin to enterprise unions, though employers do not use the term."[31]

At the TUC Annual Conference in 1999, Blair solidified New Labour's migration away from union support. He announced "in many ways we have a better, clearer relationship than ever before between trade unions and Labour. . . . You run the unions. We run the government. We will never confuse the two again."[32] As two scholars have noted, "this renunciation by New Labour of Old Labour's corporatism has left the government without any means to encourage the kind of coordination of wage bargaining which appears to have played a significant part in a number of recent 'employment miracles,' Netherlands and Ireland, for example."[33]

Retaining Mrs. Thatcher's Legacy in Markets

As in the area of union relations, New Labour converged toward Conservatives in its view of the role of the state in markets. Blair wrote: "Old-fashioned state intervention did not and cannot work. But neither does naïve reliance on markets."[34] The Labour administration saw the state's role as investing in company capabilities through better education of the work force and monitoring competitiveness with legislation. The 1998 Competitiveness Act, with the objective of boosting the U.K.'s continued lagging productivity, levied strict financial penalties for anti-competitive behavior by firms. Eventually, penalties also included the incarceration of company directors.

The Labour administration carried through many programs introduced under the Conservatives. First, the privatization program was sustained. After the Paddington rail disaster in 1999 (in which a switching error caused a train collision fatal to 31 people), Labour resisted public pressure to renationalize the trains. Instead, Labour planned for further privatization, including London Transport and the air traffic control system. Second, the administration continued the Private Finance Initiatives (PFIs) program. PFIs encouraged the introduction of private sector capital into the public sector through outsourcing projects ranging from hospital construction to prison custodial services to the refurbishment of schools. Private companies would lease projects back to the public sector for a guaranteed fee over periods up to 30 years. By 2004, it was estimated that the government would be paying out £3.5 billion per year under PFIs.[35]

In conflict with Blair, the trade unions and some members of the Labour Party pushed for legislation encouraging a stakeholder rather than shareholder view of companies. But Blair maintained the status quo in the area of corporate governance. He rejected a proposal put forward by his Ministers that directors of companies be held legally responsible to interest groups beyond just shareholders. He also resisted adopting suggestions that Britain move toward the German model of multiple boards to reflect wider stakeholder concerns. Furthermore, his administration rejected a proposal from the European Commission that would have given workers statutory rights to be consulted during takeover situations. The government still regarded the active U.K. hostile takeover market as a strength—and was notably pleased with Vodafone's successful takeover of Mannesman of Germany in 2000, the first successful hostile takeover bid of a German company by a non-German firm.

In its encouragement of broad share ownership, the Labour administration went even further than the Conservatives. It introduced new tax laws encouraging employees to invest in the stock of their companies. More general tax provisions pushed savings into equity funds. By 2000, private pension funds reached over £800 billion and were growing at £50 billion a year.[36] Often, three or four shareholders were in control of at least one third of the equity of a given company. As under Thatcher, the government hoped that concentrated ownership would lead to an increase in coordinated intervention to improve firm performance and management. However, important shareholder interventions rarely took place.[37]

Reducing Social Inequality

Where the new Labour administration did deviate substantially from the 18 years of Conservative rule was in the area of welfare reform. Blair wanted to halt Britain's growing income inequality through programs directed toward the worst-off. Changes to taxes, benefits, and minimum wages were estimated to have contributed an 8% gain to the poorest 20% of households, versus a 0.5% gain for the wealthiest 20%.[38] The administration's Welfare to Work program introduced employment subsidies combined with training and counseling for low-skilled workers. While the program succeeded in improving employment, it faced criticism for ignoring regional labor demand realities and putting downward pressure on low-skill wages. More generally, critics argued that Blair was too focused on the efficiency of welfare spending and thus had failed to implement enough social reform during his first term.

Challenges for Blair's Second Term

Public services   The Blair administration was under intense pressure in its second term, which began in June 2001, to deliver promised public service improvements, especially in the education, health, and transportation sectors.[39] Like other Anglo-Saxon countries, Britain was victim to huge disparities in the literacy capabilities of its population.[40] Blair's education policy aimed to counteract the low educational levels of Britain's least literate 5% through, for example, the introduction of financial incentives for at-risk 16-year olds to stay in school. Other policies empowered the national government to intervene where local government was seen to be failing to carry out educational responsibilities. In the area of health services, Blair encouraged public-private partnership efforts, such as PFIs. After a health service crisis at the end of 1999, Blair promised to meet average EU health spending, implying increases of 6% to 9% through 2003.

Productivity Blair also needed to improve Britain's productivity growth, which had decelerated through the 1990s. Economic growth had remained strong since 1992, driven primarily by decreasing unemployment. Further economic growth would have to come from increases in output per worker since Britain's unemployment rate had reached such low levels. Many economists attributed Britain's decelerating productivity growth to low capital investment, weak education, and slow innovation. By 2001, Britain's average output per worker was just 70% of U.S. average output per worker, largely due to the "New Economy," and 80% of French average output per worker.[41]

Macroeconomic stability Most importantly, the Blair administration wanted to maintain the stability of the economy. "Boom-and-bust" appeared to be banished, but no real crisis had tested the economy in the last nine years. Critics wondered whether the British macroeconomic framework could survive on its own, and whether adoption of the euro would serve to strengthen or weaken the U.K. economy.

Although Blair was personally in favor of euro adoption, the prevailing skepticism had led him to neutralize the issue during the run up to the elections. Blair proposed holding a referendum on the euro within two years of the election, given that certain economic criteria were met. These criteria— the Treasury's "five economic tests"—required the convergence of economic cycles in the United Kingdom and euro area; the creation of sufficient economic flexibility in the euro area to cope with economic shocks; a positive impact on investment in the United Kingdom; benefit to London as a financial center; and improvement in U.K. employment.[42]

Reflecting on the last 50 years of British history, Blair had to set his policy agenda in his second term as Prime Minister. This included planning how to keep the country's economy healthy while improving conditions for the public, particularly its poorest members. Whether this included euro adoption or not was yet to be decided.

Annex

Letter criticizing Thatcher's economic policies as published in:

The Times (London), 30 March 1981, A1.

MONETARISM ATTACKED BY TOP ECONOMISTS

We, who are all present or retired members of the economic staffs of British universities, are convinced that:

There is no basis in economic theory or supporting evidence for the Government's belief that by deflating demand they will bring inflation permanently under control and thereby induce an automatic recovery in output and employment;

Present policies will deepen the depression, erode the industrial base of our economy and threaten its social and political stability;

There are alternative policies; and the time has come to reject monetarist policies and consider urgently which alternative offers the best hope of sustained economic recovery."

The letter was signed by 364 of Britain's leading academic economists, including 76 present or past professors representing 36 universities. More specifically, signatories included:

- Five former Chief Economic Advisers
- 54 Cambridge University economists
- 47 London University economists
- 13 Oxford University economists
- 21 Warwick economists

Exhibit 1 U.K. National Income Accounts *(billion current pounds)*

	1948	1971	1979	1983	1987	1992	1997	2000
Gross Domestic Product	**11.8**	**57.7**	**197.6**	**303.3**	**419.5**	**608.2**	**805.4**	**935.4**
Private Consumption	8.5	35.0	117.0	181.5	258.7	388.0	517.9	611.7
Government Consumption	1.9	10.6	39.6	66.6	85.8	129.2	148.4	174.8
Gross Fixed Capital Formation	1.5	11.2	38.2	51.5	78.8	100.3	134.2	165.6
Changes in Inventories	0.2	0.1	2.2	1.5	1.2	-1.9	4.4	1.2
Exports of Goods and Services	2.2	12.9	54.8	79.8	106.4	143.3	229.3	254.3
Imports of Goods and Services	2.4	12.1	54.2	77.4	111.4	150.7	228.8	272.2
GDP at 1995 Prices	224.7	425.8	517.0	527.3	610.1	650.3	757.9	819.9

Source: Adapted from IMF, *International Financial Statistics*, July 2001.

Exhibit 2 U.K. Balance of Payments Accounts *(billion current U.S. dollars)*

	1971	1979	1983	1987	1992	1997	2000
Current Account	**2.7**	**-0.8**	**5.3**	**-9.4**	**-18.2**	**10.8**	**-24.5**
Trade Balance	0.5	-7.0	-2.4	-19.2	-23.3	-19.5	-43.6
Exports	*22.0*	*86.0*	*92.0*	*130.5*	*189.4*	*281.3*	*283.2*
Imports	*21.5*	*93.0*	*94.3*	*149.7*	*212.7*	*300.8*	*326.8*
Net Services	1.3	8.3	5.8	10.9	9.9	20.3	16.7
Exports	*9.5*	*30.7*	*29.1*	*44.0*	*62.6*	*94.2*	*101.7*
Imports	*8.1*	*22.4*	*23.3*	*33.1*	*52.7*	*73.9*	*85.0*
Net Income	1.3	2.6	4.3	2.3	3.8	18.2	8.1
Net Transfers	-0.5	-4.7	-2.4	-3.4	-8.6	-8.3	-5.7
Capital Account	**na**	**na**	**na**	**0.5**	**0.7**	**1.3**	**2.9**
Financial Account	**1.2**	**1.0**	**-8.6**	**27.9**	**2.5**	**-25.5**	**31.2**
Net Direct Investment[a]	-0.2	-6.1	-3.0	-15.7	-3.2	-26.5	-129.6
Net Private Capital[a]	1.5	1.1	-8.6	68.6	-33.5	-40.7	142.8
Net Official Capital	-4.0	0.1	-1.7	-0.7	-1.7	-2.0	-0.4
Net Other Capital	3.9	5.8	4.8	-24.3	40.9	43.7	18.4
Net Errors and Omissions	**0.7**	**1.9**	**1.5**	**0.0**	**8.3**	**9.4**	**-4.4**
Reserves and Related Items	**-4.6**	**-2.1**	**1.8**	**-19.1**	**6.7**	**3.9**	**-5.3**

Sources: Adapted from IMF, *International Financial Statistics*, July 2001; and IMF, *Balance of Payments Yearbook*, 1969.
Note: [a]Numbers are large in 2000 because of the Vodafone / Mannesman transaction.

Exhibit 3   U.K. Government Fiscal Accounts (*million current pounds*)

	1974	1979	1983	1987	1992	1997	1999
TOTAL REVENUES AND GRANTS	**29,465**	**64,970**	**113,801**	**152,160**	**220,520**	**289,962**	**328,278**
Total as % GDP	*35%*	*33%*	*38%*	*36%*	*36%*	*36%*	*37%*
Tax Revenue	25,774	55,925	98,771	135,067	201,179	269,331	308,722
Nontax Revenue	3,627	8,659	13,499	15,484	16,956	17,660	15,888
Capital Revenue	41	207	378	672	478	1,232	492
Grants	23	179	1,153	937	1,907	1,739	3,176
TOTAL EXPENDITURES & LENDING LESS REPAYMENT	**33,293**	**77,414**	**127,173**	**155,040**	**249,738**	**306,098**	**327,983**
Total as % GDP	*40%*	*39%*	*42%*	*37%*	*41%*	*38%*	*37%*
Total Expenditure	30,335	72,319	122,405	155,738	261,542	306,579	324,393
General Public Services	2,233	5,907	4,581	5,585	8,484	11,248	13,565
Defense	4,681	10,278	16,886	19,284	23,354	21,393	23,043
Public Order and Safety	na	na	1,581	4,799	8,680	10,127	11,323
Education	840	1,871	2,731	4,359	6,736	13,020	12,102
Health	3,912	9,058	16,293	20,965	34,904	44,664	50,013
Social Security and Welfare	6,853	18,546	35,365	49,747	91,791	112,702	118,398
Housing and Community Amenities	1,008	3,015	2,163	4,907	7,173	7,263	7,271
Other Community Services	99	230	437	661	1,220	1,297	927
Economic Affairs and Services	3,927	5,662	9,715	11,242	14,300	13,486	14,097
Interest Payments	na	na	na	na	16,729	28,026	24,881
Other Expenditures	6,782	17,752	32,653	34,189	48,171	43,353	48,773
Lending Less Repayment	2,958	5,095	4,768	-698	-11,804	-481	3,590
FINANCIAL SURPLUS (+) or DEFICIT (-)	**-3,828**	**-12,444**	**-13,372**	**-2,880**	**-29,218**	**-16,136**	**295**
Surplus (+) or Deficit (-) as % GDP	*-4.6%*	*-6.3%*	*-4.4%*	*-0.7%*	*-4.8%*	*-2.0%*	*0.0%*
Financing	3,828	12,444	13,372	2,880	29,218	16,136	-295
Domestic	2,558	9,071	13,571	-2,005	20,397	18,064	2,984
Abroad	1,084	1,217	873	5,700	8,821	-1,928	-3,279
Adjustments	186	2,156	-1,072	-815	-	-	-
Gross Domestic Product	**83,610**	**197,420**	**302,620**	**419,460**	**608,170**	**805,400**	**891,000**

Sources: Adapted from IMF, *Government Finance Statistics*, 1983, 1990, and 1999; and IMF, *International Financial Statistics*, July 2001.

Exhibit 4 U.K. Economic Indicators

A Yearly Rate of Inflation

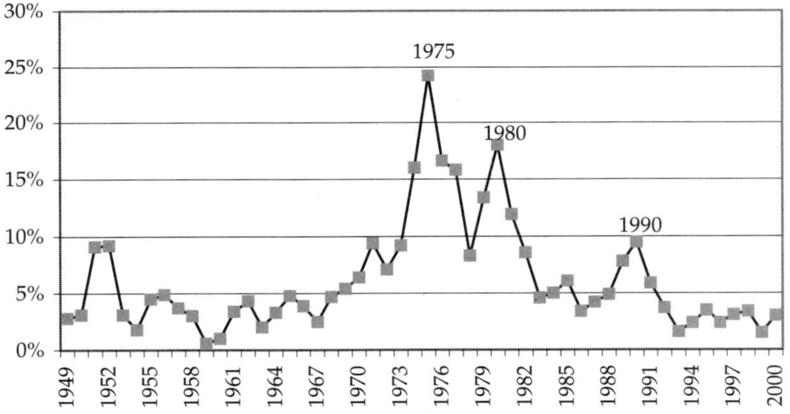
1975
1980
1990

Source: Based on data from Office for National Statistics, U.K.

B Unemployment Rate

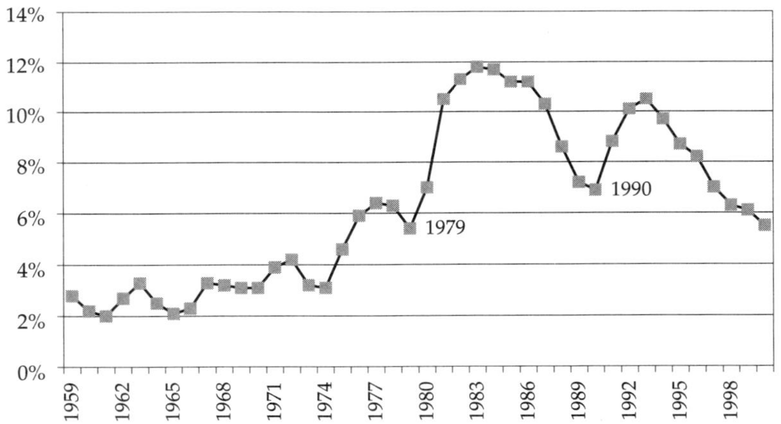
1979
1990

Sources: Based on BLS; and EIU Country Data (2000).

C Real GDP Growth *(% change year-on-year)*

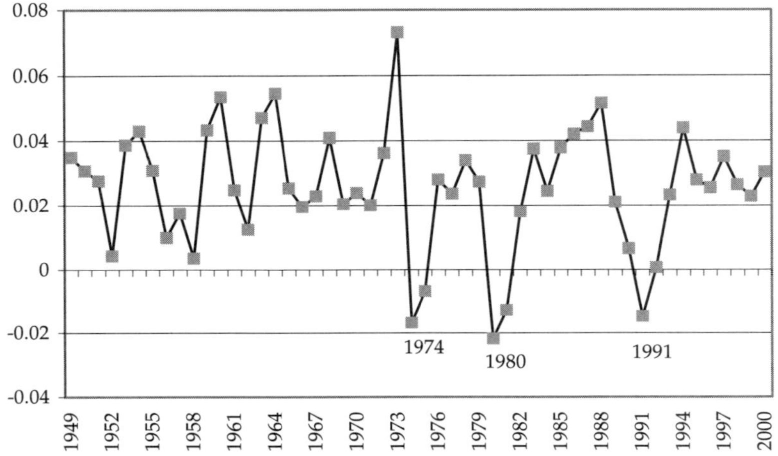
1974
1980
1991

Source: Based on IMF, *International Financial Statistics*, July 2001.

D Income Inequality

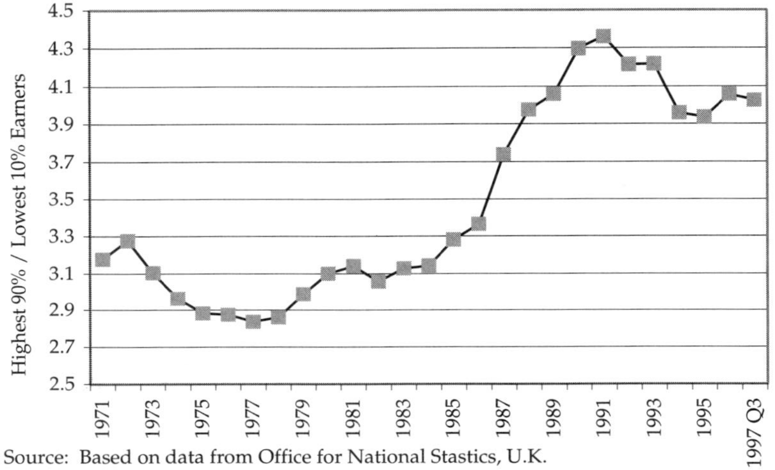
Highest 90% / Lowest 10% Earners

Source: Based on data from Office for National Stastics, U.K.

Exhibit 5   U.K. General Election Results, 1945– 2001

		Labour		Conservative		Liberal Democrat		Other	
		% vote	# seats	% vote	# seats	% vote	# seats	% vote	# seats
Labour (Attlee)	1945	47.8	393	39.8	213	9.0	12	3.4	22
	1950	46.1	315	43.5	298	9.1	9	1.3	3
Conservative (Churchill / Eden / Macmillan / Douglas-Hume)	1951	48.8	295	48.0	321	2.5	6	0.7	2
	1955	46.4	277	49.7	344	2.7	6	1.2	2
	1959	43.8	258	49.4	365	5.9	6	0.9	1
Labour (Wilson)	1964	44.1	317	43.4	304	11.2	9	1.3	0
	1966	47.9	363	41.9	253	8.6	12	1.6	2
Conservative (Heath)	1970	42.9	287	46.4	330	7.5	6	3.2	7
Labour (Wilson / Callaghan)	1974 (Feb.)	37.1	301	37.9	297	19.3	14	5.7	23
	1974 (Oct.)	39.2	319	35.8	277	18.3	13	6.7	26
Conservative (Thatcher / Major)	1979	36.9	269	43.9	339	13.8	11	5.4	16
	1983*	27.6	209	42.4	397	25.4	23	4.6	21
	1987*	31.5	229	43.3	376	23.1	22	2.1	23
	1992	34.4	271	41.9	336	18.0	20	5.7	24
Labour (Blair)	1997	44.1	418	30.7	165	16.8	46	8.4	30
	2001	40.8	413	31.8	166	18.3	52	9.1	31

Sources: Adapted from EIU, UK Country Report, July 2001, 13; Chris Cook and John Paxton, European Political Facts, 1918–1984 (New York: Facts on File Publications, 1986), 186–189; The Economist, 20 June 1987, 60; and "Tory Glory; Major exults in proving polls wrong," Newsday (Nassau and Suffolk Edition), 11 April 1992.

Exhibit 6   U.K. "Stop-Go" Cycles

Year	Policy phase	Real GDP growth rate (over prior year) %	Unemployment rate %	Change in inflation (over prior year) %	Current account BOP million current pounds	Change in foreign exchange reserves (over prior year) million current pounds
1951	**Stop**	**3.5**	**1.2**	**11.8**	**-425**	**-344**
1952	Go	-	2.0	6.7	170	-175
1956	**Stop**	**2.0**	**1.2**	**3.3**	**209**	**42**
1958	Go	-	2.1	1.5	345	284
1962	Go	-0.5	2.0	2.7	115	-183
1965	**Stop**	**3.3**	**1.4**	**4.7**	**-49**	**246**
1968	**Stop**	**4.1**	**2.4**	**4.8**	**-271**	**-114**
1971	Go	1.5	3.6	9.3	1,040	1,348
1975	**Stop**	**0.0**	**3.9**	**24.2**	**-1,732**	**-**
1977	Go	1.5	5.7	15.8	-224	-
1980	**Stop**	**-2.2**	**7.0**	**18.0**	**2,877**	**-545**
1983	Go	3.7	11.8	4.6	3,648	1,216
1990	**Stop**	**0.7**	**6.9**	**9.5**	**-17,562**	**-22**
1994	Go	4.4	9.7	2.5	-1,304	-960

Source: Adapted from 1951–1977 from Middleton, 105; 1980–1992 calculated based on data from IMF, *International Financial Statistics*, July 2001.

Exhibit 7   U.K. Privatization Program

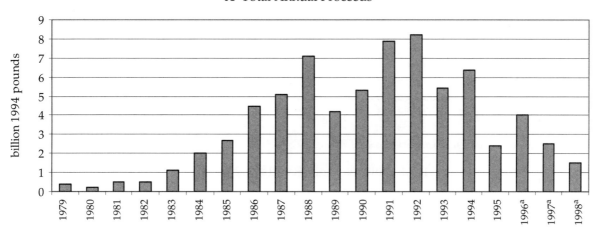

A Total Annual Proceeds

Source: Adapted from Martin, 1.

Note: [a]1995 estimates.

B Privatization by Share Offer, 1981–1991

Date		Company	Equity initially sold (%)	Proceeds (million current pounds)
Feb	1981	British Aerospace	51.6	150
Oct	1981	Cable and Wireless	50	224
Feb	1982	Amersham International	100	71
Nov	1982	Britoil	51	549
Feb	1983	Associated British Ports	51.5	22
June	1984	Enterprise Oil	100	392
July	1984	Jaguar	99	294
Nov	1984	British Telecom	50.2	3,916
Dec	1986	British Gas	97	5,434
Feb	1987	British Airways	100	900
May	1987	Rolls-Royce	100	1,363
July	1987	British Airports Authority	100	1,281
Dec	1988	British Steel	100	2,500
Dec	1989	Regional Water Companies	100	5,110
Dec	1990	Electricity Distribution Companies	100	5,092
Mar	1991	National Power and PowerGen	60	2,230
May	1991	Scottish Power and Scottish Hydro Electric	100	2,880

Source: Adapted from Lawson, 241.

Exhibit 8   Pound Sterling Exchange Rates against US Dollar and Deutsch Mark

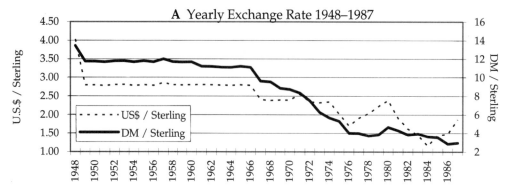

Source: Adapted from IMF, *International Financial Statistics*, July 2001.

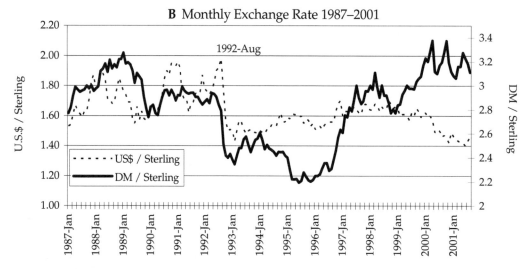

Source: Adapted from IMF, *International Financial Statistics*, October 2001.

Exhibit 9   U.K. Trade Union Density and Working Days Lost to Strike Activity

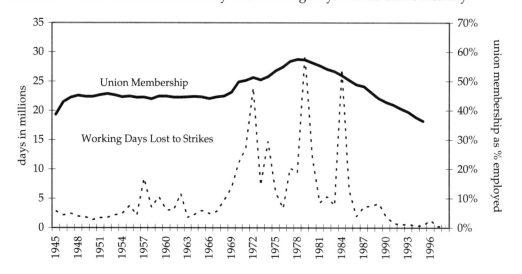

Source: Adapted from Ebbinghaus, Table UK.13; and Office for National Statistics, U.K.

Exhibit 10b   U.K. Equity Ownership

(% listed U.K. equity owned)	1963	1981	1992	2000
Rest of World	7.0%	3.6%	13.1%	32.4%
Insurance Companies	10.0%	20.5%	19.5%	21.0%
Pension Funds	6.4%	26.7%	32.4%	17.7%
Individuals	54.0%	28.2%	20.4%	16.0%
Unit Trusts	1.3%	3.6%	6.2%	1.7%
Investment Trusts	11.3%	6.8%	2.1%	2.1%
Other Financial Institutions			0.4%	4.6%
Charities	2.1%	2.2%	1.8%	1.4%
Private Non-financial Corps.	5.1%	5.1%	1.8%	1.5%
Public Sector	1.5%	3.0%	1.8%	0.0%
Banks	1.3%	0.3%	0.5%	1.4%
Total	100%	100%	100%	100%

Source: Based on data from Office for National Statistics, U.K.

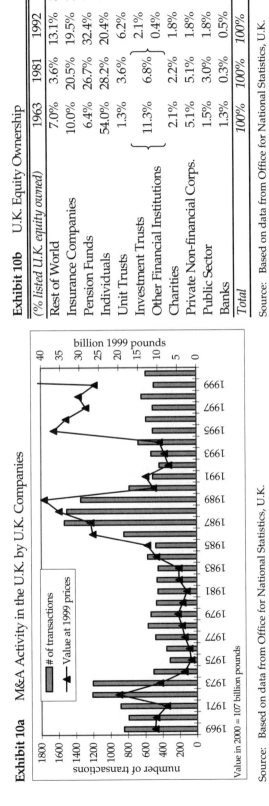

Exhibit 10a   M&A Activity in the U.K. by U.K. Companies

# of transactions
— Value at 1999 prices

Value in 2000 = 107 billion pounds

Source: Based on data from Office for National Statistics, U.K.

Exhibit 11   U.K. Tax Rates

%	1978	1979	1983	1984	1990	1993	1997	2000
Income tax								
- top rate unearned income	98	75	75	60	40	40	40	40
- top rate earnings	83	60	60	60	40	40	40	40
- basic rate	33	30	30	30	25	25	23	22
- starting rate	25	25	30	30	25	20	20	20
Value added tax	8	15	15	15	15	17.5	17.5	17.5
Corporation tax								
- main-rate	52	52	52	45	35	33	31	30
- small companies rate	42	42	38	30	25	25	21	20
Capital gains tax								
- higher rate	30	30	30	30	40	40	40	40
- lower rate	15	15	15	15	25	25	23	22
Inheritance tax (top rate)	75	75	75	60	40	40	40	40
Total taxes as % GDP[a]	34.75	35.50	38.25	38.50	37.25	na	na	na

Sources: Based on Lawson, 1085 and 1081; and Inland revenue, U.K.

Note: [a]Excluding North Sea oil taxes and revenue.

Endnotes

1   Frank Millar, "Tories miss a golden chance to hurt Labour," *Irish Times*, 3 May 2001.

2   United Kingdom, July 2001 Main Report, *EIU Country Report*, July 2001, 7.

3   For background, see the British capitalism chapters of Thomas K. McCraw, *Creating Modern Capitalism: How Entrepreneurs, Companies, and Countries Triumphed in Three Industrial Revolutions* (Cambridge, Harvard Business School Publishing, 1996).

4   Ebbinghaus and Visser, *Trade Unions in Western Europe since 1945,* 709.

5   Roger Middleton, *The British Economy since 1945* (New York: St. Martin's Press, Inc, 2000): 103, citing Paul Mosley, *The Making of Economic Policy: Theory and Evidence from Britain and the United States since 1945* (Brighton: Palgrave, 1984), 116, 148.

6   Bernhard Ebbinghaus and Jelle Visser, *Trade Unions in Western Europe since 1945* (New York: Grove's Dictionaries, Inc., 2000), 714.

7   Ronald Dore, William Lazonick, and Mary O'Sullivan, "Varieties of Capitalism in the Twentieth Century," *Oxford Review of Economic Policy* 15, no. 4 (1999): 110, 112.

8   Geoffrey Owen, "Corporate Governance in Britain: Is Incremental Reform Enough?" January 2001, 11 [part of the research project *Corporate Governance, Innovation, and Economic Performance in the EU*, available at <http://www.insead.edu/cgep/> (July 2001)] citing John Littlewood, *The Stock Market: Fifty Years of Capitalism at Work* (Financial Times Pitman Publishing, 1988), 84.

9   Middleton, *The British Economy since 1945,* 92.

10   Quoted in Will Hutton, *The State We're In,* revised edition (London: Vintage, 1995).

11   Video clip available at http://www.thatcherweb.com/multimedia/ (as of 10 October 2001).

12   Middleton, *The British Economy since 1945,* 96.

13   Sir Douglas Wass, farewell interview in *The Times* (London), 31 March 1983, as quoted in John B. Goodman and David Palmer, "Great Britain: Decline or Renewal?" HBS No. 389-011 (Boston: Harvard Business School Publishing, 1989), 8.

14   William Keegan, *Mrs. Thatcher's Economic Experiment* (Harmondsworth, 1984), 183, as cited in Middleton, *The British Economy since 1945,* 94.

15   *The Times* (London), 30 March 1981.

16   Kathleen Thelen, "Varieties of Labor Politics in the Developed Democracies," draft version of chap. 2 in *Varieties of Capitalism: The Institutional Foundations of Comparative Advantage,* ed. Peter Hall and David Soskice (Oxford University Press: 2001).

17   Peter Jenkins, *Mrs. Thatcher's Revolution: The Ending of the Socialist Era* (London: Butler & Tanner Ltd., 1987), 225.

18   Geoffrey Goodman, *The Miners' Strike* (London: Pluto, 1985), 15, as cited in Goodman and Palmer, "Great Britain: Decline or Renewal?" 10.

19   Nigel Lawson, *The View from No. 11: Memoirs of a Tory Radical* (London: Bantam Press, 1992), 161. Lawson is quoting Martin Adeney and John Lloyd, The Miners' Strike 1984-85, Routledge, pbk edn, 1988.

20   Dore, Lazonick, and O'Sullivan, "Varieties of Capitalism in the Twentieth Century," 114.

21   Owen, "Corporate Governance in Britain: Is Incremental Reform Enough?" 17.

22   Middleton, *The British Economy since 1945,* 55-57.

23   For more details about the U.K.'s privatization program, refer to Stephen Martin and David Parker, *The Impact of Privatisation: Ownership and Corporate Performance in the U.K.* (New York: Routledge, 1997).

24   Nigel Lawson, *The View from No. 11: Memoirs of a Tory Radical* (London: Bantam Press, 1992), 208.

25   "The Triumph and Tragedy of the Thatcher years," *The Financial Times*, 24 October 1993.

26 Andrew Glyn and Stewart Wood, "New Labour's Economic Policy: How Social-Democratic is the Blair Government?" 13, working draft version of chapter published in *Social Democracy in Neoliberal Times: The Left and Economic Policy Since 1980*, ed. Andrew Glyn (Oxford University Press, 2001).

27 "Lend Me Your Ears," *The Economist* (U.S. Edition), 12 May 2001.

28 "Steady as She Goes," *The Economist* (U.S. Edition), 12 May 2001.

29 Thelen, "Varieties of Labor Politics in the Developed Democracies," 42.

30 Michael Terry, "Trade Unions: Shop Stewards and the Workplace," *Industrial Relations: Theory and Practice in Britain*, ed. Paul Edwards (Oxford: Blackwell, 1995), 203-228, as quoted in Thelen, "Varieties of Labor Politics in the Developed Democracies," 44.

31 Chris Howell, "Unforgiven: British Trade Unionism in Crisis," *The Brave New World of European Labor: European Trade Unions at the Millennium*, ed. Andrew Martin and George Ross, (New York: Berghahn, 1999), 26-74, as quoted in Thelen, "Varieties of Labor Politics in the Developed Democracies," 44.

32 Blair addressing the TUC Annual Conference in 1999, as quoted in Glyn and Wood, "New Labour's Economic Policy: How Social-Democratic is the Blair Government?" 8.

33 Glyn and Wood, "New Labour's Economic Policy: How Social-Democratic is the Blair Government?" 8.

34 Ibid, 15.

35 Ibid, 16.

36 Dore, Lazonick, and O'Sullivan, "Varieties of Capitalism in the Twentieth Century," 114.

37 Owen, "Corporate Governance in Britain: Is Incremental Reform Enough?" 26. There were only 39 cases of intervention. The low incidence of intervention can be attributed to many factors. Most importantly, shareholders were often also advisors / suppliers to the companies, and did not want to jeopardize relationships.

38 Glyn and Wood, "New Labour's Economic Policy: How Social-Democratic is the Blair Government?" 9.

39 "Britain's Election Drama," *The Economist* (U.S. Edition), 12 May 2001.

40 OECD, *Literacy in the Information Age: Final Report of the International Adult Literacy Survey,* (OECD, 2000), Figure 2.1. Available at <http://www1.oecd.org/publications/e-books/8100051e.pdf> (Oct, 2001).

41 "Hunting the Snark," *The Economist* (U.S. Edition), 23 June 2001.

42 "Towards the Unknown Region," *The Economist* (U.S. Edition), 12 May 2001.

Europe: Data Supplement 1950–2003

This data supplement consists of two sections. The first section presents post-war macroeconomic data, focusing on France, Germany, Italy, the Netherlands, Spain, the United Kingdom, and, for comparative purposes, Japan and the United States. The second section includes employment, education, and social spending statistics since the 1980s, focusing on the same countries.

Professor Huw Pill and Research Associates Marie-Laure Goepfer (MBA '03) and Ingrid Vogel prepared this case. This case was developed from published sources. HBS cases are developed solely as the basis for class discussion. Cases are not intended to serve as endorsements, sources of primary data, or illustrations of effective or ineffective management.

Macroeconomic Data

Exhibit 1   Real GDP Growth *(annual average % increase)*

	1950–1960	1961–1973	1974–1983	1984–1990	1991–2000	2001	2002	2003
France	5.1%	4.8%	2.0%	2.7%	1.9%	2.1%	1.1%	0.5%
Germany[a]	na	3.7%	1.6%	3.2%	3.0%	0.8%	0.2%	-0.1%
Italy	na	4.9%	2.2%	2.9%	1.6%	1.7%	0.4%	0.4%
Netherlands	na	5.7%	1.3%	3.2%	2.9%	1.4%	0.6%	-0.9%
Spain	na	6.9%	1.5%	3.8%	2.7%	2.8%	2.0%	2.4%
United Kingdom	2.7%	2.8%	1.3%	3.2%	2.4%	2.3%	1.8%	2.2%
Japan	na	7.2%	3.6%	4.6%	1.4%	0.6%	-0.2%	2.5%
United States	3.5%	3.9%	2.3%	4.0%	3.3%	0.8%	1.9%	3.0%

Sources: Compiled from IMF, *International Financial Statistics CD-ROM*, March 2004 (for 1950–1983); and EIU Country Data, September 2004 (1984–2001).

Note: [a]Prior to 1991, Germany includes only West Germany. Post-reunification data refers to all of Germany.

Exhibit 2   Inflation *(annual average % increase in consumer price index)*

	1950–1960	1961–1973	1974–1983	1984–1990	1991–2000	2001	2002	2003
France	6.0%	4.7%	11.3%	4.1%	1.7%	1.6%	1.9%	2.1%
Germany	1.2%	3.4%	4.8%	1.6%	2.2%	2.5%	1.3%	1.1%
Italy	2.9%	4.9%	16.7%	6.9%	3.7%	2.8%	2.5%	2.7%
Netherlands	3.7%	5.4%	6.6%	1.3%	2.5%	4.5%	3.5%	2.1%
Spain	5.8%	7.3%	16.7%	7.5%	3.9%	3.6%	3.1%	3.0%
United Kingdom	3.3%	5.2%	13.7%	5.8%	3.1%	1.8%	1.6%	1.4%
Japan	3.1%	6.3%	7.8%	1.6%	0.8%	-0.7%	-0.9%	-0.3%
United States	1.8%	3.4%	8.5%	4.0%	2.8%	2.8%	1.6%	2.3%

Source: Compiled from IMF, *International Financial Statistics CD-ROM*, March 2004.

Exhibit 3   Unemployment Rate

	1960	1973	1983	1990	1995	2000	2001	2002	2003
France	1.5%	2.8%	9.0%	8.9%	11.4%	9.5%	8.7%	9.0%	9.7%
Germany	1.1%	0.7%	9.2%	7.2%	9.5%	9.6%	9.4%	9.8%	10.5%
Italy	3.7%	3.7%	7.4%	8.9%	11.5%	10.4%	9.5%	9.0%	8.6%
Netherlands	na	3.1%	9.5%	6.0%	7.1%	3.8%	3.5%	3.6%	5.3%
Spain	na	na	17.3%	16.2%	22.9%	13.9%	10.5%	11.4%	11.3%
United Kingdom	2.2%	3.2%	10.9%	6.9%	8.5%	5.4%	5.0%	5.1%	5.0%
Japan	1.7%	1.3%	2.7%	2.1%	3.2%	4.7%	5.0%	5.4%	5.3%
United States	5.5%	4.9%	9.6%	5.6%	5.6%	4.0%	4.8%	5.8%	6.0%

Sources: Compiled from U.S. Department of Labor, Bureau of Labor Statistics, Foreign Labor Statistics, <http://www.bls.gov/data/home.htm> (accessed September 9, 2002) (for 1960–1973); and EIU Country Data, September 2004 (for 1983–2003).

Exhibit 4   Productivity Increases (*annual average growth rate of constant GDP per hour worked*)

	1974–1983	1984–1990	1991–1994	1995–1999	2000	2001	2002
France	3.2%	2.7%	1.7%	1.8%	4.4%	1.9%	1.6%
Germany	2.8%	2.6%	2.7%	1.9%	2.2%	1.3%	1.3%
Italy	2.7%	2.5%	3.2%	1.4%	1.5%	0.5%	-0.9%
Netherlands	3.0%	1.6%	1.2%	1.7%	0.0%	2.8%	-1.9%
Spain	4.0%	2.8%	2.9%	0.0%	-1.1%	-1.0%	0.6%
United Kingdom	2.8%	0.9%	3.1%	2.0%	3.4%	1.2%	1.2%
Japan	2.9%	4.2%	2.2%	2.2%	2.4%	1.7%	1.6%
United States	1.1%	1.4%	1.4%	1.7%	2.4%	1.1%	2.9%

Source: Calculated by casewriter based on data from OECD Statistics Portal, <http://www.oecd.org/statsportal/> (accessed September 2004).

Exhibit 5   Productivity Comparisons with the United States, 2001

	GDP per head of population (as % of US)	Effect of % working-age population (15-64 years) to total population	Effect of % labor force to working-age population	Effect of unemploy-ment	Effect of work hours	Total effect of labor force participat'n	GDP per hour worked (as % of US)	GDP per employee (as % of US)
	(1)	(2)	(3)	(4)	(5)	(6) = (2) + (3) + (4) + (5)	(7) = (1) - (6)	(8) = (1) - (2) - (3) - (4)
Australia	76	0	0	0	0	0	76	77
Austria	80	2	-4	1	-15	-16	96	81
Belgium	78	-1	-12	-4	-16	-33	111	95
Canada	85	3	2	-2	-2	1	84	82
Czech Republic	44	2	-2	-1	4	3	41	44
Denmark	83	0	4	1	-16	-12	95	78
Finland	75	0	0	-3	-6	-9	84	78
France	77	-2	-6	-3	-15	-27	103	88
Germany	75	1	-4	-2	-21	-26	101	80
Greece	49	1	-12	-3	4	-10	59	63
Hungary	40	1	-11	0	-1	-11	51	50
Iceland	79	-2	10	2	0	10	69	69
Ireland	89	1	-9	2	-8	-14	103	94
Italy	75	1	-16	-3	-11	-30	105	94
Japan	74	1	2	0	-1	2	72	72
Korea	48	3	-6	1	12	11	37	49
Luxembourg	141	1	31	4	-11	26	116	105
Mexico	26	-2	-5	1	1	-5	31	32
Netherlands	82	1	0	2	-28	-24	106	78
New Zealand	61	-1	1	0	0	0	61	61
Norway	103	-2	6	2	-34	-29	131	97
Poland	29	1	-5	-6	.	-10	.	39
Portugal	50	1	1	0	-3	-1	51	48
Slovak Republic	36	2	-3	-6	4	-4	39	43
Spain	62	2	-9	-4	0	-12	74	73
Sweden	74	-2	2	0	-11	-11	85	74
Switzerland	82	1	10	2	-12	1	81	68
Turkey	17	0	-8	-1	.	-10	.	27
United Kingdom	74	-1	0	1	-5	-6	79	74
United States	100	0	0	0	0	0	100	100
Euro-area (12)	73	0	-7	-2	-13	-22	95	82

Source: Adapted from OECD Statistics Portal, <http://www.oecd.org/statsportal/> (accessed September 2004).

Exhibit 6   Compensation Increases per Employee (*non-public sector; annual average % increase*)

	1976–1986	1987–1990	1991–1994	1995–1999	2000	2001	2002	2003
Australia	8.5	7.1	3.0	3.7	2.8	4.1	3.9	3.2
Austria	6.7	4.5	4.9	2.2	2.7	2.3	2.4	1.9
Belgium	7.3	4.3	5.1	2.1	1.9	3.6	4.4	1.7
Canada	7.4	6.0	2.7	3.4	4.8	2.2	2.7	1.5
Czech Republic	na	na	27.1	11.1	6.4	6.7	6.7	6.8
Denmark	8.8	6.9	3.5	3.4	3.7	3.4	1.8	3.9
Finland	10.3	9.4	3.0	3.2	4.2	5.2	1.3	3.5
France	10.8	4.2	2.5	1.5	1.8	3.0	2.5	2.6
Germany	4.8	3.3	5.7	1.4	2.2	1.8	1.5	1.6
Greece	20.5	17.5	12.4	9.2	5.4	5.4	6.8	5.7
Hungary	na	na	na	15.4	16.9	14.7	11.9	10.9
Iceland	44.7	25.4	4.0	7.4	10.4	7.5	5.9	3.7
Ireland	13.6	5.0	4.4	3.4	5.4	5.8	4.3	3.9
Italy	15.6	7.9	5.9	2.9	2.9	2.8	2.2	3.3
Japan	5.2	3.1	1.8	0.1	0.3	-1.1	-2.2	-0.3
Korea	17.3	13.5	12.7	6.7	3.4	6.9	10.5	8.9
Luxembourg	5.8	4.4	5.4	2.1	5.3	3.6	2.7	2.2
Mexico	na	27.4	20.1	18.6	11.5	9.3	5.2	5.0
Netherlands	4.7	1.7	3.7	2.2	4.9	5.5	4.7	3.7
New Zealand	12.6	7.5	1.5	1.3	3.2	0.9	2.7	3.2
Norway	9.0	6.8	3.8	4.4	4.7	6.3	5.7	4.3
Poland	na	na	45.9	20.6	9.8	12.6	4.0	3.0
Portugal	19.9	13.5	11.9	5.6	6.9	5.2	3.8	3.1
Slovak Republic	na	na	na	8.1	15.0	5.4	7.1	5.7
Spain	16.7	7.8	8.3	3.5	3.9	4.4	4.2	4.8
Sweden	9.5	9.4	6.3	3.6	7.6	4.5	2.2	2.0
Switzerland	4.9	4.2	4.2	1.6	2.7	2.9	2.0	1.7
Turkey	34.6	90.3	83.7	70.0	43.1	43.6	32.0	30.5
United Kingdom	11.0	7.6	5.5	4.0	6.2	5.0	2.8	4.3
United States	6.8	4.2	3.5	3.8	6.8	2.6	2.1	3.0
Euro-area (12)	8.0	5.1	5.8	1.9	2.4	2.5	2.3	2.3

Source: Calculated by casewriter based on data from OECD Statistics Portal, <http://www.oecd.org/statsportal/> (accessed September 2004).

Exhibit 7   Government Bond Yields

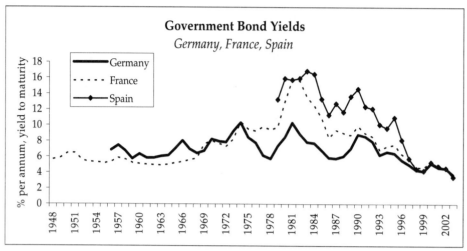

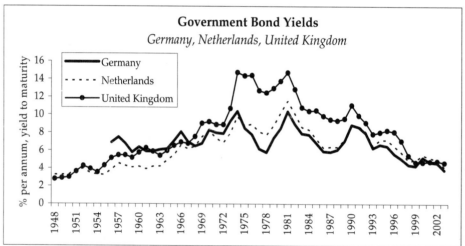

Source: Compiled from IMF, *International Financial Statistics CD-ROM*, August 2002, data on long-term government bonds of various yields. See source for more details.

Employment, Education, and Social Spending Statistics

Exhibit 8   Share of Women in Civilian Employment (%)

	1982	1985	1990	1995	2000	2001	2002
France	40.8	42.2	43.4	45.1	45.9	45.8	45.7
Germany	39.1	39.0	40.4	42.6	44.0	44.3	44.6
Italy	33.7	34.9	36.8	36.6	38.3	38.7	39.0
Netherlands	32.0	34.5	39.2	41.4	43.1	43.5	43.7
Spain	28.4	29.7	34.3	37.7	39.5	39.1	39.8
UK	39.1	41.5	43.0	43.8	44.9	44.6	44.8
Japan	39.0	39.7	40.6	40.5	40.7	40.9	40.9
US	42.7	43.5	44.6	45.7	46.2	46.2	46.2

Source: Compiled from OECD, *Labour Force Statistics Yearbook, 1982–2002* (OECD 2003).

Exhibit 9   Share of Services in Civilian Employment (%)

	1977	1983	1990	1995	1996	1997	1998	1999	2000	2001
France	53.1	58.4	64.6	69.1	69.7	70.3	70.9	71.5	72.0	72.2
Germany	49.4	53.6	57.9	60.5	61.6	62.3	62.6	63.4	63.9	64.8
Italy	45.7	51.5	58.8	59.2	60.0	60.5	60.8	61.5	62.2	62.6
Netherlands	61.7	66.9	69.1	73.7	73.8	74.1	75.0	75.4	75.4	75.9
Spain	na	na	54.7	60.9	61.7	61.7	61.4	61.7	62.1	61.9
UK	57.8	62.2	65.5	70.5	70.7	71.3	71.6	72.4	73.0	73.7
EU 15	50.7	56.1	60.9	64.5	65.1	65.6	65.9	66.6	67.0	67.6
Japan	52.8	56.0	58.7	60.8	61.2	61.6	62.7	63.2	63.7	64.6
US	65.4	68.5	70.9	73.1	73.3	73.4	73.7	74.4	74.5	75.2

Sources: Compiled from OECD, *Labour Force Statistics Yearbook, 1981–2001* (OECD 2002); *1980–2000* (OECD 2001); and *1982–2002* (OECD 2003) for Spain.

Exhibit 10   Share of Part-time Work *(less than 30 hours/week)* in Total Employment (%)

	1983	1990	1995	1996	1997	1998	1999	2000	2001	2002
France	10.3	12.2	14.2	14.0	14.8	14.7	14.6	14.2	13.8	13.7
Germany	13.4	13.4	14.2	14.9	15.8	16.6	17.1	17.6	18.3	18.8
Italy	8.0	8.9	10.5	10.5	11.3	11.2	11.8	12.2	12.2	11.9
Netherlands	18.5	28.2	29.4	29.3	29.1	30.0	30.4	32.1	33.0	33.9
Spain	na	4.4	7.0	7.5	7.9	7.7	7.8	7.7	7.8	7.6
UK	18.4	20.1	22.3	22.9	22.9	23.0	22.9	23.0	22.7	23.0
Japan	16.1	19.2	20.1	21.8	23.3	23.6	24.1	22.6	24.9	25.1
US	15.4	13.8	14.1	14.0	13.6	13.4	13.3	12.9	13.1	13.4

Source: Compiled from OECD, *Labour Force Statistics Yearbook, 1982–2002* (OECD 2003).

Exhibit 11   Share of Long-term Unemployment *(1 year and over)* in Total Unemployment *(%)*

	1983	1990	1995	1996	1997	1998	1999	2000	2001	2002
France	39.3	38.1	42.5	39.6	41.4	44.2	40.4	42.6	37.6	33.8
Germany	41.6	46.8	48.7	47.8	50.1	52.6	51.7	51.5	50.4	47.9
Italy	58.2	68.1	63.6	65.6	66.3	59.6	61.4	61.3	63.4	59.2
Netherlands	48.8	49.3	46.8	50.0	49.1	47.9	43.5	na	na	26.7
Spain	52.7	54.0	57.1	55.9	55.7	54.3	51.2	47.6	44.0	40.2
UK	45.6	34.4	43.6	39.8	38.6	32.7	29.6	28.0	27.8	23.1
Japan	12.9	19.1	18.1	19.3	21.8	20.3	22.4	25.5	26.6	30.8
US	13.3	5.5	9.7	9.5	8.7	8.0	6.8	6.0	6.1	8.5

Source: Compiled from OECD, *Labour Force Statistics Yearbook, 1982–2002* (OECD 2003).

Exhibit 12   Participation Rate in Labor Force of Population between 15 and 64 *(%)*

	1983	1990	1995	1996	1997	1998	1999	2000	2001	2002
France	66.7	66.0	66.9	67.4	67.2	67.4	67.8	68.0	68.0	68.3
Germany	66.6	67.4	70.4	70.6	70.8	71.4	71.2	71.1	71.5	71.5
Italy	58.0	59.5	57.9	58.2	58.5	59.2	59.8	60.3	60.7	61.2
Netherlands	58.8	66.7	70.1	70.9	72.1	73.0	73.9	74.6	74.9	75.6
Spain	59.2	61.7	62.6	63.2	63.9	64.5	65.3	66.7	65.8	67.1
UK	na	77.8	75.9	76.1	76.2	75.9	76.3	76.6	76.4	76.6
Japan	69.3	70.1	71.5	72.0	72.6	72.6	72.4	72.5	72.6	72.3
US	73.2	76.5	76.9	77.1	77.4	77.4	77.2	77.2	76.8	76.4

Source: Compiled from OECD, *Labour Force Statistics Yearbook, 1982–2002* (OECD 2003); ages 16–64 for UK, US, and Spain.

Exhibit 13   Participation Rate in Labor Force of Population between 15 and 24 *(%)*

	1983	1990	1995	1996	1997	1998	1999	2000	2001	2002
France	45.7	36.4	29.5	29.0	27.7	27.8	28.2	29.3	29.9	30.2
Germany	58.0	59.1	53.5	51.9	51.0	51.3	51.6	51.5	51.1	50.4
Italy	44.6	43.5	40.1	39.6	39.7	40.1	39.6	39.5	37.6	36.4
Netherlands	51.5	61.4	64.5	66.3	67.5	68.0	70.9	71.2	71.1	71.1
Spain	57.4	54.9	48.0	47.2	46.9	46.9	48.0	48.5	46.8	47.0
UK	na	78.0	69.7	70.6	70.4	69.4	69.2	69.7	68.2	68.6
Japan	44.2	44.1	47.6	48.3	48.6	48.3	47.2	47.0	46.5	45.6
US	67.1	67.3	66.3	65.5	65.4	65.9	65.5	65.8	64.5	63.3

Source: Compiled from OECD, *Labour Force Statistics Yearbook, 1982–2002* (OECD 2003); ages 16–24 for UK, US, and Spain.

Exhibit 14 Participation Rate in Labor Force of Population between 55 and 64 (%)

	1983	1990	1995	1996	1997	1998	1999	2000	2001	2002
France	42.6	38.1	36.1	36.6	36.7	36.2	37.5	37.3	38.8	41.7
Germany	41.8	39.8	42.4	44.1	45.2	45.0	43.7	43.0	43.0	43.0
Italy	44.4	42.9	39.2	39.1	38.8	39.4	40.1	40.8	41.8	na
Netherlands	33.3	30.8	30.3	31.6	32.5	34.2	36.2	38.9	39.5	42.7
Spain	44.6	40.1	36.9	37.6	38.5	39.2	38.8	40.9	41.9	42.7
UK	na	53.0	51.4	51.4	51.7	51.0	52.1	52.8	54.0	55.2
Japan	63.7	64.7	66.2	66.3	66.9	67.1	67.1	66.5	65.8	65.4
US	54.5	55.9	57.2	57.9	58.9	59.3	59.3	59.2	60.4	61.9

Source: Compiled from OECD, *Labour Force Statistics Yearbook, 1982–2002* (OECD 2003).

Exhibit 15 Educational Attainment (*% of total adult population, 2002*)

Highest level attained:	Primary	Secondary	Tertiary	Average Years of Schooling
Australia	0	69	31	13.1
Austria	0	86	14	11.3
Belgium	19	53	28	11.2
Canada	6	52	43	12.9
Czech Republic	0	88	12	12.4
Denmark	0	72	27	13.3
Finland	0	67	33	12.4
France	17	59	24	10.9
Germany	2	74	23	13.4
Greece	37	44	18	10.5
Hungary	3	83	14	11.5
Iceland	2	72	26	13.4
Ireland	21	53	25	12.7
Italy	20	69	10	9.4
Japan	0	64	36	12.6
Korea	15	59	26	11.7
Luxembourg	23	58	19	12.9
Mexico	73	21	6	7.4
Netherlands	12	64	24	13.5
New Zealand	0	70	30	10.6
Norway	0	69	31	13.8
Poland	0	88	12	11.9
Portugal	67	24	9	8.0
Slovak Republic	1	88	11	12.5
Spain	32	43	24	10.3
Sweden	8	59	33	12.4
Switzerland	3	72	25	12.8
Turkey	65	26	9	9.6
United Kingdom	0	73	27	12.7
United States	5	57	38	12.7

Source: Adapted from OECD Statistics Portal, <http://www.oecd.org/statsportal/> (accessed September 2004).

Exhibit 16a Welfare State (*public social expenditure as % GDP*)

	1980	1985	1990	1995	1998
France	21.1	26.6	26.5	29.0	28.8
Germany	20.3	21.0	20.3	26.7	27.3
Italy	18.4	21.3	23.9	23.8	25.1
The Netherlands	27.3	27.4	27.9	25.9	23.9
Spain	15.8	18.0	19.3	20.9	19.7
United Kingdom	18.2	21.3	21.6	25.8	24.7
Japan	10.1	11.0	10.8	13.5	14.7
United States	13.1	12.9	13.4	15.4	14.6

Exhibit 16b Welfare State (*public social expenditure as % GDP in 1998*)

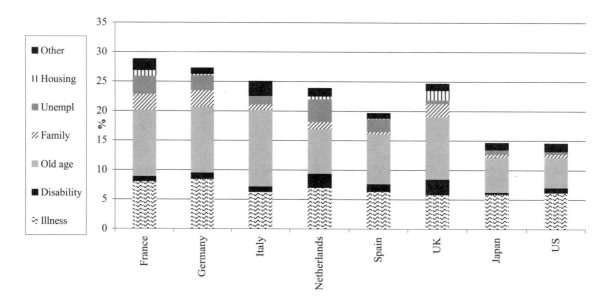

Source (16a–b): Compiled from OECD Statistics Portal, <http://www.oecd.org/statsportal/> (accessed September 2004).

Renewing Germany: Kohl's Legacy and Schröder's Dilemma

From the 1950s through the 1980s, the German economy was seen as the locomotive of European (and, on occasion, global) growth. Germany appeared to weather the stagflation of the 1970s more successfully than many other industrial economies. Reunification of East and West in 1990 at the end of the Cold War appeared to present further opportunities for growth and economic dynamism.

Yet by the time Gerhard Schröder was elected Chancellor of Germany in 1998, many saw Germany as the new "sick man of Europe"—a title assigned to Britain during the 1970s. Burdened by the unanticipated high costs of integrating the former East Germany into the Federal Republic and choked by labor market regulations and dormant financial markets, German business was no longer seen as a world-beater. Unemployment mounted to levels not seen since the 1930s as economic growth stagnated

In this context, many argued for fundamental reform of German institutions, although many of these institutions seemed to have served Germany well during most of the post-Second World War period.

Supplementary Material

Europe: Data Supplement 1950–2003

Study Questions

1. How did Germany manage the stagflation of the 1970s better than the United Kingdom? What role does institutional structure play in this comparison?
2. Are German labor markets flexible? If so, in what respects? If not (and this is seen as a problem), how was Germany so (relatively) successful in economic terms prior to reunification?
3. Does Germany need to change? In what respects? What advice would you offer to incoming Chancellor Schröder in 1998?

HUW PILL

Renewing Germany:
Kohl's Legacy and Schröder's Dilemma

On September 27, 1998, the German Social Democratic Party (SPD), in coalition with the Green Party, won its first electoral victory since 1980. Gerhard Schröder, the new Chancellor, faced the daunting task of replacing Helmut Kohl, who had governed for the preceding 16 years of German history. Kohl was the chief architect of German reunification in 1990 and one of the main drivers of European integration. Schröder knew that he had big shoes to fill. He now had to live up to his campaign promises of bringing economic stability and continuity in foreign affairs to a nation that had undergone tremendous changes over the previous decade and now faced significant economic and social challenges.

During Kohl's last term, Germany had been confronted with increasing pressures arising from globalization and the continued drive toward European integration, including the planned introduction of the euro. Over the last eight years, the country had been struggling to bear the significant costs of integrating the former German Democratic Republic. Unemployment stood at 18.2% in Eastern Germany, and 1998 GDP growth was expected to be only around 2% for all of Germany. The German pension system was seriously under-funded while the tax system seemed antiquated by international standards. Germany's capital markets were still underdeveloped relative to those of its Anglo-Saxon trading partners, and German labor laws were perceived to be exceedingly rigid. On the other hand, some observers still considered Germany a role model that had succeeded in creating a balance between a productive economy and an extensive social benefits system.

"Renewing Germany" had been Schröder's motto throughout his campaign. Now that he had won the election, Schröder had to tackle the backlog of reforms that had been created during Kohl's last term. While his top priority was to reduce unemployment for the country as a whole, he also wanted to attack the existing socioeconomic differences between Eastern and Western Germany. Schröder wondered how he should move Germany into the next century.

Michael W. Linse (MBA '02), Marie-Anne Popp (MBA '02), and Research Associate Ingrid Vogel prepared this case under the supervision of Professor Huw Pill. This case was developed from published sources. HBS cases are developed solely as the basis for class discussion. Cases are not intended to serve as endorsements, sources of primary data, or illustrations of effective or ineffective management.

Germany since 1945

Post-war Reconstruction

In the aftermath of the Second World War, Germany was severely weakened both economically and morally. With one third of its territory lost to its Eastern neighbors and most of its major cities destroyed by allied bombing, Germany faced widespread hunger and poverty. Nevertheless, Germany survived the war with both its human and physical capital relatively intact; assets hidden in caves or mines had survived air raids, and the German population remained highly skilled.

It was up to the international community to decide how to manage the country, both in terms of preventing future conflict and rebuilding its political and economic systems. U.S. President Roosevelt discarded the notorious Morgenthau Plan, which would have reduced Germany to an agricultural society. Instead, the four Allied Forces—the United States, the United Kingdom, France, and the Soviet Union—divided Germany into four zones, in each of which one power took responsibility for administrative government. The Allies were entitled to draw reparations from the zone they occupied. Given the bad experience after the First World War with reparations—which many viewed as having contributed to the rise of Nazism—only the Soviet Union made full use of this entitlement, reducing Eastern Germany's productive capacity by a further quarter on top of the damage already inflicted by allied bombing.

Differences between the victors of the war appeared quickly and soon intensified. The Western Allies were interested in having a stable Germany integrated into a stable Europe, while the Soviet Union sought to create a new Soviet satellite. The only issues the four Allies managed to agree upon were de-nazification, de-militarization, economic decentralization, and reeducation of the German people along democratic lines, although the actual meaning of "democratic" remained subject to interpretation. Despite breaking up three key industries in Western Germany – chemicals, banks, and steel (Montan) – the Western Allies had no interest in weakening Germany further. On the contrary, with the advent of the Cold War in the late 1940s, the Allies' goal was to create a strong Germany able to form a buffer between the democratic Western Europe and the communist Eastern Europe. Reconstruction in Western Germany was significantly aided by the Marshall Plan, which delivered large amounts of U.S. aid to Western Europe.

The Division of Germany

The Western Allies introduced the Deutsche Mark in June 1948 to promote stability. This had the unfortunate side effect of further isolating the eastern part of Germany. By 1949, differences between Eastern and Western Germany had become so pronounced that two separate states were formed: the Federal Republic of Germany (FRG) in the West and the German Democratic Republic (GDR) in the East. The FRG was based on principles of democracy and capitalism. In stark contrast, in the GDR, Stalin pushed for all power to be concentrated in the hands of the communist party and all industry to be transferred to public ownership. In this way, the GDR was modeled after the other "People's Democracies" established as Soviet protectorates in Eastern and Central Europe.

Germans in the GDR quickly realized the implications of the economic and political systems established in Eastern Germany and voted with their feet. Between 1949 and 1961, approximately three million East Germans crossed the border into West Germany.[1] In an attempt to stem the outflow of its labor force, the GDR closed its borders to the FRG in 1952; but this step failed to keep East Germans contained. In 1961, the leadership of the GDR took a drastic step and built the Berlin

Wall. This separated Eastern from Western Germany and isolated West Berlin as an island within East Germany for the next 30 years (see **Exhibit 1** for a map of Germany).

Strong Tradition of Economic Policy

In the West, the newly created FRG established the "Social Market Economy" (*Soziale Marktwirtschaft*) in collaboration with a group of economists called the "Freiburg School" and the then economics minister and later German Chancellor Ludwig Erhard. The social market economy was an attempt to find a balance between liberal market economics and considerations of social welfare in which the German state would play a considerable role. It was based on close cooperation between business, labor, and the government. Analysts remarked:

> Having studied or even personally witnessed the rise of external protectionism and internal interventionism and finally the switch towards central planning and political totalitarianism, the Ordoliberals [economists from the Freiburg School] were profoundly skeptical of unrestrained evolutionary processes of all kind. (...) Thus, competition had not only to be safeguarded but actually to be organized by the state — in quite the same way in which a sports race needs an organizer to invite participants and a referee to ensure that rules of fair play are observed.[2]

In general, the government limited its interference in business. For example, in contrast to other European nations at that time, relatively few industries were nationalized. In addition, anti-trust legislation in Germany was permissive, allowing the formation of large conglomerates and the reemergence of the pre-war universal banks, which had initially been split up by the Allies. In 1957, the German government set up an independent central bank (the *Bundesbank*), which viewed price stability as the prerequisite for economic growth and refused to pursue activist monetary policy in response to short-term economic fluctuations.

A comprehensive welfare system underpinned the relatively market-oriented economic system. Germany had a tradition of protecting its workers and families — a legacy of Otto von Bismarck's first welfare programs instituted in the 1880s.[3] After 1949, Germany went a step further and established one of the most extensive welfare states in Europe, with comprehensive health care, unemployment, family, and social security benefits.

The German social market economy also served to maintain a relatively narrow distribution of incomes among Germans relative to the income distributions of other developed countries (see **Exhibit 2**). First, the replacement of the *Reichsmark* with the Deutsche Mark in 1948 had already substantially reduced the wealth differences within the German population. The new currency was allotted at a 1:1 ratio with the Reichsmark, but the effective conversion rate decreased substantially for holdings exceeding 600 Reichsmark, resulting in heavy losses for holders of deposits and public debt.[4] Second, a very progressive tax system funneled income from the wealthy into the social security net. Third, collective bargaining and Germany's apprenticeship system provided certifiable skills and higher wages for a wide range of Germans, including youths.[5]

The result of the social market economy, at least initially, was lower unemployment, more price and wage stability, more peaceful labor relations, and better export performance than most other industrialized countries. The social market economy laid the foundations for the "German economic miracle," a period from 1950 to 1966 of strong economic performance with average annual GDP growth of 9%, as Germany rebuilt itself from wartime destruction.

The Role of the Bundesbank

The memory of the 1923 hyperinflation still haunted many German politicians. As a result, they established the Bundesbank with a greater degree of independence from the central government than almost any other central bank in the world. The Bundesbank's principal duty was to maintain price stability. Throughout the economic miracle and well into the 1990s, the Bundesbank did just that; it preserved the value of the Deutsche Mark, often with monetary policies that conflicted with the government's fiscal policies. Fritz Schäffer, Federal Finance Minister from 1949 to 1957, famously stated: "The road to inflation goes over my dead body,"[6] a sentiment shared by successive Bundesbank presidents.

Politics

Three political parties traditionally dominated the German political landscape: the Christian Democratic Party (CDU), the Social Democratic Party (SPD), and the Free Democratic Party (FDP).

The CDU and its sister party, the Christian Social Union (CSU), historically had the largest following, particularly during the economic miracle. These parties had traditional links to big business and to Catholic and Protestant religious groups. The CDU had no party association in the Free State of Bavaria, while the CSU put up candidates for election in Bavaria only. In parliament, however, the CDU and CSU had joint representation. The CDU / CSU supported a market economy based on price stability and low fiscal deficits. Despite their economically and fiscally conservative values, they fully subscribed to the doctrine of a socially considerate market economy supported by an extensive welfare system. In addition, the CDU / CSU emphasized family, religion, culture, and other traditional values as central tenants of their political platforms.

The SPD represented Germany's emerging working class. After the Second World War, the SPD advocated nationalization of key industries and central economic planning. But at the Bad Godesberg congress in 1959, the SPD dropped its Marxist doctrine and endorsed the CDU's social market economy. However, the SPD still maintained its close ties with Germany's labor unions. Economically, the SPD advocated a more Keynesian approach to macroeconomic management. For example, the SPD promoted macroeconomic demand stimuli in response to the 1970s oil shocks. In the 1990s, the SPD's economic policies became increasingly similar to those of the CDU.

The FDP, a centrist party, developed into a champion of civil liberties and the representative of the country's professional class and small business interests. It was the most market-oriented political party in Germany. While numerically smaller than the CDU or SPD, the FDP often held the balance of power in the Bundestag (the German lower house of parliament), and had participated in almost every cabinet since 1949, usually controlling either the economics or foreign ministries.

Two other parties—the Green Party and the Party of Democratic Socialism (PDS)—also exerted a degree of influence in German government. The Green Party emerged in the early 1980s to represent the environmental interests of the country. The PDS had its roots in the communist party of East Germany. After reunification, the PDS maintained influence in the parliaments of the states of the former GDR as the second- or third-largest party. No other political parties had consistently been able to make the 5% popular vote hurdle necessary to make it into the German parliament.

Germany in a European and World Context

After the division of Germany into separate states, the FRG became increasingly integrated into the West. It joined the European Coal and Steel Community in 1950 and NATO in 1955, and served as a founding member of the European Community in 1957.

Germany's increasing international political involvement went hand-in-hand with its growing economic power. In spite of a natural resistance toward the revival of German trade, Germany developed into a global export power in the 1950s and 1960s. Several factors made German products attractive to international buyers. First, German products were relatively cheaper than American or British products, both because of lower wages in Germany and because the Deutsche Mark was undervalued throughout the 1950s. Second, German companies could provide complex, customized engineering products that few other countries could offer. Third, German companies developed a reputation for quality, reliable delivery, and regular supply of spare parts. Finally, the Korean war boom from 1951 to 1953 and the industrial development of the rest of Western Europe triggered worldwide demand for the type of manufactured goods that Germany was positioned to produce.[7] By the early 1960s, Germany's exports exceeded those of Great Britain. By the end of the 20th century, Germany was the second-largest exporter in the world.

War Guilt

In the late 1950s and throughout the 1960s Germany started upon the long and sensitive process of coming to terms with the war crimes committed by Germans during the Second World War. Many of the collaborators of the Nazi regime were put on trial or removed from public office. Many others, particularly members of the German elite in politics, business, and bureaucracy as well as in the German military and justice system, were granted amnesty in order to prevent major upheaval.

Once the German economy had stabilized, younger generations, particularly university students, started asking uncomfortable questions about the involvement of older generations in Nazi crimes. These early investigations into the backgrounds of West Germany's political, academic, and business leaders were heavily supported by the East German government, which was interested in destabilizing the budding West German democracy. East German propaganda painted West Germany and its democratic and capitalist system as a continuation of the Nazi regime while portraying the East German political system as a clean break from Germany's National Socialist past. During the 1960s, discoveries about German public figures who had been complicit in Nazi activities prior to and during the Second World War became commonplace. University students began disclosing the identities of perpetrators of crimes in published lists that often included important members of German society.

Increasingly fervent investigations led to hardened relations between the generations that grew up before and after the Second World War. By 1968, student protests started to become less focused on exposing the Nazi pasts of German public figures. Instead, criticizing the German political and economic system as having fostered Nazism, student movements took on violent forms intended to change German society as a whole. Student leaders like Rudi Dutschke were responsible for the radicalization of the student movements (*Ausserparlamentarische Opposition*), while the Red Army Faction terrorist group (RAF)[8] declared an all-out war on German society. In the 1970s, these groups tried to destabilize German democracy with violent attacks and abductions.

Immigration

Although Germany had been at the center of the most devastating war in history, the population of Western Germany increased dramatically from 1939 to 1950, the year of the Federal Republic's first census. While the population of Western Germany just before the war stood at 43 million, it exceeded 50 million people by 1950. Almost eight million of these were refugees or victims of expulsions of ethnic Germans from Eastern Europe, mostly from Czechoslovakia, Poland, and the Soviet Union. More than 1.5 million were refugees from Eastern Germany. In total, almost one fifth of the West German population comprised displaced Germans. By 1960, this figure was closer to one quarter.[9]

Initially, the need to absorb such staggering numbers of refugees (*Flüchtlinge*) led to considerable friction within Germany, reflected in high unemployment rates and chronic housing shortages. But by the 1960s, the dynamic economy absorbed the large population surplus into the labor market and brought a sense of cohesion to West German society.

But as the economic boom continued and the Berlin Wall cut off the steady stream of East German refugees, a labor shortage emerged. To fill the gap, Germany invited citizens from other European countries, mainly Turkey and Italy, into the country as "guestworkers" (*Gastarbeiter*), selected by over 500 German recruitment offices throughout Southern Europe. Workers were usually male, between 20 and 40 years old, in good health, and without criminal records. They generally moved into jobs that Germans increasingly considered beneath them. The percentage of foreigners in the German labor force, just 1.5% in 1960, peaked at 11.9% in 1973, the year of the first OPEC oil shocks.

Guestworkers gave Germany a unique macroeconomic tool to adapt labor supply to demand fluctuations. During economic upturns, Germany increased the number of temporary one-year work permits. During recessions, work permits were simply not renewed. In the 1970s, as requests for work permit renewals were increasingly rejected, guestworkers chose to stay in Germany beyond their one-year terms and moved their families to Germany. However, guestworkers, who were now effectively immigrants, had difficulty with German naturalization laws. Since citizenship was based on blood lines rather than country of birth, even foreigners who were born in Germany and had lived in the country for decades could not become German citizens.

As the number of foreigners with permanent residence in Germany increased throughout the 1970s and 1980s, the friction with the local German population increased. A slowing economy led to rising German unemployment, and foreigners were blamed for a lack of jobs. Ironically, however, most unemployed Germans refused to take on the menial jobs vacated by foreigners who left the country. Over the next two decades, Germany continued to face the paradoxical situation of rising unemployment, an inability to fill unskilled job openings, and an unwillingness to integrate foreigners living in Germany.

The increase in "permanent" guestworkers coincided with a sharp decrease in the German birth rate. Whereas Germany had a surplus of 326,000 births over deaths in 1960, this figure dropped to a deficit of 95,000 by 1973.[10] This decrease could be traced largely to the changing role of women in German society and to the breakdown of traditional family structures. Immigrants had higher birth rates and were able to counterbalance the decrease to some extent. Even so, the German population was still aging quickly, putting significant strains on the German welfare state.

The Shocks of the 1970s

In the 1970s the OPEC oil shocks rocked the German economy. Due to a combination of factors, Germany was more exposed to the oil shocks than most other industrialized countries. First, as the incomes of Germany's trading partners declined with the rise in oil prices, demand for German goods declined throughout the world. Second, following the inflationary surge caused by higher oil prices, the immediate response of the Bundesbank, which had already been pursuing a restrictive monetary policy, was to tighten monetary policy even further. As other countries pursued loose monetary policy, the Deutsche Mark appreciated, hurting German exports further.

Nonetheless, Germany weathered the shock much better than its neighbors; between 1974 and 1983, unemployment averaged 6.9% and inflation was just 5%. However, the 1970s put a permanent end to the growth miracle of the post-war years. Not only had the oil shocks reduced demand for German products, but increased competition from American and Asian, particularly Japanese, companies had also forced German corporations to rethink their strategic positioning. Even though German productivity and production quality remained high, many Germans feared that their country was quickly falling behind. In particular, Germany was losing share to its U.S. and Japanese competitors in high tech products. It appeared that Germany's focus on stability, especially a non-confrontational relationship between unions and employers' associations, had kept unemployment and inflation in check but had also impeded the country's ability to adapt to the changing competitive environment. The German corporate elite concluded that Germany had to develop more sophisticated, skill-intensive and research-intensive products, which could not easily be replicated in countries with cheaper labor. The government decided to promote research and development and mobilized support for a shift in investment to higher tech industries.

The Challenges of the 1980s

Germany's economic performance in the early 1980s was encouraging (see **Exhibit 2**). Inflation and unemployment were low compared to other European countries such as France or the United Kingdom. In addition, Germany's GDP growth was on a par with that of the U.S. and Japan. Finally, Germany's export position in medium and low technology exports improved significantly relative to the U.S. and Japan.

One consequence of Germany's successful export economy was a constant revaluation of the Deutsche Mark. As a result, German exporters had to adjust to a new environment in which foreign competitors could compete on the basis of both lower wage costs and weaker currencies.[11] A second consequence was an increase in wages and social spending. Whereas in the 1950s wage restraint and high savings had fueled German export growth, by the 1980s German labor and German society as a whole were no longer willing to make the same sacrifices. This led to increasingly bitter wage negotiations between German unions and employers' associations. German unions demanded better wages, higher benefits, and reductions in the working week. At the same time, they were keenly aware that their demands made labor increasingly unattractive to German employers. In fact, union members secretly told the Bundesbank that they would reduce their wage demands in response to a more expansionary monetary policy. It became gradually more difficult for German unions and employers to see eye-to-eye in negotiations, and strikes became an increasingly common phenomenon.

By the late 1980s, German economic performance was mixed. Inflation remained low and GDP growth remained on a par with other European countries. However, attempts to promote entrepreneurial activity and develop leading positions in high technology industries had not been particularly successful. In addition, unemployment rose from 2.8% in 1980 to 6.3% in 1988. As unemployment grew, cries for structural changes increased. Employers demanded reductions in wages and benefits, deregulation of industries, tax reforms, and a general reduction in bureaucracy. Little progress had been made on these matters by the time the Iron Curtain came down.

German Reunification

When the Berlin Wall fell in November 1989, reunification of East and West Germany commenced almost immediately despite their extreme differences in economic and industrial structures. With regards to political considerations, quick integration was considered virtually mandatory. The economist Christopher Flockton explained:

> Clearly the policy was founded on the 'shock therapy' strategy, which may or may not have been economically the most efficient, but politically it was imperative, given the requirement to shore up the collapsing economy in the East.[12]

Reunification resulted in important economic and societal challenges. At the time of reunification, East Germany's economy was essentially bankrupt and its industry ill prepared for competition. Per capita incomes were only one third of those of West Germany.[13] At the same time, the scale of the task was tremendous; the population of East Germany was more than one quarter the population of West Germany. An expert on Germany elaborated:

> Many of the policy solutions adopted suggest the widespread belief among politicians that one economic system could just be replaced with another like equipping a car with a new engine. (…) The complexity of rearticulating and reinventing the political, economic and social structures has been underestimated. Developments since 1989 have shown that institution-building is a far more cumbersome process than policy-makers and observers had asserted and imagined. [14]

The *Treuhandanstalt*, a public privatization agency founded in 1990, played a key role in the first phase of economic restructuring. Its task was to privatize, reorganize, or, if necessary, close down the formerly state-owned firms in Eastern Germany. Describing the policies, academics remarked:

> In addition to the Treuhand policy, we can typify the strategy as involving start-up costs for social insurance and local administration, heavy direct infrastructural investment (…) and transitional assistance for the labor market. (…) Broadly, the policy subsidized new capital investment rather than, for example, labour subsidies, since it was plain that economic renewal would be carried by new investment policies responding to world conditions, rather than the subsidising of technologies and modes of working inherited from the highly distorted command economy.[15]

Reunification put strain on the economy (see **Exhibits 3–5** for German macroeconomic data). In 1991, transfer payments reached 6% of total GDP. The government financed this massive expenditure through borrowing, and the public deficit climbed to 4.4% of GDP.[16] Germany's public debt rose from DM 900 billion prior to reunification to DM 2,200 billion by 1998.[17]

Both the initial investments in Eastern Germany as well as the pent-up demand for consumer goods created a burst of economic activity. After only a few years, the boom subsided, and Germany slipped into recession. The recession was characterized by high unemployment; in the transition from a centrally planned to a social market economy, approximately one third of the East German work force became unemployed.

Despite the challenges posed by the reunification process, it appeared, in hindsight, to have been a success. The former West German economy had effectively absorbed an entire country while sustaining its global competitive position. This all happened without derailing the European integration process.

The 1990s and Beyond

After the Iron Curtain was torn down, an increasing number of asylum-seekers entered the country. Whereas the number of asylum-seekers in 1987 was less than 60,000, 1.1 million came to Germany between 1988 and 1992 – more than to all other European countries combined. A large majority of these were refugees from the disintegrating Eastern Bloc, particularly the former Yugoslavia. Since political refugees had the unconditional right under German law to claim refugee status in Germany, only few refugees were ever repatriated.[a][18] By 1998, 7.3 million foreigners lived in Germany (see **Exhibit 6**), up from four million in 1973.

Despite the influx of foreigners and the migration of 1.4 million ethnic Germans from Eastern Europe,[19] the size of the German population remained relatively stable throughout the 1980s and 1990s. Germany's birth rate, which had begun to decline in the 1960s, fell to third lowest worldwide. The long-term sustainability of the pension system was questioned as an increasingly smaller percentage of the population had to pay the pensions of an increasing pool of people over 65.[20]

Rising pension and welfare contribution payments put upward pressure on German labor costs that were already the highest among OECD countries (see **Exhibit 7**). Competitors from low wage countries—mostly Asia and increasingly Eastern Europe—were forcing German multinational companies to move production outside of Germany. This led to a heated debate about corporate under-investment in Germany (*Standortdebatte*).

Industrial Organization and Capital Markets

Industry   Historically, German industry comprised a mix of big business in capital-intensive industries such as coal and steel, automotive, chemicals, and electrical engineering, with small- to medium-sized companies that dominated the rest of the German economy. To many observers, the small- to medium-sized companies, the so-called German *Mittelstand*, formed the heart of the German economy. Many Mittelstand companies were world leaders in niche industries, usually in the manufacturing and engineering sectors. Traditionally, these companies tended to expand slowly by reinvesting their profits, all under a system of family control. In the 1990s, many Mittelstand companies entered a new era as original founders retired and either handed their companies down to the next generation or sold out.[21]

Services   The German service sector had traditionally been weak relative to other OECD countries (see **Exhibit 8**) for a number of reasons. First, after the Second World War, the frugal German population showed hesitation in paying for services. Later, a more extensive role of government inhibited the growth of a service industry through regulation and through providing services itself that were provided by the private sector in other countries. Even when Germans became increasingly wealthy in the 1980s and early 1990s and changed their attitudes toward services, entrepreneurial activity remained weak.

---

[a] In 1993, the German parliament revised the laws, making it harder for refugees to claim asylum.

Banking Debt was the predominant source of external finance for German companies. As a result, the German banking sector, characterized by powerful universal banks that combined investment and commercial banking services, was particularly important. Most companies appointed "housebanks" to act as primary lenders. Housebanks often held significant equity stakes in their largest industrial customers and were represented on their supervisory boards. According to a 1992 study, approximately 85% of the shares of Germany's 24 largest widely held companies were deposited at housebanks. Most holders of these depository shares relied on the banks to vote at annual shareholder meetings.[22]

Although large universal banks such as Deutsche Bank, Dresdner Bank, and Commerzbank wielded significant influence in the German economy, they controlled only 15% of domestic banking assets. The publicly owned banks (*Sparkassen* - savings banks) and cooperative banks (*Volksbanken* and others) together controlled 66% of banking assets. With over 4,000 banks in Western Germany alone, the German banking market was extremely fragmented.

Capital markets The power of bank financing was both a cause and a consequence of Germany's underdeveloped capital markets. The role for capital markets was very limited, as companies in need of funds would go to their housebanks. Only the largest firms made use of Germany's stock market for additional financing. By the middle of the 1990s, however, a retail shareholder culture began to emerge, jump-started by the privatization of a series of German utilities, including the IPO of Deutsche Telekom, and the establishment in 1997 of the *Neuer Markt*, a new stock exchange modeled after the U.S. Nasdaq. The Neuer Markt targeted high growth, small cap companies by offering less stringent listing requirements and lower fees. Its stricter disclosure requirements were attractive to investors.

The Neuer Markt offered the burgeoning German venture capital industry an attractive IPO venue.[23] Despite the growth of venture capital funds dedicated to Germany (see **Exhibit 9**), German entrepreneurs still faced structural and social impediments. For example, incorporation of limited liability companies was costly. Thus, entrepreneurs tended to incorporate private companies, exposing themselves to unlimited liability. This downside exposure induced entrepreneurs to invest conservatively with slow, internally financed growth. Entrepreneurial activity was also hampered by the strong social stigma of bankruptcy and its significant legal ramifications, including restrictions on directorships.[24]

Labor and Industrial Relations

The Unions

In an effort to support the development of the social market economy, German unions remained mostly non-confrontational throughout the post-World War II German economic miracle. As a result of the large immigrant streams of the 1950s and 1960s, unions initially had a weak bargaining position against big business, resulting in only moderate wage demands. With a decidedly Marxist bent, unions were instead more focused on advocating centralized planning and nationalization of key industries. In return for low wage demands, the unions insisted on co-determination, the right of workers to participate in the management of their corporations. After 1959, following the SPD's Bad Godesberg congress, German unions began to drop their Marxist agenda in favor of more practical objectives, such as achieving higher wages and a shorter workweek through collective bargaining.

Over the next 40 years, unions were able to increase significantly the average wages of German workers while reducing their average workweek (see **Exhibits 7** and **10**).

Co-determination (Mitbestimmung)

Since the 1952 Works Constitution Act, employees could participate in corporate policy-making both through works councils and employee representation on supervisory boards. Works councils represented the interests of employees vis-à-vis their employers. The councils monitored the observance of laws, wage agreements, and accident prevention regulations and had a considerable say in matters reaching from job descriptions to work processes and training. Often, employers had to consult their works councils before making any layoffs. In larger companies, employee representatives sat on supervisory boards with an equal number of shareholder representatives. This gave employees the power to participate in key decisions such as the appointment of management board members.

Collective Bargaining

Agreements on pay, working hours, and general working conditions were negotiated directly between labor and management, the so-called "social partners" in the German economic model. The negotiations were organized by region and industry, with the powerful Steelworkers' Union (*IG Metall*) kicking off the negotiation rounds and setting a precedent for other industry sectors. The wage negotiation process took into account the Bundesbank's inflation targets.

In 1998, the largest labor organization was the *Deutscher Gewerkschaftsbund* (DGB) with about eight million members in 11 unions. DGB unions were based on the industrial association principle, meaning that they enrolled workers and employees of an entire industrial or commercial sector regardless of the kind of work they did or the position they held within their company.

Unions negotiated two basic types of collective agreements with employers' associations and individual employers. The first type, wage and salary agreements, regulated pay and were renegotiated frequently. The second type, framework agreements, established employment conditions such as hours, holidays, and overtime rates and normally ran for seven years. The average statutory number of working hours per week was 48, but most employees worked less than 40. Similarly, the law prescribed a minimum of 24 paid holidays, but collective agreements generally provided for 30. Nearly all workers received additional holiday money and a Christmas bonus.

A key result of sectoral wage bargaining was that German firms competed on the basis of quality, service, and technological sophistication rather than on the basis of wage, cost, or price. Companies, particularly the cash-constrained Mittelstand companies, sought out relatively price-insensitive niches in which customers most valued the ability to make incremental customizations to existing technology. As one German observer of the system commented:

> With its centralized unions and decentralized works councils, the dual system of employee representation offers critical advantages. By extending collective bargaining agreements across entire industries and regions, it discourages employers from competing on the basis of labor costs. (…) It saves resources by requiring management carefully to justify decisions involving organizational change processes by involving works councils in the early planning stages, thus allowing them to garner employee acceptance of those changes.[25]

Social Security

Social security payments were a major component of employers' wage costs, as most potential financial hardships – unemployment, sickness, and injury – were cushioned by the welfare system. As a share of GDP, social security contributions had risen from 8–10% in the 1950s and 10–12% in the 1960s to more than 17% in the 1980s and 1990s.[26] A vicious cycle of rising unemployment and increasing contributions made labor expensive and, in turn, stopped companies from hiring or encouraged outsourcing. This was exacerbated by the soaring costs of medical treatment. The increasing cost of social security to employers and the under-funded pay-as-you-go pension system posed a threat to Germany's international competitiveness and employment outlook.

Education and Training

While the German education and apprenticeship system was a role model for the world in the 1970s and into the 1980s, it had lost some of its shine in the 1990s. Nevertheless, it was still well respected in the primary and secondary education areas. The higher education and job training model was based on free university education and an apprenticeship system that arose out of the German trade guilds of the Middle Ages.

The Apprenticeship System

Roughly two-thirds of German youths went through the apprenticeship system in the 1980s. An apprenticeship comprised both on-the-job training and classroom work in a vocational school (*Berufsschule*). German companies employed apprentices for two to three years and trained them for a particular profession such as electrician or car mechanic. In parallel, students attended the state-sponsored Berufsschulen for one or two days per week. Apprentices accepted low wages and, in return, received intermediate-level skill certifications after the completion of their apprenticeships. While apprenticeship positions were traditionally offered in the manufacturing sector, the growth of the service sector led to additional apprenticeships in areas such as banking, tourism, and health care.

The German government left the administration of the apprenticeship system largely to the private sector. The certification process and the specific skills necessary to receive a certification were supervised by employee unions and by trade chambers (*Handelskammern*), which functioned as private-interest industry associations. The interests of chambers and unions were generally opposed: Unions tried to keep the standards for skill certification as general as possible while chambers tried to ensure that the learned skills remained specific to their member firms. After completing their apprenticeships, workers usually shopped their skills to other firms, making general skill certifications more valuable for apprentices.

The German apprenticeship system developed in a unique environment. First, the absence of hostile takeovers and the predominance of bank financing allowed German companies to take a long-term business perspective. Second, since German companies tended to compete on the basis of quality and technological sophistication, they were much more willing to make investments in apprenticeship training, which improved the quality of the workforce in the long run. Third, trade chambers had the credibility to provide a certification that was perceived to be of high quality by employers and employees alike. They were also able to pool information across employers and maintain up-to-date skills standards. Other countries such as the United Kingdom and the United States never had an established system of trade chambers and in turn had difficulties establishing a

German-style apprenticeship system. In the United Kingdom, for example, private enterprises were generally hostile to the trade chambers the government tried to establish because the chambers were viewed as intrusive agents of the state.

The apprenticeship system allowed Germany to develop a highly skilled labor force with high wages. The virtuous cycle of high skills and high wages led to a high standard of living and low youth unemployment rates. Through the apprenticeship system, Germany invested in skills at a time when the return on skills was steadily rising. In the 1970s, highly skilled workers became more valuable as both the international product and financial markets became more liberalized and increasingly technologically sophisticated. Germany's highly skilled labor force significantly contributed to its export success as demand for Germany's complex products grew in response to European and worldwide industrialization.

However, the apprenticeship system also had its drawbacks, which became increasingly apparent in the 1990s when the total number of apprenticeships offered began to drop (see **Exhibit 11**). The high quality labor pool was expensive compared to labor from Ireland, Eastern Europe, or Asia. In addition, the apprenticeship system engendered a degree of inflexibility. The skill certification process led German workers to identify socially with their occupation (*Beruf*) and often inhibited teamwork and prevented cross-functional and cross-industry mobility. The more narrowly defined the skill certification, the less likely a worker was to switch industries.

The reduced power of unions posed a threat to the German apprenticeship system. Companies began to compete on price rather than quality, effectively reducing employers' incentives to invest in the long-run skills formation of their employees. As high skilled jobs received relatively lower wages, students lost the incentive to work hard to get an apprenticeship position.

After reunification, Germany had been unsuccessful at implementing the apprenticeship system in the former East Germany. Most companies in former East Germany did not have the capability to offer programs that met the standards set by trade chambers. As a result, many of their apprenticeships did not result in the level of skill development that similar programs produced in the West. Ultimately, the apprenticeships in Eastern Germany did not pay for themselves, and the German government stepped in with subsidies. In fact, in 1997, federal or state government sources either wholly or partly financed 79% of the new apprenticeship places offered in Eastern Germany.[27]

On balance, the German apprenticeship system had raised the skill level of the population and contributed to the German economic success story. However, it had developed in an environment that was now quickly changing. As equity markets became more global, it was unclear whether Germany's corporate leaders would still be willing to make long-term investments in training.

The University System

The German university system also became a political issue during the 1990s for a number of reasons. German universities were overcrowded and under-funded. Compared to their international peers, German university students spent longer studying for their degrees but were less well prepared for the job market once they graduated. They also avoided emerging opportunities in joining or founding start-ups since programs in entrepreneurship were weak. Fundamental research at German universities was increasingly uncompetitive with international research, particularly research done at U.S. institutions. The university system fostered an ivory tower approach to science where research was pursued for its own sake rather than with an aim to commercializing new discoveries. This ivory tower approach was exacerbated by the fact that, unlike in the United States, for example, universities put severe restrictions on outside earnings of university professors.[28] Lastly, the quality of education was compromised by a bureaucratic university system in which it was virtually impossible for a university employee to get fired.

While many of the problems of the German higher education system were publicly acknowledged, it was difficult to make changes to the system. The primary decision-making power with respect to educational reforms was at the state level. It was nearly impossible to develop a reform consensus among the German states. However, individual states such as Bavaria were pursuing innovative programs that were showing promising results. In addition, several private universities had developed throughout Germany during the 1980s and 1990s and were putting pressure on the traditional German university system.

Conclusion

Schröder had a number of immediate concerns. German unemployment was high and the economy was in trouble, particularly in the former East Germany. At the same time, Schröder was pressing forward with European integration and promoting the expansion of the European Union into Eastern Europe. Schröder knew that, while these issues were important and currently pressing, other internal and external factors would ultimately force even more wide-ranging changes to the traditional German model. For example, would the increasingly global financial markets and the declining power of German banks force German companies to change their long-term management perspective, with implications for the German apprenticeship system and German labor relations? Would the international product markets lead to increasing takeovers of German companies by foreign competitors? Would resistance to bureaucracy and changes to the higher education system lead to an unprecedented period of entrepreneurship in Germany?

Schröder had to consider whether adaptations to parts of the German model were possible without changing the entire system. If some aspects of the Anglo-Saxon model were introduced in Germany, could the rest of the system survive? What essential elements of the German model did Schröder need to protect and where should he foster change?

Exhibit 1   Map of Germany

Source: Reproduced from *Facts on File, Inc.* October 5, 1990, p. 735.

Note: Czechoslovakia is now the Czech Republic and Slovakia.

Exhibit 2   German General Economic Indicators

	1980	1985	1989	1990	1991	1992	1993	1994	1995	1996	1997	1998
% change over prior year												
Real GDP Growth	1.0	2.0	3.6	5.7	5.1	2.2	-1.1	2.3	1.7	0.8	1.4	2.0
Real Per Capita GDP Growth	0.8	2.4	3.0	4.7	4.2	1.6	-1.9	1.9	1.5	0.4	1.2	1.9
Consumer Price Inflation	5.4	2.1	2.8	2.7	1.5	5.1	4.4	2.8	1.7	1.4	1.9	0.9
%GDP												
Investment/GDP	27.2	23.4	25.0	25.5	25.7	25.7	24.7	25.2	24.7	23.8	23.4	24.1
Current Account/GDP	n.a.	2.6	4.3	2.9	-1.0	-0.9	-0.7	-1.0	-0.8	-0.3	-0.1	-0.3
Fiscal Surplus (+) or Deficit (-)/GDP	-1.8	-1.1	-0.1	-1.6	-2.1	-2.3	-2.4	-1.3	-1.8	-2.1	-1.3	-0.9
units as shown												
Population (millions)	78.2	77.7	78.4	79.1	79.8	80.3	81.0	81.3	81.5	81.8	82.0	82.1
Unemployment (%)	3.9	9.3	7.9	7.2	8.3	8.1	9.6	9.3	9.9	10.8	11.7	10.7
Exchange Rate (DM per U.S. dollar, period average)	1.41	2.57	1.78	1.54	1.58	1.51	1.67	1.65	1.50	1.54	1.73	1.75

Sources: Created by casewriter based on EIU Country Data, 2002; and International Monetary Fund, *International Finance Statistics Yearbook CD-ROM*, May 2002.
Note: All data, excluding population, prior to 1991 includes FRG only. Data from 1991 onwards is for all Germany.

Exhibit 3   German National Income Accounts (*billions constant 1996 U.S. dollars*)

	1980	1985	1989	1990	1991	1992	1993	1994	1995	1996	1997	1998
GDP	**1,712**	**1,812**	**2,023**	**2,138**	**2,246**	**2,297**	**2,272**	**2,325**	**2,365**	**2,383**	**2,417**	**2,464**
Private consumption	985	1,015	1,147	1,209	1,277	1,311	1,313	1,327	1,354	1,368	1,376	1,400
Government consumption	376	398	416	425	427	449	449	460	467	475	477	483
Gross fixed investment	466	425	505	545	578	590	561	586	584	566	565	593
Exports	289	371	430	478	538	534	504	543	574	603	671	717
Imports	318	340	414	456	516	524	495	531	561	578	626	682

Sources: Created by casewriter based on EIU Country Data, 2002; and International Monetary Fund, *International Finance Statistics Yearbook CD-ROM*, May 2002.
Notes: GDP does not equal sum of components because of rebasing to 1996, which alters the relative importance of individual components.
Data prior to 1991 includes FRG only. Data from 1991 onwards is for all Germany.

Exhibit 4   German Balance of Payments (*billions current U.S. dollars*)

	1980	1985	1986	1987	1988	1989	1990	1991	1992	1993	1994	1995	1996	1997	1998
Current Account	**-13.3**	**17.6**	**40.9**	**46.4**	**50.4**	**57.0**	**48.3**	**-17.7**	**-19.1**	**-13.9**	**-20.9**	**-18.9**	**-8.0**	**-2.9**	**-4.6**
Trade Balance	7.9	28.4	54.7	68.0	76.3	75.0	68.5	19.4	28.2	41.2	50.9	65.1	69.4	70.8	78.9
Exports	191.2	182.7	241.5	291.5	322.1	340.1	411.0	404.0	430.5	382.7	430.5	523.6	522.6	510.7	542.8
Imports	183.2	154.3	186.8	223.4	245.8	265.1	342.5	384.5	402.3	341.5	379.6	458.5	453.2	439.9	463.9
Net Services	-9.3	-3.0	-4.4	-7.9	-13.2	-12.6	-17.3	-21.2	-30.7	-33.1	-39.7	-45.4	-44.3	-41.9	-46.4
Net Income	0.9	2.8	4.1	3.3	7.0	14.3	20.8	21.7	18.0	13.3	6.8	0.3	0.9	-1.4	-6.7
Net Transfers	-12.9	-10.7	-13.4	-17.1	-19.9	-19.7	-23.7	-37.6	-34.7	-35.3	-39.0	-39.0	-34.0	-30.4	-30.3
Capital Account	**-0.9**	**-0.2**	**0.0**	**-0.1**	**0.0**	**0.1**	**-1.3**	**-0.6**	**0.6**	**0.5**	**0.1**	**-2.7**	**-2.2**	**0.0**	**0.7**
Financial Account	**5.7**	**-18.3**	**-37.0**	**-24.0**	**-67.6**	**-59.1**	**-54.8**	**5.2**	**51.8**	**16.2**	**30.4**	**44.0**	**16.1**	**0.5**	**8.4**
Net Direct Investment	-4.4	-4.8	-9.5	-7.9	-11.1	-8.1	-21.7	-19.6	-17.0	-13.3	-15.3	-27.1	-44.3	-30.0	-72.3
Net Portfolio Investment	-3.7	1.8	23.4	4.5	-36.3	-2.4	-1.7	23.9	32.2	120.4	-30.8	35.1	63.0	0.8	3.7
Net Other	13.8	-15.3	-50.9	-20.5	-20.2	-48.5	-31.4	0.9	36.6	-90.9	76.6	36.0	-2.6	29.7	76.9
Net Errors and Omissions	**-1.1**	**3.1**	**1.5**	**-0.9**	**1.6**	**4.8**	**15.1**	**6.9**	**3.9**	**-17.0**	**-11.7**	**-15.1**	**-7.2**	**-1.4**	**-0.5**
Reserves & Related Items	**9.6**	**-2.2**	**-5.4**	**-21.5**	**15.6**	**-2.9**	**-7.3**	**6.2**	**-37.2**	**14.2**	**2.0**	**-7.2**	**1.2**	**3.8**	**-4.0**

Sources: Created by casewriter based on EIU Country Data, 2002; and International Monetary Fund, *International Finance Statistics Yearbook CD-ROM*, May 2002.

Note: Data prior to 1991 includes FRG only. Data from 1991 onwards is for all Germany.

Exhibit 5 German Central Government Finance (*billions current DM*)

	1980	1985	1989	1990	1991	1992	1993	1994	1995	1996	1997	1998
Total Revenue	**425.8**	**554.4**	**659.8**	**701.6**	**811.9**	**989.7**	**1,022.7**	**1,104.7**	**1,130.8**	**1,139.8**	**1,166.7**	**1,194.5**
% GDP	*29%*	*30%*	*30%*	*29%*	*28%*	*31%*	*32%*	*33%*	*32%*	*32%*	*32%*	*32%*
Tax Revenue	407.2	509.0	618.9	654.7	769.2	855.2	871.2	930.8	965.2	955.1	973.0	993.5
Nontax Revenue	16.6	42.1	30.7	44.0	38.9	129.0	145.5	166.6	156.8	174.3	181.3	189.4
Capital Revenue	0.1	0.2	0.3	0.3	0.4	1.0	0.9	2.1	2.7	3.7	6.0	5.2
Grants	2.5	3.1	2.8	2.6	3.5	4.5	5.1	5.2	6.1	6.7	6.4	6.3
Total Expenditure	**447.5**	**564.6**	**656.1**	**716.3**	**860.7**	**1,045.5**	**1,084.3**	**1,142.8**	**1,188.0**	**1,213.2**	**1,214.7**	**1,233.9**
% GDP	*30%*	*31%*	*30%*	*29%*	*29%*	*33%*	*34%*	*34%*	*34%*	*34%*	*33%*	*33%*
General Public Services	18.9	24.3	23.4	49.8	71.0	34.4	37.1	35.0	33.2	32.6	na	na
Defense	40.9	50.9	54.5	55.2	55.5	54.7	51.2	48.4	47.7	47.2	na	na
Public Order & Safety	0.0	0.0	2.3	2.3	2.8	3.3	3.6	3.8	4.0	4.2	na	na
Education	4.0	3.6	4.1	4.7	6.8	7.2	6.9	6.5	6.7	6.6	na	na
Health	85.2	103.0	118.2	128.0	144.5	189.3	189.7	205.5	217.3	229.2	na	na
Social Security & Welfare	220.3	276.9	317.8	335.9	389.8	485.3	531.9	557.3	594.9	607.0	na	na
Housing and Community Amenities	1.8	1.7	2.4	3.0	5.0	5.4	3.7	5.6	6.3	5.7	na	na
Economic Affairs and Services	38.9	40.0	57.0	58.2	83.7	93.1	87.3	88.0	96.3	89.5	na	na
Other	36.0	64.3	75.3	79.2	101.7	172.8	172.8	192.6	181.7	191.3	na	na
Interest portion of other	*na*	*na*	*32.6*	*34.9*	*44.3*	*65.0*	*62.8*	*73.0*	*86.3*	*86.2*	*85.8*	*86.3*
Lending Minus Repayment	**5.2**	**7.4**	**8.0**	**9.7**	**12.0**	**13.8**	**12.1**	**15.8**	**3.6**	**3.0**	**-3.0**	**-18.0**
Overall Deficit/Surplus	**-26.9**	**-20.0**	**-1.7**	**-39.6**	**-62.3**	**-73.4**	**-78.8**	**-44.8**	**-61.8**	**-74.2**	**-49.0**	**-35.1**
Adjustment to Deficit / Surplus	0.0	-2.4	2.7	-15.2	-1.5	-3.8	-5.1	9.2	-1.0	2.3	-4.0	-13.7
% GDP	*-1.8%*	*-1.1%*	*-0.1%*	*-1.6%*	*-2.1%*	*-2.3%*	*-2.4%*	*-1.3%*	*-1.8%*	*-2.1%*	*-1.3%*	*-0.9%*
Financing	**26.9**	**20.0**	**1.7**	**39.6**	**62.3**	**73.4**	**78.8**	**44.8**	**61.8**	**74.2**	**49.0**	**35.1**
Abroad	20.8	18.1	21.6	13.3	45.1	54.6	107.9	-23.0	58.5	54.3	79.9	80.3
Domestic	6.1	1.9	-20.0	26.2	17.2	18.8	-29.2	67.8	3.4	19.9	-30.9	-45.2
GDP	*1,471*	*1,826*	*2,224*	*2,431*	*2,938*	*3,155*	*3,235*	*3,394*	*3,523*	*3,586*	*3,667*	*3,784*

Source: Created by casewriter based on data from International Monetary Fund, *Government Finance Statistics Yearbook*, 1990 and 2001.

Note: Data prior to 1991 includes FRG only. Data from 1991 onwards is for all Germany.

Exhibit 6   Foreigners in Germany by Major Countries *(1998 data, total foreigners = 7.3 millions)*

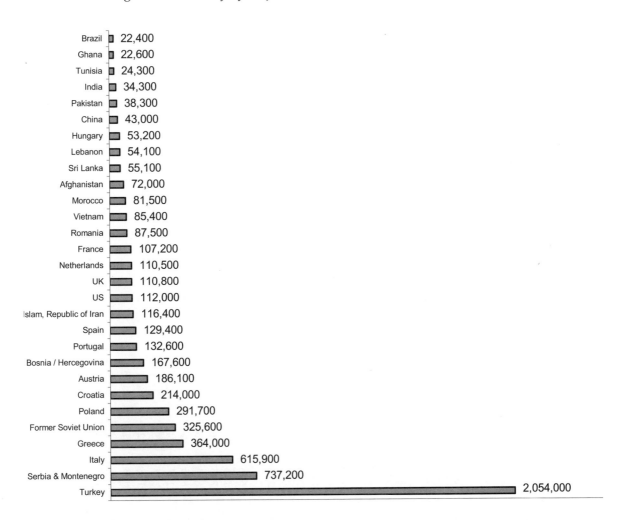

Source: Adapted from Kappler, *Facts about Germany*, 2001.

Exhibit 7   Cross-Country Comparison of Hourly Compensation Costs for Production Workers (*current U.S. dollars*)

	1975	1980	1985	1990	1995	1999
United States	6.36	9.87	13.01	14.91	17.19	19.2
Canada	5.96	8.67	10.95	15.95	16.1	15.6
Mexico	1.47	2.21	1.59	1.58	1.51	2.12
Australia	5.62	8.47	8.2	13.07	15.27	15.89
Hong Kong	0.76	1.51	1.73	3.2	4.82	5.44
Japan	3	5.52	6.34	12.8	23.82	20.89
Korea	0.32	0.96	1.23	3.71	7.29	6.71
New Zealand	3.15	5.22	4.38	8.17	9.91	9.14
Singapore	0.84	1.49	2.47	3.78	7.33	7.18
Taiwan	0.4	1	1.5	3.93	5.94	5.62
Austria	4.51	8.88	7.58	17.75	25.32	21.83
Belgium	6.41	13.11	8.97	19.17	26.65	22.82
Denmark	6.28	10.83	8.13	18.04	24.07	22.96
Finland	4.61	8.24	8.16	21.03	24.1	21.1
France	4.52	8.94	7.52	15.49	20.01	17.98
Germany, Former West	**6.31**	**12.25**	**9.53**	**21.88**	**31.58**	**26.93**
Germany, Unified					**30.65**	**26.18**
Greece	1.69	3.73	3.66	6.76	9.17 ..	
Ireland	3.03	5.95	5.92	11.66	13.61	13.57
Italy	4.67	8.15	7.63	17.45	16.22	16.6
Luxembourg	6.5	12.03	7.81	16.74	23.35 ..	
Netherlands	6.58	12.06	8.75	18.06	24.12	20.94
Norway	6.77	11.59	10.37	21.47	24.38	23.91
Portugal	1.58	2.06	1.53	3.77	5.37 ..	
Spain	2.53	5.89	4.66	11.38	12.88	12.11
Sweden	7.18	12.51	9.66	20.93	21.44	21.58
Switzerland	6.09	11.09	9.66	20.86	29.3	23.56
United Kingdom	3.37	7.56	6.27	12.7	13.67	16.56

Labor Costs Comparison, 1999

Country	U.S. Dollars
Germany, Former West	26.9
Germany, Unified	26.2
Sweden	21.6
Netherlands	20.9
Japan	20.9
United States	19.2
France	18.0
Italy	16.6
United Kingdom	16.6
Ireland	13.6
Spain	12.1
Korea	6.7

Source: Created by casewriter based on data from U.S. Bureau of Labor Statistics, June 2001.

Exhibit 8   Cross-Country Comparison of Civilian Employment in Service Sector, 1960–98
(% of total civilian employment)

	U.S.	Canada	Australia	Japan	France	**Germany**	Italy	Netherlands	Sweden	UK
	%	%	%	%	%	**%**	%	%	%	%
1960	58	55	na	42	39	**40**	33	51	45	49
1965	60	57	55	45	44	**42**	37	52	47	51
1970	62	63	57	47	48	**43**	40	56	54	54
1975	66	66	62	52	52	**n.a.**	44	61	58	58
1980	67	na	65	55	56	**52**	48	65	63	61
1985	70	na	69	57	62	**55**	55	68	66	66
1990	72	72	71	59	65	**58**	59	70	68	68
1995	74	75	73	61	70	**62**	59	73	72	71
1998	75	75	74	63	72	**64**	61	75	72	72

Source: Adapted from Bureau of Labor Statistics, 2002 <ftp://ftp.bls.gov/pub/special.requests/ForeignLabor/flslforc.txt>
          May 2002.

Exhibit 9   Private Equity Funds under Management in Germany *(millions current DM)*

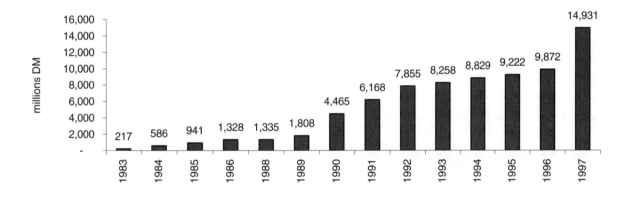

Source: Adapted from Kuemmerle.
Note: No data for 1987.

Exhibit 10   Cross-Country Comparison of Working Conditions

A Annual total hours worked *(production workers in manufacturing industry)*

	1980	1990	1996	1998
Japan	2,162	2,214	1,993	1,947
United States	1,893	1,948	1,986	1,991
France	1,759	1,683	1,679	1,672
Germany	**1,719**	**1,598**	**1,517**	**1,517**
United Kingdom	1,883	1,953	1,934	1,925

B Annual leave and public holidays as of 2000

	Average annual leave entitlement	Statutory minimum annual leave	Public Holidays per Year
France	na	25	11
Germany (west)	**29.2**	**20**	**9-12**
Ireland	20	20	9
Italy	28	20	12
Netherlands	31.4	20	8
Spain	na	25	12-14
Sweden	25	25	11
United Kingdom	25	20	8
EU average	*25.6*	*22*	*10.8*
Japan	17.8	10	15
United States	16.9	0	10

Source: Adapted from European Industrial Relations Observatory Online,
<http://www.eiro.eurofound.ie/2001/11/feature/tn0111148f.html> May 2002.

Exhibit 11   Apprenticeships in Germany

A Apprenticeship Training in Western Germany

	Apprenticeship Places	Youth seeking apprenticeships	Places / Seekers (%)
1972	584,000	585,000	99.8
1982	651,000	665,000	97.9
1987	690,000	680,000	101.5
1992	623,000	511,000	121.9
1997	487,000	494,000	98.6

B Apprenticeship Training in Eastern Germany

	Apprenticeship Places	Youth seeking apprenticeships	Places / Seekers (%)
1992	98,000	96,000	102.1
1993	102,000	102,000	100.0
1994	119,000	119,000	100.0
1995	124,000	128,000	96.9
1996	126,000	138,000	91.3
1997	126,000	148,000	85.1

Source: Adapted from Culpepper, "The Future of High Skill Equilibrium in Germany," 1999, pp. 49–51.
Note: Table 2, "places offered" includes subsidized in-firm places and apprenticeships in training centers that are not part of a firm contract. The figures are not, therefore, comparable directly with those in Table 1.

Bibliography

Dwight Crane and Ulrike Schaede, "Changing Corporate Governance: The Financial System in Germany," Harvard Business School Working Paper, September 10, 2001.

Pepper Culpepper, "The German Skills Machine: Sustaining Comparative Advantage in a Global Environment," 1999.

Pepper Culpepper, "The Future of the High-Skill Equilibrium in Germany," *Oxford Review of Economic Policy*, Vol. 15 no 1, spring 1999.

Alexander Dyck, "Germany in the 1990s: Managing Reunification," Harvard Business School Case 793-033 (Boston, MA: Harvard Business School Publishing, 1992).

Herbert Giersch, Karl-Heinz Paqué, and Holger Schmieding, *The Fading Miracle – Four Decades of Market Economy in Germany* (Cambridge, UK: Cambridge University Press, 1992).

John B. Goodman and Andrew Tauber, "West Germany: The Search for Stability," Harvard Business School Case 389-146 (Boston, MA: Harvard Business School Publishing, 1989).

Hannelore Hamel (editor), *Soziale Marktwirtschaft – Sozialistische Planwirtschaft* (Muenchen: Verlag Franz Vahlen, 1989).

Richard Hauser (publisher) "Die Zukunft des Sozialstaats," *Zeitschrift für Wirtschafts- und Sozialwissenschaften, Schriften des Vereins für Sozialpolitik, Band 271, Evolution of the Welfare State*, 1998.
- Dennis J. Snower, "The Evolution of the Welfare State."
- Hans-Werner Sinn, "Sozialstaat im Wandel."

Arno Kappler (editor), *Facts about Germany* (Frankfurt/Main: The German Federal Press and Information Bureau, Societäts-Verlag, 2000).

Walter Kuemmerle, "Comparing Catalysts of Change: Evolution and Institutional Differences in the Venture Capital Industries in the U.S., Japan and Germany," Harvard Business School Working Paper, June 12, 2001.

Walter Kuemmerle, Frederick M. Paul, and Henrik Freye "Survey of Private Equity in Germany – Summary of Results and Analysis," Harvard Business School Working Paper, 1998.

Klaus Larres (editor), *Germany since Unification* (London: Macmillan Press, 1998)
- Christopher Flockton "The German Economy since 1989/90."
- Till Geiger "Believing the Miracle Cure: The Economic Transition Process in Germany and East-Central Europe."

Klaus Larres and Panikos Panayi (editors), *The Federal Republic of Germany since 1949* (London: Longman, 1996).
- Hartmut Berghoff "Population Change and its Repercussions on the Social History of the FRG."
- Richard Overy "The Economy of the Federal Republic since 1949."

Ulrike Schaede and Bruce R. Scott, "Germany 2000: Financial System, Corporate Governance, and Economic Performance," Harvard Business School Case 701-042 (Boston, MA: Harvard Business School Publishing, 2001).

Kirsten S. Wever, *Negotiating Competitiveness – Employment Relations and Organizational Innovation in Germany and the United States* (Boston, MA: Harvard Business School Press, 1995).

Goettrik Wewer (editor), *Bilanz der Aera Kohl*, (Opladen: Leske + Burdich, 1998).

A. Zischka, *War es ein Wunder? Zwei Jahrzehnte deutschen Wiederaufstiegs* (Hamburg: 1966).

Endnotes

1   Kappler, 2000, p.122

2   Giersch / Paqué / Schmieding, 1992, p. 30

3   Prussian miners were covered for accident and health insurance beginning in 1854 while all Prussian employers became legally liable for work-related injuries in 1871. Otto von Bismarck introduced sickness insurance in 1883, accident insurance in 1884, and pension rights for employees over the age of 70 in 1889. See Hauser/Snower, 1998

4   Schaede / Scott, 2001, p. 3

5   Culpepper, 1999

6   Zischka, 1966, p. 519

7   Larres & Panayi / Overy, 1996, p. 16

8   The *Rote Armee Fraktion* or Red Army Faction (RAF), also known as the Baader-Meinhof Gang, was a collection of terrorist cells formed in the early 1970s to undermine German society. In the 1970s the RAF was responsible for a series of bank robberies, assassinations of business and political leaders, and raids on U.S. military installations, including the kidnapping and subsequent execution of Hanns Martin Schleyer, the head of the German Industries Federation. Members of the RAF also cooperated with Palestinian terrorists in the murder of Israeli athletes at the Munich Olympics and the hijacking of an El Al plane in 1976. By the late 1970s, most activists of the Red Army Faction had been either imprisoned or killed.

9   Larres & Panayi / Berghoff, 1996

10   Larres & Panayi / Berghoff, 1996, p. 39 and p. 54

11   Larres & Panayi / Overy, 1996, p. 14

12   Larres / Flockton, 1998, p. 72

13   Dyck, 1992, p. 14

14   Larres / Geiger, 1998, p. 175

15   Larres / Flockton, 1998, p. 72

16   Dyck, 1992, p. 11

17   Sinn, 1998, p. 17–18

18   Berghoff, p. 69

19   Statistische Jahrbücher der Bundesrepublik Deutschland

20   Sinn, 1998, p.15

21   The *Institut für Mittelstandsforschung* estimated that 380,000 *Mittelstand* companies, representing four million employees, were likely to undergo a change in leadership at the beginning of the 21st century.

22   Schaede, Scott, 2001, p. 9

23   Kuemmerle, Paul, Freye, 1998

24   Kuemmerle, 2001, p. 14–15

25   Wever, 1995, p.16-17

26   Giersch / Paqué / Schmieding, 1992, p. 219

27   Culpepper, Oxford Review of Economic Policy, 1999, p. 50

28   Kuemmerle, 2001, p. 15

The Netherlands: Is the Polder Model Sinking?

The Netherlands suffered economic crisis in the late 1970s and early 1980s, despite (or perhaps because of) its access to North Sea gas. In response to mounting inflation and unemployment, a tripartite agreement between employers, unions, and government was reached as Wassenaar in 1982.

This agreement laid the basis for macroeconomic stabilization in the 1980s. At the same time, a variety of structural reforms were introduced centered on improving the flexibility of the labor market by increasing part-time work. The results appeared impressive: by the mid 1990s, the Netherlands was enjoying strong economic growth and unemployment rates of below 3%, much lower than its large continental European neighbors and even better than the United States at the height of the New Economy boom. U.S. President Clinton saw much to admire and even to emulate in the Netherlands.

However, many observers doubted the sustainability of this so-called "polder model." Low unemployment had been achieved in part by reducing participation rates. Some doubted whether a declining working population could sustain the Dutch standard of living. At the same time, the Netherlands was not a leader in technological development. Some observers were concerned whether the country could compete effectively in the new global information economy.

Supplementary Material

Europe: Data Supplement 1950–2003

Study Questions

1. What is the "Dutch Disease?" Is it the cause of the Netherlands' economic problems in the 1970s?
2. Why did employers and business sign the Wassenaar agreement when market conditions (i.e., high unemployment) appeared to offer scope to reduce wages through the market mechanism?
3. Why did trade unions agree to increased labor market flexibility through greater part-time work? Do labor unions aid or hinder economic stability and growth in the Netherlands?
4. Is the polder model sustainable? How, if at all, should it be amended in 2002?
5. Given its apparent (relative and absolute) success in the 1990s, is the polder model an appropriate approach for Europe as a whole? How does the Irish experience influence your answer?

HUW PILL

The Netherlands: Is the Polder Model Sinking?

Should the Netherlands go all the way? Should it change to the type of market economy that exists in the United States? [...] The Anglo-Saxon model has its own problems. Maximising utility in the short term leads to too few savings and insufficient investment. Americans have not invested enough in public provisions like infrastructure and education. In the Rhineland, savings are considerable and investments are on an altogether higher level. Social security will have to be trimmed but the essentials of the system can be retained, provided public expenditure is kept durably under control.

A synthesis of the Anglo-Saxon and Rhineland models ought to be possible. A "Mid-Atlantic" model really would unite the positive elements of both.[1]

— European Commissioner Frits Bolkestein, December 2000

In May 2001, Wim Kok entered his eighth year as Dutch prime minister. As head of the so-called "purple" government coalition (uniting left-wing labor politicians with right wing liberals), he was credited with transforming the Netherlands from "the sick man of Europe" into one of the best performing economies in the world. In 2000, unemployment stood at less than 3%, inflation hovered around 2%, and GDP grew by over 4%.

The dramatic improvement in macroeconomic conditions was typically attributed to the so-called Dutch "polder model." Polders are pieces of land raised from below the sea through draining water and building dykes. They are important features in the Netherlands – a country with one-quarter of its land below sea level. Building polders is a complicated undertaking, requiring a strong governing authority and private cooperation and consultation.[2]

In the early 1980s, Dutch government, business, and labor representatives, including Kok as head of the labor union, adopted this cooperative model for macroeconomic policymaking, formalizing a consensual relationship among policy makers, unions, and employers. Under the arrangement, unions moderated wage demands, businesses emphasized job creation, and government agreed to lower taxes and balance the budget. In consequence, economic conditions improved while the generous Dutch welfare system was maintained. At the G-7 conference in 1997, U.S. President Bill Clinton and U.K. Prime Minister Tony Blair expressed optimism that the polder model represented a path to the oft-discussed "third way."

Yet, at the beginning of the new millennium, a number of economists were questioning the sustainability of the polder model. The Netherlands was facing low labor participation rates, a slowdown in investment, and growing criticism of wage moderation policies. It was time for the

---

Research Associate Marie-Laure Goepfer, Mathijs Robbens (MBA '02), and Research Associate Ingrid Vogel prepared this case under the supervision of Professor Huw Pill. This case was developed from published sources. HBS cases are developed solely as the basis for class discussion. Cases are not intended to serve as endorsements, sources of primary data, or illustrations of effective or ineffective management.

Netherlands to reevaluate the polder model and consider making some changes to its policies (see **Exhibits 2 through 5** for basic macroeconomic data).

History, Geography, and Social Characteristics

A Small, Open Country

The Netherlands is one of the smallest countries in Europe. Surrounded by the North Sea, Germany, and Belgium, it is divided by the estuaries of the Rhine, Maas, and Schelde rivers. The country comprises mainly coastal lowlands, with one fourth of its area below sea level (see **Exhibit 1**).

Historically, the Netherlands benefited from its unique position close to the sea and straddling the trading routes provided by the river deltas. In the 17th century, the country became the foremost commercial, maritime, and cultural power of Europe. During this Dutch "golden age," the Netherlands established some of the world's largest trading bases, and Amsterdam became the financial center of Europe.

But by the 19th century, the relative importance of the Netherlands had declined. First, the country was weakened after a series of wars with Spain, France, and England in the 18th century. Next, the Netherlands, continuing to focus on its extensive colonies and dynamic agricultural sector, began to industrialize only in 1840—well after most of the rest of Europe. The Dutch economy remained agriculturally based and poorer than its neighbors into the 20th century.

Dutch Society and Pillarization

From the late 1800s until 1950, Dutch society consisted of four groups, distinguished along confessional and political lines: liberals, social democrats, Protestants, and Catholics. Segmentation, also called "pillarization," existed not only in political parties, but also in schools, health insurance companies, trade unions, the press, and even broadcasting organizations. The size of each "pillar" in Dutch society was similar and remained stable over time.

Although pillarization was sometimes blamed for fostering separation, it actually played an important role in establishing and sustaining a strong degree of cohesion and cooperation within Dutch society. First, it kept society from dividing along social class lines since owners, managers, and workers tended to cooperate within their pillar. The elites of each pillar were charged with maintaining an atmosphere of cooperation, negotiation, consensus, and non-aggression within their respective pillars. More importantly, since no pillar had a majority, the elites formed a cross-pillar consultative umbrella under which coalitions could be forged.[3] A similar structure and reliance on coalitions emerged in the political landscape, since no single party could capture an overall majority.

Unions and Employer Organizations

Unions   Dutch labor unions were also characterized by a willingness to cooperate. Relative to the rest of Europe, Dutch unions had emerged late, following the country's delayed industrial development. In 1906, Dutch socialists formed the Dutch Association of Unions (NVV), modeled after existing union structures in Germany and the United Kingdom. Shortly after, Catholics and Protestants created the Dutch Catholic Union (NKV) and the National Christian Union (CNV), which were more conservative and willing to cooperate with employers' organizations. In response to fierce competition among unions, the socialist unions were disciplined by potential losses of non-ideological members and ultimately became more moderate and cooperative.

The government supported Dutch labor unions in several ways. In 1919, the High Council of Labor was established as a point of contact between government, labor, and employer organizations. In 1927, under pressure to improve workers' conditions through wage bargaining rules and protective legislation, the parliament put in place the first Collective Agreement Act (CAO). The CAO had a legally binding status and contained a "non-strike" clause.

Despite government support, union membership was low. Although the percentage of employees who belonged to unions increased from 16% in 1914 to 42% in 1950, it still remained lower than in many other European countries (see **Exhibit 6**).

Employers In 1899, employers in the textile industry established the first employers' association (VNW) in response to their concern that the government would introduce overly generous social provisions. Like the labor unions, employers' associations were divided along confessional lines and were known to be moderate and conflict averse. Catholic and Protestant employers formed the VNO-NCW, a federative alliance, in 1967.[4]

1945-1963: The Shaping of a Consensus Model

In May 1940, Germany invaded, defeated, and occupied the Netherlands in less than a week. Although Dutch infrastructure was left mostly intact, Germany exploited the country to support its war efforts, and the Netherlands emerged from a five-year occupation in poor economic condition. Dutch business lost autonomy by becoming tightly integrated into the German economy, and a mass migration of Dutch workers into Germany left the Netherlands with a diminished labor supply. The Netherlands' economic situation was only worsened when uprisings by the indigenous population forced the country to release its colonies in the late 1940s (notably what is now Indonesia).

In response to this malaise, a number of new political parties were formed. In 1946, a broad coalition formed a new labor party (PvdA). Two years later, liberal conservatives of the upper middle class established the liberal party (VVD). The confessional parties merged into the Christian Democratic Party (CDA), a centrist and moderately conservative party that played an important role in all governing coalitions until 1994. As of the 1960s, the VVD also participated regularly in these governing coalitions. See **Exhibit 7** for an overview of coalitions since 1945.

The poor state of the Netherlands after the war and the need for reconstruction created a sense of cohesion throughout Dutch society and led to agreement on the need for institutionalized cooperation. As such, the Labor Foundation was established in 1945 to provide a forum for employers and employees to share and resolve opinions about fundamental economic policy issues, including wages, social insurance, and hiring and firing procedures. The Labor Foundation also provided a vehicle for the "social partners" (unions and employers) to communicate with the government. For example, the government would convert wage decisions of the social partners into general wage guidelines, which led to a centralized bargaining system called "the guided wage policies." It was often the case that the social partners agreed to lower wages.

In the same year, the Central Planning Bureau (CPB) was created to supply the government, the social partners, and the public with objective economic forecasts. Over the years, the CPB developed as a neutral authority whose forecasts and advice were accepted and taken into account by all parties.

In 1950, the Social Economic Council was established as a tripartite organization including employer and union representatives as well as independent experts appointed by the government. This organization, composed of 45 members, became the official advisory board of the government on social and economic issues (see **Exhibit 8**).

These three institutions laid the foundation for the emergence of the so-called Dutch consultation model. The close proximity of all participants and their regular and informal meetings fostered a cohesive and cooperative social structure. As Jacques Schraven, president of the VNO-NCW employers' federation in 2001, remarked:

> A key element of the Dutch model is the infrastructure for deliberation. Through bodies like the Labor Foundation, the Social Economic Council, and the Central Planning Bureau, we have a platform that we can use for social discussion when needed. When I was abroad working for Shell, I thought of this system as slow and not responsive enough; now I realize that it often helps and facilitates getting to solutions. For example, I meet with the leader of the labor union, Lodewijk de Waal, all the time - informal discussions have become normal in labor relations in the Netherlands.[5]

This opinion was shared by Lodewijk de Waal, president of the labor union in 2001:

> In the Netherlands we all know each other. We are all working between Amsterdam, the Hague, Rotterdam, and Utrecht. We live near each other, and we see each other all time. Little hierarchy exists in this country; the prime minister looks like everybody and sometimes even rides his bike in the street. This helps us reach agreement.[6]

Post-War Monetary Policies

While the Labor Foundation kept wages moderate, the Central Bank kept prices stable. Postwar Dutch economists believed that long-term economic growth was better served by a strong currency, thus avoiding high inflation that would have required high interest rates to correct. Consequently, the strength of the guilder became a top priority in the postwar monetary and economic policies in the Netherlands, and the Central Bank was assigned the duty to sustain the value of the guilder (see **Exhibit 9**).

The Netherlands became a country of moderate wage growth and stable prices throughout the 1950s. Dutch nominal wages grew much less than those of its trade partners, and the price level stayed steady. As a result, the international competitiveness of Dutch industry increased, and Dutch exports grew by an average annual rate of 8.3% between 1951 and 1963. Over the same period, GDP grew by an average annual 4.4%.[7]

1959-1973: Flaws in the Consensus and Wage Moderation Model

"Dutch Disease" and its Effects on the Dutch Economy

In 1959, the Netherlands discovered the Slochteren natural gas field, at the time believed to be the world's second largest. The Dutch government immediately embarked on an aggressive energy-import substitution strategy. New industries, such as aluminum, were developed almost from scratch. Other industries, such as chemicals, were boosted by access to cheap gas. As a result, between 1963 and 1973, the Netherlands became one of the most energy intensive economies in the world.

On the one hand, the exploitation of gas resources brought substantial revenues to the government. But, on the other hand, it also caused wage costs and the real exchange rate to increase, which hurt Dutch manufacturing competitiveness and thus harmed the traditional industrial sector. This phenomenon became known as "Dutch disease," characterized by three primary economic effects:

Resource movement Resources (labor and capital) shifted from the Dutch traditional manufacturing sector into the booming energy sector. The shortage of skilled labor in traditional industries pushed wages up.

At the same time, employers from the booming oil and natural gas sector lobbied for more wage differentiation and decentralization. They demanded indexation of wages to industry specific productivity rather than national figures in order to create scope to offer higher wages and thus attract skilled workers. But initially, the Netherlands' centralized wage bargaining structure was maintained, and wage levels were boosted across all industries.

Ultimately, the successful "guided wage policies" system responsible for the growth of the Dutch economy in the 1950s and early 1960s collapsed. In 1964, real wages climbed by more than 15%—driven by the demands of the energy sector—threatening the international price competitiveness of the Dutch economy.

Spending effect The additional income generated by the energy sector boom increased consumer spending on non-traded goods and services such as real estate, education, health, and construction. Increased demand combined with high wage costs pushed up the price of Dutch non-traded goods, and inflation jumped from less than 2% in the early 1960s to more than 8% in 1972.

Real appreciation of the guilder The sudden flow of foreign funds into the Dutch economy through gas sales strengthened the currency. Although the nominal rate of the guilder stayed fixed against the Deutsch Mark (under the Bretton Woods system) the real exchange rate appreciated as Dutch inflation rose above German rates. As a result, exports of the traditional Dutch manufacturing industries such as shipbuilding, shoe making, clothing, and electronics declined. At the same time, imported goods became more attractive due to a decrease in their relative price. Local production was disadvantaged, and the import substitution policies that the government had started to implement were discouraged.

De-pillarization and the Rise of the Welfare State

"Dutch disease" jeopardized the segmentation of Dutch society along ideological pillars, with consequences for the political and labor landscapes. Confessional and political pillars abandoned their inward focus and increased cooperation at multiple levels. As such, barriers that had prevented Catholic and Protestant workers from voting for the social democratic party disappeared, and the left-wing movement strengthened. At the same time, popular theories emerged suggesting that government could shape its "makeable society" at will. High government revenues combined with the strong left-wing movement stimulated the emergence of a generous welfare state. Multiple social laws, such as General Assistance (1965), Disability Insurance (1969), and sickness benefits (1967) were introduced.

From 1962 to 1971, government expenditure almost tripled, driven in large part by increases in education, health care, and subsidized housing budgets. In 1970, government transfers as a percentage of GDP reached 22.5%, representing almost twice the level in 1960 and one of the highest in Europe[8] (see **Exhibit 10**). Public employment as a percentage of total employment in the services sector rose from 24% in 1930 to 38% in 1960. In order to sustain such a high level of expenditure, the government increased tax rates, particularly on the wealthy: With a 72% tax rate on the highest income bracket, wealth was significantly redistributed. As Hans Hillen, parliament member for the Christian Democrats, recalled:

> The welfare state was not just created by the Socialists. The Christian Democrats were seduced by these ideas as well. Progressive ideas were widely embraced at that time. We thought we could take over responsibilities as a government and we felt confident as we benefited from the inflow of gas revenues.[9]

1973–1982: Oil Shock and Economic Crisis

Initially, the oil shock of 1973 boosted the Dutch government's confidence further. As oil prices rose from $3.01 in July 1973 to $11.65 per barrel in January 1974, the price of energy substitutes such as natural gas rose also. A second oil shock boosted oil prices by 1980 to an average $36.68 per barrel.[10] Most of Europe immediately fell into economic crisis conditions with growing volatility and mounting unemployment, inflation, and fiscal deficits. Most European governments reacted to the oil shock by initiating expansionary demand policies to promote employment. But as inflation soared in response, some governments shifted to tight monetary policies, which worsened unemployment.

External Shocks: The Worsening of the "Dutch Disease"

In the short term, the first oil shock affected the Netherlands positively. By 1976, the Slochteren natural gas field was estimated to have saved the country $3.5 billion in gas imports. In the same year, $2 billion in gas export revenues were raised.

Over the longer run, however, the boom in oil prices exacerbated the "Dutch disease" and ultimately effected the Dutch economy more adversely than any other European country: The growth rate of Dutch GDP fell from an annual 5% in 1960–1973 to 3% in 1973–1979; the unemployment rate increased from 5% in 1974 to more than 12% in 1983; and the trade balance was at a deficit in 1978 for the first time since the 1960s.

The crisis hit the traditional industrial sector hardest, where output stagnated in the 1970s and grew only slowly into the 1980s. The growth of labor productivity in the sector decreased from an annual 6.4% in 1960-1973 to 0% in 1973–1979. More than 50% of workers in labor-intensive sectors lost their jobs by 1984, bringing down employment in the manufacturing sector as a percentage of total employment from 26% in 1973 to 19% in 1987.[11]

On the other hand, the Dutch agriculture and service sectors remained healthy throughout the crisis. Between 1973 and 1987, employment in agriculture stabilized at around 5% of total employment. With a shift toward higher value added products, agricultural labor productivity grew well above European rates. The improvements in productivity compensated for the rise in wages and real exchange rates. Employment in services grew from 31% of total employment in 1973 to 36% in 1987. As mostly non-traded goods, services suffered less than the traditional industry sector from the loss of Dutch international competitiveness.

Internal Shocks: Expansionary Policies and Crisis of the Welfare State

They wanted a Mercedes Benz when they could only afford a Volkswagen.[12]

Matt Marshall, *The Bank*, 1999

The economic crisis was exacerbated by the socioeconomic policies inherited from the 1960s and those put in place by the new government headed by socialist leader Joop den Uyl. In an attempt to stimulate the Dutch economy after the negative implications of the first oil shock, he introduced a set of generous social security benefits and industrial subsidies. Wim Duisenberg, Den Uyl's finance minister, even proposed sending a ten-guilder check to each Dutch citizen to boost purchasing power. As Jacques Schraven, president of the employers' federation, recalled:

> In those days Den Uyl's government thought they could model and engineer society the way they wanted it to be. Consequently they interfered on wage and price levels which led to an inflationary spiral. [...] Den Uyl used to speak of 'leuke dingen voor de mensen' which literally means: nice things for the people. These nice things were paid for from two sources: very high taxes and large gas revenues.[13]

Policymakers at that time justified these expansionary governmental programs with Keynesian ideology; through substantial spending, the government hoped to stimulate growth and boost consumer demand. The government also anticipated continued high gas revenues. As a senior official from Duisenberg's finance ministry later acknowledged:

> We were a sheikdom. In 1973, the IMF and OECD were telling us to increase our budget. We had a very strong balance of payments at that time. We were urged by the international community to pick up the slack that everyone else was creating. That year also coincided with the first left-led government budget in the Netherlands for a long time. There you have the recipe for a very expansive budget policy.[14]

Predictably, the government deficit grew; but officials' hands were tied since "automatic links" were built into most government expenditures. For example, social security benefits, pensions, and public sector salaries were linked to private sector wages, which in turn increased with the cost of living and labor productivity. As inflation fed itself and rising unemployment led to increased social benefits expenditures, public spending exploded from 42% of GDP in 1970 to 61% in 1983. This compared to a European Union average of 50%.[15] As Nout Wellink, a senior official at the Ministry of

Finance at the time, reported in 1975: "It was crazy. The public sector was taking over. It was going to take 52% the next year, then 54% the following year, and then keep going like that every year."[16]

The Dutch economy rapidly deteriorated. In 1983, with an unemployment rate of 12%, a record government budget deficit equivalent to 6% of GDP, and an increase in government borrowing from 8 billion to 30 billion guilders, the Netherlands became known as "the sick man of Europe."

1982–1994: The Turnaround of the Economy

When you are almost under water you have to pump.

The situation in 1982 was so tough that we really did not have a choice but to do a series of sensible things.

— Ed de Haas, Senior Executive, Philips Electronics

The Birth of the Polder Model

The Netherlands was ready for a change. In 1982, after the failure of successive cabinets to address the crisis adequately, a coalition of Christian Democrats (CDA) and Liberals (VVD) came to power. Ruud Lubbers, a shrewd political tactician and mediator, led the new government with a no-nonsense strategy for resolving the crisis. Lubbers declared that the government was "here to govern"[17] and proposed four major steps for economic turnaround: reforming the social system by rebuilding consensus in the labor arena; reducing the deficit by restructuring public finances; promoting long-term growth by restoring monetary stability; and improving the functioning of the economy by liberalizing the markets.

Lubbers understood that this model would succeed only with the cooperation of the unions, the government, employers, and the Central Bank. The Herald Tribune described the new model as: "A novel deal between industrialists and labor unions has found a way to maintain many European-style social benefits while doing U.S.-style downsizing, privatizing, and loosening of labor rules."[18]

Labor Policies: Rebuilding Consensus and Reforming the Social System

Lubbers' first steps as prime minister included suspending automatic inflation indexation of pensions and social benefits and freezing public sector salaries and the minimum wage. In addition, the government made an indirect threat to take over private sector wage bargaining, as had already happened in Belgium and France. Employers, keen to limit government involvement in wage negotiations, were quick to attempt to establish a relationship with unions. Unions had seen their membership decline with soaring unemployment, and had little choice but to concede. In 1982, cooperation between the employers' associations and the unions, led by Wim Kok, gave birth to the Wassenaar General Agreement, which exchanged wage moderation for a reduction in the workweek from 40 to 38 hours.[19]

"Jobs for wages" became the new motto as unions hoped to stimulate employment with workweek reduction. In 2001, representatives from employers' associations, unions, the Central Bank, and the political arena reflected on the sentiment of broad support for social responsibility at the time:

The most important thing in 1982 was that the unions and employers' federation decided to work together again. After the unions hitched a ride in Den Uyl's car in the 70s, they came to realize that by capturing too much of the pie, they were harming themselves in terms of unemployment and loss of members. Kok clearly was a clever union leader and he was instrumental in opening the dialogue.

—Jacques Schraven, president of the VNO-NCW employers' federation[20]

The credit goes to the employers for the Wassenaar agreement. We were weak and the alternative was a wage freeze. When we saw that they wanted to cooperate with us in this situation we started to believe in their good faith.

—Lodewijk de Waal, president of the FNV labor union[21]

We needed the crisis. We were standing in front of the wall. As soon as we realized this, the motto became 'we should create jobs' and everybody had come to realize that Wassenaar was a package of measures that would bring the solution.

—Age Bakker, deputy executive director, Dutch Central Bank[22]

Workers in the factories saw what was happening to the economy and understood that something had to change. Wim Kok, as the labor union leader, was very pragmatic.

—Hans Hillen, Christian Democrat (CDA) member of parliament[23]

Wage moderation had a positive impact on the cost position and investment capacity of Dutch businesses, especially in comparison with other European countries. Between 1983 and 1995, wage costs per unit of product remained stable in the Netherlands, as opposed to a rise of 2% per year in France and 2.6% in Germany.[24] This was driven in part by increases in productivity. As Philips Electronics Senior Executive De Haas argued:

The contribution of the collective reduction of working hours to the solution of unemployment remained mainly restricted to jobs requiring low qualifications. At the same time the already existing scarcity of other categories of personnel had become greater.[25]

Instead of hiring new full-time staff, employers increased part-time opportunities (see **Exhibit 11**). In the words of De Haas: "Collective working hour reduction undermined competitiveness. More flexible forms of working became a priority."[26] After 1987, sixty percent of all jobs created were for positions requiring less than 35 hours a week, and part-time labor as a percentage of employment increased from 17% in 1979 to 28% in 1990.[27] As workers settled on part-time jobs, unemployment dropped from more than 12% in 1982 to less than 8% in 1994.

The increase in part-time opportunities had a significant impact on the structure of the labor force, since nearly three-quarters of all part-time jobs were filled by women. From 1977 to 1996, the participation of women in the Dutch labor force increased from 28% (well below the European average at the time) to 41%.

Most part-time jobs opened in low wage areas, such as retail, personal services, and hotel, restaurant, and catering businesses. This contributed to wage moderation and the boom of the service economy at the end of 1980s.[28]

Fiscal Policies: Reducing the Budget Deficit and Creating New Incentives for Employment

The second component of Lubbers' economic strategy addressed the catastrophic state of public finances. Instead of reducing the deficit by increasing taxes as his predecessor had done, Lubbers took a series of steps to reduce costs. He decreased public spending on education and defense and cut subsidies introduced in 1975 to public and private companies. More importantly, in 1982 he introduced a radical package decreasing the real wages of civil servants and lowering the level and duration of social security benefits.

Despite the largest-ever postwar strike in response, the unions lacked a truly determined resistance, and the government prevailed with its new policies.[29] In consequence, the real incomes of the elderly, sick, and disabled members of society fell by around 10% in the first half of the 1980s. On the positive side, the government succeeded with its overall fiscal goal as the budget deficit decreased from 30 billion guilders in 1983 to 7 million 1986.[30] As Jacques Schraven, president of VNO-NCW, recalled:

> In the 1980s the 'Malieveld'[a] was very muddy because of all the demonstrations against the government's austerity measures. This seemed a controversial period, but in comparison to other countries the conflict was relatively moderate.[31]

Lubbers also reformed the taxation system to improve incentives for employers to create jobs and for workers to take jobs. As such, taxes were shifted from labor to consumption through a Value Added Tax (VAT). The Lubbers government reduced the tax rate on the highest income bracket and lowered taxes and social security contributions for all workers, particularly those with lower wages. People that had been excluded from the job market, including industrial workers who had suffered from the downturn of their sectors in the 1970s, were able to reintegrate.

In addition, the marginal corporate tax rate was reduced in an effort to boost the declining profitability of Dutch industry, restore its competitiveness, and promote job creation. In total, the share of taxes and premiums in GDP decreased by 12% between 1982 and 1995.[32]

Monetary Policies: Restoring the Stability of the Guilder

Lubbers also took extreme measures with regards to monetary policy. In 1983, in order to boost internal demand and promote exports, the Lubbers cabinet devalued the guilder against the Deutsch Mark by 2% within the European Exchange Rate Mechanism (ERM). However, the benefits of devaluation were at best short lived. After 1983, the Netherlands was the only European country not to devalue again against the Deutsch Mark. As Age Bakker, a senior officer at the Dutch Central Bank, recalled:

> We had to decide which way to go. We looked at Germany and the United Kingdom. The United Kingdom did not seem a good model because of its policies of "Stop and Go," whereas Germany was a symbol of stability, especially as it had been able to keep very low inflation rates. We were looking for an external anchor that would help us import stability and discipline.

---

[a] The "Malieveld" is a large open field in the middle of the Hague used for large public gatherings or events.

Pegging [the exchange rate] was an important factor in disciplining unions and employers, as we made very clear that we would not step in with another devaluation of the guilder to increase Dutch competitiveness.[33]

Utilizing a narrow currency band within the ERM allowed the Dutch economy to benefit from the Bundesbank's strict anti-inflationary and tight monetary policies. The Dutch Central Bank followed German interest rate changes, regardless of monetary or economic conditions in the Netherlands. Critics complained that the Netherlands gave away too much of its monetary policy decision-making authority and joked that the Dutch Central Bank chose to "make policies only on Thursday afternoon," following the announcement of the Bundesbank interest rates at Thursday lunchtime. But the policy proved effective as Dutch inflation decreased from an annual 8% in the period 1974–1983 to 1% in 1984–1990, and remained one of the lowest in the European Union throughout the 1990s.[34]

Ultimately, low inflation and growing international confidence in the Dutch economy led to improved international price competitiveness, especially in relation to Germany. The combination of a strong currency and low inflation led to low interest rates, which resulted in a solid base for the sustainable real growth of the economy into the 1990s.

Liberalization of Markets: Privatizing and Deregulating

The fourth component of Lubbers' economic plan involved gradually liberalizing the economy through privatization and deregulation. The new government no longer ascribed to the1960s theory of a "makeable society" which justified soaring public expenditure and a high degree of intervention. Instead, it was believed that society and the economy would thrive without government involvement.[35]

To this end, in 1982 the Lubbers cabinet launched a program of privatization of state-owned firms. The purpose of the privatization was two-fold: to strengthen the supply side of the economy by promoting efficiency and to generate funds to reduce the government deficit. The privatization program was relatively slow. Utilities, such as the postal service and postal bank, were first converted into state-owned firms. After some time, the government gradually sold its shares through consecutive public offerings.[36] In key industries like energy, transportation, and aviation, the government retained important ownership positions with "golden shares." In complement to the privatization program, the government reduced transfers to ailing industries and promoted technological change and high growth industries.[37]

Lubbers also liberalized Dutch financial markets. First, regulations against mergers in the Dutch banking sector were lifted. As a result, universal banks combining banking and insurance services emerged, and three financial groups—Rabobank, ABN AMRO, and ING Group—came to dominate Dutch banking. Second, domestic capital markets were deregulated, by, for example, allowing subsidiaries of foreign banks to act as lead managers in Dutch capital markets. Dutch bond and stock markets became much more attractive to foreign investors, and the turnover of bonds on the Amsterdam Stock Exchange exploded. The investment of pension funds in capital markets also increased dramatically.

Finally, the government attracted foreign investors, especially into areas with high unemployment, through further deregulation and tax and investment incentives. Rules on mergers, takeovers, and acquisitions were changed to allow 100% foreign ownership in ailing sectors. The

Dutch actively promoted foreign investment through dedicated national and regional agencies. By 1995, the Netherlands had become the fifth largest recipient worldwide of U.S. direct investment.

1994–2000: A New Coalition Under Kok's Leadership

Elections in August 1994 brought a new coalition uniting Social Democrats, Liberals, and Democrats to power. The so-called "purple" coalition ended the dominance of the Christian Democrats (CDA) and marked the emergence of Labor as the leading party. Wim Kok, as head of the Labor party, became the new Dutch prime minister.

One of Kok's first challenges was bringing the Dutch economy in line with the strict economic convergence criteria defined in the 1992 Maastricht treaty for Economic and Monetary Union (EMU) membership. This required lowering the budget deficit to 3% of GDP. Rather than focusing on the deficit as a percentage of GDP as his predecessors had done, Kok set absolute public expenditure targets. Such targets created more predictability by avoiding the cyclical influence of GDP. Expenditure cuts were achieved through a series of reforms to social benefits, and in the late 1990s, the Netherlands met the 3% target. By 1999, the country even enjoyed a budget surplus.

Also during his first term, Kok, who had been leader of the unions during the negotiation of the 1982 Wassenaar Agreement, focused on labor issues. The social partners negotiated new agreements, such as "A New Course" which further promoted flexibility. Under this agreement, employers agreed to give up resistance to further collective working hour reductions in exchange for more decentralized wage bargaining.[38] Reflecting the move away from centralization, the motto became "custom work and diversity." As the agreement described:

> The world is undergoing tremendous changes, with economic, community and social developments going hand in hand. Existing structures are no longer necessarily a given; a new equilibrium must be found. For the rest of the century, collective bargaining will be dominated by the concepts of custom work and diversity. The needs of both companies and employees will give rise to a greater differentiation and more options within various schemes.[39]

In 1996, a new agreement called "Flexibility and Security" aimed to increase labor flexibility while preserving job security by incorporating temporary workers within collective labor agreements. Specific training and development systems were introduced for temporary workers, as well as the right of continued employment and pension insurance after 24 months of service. As Lodewijk de Waal, president of the FNV labor union, recalled:

> Including flexible workers into the system was behind the Flexibility and Security Agreement. Before 1996 we just tried to push temporary workers out of the country exactly like many other unions in the world. But we changed our strategy by concluding a collective bargaining agreement that gave flexible workers more rights and included them in benefit schemes.[40]

With the Flexibility and Security Agreement, temporary jobs as a percentage of total jobs increased to 12% by 1997 (see **Exhibit 12**). Since temporary workers tended to receive less pay, they kept the overall Dutch wage level low, which helped improved the country's competitiveness.

In the late 1990s, the Netherlands had one of the best performing economies in Europe. In 1998, it was among the first countries to qualify for the EMU and enjoyed strong GDP growth of approximately 4%. Controlled government spending combined with guilder stability kept the inflation rate below 2% from 1994 to 1999. In 2000, the Netherlands reached an unemployment rate of 2.6%, compared to 4% in the United States, 5.5% in the United Kingdom, 8.3% in Germany, and 10.7% in Italy. In the same year, of all foreign headquarters established in Europe, close to 60% were established in the Netherlands.[41] In 1997, the Netherlands was considered by many to be the world's most attractive country for investment in the following five years.[42]

Going forward: Challenges Facing Kok's Government

In 2001 a growing number of economists were unconvinced that the Dutch success story was sustainable. They questioned whether the polder model was still appropriate, and if not, in what direction the Netherlands should head.

Hidden Unemployment

A major concern of Kok's government was the low labor participation rate: only 61% of the Dutch population participated in the labor force, compared to approximately 70% in other European nations. Critics of the Dutch welfare system were quick to link this low level with the astoundingly high proportion of the population – almost 8% in 2000 – receiving disability allowances (see **Exhibit 13** for 1990 sickness and disability data).[43] In 1999, Frits Bolkestein, former leader of the liberal party (VVD), commented:

> Officially 13% of the working population is now disabled. If a genuine figure, that would make the Netherlands the unhealthiest place in north-west Europe despite having the highest life expectancy.[44]

Accounting for these and other factors, a 1997 study by consulting firm McKinsey & Company estimated a "real" Dutch unemployment rate of 20 to 23%,[45] as opposed to an official unemployment rate of 5.6%.

The labor participation rate was further impacted by the fact that relatively few women, senior citizens, and lower skilled people were in the work force. Despite an increase over the prior decade, only 60% of Dutch women were active in the labor force in 2000, compared to over 70% in other Northern European countries. In 1999, in part due to early retirement policies, only 36% of people between 55 and 64 years old were employed. With the aging of the Dutch population, this put pressure on the Dutch public pension system.

Wage Moderation: Competitive Advantage or Obstacle?

In the past five years, the fall in unemployment had boosted consumer confidence and spending. This, in turn, created a shift into domestic demand-driven growth.[46] Given the shift toward domestic sources of growth, observers questioned whether wage moderation still provided a competitive advantage to the Netherlands.

It was argued that wage moderation created disincentives for both lower skilled and highly skilled workers. The combination of a generous welfare system and low salaries meant that lower skilled workers often did better out of work. Conservative political forces pushed for wider margins between wages and social benefits to force people to exit the so-called "poverty trap."[47] At the same time, highly skilled labor could receive more attractive pay packages working outside of the Netherlands. Negotiator Ed de Haas of Philips Electronics noted:

Philips needs to have 'knowledge people' from technical universities but it is not easy to attract these people in the Netherlands. As a a result we gradually move abroad; in a couple of years we will have our largest knowledge center in Bangalore.[48]

Also questioning wage moderation, Wim Boonstra, senior executive at Rabobank, pointed out:

In the Netherlands we are very good at distributing wealth evenly, but we should be aware that this might prevent us from creating maximum value.[49]

Union leader Lodewijk de Waal, however, still saw plenty of room to continue wage moderation:

Now that unemployment is at its minimum, wage levels should of course go up. However, there is still a large pool of people to be activated in the Netherlands. Our labor participation can go up by at least 10%. This means that, if we do our job well, we can continue with policies of wage moderation. You can think about changing our disability law or you could even treat the pension age differently.[50]

Productivity Growth and Investments Levels

Although the absolute productivity level in the Netherlands was high, the growth of productivity in the past three years was slow compared to France, the United Kingdom, the United States, and Japan. Economists related this to low levels of investment, especially in research and development. In 2000, Dutch corporate spending on R&D as a percentage of GDP was only 1.1%, compared to 2.1% in Japan, 2.0% in the United States, and 1.3% in Germany.[51] In the long run, it was feared that this would undermine Dutch competitiveness. Other indicators of low levels of innovation and knowledge-based development included the small number of entrepreneurs in the country and the relatively few Dutch medium-sized companies that were able to achieve high growth rates (see **Exhibit 14**).

Kok had just one year before the next elections in which to determine what reforms to implement to move the country forward. Many observers questioned the viability of the polder model, especially in light of tighter European integration (beginning with the introduction of the euro, the new European currency, in December 2001). Critics from his socialist party complained that Kok emphasized economic issues at the expense of social issues. However, electoral support for Kok, remained strong. Nonetheless, he clearly faced a demanding agenda.

Exhibit 1 Map of the Netherlands

Source: Dutch ministry of foreign affairs. <http://www.minbuza.nl>.

Exhibit 2   Netherlands General Economic Indicators

	1982	1984	1986	1988	1990	1992	1994	1996	1998	2000
% change over prior year										
Real GDP Growth	-1.2	3.3	2.7	3.1	4.1	1.7	2.6	3.0	4.3	3.5
Real Per Capita GDP Growth	-1.7	2.9	2.2	2.4	3.5	0.9	1.9	2.6	3.8	2.8
Consumer Price Inflation	6.0	3.2	0.3	0.9	2.5	3.2	2.8	2.0	2.0	2.5
%GDP										
Investment/GDP	19.8	20.2	21.6	22.6	22.5	21.6	20.3	21.1	21.5	22.7
Current Account/GDP	3.5	4.9	2.4	2.9	2.7	2.1	5.0	5.2	3.6	4.9
Public Debt/GDP	n.a.	64.2	70.6	76.0	75.6	76.4	74.0	75.2	66.8	56.3
Fiscal Surplus (+) or Deficit (-)/GDP	n.a.	-6.2	-5.7	-5.1	-5.7	-4.4	-4.2	-1.8	-0.8	2.2
units as shown										
Official Unemployment (%)	7.5	9.5	8.1	7.8	6.0	5.3	7.5	6.6	4.2	2.6
Official Exchange Rate (Guilders/$U.S.)	2.6	3.5	2.2	2.0	1.7	1.8	1.7	1.7	1.9	..

Source: Created by casewriters based on data from EIU Country Data, June 2002.

Exhibit 3   Netherlands National Income Accounts *(billions of current guilders through 1998; billions of euro beginning 1999)*

	1950	1965	1968	1971	1979	1983	1987	1992	1998	1999	2000
Gross Domestic Product	**18.8**	**67.8**	**89.8**	**136.5**	**316.0**	**381.0**	**440.6**	**566.1**	**750.5**	**373.6**	**401.1**
Private Consumption	12.8	39.5	51.0	78.9	192.4	229.7	267.9	340.9	445.2	186.8	199.9
Government Spending	2.3	10.5	14.2	21.8	57.2	66.6	69.8	83.0	102.2	85.6	91.2
Fixed Investment	3.8	17.0	24.0	34.6	66.5	69.5	91.6	113.3	150.0	83.7	90.9
Changes in Inventories	1.2	1.3	0.6	1.5	1.5	0.6	-0.4	3.1	2.0	0.8	-0.4
Exports	7.7	30.8	39.0	62.0	155.1	219.8	219.3	294.9	414.7	226.4	269.7
Imports	9.1	31.3	39.0	62.4	156.7	205.2	207.6	269.2	364.4	209.6	250.1
GDP at 1995 Prices	*n.a.*	*228.4*	*264.6*	*369.4*	*455.1*	*465.9*	*517.2*	*601.9*	*708.9*	*349.6*	*362.1*

Source: Created by casewriters based on data from IMF, *International Financial Statistics Yearbook CD-ROM*, January 2002.

Note: Guilder / Euro exchange rate equals approximately 2.20.

Exhibit 4   Netherlands Balance of Payments (*millions of current U.S. dollars*)

	1968	1971	1979	1983	1987	1992	1997	1998	1999	2000
Current Account	**754**	**524**	**350**	**5,089**	**4,187**	**6,847**	**25,159**	**13,373**	**15,171**	**13,764**
Trade Balance	-307	-413	-605	5,553	6,252	12,309	20,937	21,055	17,933	18,545
Exports	*8,299*	*13,486*	*63,398*	*64,534*	*92,146*	*137,332*	*188,988*	*196,277*	*197,359*	*205,653*
Imports	*8,606*	*13,898*	*64,003*	*58,982*	*85,894*	*125,024*	*168,051*	*175,222*	*179,426*	*187,107*
Net Services	259	239	-575	-597	-1,340	-177	3,273	2,476	2,496	-218
Net Income	871	782	2,282	1,113	1,327	-929	7,069	-2,977	1,091	1,631
Net Transfers	-68	-84	-752	-979	-2,052	-4,356	-6,120	-7,182	-6,348	-6,193
Capital Account	**6**	**25**	**-216**	**-148**	**-233**	**-631**	**-1,297**	**-420**	**-214**	**661**
Financial Account	**-923**	**-476**	**-816**	**-4,896**	**-1,283**	**-7,279**	**-14,478**	**-7,449**	**-24,940**	**-2,933**
Net Direct Investment	-710	-566	-4,567	-2,477	-5,629	-6,589	-13,549	458	-16,478	-20,671
Net Portfolio Flows	40	314	2,574	-164	2,660	-9,469	-21,633	-31,185	-508	-563
Net Other	-253	-223	1,177	-2,255	1,686	8,780	20,703	23,278	-7,954	18,301
Public	*-107*	*7*	*-871*	*-85*	*-465*	*-816*	*-348*	*1,395*	*-1,105*	*-2,408*
Private	*-146*	*-230*	*2,048*	*-2,170*	*2,151*	*9,596*	*21,052*	*21,882*	*-6,849*	*20,709*
Net Errors & Omissions	**5**	**111**	**-297**	**-202**	**22**	**7,181**	**-12,091**	**-7,842**	**5,372**	**-11,271**
Reserves & Related Items	**158**	**-185**	**980**	**157**	**-2,693**	**-6,118**	**2,708**	**2,339**	**4,611**	**-220**

Source: Created by casewriter based on IMF, *International Financial Statistics Yearbook CD-ROM*, January 2002.

Exhibit 5   Netherlands Government Finance *(billions of current guilders through 1998; billions of euro beginning 1999)*

A   Consolidated Central Government Deficit

	1968	1971	1979	1983	1987	1992	1997	1998	1999	2000
Total Revenue	**24.2**	**37.6**	**105.8**	**127.4**	**161.9**	**182.8**	**197.3**	**210.7**	**105.3**	**108.3**
% GDP	*27%*	*28%*	*32%*	*32%*	*35%*	*31%*	*27%*	*27%*	*28%*	*27%*
Total Expenditure	**26.4**	**39.2**	**118.9**	**157.8**	**176.9**	**203.7**	**208.3**	**213.9**	**111.1**	**108.7**
% GDP	*29%*	*29%*	*36%*	*39%*	*39%*	*35%*	*28%*	*28%*	*30%*	*27%*
Overall Deficit/Surplus	**-2.2**	**-1.7**	**-13.1**	**-30.3**	**-15.0**	**-20.8**	**-10.9**	**-3.2**	**-5.8**	**-0.4**
% GDP	*-2%*	*-1%*	*-3.9%*	*-7.5%*	*-3.3%*	*-3.5%*	*-1.5%*	*-0.4%*	*-1.6%*	*-0.1%*
GDP	*89.8*	*136.5*	*333.2*	*403.3*	*459.0*	*589.4*	*734.9*	*776.2*	*373.6*	*401.1*

Source: Created by casewriters based on data from International Monetary Fund, *International Financial Statistics Yearbook CD-ROM*, May 2002.

Note: Guilder / Euro exchange rate equals approximately 2.20.

B   Components of Expenditure

	1979	1983	1987	1990	1992	1997
Total Expenditure	**100%**	**100%**	**100%**	**100%**	**100%**	**100%**
General Public Services	7%	5%	7%	6%	7%	6%
Defense	6%	5%	5%	5%	5%	4%
Public Order & Safety	na	2%	2%	2%	2%	3%
Education	14%	11%	10%	11%	11%	10%
Health	12%	11%	11%	12%	14%	15%
Social Security & Welfare	37%	38%	35%	38%	37%	37%
Housing and Community Amenities	3%	3%	4%	4%	4%	2%
Economic Affairs and Services	10%	10%	11%	7%	6%	6%
Other	12%	13%	14%	14%	15%	17%
of which interest payments	*3%*	*6%*	*8%*	*8%*	*9%*	*9%*

Source: Created by casewriters based on data from International Monetary Fund, *Government Finance Statistics Yearbook*, 1977, 1986, and 2001.

Exhibit 6   Comparative Union Density

Union membership as a % of the total number of employees

%	1900	1914	1925	1938	1950	1963	1975	1990
Netherlands	< 5	16	23	31	42	42	38	24
Germany	4	17	28	-	35	37	35	32
UK	17	27	32	37	46	49	56	43
France	5	4	8	34	24	21	23	8
Denmark	12	20	36	38	54	65	76	82
Sweden	4	13	31	55	66	74	85	83
Norway	4	14	20	57	57	57	72	61

Source: Adapted from van Zanden, *The Economic History of the Netherlands*, p. 75.

Exhibit 7   Prime Ministers and Governments since 1945

Prime Minister	Government Coalition	Period
Wim Kok	PvdA, VVD, D66	1998-
Wim Kok	PvdA, VVD, D66	1994-1998
Ruud Lubbers	CDA, PvdA	1989-1994
Ruud Lubbers	CDA, VVD	1986-1989
Ruud Lubbers	CDA, VVD	1982-1986
Andries van Agt	CDA, D66	1982
Andries van Agt	CDA, PvdA, D66	1981-1982
Andries van Agt	CDA, VVD	1977-1981
Joop den Uyl	PvdA, KVP, ARP, D66, PPR[a]	1973-1977
Barend Willem Biesheuvel	KVP, ARP, VVD, CHU	1972
Barend Willem Biesheuvel	KVP, ARP, VVD, CHU, DS'70	1971-1972
Petrus de Jong	KVP, ARP, VVD, CHU	1967-1971
Jelle Zijlstra	KVP, ARP	1966-1967
Jozef Cals	KVP, PvdA, ARP	1965-1966
Victor Marijnen	KVP, VVD, ARP, CHU	1963-1965
Jan Eduard de Quay	KVP, VVD, ARP, CHU	1959-1963
Louis Joseph Beel	KVP, ARP, CHU	1958-1959
Willem Drees	PvdA, KVP, ARP, CHU	1956-1958
Willem Drees	PvdA, KVP, ARP, CHU	1952-1956
Willem Drees	PvdA, KVP, CHU, VVD	1951-1952
Willem Drees	PvdA, KVP, CHU, VVD	1948-1951
Louis Joseph Beel	KVP, PvdA	1946-1948
Willem Schermerhorn/Willem Drees	PvdA, KVP, ARP	1945-1946

Source: Created by casewriters.
Note: [a]KVP, ARP and CHU merged to form CDA in 1977.

Exhibit 8   Schematic Overview of Institutions Participating in Social Dialogue

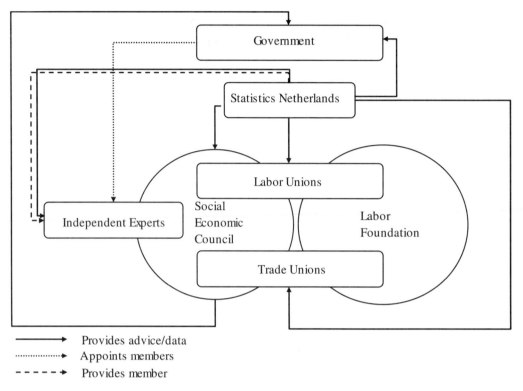

        ──────▶   Provides advice/data
        ·············▶   Appoints members
        ─ ─ ─ ─▶   Provides member

Source: Created by casewriters based on interviews.

Exhibit 9   Guilder Exchange Rates against U.S. Dollar and Deutsch Mark

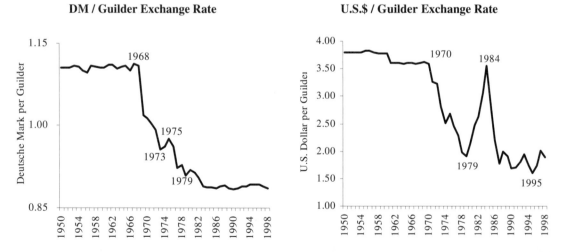

Source: Created by casewriters based on IMF, *International Financial Statistics Yearbook CD-ROM,* January 2002.

Exhibit 10   Social Transfers and Benefits

A Social Transfers

as % of GDP	1950	1960	1970	1980	1990
Germany	12.4	18.1	19.5	27.7	25.3
UK	5.7	10.2	13.2	16.4	16.2
France	11.3	13.4	16.7	22.6	27.4
Italy	9.3	13.1	16.9	21.2	22.8
Denmark	5.8	12.3	19.1	27.4	29
Netherlands	6.6	11.7	22.5	28.3	25.6

Source: Adapted from van Zanden, *The Economic History of the Netherlands,* p. 63.

Note: Figures for 1950 and 1990 are not strictly comparable with the other data.

B Social Security Beneficiaries

	1970	1975	1980	1985	1990	1995	1996	1997	1998
Social security beneficiaries (000)	2,030	2,520	3,059	3,733	3,991	4,183	4,167	4,134	4,073
Total people employed (000)	4,592	4,500	4,624	4,486	4,858	5,074	5,198	5,328	5,474
Benefits/ Employment ratio (%)	44.2	56.0	66.2	83.2	82.2	82.4	80.2	77.6	74.4
of which: recipients as a % of employed people									
Old age and survivors benefits	28.9	32.7	35.4	39.7	40.3	41.0	40.5	40.0	39.3
Sickness	3.2	3.5	3.6	3.7	3.8	3.7	3.6	3.4	2.7
Disability	9.0	12.8	19.5	21.1	23.4	20.9	19.7	19.6	19.4
Unemployment	1.6	4.4	5.2	14.7	11.1	13.7	13.2	11.8	10.3
Other social assistance	1.5	2.6	2.4	4.0	3.6	3.2	3.2	2.9	2.6

Source: Adapted from A. Lans Bovenberg, "Reforming Social Insurance in the Netherlands," *International Tax and Public Finance,* 7, 2000, p. 353.

Exhibit 11   Netherlands Prices, Wages, and Production

Annual Increase (%)	Average Collectively Agreed Pay Increases	Average Nominal Earnings	Inflation	Average Real Earnings	Labor Productivity
1970-1979	9.8	9.0	7.2	1.8	n.a.
1980-1989	3.0	2.8	3.0	-0.2	n.a.
1990	2.9	5.0	2.6	2.4	2.0
1991	4.2	3.3	4.0	0.2	0.8
1992	4.4	3.7	3.7	0.5	0.4
1993	3.3	3.2	2.1	0.6	-0.1
1994	1.5	2.3	2.7	-0.4	4.4
1995	1.3	2.8	2.0	0.8	1.1
1996	2.1	2.6	2.1	0.6	-0.3
1997	2.7	2.0	2.2	-0.2	1.0
1998	3.3	3.3	2.0	1.5	0.9
1999	2.9	1.8	2.2	-0.3	0.8

Source: Adapted from European Industrial Relations Observatory, "Comparative on Wage Policy in the Netherlands," 2000. <www.eiro.eurofound.ie/2000/07/word/nl0005190s.doc>

Exhibit 12   Flexibility in the Dutch labor market

A Temporary jobs and temporary work agencies (TWAs) (1997–1998)

	Temporary jobs	TWA workers	Revenue/ agency	Avg. Employment Duration
	% total jobs	*% labor force*	*m $U.S.*	*months*
Denmark	11	0.25	1.1	7-12
Germany	11	0.5	1.6	25-36
Spain	24	0.75	2.8	4-6
United States	2.4	2.25	8.4	na
United Kingdom	7.5	3	3.5	7-12
Netherlands	12	4.5	13.3	7-12

B Employment by sectors and type of labor contracts (1997)

As % Total Employment	Full time	Part time	Temporary
Industry	79%	12%	9%
Trade, hotel, restaurants and repair services	54%	30%	16%
Transport and communication	70%	17%	13%
Financial and business services	60%	26%	13%
Government and education	60%	34%	6%
Health care, culture and other services	29%	58%	12%
Total	58%	30%	12%

Source (A&B): Adapted from Theo Dunnewijk, "Temporary Work Agencies in the Netherlands: Emergence and Perspective," Central Planning Bureau Report 2001/1. <http://www.cpb.nl/nl/cpbreport/2001_1/s2_3.pdf>.

Exhibit 13   Population on Sickness and Disability Benefits (1990), *(% of working population)*

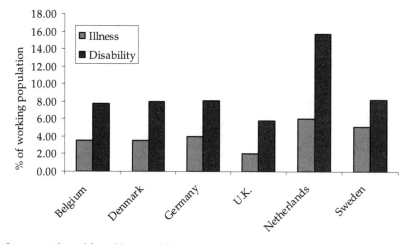

Source: Adapted from Visser and Hemerijk, A Dutch Miracle, 1997, p. 118.

Exhibit 14   Productivity, Investment Growth, and R&D in the Netherlands

A Growth Rates of GDP, Inputs, and Total Factor Productivity

avg. annual % increase	GDP	Persons employed	Hours per person	Capital Stock	R&D Stock	Total Factor Productivity
1947-73	5.07	1.51	-0.89	4.52	4.74	2.50
1973-79	2.68	0.92	-1.38	3.85	4.92	1.10
1979-87	1.22	0.56	-1.85	2.31	2.56	0.74
1987-94	2.54	1.73	-0.69	2.8	3.14	0.16

Source: Adapted from Bart van Ark and Herman de Jong, "Accounting for Economic Growth in the Netherlands since 1913," Groningen Growth and Development Centre, Working Paper GD-26, 1996, p. 211.
Note: R&D Stock is measured as number of U.S. patents granted to inhabitants of the Netherlands.

B Corporate Spending on R&D (2000) (as % GDP)

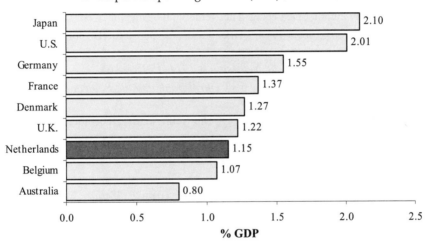

C Businesses Experiencing Rapid Growth (2000)
(as % number of medium-sized enterprises, i.e. with 100-1000 employees)

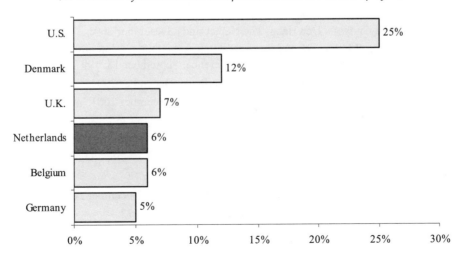

Source (B&C): Adapted from SER, 2000, p. 17.

Endnotes

[1] Frits Bolkestein, Commissioner, European Commission, Speech, December 5, 2000, Brussels. <http://europa.eu.int/comm/internal_market/en/speeches/bolkestein.htm>

[2] "Model Makers," The Economist, May 4, 2002.

[3] Frank van Empel, *The Dutch Model: The Power of Consultation in the Netherlands* (The Hauge: Labour Foundation, 1997), p.12.

[4] Johannes de Vries, *Netherlands Economy in the 20th Century: An Examination of the Most Characteristic Features in the Period 1900–1970* (Assen: Van Gorcum, 1978), p. 23–24.

[5] Jacques Schraven, interview by authors, Den Haag, The Netherlands, December 2001.

[6] Lodewijk de Waal, interview by authors, Amsterdam, The Netherlands, December 2001.

[7] Jan L. van Zanden, *The Economic History of the Netherlands 1914-1995* (Routledge, an imprint of Taylor & Francis Books, Ltd, 1997), p. 135.

[8] De Vries, *Netherlands Economy in the 20th Century*, p.113.

[9] Hans Hillen, interview by authors, Den Haag, The Netherlands, December 2001.

[10] "Controlling International Oil: 1920-1974," HBS Case No. 383-096 (Boston: Harvard Business School Publishing, 1996).

[11] Van Zanden, *The Economic History of the Netherlands 1914–1995*, p.163.

[12] Matt Marshall, *The Bank: The Birth of Europe's Central Bank and the Rebirth of Europe's Power* (London: Random House Business Books, 1999), p.25.

[13] Jacques Schraven, interview by authors, Den Haag, The Netherlands, December 2001.

[14] Marshall, *The Bank*, p. 24.

[15] EIU Country Profile, The Netherlands, 2000, p.23.

[16] Marshall, *The Bank*.

[17] Jelle Visser and Anton Hermerijck, *A Dutch Miracle: Job Growth, Welfare Reforms, and Corporatism in the Netherlands* (Amsterdam: Amsterdam University Press, 1997), p. 100.

[18] *The International Herald Tribune*, 1997.

[19] Visser and Hermerijck, *A Dutch Miracle*, p. 100–113.

[20] Jacques Schraven, interview by authors, Den Haag, The Netherlands, December 2001.

[21] Lodewijk de Waal, interview by authors, Amsterdam, The Netherlands, December 2001.

[22] Age Bakker, interview by authors, Amsterdam, The Netherlands, December 2001.

[23] Hans Hillen, interview by authors, Den Haag, The Netherlands, December 2001.

[24] Hans Blankert, "The Tulip Model: The Process to Revitalize the Dutch Economy," Speech of the president of the VNO-CNW at the Regional European IOE Conference, September 18, 1997.

[25] Ed De Haas, interview by authors, Eindoven, The Netherlands, December 2001.

[26] Ed De Haas, interview by authors, Eindoven, The Netherlands, December 2001.

[27] Visser and Hermerijck, *A Dutch Miracle*, p. 30.

[28] Visser and Hermerijck, *A Dutch Miracle*, p. 35.

[29] Visser and Hermerijck, *A Dutch Miracle*, p.101.

[30] Van Zanden, *The Economic History of the Netherlands 1914–1995*, p. 70.

[31] Jacques Schraven, interview by authors, Den Haag, The Netherlands, December 2001.

[32] Van Zanden, *The Economic History of the Netherlands 1914–1995*, p.172.

[33] Age Bakker, interview by authors, Amsterdam, The Netherlands, December 2001.

[34] International Monetary Fund, *International Finance Statistics Yearbook*, 2001.

[35] Marshall, *The Bank*, pp. 32-33.

[36] Van Zanden, *The Economic History of the Netherlands 1914–1995*, p. 172.

[37] Van Zanden, *The Economic History of the Netherlands 1914–1995*, p.172.

[38] Visser and Hermerijck, *A Dutch Miracle*, p. 35.

[39] Stichting Van de Arbeid, *A New Course: Agenda for the 1994 Negotiations on Collective Labour Agreements in a Medium-term Perspective*, 1993.

[40] Lodewijk de Waal, interview by authors, Amsterdam, The Netherlands, December 2001.

[41] The U.S. State Department, Country Commercial Guide: The Netherlands, 2001.

[42] EIU Country Report, 1997.

[43] Social Economic Council (SER), *Medium-Term Social and Economic Policy, 2000–2004* (The Hague: Social Economic Council Information Division, 2000), p. 7.

[44] Frits Bolkestein "The Dutch Model: The High Road that Leads out of the Low Countries," *The Economist*, May 22, 1999.

[45] Van Empel, *The Dutch Model*, p. 6.

[46] Hans Labohm and Charles Wijnker, *The Netherlands Polder Model: Does it Offer any Clues for the Solution of Europe's Socioeconomic Flaws?* (Amsterdam: Dutch Central Bank, 2000).

[47] Frits Bolkestein, "The Dutch Model."

[48] Ed De Haas, interview by authors, Eindoven, The Netherlands, December 2001.

[49] Wim Boonstra, interview by authors, Eindoven, The Netherlands, December 2001.

[50] Lodewijk de Waal, interview by authors, Amsterdam, The Netherlands, December 2001.

[51] SER, *Medium-Term Social and Economic Policy*, p. 17.

The EU's 13th Directive on Takeover Bids: Unlucky for Some?

In the late 1990s, the United States boomed in the context of the so-called New Economy. The countries of the European Union—despite their progress with integration in the form of the Single Market 1992 program and the adoption of a single currency in January 1999—appeared to languish behind the United States and looked for ways to stimulate faster growth.

Many observers pointed to the need for structural reform and, in particular, the creation of American-style deep and liquid continent-wide capital markets that would act as the catalyst for managerial change. By subjecting incumbent managers to the pressure of hostile takeovers, greater discipline and improved efficiency would result.

However, hostile takeovers were anathema to the bank-centered systems of corporate governance typical of continental Europe in general, and Germany in particular. The EU Commission introduced a draft takeover directive in 1989. After a tortuous process through the labyrinthine corridors of many European institutions, the directive was ultimately rejected on the basis of a tied vote in the European Parliament. This rejection had been engineered by the German Christian Democrats—a supposedly right-of-center party supported by German business.

Supplementary Material

Europe: Data Supplement 1950–2003

Study Questions

1. Does Europe need a takeover directive? Why or why not?
2. How does the EU work? Does the institutional structure of the EU make sense?
3. After the failure of the European Parliament to approve the directive, should EU Commissioner Bolkenstein introduce a new takeover directive? Of what type?
4. Will the creation of American-style capital markets allow Europe to emulate American economic performance? In the light of the collapse of the internet bubble in 2000-2001 and the subsequent Enron scandal, is attempting such emulation sensible?

HUW PILL
INGRID VOGEL

The EU's 13th Directive on Takeover Bids: Unlucky for Some?

Integrating European Union financial markets will hugely improve prospects of the EU meeting its target of becoming the most dynamic and competitive economy in the world by 2010. At the halfway stage in our timetable for implementing the Financial Services Action Plan, that prize is within reach. The pace of progress has increased significantly in the last few months. But this is a marathon, not a sprint—there can be no letup.[1]

— European Commissioner for the Internal Market Frits Bolkestein, 2002

The Takeover Directive[a] was the 13th directive of the European Union's program of financial market integration. In mid-2002, after more than 13 long years of negotiations and revisions, the passage of the directive had already proved to require the endurance and patience of a marathon. But the finishing line remained out of sight. One of the most critical elements of the EU's plan for a single market in financial services, the Takeover Directive was also one of the most contentious.

The goal of the Takeover Directive was to create the legal framework for consistent takeover rules across the EU (see **Exhibit 1** for EU map) and thereby encourage a more active takeover market. According to advocates of the directive, facilitating takeovers would help reorder the European economy, just as had happened in the United States in the 1980s and 1990s, by creating a competitive market for corporate control and thus encouraging corporate restructuring.[2] A Brussels lobbying group argued that takeovers were vital since "European industry must be able to restructure [in order] to meet the challenges of a free open economy and the international competition it must face."[3]

Intense debate focused on the provisions of the directive. The rules would have to be implemented in both Anglo-Saxon economies (such as the United Kingdom), where shareholder rights were paramount, and more traditional Continental European countries (such as Germany and the Netherlands) with their long history of stakeholder-dominated corporate governance. Just as challenging, the directive would need to address the obstacles to takeovers erected by many European governments to protect national interests such as employment and control of strategic industries like energy. Moreover, it would have to contend with companies that had instituted measures to maintain stable ownership and entrench management. Not surprisingly, the directive

---

[a] A European Union directive is a type of EU legislation (the other two types are regulations and decisions). An EU directive is an instruction from the EU level to national legislations to implement certain principles. An EU directive, once implemented, takes precedence over the national laws of the EU Member States.

Professor Huw Pill and Research Associate Ingrid Vogel prepared this case from published sources. Cases are not intended to serve as endorsements, sources of primary data, or illustrations of effective or ineffective management.

elicited vigorous reactions from EU Member States, each with definite opinions on what provisions it should and should not include.

In June 2001, all parties seemed to have finally reached agreement through the EU's standard law-making procedure (see **Exhibit 2**). One month later, the European Parliament was set to vote on the directive, in what most believed would be a clear victory. To the surprise of the European Commission, however, the vote was tied, forcing the directive to fail. This result was largely blamed on the Germans, whom Commissioner Frits Bolkestein harshly condemned as demonstrating "a retreat from modern corporatist philosophy."[4] Bolkestein asserted it was "tragic to see how Europe's broader interests [could] be frustrated by such narrow concerns."[5]

Under pressure to deliver on its promise of integrated financial markets—and to recover from its unexpected and embarrassing failure to gain Parliament's approval—the Commission sought to make the Takeover Directive a success. To this end, the Commission needed to redraft the directive to accommodate the demands of the Member States. The new proposal was due to be released at the end of September 2002 when, after the German national elections, the intense politicization of the takeover debate was expected to abate. But many observers questioned whether the 13th directive would, or even should, ever succeed. Others argued that to ensure its passage, the Commission would have to "water down" the directive to such an extent that it would be rendered useless.[6]

Toward a Single Market

An integrated capital market will be of great macroeconomic benefit to the EU. The cost of capital will fall—so GDP will rise, some say by half of 1% a year, on a sustainable basis. If GDP increases, so will jobs . . . . but most importantly, delivering this [Financial Services Action] plan matters to every European citizen. There are major social benefits, and we must spread this message much more widely. That is why we want one set of rules, not 15. This means increasing competition and financial innovation and scrapping useless cross-border bureaucracy.[7]

— European Commission President Romano Prodi, 2002

In 1986, the Single European Act was signed by the then-12 members of the European Community (EC), amending the 1957 Treaty of Rome that lay at the foundation of the EC (see **Appendix**). The goal of the act was the creation of a European-wide internal market, the "Single Market," by 1992, within which goods, capital, services, and people could circulate freely (see **Exhibit 3** for comparative macroeconomic data on the EU, the euro area, the United States, and Japan). Europe would benefit from increased competition, economies of scale and scope, and deepened financial markets. Harmonizing takeover rules within the EU was considered one of many necessary components of achieving the Single Market, since this would facilitate the creation of a continent-wide market for corporate control. By 1992, Europe had come a long way toward creating the Single Market, but the Takeover Directive remained in an embryonic state.

In 1988, the "Delors Report" (named after then-President of the European Commission Jacques Delors) asserted that the creation of the Single Market required the adoption of a single currency, and thus European monetary union. A target date of January 1, 1999 was set for the irrevocable fixing of European exchange rates and the introduction of the euro.

The introduction of the euro intensified market-driven modernization of EU securities and derivatives markets, ultimately leading to more affordable and flexible financing arrangements for small and large corporate borrowers. Issuing and trading securities across the EU was facilitated, deepening and widening capital markets.

The deeper and more liquid European capital markets made harmonization of company law across Europe—and, in particular, the creation of a level playing field for cross-border takeovers— even more important. At the same time, the possible benefits of such rules expanded. The Financial Services Action Plan (FSAP), adopted in 1999, recognized that carefully targeted regulatory measures at the EU level could generate further liquidity, risk spreading, and development of equity markets (such as the *Neuer Markt* in Germany). The plan identified a series of policy objectives and specific measures to improve the Single Market for financial services through 2005.[8] New initiatives were started and existing efforts reprioritized. The Takeover Directive became a top priority, and European institutions were encouraged to work toward its passage.

By mid-2002, EU institutions were making significant progress toward achieving the measures outlined in the FSAP. A number of initiatives updating accounting and disclosure standards and integrating securities and derivatives markets were close to being adopted (see **Exhibit 4**). But the Takeover Directive remained stalled.

The Long and Tortured History of the EU Takeover Directive

Despite its high profile and newly assigned importance, the controversy surrounding the Takeover Directive persisted. Its troubled history was often blamed on the opposition of the Germans to a market-based system of corporate control, but the situation was, in reality, much more complex.[a]

Adopting an EU Directive: The Process

First Reading

The Takeover Directive was originally conceived in 1985 as part of developing the Single European Act. But it was only at the beginning of 1989 that the Commission presented the "Thirteenth Council Directive on company law concerning takeover and other general bids" to the Council of the EU and the European Parliament (see **Exhibit 5** for a list of the other company law directives). In 1990, after suggestions from Parliament, the European Commission presented an amended proposal, which nonetheless remained unsatisfactory to most Member States.[9]

On the one hand, the United Kingdom, with its own successful self-regulatory "City Code" operated by the Takeover Panel, feared the shift toward a legislative system could hamper its already active takeover market by introducing scope for legal challenges and tactical delays. On the other hand, Germany and the Netherlands objected to encouraging takeovers in principle, favoring their existing stakeholder systems.[10] Other countries were opposed to the overly detailed text of the proposal.

The Commission set out to revise the directive again. In 1993, in an unusual move, questionnaires were sent to Member States asking them to identify issues of importance. Responses encouraged the

---

[a] The following section, "Adopting an EU Directive: The Process," addresses the timing and formal law-making procedure of the directive. The next section, "The Takeover Directive Debate," introduces the content of the proposal and outlines the source of the controversy.

Commission to adopt a framework proposal that outlined key provisions while allowing Member States to implement the provisions in accordance with their own "traditions and practices."[11] Along these lines, in early 1996, a second proposal for the 13th directive was presented to the Council and Parliament. Parliament endorsed the new framework proposal but suggested several amendments in mid-1997, which were incorporated by the Commission several months later.

In October 1998, German Chancellor Gerhard Schroeder took office. Although a Social Democrat (the main left-of-center German political party), Schroeder wanted to prove himself business friendly.[12] In a reversal of Germany's stance of the early 1990s, liberalizing takeover rules across Europe became a high priority. Schroeder involved himself directly in formulating and promoting the Takeover Directive when Germany assumed the six-month rotating presidency of the Council of the EU in January 1999. The United Kingdom, pleased that the new proposed directive resembled its own takeover code, also began to support the directive actively. By the Council's June 1999 meeting, the time appeared ripe for its passage. However, an unrelated conflict between Spain and the United Kingdom over the sovereignty of Gibraltar resulted in Spain's blocking every measure discussed at the Council, including the Takeover Directive.

Second Reading

In June 2000, the Gibraltar question was finally resolved. This allowed the Council to adopt its common position on the 13th directive. The text was then sent to the European Parliament for a second reading. The Council and the Commission hoped for a swift vote in favor of the directive, since most Member States were in agreement with its provisions. But discussions in Parliament went far from smoothly. In 1999, Member of European Parliament Klaus-Heiner Lehne, representing the right-of-center Christian Democratic Union from Germany, had been appointed rapporteur[a] for the Takeover Directive by the Parliament's Committee on Legal Affairs and the Internal Market. Lehne was opposed to many of the directive's key provisions, and as rapporteur was able to take a leading role in expressing those opinions through drafting amendments and guiding discussions. The German government tried to convince him to change his views, but to no avail. In November 2000, after much debate, Parliament presented the Commission with 20 amendments that would significantly alter the nature of the directive by making takeovers much more difficult (see next section for details).[13]

Less than a year later, the German stance on the directive took a dramatic turn. In February 2000, British telecommunications company Vodafone acquired German mobile-phone company Mannesman in a hostile takeover. At the end of 2000, American Ford Motor Company indicated interest in acquiring German auto manufacturer Volkswagen (VW). Many Germans worried that foreign investors would continue to feed on prime German companies, especially with the imminent January 2002 removal of the capital gains tax on sales of large corporate shareholdings. This tax law change was expected to lead to the unwinding of many of Germany's complicated cross-shareholding structures, which had served as an effective defense against takeovers in the past.[14]

VW felt it would become a particularly vulnerable target with passage of the Takeover Directive. The company worried the directive would call into question a state law that limited any single shareholder's voting control to 20%, regardless of capital held—effectively relieving management from the threat of a hostile takeover.[15] In April 2001, VW management and labor leaders called a

---

[a] The rapporteur is appointed by a parliamentary committee to assess a subject in detail and make a recommendation to the committee. The committee then addresses Parliament in its entirety.

meeting with Chancellor Schroeder to express their concerns. Schroeder had been a VW board member for eight years and had served as governor of the state of Lower Saxony, where VW was based. He also had relied heavily on labor for his political success. Schroeder quickly changed his position and began to lobby against the directive, seeking out key members of European Parliament, including Lehne, and other EU governments.

Conciliation and the Vote

The directive faced another complication immediately following the German government's U-turn. The Commission and the Council chose not to accept the most significant amendments presented by Parliament the previous year. As a result, a conciliation procedure, a last resort in European law making, had to be initiated.[16] The president of the Council in conjunction with the president of the European Parliament selected 15 participants from each body to negotiate a new proposal.[a] In June 2001, these 30 members came to agreement on a compromise text of the directive. One month later, the new text was presented to the European Parliament for a final vote. As with almost all other legislation that had been subject to the conciliation procedure, it was expected that the Takeover Directive would now finally pass, since the views of the conciliation committee were supposedly representative of the views of the entire Parliament and the Council.

But with a tie of 273 in favor and 273 against, the Directive failed.[b] According to some groups angered by the result, the Germans, with 99 out of the 626 parliamentary seats (see **Exhibits 6a** and **6b**), had launched a massive campaign to ensure this result in pursuit of national interests. Those voting against the directive, including even Green and Socialist party members, were accused of allowing themselves to be "manipulated by the power of the German industrial lobby and duped by the opportunistic campaign by the German government."[17] Other groups demonized Lehne personally as having single-handedly destroyed the directive's chance of passage.

Others, including the Commission, chastised Parliament members for voting for "narrow national interests"[18] (see **Exhibit 7**). A majority of Italians voted in unison against the directive, purportedly because they were upset by the recent hostile bid by French state-owned Electricite de France for Montedison, a privatized Italian power generator.[19] Most Dutch, in support of the position of Dutch industrial companies, also voted against the Takeover Directive. The Belgians, whose industrial companies expressed favor for the directive, were suspected of voting predominately against it in exchange for votes on another, unrelated matter. Another apparently coordinated effort led most U.K. members to vote in the directive's favor as demanded by financial interests in the City of London.[20] *The Wall Street Journal* commented: "Despite talk of a 'single market' and a 'new Europe,' EU members still make decisions of pan-European importance based solely on domestic political considerations, including appeals by influential domestic lobbies."[21]

The tortured history of the Takeover Directive highlighted a number of problems with the EU's legislative process. Not only did there appear to be a tendency toward nationalism obstructing the broader goals of the EU, but also, decision makers often seemed to be making decisions reactively.

---

[a] Lehne felt that the conciliation committee selected from Parliament was not representative. It included many members who had not participated in the original debate. Furthermore, more than one-third of the committee comprised U.K. members.

[b] European Parliament President Nicole Fontaine, who had been rapporteur on the Takeover Directive in an earlier stage, originally declared that the directive had passed. An adviser from the legal department corrected her ("Back to Blocker: Germany's U-Turn on the Takeover Law," *The Wall Street Journal*, June 18, 2002). As president, she could have chosen to cast the decisive vote. However, she chose not to.

More significantly, the process was slow and required negotiation of a labyrinth of European institutions. Even legislation assigned the highest priority could not be agreed upon.

After 12 long years of heated debate and despite a recent top-priority assignment, the Takeover Directive had failed. As summarized succinctly by a lobbyist at the European Banking Federation, "it represents the typical EU problem of 'yes, it's a good idea—but not today.'"[22]

The Takeover Directive Debate

Parliament's criticisms of the Takeover Directive, led by Lehne, related to its controversial contents. On the one hand, providing legal certainty for takeovers across the EU was considered important,[23] especially given the recent increase in takeover activity. Furthermore, Parliament members agreed that consistent regulation of takeovers across the EU was necessary to create an integrated capital market, which in turn was a crucial component of the Single Market.

On the other hand, members of European Parliament debated the specific provisions of the proposed "consistent" and "legally certain" takeover environment. More significantly, many questioned the fundamental issue of whether promoting an active takeover market was in fact desirable. Critics of the directive pointed out the lack of empirical support for the assertion that takeovers were value enhancing. They argued that in many cases, company stakeholders—often including target and acquiring shareholders—were actually made worse off by takeovers.

Stakeholder versus Shareholder View

We believe that the interests of company employees, as well as those of its shareholders, must be taken into account through the provision of a proper information and consultation procedure. When the directive is so modified, bringing it in line with existing and pending European company legislation, then it will have our support, and I believe it will have a good chance of being adopted speedily.[24]

— Head of the European Trade Union Confederation, the primary labor lobbying organization, based in Brussels

Many of those involved in the debate were particularly concerned about the effect of takeovers on employees. Although it required companies to disclose offer documents to employees after the offer became public, the proposed Takeover Directive completely excluded employees from the decision-making process. In countries like Germany, where employee representatives held half of the seats on supervisory boards and had, therefore, always had an influential voice in important company decisions, this exclusion would represent a severe break from tradition.[a]

The Takeover Directive had its foundations in the Anglo-Saxon shareholder-dominated model of corporate governance. Under this model, owners, including minority shareholders, had the absolute and final authority for decision making. The role of nonshareholder stakeholders was marginal. With minority shareholder protections, the system encouraged dispersed ownership, which led to more availability of equity capital and more liquid financial markets.

---

[a] In fact, under German law, excluding workers from important decisions would be unconstitutional, since codetermination rights were guaranteed under Germany's basic law (for more information, refer to HBS Case No. 702-087, "Renewing Germany: Kohl's Legacy and Schroeder's Dilemma"). An EU directive would, however, take precedence, and German law would have to be amended.

In contrast, under the stakeholder-dominated model of corporate governance typical of Continental Europe, directors were expected to look after the interests of employees, bankers, suppliers, customers, and the community at large, in addition to the interests of shareholders. Proponents of the stakeholder approach envisaged the possibility that a company might accept a lower bid for a subsidiary because the buyer was a better owner or a better employer. Under the stakeholder model, share ownership tended to be more concentrated and markets less liquid (see **Exhibit 8**), which was viewed as a stabilizing force that reduced volatility and encouraged development of cooperative relationships.

Many Europeans wanted to avoid migrating toward the Anglo-Saxon model of capitalism in which takeovers were regarded as discipline over bad management. Noting the 2001 accounting fiasco at U.S. energy company Enron and the Internet bubble of the late 1990s, they argued that such aggressive capitalism encouraged a "short-termist" view detrimental to a company's future and, by implication, the economic stability of an entire country or group of countries.

Proponents of stakeholder capitalism cited Germany as an example of a country in which the ability of companies to take a longer-term perspective had yielded positive results. They focused on Germany's successful growth during the post-war period, which they claimed could be attributed to "three ingredients: management ability to take a long-term view, harmonious labor relations, and the disciplinary function of German banks."[25] Under this system, banks, rather than shareholders, exercised supervisory authority over company management. Underperforming managers were typically replaced by bank appointees.

In response, those favoring the Takeover Directive, in line with the logic of the Single Market program and the FSAP, argued that the increasing internationalization of capital markets would force harmonization of company law across Europe (and, indeed, the world). The German model, which had served the country well for much of the post-war era, would inevitably converge with the Anglo-Saxon approach.

A "Level Playing Field" with the United States

The second major argument against the proposed Takeover Directive concerned the absence of a "level playing field" with the United States. Unlike in the United States, the proposed Takeover Directive (which was modeled after the U.K.'s national takeover code) embodied the *strict neutrality* rule. Under strict neutrality, company boards were forbidden from erecting any defense against hostile tender offers without explicit majority shareholder consent. The strict neutrality rule had at its core the principal-agent theory of corporate law, under which directors, as the agents of shareholders, were required to act in shareholders', rather than their own, best interests in managing a corporation. Deciding on takeover bids would subject directors to a conflict in this interest, so they were prevented from taking action.[26] A movement toward strict neutrality would represent a significant change for most EU Member States.[a]

In contrast, the state of Delaware (considered the top company law authority in the United States) adopted a *modified business judgment* approach to takeover bids. This approach recognized the potential collective action problem in getting dispersed minority shareholders to react to takeover offers. Under the modified business judgment approach, boards of management were allowed to act

---

[a] For example, in 1999, Italian luxury goods company Gucci managed to fend off French LVMH Moet Hennessey Louis Vuitton by selling a 42% stake in itself to French retail group Pinault Printemps Redoubt without shareholder consent. The incumbent Gucci management was thereby protected.

on the behalf of shareholders, without their explicit consent, in response to takeover offers. Defensive measures taken at management initiative such as "poison pills" (see **Exhibit 9**) were permitted if they were "reasonable in relation to the threat posed."[27] In fact, such defensive measures often increased the price paid for target companies.[28] This system was effective in the United States in large part because company boards were legally liable for their decisions and courts were "willing and able to intervene effectively" to challenge board actions.[29] Whether the legal framework in the EU would support such an approach was unclear.

In the words of a legal academic, the significant difference in takeover frameworks across the Atlantic that would follow from adoption of the Takeover Directive "raises the prospect that American companies could take over their European counterparts more easily, and pay less for doing so, than the other way around. The strong value of the dollar against the euro makes this threat even more pronounced."[30] Others contradicted this view, pointing to data showing that in 2000, European companies spent more on U.S. acquisitions than North American companies invested in Europe (see **Exhibit 10**). They also noted that only 2% of all takeover activity in Europe was hostile.[31]

Critics argued: "European politicians see business as national assets, rather than enterprises to be run with the aim of maximizing shareholder value."[32] They predicted that a strict neutrality rule would simply encourage companies and countries to adopt alternative barriers to takeovers that might be more costly but would nevertheless remain effective even with the Takeover Directive. Companies might be encouraged to retain or erect new complicated cross-ownership structures, and governments might choose to maintain or implement unfavorable tax treatment for selling shareholders, restrictions on intellectual property transfers, restrictive labor laws, or stricter interpretation of antitrust laws.[33]

A "Level Playing Field" within Europe

The third issue concerned creation of a level playing field within Europe. Many European companies had erected defenses against takeovers that would remain unaffected by the proposed Takeover Directive. For example, to protect privatized companies, particularly those in the energy, communication, defense, and transportation sectors, many countries had instituted "golden shares." Golden shares, first created by former U.K. Prime Minister Margaret Thatcher, gave national governments a casting vote over takeovers and other major decisions in privatized firms in which they no longer held a majority stake. Countries including France, Portugal, Spain, and the United Kingdom all used golden shares. Other countries, including Germany, had never instituted these largely symbolic shares and felt it would be unfair to subject their own "privatized national champions"[34] to hostile takeovers without similar companies in other countries being subjected to the same threat.

A similar argument concerned the use of shares with multiple voting rights. Multiple voting rights were particularly prevalent in Sweden, where the Wallenberg family exercised disproportionate control over a large number of corporations in relation to its invested capital. For example, with just 7% of the capital, the family held a majority of votes in telecommunications equipment manufacturer Ericsson.[35] Voting right differences were also prevalent in the Netherlands, where companies commonly issued nonlisted risk-bearing voting shares to a trust, which, in turn, issued listed nonvoting depository receipts to the public. In such cases, restrictions on defensive tactics enforced by the Takeover Directive would become irrelevant as the entrenched control group, with its majority of votes (even if a minority of capital), could simply approve impediments regardless of the wishes of the broader shareholder base. Again, German companies felt exposed relative to their counterparts in other European countries, since Germany had abolished multiple voting share structures in 1998.[a]

Under both the golden share and multiple voting right scenarios, the objective of the directive would potentially go unfulfilled as companies remained impregnable and incumbent managers remained entrenched and free of market discipline.

Proposals for the Revised Takeover Directive

Following the directive's failure to pass in the European Parliament, the European Commission appointed a group of European company law experts to write a report addressing concerns about the proposed Takeover Directive.[36] This report, published in January 2002, was intended to serve as the basis for a new, and hopefully final, draft of the Takeover Directive.

Shareholder Decision Making

The report reinforced the directive's commitment to exclusive shareholder decision-making authority. It suggested no additional rights for employees or other stakeholders in responding to tender offers and suggested that their concerns be addressed in a different forum, such as through labor and environmental laws. In addition, the report continued to suggest forbidding company boards from mounting takeover defenses without shareholder consent. Critics' fears of a wave of European companies falling prey to U.S. investors while U.S. companies remained impenetrable to European investors were not allayed.

Many participants in the debate had hoped for a compromise on the strict neutrality rule. They claimed minority shareholders would be unable to authorize boards to thwart takeover attempts given the small window of time available. They recommended addressing this collective action problem by giving shareholders the opportunity *ex ante* to allow boards to erect defensive measures. Shareholders could then elect to veto defensive actions case by case through a specified process.[37]

The company law experts relented to concerns about strict neutrality only to the extent of suggesting "it could be considered whether to allow Member States to provide the benefits of the application of the principles of shareholder decision-making . . . only [to] European listed companies making general takeover bids for other European listed companies."[38]

Proportionality Between Risk-Bearing Capital and Control

Other suggestions of the report were more surprising. Shocking many observers who had expected a watered-down proposal, the report suggested a completely new second basic guiding principle for the Takeover Directive that threatened existing national prerogatives: proportionality between risk bearing and control. In the report, the group reasoned: "In open capital markets major (institutional) investors would normally prefer to invest where bearing the ultimate economic risk of the company confers proportionate control rights. The cost of capital of such companies is normally lower and they will be better able to raise capital on the securities markets."[39] In support of this

---

[a] In Germany, however, there were some peculiarities. VW, as described in the preceding section, had limited individual shareholder voting rights to 20%; several other companies, including Porsche, only listed nonvoting shares in order to preserve family ownership.

principle, the report proposed that shareholders have the right to vote on whether to allow the board to defend against a takeover in proportion to the amount of risk-bearing capital held, regardless of the voting rights associated with the share. This would apply even if shares had diminished voting rights at the time of purchase.

Along the same lines, a breakthrough threshold of a maximum 75% was proposed. In other words, once a bidder acquired 75% of the shares of a company (or a lower percentage as defined by the country adopting the Takeover Directive), the bidder would have the right to acquire the rest. As such, the bidder would be able to break through mechanisms and structures designed to frustrate bids, such as golden shares.[40]

Not surprisingly, a flurry of activity followed the publication of these proposals. According to the head of the Federation of European Securities Exchanges in Brussels, "the lobbyists began to lobby the lobbyists."[41] Groups supporting the rights of companies with multiple voting rights (in essence, representatives of the Swedish Wallenberg family) visited him and other Brussels-based associations to demand removal of the one-share-one-vote proposal. They argued that the new proposal was tantamount to expropriation.

The *Financial Times* questioned how holders of shares with multiple votes would be compensated:

> It is hard to see how corporate Europe can move from unequal voting structures to one-share-one-vote unless there is some proposal to compensate block holders whose control rights are being confiscated. But if the block holder is monitoring the corporate performance effectively, how would an outside bidder be able to afford to pay a premium to take control via a takeover? If, in contrast, the block holders are extracting private benefits of control at the expense of minorities, a hostile bidder will clearly be able to pay a premium, because the company would be more valuable if the rip-offs stopped. But do block holders deserve to be compensated for giving up the right to loot the company?[42]

By spring 2002, rumor had it that powerful lobbyists had been successful in convincing the Commission not to adopt the one-share-one-vote proposal or the breakthrough rule.[43] Instead, some of critics' concerns about the uneven playing field within Europe created by the directive were being allayed through other channels. On June 4, 2002, the fate of golden shares was under threat as the European Court of Justice ruled that national governments could only retain the right of veto over takeovers or other key decisions if doing so was "strictly in the national strategic interest."[44]

German Member of European Parliament Lehne, pleased that the proposals had addressed many of his concerns, expressed his support for the report:

> Last year, everyone accused me of being protectionist. But this year, it's exactly the opposite. I'm in favor of the new proposal. But now we have the ironic situation that the British government, the Swedish government, the German government, the French government, and some other governments are saying "no, we don't want that." One because of Volkswagen, the other because of the Wallenbergs, the next because of airports, another because of their telephone company, and so on.[a] So, everybody is talking about the liquid and

---

[a] The United Kingdom retained a golden share in the British Airport Authority after its 1987 privatization. The European Commission filed a case in 2000 to challenge this golden share that ensured that Heathrow, Gatwick, and Stansted airports could not be sold off without government approval. Likewise, Spain retained a golden share in Telefonica, which helped the government press management to forgo a planned merger with Dutch KPN Telecom.

deep capital markets within the European Union, but once discussion starts to get serious, they all fall back into their old protectionist behavior.[45]

Concluding Remarks

Although the Takeover Directive caused much turmoil, there were several positive outcomes of the debate. First, many countries, in anticipation of the directive's eventual passage, had adopted their own takeover codes modeled, to some extent, after the latest draft of the Takeover Directive. Although significant differences remained (such as avoidance of strict neutrality in Germany's code adopted in January 2002), takeover rules across Europe were at least being clarified.

A second outcome was the scrutiny the European law-making process was being put under as a result of the Takeover Directive's tortured history. The European Commission's 2001 Lamfalussy Report,[46] produced by a committee of "wise men," recommended new processes for decision making for securities and financial market legislation. These would involve more transparency and input from experts rather than politicians. They would also offer opportunities to expedite the process and approve legislation in pieces, so that less controversial elements could be passed and implemented more quickly.[47]

The Future of the Takeover Directive

The outlook was generally positive that a Takeover Directive would finally be signed by the end of 2003. According to lobbyists, there was a "groundswell of support" behind its passage.[48] In addition, there was tremendous pressure on the European Commission—particularly individuals within the Commission who had staked their careers on the Takeover Directive—to deliver. Another failure was out of the question.

As such, the Commission was waiting to issue the new draft of the directive until it was absolutely certain of its ability to pass. To ensure its success, the Commission was conducting numerous off-the-record discussions with experts and key decision makers. In addition, the Commission recognized the importance of timing its release strategically. Although the Commission had originally promised a new draft by June 2002, by the middle of September 2002 the new draft was still not available. Rumors indicated it would be released only after the German national elections of September 22, 2002; German Chancellor Schroeder had continued to politicize the Takeover Directive debate in his campaign for reelection. According to *The Wall Street Journal*: ". . . he told cheering workers in a cavernous VW factory hall in Kassel, Germany . . . [that] 'Whoever tries to destroy this Volkswagen culture can count on the resistance of this government.'"[49]

There was still much speculation as to what provisions the new Takeover Directive would include. Indeed, many members of European Parliament and decision makers in Member States were still threatening not to support the new draft, which was certain to continue to uphold the Anglo-Saxon shareholder-dominated model of corporate governance. Whether their voice would be strong enough to change the direction of the Takeover Directive was still to be tested.

Exhibit 1   Map of the European Union (as of 2002)

EU Member States:		The Euro Area:		Enlargement Candidates:	
Austria	Italy	Austria	Ireland	Hungary	Lithuania
Belgium	Luxembourg	Belgium	Italy	Poland	Malta
Denmark	Netherlands	Finland	Luxembourg	Estonia	Slovakia
Finland	Portugal	France	Netherlands	Czech Republic	Bulgaria
France	Spain	Germany	Portugal	Slovenia	Romania
Germany	Sweden	Greece	Spain	Cyprus	Turkey *(recognized as*
Greece	U.K.			Latvia	*applicant)*
Ireland					

Source: European Union On-line, <http://europa.eu.int/comm/mediatheque/multimedia/select/maps_en.html> (accessed September 26, 2002).

Exhibit 2 Law Making within the EU: Codecision Procedure

The codecision procedure is used for all legislation concerning creation of the Single Market.

European Parliament: consists of 626 elected members from EU Member States. Elections are held nationally every five years. Parliament's role is as legislative decision maker. It also holds supervisory power over the European Commission.

Council of the European Union: consists of ministerial level representatives from each Member State empowered to act with binding effect. Representatives vary according to subject under discussion. The presidency of the Council is held in turn by each Member State for six months. The Council's main task is to lay down and implement legislation. (This should not be confused with the Council of Europe.)

European Commission: consists of 20 members (2 from Germany, France, Italy, the U.K., and Spain; 1 from other Member States) appointed by governments of Member States and approved by Parliament for five-year terms. They neither seek nor take instructions from any government. The Commission has primary responsibility for presenting proposals and drafts on Community policy.

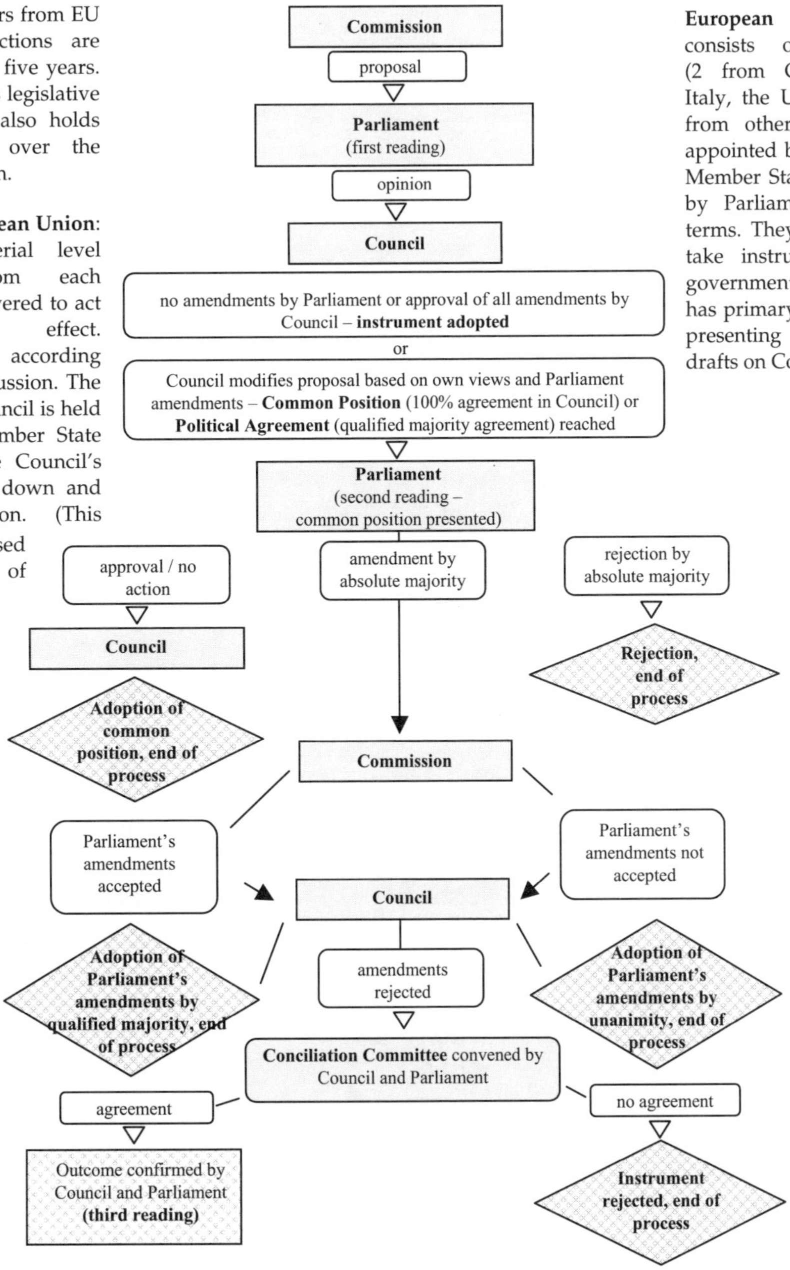

Source: Adapted from Klaus-Dieter Borchardt, *The ABC of Community Law* (European Commission, Brussels, 2000), p. 79.

Exhibit 3   EU-15, Euro Area, U.S., and Japan Comparative Macroeconomic Data for 2000

	Unit	EU-15	Euro Area	U.S.	Japan
Area	thousands k^2	3191	2496	9373	378
Population and labor force					
Total population	millions	377.2	304.7	282.5	127.0
Labor force participation rate	%		68.0	77.2	62.4
Unemployment rate	%	8.1	8.5	4.0	4.6
GDP					
GDP (conversion at PPP)	billions euro	8,147.5	6,567.7	8,704.6	2,916.9
GDP per capita (conversion at PPP)	thousands euro	21.6	21.6	30.8	23.0
Value added by sector of activity					
Agriculture, fishing, forestry	% of total	...	2.4	1.4	1.3
Industry (including construction)	% of total	...	27.9	21.6	27.9
Services (including nonmarket services)	% of total	...	69.7	77.0	70.8
Households					
Gross disposable income per capita (DI) (conversion at market exchange rates)	thousands euro	...	13.2	26.9	27.0
Gross saving	% DI	...	14.8	11.2	16.3
Gross fixed capital formation	% DI	...	11.0	6.0	7.9
Investment in financial assets	% DI	...	12.5	3.5	8.9
Financial assets held	% DI	...	335.9	475.0	431.8
Gross debt outstanding	% DI	...	81.3	100.7	103.9
Nonfinancial corporations					
Gross saving	% GDP	...	8.9	9.8	13.8
Gross fixed capital formation	% GDP	...	11.7	11.8	15.5
Net issuance of shares and other equity	% GDP	...	6.5	-1.6	1.7
Financial assets held	% GDP	...	140.7	103.8	144.2
Gross debt outstanding	% GDP	...	70.8	66.1	126.6
General government					
Expenditure	% GDP	...	48.7	30.6	39.0
Surplus (+) or deficit (-)	% GDP	...	-0.9	1.4	-7.4
Gross debt outstanding	% GDP	...	70.1	45.2	120.0
External					
Exports of goods and services	% GDP	...	19.3	10.8	11.1
Imports of goods and services	% GDP	...	19.2	14.6	9.7
Current account balance	% GDP	...	-1.1	-4.2	2.5
Net direct and portfolio investment	% GDP	...	-1.3	4.3	-1.2
Monetary and financial indicators					
CPI inflation (2001)	annual % change	...	2.1	1.6	-0.7
Broad monetary aggregate	annual % change	...	5.0	8.8	2.1
Credit (conversion at market exchange rates)	billions euro	...	8,961.9	9,046.9	6,854.3
Total amount outstanding of debt securities (conversion at market exchange rates)[a]	billions euro	...	7,092.8	14,090.3	8,228.2

Source: Adapted from European Central Bank, "Key Characteristics of the Euro Area, the United States and Japan," September 2002, <http://www.ecb.int/stats/comparison/comparison.pdf> (accessed October 1, 2002).

Note: [a] Euro area data for total amount outstanding of debt securities excludes Greece.

Exhibit 4 Progress on Measures of the Financial Services Action Plan, as of July 2002
(+ *indicates progress being made* / - *indicates no progress*)

A Strategic Objective 1: A Single EU Wholesale Market

Measure	Plan time frame (P=Proposal, A=Adoption)	Revised time frame (P=Proposal, A=Adoption)	+ / -
Raising capital on an EU-wide basis			
Directive on Prospectuses	A 2002	A 2003	+
Updating the Regular Reporting Requirements	P 2001/A 2002	P end-2002 / A 2003	-
Establishing a common legal framework for integrated securities and derivatives markets			
Directive on Market Abuse	A 2003	A end-2002	+
Directive to upgrade the Investment Services Directive		P Dec 2002 / A Jun 2003	+
Toward a single set of financial statements			
Modernization of accounting provisions of the 4th and 7th Company Law Directives	P 2000 / A 2002	P May 2002 / A early 2003	+
Containing systemic risk in securities settlement			
Implementation Settlement Finality Directive	Commission report to Council end-2002	Commission report to Council Dec 2002	+
Toward a secure and transparent environment for cross-border restructuring			
Directive on Takeover Bids	A 2000	P 2002 / A 2003	-
Follow-up: Report of High Level Group of Company Law Experts		2002 / 2003	+
Proposal for a 10th Company Law Directive	P fall 1999 / A 2002	P Sep 2002 / A 2003	+
Proposal for a 14th Company Law Directive	P fall 1999 / A 2002	P before 2003	-
A Single Market that works for investors			
Directive on Prudential Supervision of Supplementary Pension Funds	A Jan 2002	A Dec 2002	-
Communication on Clearing and Settlement	*not part of plan*	Issued in May 2002	+

Exhibit 4 (continued)

B Other Objectives

Measure	Plan time frame (P=Proposal, A=Adoption)	Revised time frame (P=Proposal, A=Adoption)	+ / -
Strategic Objective 2: Open and Secure Retail Markets			
Directive on Insurance Intermediaries	A 2002	A 2002	+
EU legal framework for payments in the Internal Market		P 2003	+
Follow-up to FIN-NET	Ongoing	Permanent	+
Follow up to Commission's Action Plan to prevent fraud and counterfeiting in payment systems			+
Work on Insurance Guarantee Schemes	not part of plan	Ongoing until 2003	+
Strategic Objective 3: State-of-the-art Prudential Rules and Supervision			
Amend the Directives Governing the Capital Framework for Banks and Investment Firms	P spring 2000 / A 2002	P 2004 / A 2005	+
Directive on Prudential Rules for Financial Conglomerates	A 2002	A Dec 2002	+
Reinsurance Supervision	not part of plan	Ongoing until 2003	+
Fundamental review of the solvency system in insurance	not part of plan	Ongoing until 2005	+
Third Money Laundering Directive	not part of plan	Proposal end 2003	+
Objective: Wider Conditions for an Optimal Single Financial Market			
Adopt a Directive on taxation of savings income in the form of interest payments	Political Agreement Nov 1999 / A 2000	P Jul 2001 / A Dec 2002	+
Implementation of the December 1997 Code of Conduct on business taxation	Ongoing examination	Ongoing examination	+
Commission initiative on taxation of cross-border occupational pensions	P end-1999 / A 2002	Issued Apr 2001	+

Source: Adapted from European Commission, "Financial Services, An Improving Climate – But Quite Some Way to Go, Sixth Progress Report," COM(2002)267, June 3, 2002.

Exhibit 5   The EU's 13 Company Law Directives

Directive	Date	Notes
1 Disclosure Directive	1968 (currently being updated)	Laid out substantial disclosure requirements for setting up companies to ensure that third parties were given full details.
2 Capital Directive	1976 (currently being updated)	Required a minimum amount of authorized capital as security for creditors for public limited liability companies.
3 Merger Directive	1978	Ensured harmonized standards of protection of third parties in mergers of domestic public limited liability companies.
4 Accounts Directive	1978, 1990 (currently being updated)	Adopted a hybrid of German, French, and U.K. law on the annual accounts of companies.
5 Structure Directive	not passed	Sought to introduce requirements for the structure of boards of companies.
6 Division Directive	1982	-
7 Consolidated Accounts Directive	1983 (currently being updated)	-
8 Statutory Audits Directive	1984	Presented guidelines on the approval of persons responsible for carrying out the statutory audits of accounting documents.
9 Groups Directive	withdrawn (1st draft 1979, 2nd draft 1984)	-
10 Cross-Border Mergers	not passed (presented 1985, new proposal expected September 2002)	Sought to ensure harmonized standards of protection of third parties in cross-border mergers of public limited liability companies.
11 Branches Directive	1989	Outlined disclosure requirements of branches opened in a Member State by companies governed by the laws of another state.
12 Single Member Companies Directive	1989	-
13 Takeover Directive	not passed (new proposal expected September 2002)	Sought to establish rules on takeover and other general bids.

Source: Adapted from European Commission Web site, <http://www.europa.eu.int/comm/internal_market/en/company/company/official/index.htm> (accessed October 1, 2002).

Exhibit 6a   Structure of the European Parliament

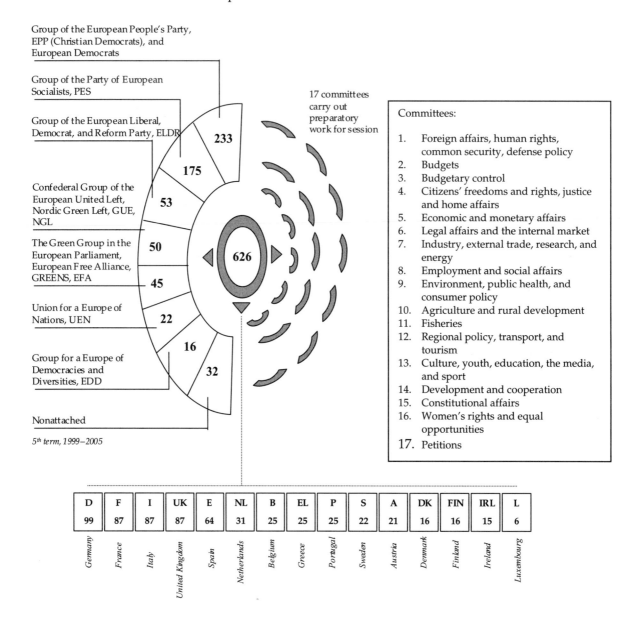

Group of the European People's Party,
EPP (Christian Democrats), and
European Democrats

Group of the Party of European
Socialists, PES

Group of the European Liberal,
Democrat, and Reform Party, ELDR

Confederal Group of the
European United Left,
Nordic Green Left, GUE,
NGL

The Green Group in the
European Parliament,
European Free Alliance,
GREENS, EFA

Union for a Europe of
Nations, UEN

Group for a Europe of
Democracies and
Diversities, EDD

Nonattached

5th term, 1999–2005

233
175
53
50
45
22
16
32
626

17 committees
carry out
preparatory
work for session

Committees:

1. Foreign affairs, human rights,
   common security, defense policy
2. Budgets
3. Budgetary control
4. Citizens' freedoms and rights, justice
   and home affairs
5. Economic and monetary affairs
6. Legal affairs and the internal market
7. Industry, external trade, research, and
   energy
8. Employment and social affairs
9. Environment, public health, and
   consumer policy
10. Agriculture and rural development
11. Fisheries
12. Regional policy, transport, and
    tourism
13. Culture, youth, education, the media,
    and sport
14. Development and cooperation
15. Constitutional affairs
16. Women's rights and equal
    opportunities
17. Petitions

D	F	I	UK	E	NL	B	EL	P	S	A	DK	FIN	IRL	L
99	87	87	87	64	31	25	25	25	22	21	16	16	15	6
Germany	*France*	*Italy*	*United Kingdom*	*Spain*	*Netherlands*	*Belgium*	*Greece*	*Portugal*	*Sweden*	*Austria*	*Denmark*	*Finland*	*Ireland*	*Luxembourg*

Sources: Adapted from Klaus-Dieter Borchardt, *The ABC of Community Law* (European Commission, Brussels, 2000), p. 34; and European Parliament Web site <http://www.europarl.eu.int/presentation/default_en.htm> (accessed September 25, 2002).

Exhibit 6b   Composition of the European Parliament by Political Group and Nationality

	EPP and European Democrats	PES	ELDR	GUE and NGL	Greens and EFA	UEN	EDD	Nonattached	Total
Germany	53	35		7	4				**99**
France	21	18		15	9	3	9	12	**87**
Italy	35	16	8	6	2	10		10	**87**
U.K.	37	29	11		6		2	2	**87**
Spain	28	24	3	4	4			1	**64**
Netherlands	9	6	8	1	4		3		**31**
Belgium	5	5	6		7			2	**25**
Greece	9	9		7					**25**
Portugal	9	12		2		2			**25**
Sweden	7	6	4	3	2				**22**
Austria	7	7			2			5	**21**
Denmark	1	2	6	4		1	2		**16**
Finland	5	3	5	1	2				**16**
Ireland	5	1	1		2	6			**15**
Luxembourg	2	2	1		1				**6**
Total	**233**	**175**	**53**	**50**	**45**	**22**	**16**	**32**	**626**

For full party names, refer to **Exhibit 6a**.

Source: Adapted from European Parliament Web site, <http://www.europarl.eu.int/presentation/default_en.htm>
(accessed September 25, 2002).

Exhibit 7   Outcome of the Parliamentary Vote on the Takeover Directive, July 4, 2001

Votes For:

	EPP and European Democrats	PES	ELDR	GUE and NGL	Greens and EFA	UEN	EDD	Non-attached	Total
Germany	1	0	0	0	0	0	0	0	1
France	15	16	0	0	0	3	6	5	45
Italy	2	12	4	1	0	6	0	7	32
U.K.	33	27	10	0	2	0	0	0	72
Spain	20	0	3	0	3	0	0	0	26
Netherlands	0	1	8	0	0	0	0	0	9
Belgium	0	0	5	0	0	0	0	0	5
Greece	1	1	0	0	0	0	0	0	2
Portugal	9	8	0	0	0	2	0	0	19
Sweden	7	6	4	0	2	0	0	0	19
Austria	0	0	0	0	0	0	0	4	4
Denmark	1	3	5	0	0	1	3	0	13
Finland	3	3	4	0	1	0	0	0	11
Ireland	4	1	1	0	0	4	0	0	10
Luxembourg	2	2	1	0	0	0	0	0	5
Total	98	80	45	1	8	16	9	16	273

Votes Against:

	EPP and European Democrats	PES	ELDR	GUE and NGL	Greens and EFA	UEN	EDD	Non-attached	Total
Germany	51	34	0	5	5	0	0	0	95
France	4	4	0	9	9	0	0	0	26
Italy	29	0	0	4	0	0	0	3	36
U.K.	0	0	0	0	4	0	2	0	6
Spain	4	22	0	4	1	0	0	0	31
Netherlands	9	5	0	1	4	0	3	0	22
Belgium	6	4	0	0	5	0	0	1	16
Greece	8	7	0	6	0	0	0	0	21
Portugal	0	1	0	0	0	0	0	0	1
Sweden	0	0	0	0	0	0	0	0	0
Austria	6	7	0	0	1	0	0	0	14
Denmark	0	0	0	0	0	0	0	0	0
Finland	1	0	0	1	0	0	0	0	2
Ireland	1	0	0	0	1	0	0	0	2
Luxembourg	0	0	0	0	1	0	0	0	1
Total	119	84	0	30	31	0	5	4	273

Source: Adapted from European Parliament Web site, < http://www3.europarl.eu.int/omk/omnsapir.so/calendar?APP= PV1&LANGUE=EN> (accessed October 17, 2002).

Note: The vote also included 22 abstentions and a remainder of no votes. (For full party names, refer to **Exhibit 6a**.)

Exhibit 8   Ownership Concentration and Market Capitalization of Domestic Listed Companies

Nation	Number of Domestic Listed Companies, 2000	% of Companies: No Holder with Majority Control	% of Companies: No Holder with at Least 25%	Market Capitalization as % of GDP (excludes investment funds)		
				1990	1995	2000
Austria	97	32.0	14.0	17	14	16
Belgium	161	34.3	6.4	33	37	80
Denmark	225	na	na	29	32	69
Finland	154	na	na	17	35	243
France	808	na	na	26	33	112
Germany	744	35.8	17.5	22	24	68
Greece	309	na	na	18	14	96
Ireland	76	na	na	na	39	87
Italy	291	43.9	34.2	14	19	72
Luxembourg	54	na	na	101	176	179
Netherlands	234	60.6	19.6	42	72	175
Portugal	109	na	na	13	18	58
Spain	1019	67.4	32.9	23	27	90
Sweden	292	73.7	35.8	40	75	144
U.K.	1926	97.6	84.1	87	122	185

Source: Adapted from European Commission Internal Market Directorate General, "Comparative Study of Corporate Governance Codes Relevant to the European Union and its Member States," Table K, p. 31, <http://europa.eu.int/comm/internal_market/en/company/company/news/corp-gov-codes-rpt-part1_en.pdf> (accessed September 24, 2002).

Exhibit 9   List of Takeover Defense Measures

"White Knight"	Seeking a friendly acquirer
"Poison Pill"	Implementing rights plans that entitle existing shareholders to large amounts of stock, debt securities, or cash if a hostile bidder gains control
"Sale of Crown Jewels"	Selling the corporation's most valuable assets
"Lock-up Options"	Granting preferential options on stock or assets to white knights or other persons other than the hostile bidder
"Green Mail"	Paying off the hostile bidder in return for it agreeing to go away
"Pac Man Defense"	Launching a bid for the bidder itself
"Golden Parachutes"	Binding the target company contractually to make large severance payments to incumbent managers in the event of a change of control

Source: Adapted from Christian Kirchner and Richard W. Painter, "Takeover Defenses under Delaware Law, the Proposed Thirteenth EU Directive and the New German Takeover Law: Comparison and Recommendations for Reform," *American Journal of Comparative Law,* 2002.

Exhibit 10   Investment Activity

A Foreign Direct Investment in the United States *(billions U.S. dollars)*

	FDI stock					FDI inflows				
	1997	**1998**	**1999**	**2000**	**2001**	**1997**	**1998**	**1999**	**2000**	**2001**
All countries	681.8	778.4	955.7	1,214.3	1,321.1	103.4	174.4	283.4	300.9	124.4
EU	386.8	465.6	582.0	760.0	808.3	65.8	147.9	220.3	221.7	59.1
as % total	*57%*	*60%*	*61%*	*63%*	*61%*	*64%*	*85%*	*78%*	*74%*	*47%*

B Foreign Direct Investment from the United States *(billions U.S. dollars)*

	FDI stocks					FDI outflows				
	1997	**1998**	**1999**	**2000**	**2001**	**1997**	**1998**	**1999**	**2000**	**2001**
All countries	871.3	1,000.7	1,173.1	1,293.4	1,381.7	95.8	131.0	174.6	165.0	114.0
EU	378.4	462.6	549.8	604.4	640.8	46.9	75.8	87.4	82.8	46.6
as % total	*43%*	*46%*	*47%*	*47%*	*46%*	*49%*	*58%*	*50%*	*50%*	*41%*

Source (A-B):   Adapted from U.S. Department of Commerce, Bureau of Economic Analysis, "Survey of Current Business," September 2002, <http://www.bea.doc.gov/bea/pub/0902cont.htm> (accessed September 24, 2002).

C Mergers and Acquisitions (2000)

Foreign Acquisitions of U.S. Companies in the United States *(billions U.S. dollars)*

Number of cross-border deals: 1,248; Value: 299.2

Top foreign acquirers	Value of transactions	Number of transactions
UK	77.7	313
Germany	47.9	138
Netherlands	38.7	71
France	28.3	87

Foreign Acquisitions in Europe *(billions U.S. dollars)*

Top non-EU acquirers	Value of transactions	Number of transactions
U.S.	98.7	1,035
Japan	8.6	47
Canada	3.1	78
South Africa	2.5	32

Source: Adapted from Irene Haikonen, "The European Union and World Trade: Basic Statistics on European Union Trade for Years 2000 and 2001; Comparison with the United States, Japan, and Regional Trading Areas," March 2002, <http://www.eurunion.org/profile/statistics2002a.pdf> (accessed September 24, 2002).

Appendix: European Union Milestones

1948: After the end of World War II, Europe sought ways to prevent another outbreak of conflict. France, Belgium, Luxembourg, the Netherlands, and the United Kingdom signed the **Brussels Treaty** agreeing on military assistance and economic, social, and cultural cooperation. A year later they set up the **Council of Europe** with the primary objective of protecting human rights, pluralist democracy, and the rule of law.

1951: France, Germany, Italy, Belgium, Luxembourg, and the Netherlands signed the **Treaty of Paris** establishing the **European Coal and Steel Community (ECSC),** based on the idea that pooling coal and steel resources would help avoid further European conflict. The predecessors of the **European Commission** and the **European Parliament** were set up, as well as the **Council of Ministers** and the **Court of Justice**.

1957: France, Germany, Italy, and the Benelux countries signed the **Treaty of Rome,** the foundation of the European Community. It set up the **European Economic Community (EEC)** and the **European Atomic Energy Community (Euratom),** which worked alongside the ECSC.

1960: Austria, Denmark, Norway, Portugal, Sweden, Switzerland, and the United Kingdom set up the **European Free Trade Association (EFTA)**. Finland, Iceland, and Liechtenstein joined later. Like the EEC, EFTA aimed to establish free trade in Western Europe. Eighteen months after EFTA was set up, the United Kingdom applied to join the EEC but was vetoed by French President Charles de Gaulle. Eventually, all but three of EFTA's members ended up leaving the EFTA to join the EEC.

1965: The EEC, the ECSC, and Euratom were merged into the **European Community** (effective 1967). A single Council of Ministers and European Commission for the unified communities was established.

1973: Denmark, Ireland, and the United Kingdom joined the European Community.

1979: The **European Monetary System (EMS)** entered force. The EMS was made up of the **European Currency Unit (ECU)** and the **Exchange Rate Mechanism (ERM)**, a system that gave national currencies a central exchange rate against the ECU. Each currency could fluctuate above and below this rate within certain boundaries. All the community's members apart from the United Kingdom joined the ERM at this time. In this year, Europeans voted in the first direct elections to the European Parliament.

1981: Greece joined the EEC as its 10th member.

1986: Spain and Portugal joined the EEC, taking the community's number up to 12. **The Single European Act**, which modified the Treaty of Rome, was signed. It set up a framework for the **Single European Market** by increasing the European Commission's powers and introducing qualified majority voting for a number of issues.

1991: European leaders met in the Dutch town of **Maastricht** to draft the **Treaty of the European Union,** a major amendment to the 1957 Treaty of Rome and the agreement that officially changed the European Community into the **European Union**. The treaty established a timetable for economic and monetary union and laid out the convergence criteria that countries had to meet to adopt the single currency.

Appendix (continued)

In the social chapter of the agreement, Europe for the first time addressed policies covering issues such as workers' pay and workplace health and safety. The United Kingdom opted out of these commitments.

Maastricht also made the citizens of the 12 Member States **European citizens**, giving them the right to move freely and live in any Member State and to vote in local and European elections in any EU country. Work also began on eastward expansion.

1995: Austria, Finland, and Sweden joined the EU, bringing membership up to 15. The **Schengen** agreement came into force, removing intra-European border controls (excluding in the United Kingdom and Ireland, which opted out because of terrorism fears).

1997: The heads of government met in **Amsterdam** to draft a new agreement that updated the Maastricht Treaty and started to get the EU ready for eastward expansion.

Amsterdam aimed to make the EU more democratically accountable and extended Parliament's powers. Qualified majority voting was introduced into new areas, reducing individual countries' powers to veto new measures. The treaty allowed for closer cooperation between countries that wanted to forge ahead on certain issues.

1998: The EU opened negotiations with Hungary, Poland, Estonia, the Czech Republic, Slovenia, and Cyprus to join the EU. A year later, at the **Helsinki summit** in December 1999, Romania, Slovakia, Latvia, Lithuania, Bulgaria, and Malta formed the second wave of candidate countries. Turkey was recognized as an applicant country.

1999: Germany, France, Italy, Spain, Portugal, the Netherlands, Austria, Finland, Ireland, Belgium, and Luxembourg adopted the **euro** as their official currency on January 1, 1999. Greece joined them two years later, but Sweden, Denmark, and the United Kingdom stayed out. The euro was introduced in physical form on January 1, 2002.

2000: Agreement was reached on the **Treaty of Nice**, outlining the key institutional principles for decision making in an enlarged EU: the number of votes each country would have in the Council of Ministers, and how many representatives each country would send to the European Parliament. In October 2002, the treaty appeared to be heading toward ratification. The enlargement candidate countries most likely to join the EU in 2004 included Cyprus, the Czech Republic, Estonia, Hungary, Latvia, Lithuania, Poland, Malta, Slovakia, and Slovenia.

Sources: This section is drawn in large part from British Broadcasting Corp. sources, the European Union On-line, and the Council of Europe Web sites available at: <http://news.bbc.co.uk/hi/english/static/in_depth/europe/2001/ inside_europe/milestones/2004.stm> (accessed September 16, 2002); at <http://europa.eu.int/comm/ mediatheque/multimedia/select/maps_en.html> (accessed September 26, 2002); and at <http://www.coe.int/ T/E/Communication_and_Research/Contacts_with_the_public/About_Council_of_ Europe/An_overview/> (accessed October 16, 2002).

Endnotes

[1] Quote of European Commissioner of Internal Markets Frits Bolkestein at a press conference associated with release of the report, "Financial Services, An Improving Climate – But Quite Some Way to Go, Sixth Progress Report," European Commission, COM(2002)267, June 3, 2002, <http://europa.eu.int/comm/internal_market/en/finances/actionplan/index.htm> (accessed September 12, 2002).

[2] "Back to Blocker: Germany's U-Turn on the Takeover Law," *The Wall Street Journal Europe*, June 18, 2002.

[3] Practitioners Working Group on Takeovers (comprised of Federation of European Securities Exchanges, European Banking Federation, and U.K. Takeover Panel), "Position Paper," January 4, 2002.

[4] Daniel Dombey and Hugh Williamson, "Berlin glee greets demise of EU takeover directive," *Financial Times*, July 6, 2001.

[5] "EU's Bolkestein says takeover vote setback to capital market integration by 2005," *AFX News: World Reporter*, July 4, 2001.

[6] Burçak Inel, adviser, Financial Markets, European Banking Federation, interview by casewriter, Brussels, May 2002.

[7] Quote of European Commission President Romano Prodi at a press conference associated with release of the report "Financial Services, An Improving Climate – But Quite Some Way to Go, Sixth Progress Report," European Commission, COM(2002)267, June 3, 2002, <http://europa.eu.int/comm/internal_market/en/finances/actionplan/index.htm> (accessed September 12, 2002).

[8] "Financial services: Commission outlines Action Plan for single financial market," European Commission, May 1999, <http://europa.eu.int/comm/internal_market/en/finances/general/action.htm> (accessed September 16, 2002).

[9] The timeline of the directive is drawn from "Report of the High Level Group of Company Law Experts on Issues Related to Takeover Bids," European Commission, January 10, 2002, pp. 13–15.

[10] Officially, the Dutch objected to the fact that the proposal abolished Dutch legal devices against takeovers while leaving untouched defensive devices in other countries.

[11] "Report of the High Level Group of Company Law Experts on Issues Related to Takeover Bids," European Commission, January 10, 2002, p. 14.

[12] "Back to Blocker: Germany's U-Turn on the Takeover Law," *The Wall Street Journal Europe*, June 18, 2002.

[13] His report is available at: <http://www2.europarl.eu.int/omk/sipade2?PUBREF=-//EP//NONSGML+REPORT+A5-2000-0368+0+DOC+PDF+V0//EN&L=EN&LEVEL=3&NAV=S&LSTDOC=Y> (accessed September 17, 2002).

[14] "Frankfurt Voice," Deutsche Bank Research, February 7, 2002.

[15] John Lippert and Kevin O'Brien, "Volkswagen vs. Investors: Critics gripe that Chairman Ferdinand Piech has ignored growing shareholder complaints," *Bloomberg Markets*, <http://www.bloomberg.com/marketsmagazine/toc_0108.html> (accessed October, 2002).

[16] This process can be likened to the House Senate Conference in the United States.

[17] Letter to the editor from Arlene McCarthy, U.K. member of European Parliament, "MEPs Failed Takeover Bid," *The Guardian*, July 6, 2001.

[18] "EU's Bolkestein says takeover vote setback to capital market integration by 2005," *AFX News: World Reporter*, July 4, 2001.

[19] "Back to Blocker: Germany's U-Turn on the Takeover Law," *The Wall Street Journal Europe*, June 18, 2002.

[20] Lord McIntosh of Haringey stated "I am pleased to report that all parties from the United Kingdom, including Conservatives, Liberal Democrats, and Labour MEPs, supported the directive when it came before European Parliament. I believe we are all united on that front." Transcript of July 19, 2001 meeting of U.K. Parliament, <http://www.parliament.the-stationery-office.co.uk/pa/ld200102/ldhansrd/vo01709/text/10719-03> (accessed April 2001). In fact, several U.K. members of European Parliament voted against the directive.

[21] "Back to Blocker: Germany's U-Turn on the Takeover Law," *The Wall Street Journal Europe*, June 18, 2002.

[22] Michael Vercnocke, European Banking Federation, interview by casewriter, May 2002.

[23] Critics noted, however, that Parliament rejected proposals to clarify jurisdictional issues related to the directive, i.e., establishing who would be responsible for regulatory and supervisory authority for takeovers.

[24] Emilio Gabaglio, General Secretary, European Trade Union Confederation, "Letters to the Editor: Supporting the EU Takeover Directive," *Financial Times*, July 6, 2001.

[25] Roberta S. Karmel, "The Failed European Union Takeover Directive," *New York Law Journal*, August 16, 2001.

26 For a clear discussion of the difference between "strict neutrality" and "modified business judgment" in the context of the EU Takeover Directive, refer to Christian Kirchner and Richard W. Painter, "European Takeover Law – Towards a European Modified Business Judgment Rule for Takeover Law," *European Business Organization Law Review* 2, 2000, p. 357.

27 Christian Kirchner and Richard W. Painter, "European Takeover Law – Towards a European Modified Business Judgment Rule for Takeover Law," *European Business Organization Law Review* 2, 2000.

28 See FN 19 in Christina Kirchner and Richard W. Painter, "European Takeover Law – Towards a European Modified Business Judgment Rule for Takeover Law," *European Business Organization Law Review* 2, 2000, p. 357.

29 Quote of Jaap Winters, the chairman of the High Level Group of Company Law Experts producing the Issues Related to Takeover Bids report, in "Proposals for EU takeover law far-reaching, unlikely to win approval," *AFX News: FOCUS,* January 11, 2002.

30 Richard W. Painter, "Don't Disadvantage Europe: The European Parliament made the right call in rejecting the strict neutrality rule," *The Wall Street Journal,* Editorials and Opinions, July 19, 2001.

31 Refer to "Frankfurt Voice," Deutsche Bank Research, February 7, 2002, which includes discussion of the incidence of hostile versus friendly takeovers in Germany.

32 Tom Bergin, "EU merger law not seen halting political meddling," *Reuters News,* August 7, 2002.

33 These are also discussed in the Kirchner, Painter articles cited above.

34 Terminology used in: Andrew Osborn, "Golden Shares Lose Glitter," *The Guardian,* June 5, 2002, <http://www.guardian.co.uk/eu/story/0,7369,727525,00.html> (accessed September 18, 2002).

35 Paul Betts, "A Helping of Euro Fudge," *Financial Times,* June 5, 2002, p. 6.

36 "Report of the High Level Group of Company Law Experts on Issues Related to Takeover Bids," European Commission, January 10, 2002.

37 Klaus-Heiner Lehne, member of European Parliament, interview by casewriter, Strasbourg, May 2002.

38 "Report of the High Level Group of Company Law Experts on Issues Related to Takeover Bids," European Commission, January 10, 2002, p. 6.

39 "Report of the High Level Group of Company Law Experts on Issues Related to Takeover Bids," European Commission, January 10, 2002, p. 7.

40 "Proposals for EU takeover law far-reaching, unlikely to win approval," *AFX News: FOCUS,* January 11, 2002.

41 Paul Arlman, secretary general, Federation of European Securities Exchanges, interview by casewriter, Brussels, May 2002.

42 "Inside track, hostile developments – moves toward relaxing Europe's laws on hostile takeovers are likely to be gradual," *Financial Times,* May 1, 2002, p. 14.

43 Paul Betts, "A Helping of Euro Fudge," *Financial Times,* June 5, 2002, p. 6.

44 Andrew Osborn, "Golden Shares Lose Glitter," *The Guardian,* June 5, 2002, <http://www.guardian.co.uk/eu/story/0,7369,727525,00.html> (accessed September 19, 2002).

45 Klaus-Heiner Lehne, member of European Parliament, interview by casewriter, Strasbourg, May 2002.

46 The report is available at: <http://europa.eu.int/comm/internal_market/en/finances/general/lamfalussyen.pdf> (accessed September 20, 2002).

47 Frédéric de Brouwer, legal adviser, European Banking Federation, interview by casewriter, Brussels, May 2002.

48 Paul Arlman, secretary general, Federation of European Securities Exchanges, interview by casewriter, Brussels, May 2002.

49 "Back to Blocker: Germany's U-Turn on the Takeover Law," *The Wall Street Journal Europe,* June 18, 2002.

The Global Economy: Globalization Meets National Institutions

Spain: Straddling the Atlantic

A brutal civil war left Spain deeply divided and governed by a right-wing dictator who was not admired in Europe or America. Many young Spaniards emigrated to Latin America. Yet, during the post-World War II period Spain grew at a pace more similar to that of other European countries.

After Franco's death, Spain's transition to democracy focused the country on Europe. With full membership in the European Community came higher rates of GDP growth, a modernization of the educational system, aggressive social legislation, and a new sense of identity. But it also brought some of the highest unemployment rates seen since the Great Depression and a renewal of regional tensions, which in the case of the Basque Country produced the brutal terrorist organization ETA.

In response to these threats the appeal of center-right parties increased, leading to the election of Jose María Aznar in 1996. One of Aznar's most noteworthy policies was his alignment with U.S. President George Bush's antiterrorist policies, which included the invasion of Iraq. In spite of many successes of the Aznar administration, the socialists returned to power in April 2004, with a promise to withdraw from Iraq.

Supplementary Material

Europe: Data Supplement 1950–2003

Study Questions

1. How did Spain leave behind a history of civil war and internal divisions to become a prosperous European democracy?
2. What effects has Europe had on Spain? Any of them negative? Could these have been avoided? How?
3. What is your evaluation of Aznar's reforms? Are they sustainable? How do they fit with Spain's overall development strategy?
4. Are there any lessons that we can draw for other countries trying to join Europe (e.g., Turkey)?

RAFAEL DI TELLA

Spain: Straddling the Atlantic

On March 11, 2004, just three days before the country's general election was to be held, Spain fell victim to the worst terrorist attack in recent history in all of Western Europe.[1] Almost 200 people were killed and 1,500 injured in a series of coordinated bomb attacks at three commuter-rail stations during morning rush hour in the capital city of Madrid. Incumbent Prime Minster José María Aznar of the center-right Popular Party (PP), who had taken a hard line against Basque separatists over his eight-year rule, agreed with initial intelligence reports implicating Basque terrorist group ETA, whose earlier plans to disrupt the elections through a series of bombings in Madrid had been foiled several weeks before.

When convincing evidence against al-Qaeda became public knowledge, Spaniards felt cheated. They perceived the PP to have misrepresented the tragedy in order to win the election. An attack by ETA, responsible for almost 800 deaths over the previous 30 years, would help to strengthen public support for the PP with its tough stance against domestic terrorism. In contrast, terror linked to al-Qaeda might call into question the prudence of their decision to align Spain so closely with U.S. President George W. Bush in the 2003 U.S.-led war in Iraq. Unlike France and Germany, the PP had supported the war with 1,300 troops, despite polls that consistently showed 90% of Spaniards to be against Spain's involvement in the war.[2]

In the weeks before the March 14 general election, political analysts had expected what they considered a fairly apathetic electorate to reinstate the PP. But in the wake of the terrorist bombing, Spanish voters mobilized to ensure the victory of the Socialist Workers' Party (PSOE), led by José Luis Rodríguez Zapatero.[3]

Zapatero faced a number of challenging issues in addition to international terrorism. First, he sought to influence Spain's position within the European Union (EU). Spain, ruled under a dictatorship by General Francisco Franco from 1939 until his death in 1975, was a late-comer to the European Community (the predecessor to the EU), joining only in 1986. The country subsequently became a founding member of European Monetary Union (EMU), which took effect in 1999. In recent years, the country had begun to adopt a less accommodating position within the EU. For example, in late 2003, Spain under the PP, in an alliance with Poland, was blamed for contributing to the collapse of negotiations around creating an EU-wide constitution. Zapatero vowed to return Spain to its more mainstream role in the EU. (See **Exhibits 1–4** for basic economic statistics).[4]

Professor Rafael Di Tella and Research Associate Ingrid Vogel prepared this case. This case was developed from published sources. HBS cases are developed solely as the basis for class discussion. Cases are not intended to serve as endorsements, sources of primary data, or illustrations of effective or ineffective management.

Zapatero also faced a number of pressing domestic issues, including Spanish unemployment levels persistently higher than in the rest of Europe and Basque demands for further regional autonomy. The non-violent Basque Nationalist Party that dominated politics in the region was promoting plans for a referendum to move unilaterally toward *de facto* independence. If the referendum were to move forward and the result were positive, the Spanish government could be forced to defend its constitution ensuring an undivided state through dramatic measures.

Spain Profile and Background[5]

Spain is Western Europe's second-largest country, comprised of 17 administrative regions (in addition to two cities) with varying degrees of autonomy (see **Exhibit 5**). Tensions for further devolution remain in the Basque Country, Catalonia, and Galicia, where citizens consider themselves linguistically, ethnically, and historically distinct. After Queen Isabel "the Catholic" sponsored Christopher Columbus' voyage to the New World in 1492, Spain became one of Europe's wealthiest and most influential countries. However, Spain lost its position over subsequent centuries as continual controversies involving the monarchy hampered economic progress and distracted the country from taking part in the mercantile and industrial revolutions transforming the rest of "enlightened" Europe.

In 1931, Spain established the Second Republic. The government—initially dominated by Spain's Socialist Party (PSOE)—embarked on a major reform of the structure of Spanish society including breaking up Spain's large estates, dividing church and state, and adopting antimilitarist stance.[6] With their interests and their ideals threatened, the landed aristocracy, the church, the military, and the monarchists rallied against the government. A new fascist party, the Falange, gained political momentum, in part buoyed by the success of fascism in Italy and the rise of the Nazis in Germany.[7] In 1936, after the left-wing government outlawed the Falange, granted Catalonia political and administrative autonomy, and transferred right-wing military leaders (including Spain's future dictator Francisco Franco) to foreign posts, members of the army began plotting an overthrow.

In July 1936, the Spanish Civil War broke out between the Russian-supported Republicans—representing those in favor of the elected left-wing coalition government—and the Hitler- and Mussolini-supported Nationalists—representing the opposition. In 1939, the rebel Nationalists emerged victorious, and General Francisco Franco became Spain's Head of Government and State.[8] Historians estimated that more than 500,000 people were killed during the war, with atrocities having been committed by both sides.[9] Picasso's masterpiece "Guernica" illustrates one of them: the bombing of civilians in a little Basque village with the help of the German Luftwaffe. Another several hundred thousand were estimated to have been forced into exile. After Franco became Spain's new ruler, his regime continued to persecute political opponents. Estimates of the number of political prisoners killed in the five years after the war through overwork, starvation, or firing squads varied widely.[10] Official figures stood around 35,000, while many historians estimated figures closer to 200,000.

Spain under Franco

Franco merged the many disparate supporters of the Nationalist forces under the *Movimiento Nacional*, the only legal political group in Franco's Spain. The ideology of the fascist Falange division of the party dominated the government's social, political, and economic agendas in the early years.

Franco's social agenda was marked by censorship, restrictions on religious freedom, and reduced women's rights.[11] The regime's political agenda focused on creating an independent, highly centralized state through forbidding regional governmental bodies and restricting the use of vernacular languages. The Falangists outlawed labor unions and established vertical syndicates that both owners and employees were required to join. They also set up the *Instituto Nacional de Industria* (INI) to ensure state control of vital sectors of the economy and instituted heavy government regulation, including controls on prices, wages, imports, and supply allocations.

The Falangist tendency toward insularity was reinforced after the conclusion of World War II. Spain had remained neutral but had actively supported Germany with troops on the Eastern Front. The international community hoped to depose Western Europe's remaining dictator through a strategy of ostracism.[a] Around the world, Spain's diplomatic ties were cut. In 1946, the newly created United Nations (UN) recommended a trade boycott of Spain and, six months later, the Marshall Plan excluded Spain from plans for aid for the rebuilding effort in Europe. Real income per capita in Spain fell to 19th century levels. As Spain entered the *"años de hambre"* (years of hunger), the country relied on loans from Argentina's President General Juan Perón.

By the late 1940s, it was clear that efforts to weaken Franco through isolation were failing. Instead, the Cold War pitting the Communist world against the West raised Spain's standing as an important ally. In the early 1950s, recognizing the strategic significance of the Iberian Peninsula as well as Franco's anti-communist credentials, the United States provided Spain with an aid package and helped repeal the UN blockade in exchange for military bases. In 1955, Spain's membership application to the UN was approved. The European Community (EC), however, continued to reject appeals for association from the non-democratic country.

As Spain's external opportunities broadened, the Falangist economists in charge continued to maintain their isolationist economic strategy, refusing to open Spain's economy to foreign trade and investment. This strategy was blamed for the ensuing foreign-exchange account deficit, inflation approaching double digits, and falling real wages. With the country close to bankruptcy and growing signs of unrest among students and workers, Franco finally recognized the need for change.[12]

Economic Miracle and the Seeds of Discontent

In 1957, Franco appointed a group of neoliberal technocrats to replace his Falangist economic advisors. The group was dominated by men from wealthy backgrounds with successful business or academic careers who were also members of the Roman Catholic elite lay organization Opus Dei. The overriding objective of Opus Dei was the retention of Catholic values in everyday life. Members believed that resolving Spain's economic problems and improving its standard of living would help delay demands for the restoration of democracy and therefore bolster Franco's regime, under which the Catholic Church enjoyed significant influence.[13] In 1959, the group unveiled its Stabilization Plan, which had the objectives of addressing Spain's immediate inflationary problems with necessary fiscal and monetary measures while supporting longer-term growth through opening the economy to foreign trade and investment. The government complemented the plan with the introduction of financial incentives for Spaniards to seek work abroad and measures to encourage tourism such as abolishing visa requirements for Western European vacationers. Spain joined the IMF, World Bank, and OECD, but was still denied full access to the EC.[14]

---

[a] Portugal also was ruled under a military dictatorship (by Antonio Oliveira Salazar who became incapacitated in 1968).

Although real incomes dropped and unemployment rose dramatically in response to contractionary measures, the country was successful achieving its longer-term goal of growth supported by economic liberalization. Between 1961 and 1973, Spain's GDP increased 7% per year—faster than any economy in the non-communist world except Japan's. By 1964, per capita GDP surpassed $500, the UN threshold for defining developing nations at the time.[15] (See **Exhibit 6** for comparisons of GDP per capita in Spain with other countries.) By 1973, Spain became the world's ninth industrial power and, a few years later, GDP per capita reached 81% of the EC average (see **Exhibit 7**).[16] The imports needed to support Spain's industrialization were funded through tourism, foreign investment, and the remittances of more than 1 million Spanish workers abroad.

By the early 1970s, Spain's economic boom started to show signs of slowing. Tourism declined and Spanish workers abroad began to lose their jobs as growth in the rest of Europe faltered. Foreign investment likewise fell. The OPEC oil price increases in 1973 and 1974 delivered the definitive blow to Spain's economy, which depended on imported oil for two-thirds of its energy production. In 1974 with the cost of living up 17%, Spain joined the worldwide recession.[17]

Labor agitation and student protest heightened amidst the return of economic hardship and anticipation of aging Franco's impending demise. Many industrialists, eager to improve business through membership in the EC, joined the growing movement in favor of regime change. A new generation of leadership in the Catholic Church also began to work toward democracy. In 1973, the Church officially spoke against its decision to have taken sides in the Civil War.[18] The same year, in the most dramatic display against the future of Franco's regime, Basque separatist group *Euskadi Ta Askatasuna* (Basque Homeland and Liberty Group, ETA) assassinated Franco's carefully chosen successor as Head of Government, Luis Carrero Blanco—considered a formidable, hard-line Francoist who would maintain Franco's policies. Franco was forced to appoint Carlos Arias Navarro, thought to be an ineffective and uncharismatic politician, as prime minister in place of Carrero Blanco.[19]

Transition to Democracy

On November 20, 1975, in the depths of the worldwide recession and growing civil discontent, Franco died. Although seeds of democracy had been planted in the years preceding his death, there was still overwhelming concern that hard-line Francoists would prevent the emergence of a democratic Spain. Historians—recognizing that a dictatorial regime had never before been successfully transformed into a full democracy without civil war, revolutionary overthrow, or defeat by a foreign power[20]—summarized the pessimism surrounding Spain's future:

> Of the many prophesies circulating on that chilly November morning, one of the gloomiest yet most possible was that the government would sooner or later be overwhelmed by an outburst of popular frustration. At that point, the armed forces—which had much to loose and little to gain from the introduction of democracy—would step in to 'restore order'…From then on…Spain would settle in to a pattern well known to the Latin American nations (and which was in fact set in Spain during the last century)—phases of limited reform alternating with outbursts of savage repression.[21]

The public was particularly skeptical of Franco's appointed successor as Head of State.[22] Prince Juan Carlos, son of Spain's exiled King Juan de Borbón, had been groomed as Franco's heir since the age of 10. He attended Spain's three military academies and had performed various internships in the administration. After his official appointment in 1969 as future king, Juan Carlos gave a public speech swearing loyalty to the principles of Franco's regime. Indeed, his first act as King was to confirm the continuation of Arias as prime minister.[23]

In July 1976, unable to appease either the Francoists or the liberal opposition, Arias confirmed his reputation as ineffective. Juan Carlos asked him to resign and replaced him with Adolfo Suárez Gonzalez, who had served under Franco as secretary general of the *Movimiento Nacional*. Pessimism increased. The general sentiment was summarized by the later notorious newspaper headline: "What a Mistake! What an Immense Mistake!"[24]

Unknown to most observers, Juan Carlos' choice of Suárez as prime minister was the result of months of careful planning. During Franco's last months, Juan Carlos had secretly met with a number of politicians and officials for their views on how Spain could best be transformed into a democracy. Suárez had presented a detailed and realistic appraisal and seemed to Juan Carlos to have the personal appeal and knowledge necessary to achieve change.[25]

Initiating Change – The Moncloa Pacts

Suárez moved fast, initiating a *ruptura pactada* (negotiated break) under which the authoritarian regime would transform itself by legal means through its own institutions (there was insufficient support for calls from Spain's Communist Party (PCE) for a radical rupture immediately dismantling Franco's regime).[26] In September 1976, Suárez announced the Law for Political Reform bill that would introduce universal suffrage and a two-chamber Parliament as well as establish the framework for elections. Members of Spain's governing council, the *Cortes*, were encouraged to vote in favor of the bill in several ways. The proceedings were to be televised, with members recording their votes individually. Members were warned that their votes would impact the composition of committees as well as how the future administration would treat pensions and untaxed accounts.[27] In November, the *Cortes*, voted in favor of the bill, thereby dissolving itself. In a referendum several weeks later, with an electoral turnout of 78%, 94% of those voting approved the transition to democracy.

In March 1977, Franco's worker syndicates were replaced by independent trade unions and the right to strike was restored. In April, the *Movimiento Nacional* was disbanded and an election date of June 15 was set to form Spain's new Parliament.

Political parties began to organize in preparation for the elections. The PSOE, which had been established in 1879 and had been operating in secrecy during Franco's regime, became legalized in February. Suárez faced a bigger challenge in deciding how to treat Spain's Communist Party. Before his swearing in, Suárez had promised to maintain the ban on the PCE to avoid possible reaction from the armed forces. But after his appointment, Suárez realized that by not legalizing the party he risked questions about the legitimacy of his government.[28] In April, Suárez legalized the PCE in return for the party's promise to accept Spain's reform program and institutions, including the monarchy.[29] Juan Carlos used his influence with the military to help avert any possible coup attempt.[30]

The results of the election demonstrated the moderation of the electorate. Spain's extreme parties—the PCE on the left and the neo-Francoist *Alianza Popular* (AP) on the right—obtained only 9.4% and 8.2% of the vote, respectively. The *Union de Centro Democrático* (UCD), a diverse moderately right-wing coalition led by Suárez, emerged with 34.5% of the vote. The PSOE won 29.4% of the vote, while Basque and Catalán regional parties accounted for much of the balance (see **Exhibit 8**).[31]

The new government's most important task was drafting a constitution. In August, a Constitutional Committee was established representing all major national parties as well as the more influential regional parties. Suárez paved the way for successful constitutional negotiations by first working toward a series of agreements among adversaries. The first and most important of these was the "Moncloa Pacts," named after the prime minister's official residence where leaders of Spain's major political parties met and agreed to share the political costs of reform. The Moncloa Pacts, signed in October 1977, pledged continued reform of political institutions in exchange for support of an austerity program necessary to update Spain's economy and address its deepening economic crisis. The government promised to initiate social reform (such as increasing unemployment benefits), work toward the creation of new jobs, democratize the education system, and overhaul Spain's regressive taxation system. In exchange, the parties on the left promised to accept more restrictive monetary and expenditure policies and a ceiling on wage increases, as well as to work with labor unions to gain their acceptance of the measures and to reduce strike activity.[32]

The development of the new constitution continued this trend of accommodation. The first set of trade-offs related to the monarchy. The right wanted a short constitution institutionalizing the monarchy and specifying few rights. The left agreed to a monarchy, but only with strictly limited powers. The result was a parliamentary monarchy guaranteeing its citizens equality before the law and a full range of individual liberties. The next set of trade-offs related to the economy. The left agreed to the right's demands for a "free-market economy," but only in exchange for the institutionalization of government intervention when appropriate. The Catholic Church proved another delicate topic. While the right wanted to maintain the strong link between the Catholic Church and the state, the left insisted on religious freedom and no special role for the Church. In the end, the left agreed to allow mention of the Catholic Church in the text of the constitution (in the context of cooperating with other denominations) as well as the retention of some Catholic values in Spanish law, such as prohibitions against divorce and abortion. Compromise was also forged on the regional issue. The Basque Country and Catalonia sought special recognition along the lines granted by the Republicans during the Second Republic. The right, the military, and other regions were strongly opposed. In the end, the constitution agreed to a general decentralization, but stressed the indivisibility of the country. The constitution also specified the role of the military, charging it with defense of the constitution and with the independence and territorial integrity of Spain.[33]

The result was a lengthy and, as some historians argued, sometimes vague and contradictory constitution—among the most liberal in Western Europe.[34] It was approved by Parliament in October 1978 and by the public in a referendum two months later.

Democracy Tested

In March 1979, new national elections were held. Both the UCD and the PSOE increased their influence slightly, winning 168 and 121 seats of 350 in the lower house, respectively. Although the PSOE had abandoned the term "Marxism" from its platform in preparation for the election, it was thought that many voters still feared that a PSOE victory would incite a military coup.

No longer united by a singular goal of transition to democracy and under pressure from a second round of oil price hikes, the various factions within the UCD coalition began to diverge. Taking advantage of the governmental disarray, Basque terrorism intensified. Discontent with Suárez's leadership grew, and in January 1981, he resigned as prime minister.

In the period before his successor was sworn in, the fragility of Spain's new democracy was dramatically highlighted. On February 23, a group of military leaders, dissatisfied with the government's inability to suppress terrorism and still angered by the earlier decision to legalize the PCE, attempted a coup.[35] Hoping for support from King Juan Carlos, they stormed parliament with 300 troops and held at gunpoint most of Spain's notable politicians. After the King made his resistance to the coup clear, many of the military leaders backed down and the coup ultimately failed. Subsequently, millions of Spaniards took to the streets to demonstrate in favor of democracy.

With the UCD in disarray, the Socialists (PSOE), under the leadership of Felipe González Marquez, won the October 1982 elections, garnering 202 of 350 seats in the lower house. Most historians consider the transfer of power that occurred from the UCD to the PSOE without bloodshed or military intervention to be the defining milestone for the completion of the transition to democracy in Spain.[36] But fear of possible future coups remained. PSOE officials, claiming they were "frightened of reviving the brutal passions of the civil war," chose not to honor the wishes of relatives of those who had disappeared under Franco's rule to exhume mass graves expected to contain 30,000 bodies. In fact, the victims of Franco's oppression had not yet been acknowledged, compensated, properly buried, or honored in any way. Historians later noted: "Spain's transition to democracy was carried out leaving aside the internationally recognized duty of all states to investigate serious and systematic violations of fundamental rights."[37] It was also claimed that senior PSOE officials, determined to prove that social order could be maintained under a democracy without military intervention, surreptitiously set up the Antiterrorist Liberation Groups (GAL), responsible for the deaths of 28 suspected ETA members.[38] It was argued that, ironically, GAL had been a major force in ensuring the survival of ETA, with state-sponsored terrorism providing strong propaganda for supporters of the radical nationalist terrorism movement.[39]

Democratic Spain

For Spain, EU membership never centered on money. The bargaining did: we open our market to your modern industries; you must help us to develop so that we can compete. But the aim was political. Membership was an aid, a guarantee, but above all a symbol, of European normality; freedom, democracy, social progress.[40]

The PSOE inherited a weak economy. Inflation stood at 16%, economic growth was negative, foreign exchange reserves were depleted, and the current account was severely out of balance. Rather than embark on a traditional socialist program of redistribution of income, increased state intervention in the economy, or nationalization of industry, the government adopted a pragmatic, orthodox approach to economic reform—both to improve Spain's immediate economic situation and to improve the outlook for EC accession. With a solid majority in both houses of Parliament, the PSOE was able to implement unpopular, market-based austerity measures such as scaling down inefficient state enterprises; bringing the social security system closer to balance through reduced benefits and increased payroll contributions; liberalizing foreign investment in Spain and Spanish investment abroad; raising the prices of electricity, gasoline, and public transportation; and increasing labor market flexibility through, for example, limiting wage growth.[41] Prime Minister González noted: "It is true, as the unions contend, that workers' salaries have risen more slowly than the owners' income. That is the way it is all over Europe, and that is the way it should be in the early stages of recovery. Only this way can profits be invested in productive sectors of the economy."[42] Even so, Spain's labor costs increased by 2.6% per year between 1973 and 1985, compared with 1.7% in the rest of Europe.[43]

The PSOE's goal to integrate Spain with the rest of Europe followed years of complicated and protracted negotiations. After multiple failed attempts to join the EC as a full member under Franco's authoritarian rule, Spain had applied to the EC as a democracy in 1977. But the country faced new obstacles. On the one hand, the UCD government had been reluctant to introduce a value-added tax as well as to curtail subsidies and end protectionism—steps considered necessary for countries in preparation for accession.[44] On the other hand, EC member countries feared the impact the free movement of labor from Spain, with its high levels of unemployment, would have on their own employment levels. Furthermore, France and Italy wanted to protect their growers from competitive pressure from Spain's agricultural sector and wanted to avoid providing free access to EC waters to Spain's fishing fleet, which was larger than the entire EC fleet combined.[45] More generally, the level of economic development in Spain was much lower than in EC member countries, which implied that Spain would be a net drawer from the already strained EC budget.

However, the EC's many misgivings were somewhat tempered by the PSOE's ambitious economic agenda that was modernizing its economic and social structure. Finally, in the first half of 1985, outstanding EC budgetary issues were resolved and negotiations with Spain on agricultural and fishery issues completed. Spain was set to join the EC on January 1, 1986.[46]

An economic boom followed the PSOE's EC convergence program, aided in part by a continuing fall in oil prices, increased tourism, and foreign investment inflows. Inflation was reduced from 15% in 1982 to 4.5% in 1987. The budget deficit fell from its peak of 6.5% of GDP in 1985 to 3.1% in 1987. GDP growth recovered dramatically, from a negative rate in 1982 to 3.3% in 1986 and 5.5% in 1987. Industrial output rose 3.1% in 1986 and 5.2% in 1987.[47]

In spite of these improvements, unemployment grew from 4.6% in 1975 to 21% in 1987 while wages increased more slowly than inflation or corporate profits. Strike activity increased sharply with widespread participation, including teachers, doctors, miners, and factory workers. In 1988, after the expiration of the latest social pact between the government and unions[48] and the failure to negotiate a new pact, Spain held its first nationwide general strike since the 1930s. González offered several concessions to end the strike, including raising pensions and increasing unemployment insurance, marking the beginning of a cycle of expansion of social spending and of major developments in social services.

For Spaniards, "becoming European" implied adopting EC discourse on fighting poverty and social exclusion, promoting gender equality, reconciling family and work life, and introducing active employment policies.[49] With only 18% of Spain's GDP used for social protection spending in 1980, compared with an average 24% in the EC, Spain had a long way to go to achieve a welfare state (see **Exhibits 9a–d**). The PSOE introduced a national healthcare system which came to cover 99.9% of the population and expanded unemployment protection. (See **Annex** for a full timeline of social reform.) Over time, powers over social services were universalized and devolved to Spain's autonomous regions and principalities, many of which kept offices in Brussels and Strasbourg, home of EC decision making.

Spain continued its trend toward international integration. Several months after becoming an EC member, Spain held a referendum on its participation in the North Atlantic Treaty Organization (NATO).[50] Despite strong anti-NATO sentiment stemming in large part from a general distrust of the United States for its support during Franco's dictatorship, the public voted to keep Spain in the alliance. In 1992, Spain's profile was enhanced as it hosted the Olympic Games in Barcelona and the World Exhibit in Sevilla.

The Problem of Unemployment

Spain was forced to devalue its currency in November 1992 and May 1993 within the European Exchange Rate Mechanism after a speculative attack on a number of member currencies, including the peseta. The more competitive peseta, however, did not prevent the country from entering a deep recession worse than in the rest of Europe.

In 1994, Spanish unemployment peaked at over 24%, much higher than the European average of 10%. Possible explanations for Spain's persistent and high unemployment abounded. In the early years, unemployment was linked to return migration. Subsequently, observers blamed Spain's changing demographics: the decline in agricultural employment, the high birth rate in the 1950s and 1960s, and the increase of women entering the work force.[51] Data indicated that Spain devoted far fewer resources to public employment services, such as retraining to address labor skill mismatches, than other European countries.[52] Other observers blamed high unemployment benefits: In 1994, 82% of those unemployed received benefits, compared with 39% in 1983. Still other observers pointed out that unemployment levels varied widely across Spain's regions (34.5% in Andalucia in 1994 compared with 16% in Aragón) while workers refused to relocate. Another argument referred to Spain's large black market, which some observers argued could account for anywhere between 3 and 15 percentage points of the unemployment rate.

Another popular explanation was Spain's rigid labor markets. It was argued that wage rates did not moderate in response to changes in unemployment or productivity, and that companies were forced to reduce staff as wage growth outpaced inflation and productivity growth.[53] However, some studies showed Spanish productivity increases to be in excess of labor cost increases between 1973 and 1995.[54] It was also argued that Spain's overly protective employment legislation led to inefficiencies. Multiple studies identified Spain as having among the highest firing costs and most cumbersome dismissal procedures in the late 1980s and mid-1990s.[55] For example, in Spain, regular workers dismissed for "objective" reasons (economic redundancy or inability to adapt to new practices after three months training) had 30 days notice and up to one year severance pay. In the case of "unjustified" dismissal, an employee could claim up to 42 months pay or could be hired with back pay. Labor courts decided whether individual dismissals were "fair" or "unfair," and collective dismissals needed administrative approval by the Labor Ministry and the agreement of worker representatives.[56] Because of the involvement of administrative and labor courts, dismissals entailed costly bureaucratic procedures. Most firms chose to avoid those costs by settling dismissal cases out of court at amounts above the legal levels.[57]

Business reinforced the view that rigid labor markets were primarily to blame to Spain's high unemployment. In a 1994 interview, the president and managing director of GM's Spanish division remarked: "Spain is the most expensive place to get rid of people. That's why even though GM will gear up production in the next few years, it doesn't have major plans for hiring. Instead, it plans to push productivity to the limit before taking on new people who might be expensive to fire later."[58]

Facing continued high unemployment, the PSOE was forced to introduce labor market reform. A first wave of reform had been implemented in 1984, when the increased use of temporary contracts was allowed. Temporary contracts came to account for 90% of new hires, reaching a 30% employment share by the mid-1990s.[59] In 1994, the PSOE increased restrictions on the use of fixed-term contracts while easing employment protection legislation for regular contracts, through, for example, making procedural requirements for dismissals less time-consuming. According to an OECD study, between 1990 and 1998, Spain's employment protection legislation for regular contracts fell from second strictest among 20 countries to eighth strictest. For fixed-term contracts, Spain increased from sixth to second strictest.[60]

Further European Integration

The negative impact of high unemployment and the recession on the PSOE's credibility was compounded by a corruption scandal. The moderately right-wing *Partido Popular* (PP) led by José María Aznar López won the general election of 1996, bringing an uninterrupted period of 13 years of socialist rule to an end. Aznar set Spain a formidable challenge in achieving further European integration. Spain's economic performance in 1997 would be measured against Maastricht convergence criteria to determine whether the country would be allowed to join European Monetary Union (EMU) as a founding member. The criteria required Spain to reduce its budget deficit from 6.4% to below 3% of GDP, its public debt from 65.7% to 60% of GDP (or be approaching the 60% level at a "satisfactory" pace), inflation from 4% to less than 1.5% over the average rate of the EU's three best inflation performers, average long-term interest rates to less than 2% over the average interest rates in the same three best inflation performers, and to have maintained a fairly stable currency over the prior two years.[61] Italy had suggested to Spain that the countries work together politically to force a delay on EMU or more flexibility in the criteria. Despite the fact that many observers considered Spain an outside candidate for EMU entry, Aznar rejected the suggestion, stating: "I am absolutely confident that Spain will be part of EMU from the beginning, and that it will stay inside afterwards."[62]

Spain met the criteria (see **Exhibit 10**) and was admitted, along with ten other countries, as a founding member of EMU.[a] On January 1, 1999, Spain adopted the euro as its currency and deferred monetary policy to the European Central Bank (ECB). Skeptics wondered how Spain, with its high unemployment rates, would tolerate sacrificing monetary independence.

Integration with Europe had economic benefits for Spain, including lower interest rates, receipt of structural and cohesion funds, and increased trade. Structural funds were designed to assist regions within EU countries with GDP per capita less than 75% of the EU average in promoting development (such as through improving physical infrastructure), adjusting to industrial decline, and improving labor force productivity. Cohesion funds, established in 1993 after the Maastricht treaty was ratified, were designed to compensate countries with GDP per capita less than 90% of the EU average for their efforts to comply with the criteria for participation in the European single currency.[63] Together, these funds accounted for approximately one-third of the EU budget. Between 1989 and 1993, structural funds accounted for 0.7% of Spain's GDP. Between 1994 and 1999, the contribution of structural and cohesion funds to Spain's GDP was 1.5%.[64] In 2000, Spain anticipated a net receipt in 2001 of $8 billion from the EU budget (see **Exhibit 11**).[65] The impact of these funds on convergence was mixed: In 2001, Spain's per capita GDP reached 87% of the EU average—but disparities across Spain's regions persisted (see **Exhibit 12**) and seemed to be widening.[66] The funds gave EU decision makers an avenue to influence the development and character of Spain's welfare state, which still lagged behind the rest of Europe.[67]

European integration also brought about significantly increased trade (see **Exhibit 13**). Spain entered an intense period of trade reform upon joining the EU as tariff structures were brought into line with EU requirements. The sum of imports and exports rose from 27% of GDP in 1970 to 62% in 2000.[68] Fears of a more advanced European industrial sector decimating Spain's less competitive industrial sector did not materialize. In fact, Spain's exports of intermediate goods (excluding food and energy) rose dramatically.

The Return of the Left

In the wake of its success with EMU and with the PSOE in disarray, the PP won the 2000 nation elections with an outright majority. The economy continued to do well with GDP growth averaging 4% per year. In terms of real growth of exports and output, the country was outperforming the rest of

---

[a] The others were Austria, Belgium, Finland, France, Germany, Ireland, Italy, Luxembourg, the Netherlands, and Portugal.

the euro area.[69] Yet, despite Spain's economic success, Aznar was criticized for losing touch with the Spanish people and for becoming "increasingly imperious" in his second term.[70]

First, in 2002, the PP rejected requests for parliamentary funding to help recover and identify victims of Franco's regime buried in mass graves. A PP spokesman remarked: "This issue is closed for us. We don't have to look at the past."[71] This rejection followed Aznar's refusal in 1998 to support a Spanish judge's decision to seek the extradition to Spain from the United Kingdom of former Chilean dictator Augusto Pinochet for genocide, terrorism, and torture of Spanish nationals.[72] Second, unlike France and Germany, Aznar supported the 2003 U.S.-led war in Iraq, despite opposition from over 90% of the Spanish people. The PP government further aligned Spain away from France and Germany in negotiations surrounding the EU Constitution in December 2003. France and Germany sought to modify voting rights in the European Council of Ministers to prepare the EU for pending enlargement.[a] Instead of relying on the number of votes granted in the 2000 Treaty of Nice (under which Spain and Poland each had 27 votes compared with 29 for Germany, Britain, France, and Italy), France and Germany proposed requiring a simple majority of countries representing at least 60% of the total EU population.[73] Spain and Poland argued that gave too much power to the most populous countries. No agreement could be met, and negotiations collapsed.[74]

Aznar also faced the challenge of increased Basque terrorist activity. In response, he adopted a hard line against terrorism. In 1997, all 23 members of Herri Batasuna, the political arm of ETA (with two seats in the lower house), were given seven years in prison for collaboration with the armed group. ETA, which had been created in 1959 after a group of student activists became dissatisfied with the inability to advance the "Basque cause" through legal methods under Franco's regime, demanded full independence for the Basque Country (they were not satisfied with the partial autonomy granted under Spain's 1978 Constitution) and union with Navarre. In 1999, the organization, thought to have 20 principal organizers with several hundred supporters, vowed to intensify attacks on Spanish targets.[75] Terrorism continued even after the non-violent Basque Nationalist Party (PNV) formally proposed a quasi-independent status for the Basque Country which created a framework of joint sovereignty with Spain. The September 2002 proposal would allow the Basque Country to secede fully from Spain at a later stage. The PNV planned to hold a regional referendum on the proposal in May 2005.

Despite Aznar's controversial decisions in his second term, polls in the months prior to the 2004 election showed the PP, led by Manuel Rajoy (Aznar had promised to act as prime minister for no more than two terms), as the favorite to win the election over the PSOE. However, this all turned around with the unprecedented terrorist attack of March 11, 2004. Voters, frustrated by the PP's handling of information surrounding the attacks, mobilized to ensure regime change.

The PSOE, led by José Luis Rodríguez Zapatero, won the national election with 43% of the vote. After eight years, the party returned to power vowing to carry through campaign promises to withdraw Spanish troops from Iraq—resulting in strained relations with the United States. He aimed to further realign Spain with France and Germany by working toward ratification of the EU Constitution. It remained to be seen how he would address domestic issues such as Basque terrorism, the impending PNV referendum on Basque independence, continued high unemployment, and the further evolution of Spain's welfare state.

---

[a] The European Council of Ministers functions as the EU's main decision-making body. It passes European laws and approves the EU budget, both in coordination with the European Parliament.

Annex   Timeline of Major Social Policy Developments in Spain (1978–2001)

1978: Democratic Constitution. Old Institute for Social Provision turned into 4 National Institutes for Social Security, Health, Social Services, and Unemployment. Unions and employer's associations gain representatives in their management committees.

1981: Law on Social Integration of the Disabled (LISMI) is passed. Powers on health care transferred to Catalonia. Ministry of Health becomes independent from Ministry of Labor. Divorce legalized. Female participation in labor force increases.

1983: National Institute for Women created as a consultative body.

1984: Decree on Basic Health Structures (reform of primary care). Powers on health care transferred to Andalusia. First wave of labor market flexibility reforms.

1985: Restrictive reform on pensions. Minimum contributory period increased from 10 to 15 years. Number salaried years used to calculate initial amount increased from 2 to 8.

1986: General Health Law: creation of National Health System. Powers on health care transferred to Basque Country and Valencia.

1988: Unions frustrated and go on general strike. Pensions indexed to past inflation. Expansion of unemployment protection. Ministry of Social Services created.

1989: Decree of universalization of health care coverage. By 1993, social services decentralized to all regions, and health care comes to be financed out of state revenues. Regions decide to establish minimum wage.

1990: Reform of family allowances. Program becomes universal and targeted to low-income families. Powers on health care transferred to Galicia and Navarre.

1991: Parliamentary Commission propose introduction of cost-containment measures in healthcare (not adopted). Non-contributory pensions for elderly and disabled established to universalize coverage of pension systems.

1992: Restrictive reform of unemployment subsidies: reduced time span of benefit and its amount and increased required contributory period.

1993: List of pharmaceuticals not financed publicly established. Second wave of labor market flexibility reforms start to be implemented. Part-time jobs fostered. Private non-profit employment agencies allowed.

1994: Powers on health care transferred to Canary Islands. Pensions indexed to expected inflation.

1995: Decree on health care services. A positive and negative list of services provided by the NHS is established. Positive list includes new services. Reform of maternity benefits. Replacement rate increased to 100% of previous salaries. Parental leave becomes more generous.

1996: Decree on autonomy of management of healthcare instits. Decree on flexibility of pharmaceutical services (opening hours and establishment of new community pharmacies). Social pact on reform of pension system.

1997: Number of salaried years to calculate pension increased from 8 to 15. Agreement on territorial financing of healthcare. Social pact on labor market policies decrease redundancy payments and create new conditions to foster creation of permanent jobs. Improvement in lowest widower and orphan pensions and more generous treatment of short-term careers.

1998: Fiscal reform lowers taxes. Exemptions for families increased. Concept of "large family" widened. Improvement in social protection of part-time workers.

1999: Health care becomes financed totally out of taxes. Introduction of managed competition. Cost-control measures on pharmaceuticals. Part-time and fixed-term jobs granted same social security rights as full-time contracts. New partial retirement scheme introduced. Law on conciliation of work and family passed. Social expenditure increased in budget for 2000, devoted to improvement of lowest pensions and activation policies.

2000: Moderate increase in family subsidies. Improvement in health protection for immigrants (a few months later, restricted). Fiscal deductions and maximum yearly amounts of private pension plans increased.

2001: Devolution of health care powers to remaining 10 autonomous regions planned by 2002. Reform of legislation on social reinsertion and reeducation. Social actors unable to reach agreement on labor market reform. Family Support Plan (housing subsidies and fiscal exemptions proportional to family size) approved. Social pact on pensions signed between government, employer's association, and main union–redundancy payments lowered.

Source: Adapted from Ana Guillén, Santiago Alvarez, Pedro Adão e Silva, "Redesigning the Spanish and Portuguese Welfare States: The Impact of Accession into the European Union," Harvard University Center for European Studies Working Paper No. 85, presented November 2–3, 2001.

Exhibit 1a Spain General Economic Indicators

	1975	1976	1980	1985	1990	1995	2000	2001	2002	2003
% change over prior year										
Real GDP Growth	na	3.3	2.2	2.3	3.8	2.8	4.1	2.8	1.8	2.4
Real Per Capita GDP Growth	na	2.4	1.7	1.2	3.6	1.3	3.4	2.4	1.3	1.8
Consumer Price Inflation	16.9	17.6	15.5	8.8	6.7	4.7	3.4	3.6	3.1	3.0
% GDP										
Current Account/GDP	-3.6	-4.1	-2.5	1.6	-3.5	0.1	-3.4	-2.8	-2.4	-2.8
Public Debt/GDP	11.6	12.5	19.4	37.5	44.8	65.5	72.4	68.4	65.9	62.4
Fiscal Surplus (+) or Fiscal Deficit (-)/GDP	0.1	-0.2	-2.4	-6.2	-4.1	-7.3	-0.6	-0.1	0.0	-0.3
units as shown										
Unemployment (% total)	na	na	11.1	21.0	16.0	22.7	13.9	10.5	11.4	11.3
Employment in Agriculture (% total)	na	na	19.3	18.3	11.5	8.9	6.6	6.4	na	na
Employment in Industry (% total)	na	na	36.0	31.7	33.8	30.2	31.3	31.6	na	na
Employment in Services (% total)	na	na	44.6	49.7	54.7	60.9	62.0	61.9	na	na
Rural Population (% total)	30.4	29.8	27.2	25.8	24.6	23.5	22.4	22.2	21.9	na
Stock of foreign reserves and gold (bns USD)	na	na	na	14.9	56.0	38.7	35.6	34.2	40.3	26.8
Exchange rate (period average; pesetas per USD to 1998, euros per USD after)	57.4	66.9	71.7	170.0	101.9	124.7	1.09	1.12	1.06	0.89

Sources: Compiled from World Bank, World Development Indicators Database, September 2004; EIU Country Data, September 2004; IMF, *International Financial Statistics CD-ROM*, February 2004; and European Monetary Institute Convergence Report, March 1998.

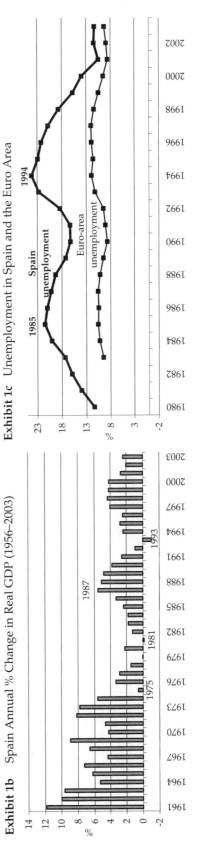

Exhibit 1b Spain Annual % Change in Real GDP (1956–2003)

Source: Compiled from World Bank, World Development Indicators Online, October 2004.

Exhibit 1c Unemployment in Spain and the Euro Area

Source: Compiled from EIU Country Data, September 2004.

Exhibit 2 Spain National Income Accounts (*bns current pesetas 1955–1998; bns euros 1999–2003*)

as % GDP	1955	1960	1965	1970	1975	1980	1985	1990	1995	1997	1999	2001	2003
GDP (bns current)	376	621	1,399	2,630	6,039	15,168	28,201	50,145	72,842	82,218	565	653	741
Private Consumption	72%	69%	76%	65%	65%	66%	64%	62%	60%	59%	59%	58%	58%
Government Spending	9%	9%	7%	9%	10%	13%	15%	16%	18%	18%	17%	18%	18%
Fixed Investment	20%	19%	22%	26%	26%	22%	19%	24%	22%	22%	24%	25%	25%
Changes in Inventories	1%	0%	3%	1%	2%	1%	0%	1%	0%	0%	0%	0%	0%
Exports	5%	11%	6%	13%	14%	16%	23%	17%	23%	27%	28%	30%	28%
Imports	7%	8%	14%	14%	17%	18%	21%	20%	23%	26%	29%	32%	30%
Total	100%	100%	100%	100%	100%	100%	100%	100%	100%	100%	100%	100%	100%
GDP at Constant 1986 Prices	8,278	10,099	15,147	20,512	26,572	29,027	31,322	39,018	41,707	44,224	663	710	741

Source: Compiled from IMF, *International Financial Statistics CD-ROM*, February 2004.

Exhibit 3 Spain Balance of Payments (*bns current U.S. dollars*)

	1975	1980	1985	1990	1995	2000	2001	2002
Current Account	**-3.89**	**-5.58**	**2.79**	**-18.01**	**0.79**	**-19.24**	**-16.40**	**-15.94**
Trade Balance	-7.39	-11.73	-4.76	-29.16	-18.42	-34.82	-32.54	-33.10
Exports	7.82	20.55	24.85	55.66	93.44	116.21	117.94	125.80
Imports	-15.21	-32.27	-29.61	-84.82	-111.85	-151.03	-150.47	-158.89
Net Services	2.90	5.86	8.17	11.88	18.70	22.26	24.21	24.87
Net Income	-0.17	-1.36	-1.69	-3.53	-4.13	-8.25	-9.75	-9.89
Net Transfers	0.77	1.65	1.06	2.80	4.64	1.58	1.67	2.18
Capital Account	**0.38**	**0.41**	**0.07**	**1.45**	**6.00**	**4.79**	**4.97**	**7.07**
Financial Account	**2.64**	**5.25**	**-3.22**	**22.97**	**-7.95**	**16.94**	**16.60**	**18.84**
Net Direct Investment	0.51	1.18	1.72	10.46	2.09	-16.93	-5.13	2.62
Net Portfolio Flows	-0.09	0.00	0.23	9.02	21.16	-1.17	-17.80	6.63
Net Other	2.21	4.07	-5.17	3.48	-31.20	35.05	39.53	9.59
Public	-0.01	0.13	-0.19	0.32	1.04	-7.33	15.10	7.15
Private	2.22	3.94	-4.97	3.16	-32.25	42.38	24.43	2.44
Net Errors and Omissions	**0.05**	**-0.87**	**-1.91**	**0.78**	**-5.26**	**-5.38**	**-6.51**	**-6.28**
Change in Official Reserves	**-0.83**	**-0.80**	**-2.28**	**7.19**	**-6.41**	**-2.88**	**-1.34**	**3.69**

Source: Compiled from IMF, *International Financial Statistics CD-ROM*, February 2004.

Exhibit 4   Spain Government Finances *(bns current pesetas 1965–1998; bns current euros 1999–2003)*

	1965	1970	1975	1980	1985	1990	1995	2000	2001	2002
Revenue	156	327	758	2,179	4,440	10,203	14,077	119	125	105
Expenditure	157	326	766	2,553	5,926	11,375	17,242	121	128	116
Lending Minus Repayment	25	20	103	182	234	102	442	0	2	2
Deficit (-) or Surplus (+)	-27	-20	-111	-556	-1,720	-1,274	-3,606	-2	-5	-13
Total Financing	27	19	111	556	1,719	1,274	3,606	2	5	13
Total Debt by Residence	210	366	700	2,317	11,391	19,491	38,678	309	307	310
Domestic	196	344	666	2,183	10,676	18,269	29,952	188	178	173
Foreign	14	22	33	134	715	1,221	8,726	121	130	137

Source: Compiled from IMF, *International Financial Statistics CD-ROM*, February 2004.

Exhibit 5   Map of Spain

Source: Adapted from University of Texas Perry Castaneda map collection online, <http://www.lib.utexas.edu/maps/spain.html> (accessed September 2004).

Exhibit 6   Comparison of Country GDP per Capita with Spain over Time

Country GDP/capita over Spain GDP/capita (current U.S.$)	1954	1960	1966	1972	1978	1984	1990	1996	2002
Europe									
France	**3.6**	**3.5**	**2.6**	**2.4**	**2.2**	**2.2**	**1.6**	**1.7**	**1.5**
Germany	**1.8**	**2.9**	**1.9**	**2.2**	**2.2**	**2.0**	**1.6**	**1.9**	**1.5**
Italy	**1.5**	**2.0**	**1.6**	**1.6**	**1.3**	**1.7**	**1.5**	**1.4**	**1.3**
United Kingdom	**3.3**	**3.6**	**2.3**	**1.8**	**1.4**	**1.8**	**1.3**	**1.3**	**1.7**
Latin America									
Argentina	**3.3**	na	**1.46**	0.86	0.51	0.62	0.33	0.51	0.18
Bolivia	na	0.51	0.35	0.23	0.12	0.11	0.06	0.06	0.06
Brazil	na	0.54	0.36	0.36	0.42	0.37	0.24	0.31	0.16
Chile	na	**1.43**	0.92	0.72	0.34	0.38	0.18	0.31	0.26
Costa Rica	**1.1**	**1.12**	0.50	0.41	0.39	0.33	0.14	0.22	0.27
Mexico	0.8	0.91	0.63	0.51	0.38	0.56	0.24	0.23	0.40
Uruguay	na	1.25	0.64	0.47	0.41	0.38	0.23	0.41	0.23
Venezuela	**2.5**	**3.02**	**1.28**	0.88	0.82	0.84	0.19	0.20	0.24
Others									
Japan	0.8	**1.24**	**1.24**	**1.77**	**2.07**	**2.51**	**1.88**	**2.41**	**1.97**
United States	**7.6**	**7.42**	**4.58**	**3.58**	**2.46**	**3.87**	**1.76**	**1.86**	**2.26**

Sources: Calculated based on data from World Bank, World Development Indicators Database, September 2004 (for 1960–2002); and IMF, *International Financial Statistics CD-ROM*, February 2004 (for 1954 and Germany 1954–1966).

Exhibit 7   Spain per Capita Income as % EU Average

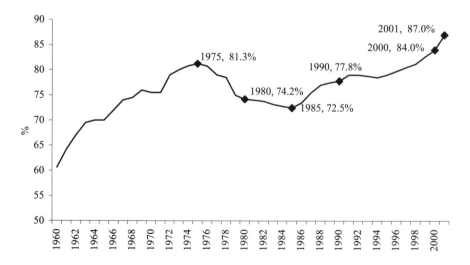

Sources: Adapted from Royo and Manuel, 2001, p. 22 (for 1960–2000); and Aninat, 2001 (for 2001).

Exhibit 8   Spain Election Results (1977–2004)

	6/15/77		3/1/79		10/28/82		6/22/86		10/29/89		6/6/93		3/3/96		3/12/00		3/14/04	
Voter turnout (%)	78.8		68.3		80.0		70.5		69.7		76.4		77.4		68.7		75.7	
	%vote	seats	%vote	seats	%vote	seats	%vote	seats	%vote	seats	%vote	seats	%vote	seats	%vote	seats	%vote	seats
Unión de Centro Democrático (UCD)	**34.5**	**165**	**35.0**	**168**	**6.8**	**11**	-	-	-	-	-	-	-	-	-	-	-	-
Centro Democrático y Social (CDS)					2.9	2	9.2	19	7.9	14	-	-	-	-	-	-	-	-
Partido Soc. Obrero Español (PSOE)	**29.4**	**118**	**30.5**	**121**	**48.3**	**202**	**44.1**	**184**	**39.6**	**175**	**38.8**	**159**	**37.6**	**141**	**34.2**	**125**	**42.6**	**164**
Partido Comunista de España (PCE)	9.4	20	10.8	23	4.0	4	-	-	-	-	-	-	-	-	-	-	-	-
Izquierda Unida (IU) (w/EUiA in 2000)							4.6	7	9.1	17	9.6	18	10.5	21	5.4	8	5.1	5
Alianza Popular (AP)	8.2	16			-	-	-	-	-	-	-	-	-	-	-	-	-	-
Coalición Democrática (CD)			6.0	9	-	-	-	-	-	-	-	-	-	-	-	-	-	-
Alianza Pop.-Part.Demócr.Pop.(AP-PDP)							26.0	105	-	-	-	-	-	-	-	-	-	-
Coalición Popular (CP)					26.5	107	-	-	-	-	-	-	-	-	-	-	-	-
Partido Popular (PP)	-	-	-	-	-	-	-	-	**25.8**	**107**	**34.8**	**141**	**38.8**	**156**	**44.5**	**183**	**37.7**	**148**
Regional Parties																		
Catalonia: CiU / UC-DCC / EC-FED / PDC / ERC / IC-V	4.6	14	3.4	9	4.4	13	5.4	18	5.4	18	5.7	18	5.3	17	5.5	17	5.7	18
Basque Country: HB / PNV / EAJ / EE / EA	1.9	9	3.0	11	3.4	11	3.2	13	3.5	13	2.7	8	2.5	8	1.9	8	1.9	8
Galicia: CG / GNG	-	-	-	-	-	-	0.4	1	0.2	-	0.5	-	0.9	2	1.3	3	0.8	2
Andalucía: PA / PSA	-	-	1.8	5	0.4	-	0.5	-	1.0	2	0.4	-	0.5	-	0.9	1	0.7	-
Valencia: UV	-	-	-	-	-	-	0.3	1	0.7	2	0.5	1	0.4	1	0.2	-	-	-
Aragon: CAIC / PAR / ChA	0.2	1	0.2	1	-	-	0.4	1	0.4	1	0.6	1	0.2	-	0.5	1	0.4	1
Canary Islands: AIC / UPC / CC	-	-	0.3	1	0.2	-	0.3	1	0.3	1	0.9	4	0.9	4	1.1	4	0.9	3
Navarra: UPN / Na-Bai	-	-	0.2	1	-	-	-	-	-	-	-	-	-	-	-	-	0.2	1
Others	11.8	7	8.8	1	3.1	-	5.6	-	6.1	-	5.5	-	2.4	-	4.5	-	4.0	-
Total	**100**	**350**	**100**	**350**	**100**	**350**	**100**	**350**	**100**	**350**	**100**	**350**	**100**	**350**	**100**	**350**	**100**	**350**

Source: Compiled from <http://electionresources.org/es/congress.php?election=2004&province=> (accessed August 19, 2004).

Note: Includes all parties that had at least 5% of the vote in any national election, plus all regional parties with at least 0.2% of the vote.

Exhibit 9   Social Protection in Spain

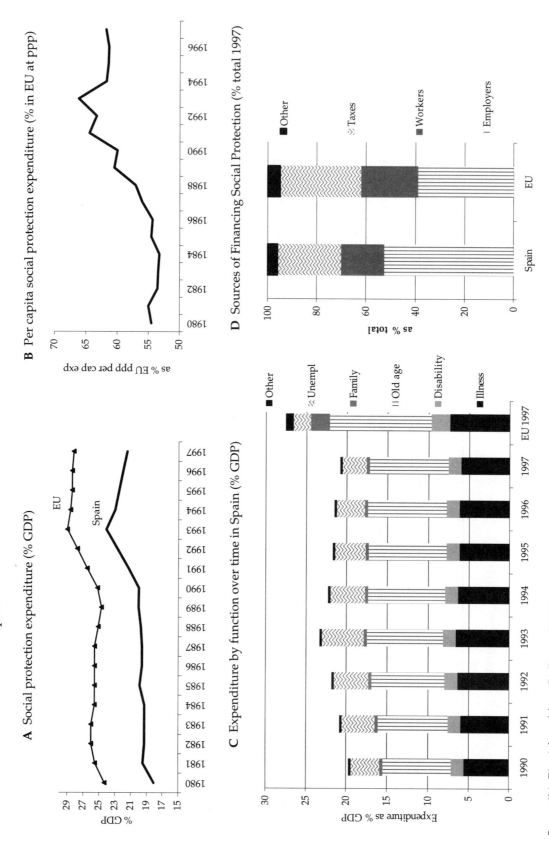

A Social protection expenditure (% GDP)

B Per capita social protection expenditure (% in EU at ppp)

C Expenditure by function over time in Spain (% GDP)

D Sources of Financing Social Protection (% total 1997)

Source (9A–D):   Adapted from Guillen, et al, 2001.

Exhibit 10   Spain Compliance with EMU Convergence Criteria

	a) Inflation		b) Long-term Interest Rates		c) Government Deficit (-) (% GDP)		d) Government Debt (% GDP)	
	Spain	Ref. Value[a]	Spain	Ref. Value[a]	Spain	Ref. Value	Spain	Ref. Value
1990	6.7	*3.6*	14.7	*10.8*	-4.1	*-3*	44.8	*60*
1991	5.9	*4.3*	12.4	*10.5*	-4.2	*-3*	46.4	*60*
1992	5.9	*3.8*	12.2	*10.9*	-3.8	*-3*	48.0	*60*
1993	4.6	*3.3*	10.2	*8.9*	-6.9	*-3*	60.0	*60*
1994	4.7	*3.3*	9.7	*9.6*	-6.3	*-3*	62.6	*60*
1995	4.7	*3.2*	11	*9.4*	-7.3	*-3*	65.5	*60*
1996	3.6	2.5	8.7	9.1	-4.6	-3	70.1	60
1997	1.8	2.7	6.4	7.8	-2.6	-3	68.8	60

e) Exchange Rate Stability (Mar 1, 1996 – Feb 27, 1998)

Maximum deviations of the Spanish peseta from central rates against the following other currencies in the European Exchange Rate Mechanism:[b]

%	Upward	Downward
Belgian franc	2.0	(0.2)
Danish krone	3.5	0.2
Deutsche Mark	2.4	(0.1)
French franc	3.3	0.2
Irish pound	5.1	(9.7)
Italian lira	1.4	(0.9)
Dutch guilder	1.7	(0.5)
Austrian schilling	2.4	(0.1)
Portuguese escudo	2.4	(1.7)
Finnish markka	0.2	(2.1)

Sources: Compiled from European Monetary Institute, Convergence Report, March 1998; and EIU Country Data, September 2004.

Notes: [a] Values for 1990–1995 are non-official approximations derived by casewriter using EIU Country Data.

[b] Until 1993, Spain (as well as Portugal) was allowed to deviate ± 6% from its central rate against other currencies, while other currencies were allowed to deviate ± 2.25%. After the European currency crisis in 1993, all bands were increased to ± 15%. Daily data; deviations from Finish markka refer to Ocotber 14, 1996 and on; deviations against Italian lira refer to November 25, 1996 and on. Spain had been a member in European Exchange Rate Mechanism (ERM) since June 19, 1989.

Exhibit 11   Spain Position within the European Union Budget

		1993 ecus	1994 ecus	1995 ecus	1996 ecus	1997 ecus	1998 ecus	1999 euros	2000 euros	2001 euros	2002 euros	2003 euros
Spain's total contributions to EU budget	billions	5.2	4.7	3.6	4.5	5.4	5.8	6.2	6.4	6.6	6.6	7.4
as % total contributions by EU members		*8.1%*	*7.4%*	*5.4%*	*6.4%*	*7.1%*	*7.0%*	*7.6%*	*7.3%*	*8.2%*	*8.4%*	*8.9%*
Structural funds dedicated to Spain		3.7	3.2	6.1	6.3	6.4	6.8	7.4	5.1	7.1	8.8	9.0
as % total structural funds dispersed		*19.4%*	*20.6%*	*31.9%*	*25.8%*	*24.5%*	*24.1%*	*27.8%*	*18.5%*	*31.8%*	*38.0%*	*31.7%*
Spain's total receipts from EU budget		8.2	7.9	10.9	10.7	11.3	12.4	13.0	10.9	13.6	15.2	15.9
as % total funds dispersed		*12.8%*	*13.1%*	*16.3%*	*13.9%*	*14.1%*	*15.4%*	*16.1%*	*13.1%*	*17.1%*	*17.9%*	*17.5%*
Net flow of EU funds to Spain		3.0	3.2	7.3	6.2	5.9	6.6	6.8	4.5	7.0	8.6	8.5

Source: Compiled from European Commission Budgets 1999 and 2003.

Exhibit 12   Spain's Regional Disparities

	Index of avg wages and salary (2002)	Index of avg expenditure per person (2003)	% households with computer	% households with internet access
Average Spain	**1.00**	**1.00**	**43**	**25**
Andalucia	0.91	0.89	38	21
Aragon	0.99	1.04	43	26
Asturias	0.98	0.97	42	21
Belars	0.89	1.15	44	30
Canarias	0.84	0.90	48	29
Cantabria	0.91	1.09	39	23
Castilla y Leon	0.84	0.94	39	21
Castilla-La Mancha	0.93	0.82	35	15
Cataluna	1.07	1.08	52	33
Comunidad Valencia	0.89	0.97	40	23
Extremadura	0.81	0.78	32	14
Galicia	0.87	0.93	35	17
Madrid	1.20	1.19	51	32
Murcia	0.81	0.90	42	22
Navarra	1.10	1.22	46	27
Pais Vasco	1.16	1.13	46	32
Rioja	0.91	1.03	40	21
Ceuta / Melilla	na	na	44/41	27/32

Source: Compiled from Spain National Statistics Institute, *2004 Yearbook.*

Exhibit 13   Spain Exports and Imports as % GDP

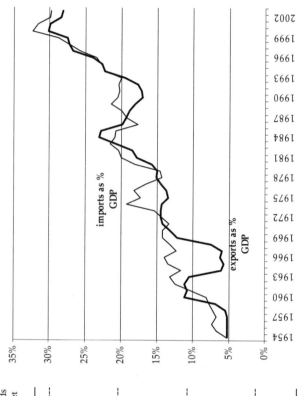

Source: Compiled from IMF, *International Financial Statistics CD-ROM,* February 2004.

Endnotes

1 "Terror Before an Election: Terrorist Bombs in Spain," *The Economist,* March 13, 2004.

2 "From A to Z," *The Economist,* June 26, 2004.

3 Leslie Crawford, "Baptism of Ire," *Financial Times,* July 14, 2004.

4 Barry R. Weingast, "Constructing Self-Enforcing Democracy in Spain," in eds. Irwin L. Morris,   Joe A. Oppenheimer, and Karol Edwar Soltan, *Politics from Anarchy to Democracy: Rational Choice in Political Science* (Stanford University Press, April 2004).

5 This section is largely drawn from John Hooper, *The Spaniards: A Portrait of the New Spain* (Viking: Middlesex, England, 1986), pp. 204–210; and Economic Intelligence Unit, *Country Report Spain 2004/2005,* 2004.

6 Juan J. Linz and Miguel Jerez with Susana Corzo, "Ministers and Regimes in Spain: From First to Second Restoration, 1874–2001," Minda de Gunzburg Center for European Studies at Harvard University, Working Paper Series, Number 101, available at <http://www.ces.fas.harvard.edu/publications/> (accessed October 4, 2004).

7 A coalition between the conservative Catholic party CEDA and the more central Radical Party won the 1933 election and overturned many of the PSOE's earlier reforms. In early 1936 with elections imminent, a left-wing coalition called the Popular Front formed, which included, among others, liberal republicans, the PSOE, and the Communist Party (PCE).

8 Franco officially became Head of State in 1947 pending choice of a king.

9 Renwick McLean, "A Demand for Light on Spain's Dark Past: State Urged to Help ID Franco's Victims," *The New York Times,* June 16, 2004.

10 192,000 from Gwynne Dyer, "Out of War, Dictatorship, the Miracle of Modern Spain," *The San Diego Union-Tribune,* March 26, 1989. 200,000 from David Sharrock, "Spain Confronts its Civil War Memories," *The Times,* September 17, 2002. Lower numbers are much more common in many other sources.

11 Hooper, 1986, p. 194.

12 Hooper, 1986, p.25.

13 Hooper, 1986.

14 In 1970, Spain entered into a limited preferential trade agreement with the EC.

15 Hooper, 1986.

16 Miguel Sebastian, "Spain in the EU: Fifteen Years May not Be Enough," Minda de Gunzburg Center for European Studies at Harvard University, Working Paper Series, Number 96, 2001, available at < http://www.ces.fas.harvard.edu/publications/> (accessed October 4, 2004).

17 Hooper, 1986.

18 Weingast, 2004, p. 27.

19 Hooper, 1986, p. 37.

20 Complete meaning pluralistic and parliamentary. From Federal Research Division of the Library of Congress, "Spain," available at <http://countrystudies.us/spain/> (accessed October 4, 2004).

21 Hooper, 1986, p. 36.

22 Hooper, 1986, p. 36.

23 Library of Congress, "Spain."

24 Hooper, 1986.

25 Hooper, 1986.

26 Juan J. Linz, "The Transition from Authoritarian Regimes to Democratic Political Systems and the Problems of Consolidation of Political Democracy," International Forum, 151–121 Seoul: International Cultural Society of Korea, 1985, available at <http://www.cepchile.cl/dms/lang_1/doc_1333.html> (accessed August 16, 2004).

27 Hooper, 1986.

28 Weingast, 2004.

29 Weingast, 2004, pp. 32–33.

30 Library of Congress, "Spain."

31 Manuel José, "Election Resources on the Internet," available at
    <http://electionresources.org/es/index_en.html> (accessed October 4, 2004).

32 Weingast, 2004, p. 36 and Library of Congress, "Spain."

33 Weingast, 2004, p. 37.

34 Hooper, 1986, p. 43.

35 Library of Congress, "Spain."

36 Weingast, 2004; Hooper, 1986; and Library of Congress, "Spain."

37 Giles Tremlett, "Spain poised to seek the graves of Franco's disappeared in Madrid," *The Guardian*, August
    23, 2002.

38 GAL was disbanded in 1986 after France agreed to stricter extradition guidelines for suspected Basque
    terrorists. For more on this, see International Policy Institute for Counter Terrorism materials, including
    website available at <http://www.ict.org.il/,> (accessed October 4, 2004).

39 Paddy Woodworth, *Dirty War, Clean Hands -- ETA, the GAL and Spanish Democracy* (Cork University Press,
    2001).

40 "Spain Survey: The Wide World," *The Economist*, November 25, 2000.

41 Library of Congress, "Spain."

42 Donald Share, *Dilemmas of Social Democracy: The Spanish Socialist Workers Party in the 1980s* (New York;
    Westport, CT; London: Greenwood Press, 1989), p. 101.

43 Juan J. Dolado and Juan F. Jimeno, "The Causes of Spanish Unemployment: A Structural VAR Approach,"
    European Economic Review 41, 1997.

44 Article 99 of the Treaty of Rome called for the harmonization of indirect taxation to ensure "the proper
    functioning of the internal market." In 1967, two directives required the adoption of VAT by all member
    states.

45 Sebastián Royo and Paul Christopher Manuel, "Reconsidering Economic Relations and Political Citizenship
    in the New Iberia of the New Europe: Some Lessons from the Fifteenth Anniversary of the Accession of
    Portugal and Spain to the European Union," Minda de Gunzburg Center for European Studies at Harvard
    University, Working Paper Series, Number 94, 2001, available at
    <http://www.ces.fas.harvard.edu/publications/> (accessed October 4, 2004).

46 Royo and Manuel, 2001.

47 Library of Congress, "Spain"; fiscal numbers from Ángel Luis Gómez Jiménez and José María Roldán Alegre,
    "Analysis of Fiscal Policy in Spain: A Macroeconomic Perspective (1988–1994)," Banco de España, Servicio de
    Estudios, Estudios Económicos, Number 53, 1996, available at
    <http://www.bde.es/informes/be/sazul/azul53e.pdf> (accessed October 4, 2004).

48 The Economic and Social Agreement was signed on October 9, 1984 by the Government, the UGT workers'
    confederation and the CEOE and CEPYME employers' organizations to establish the outlines of economic
    and social policy for 1985 and 1986. It also included agreed commitments on pay increases, productivity and
    absenteeism, the structure and duration of agreements, and procedures for settling industrial disputes. See
    <http://www.eurofound.eu.int/emire/SPAIN/ECONOMICANDSOCIALAGREEMENTOF1984-ES.html>
    (accessed October 4, 2004).

49 Ana Guillen, Santiago Alvarez and Pedro Adlao e Silva, "Redesigning the Spanish and Portuguese Welfare
    States: The Impact of Accession into the European Union," Minda de Gunzburg Center for European Studies
    at Harvard University, Working Paper Series, Number 85, 2001, available at
    <http://www.ces.fas.harvard.edu/publications/> (accessed October 4, 2004).

50 NATO is the alliance of countries in North America and Europe founded in 1949 to safeguard the securities and freedoms of member countries through political and military means.

51 Refer to Jeffrey Franks, "Explaining Unemployment in Spain: Structural Change, Cyclical Fluctuations, and Labor Market Rigidities," IMF Working Paper No. 94/102, September 1, 1994.

52 Reference to an OECD study which shows that Spain had 713 unemployed people per public employment staff member in 1988, compared with 86 in Germany, 53 in the United Kingdom, and 14 in Sweden is made in Juan J. Dolado and Juan F. Jimeno, "The Causes of Spanish Unemployment: A Structural VAR Approach," European Economic Review 41, 1997.

53 For more information on unemployment related to birth rate, return migration, and high real labor costs, see European Union organization European Foundation for the Improvement of Living and Working Conditions materials, including <http://www.eurofound.eu.int/emire/SPAIN/UNEMPLOYMENT-ES.html> (accessed October 4, 2004).

54 Dolado and Jimeno, "The Causes of Spanish Unemployment" 1997, shows an average yearly increase of 1.9% for labor costs and 2.6% for productivity over the period.

55 Refer to OECD, *Employment Outlook,* 1999.

56 OECD, *Employment Outlook,* 1999.

57 Dolado and Jimeno, "The Causes of Spanish Unemployment" 1997.

58 Audrey Choi and Carlta Vitzthum, "GM's Success in Figueruelas Shows How Spain May Make Itself a Better Home for Auto Makers," *The Wall Street Journal,* April 29. 1994.

59 Gilles Saint-Paul, "Flexibility vs. Rigidity: Does Spain Have the Worst of Both Worlds," IZA Discussion Paper Series DP No. 144, April 2000.

60 See Giuseppe Nicoletti, Stefano Scarpetta and Olivier Boylaud, "Summary Indicators of Product Market Regulation with an Extension to Employment Protection Legislation," OECD Economics Department Working Papers No. 226, April 2000.

61 "Spain: Get a Move On," *The Economist,* September 28, 1996.

62 "The Maastricht Conundrum," *The Economist,* December 14, 1996.

63 For more about the impact of the funds on inequality, see Pere Gomis-Porqueras and Enrique Garcilazo, "EU Structural and Cohesion Funds in Spain and Portugal: Is Regional and National Inequality Increasing?" University of Miami Salvador da Madariaga Institute, Working Paper Series Vol. 3 No. 11, December 2003, available at <http://www.miami.edu/eucenter/gomis.pdf> (accessed October 4, 2004).

64 Sebastian, "Spain in the EU," 2001.

65 "Spain Survey: The Wide World," *The Economist,* November 25, 2000.

66 Gomis-Porqueras and Garcilazo, "EU Structural and Cohesion Funds in Spain and Portugal," 2003.

67 Guillen, 2001, p. 25.

68 Eduardo Aninat, Deputy Managing Director, International Monetary Fund, "Reflections on Globalization, Spain, and the IMF," speech given at General Meeting of ELKARGI in San Sebastian, Spain, June 29, 2001, available at <http://www.imf.org/external/np/speeches/2001/062901.htm> (accessed October 4, 2004).

69 Aninat, 2001.

70 Economist Intelligence Unite, Spain Country Report, 2004.

71 CNN Madrid Bureau Chief Al Goodman, "Spanish Poetry Icon to be Exhumed," *CNN,* September 4, 2003, available at <http://www.cnn.com/2003/WORLD/europe/09/04/spain.lorca/> (accessed October 4, 2004).

72 Hugh O'Shaughnessy, "Secret UK Deal Freed Pinochet," *The Observer,* January 7, 2001, available at <http://observer.guardian.co.uk/international/story/0,6903,418797,00.html> (accessed October 4, 2004).

73 "Poland Threatens Veto in EU Row," *BBC News,* December 11, 2003, available at <http://news.bbc.co.uk/2/hi/europe/3308917.stm> (accessed October 4, 2004).

74 "Poland Doubtful over EU Constitution," AFP, May 25, 2004, available at
    <http://www.eubusiness.com/afp/040525084418.t3dfha9u> (accessed October 4, 2004).

75 See International Policy Institute for Counter Terrorism website at <http://www.ict.org.il/> (accessed
    October 4, 2004).

Brazil 2003: Inflation Targeting and Debt Dynamics

In October 2002, Brazilians elected a left-wing president, Luís Inácio Lula da Silva, for the first time in that country's history. As markets faltered in response, Lula sought to reaffirm his commitment to fiscal discipline, a floating exchange rate, and inflation targeting. By August 2003, however, his attempt to change market sentiment was coming under threat as the country faced a looming recession. Skeptics began to worry that the new government would be forced to resort to printing money to meet its campaign promises. Furthermore, after Argentina's massive default on its public debt at the end of 2001, observers were questioning the sustainability of Brazil's debt situation. Lula was under intense pressure to deliver results immediately and implement measures that would help spur the economy.

Study Questions

1. Would you buy a Brazilian bond July 2002? How would you make your decision? What other information would you like to have?
2. How about July 2003—would you buy a Brazilian bond? What has changed?
3. What is inflation targeting? What are the alternatives?
4. Is inflation targeting a good strategy for emerging markets such as Brazil?

LAURA ALFARO
RAFAEL DI TELLA

Brazil 2003: Inflation Targeting and Debt Dynamics

The PT [Workers' Party] follows socialist ideology, and socialism is the final objective of the party.[1]

—Lula, 1989

I am going to call up the bankers and say: "Look, I recognize our debt, but, between paying interest to you guys and filling the bellies of the people, I am going to stick with the Brazilian people. As long as there are children dying of hunger in Brazil, I will not have the means to pay down the debt."[2]

—Lula, 1998

Brazil has changed. The union movement has changed. I have changed.[3]

—Lula, 2002

In October 2002, Brazilians elected a left-wing president, Luís Inácio "Lula" da Silva, for the first time in that country's history. Lula, who had emerged from humble origins to become a leader in the trade union movement and founder of the PT (*Partido dos Trabalhadores*, Workers' Party), was expected to herald a new era in Brazilian politics. In his 2002 presidential campaign, he promised to improve opportunities for the poor in one of the world's most unequal societies. Despite his radical past, during which he argued for socialism and the repudiation of Brazil's public debt, he promised to pursue social reform under the orthodox economic policy framework inherited from the administration of his centrist predecessor, President Fernando Henrique Cardoso.

But markets remained skeptical and worried that Lula had committed to Cardoso's framework of fiscal discipline, a floating exchange rate, and inflation targeting only to win the election. Amid growing uncertainty surrounding what radical changes the PT might in fact implement once in office, the stock market fell, the country risk premium increased, prices crept higher, and the currency weakened dramatically in the last months of 2002. Brazil's central bank was forced to respond by raising interest rates to their highest levels in more than three years.

Upon taking office in January 2003, Lula attempted to change market sentiment, embarking on an aggressive plan to generate a large primary fiscal surplus that would help ensure debt repayment and promote macroeconomic stability. He also implemented a popular "Zero Hunger" program and began work toward important pension, tax, and bankruptcy reforms.

By mid-2003, however, his attempt to change market sentiment was coming under threat as the country faced a looming recession. Skeptics began to worry that the new PT government would be

Professors Laura Alfaro and Rafael Di Tella and Research Associate Ingrid Vogel prepared this case. Andrea Fernandez (MBA '04) provided some helpful assistance. This case was developed from published sources. HBS cases are developed solely as the basis for class discussion. Cases are not intended to serve as endorsements, sources of primary data, or illustrations of effective or ineffective management.

forced to steer away from orthodox policies to meet its campaign promises. Furthermore, after Argentina's massive default on its public debt at the end of 2001, observers were questioning the sustainability of Brazil's debt situation. Lula was under intense pressure to deliver results immediately and implement measures that would help spur the economy.

Lula's vice president, José Alencar, pointed to the interest rate as one such measure. He argued that the high rates imposed by the Central Bank of Brazil under the inflation-targeting framework placed the country at a competitive disadvantage and stymied growth:

> Interest rates should be reduced in a more consistent way since we are now starting to experience deflation. When the government first took office, yes, there was a risk of inflation rekindling, but now the situation has changed. The country needs to return to a path of growth so that the current economic environment isn't further aggravated. We already have lost two decades, and this should not be allowed to happen again.[4]

Despite Lula's emphasizing his commitment to the autonomy of Brazil's central bank in setting the interest rate, critics were demanding a rate reduction at the bank's monthly meeting, which was due to take place on August 20. But the central bank had stated it would loosen monetary policy only gradually, as it feared that abrupt moves could bring back inflationary pressures in the short term and compromise sustainable growth in the medium term. It also needed to maintain its credibility as focused on fighting inflation.

In mid-August 2003, all eyes were on Brazil: Would the central bank reduce its benchmark interest rate (the Selic)[a] amid signs that inflation had been contained around 15% and the exchange rate stabilized? And by enough to ease Brazil's growing debt burden? Or would it remain cautious and seek to reaffirm its independence by choosing to maintain the rate at a high 24.5%?

Brazil Before Inflation Targeting[5]

As the world's eighth-largest economy in terms of purchasing-power parity and fifth-largest country in terms of both population and land area, Brazil was considered to have enormous potential for becoming an important world economic power. But the country seemed to have problems in fulfilling that potential. For almost 40 years, Brazil had followed an import-substitution strategy characterized by massive government investment targeting key industries and protection against international competition through high tariff and nontariff barriers. For decades, the strategy appeared to be successful: Brazil grew by 7% per year between 1950 and 1980 (from 1964 under repressive military rule) and created a large and diversified industrial sector. It also, however, left the country with the largest external debt in the developing world and a tendency for high inflation. When oil prices shot up in 1979 and interest rates rose in response, the Brazilian economy crumbled. In 1981, gross domestic product (GDP) fell by more than 4% while fiscal deficits increased, inflation skyrocketed, and public and private investment fell. Along with most of Latin America, Brazil defaulted on its debt in 1982.[b] In 1985, the military regime finally lost its hold.

With the return of democracy, hopes for Brazil rose anew. But a series of stabilization programs that aimed to solve the problem of triple-digit inflation all failed, and the 1980s became known as the "lost decade." Finally, in 1993, Finance Minister Fernando Henrique Cardoso announced the Real

---

[a] The Selic interest rate is the interest rate for overnight interbank loans collateralized by government bonds registered with and traded on the *Sistema Especial de Liquidação e Custódia*.

[b] Although Brazil did not repudiate its debt, it stopped paying interest.

Plan. This new stabilization plan introduced the *real* as Brazil's currency, which was tied to the dollar through a crawling peg. Inflation dropped dramatically, from 50% per month in mid-1994 to approximately 2% per month by the end of 1994. On the basis of this success, Cardoso easily won the presidential elections in 1994.

Upon taking office, Cardoso introduced a development model based on opening Brazil's closed economy through privatization, deregulation, trade liberalization, and encouragement of foreign direct investment (FDI). A period of price stability and economic growth followed but was accompanied by underlying problems. The appreciation of the real led to increasing current account deficits. Furthermore, nonfinancial primary fiscal deficits persisted from 1995–1999 after failed attempts by the government to reform the tax system and introduce public spending reductions, particularly on wages and pensions. The external imbalance and fiscal deficits were partly financed by FDI, medium- and long-term debt in the international bond market, and substantial inflows of short-term portfolio capital attracted by high interest rates. As a result, Brazil's net-public-debt-to-GDP ratio increased from 30% at the start of 1995 to 42% at the start of 1999. (See **Exhibits 1–4** for basic macroeconomic data.)

Brazil had again become vulnerable to volatility in global capital markets. The Asian crisis in mid-1997 led to a first wave of speculative attacks against the real. In response, the central bank sharply increased interest rates. The Russian crisis in mid-1998 put further pressure on Brazil's crawling peg and led to a halt in capital flows to the country. The central bank was forced to raise rates even higher. In October 1998, Cardoso was reelected for a second term on the basis of promises to continue to defend the currency. Toward this end, he secured a $42 billion assistance package from the International Monetary Fund (IMF). In December 1998, however, the government failed to gain sufficient congressional support for IMF austerity measures, and investors began to lose confidence in the country. In early January 1999, full-scale capital flight ensued—with speculative capital fleeing the country at a rate of $200 million per day—after the state of Minais Gerais defaulted on debt payments. After a second state declared it would also default, capital flight peaked at $1 billion in one day, and Brazil could no longer defend its currency. On January 12, the central bank, hoping to implement a managed float, devalued the real by 8%. Three days later, the central bank was forced to float the currency fully.

In early March 1999, the real plummeted to 2.16 to the dollar, from 1.21 in early January (see **Exhibit 5**). Financial analysts were predicting deterioration of all macroeconomic fundamentals, including inflation's escalating to annual rates of 30% to 80% and negative GDP growth of –3% to –6%.[6] In response, in March 1999, Brazil's central bank announced that its goal was to bring inflation down to a single-digit annualized rate by the last quarter of 1999 (see **Exhibit 6**). To this end, it raised the basic short-term interest rate (the Selic) from 39% to 45% (see **Exhibit 7**). On July 1, the central bank formally adopted a new strategy: a full-fledged inflation-targeting framework behind a floating currency.

Inflation Targeting Worldwide

Inflation targeting was introduced in the 1990s—initially in industrial countries and later in emerging-market economies—with the objective of keeping inflation close to a long-run low level. During this period, there was a strengthening belief among economists and central bankers that low inflation helped to promote economic efficiency and growth in the long run.[7] New Zealand was first, in 1990, to formally introduce a clear and credible commitment to a specific inflation target. The country had a poor economic track record relative to other Organization for Economic Cooperation and Development (OECD) members, with a decade of inflation rates at the upper end of the OECD range (in excess of 10%) combined with growth rates at the bottom of the range. After a foreign exchange crisis forced New Zealand to break its peg to the U.S. dollar in 1985, the government asked the central bank to focus strictly on maintaining low inflation rather than a mix of objectives including low inflation, high employment, and growth. After five years, a formalized inflation-targeting framework was officially introduced.[8] Other countries followed with their own systems: Canada in 1991, the United Kingdom in 1992, Sweden in 1993, and Australia later in 1993. By 2003, 20 countries in total were classified as having adopted full-fledged inflation-targeting frameworks (see **Exhibit 11**),[9] while the central banks of more than 40 countries had the explicit aim of achieving low and stable inflation.

Alternatives to Inflation Targeting

Inflation targeting was only one of a number of monetary regimes on which central banks could base their policy decisions. Some economists argued that central banks should target the growth rate of nominal GDP. It was argued, though, that this approach suffered from weaknesses when compared to inflation targeting: price information was more frequently published, more timely, and more accurately reported than output information; inflation targeting was more capable of delivering short-term stability; the concept of inflation was more easily understood by the public than nominal GDP (which could be confused with real GDP); and a nominal GDP target would be subject to more political contention.[10]

Alternatively, some economists were in favor of a "just do it" approach of monetary policy without explicit targets. The United States appeared to have experienced success under a strategy of responding to signs of future inflation with "preemptive strikes," without any strict or announced inflation target.[11] U.S. monetary policy makers would officially deny that they targeted indicators other than inflation. However, critics cited the Federal Reserve Bank's announcement after the 1987 stock market crash that it would increase liquidity as evidence that it was using the stock market as a target.

More common than GDP targeting or a "just do it" approach were strategies aiming to control the evolution of the price level. Economists described that in doing so, central banks essentially had three options: the adoption of an exchange rate anchor, a monetary anchor, or an inflation-targeting framework.[12] With an exchange rate target, countries relied on a peg to a stable currency to control inflation. The target had the advantage of being simple to implement and monitor, and something over which the central bank had direct control. At the most extreme, countries could implement a currency board[a] or directly adopt the stable currency as its own, such as through dollarization. As such, monetary policy would be relinquished completely. Maintaining a fixed exchange rate constrained the central bank's ability to respond to shocks and (not relevant in the case of dollarization) was difficult under the growing and unstable cross-border movement of capital.[13]

Targeting a monetary aggregate became popular in the 1970s after most industrial countries adopted flexible exchange rate regimes. Under this approach, the central bank sought to control inflation by aiming for particular rates of monetary growth that could be expected to deliver desired rates of inflation. In contrast to exchange rate targeting, monetary targeting allowed central bankers to adjust monetary policy to domestic conditions. After continued failure to meet targets and persistent instability in the relationship between monetary growth and inflation, however, monetary targets began to be replaced by inflation targeting.[14]

---

[a] Under a currency board, a central bank had to convert currency on demand at a fixed exchange rate, and money supply was restricted to the level of hard-currency reserves. For more details, see "Argentina's Convertibility Plan," HBS Case No. 702-002.

Inflation Targeting Defined

Full-fledged inflation-targeting frameworks included a number of important components. First, countries made an explicit institutional commitment to meet a specified numerical inflation rate target or target range within a specified time frame. This became the primary goal of monetary policy, to which other goals were subordinated. Second, monetary-policy strategy was made transparent through communication with the public and the markets about the plans, objectives, and decisions of the monetary authorities. Third, countries publicly announced their targets on a regular basis. As such, the targets provided an anchor for private market expectations as well as for monetary authorities. Fourth, countries had institutional arrangements in place to ensure that the central bank would be held accountable for reaching specified targets. In New Zealand, for example, the finance minister retained the right to dismiss the central bank governor in the case of missed targets.[15]

Since inflation targeting required credibility in pursuit of inflation objectives, most countries granted operational independence to their central banks. Although in many cases the government was responsible for setting the target, the central bank was free to pursue the target independently.

Central banks had to develop models to predict the effects of given actions (e.g., changes to interest rates) on inflation. Inflation forecasts were assumed to have a *predictable* relationship with inflation; were *controllable* in that monetary authority instruments were capable of affecting projected inflation outcomes; and were a *lead indicator* of future inflation since they were explicitly forward looking.[16] An important feature of inflation targeting was that monetary authorities were required to consider inflation in subsequent periods in addition to in the immediate period. Monetary authorities could conceivably affect inflation in the immediate period through measures, such as appreciating the exchange rate, that were unsustainable. Given longer-term inflation targets, however, monetary authorities would be deterred from implementing them. This was particularly relevant given the long lags (up to two years in some cases) in the effect of monetary policy on the price level.[17]

For the most part, reviews of inflation targeting were positive. Many economists argued that countries adopting inflation targeting experienced low and stable inflation rates without inordinately sacrificing economic growth or destabilizing their economies.[18] Ben Bernanke, a governor of the U.S. Federal Reserve Board, stated: "Central banks that have switched to inflation targeting have generally been pleased with the results they have obtained. The strongest evidence on that score is that, thus far at least, none of the several dozen adopters of inflation targeting has abandoned the approach."[19] Other economists pointed out that the positive performance of countries adopting inflation targeting could be explained by external factors, such as an overall low inflationary international environment over the period.[20] These economists conceded, however, that inflation targeting appeared to do no harm and even possibly had other benefits, such as promoting more open and transparent policymaking. As Bernanke stated, inflation targeting made "the role of the Central Bank more consistent with the principles of a democratic society."[21]

Challenges in Emerging-Market Economies

Many economists noted that emerging-market economies faced special challenges in implementing inflation-targeting frameworks. Fundamental issues included a tendency toward fiscal indiscipline, high rates of dollarization, credibility problems, and vulnerability to external shocks.

Inflation targeting required fiscal discipline—a feature considered lacking in general in many emerging-market economies. If fiscal deficits were to become too large, countries might be forced to borrow heavily and erode existing debt through price increases.[22] Even just the possibility that such a scenario could occur in the future served to increase expected inflation in the present. Hence, in order to keep inflation at a long-run low level, it was a prerequisite that governments incorporated fiscal discipline into their primary objectives.[23]

A high degree of liability dollarization (with obligations of banks, corporations, and governments denominated in dollars while revenues were largely denominated in local currency) was also pointed out as a problem.[24] The exchange rate flexibility required by inflation targeting could cause financial instability by allowing large and sudden currency depreciations to increase the burden of dollar-denominated debt dramatically. Emerging-market economies could not, therefore, afford to ignore the exchange rate completely when conducting monetary policy. As such, however, those countries operating under an inflation-targeting framework ran the risk of transforming the exchange rate into the nominal anchor for monetary policy, even if only in the eyes of the public. This was especially true since in countries with poor histories of monetary stability, the exchange rate tended to be a focal point for inflationary expectations.[25]

Emerging-market economies were also seen to suffer from weak institutions and low credibility—in their financial systems as well as both fiscal and monetary policymaking. As elaborated by Brazil's former central bank governor, Arminio Fraga:

> Institutions in emerging economies tend to be weaker than in developed economies. Central banks are no exception. In this context, the adoption of inflation targeting represents an effort to enhance the credibility of the monetary authority as committed to price stability. . . . Given the history of low credibility, private agents assign some positive probability that the central bank will renege on its commitment to the targets. As a result, the expected inflation and consequently the actual inflation tend to be higher than with a perfectly credible monetary authority.[26]

Because of credibility problems, emerging-market economies tended to adopt more formal frameworks for inflation targeting, and their central banks were reluctant to miss inflation targets even temporarily for fear of undermining anti-inflationary credibility. One economist pointed out that inflation targeting was designed to introduce some flexibility into monetary policymaking (e.g., in comparison to fixed exchange rates) but that "credibility problems will force precisely those emerging markets where a flexible approach to inflation targeting is most valuable to adopt a relatively rigid version."[27]

The vulnerability of emerging-market economies to large external shocks led to high volatility of the exchange rate and contributed to the problems associated with high degrees of dollarization. It also made inflation forecasting more difficult, thereby compounding credibility problems.[28] First, commodity items comprised a large proportion of the consumer price inflation basket of lower-income countries. With very high price volatility and reliance on the external environment, commodity items could, in the words of one economist, "wreak havoc with the forecastability of consumer price inflation."[29] Second, domestic financial conditions of emerging-market economies were highly sensitive to international capital flows. So-called sudden stops in capital flows to emerging-market economies could easily destabilize these economies, resulting in high inflation.[30]

Many economists argued that higher volatility of inflation results in emerging-market economies, combined with the intrinsic limits of forecasting models, justified the use of bands around inflation targets and a clear process to adjust targets. Fraga outlined the credibility trade-off: "The target is adjusted in order to take into account primary effects of change in relative prices and of past inertia that will be accommodated. The new target is publicly announced. Although there is a credibility loss stemming from the target change itself, the gains in terms of transparency and communication are more significant."[31]

Brazil's Inflation-Targeting Framework

Unlike the gradualist approaches of its inflation-targeting Latin American neighbors, Brazil developed the technical and institutional infrastructure required for its full-fledged inflation-targeting regime in just four months. Under this "big bang" approach, targets were set immediately at single-digit levels.[32] Specifically, on July 1, 1999, Brazil formally adopted the new monetary policy framework and set year-end inflation targets (based on the IPCA Broad Consumer Price Index) for the current and following two years at 8% for 1999, 6% for 2000, and 4% for 2001, with a tolerance interval of ± 2%.

Transparency and accountability were important parts of the framework. The central bank's Monetary Policy Committee (Copom) met at regular monthly intervals to set interest rates and announced decisions immediately. It published the minutes of its monthly meetings and a quarterly inflation report that provided detailed information on economic conditions. In the case of breached targets, the central bank governor was required to issue an open letter addressed to the minister of finance explaining the underlying causes and planned corrective measures.[33]

The central bank built models of the transmission mechanism of monetary policy to prices. Given the problems associated with exchange rate volatility, the central bank intervened in exchange rate markets when necessary. It did so as transparently as possible in order to avoid losses in credibility of the central bank's commitment to inflation targeting. Accordingly, the central bank defined the most important transmission channels to inflation as working through aggregate demand (total spending in the economy) and the exchange rate. Permanent changes in the Selic were estimated to take between one and two quarters to impact aggregate demand, which, in turn, took an additional quarter to be perceived in consumer price inflation. The exchange rate channel was estimated to have a shorter transmission lag lasting just one quarter. The pass-through to the overall inflation index of currency depreciation was estimated to be smaller than the pass-through of aggregate demand.[34] (See **Exhibit 15** for a diagram of the transmission mechanism.)

Brazil's Initial Performance under the Framework

Brazil's economy, for the most part, performed well under the inflation-targeting framework in its initial years. The central bank met its inflation targets of 8% in 1999 and 6% in 2000, with actual inflation registering 8.9% and 6.0%, respectively. At the same time, the economy grew by 0.8% in 1999 (an improvement over analyst expectations of negative growth) and by 4.3% in 2000. Growth was prompted by numerous factors: the Selic had fallen from a peak of 45% in March 1999 to 19% by the end of 1999 and to 15.75% by the end of 2000; confidence in Brazil improved, reflected by a fall in the country risk premium from 15% in January 1999 to around 7.5% at the end of 1999 and in 2000 (see **Exhibit 8**); and the currency stayed relatively steady, fluctuating between 1.7 and 2.0 reais to the dollar throughout both years. In support of the inflation-targeting framework, the country succeeded in generating a primary fiscal surplus of 3.1% in 1999. On the negative side, real wages fell by 5% in 1999 and by 1% in 2000, and unemployment officially stood at a relatively high 14% (unofficial estimates were much higher). In addition, Brazilian companies with large dollar debts became worried that under the new framework the central bank would no longer target the exchange rate, in particular since at its weakest it had depreciated more than 80% against the dollar.

Brazil's economic success faltered in 2001. That year, the country experienced economic growth of only 1.4% and missed its inflation target of 4%, with inflation registering 7.7%. In its formal open letter of explanation to the finance minister, the central bank cited contagion from Argentina's economic crisis. The central bank argued that the loss of confidence that Argentina's impending default brought to the Latin American region as a whole, combined with a deceleration in the world economy and the 9/11 terrorist attack on the United States, led to a significant depreciation of the real,[35] which peaked at 2.78 to the dollar (representing an accumulated depreciation over the year of 43%) in mid-October before falling back to 2.32 by the end of the year. The central bank continued to anticipate a downward trend in inflation, however, concluding that "shocks are not expected to reoccur with the same magnitude."[36]

Electoral Uncertainty

The central bank was wrong: An even bigger shock hit the Brazilian economy in 2002. After a relatively mild first half of the year, uncertainties regarding the presidential elections of October 2002 brought turmoil to the economy in the second half. As PT (Workers' Party) candidate Luís Inácio "Lula" da Silva began to lead against his center-right government-backed opponent in the electoral polls, markets reacted with skepticism. Brazilian bonds were downgraded, and the country risk premium climbed to above 20%. Meanwhile, the currency was approaching 4 reais to the dollar— representing a loss in value exceeding two-thirds since the beginning of the year. As the private sector holding dollar debt was collapsing, the government was forced to impose emergency economic measures, including lowering reserve requirements, tapping into a line of credit with the IMF, and buying back $3 billion of foreign debt.

Multibillionaire investor George Soros, who was heavily invested in Brazil, warned that a victory by Lula would "unleash chaos," including market expectations of default on Brazil's $260 billion in public debt.[37] He argued that because of this, Lula was sure to lose the presidential race. In Brazil's leading financial newspaper, *Folha de São Paulo*, Soros commented: "In ancient Rome, only the Romans voted. In modern global capitalism, only U.S. financial agents vote, not Brazilians." As Wall Street appeared to band together in support of the government-backed candidate, Lula accused international speculators of committing "economic terrorism" against his campaign.[38]

Luís Inácio "Lula" da Silva

Lula spent most of his adult life labeled as a revolutionary and radical militant committed to reversing Brazil's enormously unequal society, in which the poorest 50% of the population accounted for only 10% of national income, through anticapitalist methods. He appeared to have a personal rather than simply an ideological commitment to reducing inequality in the country. (See **Exhibit 12** for comparative data on social indicators.)

Unlike other Brazilian politicians, most of whom were a part of the Brazilian "elite," Lula grew up in extreme poverty. He was the seventh of eight children, born in 1945 to farm workers in the arid and impoverished northeastern Brazilian state of Pernambuco. When Lula was seven years old, his family migrated to the state of São Paulo, where Lula worked as a street vendor, shoeshine, and delivery boy. After finishing elementary school at the age of 12, Lula embarked on a two-year technical degree as a machine operator. Upon graduation, he obtained a permanent job at a metalworks where, four years later, he lost a finger in a workplace accident.[39]

While the factory was Lula's opening to politics, an older brother was the impetus. Lula refused to follow his brother's lead in becoming a member of the then-banned Communist Party but eventually agreed to his suggestions to become active in the metalworkers union in the automaking hub of São

Bernardo do Campo, outside São Paulo. In 1972, he was elected first secretary of the syndicate. In 1975, after demonstrating superior negotiating and leadership skills and a pragmatic approach to obtaining jobs and benefits, he was elected its president with 98% of the vote. Under his direction, the union held a huge wave of strikes that, with participation in excess of 100,000 workers, solidified the labor movement and challenged Brazil's military dictatorship. In 1980, the military regime imprisoned him for 31 days. Later that year, with the government's easing of political restrictions, Lula founded the leftist *Partido dos Trabalhadores* (PT, Workers' Party). These struggles for democracy endeared him to the liberal and intellectual elite.[40]

Previous Elections

In 1982, in the first elections allowed by the military dictatorship, Lula finished fourth in the race for governor of São Paulo. In 1986, he was elected to the legislature, where he was argued to be ineffectual because of his insistence on pursuing extremist positions.[41] In 1989, Lula ran for president for the first time. He surprised the world when he came close to winning—garnering 47% of the vote in the runoff election—despite his persona as an extremist revolutionary and rumors generating a "red scare" with the specter of government confiscation and reallocation of private property.

In 1994 and 1998, Lula ran for president again, both times against Fernando Henrique Cardoso. In 1994, he mistakenly campaigned on anticipated failure of the Real Plan and won only 27% of the vote. In 1998, he did only marginally better, with 31% of the vote. It was argued that the threat of intensified economic crisis had deterred voters from the leftist candidate promising to default on the public debt and undo free-market reform.

Most analysts believed his third failed challenge for the presidency in October 1998 would be his last, but Lula was selected as the PT's candidate once more in 2002. Although he struggled to appeal to centrist voters, the economic crisis and political scandals involving the ruling party boosted the PT's appeal as a protest vote for those disillusioned with the austerity measures of the Cardoso government. Perhaps most importantly, Lula gave up his radical rhetoric for a campaign message of "peace and love" in an attempt to appeal to the center ground and the international community.[42]

Lula Wins the Election

Lula's change of tack proved successful. In the October 6, 2002 election, he won 47% of the vote, more than any other candidate but just shy of the 50% plus one vote required for an outright win. The runoff, against government-backed candidate José Serra, was scheduled for October 27. Markets remained unconvinced by his apparent transformation to capitalism and reacted poorly to the continued uncertainty surrounding the election. Specifically, investors feared that Lula cared little about corporate profits and could lead the country to default on its foreign debt. In mid-October, the real climbed to 3.96, just shy of the psychological barrier of 4 reais per dollar, prompting the Central Bank of Brazil to call an extraordinary meeting of the Copom. In an effort to halt a further plunge of the currency and rein in inflation, the Copom raised the Selic overnight rate from 18% to 21%—its highest rate and steepest increase in more than three years. Brazilian stocks fell 4.6% in response. In addition, the country risk premium climbed to almost 23% and foreign investment slowed.

Serra made a televised statement attacking Lula for what he said were contradictory pledges of change to common people and continuity to businesses: "If Lula is elected, we will be facing two possibilities. If he fulfills the recently assumed commitments to businessmen, it will be the biggest election fraud. And, if he tries to fulfill his 'magical' promises to the population, it will be the ruin of Brazil."[43]

Despite such dire warnings, Lula received a decisive 61% of the vote in the runoff election and was set to assume the presidency on January 1, 2003. Lula reaffirmed his willingness to stand by market-friendly policies: He voiced commitment to fiscal discipline, pledged that Brazil would honor its obligations to international lenders, and appointed a credible economic team. Lula chose highly regarded Antonio Palocci Filho, a former physician and moderate PT mayor known for his caution and pragmatism, to become finance minister. Henrique Meirelles, an experienced commercial banker, was selected to replace popular central bank president Arminio Fraga. Despite Lula's previous promise that he would not appoint a "mini-Fraga," Meirelles was expected to retain many of the advisers of his predecessor. Markets calmed somewhat, and the real gained strength against the dollar in response.

But skepticism persisted in the last few months of 2002 amid continued mixed signals from the future president. Some observers were uneasy about Lula's close relationships with Cuba's Fidel Castro and Venezuela's President Hugo Chavez.[44] They also questioned how Lula would fulfill his campaign promises to double the minimum wage, create jobs, improve health care, and carry out land reform. Some worried that he would be forced to resort to unorthodox economic policies, such as defaulting on the external debt or printing money and thereby rekindling runaway inflation. As a result, the central bank raised the Selic twice more at its regularly scheduled meetings in 2002, to 22% in November and to 25% in December.

Debt Dynamics

Lula inherited a weakly performing economy. As in 2001, Brazil missed its 2002 inflation target, this time with an actual rate of 12.5% versus its target of 3.5%. (See **Exhibit 13** for an inflation components breakdown and **Exhibit 10** for data on money growth.) As a result, the 2003 inflation target was raised to 8.5% (from 4%) and the 2004 target to 5.5% (from 3.75%).[45] GDP growth was only 1.5%. Official unemployment remained high at 12% in 2002 (unofficial numbers were much higher). Furthermore, the net-public-debt-to-GDP ratio had increased from 42% at the beginning of 1999 to 57% at the end of 2002.

In the aftermath of Argentina's massive default in early 2002, many observers were questioning the sustainability of Brazil's growing public debt. In order for the debt-to-GDP ratio to remain stable or decrease, the primary surplus plus increases in GDP needed to be large enough to cover interest payments on the debt and any hidden liabilities. Depending on assumptions about inflation, interest rates, the exchange rate, the primary surplus, GDP growth, hidden liabilities, and how much should be netted from gross debt, some economists predicted Brazil would be forced into a massive debt restructuring while others predicted a healthy, consistently declining net-public-debt-to-GDP ratio.[46]

Since approximately 48% (425 billion reais) of Brazil's net debt of 881 billion reais was linked to the Selic at the end of 2002, central bank decisions surrounding the interest rate had a significant impact on Brazil's debt burden. With another 42% (373 billion reais) of the net debt linked to foreign currencies, a fall in the real also served to increase the debt-to-GDP ratio dramatically. The Central Bank of Brazil estimated that the exchange rate depreciation of 52.3% against the dollar in 2002 led to a 148 billion real increase in the debt.[47] (See **Exhibit 14** for more details about and data on debt dynamics.)

Lula Initiates Change

In an effort to improve Brazil's economic situation, Lula's government implemented a number of measures. Palocci raised Brazil's primary fiscal surplus target from 3.75% of GDP, as agreed on with the IMF, to 4.25%. At the same time, the government was working toward congressional approval of four important and sensitive reform packages.

The government's first- and highest-priority reform package involved the public pension system, thought to be among the most generous in the world, which was estimated to be running a deficit of more than 4% of GDP while benefiting only 2.5 million people. Previous governments had attempted such reform in the past, but to no avail—largely because of resistance from the PT itself. The second priority was a planned tax reform. The reform would aim to make Brazil's tax system easier to administer and would promote social justice through making some taxes progressive. Third, the government wanted to rewrite bankruptcy laws in favor of creditors—such as through making collateral easier and quicker to recover—in order to enable banks to lend at lower rates and expand credit. Banks would benefit from provisions clarifying bankruptcy proceedings, while distressed companies would find it easier to emerge intact from bankruptcy under the proposed laws.

The government's fourth legislative priority centered on granting the nominally autonomous central bank full independence to set short-term interest rates and pursue its inflation-targeting objectives. Proponents argued that granting the central bank formal independence would strengthen Brazil's institutional framework and boost market confidence. Under proposed legislation, the central bank president and directors would have fixed terms that did not coincide with changes in government. In addition, the central bank would no longer report to the finance ministry.[48]

Confronting an Incipient Recession

Lula's approval ratings soared with his early success in establishing credibility and working toward major reform. Between January 2003 and July 2003, polls showed that between 74% and 84% of Brazilians approved of his "personal performance."[49] In July 2003, the country risk premium fell to an average 775 basis points from a high of 2,300 during the election period. Despite dour predictions prior to the election, Brazil avoided large-scale capital flight. By mid-August 2003, with the exchange rate having appreciated significantly over the year while inflation remained high, it appeared that Brazil's debt situation would show improvement in the short term. In addition, the government hoped to raise 1.7 billion reais in 2004 from the proposed changes to public pensions, enough to cover the cost of Lula's Zero Hunger antipoverty program. Recognizing that nearly a quarter of the population lived on less than half the minimum wage of $80 a month and 15% lacked enough money for proper nutrition, Lula also began work on other antipoverty and redistributional initiatives. He planned to coordinate several dozen programs that transferred money to the poor in an effort to improve their reach and efficiency. Under the reorganization, local groups were to be given a more significant role in identifying beneficiaries and monitoring the programs.

Many critics, however, complained that Lula failed to do enough for the poor. Specifically, they claimed that the Zero Hunger program was ineffectual and simply a public relations tool. Furthermore, the latest GDP growth numbers threatened to halt the momentum behind Lula's reform campaign; the economy was anticipated to retract for a second consecutive quarter. (See **Exhibit 9** for industrial production data.) With recession looming, observers worried that Lula's popularity would erode and with it the political strength required to sustain austerity and push reforms through a reluctant Congress. It was feared that representatives of various vested interests might seize the opportunity to challenge free-market reforms introduced by former President Cardoso. Some state governors (who often had significant influence in the capital) were already starting to press for a relaxation of the fiscal-responsibility law, which had put an end to the spending excesses of local government.

The Decision

The central bank was under increasing pressure to respond to Brazil's slowed growth at its regularly scheduled August meeting by lowering the Selic overnight rate. The central bank had been forced to increase the rate to 25.5% in January 2003 and 26.5% in February 2003 in the face of mounting inflation. Although the rate was then reduced to 26% in June and 24.5% in July, many critics, including PL Vice President José Alencar, complained that the rate was too high and put Brazil at a competitive disadvantage vis-à-vis its neighbors. Consistent with Alencar's position, some observers praised Brazil for responding to shocks in the past by increasing its inflation targets. Referring to a past episode, one economist wrote:

> The procedure followed by the Banco Central do Brasil has several very important advantages and is a textbook case for central bank response to shocks. First, the procedure has tremendous transparency. . . . Second, the central bank recognized that not adjusting the inflation target was just not credible because the market and the public clearly recognized that inflation would overshoot the initial target. Thus adjusting the target was absolutely necessary to retain credibility for the central bank, because to do otherwise would have just signaled to the markets that the central bank was unwilling to be transparent. Third, by discussing alternative paths for the inflation rate and why the particular path using the adjusted target was chosen, the central bank is able to demonstrate that it is not . . . an "inflation nutter" who only cares about controlling inflation and not about output fluctuations. By its procedure of outlining that lower inflation paths would lead to large output losses, the Banco Central do Brasil demonstrated that it is not out of touch with the concerns of the public because it indeed does care about output losses, just as the public and the politicians do.[50]

Some market participants, aware that Lula retained the power to withdraw support for the central bank president or even fire him, were demanding that the government intervene to assure lower rates. Lula, however, stood firm in his conviction that the central bank should remain independent. He continued to defend central bank president Meirelles, as he had when Vice President Alencar attacked him for failing to reduce rates in May.

In fact, inflation targeting itself was being lambasted. Critics complained that it did not work in an economy vulnerable to buffeting from the outside world. Others thought that the targets were too ambitious and the central bank too rigid in trying to meet them. They also pointed out that a long time lag existed between monetary policy and its effect on prices. Still other critics of inflation targeting contended that since inflation was not directly under the control of the central bank, it was not a sensible target. Furthermore, they argued that in emerging-market economies, there was always going to be a tendency to look at and respond to changes in the exchange rate, regardless of any inflation-targeting commitment.

The central bank faced a challenging decision. Most indications showed that inflation had been contained and the exchange rate stabilized. Furthermore, Brazil required lower rates to be able to continue to pay down its debt. But the Copom had an aggressive inflation target to meet, and a third consecutive year of missed targets could seriously threaten the credibility of the institution. It also needed to make its independence in decision making clear, particularly as high-ranking government officials were so publicly critical.

Exhibit 1 Brazil General Economic Indicators

% change pa	1990	1991	1992	1993	1994	1995	1996	1997	1998	1999	2000	2001	2002
Real GDP Growth	n.a.	1.1	-0.6	4.9	5.8	4.2	2.7	3.3	0.2	0.8	4.3	1.4	1.5
Real Per Capita GDP Growth	n.a.	-0.5	-2.1	3.3	4.3	2.8	1.3	2.0	-1.0	-0.3	3.3	0.4	0.6
Consumer Price Inflation	1,621.0	433.3	1,112.5	2,477.3	916.5	22.4	9.6	5.2	1.7	8.9	6.0	7.7	12.5
Stock Market Index ($ value)	n.a.	n.a.	n.a.	n.a.	-83.7	-14.1	53.3	34.9	-38.6	70.2	-18.3	-25.0	-45.5
Average Real Wage Increase	n.a.	n.a.	n.a.	n.a.	5.8	10.3	7.4	2.1	-0.4	-5.4	-0.5	-8.2	-2.2
M1 Growth	n.a.	400.0	960.0	2,000.0	2,194.7	25.7	29.9	22.4	7.5	13.6	18.9	12.8	28.3
units as shown													
Nominal Exchange Rate (reais per dollar, end-period)	n.a.	n.a.	n.a.	n.a.	0.8	1.0	1.0	1.1	1.2	1.8	2.0	2.3	3.5
Real Ex. Rate (increase = appreciation, 1997=100)	109.5	89.2	78.7	80.6	85.8	93.5	98.7	100.0	96.8	63.9	69.4	58.2	52.9
Unemployment (%)	8.0	9.0	10.6	9.9	9.5	8.7	10.1	10.6	14.2	14.1	13.3	11.3	11.7
Primary Public Sector Surplus (+) or Deficit (-) (% GDP)	-5.8	-0.4	-3.8	-9.3	-6.1	n.a.	n.a.	-0.9	-0.1	3.2	3.4	3.6	3.9
International Reserves (current $ bns, year-end)	9.2	8.8	23.3	31.7	38.5	51.5	59.7	51.7	43.9	35.7	33.0	35.9	37.8
Net-Debt-to-GDP ratio (year-end)	n.a.	n.a.	n.a.	n.a.	29.2	30.5	33.3	34.3	41.7	48.7	48.8	52.6	56.5
Foreign Debt (current $ bns, year-end)	120.0	121.0	129.1	144.1	152.4	160.5	181.3	198.0	241.0	243.7	238.8	226.4	227.1

Sources: Created by casewriter based on data from Economist Intelligence Unit (EIU) Country Data, August 2003; Ministerio Da Fazenda, *Boletim de Acompanhamento Fiscal,* September 2003; and *Banco Central do Brasil Annual Report,* 2002 and 1997.

Exhibit 2 Brazil National Income Accounts (*billions of constant 1996 U.S. dollars*)

	1990	1991	1992	1993	1994	1995	1996	1997	1998	1999	2000	2001	2002
Gross Domestic Product	**100%**	**100%**	**100%**	**100%**	**100%**	**100%**	**100%**	**100%**	**100%**	**100%**	**100%**	**100%**	**100%**
Household Consumption	59%	59%	59%	58%	59%	62%	63%	62%	62%	61%	61%	61%	59%
Government Consumption	20%	20%	21%	20%	19%	19%	18%	18%	19%	19%	18%	18%	18%
Gross Fixed Investment	19%	20%	18%	19%	20%	21%	21%	22%	22%	20%	21%	20%	19%
Exports	7%	6%	7%	8%	8%	7%	7%	7%	8%	8%	9%	10%	10%
Imports	4%	5%	5%	6%	7%	9%	9%	10%	10%	9%	9%	9%	8%
Real GDP (constant 1996 US$ bns)	648.9	655.7	652.0	684.1	724.0	754.7	775.0	800.7	801.9	808.1	843.1	854.7	867.6
Nominal GDP (current US$ bns)	465.0	407.7	390.9	438.4	546.2	704.2	775.0	807.7	787.7	536.6	601.7	510.6	452.4

Source: Created by casewriter based on data from EIU Country Data, November 2003.

Note: GDP does not equal sum of components because of rebasing to 1996, which alters the relative importance of individual components.

Exhibit 3   Brazil Balance of Payments (millions of current U.S. dollars)

	1990	1991	1992	1993	1994	1995	1996	1997	1998	1999	2000	2001	2002
Current Account	-3,823	-1,450	6,089	20	-1,153	-18,136	-23,248	-30,491	-33,829	-25,400	-24,225	-23,215	-7,696
Trade Balance	10,747	10,578	15,239	14,329	10,861	-3,157	-5,453	-6,652	-6,603	-1,261	-698	2,650	13,143
Exports	31,408	31,619	35,793	39,630	44,102	46,506	47,851	53,189	51,136	48,011	55,086	58,223	60,362
Imports	-20,661	-21,041	-20,554	-25,301	-33,241	-49,663	-53,304	-59,841	-57,739	-49,272	-55,783	-55,572	-47,219
Net Services	-3,761	-3,891	-3,342	-5,590	-5,346	-7,495	-8,059	-9,309	-9,045	-6,983	-7,162	-7,759	-5,038
Net Income	-11,608	-9,651	-7,997	-10,322	-9,091	-11,105	-12,177	-16,344	-19,617	-18,844	-17,886	-19,743	-18,191
Net Transfers	799	1,514	2,189	1,603	2,423	3,621	2,441	1,814	1,436	1,688	1,521	1,638	2,390
Capital Account	35	42	54	81	173	352	494	482	375	339	273	-36	433
Financial Account	-5,441	-4,868	5,889	7,604	8,020	29,306	33,428	24,918	20,063	8,056	29,376	20,331	-3,102
Net Direct Investment	324	89	1,924	801	2,035	3,475	11,667	18,608	29,192	26,886	30,498	24,715	14,084
Net Portfolio Investment	512	3,808	7,366	12,322	44,732	9,235	20,832	10,058	18,419	3,800	6,955	77	-5,119
Net Government	-3,438	-3,897	-2,289	-2,767	-36,154	-1,652	-3,817	381	-1,728	-4,949	1,514	1,149	-1,626
Net Other	-2,839	-4,868	-1,112	-2,752	-2,593	18,248	4,746	-4,129	-25,820	-17,681	-9,590	-5,609	-10,441
Net Errors and Omissions	-296	852	-1,393	-815	-442	1,447	-1,992	-3,160	-2,911	240	2,557	-498	-901
Balance/Change in Official Reserves	-9,525	-5,424	10,639	6,890	6,598	12,969	8,682	-8,251	-16,302	-16,765	7,981	-3,418	-11,266
Nominal GDP (current US$ bns)	465.0	407.7	390.9	438.4	546.2	704.2	775.0	807.7	787.7	536.6	601.7	510.6	452.4

Source: Created by casewriter based on data from IMF, International Financial Statistics CD-ROM, November 2003.

Exhibit 4   Brazil Government Finance

as % current GDP	1997	1998	1999	2000	2001	2002	2003		
							June	July	August
Primary Revenue of the Central Government	15.7	17.3	18.5	18.1	19.1	20.5	20.1	20.0	19.9
Primary Expenses of the Central Government	15.5	16.5	16.5	16.3	17.3	18.1	17.3	17.1	17.0
Social Security	*-0.3*	*-0.8*	*-1.0*	*-0.9*	*-1.1*	*-1.3*	*-1.4*	*-1.4*	*-1.5*
Errors and Omissions	-0.5	-0.3	0.3	0.0	0.0	0.0	0.0	0.0	0.0
Primary Result of the Central Government	-0.3	0.5	2.3	1.8	1.8	2.4	2.8	2.9	2.9
Primary Result of the State Governments	-0.7	-0.4	0.2	0.4	0.6	0.6	0.8	0.7	0.7
Primary Result of the Municipal Governments	n.a.	0.2	0.1	0.1	0.3	0.2	0.1	0.1	0.1
Primary Result of the State Enterprises	0.1	-0.4	0.6	1.1	0.9	0.7	0.7	0.7	0.6
Primary Result of the Public Sector	**-0.9**	**-0.1**	**3.2**	**3.4**	**3.6**	**3.9**	**4.4**	**4.4**	**4.3**
Interest Payments	5.2	7.8	12.4	7.9	8.8	14.4	11.0	9.3	11.0
Nominal Result of the Public Sector	-6.1	-7.9	-9.2	-4.5	-5.2	-10.5	-6.6	-4.9	-6.7
Central Government	*-2.6*	*-5.2*	*-6.1*	*-3.1*	*-3.7*	*-6.6*	*-2.8*	*-1.8*	*-3.3*
State Governments	*-3.0*	*-1.8*	*-2.7*	*-1.8*	*-1.9*	*-3.3*	*-3.4*	*-2.9*	*-2.9*
Municipal Governments	*n.a.*	*-0.2*	*-0.5*	*-0.3*	*-0.1*	*-0.6*	*-0.6*	*-0.6*	*-0.6*
State Enterprises	*-0.5*	*-0.5*	*0.1*	*0.7*	*0.6*	*0.0*	*0.3*	*0.5*	*0.2*
Harmonized Nominal Result of the Public Sector[a]	n.a.	-7.5	-5.8	-3.6	-3.6	-4.7	-5.5	-6.0	-6.2
Central Government	n.a.	-4.9	-2.7	-2.3	-2.1	-0.8	-1.7	-2.9	-2.9
Privatizations	2.1	2.9	0.6	1.8	0.2	0.3	n.a.	n.a.	n.a.

Source: Compiled from Ministry of Finance of Brazil, *Boletim de Acompanhamento Fiscal*, September 2003.

Note: [a]Excludes effect of exchange rate on the stock of internal, real-denominated debt indexed to the exchange rate.

Exhibit 5   Real/Dollar Exchange Rate

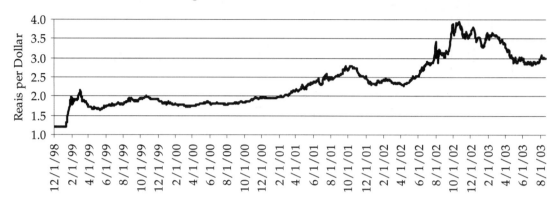

Source: Compiled from Banco Central do Brasil data.

Exhibit 6   Brazil Monthly CPI (% change over previous year, period average)

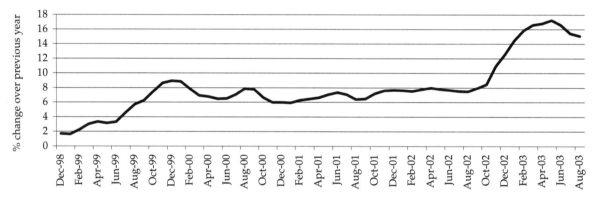

Source: Compiled from EIU Country Data, November 2003.

Exhibit 7   Selic Rate, as Set by Copom

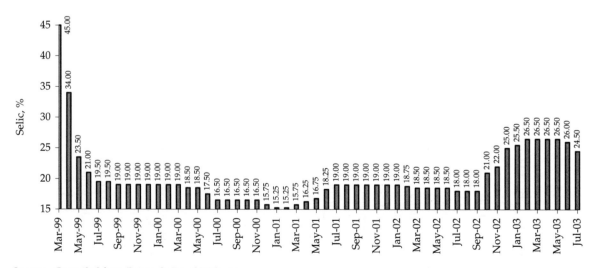

Source: Compiled from Banco do Brasil Web site.

Exhibit 8 J.P. Morgan Emerging Market Bond Index, Brazil

Source: Compiled from JP Morgan data.

Exhibit 9 Monthly Industrial Production Index (1996=100, seasonally adjusted)

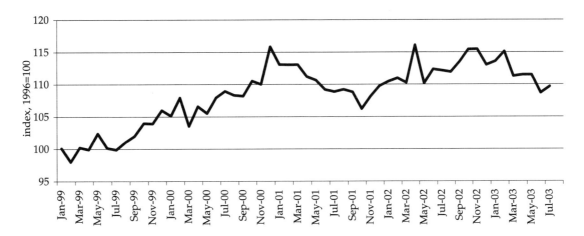

Source: Created by casewriter based on data from EIU Country Data, November 2003.

Exhibit 10 Money Growth in Brazil (% change over previous year)

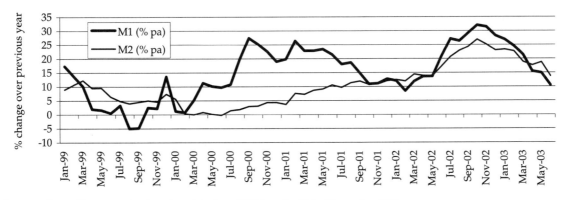

Source: Created by casewriter based on data from EIU Country Data, November 2003.

Exhibit 11   List of Countries Adopting Inflation Targeting (as of June 2003)

	Date of Adoption Inflation Targeting	Initial Target	Inflation Right Before IT Adoption	Inflation 12 Months After IT Adoption
Developed Economies				
New Zealand	Mar-90	3%–5%	7.03	4.52
Canada	Feb-91	3%–5%	6.83	1.68
United Kingdom	Oct-92	1%–4%	3.57	1.35
Sweden	Jan-93	2% (± 1%)	1.76	1.7
Australia	Apr-93	2%–3%	1.22	1.74
Switzerland	Jan-00	<= 2%	1.63	0.9
Norway	Mar-01	2.5	3.64	1.1
Iceland	Mar-01	2.5% (−1.5%+3.5%)	4.05	8.72
Average		*2.8*	*3.72*	*2.71*
Median		*2.5*	*3.61*	*1.69*
Emerging-Market Economies				
Chile	Jan-91	15%–20%	27.31	19.47
Israel	Jan-92	14%–15%	18.03	10.74
Peru	Jan-94	15%–20%	39.49	13.71
Czech Republic	Jan-98	5.5%–6.5%	9.98	3.5
South Korea	Jan-98	9%(± 1%)	6.57	1.46
Poland	Oct-98	<=9.5	10.44	8.82
Mexico	Jan-99	<=13%	18.61	11.03
Brazil[a]	Jun-99	8% (± 2%)	3.15	6.51
Colombia	Sep-99	15%	9.22	9.35
South Africa[b]	Feb-00	3%–6%	2.65	7.77
Thailand	Apr-00	0%–3.5%	1.04	2.47
Hungary	Jun-01	7% (± 1%)	10.78	4.87
Average		*10.3*	*13.11*	*8.31*
Median		*9.3*	*10.21*	*8.3*

Source: Adapted from Fraga, 2003, p. 6.

Notes: [a]In Brazil, the inflation of the period previous to the adoption of inflation targeting was in part a result of the over-appreciation of the domestic currency.

[b]First target established for 2002.

Exhibit 12   Social Indicators (most recent between 1997 and 2002)

	Gini Index[a]	Infant Mortality (deaths per 1,000 live births)	Life Expectancy at Birth (in years)	Secondary School Enrollment (% gross)	Tertiary School Enrollment (% gross)	Adult Illiteracy (% people over 15)	Sanitation Facilities (% population with access)	Fixed-Line and Mobile Phone Subscribers (per 1,000 people)
Brazil	60.7	31	68.6	n.a	17%	12%	76%	385
U.S.	40.8	7	78.0	95%	73%	n.a.	100%	1,121
Argentina	n.a.	16	74.3	97%	48%	3%	n.a.	416
Chile	57.5	10	75.9	75%	38%	4%	96%	575
Ecuador	43.7	24	70.4	57%	na	8%	86%	170
Mexico	51.9	24	73.6	75%	21%	8%	74%	354
Venezuela	49.5	19	73.7	59%	29%	7%	68%	373

Source: Compiled from World Bank, *World Development Indicators Database Online,* December 2003.

Note: [a]The Gini Index measures the degree of income inequality. A higher number represents more inequality.

Exhibit 13   Contributors to Inflation

	2001		2002	
	As % Contribution	Percentage Point Contribution to Total Inflation	As % Contribution	Percentage Point Contribution to Total Inflation
Exchange Rate Pass-through	38%	2.9	46.4%	5.82
Market-Price Inflation (Excluding Exchange Rate Pass-through, Inertia, and Expectations)	28%	2.4	18.2%	2.28
Contract-Price Inflation (Excluding Exchange Rate Pass-through, Inertia, and Expectations)	24%	1.7	14.8%	1.85
Expectations	n.a.	n.a.	13.2%	1.65
Inflation Inertia	10%	0.7	7.4%	0.93
Total	**100%**	**7.7**	**100%**	**12.53**

Source: Adapted from Banco Central do Brasil Web site.

Exhibit 14   Debt Dynamics in Brazil

	All values in billions reais, unless noted	2001	2002	2003 est.
a	Total net debt	660.9	881.1	1,093
b	**Foreign currency-linked debt** as % total net debt		42.4%	42%
c=a*b	Value		373.4	463
d	Interest rate (avg LIBOR + avg sovereign spread)		15.4%	10%
e	Depreciation (avg monthly year-to-date against dollar		26.1%	-12%
f=d+e	Total interest rate		42%	-2%
g=c*f	*Interest cost*		155.2	-9
h	**Selic-linked debt** as % total net debt		48.3%	48%
i=a*h	Value		425.9	528
j	Interest rate (avg Selic rate)		17.9%	25%
k=i*j	*Interest cost*		76.3	130
l	**Inflation-linked debt** as % total net debt		9.3%	9%
m=a*l	Value		81.8	101
n	Interest rate (avg TIPS + avg sovereign spread)		15.6%	11%
o	Inflation		12.5%	15%
p=n+o	Total interest rate		28.1%	26%
q=m*p	*Interest cost*		23.0	26
r=g+k+q	Total interest cost		254.4	148
s	Minus primary surplus		52.9	65
t	Plus hidden liabilities		9.9	12
u=r-s+t	Equals increase in debt		211.5	94
v	Nominal GDP	1,200	1,322	1,536
w	Nominal GDP used by BCB for debt calculations	1,257	1,559	1,812
x	Real economic growth	1.4%	1.5%	1.25%
y=a/w	Total net debt as % GDP	52.6%	56.5%	
z=(a$_{prior\ year}$+u)/w – y$_{prior\ year}$	Change in debt/GDP ratio		3.4%	-2.7%
aa=y$_{prior\ year}$ = z	Calculated total net debt as % GDP		56.0%	53.8%

Source: Casewriter calculations, based on debt model presented in Williamson (2002).

Notes: a: From BCB Annual Report; 2003e = a2002+u2002.

b: Calculated from BCB Annual Report as 100% external debt + % of FX-linked debt in domestic debt; 2003 proportions assumed consistent - although not equivalent to c+g.

e: Not a cash cost, but a revaluation effect; this is just an approximation, since some foreign debt is not dollar-linked.

h: Calculated from BCB Annual Report as % of Selic-linked debt (plus most "other" debt) in domestic debt.

l: Calculated from BCB Annual Report as % of IGP- and IPCA-linked debt in domestic debt.

n: TIPS are U.S. inflation-protected securities.

o: Yearly inflation; not a cash cost but a revaluation effect.

s: 4% of GDP in 2002; 4.25% of GDP in 2003.

t: 0.75% GDP (as in Williamson and Goldfajn).

v: From BCB Annual Report: Annual nominal GDP at December prices deflated by the centered IGP-DI based on a series published by the IBGE (therefore recognizing the significance of inflation over the year); 2003 estimated as GDP 2002 * (1+ inflation 2003 + GDP growth 2003).

w: From BCB Annual Report; 2003 estimated as GDP 2002 * (1+ inflation 2003 + GDP growth 2003).

Exhibit 15   Transmission Mechanism, as Defined by Banco Central do Brasil

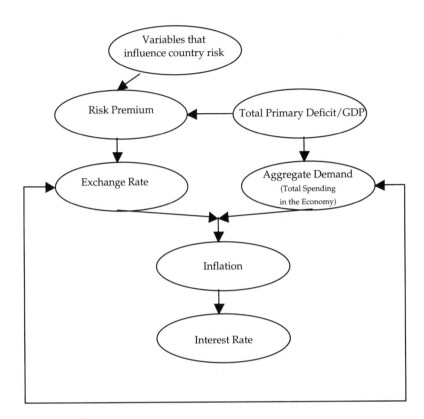

Source: Adapted from Joel Bogdanski, Alexandre Antonio Tombini, and Sergio Ribeiro da Costa
Werlang, "Implementing Inflation Targeting in Brazil," paper presented at the IMF Seminar
on Implementing Inflation Targets, March 20, 2000, available at <http://www.imf.org/
external/pubs/ft/seminar/2000/targets/werlang.pdf> (May 13, 2004).   For quantitative
model behind diagram, see source.

Endnotes

1   As quoted in "Eleições 2002: La Muda a História, Vinte Anos na Oposição," *Veja*, October 30, 2002, pp. 39–41 (translated by casewriter).

2   As quoted in "Eleições 2002: La Muda a História, Vinte Anos na Oposição," *Veja*, October 30, 2002, pp. 39–41 (translated by casewriter).

3   As quoted in "Os Quatro Presidenciáveis: Um Flagrante de Lula, Serra, Ciro, e Garotinho no Calor da Campanha," *Veja*, September 25, 2002, p. 88 (translated by casewriter).

4   Heliana Frazão, "Vice-Presidente Critica Juros Altos e Diz Que 2003 É um 'Ano Perdido,'" *O Globo*, August 18, 2003.

5   This discussion draws largely on Laura Alfaro, "Brazil: Embracing Globalization?" HBS Case No. 701-014 (Boston: Harvard Business School Publishing, 2001). It also uses information from the Embassy of Brazil in the United States, available at <www.brasilemb.org> (November 2003).

6   Arminio Fraga, "Monetary Policy During the Transition to a Floating Exchange Rate: Brazil's Recent Experience," *Finance & Development*, Vol. 27, No. 1, March 2000.

7   For more on this, see Ben S. Bernanke, Thomas Laubach, Frederic S. Mishkin, and Adam S. Posen, *Inflation Targeting: Lessons from the International Experience* (Princeton, NJ: Princeton University Press, 1999), p. 16.

8   Between 1985 and 1990, New Zealand targeted inflation under a looser framework. For more on New Zealand's experience, see Reserve Bank of New Zealand Web site, particularly <http://www.rbnz.govt.nz/speeches/0076721.html> (accessed December 2003).

9   Arminio Fraga, Ilan Goldfajn, and André Minella, "Inflation Targeting in Emerging Market Economies," *NBER Macroeconomics Annual 2003*, Vol. 18, June 2003, p. 6.

10 Bernanke, et al., *Inflation Targeting*, pp. 301–308.

11 Bernanke, et al., *Inflation Targeting*, pp. 301–308.

12 "The Move to Inflation Targeting," *Finance & Development: Back to Basics*, June 2003.

13 Bernanke, et al., *Inflation Targeting*, p. 303.

14 For more on monetary growth targets, see Michael G. Rukstad, "Paul Volcker and the Federal Reserve: 1979–1982," HBS Case No. 386-055; and Huw Pill, "Fighting the Last War (A): Controlling British Inflation, 1973–1992," HBS Case No. 797-048.

15 Frederic S. Mishkin, "Inflation Targeting in Emerging-Market Countries," *AEA Papers and Proceedings*, Vol. 90, No. 2, May 2000, pp. 105–109; and Barry Eichengreen, "Can Emerging Markets Float? Should They Inflation Target?" Banco Central do Brasil Working Paper Series, No. 36, February 2002.

16 As in the introduction to Andrew G. Haldane, *Targeting Inflation: A Conference of Central Banks on the Use of Inflation Targets Organized by the Bank of England* (London: Bank of England, 1995), p. 5.

17 This is discussed in more detail in Alex Bowen, "British Experience with Inflation Targetry," in Leonardo Leiderman and Lars E. O. Svensson, eds., *Inflation Targets* (London: Centre for Economic Policy Research, 1995), pp. 53–68.

18 Vittorio Corbo and Klaus Schmidt-Hebbel, "Inflation Targeting in Latin America," Central Bank of Chile Working Papers, No. 105, September 2001; and "The Move to Inflation Targeting," June 2003.

19 Ben S. Bernanke, "A Perspective on Inflation Targeting," *Business Economics*, Vol. 38, Iss. 3, July 1, 2003.

20 For example, Laurence Ball and Niamh Sheridan, "Does Inflation Targeting Matter?" NBER Working Paper No. 9577, March 2003, which argues it can be explained by regression to the mean.

21 Bernanke, et al., *Inflation Targeting*.

22 Frederic S. Mishkin, "Inflation Targeting in Emerging-Market Countries," *AEA Papers and Proceedings*, Vol. 90, No. 2, May 2000, p. 107.

[23] Fraga, et al., "Inflation Targeting in Emerging Market Economies," p. 24.

[24] Mishkin, "Inflation Targeting in Emerging-Market Countries," May 2000, p. 107; discussed more fully and technically in Fraga, et al., "Inflation Targeting in Emerging Market Economies," and Eichengreen, "Can Emerging Markets Float? Should They Inflation Target?" pp. 27–34.

[25] Fraga, et al., "Inflation Targeting in Emerging Market Economies," p. 29.

[26] Fraga, et al., "Inflation Targeting in Emerging Market Economies," pp. 14–15.

[27] Eichengreen, "Can Emerging Markets Float? Should They Inflation Target?" p. 41.

[28] Eichengreen, "Can Emerging Markets Float? Should They Inflation Target?" pp. 23–27.

[29] Eichengreen, "Can Emerging Markets Float? Should They Inflation Target?" p. 25.

[30] Guillermo Calvo, Leonardo Leiderman, and Carmen Reinhart, "Inflows of Capital to Developing Countries in the 1990s," *The Journal of Economic Perspectives*, 10 (1996): 123–139; and Guillermo Calvo and Carmen Reinhart, "When Capital Flows Come to a Sudden Stop: Consequences and Policy," in Peter B. Kenen and Alexander K. Swoboda (eds.), *Reforming the International Monetary and Financial System* (Washington, DC: International Monetary Fund, 2000).

[31] Fraga, et al., "Inflation Targeting in Emerging Market Economies"; Eichengreen, "Can Emerging Markets Float? Should They Inflation Target?" p. 23, also discusses this.

[32] Klaus Schmidt-Hebbel and Alejandro Werner, "Inflation Targeting in Brazil, Chile, and Mexico: Performance, Credibility, and the Exchange Rate," Working Papers, Central Bank of Chile, 2002.

[33] Open letters are available on Brazil's central bank Web site, <www.bcb.gov.br>.

[34] Joel Bogdanski, Paulo Springer de Freitas, Ilan Goldfajn, and Alexandre Antonio Tombini, "Inflation Targeting in Brazil: Shocks, Backward-looking Prices, and IMF Conditionality," BIS Paper No. 12, November 2001, pp. 356–384. This is actually more complicated—requires that expectations remain consistent with the model and that the policy change is a sufficiently small departure from the initial position.

[35] Open letter available on BCB Web site, "Open Letter, January 16, 2002, From Arminio Fraga Neto to Finance Minister," <www.bcb.gov.br> (accessed December 2003).

[36] Ibid., p. 11.

[37] Mario Osava, "Politics–Brazil: Potential Lula Victory Shakes up Investors," *Inter Press Service*, June 21, 2002.

[38] "Front-Runner's Edge in Brazil Worries Foreign Investors," *The Boston Globe*, September 22, 2002.

[39] This section draws on a number of popular sources, including Mario Osava, "Elections–Brazil: Lula, From Revolutionary to Social Democrat," *Inter Press Service*, October 4, 2002; Ray Collitt and Richard Lapper, "Victory in Sight for Brazil's Lula," *The Financial Times*, September 27, 2002; Gabriella Gamini, "Poor Boy from the Factory Floor – The Favourite – Brazil Election," *The Times*, October 3, 2002; and Jonathan Karp, "A da Silva Landslide is Expected in Brazil: Exit Polls Show Him with 63% of the Ballot in Runoff Against Serra," *The Wall Street Journal*, October 28, 2002.

[40] Ibid.

[41] Francisco Figueroa, "Lula: Proletarian in Armani Suit," EFE News Service, October 4, 2002.

[42] "Brazil Risk: Political Stability Risk," Economist Intelligence Unit Riskwire, August 29, 2003.

[43] As quoted in Andrei Khalip, "Brazil Lula Set for Runoff Win, Rival on Warpath," *Reuters News*, October 20, 2002.

[44] The two were front row guests at his inauguration, as discussed in Clinton Porteous, "Lula's Revolution: Tackling the Social Time Bomb of Brazil," *Australian Financial Review*, January 24, 2003.

[45] The change is outlined in the Open Letter from the Governor of the Central Bank of Brazil to the Finance Minister, January 21, 2003, available at <www.bcb.gov.br> (accessed December 2003).

[46] John Williamson, "Is Brazil Next," International Economics Policy Briefs, No. PB 02-7, August 2002; Ilan Goldfjan, "Are There Reasons to Doubt Fiscal Sustainability in Brazil?" Banco Central do Brasil Technical Note No. 25, July 2002; Carlo A. Favero and Francesco Giavazzi, "Why Are Brazil's Interest Rates So High?"

Working Papers from IGIER (Innocenzo Gasparini Institute for Economic Research), No. 224, Bocconi University, July 2002; and Morris Goldstein, "Debt Sustainability, Brazil, and the IMF," Institute for International Economics, Working Paper No. WP 03–1, February 2003. Williamson uses a net-debt-to-GDP ratio of 66% and presents a mixed message; under multiple equilibria, could go either way. Goldfjan uses the BCB's net-debt-to-GDP ratio of 58% and presents a more optimistic picture. Favero and Giavazzi are much less optimistic. They use a much higher debt figure, do not augment the primary surplus to allow for the income that the government receives on the assets that they have netted out, and project a continuing real depreciation of the real. Goldstein is less optimistic as well.

[47] As presented in the 2002 Annual Report of the Banco Central do Brasil, p. 98. Not all foreign-currency-linked debt was dollar denominated, explaining the difference between the central bank's estimate of 148 billion reais and 197 billion reais, which would result from 373 billion reais x 0.523.

[48] "Lula 'twixt Inflation and Recession," *The Economist,* June 21, 2003.

[49] As polled by Sensus Opinion Research Institute.

[50] Frederic S. Mishkin, "Comments on Fraga, Goldfajn and Minella, 'Inflation Targeting in Emerging Market Economies,'" NBER, August 14, 2003.

Korea: On the Back of a Tiger

Under President Park Chun Lee (1961–1979), Korea achieved very rapid rates of economic growth, transforming itself from a war-torn poor country similar to its North Korean rival into a leading "Asian tiger." Much of this economic success was attributed to Park's development strategy, which mimicked Japan's attempt to mobilize domestic capital through the banking system and direct it to investment in heavy industry.

After a setback in the late 1970s and early 1980s, Park's successors tried to liberalize certain aspects of the heavily regulated and government-directed system. Although economic growth slowed from its heady earlier rates (particularly in the early 1980s), Korea continued to perform strongly.

In the 1990s, in part to satisfy the demands of the OECD—the rich countries' club, to which Korea aspired to membership—financial liberalization, especially of the capital account of the balance of payments, was introduced. Such liberalization exposed Korea to the international capital market. As financial crisis spread through Asia in 1997 following the collapse of the Thai bath in July of that year, Korea was faced with new problems.

Study Questions

1. How did Korea achieve its "economic miracle?"
2. If Park's strategy up to 1979 was so successful, why did his successors want to change it?
3. Was the financial crisis of 1997 inevitable? What were the main causes of the crisis?
4. How should Korea address the crisis? Does Korea need to change in a fundamental way? If so, how? If no, why not?

YASHENG HUANG

Korea: On the Back of a Tiger

December 28, 1999. Investor exuberance echoed around the corners of the Korea Stock Exchange as the market signaled its final day of trading for the year. Reflecting the euphoric state of the nation, the Korea Stock Price Index (KOSPI) had rebounded strongly since hitting rock bottom two years earlier. The economy made a robust recovery in 1999, growing by 10.7%, in sharp contrast to the 5.8% decline in 1998. "New millennium, new hope," remarked President Kim Dae Jung in his speech to the Korean public marking the opening of business for the year 2000.[1]

Only two years earlier, a financial crisis had swept the nation. On December 3rd, 1997, the International Monetary Fund (IMF), supported by the United States, Japan, and the leading economies of Europe, extended a loan up to US$55 billion to the Republic of Korea (Korea)—the largest financial bailout in history. The financial crisis occurred as foreign banks were assessing anew their exposure in Korea in the wake of the currency storms sweeping Thailand, Malaysia, Indonesia, and Hong Kong, leaving shattered economies in their trails. Korea, one of the world's largest external debtors, was battered as foreign bankers refused to extend the maturing debt. Its foreign exchange reserves plunged to US$8.9 billion in December 1997, a level barely large enough to support 22 days of import requirements. It was a humbling blow. Declaring that "we have lost our economic sovereignty," President Kim Young Sam asked Koreans to endure "bone-carving pain" in the years to follow. Many Koreans rallied to the cause. Women donated their gold jewelry to boost the state's gold reserves; others boycotted imports.

Korea, inducted into the OECD club of rich nations in October 1996, was the eleventh largest economy in the world and the pride of the East Asian economic tigers for having engineered a modern economic miracle. An important component of Korea's economic development strategy was its heavy reliance on both domestic and foreign debt. In the wake of the financial crisis, many began to ask probing questions. Why did the same growth strategy that had brought about such spectacular success earlier result in a sudden financial meltdown in 1997? What were the vulnerabilities of such a growth strategy? Had the move toward democracy helped or hindered government efforts to change strategy and to reform the economic structure? These were the questions that must have been on the mind of President Kim Dae Jung, elected to office amidst the financial crisis, as he formulated a new direction for the country.

Professor Yasheng Huang prepared this case from published sources. He received assistance from Steven Cha and Scott Sang-Won Hahn (MBAs '00). HBS cases are developed solely as the basis for class discussion. Cases are not intended to serve as endorsements, sources of primary data, or illustrations of effective or ineffective management.

Historical Background

In 2333 B.C., according to a legend, Dangun, the son of the Heavenly God and a woman from a bear-totem tribe, established the first kingdom in Korea. Korea, located on the northeastern corner of Asia, was unified during the Shilla Kingdom (57 BC–AD 935).[2] (See map in **Exhibit 1**.) Since then, the nation had preserved a homogenous culture, language, and identity associated with many religions such as shamanism, Buddhism, Confucianism, and, recently, Christianity. Korean culture emphasized deference to authority, scholarship, and harmony. The last kingdom, Cho Sun (translated as the "Land of the Morning Calm"), underscored the nation's emphasis on peace and harmony.

Japanese Rule (1910–1945)

Having experienced a total of more than 3,000 invasions, Korea was the battleground for its larger neighbors—China, Russia, and Japan. Centuries of domination by its powerful neighbors had imbued a fierce spirit of independence among the people. In the twentieth century, Korea underwent especially tumultuous times. In 1910, it was forcibly annexed by Japan, instituting colonial rule that ended in 1945. During the colonial period, many Koreans lost their lives fighting for independence. Japanese policy was to completely assimilate Korea at both political and cultural levels. Under the policy of *Nissen Ittai* (Japan and Korea as One), the use of the Korean language was forbidden; the Japanese name system and Japanese religion, Shinto, were forcibly imposed on the native population—practices that aroused enormous resentment toward the colonialists. In addition, Japanese rule created a dispossessed population, as many Koreans lost their titles to land and some Korean women were forced into prostitution for the Japanese troops, an issue that still reverberates in the Korean-Japanese relations today.

During the colonial period, textiles, chemicals, and metals developed, increasing their shares of industry at the cost of the shares of the food processing industries, as Korea became an industrial base for Japanese war preparations.[3] To increase food output, the Japanese introduced high-yield agricultural seeds and carried out land reforms that transferred land titles from absentee landlords to cultivators. They also transferred their own financial and bureaucratic systems to Korea, such as bank-centered financial intermediation, a high degree of specialization among banks, and a postal savings system.

Japan's economic programs in the colonies were designed to advance its imperialist goals. It targeted industries that complemented and supported, rather than competed with, Japan's industrial programs. Korea was highly valuable to Japan because of its rich natural resources. To exploit these natural resources, mainly located in the north, the Japanese established upstream industries there and shipped the products to Japan for downstream and for higher value-added processing.[4] The colonial policy was to achieve Japanese self-sufficiency and to reduce economic dependence on countries outside the empire. This effort led to the development of chemical and metal industries in the Japanese colonies even though, by world standards, the colonies were not necessarily low-cost producers. Thus Samuel Ho, an economic historian, commented: "These industries survived only because they received substantial government subsidies and protection …. The colonial industrial sectors had developed not according to their comparative advantages but rather to meet specific Japanese needs."[5]

The Korean War (1950–1953)

The division of the north and the south of the country was another long-lasting legacy of Japanese rule. At the end of WWII, Japanese troops north of the 38th parallel surrendered to the advancing Soviet army; troops stationed to the south surrendered to the Americans. In 1947, the United Nations set up a commission to aid Korean reunification and to observe elections for the creation of a national assembly and government. In May 1948, Dr. Syngman Rhee won the election in the South but in the same year, the North excluded the UN election commission and elected its own government.[6] Soon a devastating war erupted between the North and the South; three years of fighting ended in a stalemate and a ceasefire agreement was signed on July 27, 1953. The war inflicted a terrible human and economic toll on both sides. Altogether 1.3 million Koreans perished, including one million civilians. Forty-three percent of Korean industrial and infrastructural facilities were destroyed. The Korean war also made permanent the division between the North and the South. The South lost access to the market and raw materials in the North. Under Japanese rule, the North was more industrialized than the South, accounting for 54% of manufacturing output but only 40% of agricultural output. The North was more developed in chemicals, metals, and ceramics, while the South had larger shares of textiles, machines and tools, printing and foodstuffs. Overall, the South had a larger economy, accounting for 54% of the net commodity product (a measure of output) of the combined economy of the two Koreas before the war.[7]

The Failed Democracy (1953–1961)

After the war, President Rhee presided over an autocratic political system, which, in the words of a Korean scholar, "still carried the U.S. cachet of liberal democracy."[8] Presidential elections were held in 1952, 1956, and 1960, all of which Rhee easily won but which were usually preceded by the sudden deaths of the opposition candidates. The economic system was notoriously corrupt. Under President Rhee's strategy of import substitution, the overvalued exchange rate created an excess demand for foreign exchange, which was allocated to those businesses willing to engage in giving bribes. Yi Pyong-ch'ol, the head of Samsung, received many such favors. He was later accused of giving 64 million won (about US$1.3 million at the 1957 exchange rate) to Rhee.[9] In 1960, popular protests forced Rhee to resign and to leave the country. The National Assembly—Korea's parliament— amended the Constitution and created a parliamentary system with the president as a figurehead. The new Chang Myon government attempted to clean up the corruption, to re-organize the bureaucracy and the military, and to devalue the currency, but these efforts were politically divisive and undermined business confidence. The democratic experiment was short-lived and chaotic. On May 16, 1961, Major General Park Chung Hee staged a coup and seized power on the pretext that the democratic government had failed to establish political and economic stability. The coup ushered in a long era of military rule in Korean politics.

The Era of Park Chung Hee (1961–1979)

"In order to ensure efforts to improve the living conditions of the people in Asia, even undemocratic emergency measures may be necessary. . . . The people of Asia today fear starvation and poverty more than the oppressive duties thrust on them by totalitarianism. . . ."

—Park Chung Hee[10]

"In human life, economics precedes politics or culture."

—Park Chung Hee (from his book, *The Country, The Revolution, And I*)[11]

In 1961, Korea's per capita income barely reached US$100. The country survived mainly on the economic and military aid from the United States. In 1957, U.S. military and economic assistance amounted to US$783 million as against US$456 million in total government revenue.[12] The economy labored under the strains of Rhee's rule. The compound annual growth rate for GNP between 1953 and 1959 was 3.7% and then GNP growth slowed down every year between 1957 and 1960, from 8.7% to 2.3%.[13] The outlook was grim. Reflecting later, Park said, "I honestly felt as if I had been given a pilfered household or a bankrupt firm to manage. Around me I could find little hope."[14]

Under Park, Korea lifted itself out of poverty and created an unparalleled economic miracle. Per capita GDP doubled first between 1960 and 1968; then a second time between 1968 and 1975. Between 1961 and 1979, GNP grew around 10% every year (**Exhibit 2**). In 1962, Korea ranked ninety-ninth in the world in terms of per capita income; by 1986, it ranked forty-fourth. It took Korea less than 30 years to transform itself from a largely agrarian economy into an industrialized economy. In 1965, agriculture accounted for a large portion of Korean GNP while manufacturing accounted for a small share. By 1984, the manufacturing share had increased significantly while the agricultural share had declined. Korea's economic success is often described as "export-led." Exports grew rapidly in the 1960s and 1970s. Spectacular economic successes were accompanied by equally remarkable achievements on the social side. A common measure of income distribution is the Gini coefficient (a range from zero to one, with zero representing perfect income equality and one representing perfect inequality). During the Park era, Korea's income distribution deteriorated but was still more egalitarian than that in Latin America. (For a comparison of economic and social indicators, see **Exhibit 6**.) The "miracle on the Han"[15] was often attributed to Park's deft political management of the economy and to pursuing a well-designed development strategy.[16]

Political Development

Described as an aloof and meticulous man, Park Chung Hee was a legendary figure in Korean politics. In 1995, almost a decade after the country had become democratic, more than two-thirds of South Koreans still rated Park as the country's greatest president.[17] Park ruled Korea under extraordinarily challenging conditions. The two Koreas were technically at war and tensions occasionally flared up between the two countries separated only by a narrow demilitarized zone. The military spending was high, augmented further by an American military presence in Korea. The experience of the 1950s convinced Park that democracy was the wrong form of government to deal with the country's economic and political problems. The purpose of the military coup, as he put it, was "to suspend [democracy] temporarily while it is undergoing medical treatment."[18] After the 1961 coup, the Kennedy Administration pressured Park to restore democracy; he relented in 1963 and in the same year he narrowly won the presidential election. The country thus returned to nominal civilian rule as Park and his top lieutenants shed their military uniforms in favor of civilian dress. A Harvard political scientist, Rupert Emerson, drafted a liberal constitution, which Park promptly superseded by imposing martial law and subjecting the press to government control.

Park used his sweeping powers to effect radical changes in economic policies. Declaring that exports were vital to Korea's self-reliance, against the prevailing intellectual ethos at the time, he shifted the nation's development strategy from import substitution to export promotion through a series of drastic currency devaluations in the early 1960s. And he directed the country's financial resources to support export production. To overcome opposition from the business community, he enacted the Illicit Wealth Accumulation Act whereby he arrested all the prominent businessmen and paraded them through the streets (carrying placards such as "I am a corrupt swine.").[19] The incarcerated entrepreneurs, led by Yi Pyong-ch'ol, the head of Samsung, bargained for release by agreeing to build new industries for export and to donate shares to the state.[20] An alliance between state and business was effectively born. The Federation of Korean Industries (FKI), formed by the pardoned entrepreneurs, became a vehicle to carry out government policies.

Although government clearly towered over business, Park carefully solicited information from the business community as the basis for policy making. Government and business worked closely to hammer out export targets and to make credit and subsidy decisions through monthly export-promotion meetings, often attended by Park himself. Park made a practice of never meeting business people privately but only in large groups in which the business people acted as representatives of their industries rather than of their firms. [21] Park also reformed Korea's civil service. To attract talent and to eradicate corruption, he instituted a merit-based system and a retirement system patterned after Japan's *amakudari* ("descent from heaven") whereby retired bureaucrats often landed lucrative jobs in the private sector. Park also recruited heavily from academia. Each ministry ran its own research institute staffed by people with PhD degrees from abroad. But Park himself kept a tight reign on senior bureaucrats. He allegedly used the Korean Central Intelligence Agency to conduct surveillance of bureaucrats. On the eve of each New Year, Park would visit his cabinet ministers to discuss goals and strategies for the upcoming year. He would check their performance a year later against their promises. Ministers who achieved less than 80% of their promises were fired.[22] The pay and efficiency levels of Korean bureaucrats compared favorably with those of bureaucrats in other developing economies (**Exhibit 7**).

In 1961, Park banned all strike activities and arrested many union activists. He also created an umbrella labor organization called the Federation of Korean Trade Unions (FKTU). The FKTU acted to moderate the demands of its constituent unions, to implement government policies, and to discipline disobedient workers. The Korean Central Intelligence Agency routinely selected the leaders of the FKTU. The repressive labor policies had a tangible effect on strike activities and wages. Real manufacturing wages suffered a decrease in 1960, 1961, and then, drastically, in 1964.[23] It was not until 1966 that union membership reached its 1960 level; Korean work stoppages declined from an average of 79 per year between 1955 and 1960 to only fifteen per year between 1963 and 1971.[24]

In 1971, Park came close to losing the presidential election to an opposition candidate, Kim Dae Jung. In the wake of the election, Park declared a national emergency and promulgated the so-called Yushin (Revitalization) doctrine on the grounds of the "dangerous uncertainties of the international situation" and security threats from North Korea. He suspended the Constitution, dissolved the legislature, closed the universities, and banned all political parties. The new Constitution gave Park powers to dissolve the National Assembly and to appoint one-third of its members. Election of the President was made indirect. The Park government also began a decade-long persecution of Kim Dae Jung. During the 1970s, Kim Dae Jung was run over by a truck; kidnapped and put under house arrest in 1979; and finally sentenced to death, only to be spared with last-minute intervention from President Jimmy Carter. During this period, many other political activists were also arrested and the press was censored.[25]

Economic Development Strategy

The Korean state was heavily interventionist during the Park years. Park, a graduate of a Japanese military academy, was inspired by the success of Japan's economic development model which was characterized by export-led growth and a tightly coordinated relationship between government and business. Emulating Japan's Ministry of International Trade and Investment (MITI), Park created the Economic Planning Board ("EPB") as a super-ministry and vested it with the power to shape the nation's economy through its Five-Year Economic Development Plans. In the EPB's formative years, the agency focused on achieving national self-sufficiency, building basic national infrastructure, and supporting light industries to earn foreign exchange from exports. Subsequent plans set broad macroeconomic and social goals and delineated specific steps to achieve them.[26]

Government financial control   The EPB exercised supervision over all economic ministries, such as the budgeting functions of the Ministry of Finance (MOF) and the collection of economic statistics by the Ministry of Internal Affairs. Through the EPB, government financial control was sweeping. In the 1950s, on advice from the U.S. and the IMF, the government privatized the banks that had been taken over from the Japanese after the war. But the Park regime, staffed by U.S.-trained military officers rather than economists, created a centralized financial system. The 1962 Bank of Korea Act strengthened the MOF's control over monetary policy. The MOF could request the board of the Bank of Korea to "reconsider" previously passed resolutions and it exercised substantial authority over appointing the members of the Monetary Board. The operating budget of the Bank of Korea was subject to approval by the cabinet. In the early 1960s, the Park regime re-nationalized all commercial banks in the name of confiscating "illicit wealth." Legislation was passed to sharply curtail the voting power of the remaining large private shareholders. The government appointed all major bank officers and the government approved the banks' annual budgets. Interest rate ceilings and floors were imposed and the MOF screened and approved all loan applications. Currency was inconvertible, although it was set at a level reasonably close to a hypothetical market-determined exchange rate in the 1960s.[27] Between 1974 and 1979, the government pegged the exchange rate to the U.S. dollar.

Export promotion and import substitution   Throughout the Park era, consistent with its goal of export promotion, exporters received generous financial incentives in the form of subsidized bank loans. The benefits for the recipients of the rationed credit are reflected in the large discrepancies between the official interest rates and the unofficial—called curb—market loan rates, especially in the 1970s. In the 1960s and 1970s, the severe financial repression policies of the government led to periods of negative or low real interest rates, which created an excess demand for credit. To cover the shortage, banks turned to the discount windows of the central bank, an occasion for the central bank not just to set monetary aggregates but to direct credit to favored sectors, a practice known at the time as "window guidance." Credit availability thus became a powerful tool for the government to enforce its industrial policy objectives. (On interest rates, see **Exhibit 11**.) Exporters were also exempt from tariffs or quantitative restrictions imposed on their imported inputs. Exports grew rapidly as measured by the export/GNP ratio. In the 1960s, the annual average ratio was 23.6%; in the 1970s, the ratio more than doubled, to 53.9%. [28]

Before the 1967 reform, imports had been virtually banned. In 1967, the authorities shifted to a different protection regime. All imports were divided into prohibited, restricted, and unrestricted categories. In 1967, the ratio of restricted items to total imports was 40%. Tariffs and quotas were never as important as the approval system to protect domestic industries. In 1968, according to a World Bank study, tariffs only amounted to 9% of import value and the monetary equivalent of quotas amounted to only 4%.[29]

The other main instrument by the government to promote domestic industries was financial control. Government financial control reached its zenith in the mid-1970s when Park, using his unprecedented executive powers under the Yushin system, shifted to a stronger import substitution stance (against advice from the United States and IMF). He launched the Heavy and Chemical Industrialization Policy (HCIP) and targeted capital-intensive products, such as autos, steel, and chemicals, for development. In addition to the central bank's discount facilities, the government established the National Investment Fund (NIF) in 1974 to promote the heavy and chemical industries. Banks were required to make compulsory deposits in the NIF and the MOF designed the annual lending programs. Because of the huge capital requirements under the HCIP and in part because of the availability of cheap petro-dollars, Korea's foreign debt rose during this period. In 1975, the foreign debt/GNP ratio reached 40.5%, as compared with 28.7% in 1970, even though Korea's private savings rose from 7.4% of GDP in the 1960s to 18% in the 1970s (**Exhibit 2**).[30]

To ensure scale economies and the efficiency of capital allocation, the government encouraged firms to export capital-intensive products and it tied bank loans to export performance. As a result, capital-intensive exports grew during the HCIP period. Between 1971 and 1979, the share of heavy and chemical products of Korean merchandise exports rose while the share of labor-intensive light industry products declined (**Exhibit 5**). (However, textile and apparel products still accounted for 30% of Korean exports by 1985.[31]) An example of how the program worked is the case of Hyundai Motor Company, which successfully exported its first car model, the Pony, in 1979. Hyundai had obtained foreign exchange loans from the government to import body styling and designs from Italy and engines, transmission, and axle technology from Mitsubishi. The condition for the loan was that the Pony had to be exported.[32]

Foreign debt strategy   During the Park era, investment grew at a high rate (**Exhibit 2**). The HCIP created an investment boom. During 1973 and 1974, investment grew at 36% per year. Such a high rate of investment growth could not be funded fully by domestic savings. In the 1950s, Koreans saved very little; in 1960, the private savings rate was only 2.9% of GNP and in the 1960s, the private savings rate hovered around 9%. Initially, foreign aid—primarily from the United States—financed much of Korea's net funding needs, averaging around US$300 million per annum during the 1955-1959 period—about 16% of GNP. Over time, however, reliance on foreign aid decreased. In the early 1960s, foreign aid averaged around US$210 million per year; it dropped to $110 million between 1965 and 1969; and to just a trickle of US$28 million in the first half of the 1970s. Foreign aid completely ended in 1975.[33]

To preserve national control of its own industries, Korea restricted foreign direct investment (FDI) inflows, preferring instead debt financing. As foreign aid dried up, the Park government increasingly turned to foreign borrowing. The Foreign Capital Inducement Act had been amended in 1962 to provide government guarantees to lenders, thus removing any default risks. Throughout the Park era, foreign debt, measured as a ratio of GDP, rose dramatically. In 1962, the foreign debt/GDP ratio was a mere 3.8%; by the end of the Park reign it had risen to 35.4% (**Exhibit 4**). In contrast, the FDI/GDP ratio hovered between 1% to 2%.

Macroeconomic policy adjustment   Throughout the Park reign, the government kept a loose monetary tap. On average, M2 grew at a double-digit rate between 1961 and 1979 (**Exhibit 2**). The corporate debt/equity ratio was high; the ratio for the manufacturing sector rose from 136% in 1961 to 377% in 1980. Inflation was also high during the Park era (**Exhibit 11**). Foreign debt was used proactively to manage macroeconomic cycles. In the wake of the first oil shock, the government financed the increasing costs of fuel imports by borrowing abroad. Between 1973 and 1974, foreign debt rose by 42% but overall economic growth was maintained. In 1976, while many other non-oil producing countries were deep in recession, Korean GNP grew by 14.4%. Because foreign debt was tied to export promotion, exports grew by 49% in 1976.[34]

Corporate policy   The prime beneficiaries of the government's tight financial rein during the Park era were the large and highly diversified business groups known as chaebols. The top four chaebols—Hyundai, Samsung, Lucky-Goldstar (LG), and Daewoo, all ranking among the *Fortune* 500 in size—developed rapidly during this period. These chaebols were family-owned conglomerates.

Their organization was similar to that of the Japanese zaibatsu, i.e., they were groups of firms held together by ownership, management, and family ties. There were two significant differences, however. First, ownership and control of the chaebols were vested with the families of the groups' founders. Second, the chaebols did not control banks. State financial control meant that the chaebols were more dependent on the state than were the Japanese zaibatsu. Chaebols were highly capable firms. They were able to absorb technology from their foreign suppliers effectively and quickly. For example, Hyundai began to produce cars only in 1973, but by 1979, it was already exporting 62,592 units of its Pony model. To develop this model, Hyundai had licensed technologies from twenty-six firms in Italy, Japan, and Britain.[35]

The government supported the chaebols by bestowing cheap credit and issuing investment licenses to those chaebols with proven records of success. One indication of this policy bias was that large firms in Korea were much more heavily indebted than small firms. In 1975, for example, the average debt/equity ratio for the large manufacturing firms was 351%; for small firms, it was only 186%.[36] Chaebols grew rapidly because of favorable policy treatments. In 1976, the combined sales of the top 10 chaebols accounted for approximately 20% of GNP. This grew to 48% of GNP by 1980 (**Exhibit 9**). However, the government did not support chaebols only for the purpose of achieving economic ends; it also did so to fulfill its social and political objectives. Chaebols absorbed much of the work force in the nation. Virtually all of the chaebols promised lifetime employment, with promotions and compensations determined on the basis of seniority. Chaebols were relied upon to enforce government social programs. For example, the chaebols helped implement the Samauel ("New Town") movement, initiated by Park. Under Samauel, modern towns were constructed in rural counties to extend social welfare programs to the impoverished.[37]

The Dawning of Political and Economic Liberalization (1980-1992)

"In the 1970s, we followed the Japanese model, but in the 1980s we are looking more to the U.S.A."

— A Korean official[38]

Political Transition

In October 1979, South Korea faced a major national crisis when President Park Chung Hee was assassinated. Acting President Choi Kyu-Hah described the death of Park in the following terms: "[T]he heavens trembled and the earth shook, nature seemed to wither and the people were stricken by fright and grief."[39] In May 1980, Chun Doo Hwan, a four-star general, seized control via a coup d'état and promptly extended martial law and banned all political activities to restore political stability. In the same year, Chun ordered troops to fire on demonstrators in Kwangju, killing at least 240 people and wounding 1,800.[40] This event—later known as the Kwangju Massacre—dogged Chun's presidency to its end. In May 1981, Chun garnered 90% of the vote in an election bereft of any opposition.

Throughout the Chun era, demonstrators took to the streets to challenge his rule and the National Assembly became more assertive. In the 1985 legislative elections, the ruling party suffered a surprising setback even though it still retained a majority. In the same year, a constitutional amendment was proposed to allow the direct election of the president. By 1987, as the burning stench of tear gas had barely dissipated, winds of change swept the Korean nation on a rising popular chorus for freedom and democracy. The 1988 Olympic Games, held in Seoul, provided extra impetus for political reform as political and policy elites clamored for international respectability. Chun, true to his pledge, stepped down after his first term. A contrite Chun appeared on national TV and acknowledged his misdeeds. Afterward, he retired to seclusion in a monastery. In December 1987, Korea held its first genuinely competitive presidential election in which Roh Tae Woo, Chun's military classmate and his hand-picked successor, won the presidency. Although there were charges of electoral fraud, most observers agreed that the outcome was fair and that Roh's victory was due to the inability of the two major dissidents-turned-politicians, Kim Young Sam and Kim Dae Jung, to form a united front.

Just one year after the 1987 presidential election, in 1988, voters denied the ruling party, the Democratic Liberal Party, a majority in the National Assembly for the first time. Significantly, Roh did not attempt to use the military to change the political arrangements. Instead, he resorted to an age-tested political approach in mature democracies—crafting a coalition of parties to hold on to power. The new coalition, incorporating Kim Young Sam's Reunification Democratic Party, won the 1992 presidential election, resulting in Kim Young Sam presidency between 1992 and 1997. In contrast to the 1987 election, street demonstrations were muted and the specter of possible military intervention was completely absent.

That Korea emerged from the shadows of a military junta with tranquility is testimony to the crowning economic achievements of the country. Political scientists have long speculated that there is a transition zone in which the probability of authoritarian regimes shifting to democracy increases dramatically. In the 1980s, that zone was estimated to range from US$1,000 to US$3,000 per capita, a level Korea had reached by then. Rising incomes were associated with the emergence of a middle and professional class, which made repression more costly. As an article in *The Economist* asked in 1987: "What happens when tear gas meets the middle class in Seoul?"[41] The middle class also valued autonomy, individual welfare, and an increasing scope for decision making. Hyung-Koo Lee, Minister of Labor in the early 1990s, observed, "I couldn't care less about the construction of the Seoul-Pusan expressway when the roads in our town still remain dirty and my village doesn't have an adequate elementary school."[42] Economic success also raised awareness of the exacting social cost associated with it. In a survey of eight Asian cities in 1989, Koreans were found to be hardest working: They worked 2,300 hours a year but only took eight days off.[43] Deaths attributed to stress-related illness among Korean males were 2.3 times higher than Japanese males; the ratio was even higher for Korean females.[44]

Fine-tuning the Economic System

Korea entered the 1980s with an uncertain economic and political future. In the early years of the decade, Korea was the fourth largest debtor in the world (after Mexico, Brazil, and Argentina) and it seemed to possess all the elements for a full-blown financial crisis.[45] The assassination of General Park clouded the country's prospects. Reeling from the second oil shock and a poor harvest, output stagnated and declined. Inflation was high, at 24.9% in 1980 and 21.3% in 1981. Current account deficits rose from –2.1% of GDP in 1978 to –9.7% in 1980. (Economic data for this period are found in **Exhibit 2**.) Apart from these immediate woes, the economy began to experience structural strains from Park's developmental strategy. The income distribution worsened and business concentration was unprecedented (**Exhibit 9**). As an eerie antecedent to the events in 1997, the Korean financial community was rocked by corruption scandals--apparently involving Chun's wife—which brought the Korean money market to near collapse.[46] Elsewhere in the world, debt suspensions and rescheduling by Mexico, Argentina, Chile, and Brazil boded ill for Korea's payment prospects.[47]

Backed by two stand-by agreements with the IMF (in 1981 and 1983), Chun put into effect a far-reaching stabilization program. To restore fiscal balance, he imposed a wage freeze on public-sector employees, froze all hirings, and delayed promotions. Under a "social purification" campaign, Chun simply purged a large number of government employees. He also imposed a wage freeze on Korean labor in 1981 and restructured Korean labor unions to reduce their power. These policies produced a dramatic success. By 1986, while the Latin American economies were still mired in what was later known as the "lost decade," Korea successfully halved its budget deficit and lowered the inflation rate from 24.9% in 1980 to 4.6% in 1986. The budgetary deficit was eliminated in the second half of the 1980s. GNP grew by 9.9% between 1986 and 1989. Exports grew by 16% per year from 1980 to 1986 and the current account was in the black every year between 1986 and 1989, the longest streak in history. Foreign debt fell and the maturity structure improved. The country never needed to reschedule its debt payment, as many other high debtor nations did at the time. (On Korea's debt burdens, see **Exhibit 4** and **Exhibit 6**.)

After Chun successfully broke the high inflation that was a hallmark of the Park era, he began to initiate a number of structural reforms. Several forces propelled the movement toward economic reform. First, the huge current account surplus that had emerged since 1986 increased tensions with the United States. The United States was Korea's largest export destination, accounting for 36% of Korea's exports in 1985. With a trade deficit of US$7 billion in 1987, the United States pressured the Korean government to liberalize imports. Second, reform-minded policy advisors and academics— many of whom had been educated in the United States—advocated free market ideas. To them, financial steerage by the government was stunting the maturation of the Korean financial system, as banks, sandwiched between low deposit rates and mandated loan rates, performed poorly. They pointed to declining bank profitability and rising non-performing loans as signs of a dysfunctional financial system (**Exhibit 14**). However, Chun and his successor, Roh Tae Woo, only embraced reform selectively. They often initiated a round of liberalization in one area while imposing new controls in other areas. Reform measures were adopted on both internal and external fronts.

Internal front   The financial sector was a focal point of the reform effort. Interest rates were first raised in 1980 and then interest rate structures were streamlined. In the 1970s, Korea had a highly differentiated interest rate structure, with loans for different purposes carrying multiple rates. Export loans consistently enjoyed the lowest rates, followed by facility investments in heavy industries favored by the state. Small businesses had to pay high unofficial curb market rates as the official credit market was inaccessible to them. In 1982, loan rates were unified and real interest rates became positive and over time the curb market rates came down gradually. Because loan rates were still set by the government, interest rate differentials between official and unofficial sources of finance remained (**Exhibit 11**). In 1988, the government abolished a number of policy loans, including those supporting exports.

Between 1981 and 1983, the four national banks were privatized but the state limited each individual shareholder to only 8% of the stake. The purpose was to limit control of these banks by the chaebols and to prevent further business concentration. The government also imposed maximum quotas on bank lending to the chaebols in order to curb the chaebols' rapid growth. This policy was complemented by a requirement that banks meet minimum lending quotas to small and medium enterprises (SMEs). In addition, the government encouraged the development of capital markets in order to reduce corporate reliance on bank credit and to foster growth of direct financial intermediation mechanisms. Favorable tax treatments and preferential access to bank credit were given to corporations that went public on the stock exchange.

The effort to direct credit away from the chaebols was only partially successful. On the one hand, the chaebols' debt level came down; in 1985, the debt/equity ratio for the top 30 chaebols was 571%; by 1990, it had declined to 381%.[48] But at the same time, the chaebols acquired more financing facilities. The limitation on chaebol ownership of banks was only partially enforced and the government lowered entry barriers for non-bank financial institutions, such as merchant banks, short-term finance companies, and insurance and securities companies, most of which were owned by chaebols. The proliferation of non-bank financial institutions broke down the traditional fire wall between the financing and production functions of the chaebols. In the 1980s, firms diversified their funding channels (**Exhibit 10**).

Chun and Roh attenuated but ultimately failed to dislodge the basic character of Park's industrial policy regime. In 1980, the Fair Trade Law was passed. It was the first antitrust legislation in Korean history.[49] The Law "aimed at encouraging fair and free competition and thereby stimulating creative business activities and protecting consumers as well as promoting a balanced development of the national economy."[50] Enforcement again lagged behind the reformist rhetoric. Practically all the mergers were approved by the government and between 1981 and 1985 only five firms were accused of abusing their power.[51] In 1985, Chun introduced the Industrial Development Law, which stressed a "functional" rather than sectoral approach to industrial policy. But the Industrial Development Law appeared to strengthen the hand of the state by endowing it with wide-ranging powers to rationalize industries and corporations. The law was also used to pressure banks to rescue troubled companies as well as to force poorly performing firms to merge with strong firms.[52]

External front The Chun-Roh governments took steps to liberalize Korea's trade account. The thrust of the reform was to reduce the number of imports on the restricted list and to move more items to the so-called "automatic approval" list. The ratio of import items subject to automatic approval—called the liberalization ratio—rose several times, usually according to a pre-announced schedule, from 68.6% in 1980 to 84.8% in 1984 and to 99% in 1992. Average tariff rates, however, rose in the early 1980s, mainly to protect agriculture and then came down in the second half of the 1980s. In 1983, the average tariff rate was 13.7%; in 1990, it was 11.4%. The rising liberalization ratio and tariff reduction, however, did not entail a completely open trade account. Laws on health, safety, and public health mechanisms served as non-tariff barriers. According to the World Bank, the rapidly rising liberalization ratio overstated the extent of true import liberalization. For example, under a "surveillance system," an unrestricted import item required review by Korean industry associations to determine if the importation was injurious to domestic firms.[53] The surveillance list was abolished in 1989.

While the trade account reforms were gradually and progressively implemented, the capital account reforms took a more circuitous route. As the current account surpluses built up, in the second half of the 1980s, the authorities began to liberalize rules on capital outflows, such as permitting Korean firms to purchase real estate abroad and steadily raising the approval threshold for direct investment projects abroad. On the portfolio side, Korean institutional investors were permitted to buy foreign stocks in 1988 and Korean banks could issue foreign exchange bonds in 1990. The authorities also used its foreign exchange reserves to improve the maturity structure of its foreign debt. In 1987 and 1988, the government supplied loans to Korean financial institutions and directed them to speed up payment of short-term loans before maturity.

Capital inflow reforms were phased in more gradually. FDI restrictions were first eased, followed by an easing of restrictions on portfolio capital inflows. Because of the traditional stance against FDI, there were numerous restrictions. Majority foreign ownership was discouraged and sole foreign ownership was allowed only in areas where production was for export. In 1988, a negative list system—which spelled out sectors off-limits to FDI—replaced a positive list system, but the list covered some 150 categories. In 1992, local content, export sales, and mandatory technology transfer requirements were relaxed. However, concerned about the effect of the rising foreign presence on domestic firms, the authorities at the same time also withdrew the tax privileges enjoyed by foreign investors. In a major move in 1992, the domestic stock market was opened to foreign investors, but a 3% limit on investment by an individual foreigner and a 10% limit on total foreign investment were imposed.

The government reformed the foreign exchange system on two fronts. First, in 1988, the government accepted the obligations of Article VIII of the IMF to allow currency convertibility on current account transactions. However, numerous restrictions—such as documentation requirements and limits on the size of foreign exchange holdings—still remained on foreign exchange transactions. Second, the government reformed the exchange rate regime. In 1980, as a part of its macroeconomic adjustment program, the authorities devalued the won by 17% and introduced a more flexible exchange rate regime. Under the new regime, the exchange rate was determined on the basis of a basket of currencies and other factors affecting the Korean external position.[54] In 1990, the government adopted a managed float system, called the "market average exchange rate (MAR)." The MAR was determined on the basis of the weighted average of the inter-bank rates for the won-dollar spot transactions on the previous day. During each business day, the non-interbank rate was allowed to fluctuate within the given margins of the MAR. In a number of moves, the margin was widened from ± 0.4% in 1990 to ± 0.8% in 1992.[55]

Crusader for Reform: Kim Young Sam (1993–1997)

In the 1990s, as the Korean economy gained stature, Korean leaders themselves viewed economic reform as a way to gain respectability in the international community. Kim Young Sam, elected to office in 1992, epitomized this new breed of leaders. In March 1995, Korea applied to join the prestigious Organisation for Economic Co-operation and Development. OECD membership required Korea to open further its service and capital accounts and to undertake deep financial reforms. President Kim was eager to join the OECD before his term expired. Reflecting pride that the country had come so far, President Kim declared, in a 1995 interview with *BusinessWeek*, that Korean per capita income would reach US$10,000 in 1995 and would reach US$20,000 by the twenty-first century. "[I]t is our turn," he said, "to contribute to the world by helping developing countries in need."[56]

Determined to showcase a new Korea, Kim Young Sam even demolished the old building that had housed Korean presidents since Syngman Rhee. In his inauguration address, he proclaimed, "Misconduct and corruption are the most terrifying enemies attacking the foundations of our society."[57] He coined the phrase, "Korean disease," of which he saw signs not only in the public but also in the private sectors. In an interview, he compared the chaebols to an "octopus with their tentacles stretching throughout the economy."[58] Throughout his presidency, he thrust numerous reform decrees on a reluctant bureaucracy and business community. His manner of reform was described by one scholar as "reform authoritarianism."[59] The reform program encompassed an ambitious and broad agenda ranging from political to economic issues.

Political Reforms

In 1995, Kim Young Sam indicted his predecessors, Chun Doo Hwan and Roh Tae Woo, on charges of corruption and sedition in connection with the Kwangju Massacre. They were alleged to have together accumulated slush funds of US$1 billion in return for political patronage during their presidential terms.[60] Both were sentenced harshly but later received clemency.[61] Kim's quest to wipe out corruption extended to purges of more than 3,000 government officials, three ministers, five vice-ministers, and the mayor of Seoul.[62] Commercial bankers who had funneled funds between business and political leaders were also jailed. Virtually all chaebol leaders were summoned for lengthy hearings in widely-televised sessions in an attempt to expose their past corrupt business practices. Kim also purged many political loyalists associated with Chun and Roh, including even those who had aided his own election in 1992. He tightened laws on political contributions and disclosed his own family's wealth. To make Korean politics transparent, he outlawed the use of aliases in financial transactions. In the past, Koreans had not been required to disclose their real names or entities in financial transactions, such as lending and investing, which facilitated tax evasions and prevented the authorities from tracing the sources and uses of funds. This measure apparently touched a raw nerve. The KOSPI immediately fell by 4.5%, until then the largest single-day drop. [63]

Economic Reforms

Kim led a crusade against the chaebols, arguing that their opaque management style was undemocratic. Financial liberalization was the key to undo the chaebols' dominance. On the heels of his inauguration, Kim unveiled an ambitious "Blueprint for Financial Reform" in 1993. The reforms aimed at liberalizing all interest rates (except policy loans), reducing the interest rate subsidies on policy loans, and giving more autonomy to banks and firms. For example, the reforms ended the appointment of commercial bank managers by government, removed maturity restrictions for commercial paper and corporate bonds, eliminated credit controls on all chaebols except the top ten, and lowered the mandatory lending quota to the SMEs. The government announced the goal of seeking to ban the cross guarantees of debt—whereby subsidiaries of the chaebols guaranteed one another's debts, a source of financial advantage to the chaebols—by March 2001. Kim also outlined steps to limit the debt/equity ratios of the chaebols. He demanded that the top 30 chaebols select three to four core businesses and divest the rest. He also sought additional financial disclosures from Korean corporations and demanded consolidated financial statements from Korean companies. A broad effort was launched to reform Korea's business licensing system. The five-year plan was abolished and the all-powerful EPB was merged with the Ministry of Finance to form the Ministry of Finance and Economy (MOFE).

On the external front in the first year of Kim's presidency, the government further opened the capital account and numerous policy initiatives were enacted. Many rules on portfolio capital inflows were either abolished or simplified. For example, Korean firms were no longer required to apply for permission to issue foreign exchange-denominated bonds. Regulatory requirements were also eased. In 1993, the government abolished the requirement that overseas branches of Korean banks register with the government every three years. Banks and non-bank financial institutions were allowed to set up overseas branches to engage in overseas borrowing.

Limited liberalization on FDI inflows was enacted in 1994 and 1995. Approval procedures were simplified in 1994 and a number of manufacturing and service sectors were opened to FDI in 1995. Ceilings on stock investments by foreign investors were raised. Individual ceilings were raised from 3% to 7% and aggregate ceilings, from 10% in 1996 to 26% in 1997. The overseas branches of domestic banks were allowed to supply loans to those Korean firms engaged in trading financial futures and Korean firms were permitted to borrow abroad to finance imports of capital goods.[64] The authorities also reduced the controls on capital outflows by raising the size of the projects subject to automatic approval and by reducing the number of restricted sectors. The government further widened the margins of the currency, from ±0.8% of the MAR in 1992 to ±2.5% in 1997. [65]

Reform Outcomes

The outcomes of these reform initiatives were mixed. Kim's anti-corruption campaign was stymied by scandals within both his own administration and his own family toward the end of his reign, thus tarnishing his image as a reformer. In 1996, two ministers were charged with receiving bribes and Kim's personal assistant was arrested on charges of graft. Furthermore, there were accusations of favoritism. The Hanbo Group, a steel producer and the first chaebol to file for bankruptcy in 1997, apparently had received its business license with the help of no less than President Kim's son, while a far more capable firm, Hyundai, was consistently denied the opportunity to foray into steel production. In June 1997, as financial troubles at the country's third largest auto producer, Kia, unfolded, Finance Minister Kang Kyung Shik stated that the Korean economy needed market discipline and that "even the chaebols can fail." However, it was widely known that Minister Kang had extensive connections with Kia's rival, Samsung, which was looking to acquire Kia's facilities. Newspapers speculated that the reason why Samsung was permitted to enter the crowded automobile production sector was because it had invested heavily in Kim Young Sam's hometown of Pusan.[66]

Kim's reforms were popular among the public; at one point, his approval ratings reached 90% and there were calls to revise the Constitution to allow him to govern another term. But there was brewing discontent beneath the surface. Kim's political reforms had alienated many of the members of his own party. A growing voice opposed to Kim's reforms was from the Korean business community. With their increasing size and sophistication, the chaebols came to resent the heavy-handed paternalism by the government and began to demand more independence. The Korean Federation of Industries, in effect a government watchdog under Park, had become a mouthpiece advocating the interests of the big business.

Business leaders believed that they had no alternative but to provide illicit funds to lobby the politicians. Chung Ju-Yung, the founder of the Hyundai Group, aptly summed up this sentiment by saying, "(the) politicians are the culprits and the businessmen are accomplices."[67] The business community also opposed Kim's regulatory efforts. Kang Ho Young, an official at the FKI, stated, "Business should be left to market. There shouldn't be any regulations."[68] Compounding these political problems, the economy slowed down in 1996 (**Exhibit 2**). Given the weight of the chaebols in the Korean economy, Kim had to placate their demands. He delayed implementation of the ban on cross guarantees and the reduction of the debt/equity ratios. In the name of increasing competitiveness, the government eased the funding restrictions placed on the chaebols and accelerated approvals of non-bank financial institutions. In 1993, there were six merchant banks; in 1994, there were fifteen; and in 1996 the number increased to thirty. Because the merchant banks provided the chaebols with additional sources of funds, both the size and debt/equity ratio of the chaebols grew under Kim (**Exhibit 9**).

The result of the opening of the capital account was an increase in portfolio capital flows. Because long-term capital inflows were still restricted, short-term capital came in rapidly. During the 1994-1996 period, over 60% of private capital inflows were comprised of short-term capital. Foreign debt, after having stabilized for a number of years, began to rise again and the maturity structure deteriorated (**Exhibit 4**).

The diversification of the funding sources for firms (**Exhibit 10**) presented regulatory difficulties. In terms of loans and discounts, non-bank financial institutions accounted for 37% in 1980; by 1996, their share reached 57%. Non-bank financial institutions were subject to less governmental supervision than commercial banks. Commercial banks were regulated by the Bank of Korea and the

Office of Banking Supervision (OBS), whereas non-bank financial institutions fell under the authority of the MOFE. This lack of a consolidated regulatory structure led to different regulatory standards; the MOFE was traditionally less vigilant than the Bank of Korea and OBS in enforcing financial supervision. Also banks and the non-bank financial institutions engaged heavily in borrowing and lending activities completely outside the regulatory reach of the Korean supervisory authorities through their overseas branches. In 1996, Korea's foreign debt reached US$100 billion. However, according to an OECD study, this figure did not include the off-shore borrowing of overseas branches and subsidiaries of Korean financial and non-financial institutions. This amount, at US$50 billion in 1996, did not enter the government's balance of payment accounting of foreign debt because the borrowing was done by non-resident institutions.[69]

Other areas of financial supervision remained lax. The non-performing loan classification standard was loose as compared to that of other OECD nations. For example, non-performing loans were defined as loans in arrears for six months rather than the three months prevailing elsewhere. The Korean tax code discouraged prudential practices. Adequate provisioning for losses was penalized by the tax code: Loan loss reserves over 2% of total loans were not tax deductible. Merchant banks, in the face of the increasing riskiness of their loans, in fact decreased loss provisions, from 1.5% of total loans in 1993 to only 0.6% in 1996. In 1995, the government loosened provisioning requirements: The provisioning for doubtful loans was lowered from 100% to 75%; for securities holdings, from 100% to 30%. Accounting rules failed to enforce strictly the requirement that firms provide consolidated statements encompassing their affiliated financial institutions and subsidiaries.[70]

Korea in the Eye of the Storm

After a period of healthy economic growth, low inflation, and low unemployment, in 1996 Korea's trade deficit rose sharply, mainly because of the collapse of the price of the country's main export item, memory chips. At one point, the average unit price fell from as high as US$50 to US$4. Moreover, the real exchange rate had appreciated, but the Kim Young Sam government devalued the currency by only 8% despite calls for a sharper devaluation to restore competitiveness[71] (**Exhibit 2** and **Exhibit 3**). Despite these problems in the economy, Korea's borrowing costs in fact declined, due to the aura conferred on the country by its induction into the OECD. In 1996, the Korean banks' spread over the London Inter-Bank Offered Rate (LIBOR) narrowed, further feeding a borrowing binge.[72] Attracted by high Korean interest rates, a large amount of short-term debt came into the country and resulted in a maturity mismatch: Korean banks borrowed overseas short-term but lent the money to chaebols to finance investment projects with long gestation periods. Of the money borrowed by the merchant banks, 64% consisted of short-term loans, but 85% of their lending was long term.[73] By early 1997, signs of troubles emanated from the Korean corporate sector. Between January and April, three second-tier chaebols, Hanbo (ranked fourteenth), Sammi (twenty-sixth), and Jinro (nineteenth) filed for bankruptcies. These smaller chaebols had very high debt levels, compared to the top chaebols. The average debt-to-equity ratio for Hanbo, Sammi, and Jinro in 1995 reached 2,120%, as compared to the average ratio of 298% for Hyundai, Samsung and LG, the top three chaebols.[74]

The Financial Crisis

The Asian financial crisis first erupted in Thailand, with the collapse of the Thai baht in July 1997. Economic turmoil quickly spread to other Asian regions, attacking the Indonesian rupiah and the

Malaysian ringgit. In October, the Hong Kong stock market crashed and Taiwan promptly devalued its currency. The economic links between Korea and Southeast Asia appeared modest. Korean firms had only lost US$2 billion in Southeast Asia in the summer of 1997. The region as a whole accounted for about 9.6% of Korean exports.[75] But as the crisis took on an East Asian dimension, Standard and Poor's downgraded Korea's sovereign status. Foreign banks began to withdraw credit lines or otherwise refused to extend maturing debt and Korea's foreign exchange reserves plummeted. In October, the government devalued the won; in November the government was forced to widen the margins of the currency, from ±2.5% to ±10% of the MAR, and on December 16, the won was allowed to free float. The currency rapidly depreciated and lost some 75% of its value against the dollar in the last three months of 1997. Amidst the massive hemorrhage of foreign exchange reserves, it was revealed that only a small portion of the official foreign exchange reserves was "usable." In October and November, the Bank of Korea had deposited some US$17 billion of its foreign exchange reserves in accounts of overseas branches of Korean financial institutions to prevent them from defaulting. By the end of November, usable foreign exchange reserves stood at only US$7.2 billion.

Many in government and in the business community had initially thought that the events leading up to the crisis were just a short-term development. The Minister of Finance proclaimed that it was "unthinkable" to receive assistance from the IMF. In November, the government turned to Japan and the United States to seek help to roll over the maturing short-term debt, but the effort was unsuccessful. As the situation continued to deteriorate, the government reached an agreement with the IMF on December 3, 1997 to receive a loan up to US$55 billion. The loan consisted of US$21 billion from the IMF, US$14 billion from the World Bank and the Asian Development Bank to support structural reforms, and US$20 billion pledged by Japan, the United States, and a number of European countries as "the second line of defense." Going well beyond its traditional mandate to aid countries experiencing short-term balance of payment difficulties, the IMF imposed a sweeping program of structural reforms as a condition for its loan support. The IMF program not only specified the general direction of reforms but also dictated a detailed timetable to enforce them.[76] For example, the IMF program required Korea to allow foreign investors to acquire 55% of its listed companies by December 1997 and then 100% by the end of 1998. (See **Exhibit 15** for a summary of the IMF reforms.)

The IMF package was consummated at the most politically inopportune moment. The country was in the middle of a presidential election; the harsh and sweeping conditions contained in the package provoked a public backlash. All of the candidates criticized the package and some even suggested that the debt crisis itself was "the result of a plot by Japan and the United States to place South Korea under neocolonial economic rule by the International Monetary Fund."[77] The won continued to plummet and foreign exchange reserves drained ever more rapidly. The exchange rate had stood at 1,235 won per dollar right before the IMF agreement was reached but on December 23, the won dipped to 1,962 won per dollar. Interest rate nearly doubled in the month of December. (For exchange rate movements, money market rates and key events in 1997, see **Exhibit 13** and **Exhibit 16**.)

On the Back of a Tiger

On December 18, 1997, Korea held a presidential election. Kim Young Sam stepped down, as mandated by the Korean Constitution that stipulated a one-term presidency. Kim Dae Jung, the former political prisoner on death row, won with a margin of victory of only 1.6%. This historic moment, in which a transfer of power took place between two civilian presidents, was marred by the financial crisis enveloping the nation. Ever a populist, candidate Kim Dae Jung hawked vegetables to garner votes during the presidential campaign; he was also a harsh critic of the IMF program. At a press conference on December 22, 1997, an ashen-faced President-elect, more in the habit of the straight talk of a political dissident than that of a skilled politician, declared, "[W]e have no money. We don't know whether we'll default tomorrow or the day after tomorrow. I am totally flabbergasted."[78] The statement set off a panic among investors and bankers and the Korean stock and currency markets were battered anew.

Initially, many doubted that Kim Dae Jung was the right leader for the moment. He was often portrayed as a left-wing radical and as being reluctant to push for the much-needed labor reforms. On the other hand, there was also speculation that he was too close to the conservative oligarchy to implement real reforms. In one of his first presidential acts, he pardoned both Chun Doo Hwan and Roh Tae Woo and he formed a coalition government with the conservative United Liberal Democrats (ULD). The leader of the ULD, Kim Jong-Pil, had been the mastermind behind the 1961 coup and the founder of the Korean Central Intelligence Agency. But after he assumed the mantle at the Blue House—the presidential residence, Kim Dae Jung quickly shed his populist image and pledged to implement the IMF program in full and at a fast pace.

He strengthened the regulatory standards by making mandatory the reporting of consolidated financial statements. Currency reforms were implemented to make the won convertible on the capital account by the end of 2000. He pushed through legislation to allow layoffs and to expand the coverage of the social safety net. He even went beyond the IMF program to permit hostile takeovers by foreign firms. Kim, however, faced considerable political obstacles in his reform effort. His own party did not have control of the National Assembly (**Exhibit 8**). Although he did secure a tenuous working majority in the National Assembly, his political edge might dissipate in the National Assembly elections in April 2000. He tried to reach out to labor by establishing a tripartite committee, consisting of government, business, and labor. But labor decided to boycott the entire effort. In July 1998, workers at a Hyundai auto plant struck, protesting the firm's plan to lay off workers. The business community strongly opposed the corporate restructuring plans and the opening of the capital market to foreign investors, as laid out in the IMF program. The FKI again led the way by organizing a concerted effort to portray Kim's policy to attract FDI as unpatriotic.

To overcome the opposition, Kim resorted to some extreme measures. On the political front, he railroaded many of his reform bills through the National Assembly without consultation with the opposition. Such actions invited lawsuits from citizens accusing their deputies of dereliction of duty. On the economic front, he pressured firms to comply with his restructuring plan not by market mechanisms but by old-fashioned state intervention. He threatened to cut off loans to Lucky-Goldstar when Lucky-Goldstar refused to accept the government's restructuring plan.

In 1999, the economy made a strong recovery (**Exhibit 2**). FDI rose to a record US$ 8.8 billion and protracted and highly symbolic negotiations finally brought about the sale of Korea First Bank to Newbridge Capital of the United States. There were, however, structural problems to be tackled. The average debt/equity ratio of the five top chaebols was over 300% even though the goal was to reduce the ratio to below 200% and the five top chaebols dominated the new stock and bond issues for the year. Government financial control increased, not decreased, as noted in *The Economist*. The government had nationalized the three biggest commercial banks and was a major shareholder in three other banks. On the social front, according to a government report, income distribution worsened as the economy was being restructured.[79]

As President Kim looked to the future, he was reminded of an ancient Asian proverb, "A man on the back of a tiger finds riding difficult." Similarly, leading and managing Korea's fast-growing economy was never easy, but the task was made all the more difficult as the Korean polity became more democratic and its society became more polarized. Could President Kim complete his reform program while holding together the basic social and political fabric of this young democracy?

Exhibit 1   Map of Korea

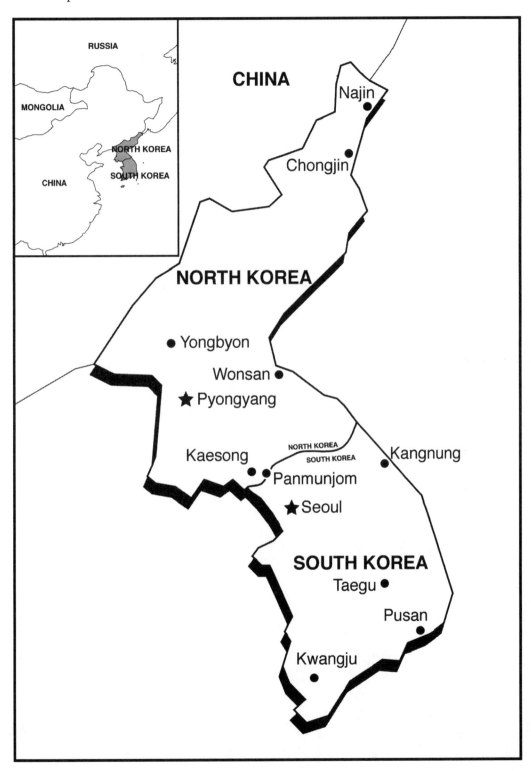

Exhibit 2   Main Economic Indicators

	1961–1969[a]	1970–1979[a]	1980–1985[a]	1986–1990[a]	1991	1992	1993	1994	1995	1996	1997	1998	1999
Real sector (Annual real changes in %)													
GDP growth	10.6	9.9	6.1	9.9	9.6	5.3	5.5	8.8	9.0	6.5	5.2	-5.8	10.7
Private consumption	8.6	8.2	5.3	7.5	9.3	6.6	6.57	10.3	9.4	9.0	6.6	-8.12	10.3
Government consumption	7.6	9.1	6.55	10.7	9.5	8.5	3.1	4.4	3.4	12.2	4.2	1.8	-0.6
Investment	26.0	12.9	3.3	15.5	15.5	-1.3	0.4	11.4	10.8	8.94	-5.29	-42.6	30.4
GDP components (%)													
Private consumption	80.0	67.8	61.7	53.1	52.5	53.2	53.7	54.4	54.7	55.9	56.7	55.3	55.9
Government consumption	11.1	10.1	10.9	10.0	10.5	10.8	10.6	10.2	9.65	10.2	10.1	10.9	10.1
Investment	19.3	28.0	29.7	32.3	40.0	37.5	35.7	36.5	37.2	38.0	34.2	20.9	26.8
Net exports	-10.5	-5.92	-2.33	4.64	-3.02	-1.5	0.5	-1.14	-1.47	-4.1	-1.0	12.9	6.8
Other indicators													
Current GDP per capita (US$)	138	741	2,000	4,258	6,792	7,162	7,787	9,012	10,856	11,402	10,360	6,913	8,680
Population (million)	28.7	35.5[b]	39.6	42.0	43.3	43.7	44.1	44.5	45.1	45.5	46.0	46.6	46.9
Nominal exchange rate (won/dollar, end of period)	227.0	439	770.4	746.8	760.8	788.4	808.1	788.7	774.7	844.2	1,695	1,205	1,145
Nominal exchange rate (won/dollar, period averages)	219.4	427.3	745.2	762.9	733.35	780.65	802.67	803.45	771.27	804.45	951.29	1,404.4	1,190
Change in real exchange rate (%)[c]	--	-8.4[d]	5.8	-6.6	-3.2	1.5	-1.6	-5.1	-9.0	2.3	16.9	43.1	--
Gross domestic savings rate (%)	--	22.9	27.5	37.8	37.3	36.4	36.2	35.5	35.5	33.8	33.4	34.0	33.7
Private savings rate (%)	7.4	18.0	26.7	27.5	30.6	29.1	28.5	26.9	25.8	23.5	22.8	25.1	24.2
Government budget balance/GDP ratio (%)	--	-1.55	-1.98	0.27	-1.62	-0.49	0.62	0.30	0.27	0.10	-1.27	-3.8	-2.9
Change in GDP deflators (%)	14.7	19.8	10.8	6.32	10.8	7.7	7.0	7.6	7.2	3.9	3.2	5.3	-1.6
Nominal M2 growth (%)	46.4	30.4	19.6	19.2	21.9	14.9	16.6	18.7	15.6	15.8	14.1	27.0	27.4
M2/GDP ratio (%)	17.7	32.5	34.4	37.3	38.8	39.4	40.6	41.2	40.8	42.7	44.9	57.5	68.1
Unemployment rate (%)	7.6	4.0	4.33	2.88	2.3	2.4	2.8	2.4	2.0	2.0	2.6	6.8	6.3

Source: Bank of Korea, *Economic Statistics Yearbook*, various years and Ministry of Finance.

Notes: (--) = not available. The period average values are used for exchange rate conversions calculations.

[a]Period averages.

[b]1972-1979.

[c](-) indicates an appreciation and (+) indicates a depreciation. Changes in Korean and U.S. deflators are used as measures of relative price changes.

[d]1972-1979.

Exhibit 3 Balance of Payments, Selected Years (US$ millions)

	1980	1981	1982	1983	1986	1987	1988	1989	1990	1991	1992	1993	1994	1995	1996	1997	1998	1999
Current account	-5,312	-4,607	-2,551	-1,524	4,709	10,058	14,505	5,360	-2,003	-8,317	-3,943	990	-3,867	-8,508	-23,005	-8,167	40,558	25,000
Trade balance	-4,613	-3,849	-2,827	-1,847	4,299	7,529	11,283	4,361	-2,450	-6,803	-1,755	2,319	-2,860	-4,444	-14,965	-3,179	41,627	28,716
--Merchandise exports	17,245	20,747	20,934	23,272	34,128	46,560	59,973	61,832	63,659	70,541	76,199	82,089	94,964	124,632	129,968	138,619	132,122	145,494
--Merchandise imports	21,859	24,596	23,762	25,120	29,829	39,031	48,690	57,471	66,109	77,344	77,954	79,771	97,824	129,076	144,933	141,798	90,495	116,778
Net service	-723	-486	265	394	1,352	2,277	2,257	444	-615	-2,153	-2,884	-2,126	-1,801	-2,979	-6,179	-3,200	628	-1,006
Net factor payment	-512	-887	-644	-793	-2,310	-1,587	-1,328	-578	-88	-164	-396	-391	-487	-1,303	-1,815	-2,454	-5,049	-4,660
Net transfers	536	615	656	724	1,369	1,839	2,293	1,132	1,150	803	1,091	1,188	1,280	218	-46	667	3,352	1,951
Capital account	6,522	5,313	3,935	2,391	-4,217	-10,369	-5,068	-2,886	2,564	6,412	6,587	2,741	10,295	16,786	23,327	1,314	-3,253	577.9
FDI outflows	-26	-48	-151	-130	-1,227	-515	-643	-598	-1,052	-1,489	-1,162	-1,340	-2,461	-3,552	-4,671	-4,449	-4,799	-4,044
FDI inflows	6	102	69	69	460	616	1,014	1,118	788	1,180	728	589	810	1,776	2,326	2,844	5,415	8,798
Portfolio outflows	--	--	--	--	--	--	-473	-709	-134	717	849	-538	-2,028	-2,284	-5,998	2,008	-1,587	1,950
Portfolio inflows	134	24	-15	546	-333	-297	-607	-2	218	2,338	4,953	10,553	8,149	13,875	21,183	12,287	-297	6,875
Other investments:[a]																		
--Assets	-492	-19	-794	-547	-682	-112	-1,463	-963	-2,425	-3,006	-3,299	-4,592	-7,369	-13,991	-13,487	-13,568	6,993	-2,390
--Liabilities	6,303	4,660	4,840	2,374	-2,213	-8,629	-2,050	-1,414	5,500	7,001	4,924	-1,455	13,632	21,450	24,571	-8,317	-13,868	-10,303
Errors and omissions	-369	-409	-1,292	-941	-539	1,197	-581	716	-1,747	762	1,064	-723	-1,782	-1,233	1,067	-5,069	-6,330	-2,612
Changes in reserves	-841	-297	-93	74	46	-886	-8,857	-3,190	1,186	1,143	-3,708	-3,008	-4,646	-7,045	-1,389	11,922	-30,975	-22,967
Current account balance/ GDP ratio (%)	-8.4	-6.6	-3.4	-1.8	4.3	7.4	8.0	2.4	-0.8	-2.8	-1.3	0.3	-1.0	-1.7	-4.4	-1.7	12.6	6.1
Export of goods and services/GDP ratio (%)	34.0	36.5	34.5	35.4	37.6	40.2	38.4	32.7	29.8	28.1	28.9	29.3	30.1	33.1	32.4	38.1	48.7	42.1

Sources: Bank of Korea, *Economic Statistics Yearbook*, various years; and International Monetary Fund, *International Financial Statistics Yearbook*. Figures for 1999 are from Ministry of Finance and Economy.

Notes: Foreign exchange reserves figures do not include gold holdings. The period average values of exchange rates are used for conversion.
[a] Reflect all other transactions with nonresidents in financial assets and liabilities. The main categories are transactions in currency and deposits, loans, and trade credits.

Exhibit 4   External Debt Developments

	1972–1979	1979	1980	1981	1982	1983	1986	1987	1988	1989	1990	1991	1992	1993	1994	1995	1996	1997	1998	1999
Foreign debt/GDP (%)	36.9	35.4	47.1	47.3	50.1	48.8	43.0	29.2	19.6	14.8	13.8	13.5	14.3	14.2	19.1	27.9	33.7	36	46.4	33.5
Foreign debt/export of goods and services (%)	134.5	126.8	138.3	129.6	145.4	137.8	114.3	72.7	51.1	45.1	46.3	47.9	49.6	48.5	63.6	84.5	104.2	94.4	95.1	97.7
Long-term foreign debt/total foreign debt (%)	74.7	68.7	64.2	69.0	66.7	70.0	80.2	76.7	72.6	70.1	69.1	71.7	73.0	74.2	59.7	43.6	42.9	60.1	79.4	72.1
Short-term foreign debt/foreign exchange reserves ratio (%)	226.8	246.3	362.6	390.5	452.9	543.4	280.4	260.5	79.3	65.4	74.7	84.2	71.6	61.9	117.4	225.2	280.8	322.5	59.1	51.4
Interest rate differential[a]	--	--	--	--	--	--	3.1	2.8	2.0	2.7	1.7	4.0	6.0	5.3	3.8	2.8	2.0	--	--	--

Sources: Debt data between 1979 and 1993 are from Asian Development Bank, *Key Indicators of Developing Asian and Pacific Countries*. Data since 1993 are from Bank of Korea webpage at www.bok.or.kr. Data on the international rate differential come from R. Barry Johnston, Salim M. Darbar, and Claudia Echeverria, *Sequencing Capital Account Liberalization: Lessons from the Experiences of Chile, Indonesia, Korea, and Thailand* (Washington, D.C.: International Monetary Fund, 1997). The 1999 data are from Ministry of Finance and Economy.

Notes: Foreign exchange reserves figures do not include gold holdings. The period average values of the exchange rate are used for conversion between won and U.S. dollar.

[a]Interest rate differential = Korean deposit rate – London Interbank Offer Rate (LIBO) on one-year U.S. deposit rate.

Exhibit 5   Percentage Shares of Heavy and Chemical Industry and of Light Industry in Manufacturing Output and Merchandise Exports, 1971–1979

	1971	1972	1973	1974	1975	1976	1977	1978	1979
Heavy & Chemical Industry									
--Export Share (%)	13.7	21.1	23.6	33.2	25.9	28.8	31.6	33.2	37.7
--Industry Share (%)	40.5	39.7	42.6	49.9	47.5	49.5	50.7	53.0	54.9
Light Industry									
--Export Share (%)	86.3	78.9	76.4	66.8	74.1	71.2	68.4	66.8	62.3
--Industry Share (%)	59.5	60.3	57.4	50.1	52.5	50.1	49.3	47.0	45.1

Source: Adapted from Alice Amsden, *Asia's Next Giant: South Korea and Late Industrialization* (New York: Oxford University Press, 1989), p. 58.

Exhibit 6 Comparative Economic and Social Indicators, Selected Years

	Korea	Taiwan	Brazil	Mexico
Real growth in GNP per capita (annual %)				
1965-1984	6.6	9.0	4.6	2.9
1985-1994	7.8	6.2	-0.4	0.9
Human development index value[a]				
1960	0.398	--	0.394	0.517
1980	0.666	--	0.673	0.758
1994	0.89	--	0.783	0.804
Manufacturing's share in GDP (%)				
1965	18	24	26	21
1984	28	37	27	24
Agriculture's share in GDP (%)				
1965	38	27	19	22
1984	14	22	13	14
Real growth of exports (annual %)				
1965-1973	32	19	10	1
1973-1984	15	16	8	19
Foreign debt/GNP ratio (%)				
1972	37.8	--	20.1	17.4
1980	47.9	20.2 (1982)	31.8	30.5
1994	15.3	10.6 (1993)	27.9	35.2
Share of public foreign debt to total foreign debt (%)				
1978	69.3	--	53.6	72.2
1980	55.2	--	53.2	58.4
Gini coefficient				
1965	0.344	0.356 (1966)	0.53 (1960)	0.555 (1963)
1982	0.357	0.308	0.57 (1983)	0.579 (1970)
Income share of the poorest 40% of the population (%)				
1964	18	11.3	8.0-11.5 (1960)	9.2-10.3 (1963)
1976	16.9	22.7 (1980)	6.8-9.9	8.0-8.2 (1977)
School enrollment by age cohort (%)				
—Primary				
1960	94	95	95	80
1985	96	100	103	115
—Secondary				
1960	27	--	11	11
1985	94	--	35 (1983)	55
—Tertiary				
1960	4.6	--	11	2.6
1985	32	--	55	16
Life expectancy at birth (years)				
1960	53.9	--	54.7	56.9
1994	71.5	--	66.4	72

Sources: Income share and school enrollment data are taken from Stephan Haggard, *Pathways from the Periphery* (Ithaca: Cornell University Press); and female life expectancy data are taken from World Bank, *World Development Report 1987* (New York: Oxford University Press, 1987). Human development index values are from UNDP, *Human Development Report 1997* (New York: Oxford University Press, 1997). GNP per capita data and debt data are from *World Development Report*, various issues. Debt data on Taiwan are from Asian Development Bank, *Key Indicators of Developing Asian and Pacific Countries 1997* (Manila: Oxford University Press).

Notes: Bracketed numbers refer to the years to which the data apply. Ranges for Brazil and Mexico for the income share data reflect different assumptions about the underreporting of income. Primary level refers to students aged 6–11; secondary level to 11–17; and tertiary level to 20–24. Totals may exceed 100% when students younger and older than the cohort are enrolled.

(--) = Data not available.

[a]Human development index is a broader measure of a country's development levels than GDP. It incorporates such factors as life expectancy, access to educational facilities, and gender equality as well as the normal economic measures.

Exhibit 7   Bureaucratic Pay and Efficiency, Selected Countries

Country	Ratio of Public to Private Sector Salaries in the Early 1990s (%)[a]		Index of Bureaucratic Efficiency[b]	
	Senior Level	Mid-level	1972	1982
Singapore	114.0	115.0	3.1	3.1
South Korea[c]	69.3	57.1	2.1	2.5
Taiwan	65.2	63.5	2.7	2.5
Malaysia	40.0	34.3	2.3	1.9
Thailand	47.1	37.2	1.4	1.6
Philippines	27.7	25.0	1.5	1.8
Chile	70.4	--	--	--
Venezuela	29.5	53.4	--	--
Uruguay	--	37.1	--	--
Argentina	24.1	28.6	--	--

Source: Adapted from World Bank, *The East Asian Miracle* (New York: Oxford University Press, 1993).

Notes: (--) = data not available.

[a]Ratios refer to the average salaries of the public sector to the average salaries of the private sector.

[b]This is based on surveys of business executives conducted by Business Environment Risk Intelligence. The surveys asked respondents to rank bureaucratic performance from 1, the lowest score, to 4, the highest score.

[c]Estimates of private sector salaries include allowances and bonuses. Data are from a survey of companies with 500 or more employees.

Exhibit 8   Parliamentary Election Results, April 1996

Party	Percentage of Votes	Percentage of Seats	Seats Won	Of Which Allocated[a]
New Korea Party (Kim Young Sam)	34.5	46.5	139	18
National Congress for New Politics (Kim Dae Jung)	25.3	26.4	79	13
United Liberal Democrats (Kim Jong Pil)	16.2	16.7	50	9
Democratic Party	11.2	5.0	15	6
Others	12.8	5.4	16	0
Total	100.0	100.0	100	46

Source: Adapted from Fitch IBCA, *Rating Report: Republic of Korea*, February 1999, p. 5.

Note: [a]In the Korean system, a number of seats were allocated according to proportional representation.

Exhibit 9   Combined Gross Sales of Chaebols as Percentages of Korean GNP, Selected Years

	1976	1980	1984	1994	1997
Top Chaebol	4.7	8.3	12.0	17.1	17.5
Top 2 Chaebols	8.1	16.3	24.0	32.6	32.4
Top 4 Chaebols	12.9	30.1	44.3	49.2	56.4
Top 6 Chaebols	16.1	38.2	56.2	57.8	65.4
Top 10 Chaebols	19.8	48.1	67.4	66.6	74.7

Source: Adapted from Kang Myung-Hyun *Chaebols Kwa Hanguk Kyongje* [Chaebols and the Korean Economy] (Seoul: Nanam Publishing, 1998), p. 252.

Exhibit 10   Sources of Funds Raised by the Corporate Sector[a] (percentage shares)

Sources	1963–1974	1974–1979	1980–1984	1985–1989	1990–1994	1995	1996
Internal funds[b]	19.9	23.0	27.4	38.3	27.3	27.9	22.6
Equity	13.7	11.3	11.3	13.6	11.3	12.6	9.1
Debt	66.4	65.6	61.4	48.0	61.4	60.5	68.3
—Of which:							
Borrowing from banks	19.2	23.8	20.8	27.7	19.7	17.7	16.0
Borrowing from nonbanks	15.7	13.9	22.5	20.0	25.7	20.3	15.8
Debt securities[c]	--	7.0	17.6	22.3	28.8	38.0	40.3
Foreign borrowing	19.0	15.2	6.2	2.5	8.3	10.1	11.7
Trade credit, government loans, and other	12.6	40.1	32.9	27.5	17.4	13.9	16.3

Sources: Leroy P. Jones and Il. Sakong, *Government, Business, and Entrepreneurship in Economic Development: Korea* (Cambridge: Harvard University Press, 1980), p. 102; and Eduardo Borensztein and Jong-Wha Lee, *Credit Allocation and Financial Crisis in Korea* (Washington, D.C.: International Monetary Fund, 1999).

Notes: [a]For the 1963–1974 period, the corporate sector refers to private firms only. Data for other periods include both private and public enterprises.

[b]Internal funds are savings, fixed capital depreciation, and capital transfers (net).

[c]Includes bonds, industrial paper, and debentures.

Exhibit 11   Interest Rates and Inflation Rates (percent)

Year	Curb Market[a]	Corporate Bonds[b]	General Loans[c]	Export Loans[d]	NIF[e]	Inflation[f]
1954	--	--	18.3	--	n.a.	31.6
1964	61.8	--	16.0	--	n.a.	32.1
1970	48.6	n.a.	24.0	--	n.a.	13.5
1975	41.3	20.1	15.5	9.0	12.0	26.3
1979	42.4	26.7	18.5	9.0	16.0	21.2
1980	44.9	30.1	20.0	15.0	19.5	24.9
1981	35.3	24.4	17.0	15.0	16.5	17.6
1982	30.6	17.3	10.0	10.0	10.0	6.7
1983	25.8	14.2	10.0	10.0	10.0	5.2
1984	24.7	14.1	10.0-11.5	10.0	10.0-11.5	5.4
1985	24.0	14.2	10.0-11.5	10.0	10.0-11.5	4.7
1986	23.1	12.8	10.0-11.5	10.0	10.0-11.5	4.6
1987	23.0	12.8	10.0-11.5	10.0	10.0-11.5	5.1
1988	22.7	14.5	10.0-11.5	10.0	10.0-11.5	6.7
1989	23.1	15.2	10-0-12.5	n.a.	10.0-11.5	5.3
1990	19.9	16.4	10.0-12.5	n.a.	10.0-11.5	9.9
1991	23.4	18.9	10.0-12.5	n.a.	10.0-11.5	10.8
1992	23.9	16.1	10.0-12.5	n.a.	10.0-11.5	7.7
1993	20.8	12.6	8.5-12.0	n.a.	9.0	7.0
1994	19.4	12.9	8.5-12.5	n.a.	n.a.	7.6
1995	20.8	11.9	9.0-12.5	n.a.	n.a.	7.2
1996	--	12.6	11.1	n.a.	n.a.	3.9
1997	--	24.3[g]	15.3	n.a.	n.a.	3.2
1998	--	8.3[g]	11.1	n.a.	n.a.	5.3
1999	--	9.9	8.6	n.a.	n.a.	-1.6

Sources: Adapted from Leory P. Jones and Il Sakong, *Government, Business, and Entrepreneurship in Economic Development: Korea* (Cambridge: Harvard University Press, 1980); Eduardo Borensztein and Jong-Wha Lee, *Credit Allocation and Financial Crisis in Korea* (Washington, D.C.: International Monetary Fund, 1999), Table 4; and Economist Intelligence Unit, *Country Profile: South Korea and North Korea*, Fourth Quarter, 1999. Figures for 1999 are provided by Ministry of Finance and Economy.

Notes: n.a. = Not applicable; (--) = Not available.

[a]Curb market loans were made by private financial institutions at rates not regulated by the state.

[b]Bonds with maturities between 1 and 3 years.

[c]General purpose loan of up to one-year maturity.

[d]Abolished in December 1988.

[e]National Investment Fund, established in 1974.

[f]Changes in GDP deflator.

[g]Referring to three-year maturity.

Exhibit 12   Comparative Debt/Equity Ratios of the Corporate Sector, 1970–1996

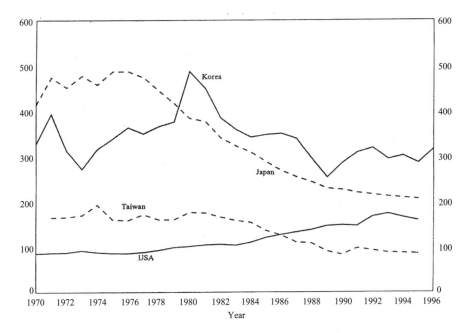

Source: Eduardo Borensztein and Jong-Wha Lee, *Credit Allocation and Financial Crisis in Korea*
          (Washington, D.C.: International Monetary Fund, 1999).

Exhibit 13   Exchange Rate Movements and Money Market Rates in 1997

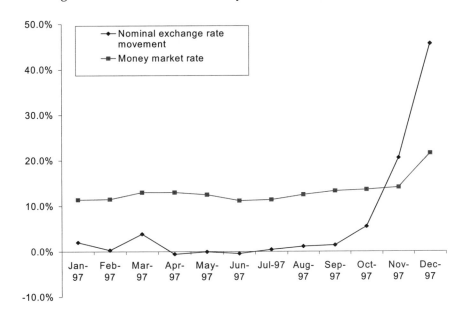

Source: International Monetary Fund, *International Financial* Statistics, various years.

Notes: Nominal exchange rate (won/dollar) movement is measured by the percentage change of the exchange rates between
          two periods. Thus a movement in the upward direction implies a depreciation and a movement in the downward
          direction means an appreciation. Exchange rates used here are the end of the period values.

Exhibit 14   Bank Performance and Chaebols' Debt Levels, Selected Years

	Bank Performance[a]		Chaebols' Debt	
	Net Profit/ Net Worth Ratio	Nonperforming Loan Ratio[b]	Share of Credit to Top 30 Chaebols[c]	Debt/Equity to the Top 30 Chaebols
1974	28.90	0.63	--	--
1977	13.49	1.67	--	--
1980	14.36	2.74	--	--
1982	5.19	6.95	--	--
1984	6.81	10.85	--	--
1985	3.90	10.22	--	571
1986	4.04	10.53	--	--
1987	4.38	8.42	27.2	--
1988	6.56	7.44	49.1	--
1989	6.06	5.86	22.8	--
1990	--	--	27.3	381
1991	--	--	41.2	403
1992	--	--	42.9	426
1993	6.36	7.4	36.8	400
1994	6.38	5.8	22.2	405
1995	4.66	5.2	23.0	390
1996	4.33	4.1	38.5	450
1997	--	--	40.3	519
1998	--	--	--	458.2
1999	--	--	--	164.1

Sources: Compiled from Organisation for Economic Co-operation and Development, *OECD Economic Surveys: Korea*; International Monetary Fund, *Republic of Korea: Selected Issues* (Washington, D.C.: International Monetary Fund, 1998); Eduardo Borensztein and Jong-Wha Lee, *Credit Allocation and Financial Crisis in Korea* (Washington, D.C.: International Monetary Fund, 1999); Pyung Joo Kim, "Financial Institutions," *Korea's Political Economy: An Institutional Perspective* (Boulder: Westview Press, 1994); and Thomas J.T. Balino and Angel Ubide, *The Korean Financial Crisis of 1997—A Strategy of Financial Sector Reform* (Washington, D.C.: International Monetary Fund, 1998). Figures for 1999 are provided by Ministry of Finance and Economy.

Notes: -- Data not available.

[a]Data before 1993 cover national banks only, i.e., seven nationwide commercial banks including the Shinhan Bank and the KorAm Bank. Data since 1993 incorporate regional banks as well.

[b]Nonperforming loan (NPL) ratio refers to the ratio of the sum of fixed, doubtful, and estimated losses to total credit outstanding.

[c]Includes loans from financial institutions, commercial paper, debentures, external bonds and other foreign debts of the corporate business sector.

Exhibit 15   International Monetary Fund Guidelines for Reform and Restructuring (1997)

Reforms	Targets
Macroeconomic policy targets	3% GDP growth in 1998
	Monetary policy: 10% inflation in 1998
	Fiscal policy: Tighten government spending and raise taxes
Financial sector restructuring	Amend the Bank of Korea Act to provide independence for the central bank
	Establish the Financial Supervisory Commission to regulate and supervise all financial institutions
	Create deposit insurance
	Immediately close 15 of the 30 major merchant banks with the largest nonperforming loans
	Ban cross guarantees of debt
Capital account liberalization	Allow foreign investors to acquire 55% of listed companies from December 1997 and 100% by the end of 1998
	Allow friendly mergers and acquisitions by foreigners
	Fully open the foreign bond market
	Allow foreign banks to buy Korean banks
Corporate governance reforms	Allow external and independent auditors to evaluate data maintained by MOFE
	Disclose all information of the Bank of Korea on foreign reserves
	Require consolidated financial statement reporting
	Relax—although not abolish—corporate takeover rules
Business reforms	End trade-related subsidies
	Liberalize labor markets to facilitate layoffs

Source: Adapted from *Korea Telecom Corporation American Depository Shares Offering Prospectus*, May 26, 1999, pp. A10–A15.

Exhibit 16   Thirty Days That Shook the World: Key Events and End-of-Day Trading Values of Won/Dollar Exchange Rates in December 1997

Events	Won/dollar[a]
DEC. 2–DEC. 5: On December 3, in the first letter of intent to the IMF, the Korean government noted both the economic progress as well its problems. In the letter, the government expressed confidence that the situation would stabilize quickly. The letter also outlined a three-year program to reform Korea's economy; this included allowing friendly mergers and acquisitions by foreigners and partially lifting foreign ownership restrictions. The letter noted the intention to set a timetable for further capital account liberalization and trade reforms. On the same day, the IMF announced a rescue package totaling US$55 billion and an agreement with Korea on the terms of the loan. Reactions were swift. All three Korean presidential candidates pledged support for the agreement, although some did so reluctantly. US Secretary of Treasury Robert Rubin commented, "We have a vital national economic and security interest in helping Korea restore market stability as soon as possible." Another senior treasury official commented, "The program's policy commitments will bring about very substantial changes in the Korean financial sector, which in turn have the potential to open up the Korean economy." Others were more negative in their assessments. Lawrence Lindsey, a research fellow at the American Enterprise Institute, said, "Absent an IMF bailout, the amount of market reform and the amount of market opening would be greater." An analyst from Merrill Lynch commented, "The market is still shrouded in skepticism about Asia in general and its ability to adjust."	Dec. 1 (M): 1187 Dec. 2 (T): 1235 Dec. 3 (W): 1196 Dec. 4 (Th): 1172.5 Dec. 5 (F): 1230
DEC. 9–DEC. 12: On December 9, the Korean government publicly appealed to the US and Japan for a speedy delivery of funds. Lim Chang Yuel, Korean minister of finance, justified this request by saying, "They [the US and Japan] are advising on policies and not really putting their money in at all. What will the Korean public's response be? You can imagine." The US swiftly rejected the plea. On December 11, Rubin commented, "They've got a strong program with the IMF, and I think the key is for them to implement that program and implement it effectively." An official at the IMF said, "If they implement the program and get on with it, they should have enough cash." A strategist from Bankers Trust reacted to the news this way, "[I]f nothing is done, and Korea has to declare a moratorium on its debt, the repercussions in international financial markets are going to be significant." Doubt also mounted about the reliability of Korean economic data. On December 9, an IMF report revealed that Korea was closer to default on December 2 than outsiders had realized and, later in the week, the government admitted that its short-term debt was US$100 billion, much higher than previously thought. A money manager commented, "They need somewhere in the vicinity of $120 billion." On December 10, Kim Dae Jung unveiled a full-page newspaper ad vowing to re-negotiate with the IMF over loan terms. On the same day, Moody's downgraded Korea's credit rating. In the meantime, the Korean government scrambled for funds. On December 11, the Korean Development Bank again sought investors for a US$2 billion bond launch after the issue had already been delayed once. A banker was puzzled by this move. He asked, "They just organized an IMF package, and suddenly they need another $2 billion right now?" On December 12, the Bank of Korea announced "a financial support package" and bought shares in two failing banks.	Dec. 8 (M): 1342.4 Dec. 9 (T): 1460 Dec. 10 (W): 1565.9 Dec.11 (Th): 1719.8 Dec. 12 (F): 1710
DEC. 16–DEC. 19: On December 16, the daily exchange rate band was removed.[a] On December 18, Kim Dae Jung was elected president. On the next day, he promised to abide by the IMF agreement. Investors, however, were not assured. "He clearly was not the IMF's favorite candidate," one investment banker said. Korea specialists had a different view. "The greatest concern in the days to come is labor and political stability in Korea," remarked Meredith Woo-Cumings, a professor of political science at Northwestern University, "and Kim Dae Jung is best positioned to handle that issue." In an amendment to the first letter of intent, dated December 18, the government noted reform progress made to date, including an accelerated pace of capital account liberalization, suspension of poorly-performing banks, imposition of restructuring requirements on the suspended banks, greater transparency, and legislation after the presidential election that would overhaul the financial sector. On December 18, Alan Greenspan and Robert Rubin met privately. They agreed that private banks had to do their part to avert a crisis. The task of communicating with the private banks fell on Rubin. Greenspan felt he had a conflict of interest as he might be perceived of using his regulatory power to extract compliance from the banks.	Dec. 15 (M): 1563.9 Dec. 16 (T): 1425 Dec. 17 (W): 1481 Dec. 18 (Th): n/a Dec. 19 (F): 1550

Exhibit 16 (Continued)

Events	Won/dollar[a]
DEC. 22-DEC.26: On December 22, President-elect Kim professed that he was "flabbergasted" about the situation. On December 23, S&P downgraded Korea's credit rating on the heels of a similar downgrading by Moody's on December 21. On December 24, Rubin telephoned senior executives at several US banks, asking them to roll over their loans. His message was that if the private sector did not help, the efforts by the IMF would fail. He also made it clear that the US would not put in more money to bail out private banks. Sophisticated New York bankers were easier to convince but it took a while to convince bankers from other regions. One banker from Chicago reportedly commented to Lawrence Summers, "This is a hell of a Christmas present." But in the end he pledged cooperation. On the same day, executives from six US banks met with William McDonough, president of the Federal Reserve Bank of New York. After the meeting, they issued a statement: "It is our firm belief that a market-oriented private sector financing initiative offers the best solution to Korea's short-run liquidity concerns." Also on Christmas Eve, British bank executives were summoned to the Bank of England to discuss the Korean situation. British bankers pledged cooperation and commented that they would have rolled over these loans "in more normal market conditions." Similar meetings between central and private bankers were held in other G7 countries. In the second letter of intent to the IMF dated December 24, Korea promised to move up its capital account liberalization schedule from the one outlined in the first letter of intent. On the same day, the IMF agreed to accelerate disbursement. The World Bank and the Asian Development Bank agreed to disburse US$5 billion immediately. In addition, 13 governments announced readiness to make available US$8 billion contingent on private banks agreeing to maturity extensions. On December 26, the head of the French bankers' association indicated that French banks were likely to extend loan maturity. On the same day, Korean TV reported a plan to sell two banks to foreigners and interest from Citibank and Chase Manhattan in an acquisition.	Dec. 22 (M): 1715 Dec. 23 (T): 1962 Dec. 24 (W): 1836 Dec. 25 (Th): n/a Dec. 26 (F): 1498
DEC. 29-DEC.31: On December 29, ten of the largest Japanese banks met to discuss helping Korea. On the same day, a meeting chaired by Citibank and convened in the offices of the New York Fed and J.P. Morgan included representatives from top US banks and from banks based in Italy, Canada, Japan, Germany, France, the UK, and Switzerland. Foreign bankers briefed attendees about positive efforts in their respective countries to alleviate Korea's short-term debt burdens. After the morning session, President McDonough said that he was pleased with the progress. The bankers issued a statement that said that they believed that the Korean economy was strong and that the current problem stemmed from a liquidity squeeze. One attendee explained, "The central banks have been explaining in blunt terms where our self interest lies." A credit analyst from Lehman Brothers remarked, "They all need to know they're not the last guy lending." Also on December 29, after a meeting in Frankfurt, 80 German banks agreed to roll over their loans to Korea. French, British, and Japanese banks reported similar plans. A banker commented on these loan deferrals, "This is strictly a voluntary operation…. This is just a group of banks trying to work out the problem." On December 29, the Korean Parliament overcame considerable political resistance and passed sweeping legislation overhauling the country's financial system. On December 30, J.P. Morgan, Chase, and Citibank met with a group of investment bankers to brief them on the Korean situation. Officials from the New York Fed attended the meeting. While bankers scrambled for a solution, the IMF's loan package provoked controversies. James Glassman, a research fellow at the American Enterprise Institute, argued, "Bad investments, like bad ideas, must be allowed to fail in the marketplace. Capitalism without bankruptcy is like Christianity without Hell."	Dec. 29 (M): 1395 Dec. 30 (T): 1550 Dec. 31 (W): 1695

Sources: The section on the Greenspan-Rubin meeting and on Rubin's telephone calls to bankers is from Bob Woodward, *Maestro: Greenspan's Fed and the American Boom* (New York: Simon & Schuster, 2000). Other information is from press reports, IMF press releases, Korean government documents, and interviews with Korean officials.

Note: [a]Before December 16, there was a daily exchange rate band of $\pm10\%$. Won was free floating since December 16.

Endnotes

1   "D.J. Kim Speaks on 'New Millennium, New Hope,' *Korea Times*, January 3, 2000, p. 1.

2   Byung-Nak Song, *The Rise of the Korean Economy* (New York: Oxford University Press, 1997), p. 32

3   Samuel Pao-San Ho, "Colonialism and development: Korea, Taiwan, and Kwantung," *The Japanese Colonial Empire*, ed. Ramon H. Myers and Mark R. Peattie (Princeton: Princeton University Press, 1984), pp. 347–398.

4   While these industries were located in Korea, the Japanese actively discouraged Koreans from engaging in manufacturing sectors. The purpose of course was to keep a division of labor within the Japanese empire that assigned a primarily agricultural role to Korea. In the 1910s and 1920s, under an "agriculture first" policy, the colonial government used the Company Regulations to screen the formation of new companies. The approval was granted selectively as a way to keep out Koreans. Manufacturing did not develop until the repeal of the Company Regulations in 1920. See Leroy Jones and Il Sakong, *Government, Business, and Entrepreneurship in Economic Development: The Korean Case* (Cambridge: Harvard University Press, 1980).

5   Ibid.

6   See John King Fairbank, Edwin O. Reischauer, and Albert M. Craig, *East Asia: Tradition and Transformation*, (Boston: Houghton Mifflin Company, 1973).

7   The figures are from ibid., p. 27.

8   Jung-en Woo, *Race to the Swift: State and Finance in Korean Industrialization* (New York: Columbia University Press, 1991).

9   Bruce Cumings, *Korea's Place in the Sun: A Modern History* (New York: W.W. Norton & Company, 1997).

10   Quoted in Stephan Haggard, *Pathways from the Periphery* (Ithaca: Cornell University Press , 1990), p. 62.

11   Quoted in Mark L. Clifford, *Troubled Tiger* (Armonk, New York: M.E. Sharpe, 1998), p. 45.

12   Cumings, *Korea's Place in the Sun: A Modern History*.

13   Haggard, *Pathways from the Periphery*.

14   Quoted in Don Oberdorfer, *The Two Koreas* (New York: Basic Books, 1997).

15   Han refers to the Han River in South Korea.

16   As stated in the *World Development Report 2000*, "East Asian economies, making active use of export subsidies and credit allocation, experienced the most powerful sustained surge of economic development the world had seen in decades." See World Bank, Don Oberdorfer, *The Two Koreas* (New York: Basic Books, 1997).

17   Oberdorfer, *The Two Koreas*.

18   Quoted in John P. Lovell, "The Military and Politics in Postwar Korea," in *Korean Politics in Transition*, ed. Edward Reynolds Wright (Seattle: University of Washington Press, 1975).

19   From Cumings, *Korea's Place in the Sun: A Modern History*.

     Seok Ki Kim, "Business Concentration and Government Policy: A Study of the Phenomenon of Business Groups in Korea, 1945-1985," Doctor of Business Administration Dissertation, (Boston: Harvard Business School, 1987).

21   See Chalmers Johnson, "Political Institutions and Economic Performance: The Government-Business Relationship in Japan, South Korea, and Taiwan," in *The Political Economy of the New Asian Industrialism*, ed. Frederic C. Deyo (Ithaca: Cornell University Press, 1987).

22   Jose Edgardo Campos and Hilton L. Root, *The Key to the Asian Miracle* (Washington, D.C.: The Brookings Institution, 1996), p. 140.

23   As an American adviser to the Korean government, David Cole, testified, "the choice in the mid-sixties was whether to concentrate on trying to do something about raising wages or expanding employment, and the choice was to expand employment." Quoted in Haggard, *Pathways from the Periphery*.

24 This section draws from Frederic C. Cumings, *Korea's Place in the Sun: A Modern History.*

25 Cumings, *Korea's Place in the Sun: A Modern History.*

26 This section draws heavily from Jones and Sakong, *Government, Business, and Entrepreneurship in Economic Development: The Korean Case;* Johnson, "Political Institutions and Economic Performance: The Government-Business Relationship in Japan, South Korea, and Taiwan," *The Political Economy of the New Asian Industrialism;* World Bank, *Korea: Managing the Industrial Transition* (Washington, D.C.: The World Bank, 1987); Alice Amsden, *Asia's Next Giant: South Korea and Late Industrialization* (New York: Oxford University Press , 1989); Joseph J. Stern et al., *Industrialization and the State: The Korean Heavy and Chemical Industry Drive* (Cambridge: Harvard Institute for International Development and Korea Development Institute, 1995); Yoon Je Cho and Joon-Kyung Kim, "Credit Policies and the Industrialization of Korea," (Washington, D.C.: The World Bank, 1995); and Jessica Gordon Nembhard, *Capital Control, Financial Regulation, and Industrial Policy in South Korea and Brazil* (Westport, CT: Praeger, 1996)..

27 Robert Wade, *Governing the Market: Economic Theory and the Role of Government in East Asian Industrialization* (Princeton: Princeton University Press, 1990).

28 Amsden, *Asia's Next Giant: South Korea and Late Industrialization.*

29 World Bank, *Korea: Managing the Industrial Transition.*

30 Susan M. Collins and Won-Am Park, "External Debt and Macroeconomic Performance in South Korea," *Developing Country Debt and the World Economy,* ed. Jeffrey D. Sachs (Chicago: University of Chicago Press, 1989), pp. 121-140.

31 Michael E. Porter, *The Competitive Advantage of Nations* (New York: The Free Press, 1990), p. 455.

32 Young-Suk Hyun and Jinjoo Lee, "Hyundai Motor Company: Self-Reliance Strategy and Growing Challenges," *Management behind Industrialization: Readings in Korean Business,* eds. Dong-Ki Kim and Linsu Kim (Seoul: Korea University Press, 1989), pp. 516-539.

33 Ibid.

34 See Amsden, *Asia's Next Giant: South Korea and Late Industrialization.*

35 Linsu Kim, *Imitation to Innovation: The Dynamics of Korea's Technological Learning* (Boston: Harvard Business School Press, 1997). Similar examples can be found in the semiconductor industry in the 1980s.

36 World Bank, *Korea: Managing the Industrial Transition,* p. 117.

37 Amsden, *Asia's Next Giant: South Korea and Late Industrialization.*

38 Quoted in Benjamin Gomes-Casseres, "State and Markets in South Korea," Harvard Business School Case Study, 1995.

39 Mark L. Clifford, *Troubled Tiger,* p. 138.

40 Doh C. Shin, *Mass Politics and Culture in Democratizing Korea* (Cambridge: Cambridge University Press, 1999), p. 202.

41 Quoted in Samuel P. Huntington, *The Third Wave: Democratization in the Late Twentieth Century* (Norman: University of Oklahoma Press, 1991), p. 366.

42 Hyung-Koo Lee, *The Korean Economy* (Albany: State University of New York Press, 1996).

43 In contrast, respondents in Bombay reported to spend 2,000 hours working and to take 40 days off. See Kim, *Imitation to Innovation: The Dynamics of Korea's Technological Learning,* pp. 78–79.

44 Ibid., pp. 71-72.

45 Susan M. Collins and Won-Am Park, "External Debt and Macroeconomic Performance in South Korea."

46 Pyung Joo Kim, "Financial Institutions," *Korea's Political Economy: An Institutional Perspective,* eds. Lee-Jay Cho and Yoon Hyung Kim (Boulder: Westview Press, 1994), pp. 273–319.

47   Brazil rescheduled its debt payment in 1983 and 1984; so did Mexico and Peru. Argentina and Venezuela rescheduled their debt payment in 1984. See Jeffrey D. Sachs, "External debt and macroeconomic performance in Latin America and East Asia," Brookings Paper on Economic Activity, Number 2 (1985).

48   International Monetary Fund, *Republic of Korea: Selected Issues* (Washington, D.C.: International Monetary Fund, 1998), p. 12.

49   Byung-Nak Song, *The Rise of the Korean Economy* (New York: Oxford University Press, 1997).

50   Ibid.

51   Amsden, *Asia's Next Giant: South Korea and Late Industrialization.*

52   International Monetary Fund, *Republic of Korea: Selected Issues.*

53   World Bank, *Korea: Managing the Industrial Transition*, p. 65.

54   Bijan B. Aghevli and Jorge Marquez-Ruarte, *A Case of Successful Adjustment: Korea's Experience During 1980-1984* (Washington, D.C.: International Monetary Fund, 1985).

55   R. Barry Johnston, Salim M. Darbar, and Claudia Echeverria, *Sequencing Capital Account Liberalization: Lessons from the Experiences of Chile, Indonesia, Korea, and Thailand* (Washington, D.C.: International Monetary Fund, 1997).

56   Quoted in "Now It Is Our Turn to Contribute to the World," *Business Week*, July 31, 1995, p. 64.

57   Quoted in "South Koreans Swear in First Civilian President," *Christian Science Monitor*, February 24, 1993, p. 8.

58   "Now It Is Our Turn to Contribute to the World," *Business Week*, July 31 1995, p. 64.

59   Young Jo Lee, "The Rise and Fall of Kim Young Sam's Embedded Reformism," *Institutional Reform and Democratic Consolidation in Korea*, eds. Larry Diamond and Doh Chull Shin (Stanford: Hoover Institution Press, 2000), pp. 97–126.

60   Clifford, *Troubled Tiger.*

61   Chun was initially sentenced to death and Roh was sentenced to 17 years in prison.

62   Clifford, *Troubled Tiger*, p. 332.

63   Ibid.

64   Johnston, Darbar, and Echeverria, *Sequencing Capital Account Liberalization.*

65   Ibid.

66   Ha-Joon Chang, "South Korea: The Misunderstood Crisis," *Tigers in Trouble*, ed. Jomo K.S. (Hong Kong: Hong Kong University Press, 1998), pp. 222–231.

67   Clifford, *Troubled Tiger*, p. 329.

68   Quoted in Michael Schuman, "Korea Retreats on Move to Curb Chaebol," *The Asian Wall Street Journal*, November 8, 1996, p. 1.

69   OECD, *OECD Economic Surveys: Korea* (Paris: OECD Publication Service, 1999), pp. 26-30.

70   Thomas J. T. Balino and Angel Ubide, *The Korean Financial Crisis of 1997—A Strategy of Financial Sector Reform* (Washington, D.C.: International Monetary Fund, 1999), p. 17.

71   Ha-Joon Chang, "South Korea: The Misunderstood Crisis."

72   Heather Smith, "Korea," *East Asia in Crisis: From Being a Miracle to Needing One?*, eds. Ross H. McLeod and Ross Garnaut (London: Routledge, 1998), pp. 66-84.

73   Ha-Joon Chang, "South Korea: The Misunderstood Crisis," p. 226.

74   OECD, *OECD Economic Surveys: Korea*, Table 30, p. 124. The average ratios refer to arithmetic values. The debt-to-equity ratio exclude financial companies.

75   The US$2 billion figure comes from Ha-Joon Chang, "South Korea: The Misunderstood Crisis" and the trade share figure comes from Taimur Baig and Ilan Goldfajn, *Financial Market Contagion in the Asian Crisis* (Washington, D.C.: International Monetary Fund, 1998).

76   For a spirited critique of the IMF actions, see Martin Feldstein, "Refocusing the IMF," *Foreign Affairs*, March/April 1998.

77   Quoted in George C. Lodge and Anthony St. George, "Collapse in Asia: 1997-1998," Harvard Business School Case Study (Boston: Harvard Business School Press, 1998).

78   Quoted in Marcus Noland, "Korea's Financial System," *Korea's Economy 1998*, ed. Joseph A.B. Winder, vol. 14 (Washington, D.C.: Korea Economic Institute of America, 1998).

79   Economist Intelligence Unit, *Country Report: South Korea and North Korea*, Fourth Quarter, 1999.

Bahtulism, Collapse, Resurrection? Financial Crisis in Asia: 1997–1998

A currency crisis in Thailand in July 1997 spread like wildfire through East Asia during the autumn of that year and into 1998. Like the famous "domino theory" that cold war strategists had postulated in the 1960s, successive capitalist Asian economies succumbed one after another. But the catalyst for these successive crises was not the spread of communist insurgency that the cold war hawks had feared. Rather Asia was falling to the pressure of capitalism itself, in the form of the international financial markets and (in)famous currency "speculators" like George Soros.

Some viewed the East Asian crisis as representing the inevitable demise of crony capitalism—a corrupt and ersatz version of the real thing. Others saw fundamentally sound and historically successful Asian countries failing in the face of irrational herding and panic decisions made by ill-informed MBAs working in New York, London, and Tokyo investment houses.

Either way, the crises presented a challenge to the existing system of global economic governance represented by the International Monetary Fund and World Bank. Action was apparently required if a global economic slowdown was to be avoided.

Study Questions

1. What is "contagion?" Does financial market contagion explain the spread of the East Asian crisis during 1997–1998?
2. Is contagion rational? As a speculator, is it possible to make money from contagion? If so, how?
3. Are countries in Asia innocent victims of irrational capital markets? How much blame should they take for the Asian crisis?
4. What—if anything—should the IMF and the international financial community have done to address the crisis? What is the logic behind using capital controls? Was the IMF response to the crisis appropriate? Is this the Washington consensus?
5. What does the future hold for Asia? What can we learn?

HUW PILL

Bahtulism, Collapse, Resurrection? Financial Crisis in Asia: 1997–1998

July 1997: *". . . this turmoil will seem, in retrospect, no more than a blip on the path of rapid East Asian economic growth. . . . At worst, currencies will float freely for a while . . . then the strong fundamentals of East Asian economies will reassert themselves."*[1]

—Martin Wolf, chief economics commentator for the Financial Times

January 1998: *". . . nobody anticipated anything like the current crisis in Asia . . . we expected [a] longer-term slowdown in growth to emerge only gradually. What we have actually seen is . . . likely to be much more of a severe real downturn than even the most negative-minded anticipated."*[2]

—Paul Krugman, MIT economist

On July 2, 1997, in response to continued speculative attack, Thai Finance Minister Thanong Bidaya took radical action. He eliminated the Thai currency's peg, allowing the *baht* to float freely for the first time since 1984. For 13 years of unparalleled economic growth, the *baht* had been pegged to a basket of foreign currencies, dominated by the U.S. dollar. Suddenly, it was subject to the vagaries of the market. Thanong had little choice—usable foreign exchange reserves were near zero, and he desperately needed to stabilize the troubled Thai financial sector. Thailand thus became the first "Tiger" country to abandon its fixed exchange rate regime—a regime that had characterized Asian monetary policy for many years. It was not the last.

Upon being allowed to float, the *baht* instantly lost 15% of its value, initiating what would become perhaps the most cataclysmic economic melt-down in Asia's modern history. The *baht* devaluation set off a chain reaction of events that neither Thanong nor anyone else had predicted. Within days, investors were pulling their funds out of Asia as rapidly as possible, causing a broad collapse of currency values and breaking the dollar peg of nearly every country hit by this "contagion." Against a backdrop of inflated real estate and asset prices (driven, at least partly, by the volume of earlier foreign capital inflows into the region), the currency devaluations had a dramatic impact. Plunging asset values highlighted the shaky debt portfolios of banks from Thailand to South Korea. Bank assets collateralized against real estate—a market characterized by overcapacity throughout Asia—proved particularly vulnerable. With large amounts of dollar-denominated foreign debt held by banks and firms, liquidity and solvency crises rapidly ensued, and real economies suffered throughout the region. The crisis led to bankrupt companies, unemployment, collapsing trade, rising food and other commodity prices, social and political unrest, and a broad loss of confidence. Cries for help

Professor Huw Pill and Don Mathis (MBA '98) prepared this case. HBS cases are developed solely as the basis for class discussion. Cases are not intended to serve as endorsements, sources of primary data, or illustrations of effective or ineffective management.

addressed to the world community (and answered principally by the IMF), did not result in a quick recovery.

Over a period of just a few months, a region of the world previously known for its "miracle" economic performance had collapsed with little warning. The Asian economic crisis raised serious questions about the management of international capital flows, IMF reforms, and emerging market development policies. (See **Exhibits 1–7** for data related to the Asian economic crisis).

Explanations of Currency Crises

Conventional Explanations

There are two conventional explanations of fixed exchange rate collapse. The first emphasizes a real overvaluation of the domestic currency which renders exports uncompetitive on international markets. The second focuses on fiscal indiscipline which leaves an exchange rate peg unsustainable.

Real Overvaluation   If a country pegs its nominal exchange rate to the U.S. dollar while domestic inflation remains higher than in the United States, then the price of domestically produced goods in dollar terms will rise more quickly than goods in the rest of the world. As international price competitiveness erodes, the volume of exports will decline while the volume of imports increases. Other things being equal, domestic output decreases, GDP growth slows, and unemployment rises. In addition, the trade balance moves into deficit. For countries that rely on trade for foreign exchange, this may lead to balance of payments problems as foreigners, fearing a country's inability to repay, refuse to lend to the country.

A balance of payments crisis, a domestic employment crisis, or a growth crisis may force the domestic government to devalue its currency to improve competitiveness or to address social and political tension.[3] Anticipating the capital loss a devaluation would impose on domestic currency holdings, investors switch into foreign currency, ultimately precipitating the devaluation.

Fiscal Indiscipline   A country running a large fiscal deficit may be forced to "print money" to finance its deficit. As domestic money supply expands, foreign exchange reserves remain finite. If the country has a fixed exchange rate, investors may choose to exchange an increasing amount of the domestic currency for foreign currency at the central bank at the fixed rate. The resulting depletion of the country's finite stock of foreign exchange reserves raises the possibility of an eventual inability to maintain the peg and a required shift to a floating exchange rate. A float would force the currency to depreciate, creating a capital gain for holders of foreign currency. Rather than allow central bank reserves to run out gradually, speculators, recognizing the inconsistency and anticipating the capital gain, purchase all central bank reserves immediately in a "speculative attack." With central bank reserves exhausted, the currency is forced to float and a deep depreciation follows.[4a]

Subsequent Explanations

The problems of real overvaluation and fiscal indiscipline were thought to be sufficient explanations for exchange rate and financial crises in emerging market economies observed during

---

[a] This explanation is distinct from a speculative attack aimed at creating a self-fulfilling crisis.

the 1970s and 1980s. However, they appeared incomplete in describing the currency crises in Europe in 1992–1993 and Mexico in 1994–1995. Subsequent explanations of currency crises place greater emphasis on the role of international capital markets and their interaction with relatively underdeveloped domestic financial markets in emerging market economies.

Failures in the International Capital Markets   During periods of low returns in industrialized economies, international banks and investment funds tend to increase capital flows to higher-return emerging market economies. Many observers question the degree to which this investment is efficiently directed and question the adequacy of investors' internal systems for assessing and monitoring the associated risks. When unanticipated problems in emerging markets arise, foreign investors may become desperate and choose suddenly to withdraw capital in favor of safer investments in the industrial world. Exchange rates and financial systems of emerging market economies, which are likely to have become increasingly dependent on foreign sources of capital, will be subject to pressures and may collapse under the strain.

The structure of the international financial markets may exacerbate this problem in several ways. For example, the performance of fund managers is often evaluated against peers rather than against objective criteria. As such, managers are motivated to copy their peers in seeking high returns in emerging markets without paying sufficient regard to the risks. The resulting "herd" behavior adds to the likelihood of dramatic and destabilizing swings between massive capital inflows and outflows. Such swings could be triggered by small—and possibly arbitrary—changes in sentiment.

Moreover, if international investors believe there is a high probability that they will be "bailed out" in the event of an adverse macroeconomic outcome such as a financial or currency crisis, they have even less incentive to assess the risks correctly. Such "moral hazard" will only serve to exacerbate the problems of inefficiently directed and poorly assessed investments.

Failures in Domestic Financial Markets   Just as failures in international capital markets can result in poorly directed and volatile lending that reduces the financial and monetary stability of recipient countries, failures in domestic financial markets are likely to be equally destabilizing. Economic liberalization programs typical of emerging market economies include deregulation of domestic financial systems and, therefore, usually require the financial institutions and markets in the reforming countries to undertake new tasks. Risk and portfolio management techniques that would be considered standard in industrialized countries may be unfamiliar. Furthermore, the banking system may simply be inadequately prepared to intermediate the vast flows of international capital that often surge into liberalizing economies. This could result in poorly directed credit expansion, culminating in bad loans and banking crises.

Such problems will only be exacerbated when the supporting institutional infrastructure is weak. Because of the important role that banks play in the payments system (vital to the functioning of a market economy), they are often widely believed to enjoy a public guarantee—even when the government claims there is no guarantee. Since domestic banks may believe that they will be "bailed out" in the event of crisis, they will discount bad outcomes and lend too aggressively to excessively risky projects in search of higher returns. Regulators are charged with controlling this "moral hazard" problem. But if they are weak, corrupt, or underinformed, they will be unable to do so.

Whatever the source of financial fragility, it is likely to render the country vulnerable to speculative attacks on exchange rate pegs. A conventional defense against capital flight in countries which might devalue is to raise interest rates (offering the capital that remains a higher return as a disincentive to flight). But where the banking system is weak and bad loans weigh heavily on bank balance sheets, higher interest rates may cause borrowers to default, precipitating a banking crisis.

Constrained in this way, the authorities are unable to defend their currency peg and are forced to float the exchange rate. However, if banks (or their borrowers) have large foreign currency denominated liabilities, the float (and consequent rapid depreciation) may itself prove an alternative catalyst for insolvency and bankruptcy.

Introduction to Countries Facing Crisis

South Korea[5]

South Korea's economic strategy, based on massive investment in manufactured goods production, appeared enormously successful in the mid-1990s. Starting in the 1980s, South Korea managed a series of economic plans designed to be outward-looking and to put producers ahead of consumers. Economic policies emphasized education and training, wage restraint, income distribution, infrastructure development, the provision of low-cost capital to selected sectors, and trade protection for new industries. Government policies aimed to assist *jaebol*—large, integrated industrial conglomerates—in becoming more competitive in the world economy. With the implementation of these plans, little room was left for democratic pluralism during most of the second half of the 20th century (post-Korean Conflict), particularly in the early stages of national development. Union activity was restricted and political opposition prohibited. President Chung Hee Park (1961–1979) observed: "For such poor people like the South Koreans, on the verge of near starvation, economics takes precedence over politics in their daily lives, and enforcing democracy is meaningless."[6]

South Korea financed its growth by borrowing from abroad rather than by relying on domestic savings. Imports of machinery and equipment to build manufacturing capacity exceeded exports, causing regular current account deficits financed by massive borrowing from the United States. South Korea was the fourth-largest debtor in the world by 1985.

South Korea's real GNP had grown at an average annual rate of 8.6% since the mid-1960s. Income per capita stood at U.S. $9,250 in 1996. Inflation averaged 6.9% between 1985 and 1993, falling to 6.2% in 1995. South Korean had become the 11th-largest economy by the mid-1990s, joining the world's advanced industrial nations.

Thailand[7]

Thailand, a constitutional monarchy established in 1932, was a strong society bound by centuries of cultural and social traditions. According to historians, Thailand was "bound together by three basic tenets: Theravada Buddhism, support for the Thai monarchy, and pride of citizenship in the only nation in Southeast Asia to have maintained its independence throughout its history, including the colonial era."[8] Thai politics, meanwhile, had been dominated by the military and a bureaucratic elite since the mid-20th century. In 1992, the last military regime was forced from power and replaced by an elected government after civil unrest resulted in the deaths of at least 50 people.

In 1987 and 1988, economic growth exceeded 6% while manufacturing increased by 8%. Expansion was taking place in many manufacturing industries. Textile production, most of it for export, increased nearly 50% annually in the late 1980s. In the early 1990s, continued growth in the export sector drove further economic growth and improvements in the country's standard of living. Investment in both private and public building projects increased on a massive scale.

The Thai economy began to show some weaknesses in the early and mid-1990s. As wage levels rose, Thailand's competitiveness fell versus other Asian export economies. While in 1995 Thailand registered a 26% growth in exports, 1996 export growth was flat. As its current account deficit rose to 8.1% of GDP by 1995, the country began to accumulate short-term debt. High short-term interest rates intended to prop up the value of the *baht* against foreign currencies served to hamper Thailand's position.

Malaysia[9]

Following race riots in 1969, Malaysia devised the New Economic Policy (NEP) which aimed to foster economic development and, as a result, civil order. Growth in the country relied heavily on exploitation of natural resources, with which Malaysia was richly endowed. During the 1950s and 1960s, Malaysia's strategy relied heavily on import substitution. In the late 1960s, recognizing that an inward-focused strategy was not viable in the country's small domestic market, the government shifted toward export-led growth through a wide range of policy instruments. In 1981, Malaysia embraced a plan for "heavy industrialization" characterized by pervasive government intervention in the marketplace. Petrochemical plants, auto manufacturing, and iron and steel mills were constructed and commodity diversification was emphasized.

In 1986, the Fifth Malaysia Plan (1986-1990) was launched, shifting the country's growth strategy. Deregulation was introduced as the private sector became the chief engine of growth. Foreign investment in export-oriented high-technology firms was encouraged. In 1990, the National Development Policy (NDP) was formulated to replace the NEP. The NDP emphasized export-oriented manufacturing industries including electronics and electrical machinery.

Malaysia's real GNP grew at an average annual rate of 8.5% from 1988 to 1995, while inflation remained moderate. Income per capita reached U.S. $4,000. In the late 1980s, the current account shifted from a surplus to a deficit, financed primarily by private inflows of capital. By July 1997, while most observers remained confident about Malaysia's opportunities for continued economic growth, some were warning that the economy was overheating.

Indonesia[10]

At the time of the crisis, Indonesia had been ruled by the authoritarian former general Soeharto for more than 30 years. His regime was characterized by political stability (if not human rights or democracy) and economic growth. Since the early 1980s, Indonesia's economy had been managed by western-educated technocrats. Their policy prescriptions included capital market liberalization, trade liberalization, tax reform, and the loosening of restrictions on foreign direct investment (FDI).

For three decades, Indonesia recorded average annual GDP growth of 6%. By 1995, Indonesia established itself as a middle-income nation with an estimated income per head of U.S. $1,030. Industry was the principal vehicle of growth, with manufacturing having expanded at a faster rate than the economy as a whole. Agriculture had also grown steadily. Nevertheless, by the end of 1995, the current account deficit was growing, inflation was on the rise, and foreign borrowing was increasing. The country's external debt had grown steadily since the mid-1960s. The economy was showing signs of overheating, and the funding needs of Indonesia's development exceeded the country's capital resources.

The Crisis Unfolds[11]

In mid-1997, Asia's economies looked as healthy to most observers as they had over the prior two decades. Analysts were still postulating how the Asian "miracle" could be emulated elsewhere in the world. They viewed the region's economic conditions as favorable: Growth was strong; unemployment was low; fiscal policy was constrained, with little evidence of government deficit spending; foreign investment, both in the form of FDI and short-term portfolio capital investment, was high; exchange rates were credibly fixed, most typically to the U.S. dollar; interest rates were higher than in the United States, Japan, or Europe; banking sectors were growing rapidly; and stock markets were buoyant.

On the negative side, public and private debt was rising. But analysts claimed the debt appeared manageable based on published data. In addition, current account deficits were increasing. But even with Thailand's current account deficit at 8% of GDP, observers were optimistic, arguing that the Thais could "still finance one of the highest rates of investment in the world without a cent of net capital inflow. One year of import stagnation and one year of export growth at its rate in the first half of the 1990s would close the current account deficit."[12]

Some analysts wondered whether the fundamental driver of Asia's rapid growth was simply resource mobilization and reallocation, akin to the self-limiting Communist "miracle" of the 1950s and 1960s.[13] Other analysts disagreed, arguing that growth was based on sustainable productivity enhancements (growth in "total factor productivity").

In summary, Asian economies continued to appear miraculous to most observers, including foreign fund managers and credit analysts. Foreign capital—in the form of short-term lending by international banks (especially European and Japanese banks), portfolio flows into the region's emerging securities markets, and FDI in productive capacity—flooded into the region on an unprecedented scale, hardly pausing to draw breath following the Mexican peso crisis of 1994-1995.

Chronology of the Crisis

January 1997   A leading **South Korean** *jaebol* (Hanbo Steel) fails, due to debts totaling in excess of U.S. $6 billion. This is the first bankruptcy of a leading Korean conglomerate in more than ten years.

February 1997   Somprasong, a **Thailand**-based company, misses scheduled payments on its foreign debt—the first Thai firm to do so.

March 1997   Recognizing the threat to its financial sector posed by bad property debt, **Thailand**'s government pledges to purchase U.S. $3.9 billion in failed property loans from financial companies. However, it later rescinds the pledge. IMF Managing Director Michel Camdessus publicly stated his view that the crisis would not develop further.

In **Malaysia**, the central bank imposes restrictions on bank loans for the purchase of property and stocks to avoid creation of an asset bubble.

In **South Korea**, Sammi Steel, another *jaebol*, fails under the burden of an apparently unsustainable debt.

April 1997 As problems with **Thailand**'s finance companies persist, Thai authorities are forced to suspend trading in their shares on the Bangkok Stock Exchange.

May 1997 In early May 1997, officials of **Japan's** central bank offer concerns about the *yen's* depreciation and hint that they may raise interest rates in order do defend their currency. While the Bank of Japan takes no immediate action, the fear of a Japanese interest rate hike may have led some investors to withdraw funds from Southeast Asia and Korea.

In **Thailand**, the *baht* is attacked by speculators, due to a slowing economy.

Spillover tremors cause the **Philippine** central bank to raise their overnight rate to 13%.

June 1997 **Thailand**'s *baht* continues to come under speculative attack as currency investors bet against its value relative to the underlying health of the economy. The Ministry of Finance responds by raising interest rates (the cost of overnight funds reaches 20% for banks and 25% for finance companies) and using foreign currency reserves to buy *baht*. Prime Minister Chavalit Yongchaiyudh announces his intent not to devalue the *baht*.

The finance minister, Amnuay Viravan, is a proponent of defending the currency at all costs, stating his belief that the *baht* will return to its parity. He warns that losing the peg and devaluing would have dire consequences: the bankruptcy of many Thai financial institutions (which hold both large foreign loan portfolios as well as significant bad real estate debt); the immediate rise in the cost of foreign imports, including many inputs critical to Thai businesses and economic expansion; and the dramatic loss of jobs with the destruction of many companies.

Amnuay resigns on June 19. The new finance minister, Mr. Thanong, faces a grave situation: foreign debt is high; the current account deficit is an unprecedented 8% of GDP; Thai exports are becoming increasingly less competitive in global markets; and the Bank of Thailand has lent over U.S. $8 billion (in *baht*) to weak financial institutions, equal to *all* of the fiscal surpluses generated by the government over the last seven years. Also, Thanong learns that a relatively inexperienced currency trader at the central bank, Paiboon Kittisrikangwan, has been misusing forward contracts in his trading—pledging existing Thai currency reserves against future contracts as a means of conducting open market transactions. Of Thailand's supposed U.S. $30 billion in foreign exchange reserves, only U.S. $1.14 billion remains available. This is barely enough to cover two days of imports.

Thanong takes several dramatic steps. First, he ends Bank of Thailand support for the most troubled financial institutions. Within two days, 16 finance companies, including the prestigious Finance One, shut down.

Meanwhile, in **South Korea**, discussion begins of a financial reform package.

July 1997 On July 2, **Thailand**'s Finance Minister Thanong floats the *baht*. Foreign investors flee as fast as possible, causing an immediate 15% collapse in the value of the *baht*.

Devaluation is driven, at least in part, by the collapse of the implicit guarantee that has existed for years between the Thai monetary authorities and the banking sector. Investors had not expected the authorities to allow financial intermediaries to fail and thus had made low assessments of the risks of investing in Thailand. After Thanong allows finance companies to fail, risk assessment swings in the opposite direction, stirring panic amongst international and domestic investors.

Thailand begins negotiations with the IMF almost immediately as the depth of its problems start becoming clear. In response, the IMF sets stringent conditions, including a radical overhaul of the

Thai economy. As a first step toward meeting their requirements, Thailand allows foreign ownership of its financial firms in excess of the previous limitation of 25%.

Meanwhile, the *baht*'s problems lead to a re-evaluation by international investors of the strength of the Asian economies overall in the so-called "bahtulism" effect. The **Philippine** central bank is forced to intervene to defend the *peso* from spill-over effects as investors flee the region. The overnight lending rate is raised to 24%, and the central bank indicates that it will allow the *peso* to move in a wider band relative to the U.S. dollar. The Philippines turns to the IMF, and is granted emergency assistance amounting to U.S. $1.1 billion.

In **Malaysia**, the currency comes under assault, and the central bank is forced to liquidate substantial foreign currency reserves to defend it. On July 14, Malaysia abandons the peg and allows the *ringgit* to float. On July 24, it hits a 38-month low of 2.6530 to the dollar. Prime Minister Mahathir Mohamad protests that the problems are the result of "rogue speculators," targeting George Soros in particular and labeling him a "moron."[a]

In **Indonesia**, the *rupiah* also suffers speculative attack, and the central bank responds by widening the trading band to 12% (up from 8%).

In **Singapore**, the currency depreciates to its lowest level against the dollar since February 1995.

Meanwhile, in **South Korea,** Kia, the nation's third largest car maker, experiences a sharp liquidity crisis and petitions the government for emergency loans.

August 1997   As August begins, **Thailand** announces an austerity plan which includes a major restructuring of the financial sector. The austerity measures include the suspension of 48 finance companies. The IMF responds with the announcement of a rescue package with loans totaling U.S. $17 billion (with capital pledged from the IMF and from other Asian nations).

Meanwhile, contagion spreads. On August 13, the **Indonesian** *rupiah* comes under speculative pressure and hits a historic low of 2,682 to the U.S. dollar. Analysts believe it would have gone lower if the central bank had not intervened in its defense. On August 14, Indonesia allows the *rupiah* to float, abandoning the managed-band trading system. Underscoring the lack of confidence in the investor community, the *rupiah* sinks to another record low of 2,755 to the U.S. dollar. The central bank responds by significantly increasing interest rates.

In addition, the currency board in **Hong Kong** comes under speculative attack.[b] The Hong Kong Monetary Authority pushes overnight interest rates higher and the Hang Seng stock market index sinks in response.

---

[a] Speculation-driven hedge funds run by Soros—famous after an attack in 1992 on the pound sterling that forced Britain out of the European Exchange Rate Mechanism—profited from the Thai baht's devaluation after taking large short positions on the currency. Some analysts argued that Soros' effect on the value of the baht was negligible, while others blamed him for ultimately forcing the central bank to float in July 1997. His funds also took positions against other Asian currencies during the crisis. Some analysts defended the role of such funds as "punishing bad monetary policies and rewarding sound economic management"—claiming that economic fundamentals were ultimately to blame for currency crises. Others argued that speculators hurt genuine investors (and economic performance more generally) by forcing central banks to drive up interest rates in prolonged standoffs (as well as by exacerbating instability).

[b] A currency board establishes a fixed exchange rate and ensures that every unit of local currency on issue is backed by the equivalent in a benchmark foreign currency. It also requires the monetary authority to convert currency on demand. The Hong Kong currency board tied Hong Kong to the U.S. dollar.

In **Malaysia**, currency speculators attack the *ringgit*, and the central bank imposes controls on lending to short-term sellers.

September 1997   The crisis shows little sign of abating. The **Philippine** peso continues to fall, hitting a record low in early September. Its downward slide is arrested by central bank intervention.

The **Malaysian** *ringgit* and stock market decline. Mahathir publicly announces that currency trading and convertibility may be restricted (international pressure causes him to back away from this position). He also announces the delay of several multi-billion dollar construction projects. At the Hong Kong IMF/World Bank annual conference on September 20, Mahathir makes a speech to the delegates in which he declares: "Currency trading is immoral and should be stopped."[14] George Soros responds, "Dr. Mahathir is a menace to his own country."[15]

In **Indonesia**, the *rupiah* begins a rapid depreciation. The government announces the launch of a reform effort, including the delay of several major infrastructure projects worth 39 trillion *rupiah*. Restrictions on foreign purchases of newly offered public companies are lifted.

In **Thailand**, planned reforms do not appear to be getting underway, and the IMF states that it is growing impatient with the progress of financial restructuring.

In **China**, meanwhile, the president announces a new long-range goal of major privatization of state-owned enterprises. He also discusses capital markets overhaul, including increased support for public offerings, mergers, and bankruptcies. Some analysts believe that China may be acting preemptively to stave off contagion from the crisis.

October 1997   In early October, the **Indonesian** *rupiah* drops to a new low of 3,845 against the U.S. dollar. Indonesia announces publicly that it will seek emergency aid from the IMF. The cost of the bail-out is set at U.S. $28 billion. Indonesia is hailed for being proactive in its announced reforms.

On October 17, **Malaysia** announces a fiscal tightening in an attempt to prevent the crisis from impacting the real economy. The stock market and the currency continue to decline.

Taiwan's currency now comes under attack. It devalues its dollar in response.

Hong Kong is finally shaken by the crisis. From Monday, October 20, through Thursday, October 23, the stock market loses 25% of its value. The fall is more severe than the 1987 crash. Many observers attribute the scare in Hong Kong to the devaluation in Taiwan. On October 27, the Hang Seng loses another 5.8%, this time sending ripples throughout the global equity markets. The Dow Jones industrial average posts its single-biggest point loss ever. Officials suspend trading to stem the losses. Stock prices in Brazil, Argentina and Mexico post their biggest single-day loss.

In **Thailand**, the legislature adopts new regulations regarding foreign ownership of financial institutions as part of a comprehensive restructuring package.

Meanwhile, the currency contagion spreads further—the **South Korean** *won*, coming under pressure, is devalued. South Korea is now firmly drawn into the crisis.

In **China**, new rules are announced which restrict the types of institutions that may hold foreign exchange as a measure to tighten control of the currency. Also, the Chinese government announces that mutual funds will be established.

November 1997   In **Thailand**, after only 11 months in power, the prime minister resigns. Meanwhile, the IMF and Thailand renegotiate elements of the bailout. The IMF agrees to a revised (and less strict) set of conditions for assistance.

In **Malaysia**, the stock markets and the currency are hit yet again.

Michel Camdessus, managing director of the IMF, states that the rescue package for **Indonesia** should end the economic destabilization in Asia. Meanwhile, Indonesia's central bank closes 16 commercial banks as part of its aid package with the IMF. Some commentators, most notably Jeffrey Sachs of Harvard University, attack this action, arguing it will lead to an unnecessary tightening of domestic credit when solvent companies are failing due to liquidity problems.[16] Meanwhile, the stock market and the *rupiah* continue to decline.

In **South Korea**, investor and public confidence is badly shaken by the October devaluation of the *won* and the ballooning trade deficit. Some economists foresee an immediate 20% devaluation if the currency moved to a floating regime. The Finance and Economy Ministry claims that panic triggered by "sheer speculative foreign press articles" is putting unnecessary pressure on the currency.

The *won* devaluation negatively impacts the holders of foreign debt, of which approximately 80% is short term. With a number of major bankruptcies having already taken place (8 of the country's 30 largest conglomerates have either declared bankruptcy or are facing severe financial strains by this point), the financial system has become burdened with billions of U.S. dollars of bad loans. Ratings agencies downgrade Korea's foreign debt, while interest rates increase dramatically. The finance minister, in an effort to avoid an IMF bailout, develops an alternative reform plan which includes asking Japan for help in rolling over maturing short-term loans and allowing the *won* to fluctuate by up to 10% per day (the previous limit was 2.5%). However, the currency and stock markets continue to fall—the stock market has fallen 28% in 1997 by this time—while the currency has lost 14% of its value, reaching a record low.

As a result of the failure of markets to respond, the finance minister is fired. The new finance minister, Lim Chang Yuel, acknowledges that recovery will be impossible without IMF assistance. Controversy erupts over the decision; the country had previously declared that it would never seek help from the IMF. In particular, controversy surrounds the IMF's projected growth rates of between 2.0% and 3.0%, just half the government's projected increase (Korea has enjoyed 8.6% average annual growth for 30 years). Initial reform efforts include easing restrictions on foreign ownership of Korean companies and allowing investment in the over-the-counter (OTC) market by foreigners.

South Korea is the world's 11th-largest economy. Its financial turmoil has raised fears of global contagion. Latin America, in particular, is worried. **Brazil** announces U.S. $18 billion in budget cutbacks and raises interest rates in an effort to reassure investors that it is prepared to defend against a currency attack. Brazil is potentially vulnerable to devaluation pressures due to negative public sector accounts, a large current account deficit, and an overvalued real currency.

December 1997   The **Philippine** *peso* declines to its lowest level in 25 years.

Thailand continues its efforts to "clean house" in the financial sector, permanently closing 56 finance companies. The IMF forecasts Thailand's economy to stagnate in 1998. The Thai *baht* hits its lowest level since the Thai central bank started keeping records in 1969.

In **Malaysia**, the *ringgit* falls to its lowest level since it was floated in 1973. Finance Minister Anwar Ibrahim announces a severe austerity program. The government revises its predictions for economic growth to 4%–5% in 1998, down from 7.5% in 1997. The proposed restructuring program contains IMF-style provisions, including: 1) reductions in fiscal outlays by 18%, including cuts in spending on large infrastructure projects; 2) restrictions on new public offerings; 3) plans to improve the foreign-exchange reserves, which were drawn down in Malaysia's effort to defend the *ringgit*; 4) plans to reduce the current account deficit to the equivalent of 3% of GNP, down from 5% of GNP in 1996; 5) allowing bad banks to fail; 6) restrictions on the issuance of new bank credits; and 7) a broad tightening of credit policies. The financial sector reforms are designed to restrict credit expansion, which has been growing at 25% per year. Banks will be allowed to terminate credit to unworthy borrowers. This is significant: Malaysia's period of rapid economic growth was partly characterized by government subsidy of expensive infrastructure and property projects. Worse, contracts for these projects were often awarded on the basis of patronage and "crony capitalism" rather than a competitive bidding process, fostering a climate of corrupt practices and competitive decline.

Malaysia's currency has suffered a 33% depreciation in value against the U.S. dollar, and the stock market has lost more than 50% in the period since July 1997. Many companies have been unable to capitalize projects in the damaged markets and have experienced severe liquidity problems, leading Malaysian financial companies to ease credit. Non-performing loans have increased accordingly, creating fears that a financial sector collapse is possible and that the real economy could be dragged down in a vicious circle of corporate and banking failures.

South Korea's currency and stock prices have lost half of their value. New information reveals that foreign-exchange reserves are dangerously low, with official reserves standing at U.S. $23.9 billion on December 2, down from U.S. $30.5 billion at the end of October. Of the U.S. $23.9 billion, only U.S. $6 billion are "usable funds." The remainder is "unusable" because it had been deposited by Korea's central bank at overseas branches and subsidiaries of domestic banks, which then used the deposits to repay non-renewed short-term debt.

The Korean authorities finally negotiate a U.S. $57 billion bail-out plan with the IMF. This leads many South Koreans to express rage and humiliation. Trade unions threaten "all-out strikes" if companies lay off workers. Newspaper editorials accuse the U.S. and Japan of using the financial crisis as leverage to force South Korea to open its markets further.

A series of reforms is launched, which include allowing the *won* to float. Foreigners are now permitted to acquire 55% of listed companies (the previous limit was 7%). The large *jaebol* are ordered to increase transparency. Restrictions on corporate takeovers are eased. Japanese products will be allowed greater access to the Korean market. Banks must meet the prudential standards of the Bank for International Settlements.

South Korean markets respond favorably to the package. However, there are several large market fluctuations, especially when prestigious Coryo Investment & Securities declares bankruptcy, marking the first failure of a Korean financial institution in over 30 years.

On December 30, several major international banks announce they will roll over South Korea's short-term debt which is coming due. Of the U.S. $100 billion total short-term figure, U.S. $15 billion is due by December 31 and U.S. $15 billion in January.

On December 18, South Korean voters elect former dissident Kim Dae-Jung as president, raising fears that the economy will be badly affected as a result. The populist Kim had been extremely critical of the IMF bailout during his campaign and declared that Korea was close to "bankruptcy." But by the end of the December, it appeared he was committed to IMF-style market-based reforms after all.

In **Indonesia**, President Soeharto takes an unprecedented 10-day home rest in mid-December, raising fears that he is ill and concerns over succession. The *rupiah* again plunges in value.[17] Between July and late December, the *rupiah* loses 58% of its value. Part of this loss is driven by revelations that the country's debt burden is higher than previously reported. Analysts estimate total debt close to U.S. $200 billion, substantially more than the government's official figure of U.S. $117 billion which analysts claim failed to include the debts of Korean-owned foreign subsidiaries.

Analysts worry that Indonesia is not taking its reform process seriously enough. Besides the regional currency crisis, Indonesia is also suffering from a severe drought, raising fears about food shortages in the midst of the economic crisis. It is feared that this could lead to civil unrest.

China, meanwhile, vows it will *not* devalue its currency. The pledge reassures analysts who fear that a Chinese devaluation would set off another round of regional devaluations and potentially cause Hong Kong to lose its peg to the U.S. dollar.

Many analysts believe the Asian currencies are now undervalued in terms of fundamental economic measures. Even so, analysts do not predict a quick rebound. Some economists remark that the downward pressure on the currency could continue.

The IMF, meanwhile, announces revised forecasts for world economic growth. Economic growth for 1998 is projected to be 3.5%, down from a forecast of 4.3% in September. The IMF warns: "A sharp slowdown in economic growth is an unavoidable consequence of the type of crisis affecting a number of the Asian economies."[18]

On December 23, government debt in Malaysia, Indonesia, and Thailand is downgraded to junk bond status.

January 1998   In **China**, a major series of reforms are announced, including a reorganization of the central bank, the closure of 150 trust companies as well as 12 informal OTC exchanges, and the granting of more autonomy for the top four state-owned commercial banks (the banks will shut down unprofitable branches and will accelerate the write-offs of bad debts).

Indonesia's commitment to economic reform increasingly is being questioned by investors and analysts. The head of Asian currency trading at a major German bank in Jakarta states: "We basically want to see if Indonesia will do anything to achieve the necessary compliance with the IMF. . . the *rupiah*'s direction hangs on this."[19] The decision to delay liquidation of PT Bank Jakarta, one of the 16 banks scheduled for closure in December (owned by Soeharto's half-brother Probosutedjo) has a further deleterious effect. Soeharto was under pressure to step down as social cohesion is threatened. Reports of panic food buying begin appearing.

The *rupiah* experiences a series of major declines in early to mid-January. Dollar buying by unhedged corporates to pay down foreign debt helps drive a vicious circle of devaluation, and the currency drops to 17,000 per U.S. dollar, less than 80% of its July 1997 value. The currency recovers by late January to 9,850/10,800. Indonesia's central bank governor explained that foreign debt holders were unhedged because: "They had come to expect a devaluation of just 5% a year, which is what we always did. The finance minister even mentioned it once in a speech."[20] In other words, corporate managers lost less in value due to the historically predictable devaluations than they would have had they hedged their exposure. Other factors causing the steep decline include growing bank liquidity problems, as well as political uncertainty after hints that Research and Technology Minister Jusuf Habibie may become President Soeharto's vice-presidential candidate in March. Habibie is widely viewed as an ardent nationalist, on occasion openly hostile to the wealthy Chinese minority.

Furthermore, he is a proponent of large-scale industrial policy, demonstrated by his support of massive projects such as a U.S. $2 billion effort to build an advanced aircraft industry.

Soeharto signs a new agreement with the IMF which does little to restore confidence. Provisions include new reforms in the financial sector which guarantee commercial bank obligations and allow foreign investment in domestic banks. In addition, a freeze on debt payments is announced pending a solution to the private sector foreign debt problem: 228 companies are currently unable to service their debt. Indonesian stocks also decline sharply in January.

In **Malaysia**, the *ringgit* drops to a new all-time low against the U.S. dollar. Figures from the Bank of International Settlements show that Malaysia's short-term debt reached 56% of total borrowings from foreign lenders, higher than the previous estimate of 30%.

The **Philippine** *peso* also hits a record low against the U.S. dollar.

Thailand announces that it is petitioning the IMF to ease further the terms of its bailout package. Prime Minister Chuan Leekpai recognizes that the budget will fall short by 100 billion *baht*, despite reduced spending. Government economists project that the Thai economy will contract in 1998 by 0.7%. As growth slows and austerity programs are implemented, they expect increases in bankruptcies, unemployment, and social unrest (Thai labor unions threatened mass protests if nothing was done to mitigate expected increases in unemployment). Thailand cuts its 1998 budget in three moves to 800 billion from 982 billion *baht*. Austerity measures include: 1) pay cuts for politicians and senior civil servants; 2) reductions in military spending; 3) a rise in the value-added tax on goods and services; and 4) an increase in excise duties on certain imported luxury goods and automobiles.

The Thai currency continues to decline, dipping through the psychological barrier of 50 to the dollar for the first time—down from 25 to the dollar when it was first floated in July 1997.

In **Hong Kong**, Chief Executive Tung Chee-hwa predicts a slowing growth rate. However, he reiterates his determination to defend the peg to the U.S. dollar.

South Korean foreign exchange reserves stabilize for the first time since the crisis began. President-elect Kim Dae-Jung says: "The real ordeal will begin from now on. . . . Frankly speaking, we're just entering a dark IMF tunnel. . . . It's very much clear that in an era of a global economy, we can't survive without foreign investment. We must change our attitude toward foreign investment. We should welcome it. . . by allowing layoffs, we'll lose 20% but save the other 80%."[21]

South Korea reaches a comprehensive agreement with global creditors to exchange U.S. $24 billion in short-term debt for government-guaranteed loans. Also, South Korea closes 10 merchant banks (out of a total of 30) with insufficient capital. The merchant banks, which are characterized by their specialty in short-term corporate lending, were responsible for making billions of dollars of bad corporate loans and investments.

In **Malaysia**, pressure in the financial sector forces the merger of Malaysian finance companies.

February 1998   The first evidence of a restoration in confidence in the Asian region occurs in early February following the Asian New Year and the beginning of the "Year of the Tiger." Equities and currency markets throughout the region post sharply higher returns. On February 2, there is widespread sentiment that the Asian crisis is over.

In **America**, the latest U.S. monthly trade report suggests that the Asian financial crisis is beginning to affect the U.S. economy. The U.S. trade deficit in December increased 24% to $10.8 billion, far more than expected. The deficit for 1997 was the largest in nine years.

Japan's Economic Planning Agency declares the economy "stagnant" with the worst performance for over 20 years. Japan's ruling party announces a package of economic reform measures, the fourth economic package since October designed to stimulate the economy. Analysts widely criticize the plan as being a half measure at best.

In **Indonesia**, the *rupiah* experiences a short-term gain on the prospect that a currency board may be adopted. However, most analysts fear that, if adopted, a currency board will quickly collapse due to insufficient reserves. The IMF threatens to withhold additional funding if Indonesia goes ahead with the plan. IMF Managing Director Michel Camdessus remarks: "In the present circumstances...if a currency board proposal were adopted, we would not be able to recommend to the IMF Board the continuation of the current program because of the risks to the Indonesian economy.... The failure of a currency board would completely undermine credibility and policy making, and seriously damage the country's growth prospects."[22]

Major rioting breaks out for the first time, and Indonesians burn shops owned by ethnic Chinese during protests against rising prices in three West Java towns. In East Java, police warn that rioters could be shot on sight. Meanwhile, the ruling Golkar party names Jusuf Habibie as vice-presidential candidate in the March indirect election.

On February 17, central bank governor Soedradjad Djiwandono is sacked by President Soeharto, over a disagreement concerning plans to create a currency board, as well as other differences in reforming the Indonesian economy. He is replaced by U.S.-trained economist Sjahril Sabirin. Banking sources expect Sabirin would back the currency board.

The **Philippines** experiences a marked improvement in its fortunes, and the *peso* rises based on improving confidence in the IMF-sponsored reforms. As dollars return, observers begin to believe the worst is over.

Concluding a series of negotiations with the IMF, **Thailand** wins concessions in its aid package. The IMF will allow the country to run a 1-2% budget deficit (in lieu of running a budget surplus) in the upcoming fiscal year and will allow the reduction in domestic interest rates which had been raised to defend against speculative attack on the *baht*. An official at the IMF remarks: "The government has control of the financial system and is creating stability."[23]

Following the first quarterly review of the country's progress under its IMF rescue program, **South Korea** agrees to expand its social safety net and raise unemployment benefits. The IMF releases an additional U.S. $2 billion to South Korea, bringing total IMF lending to U.S. $15 billion. The IMF Executive Board expresses approval of Seoul's efforts to reform the economy. Standard & Poor's upgrades South Korea's credit rating.

Meanwhile, according to the South Korean government, the nation's banks experienced a fourfold increase in their portfolio of bad loans in 1997. Some analysts worry that this figure radically understates the bad debt problem. Whereas the central bank claim the total is 6% of all loans, critics suggest it could be as high as 15% to 20%.

March 1998   The People's Constituent Assembly (MPR) in **Indonesia** reelects 76-year-old Soeharto to the presidency and approves state policy for the next five years.

The Indonesian government warns that the economy is on the brink of hyperinflation. Price levels are rising rapidly, at a pace not seen since the mid-1960s. Month-to-month inflation rose to 12.8% in February alone. Reuters calculates the year-to-year rate to be 31.8%. Food prices are rising most rapidly, resulting in several months of civil unrest. During riots, five people are killed as troops fire on mobs looting and burning food shops. According to analysts, base money figures indicate that the central bank was printing money at a time when there were shortages of food and other essential goods in the real economy. In addition, the 75% depreciation of the *rupiah* between July 1997 and March 1998 has caused a rapid rise in the price of imports.

Indonesia announces that, despite an IMF prohibition, it will subsidize imports of food and other essentials in response to inflation. The government warns that any delay by the IMF in disbursing funds from a bailout package will hurt regional currencies.

Meanwhile, the United States and other nations place significant pressure on the Indonesian government to cease plans to implement a currency board. In response, Johns Hopkins University economist Steve Hanke, adviser to Soeharto and widely seen as the architect of the proposed currency board, says Indonesia is committed to implementing an "IMF Plus" plan that includes a currency board. (Hanke has been criticized for a potential conflict of interest: He is chairman of currency trading firm Friedberg Mercantile Group and acknowledges that the firm profited from speculating against the *rupiah* and other Asian currencies in recent months).

In late March, President Soeharto makes a series of cabinet appointments which further undermine confidence in the country's commitment to implementing reform. The "Berkley Mafia," a group of Western-trained technocrats, is marginalized in the cabinet reshuffle. He appoints his daughter as social affairs minister. She presides over a major conglomerate that was forced to cancel one of its power projects because of IMF provisions and that stood to lose other infrastructure contracts if IMF-sponsored regulations designed to promote fair public tenders were introduced. Soeharto appoints Bob Hasan, a business associate and golf partner, to head the ministry of trade and industry. Hasan operates a major conglomerate that was targeted by the IMF for its dominance of the forestry industry. Fuad Bawazier is appointed finance minister. Bawazier is a board member of two state banks that made loans to Soeharto's family businesses. Finally, Ginanjar Kartasasmita, an outspoken opponent of IMF-style market liberalization, is appointed coordinating minister for economy, finance, and development.

Even so, by the end of March Indonesia's prospects appear to be improving: The government announces that it is postponing plans to implement a currency board; the World Bank announces it will coordinate an international effort to provide food and other essentials worth U.S. $1.5 billion to the country; and the IMF announces that it was making "considerable progress" with the Indonesian government towards completing a new rescue package. The new agreement would honor the Indonesian request to maintain state subsidies for food and basic medicines. If completed, this will be the third agreement between the IMF and Indonesia.

The central bank of Indonesia raises key interests rates (doubling one month rates to 45%), which encourages the IMF and other outside observers. It also abandons a proposed 5% tax on foreign currency purchases. Furthermore, 47 domestic banks facing insolvency will come under the jurisdiction of a new agency set up to rehabilitate bad banks.

In early March, **Malaysia** announces that the banking unit of Sime Darby Bhd, one of the country's top 10 banks, requires a capital infusion in excess of 1 billion *ringgit*. Furthermore, the government announces that the country's second-largest bank, government-run Bank Bumiputra Malaysia Bhd, as well as two additional finance companies may also require significant new capital injections to maintain liquidity. Currency and equity markets throughout the region are adversely affected. Observers worry about panic and the affect of destroyed market confidence.

In **Thailand**, equity and currency markets rise based on the perception that Thailand is implementing the appropriate policies, in accordance with the IMF plan, to address its economy.

South Korea also appears to be improving as it continues to make rapid progress toward economic reform. Confidence has recovered significantly, allowing the critical restructuring by foreign creditor banks of over 95% of the short-term debt which has been threatening the solvency of the South Korean financial system. More than 80% of the debt is rolled over for two- to three-year maturities. It is anticipated that this will expedite the reopening of South Korea to international capital markets.

China's new premier, Zhu Rongji, helps increase confidence by stating that China will defend the Hong Kong currency board at any cost.

April 1998   On April 1, Japan adopts the first measures of the country's "Big Bang" deregulation of the financial markets. Most restraints on foreign exchange trading are lifted and commissions on large equity transactions, previously fixed at set rates, are deregulated.

Based on poor recent economic performance, Moody's speculates about a possible downgrade for Japan. The Chairman of Sony Corporation, Norio Ohga, warns that the economy is on the brink of a collapse which could cause a world-wide recession. In response to the criticism of his handling of the economy, Prime Minister Ryutaro Hashimoto promises new efforts to reinvigorate the moribund economy, proposing larger-than-expected tax cuts totaling ¥30.5 billion.

Thailand announces that its central bank will set more stringent standards governing the accounting of bad loans by the country's banks. Sixteen commercial banks and 35 finance companies have survived the crisis thus far. One-quarter of all bank loans are currently listed as non-performing.

In **South Korea**, restrictions against foreign-led takeovers of Korean firms are lifted. Foreign brokerages and banks are permitted to open wholly owned subsidiaries in the country for the first time. In the first quarter of 1998, 10,000 Korean firms declared bankruptcy—as compared to 14,000 in the entire previous year. Debt-to-equity ratios run an average of 200% to 400% amongst the *jaebols*. South Korea also receives strong interest in a U.S. $4 billion bond sale.

Officials from North and South Korea meet in Beijing on April 11 and 12, marking the first official bilateral contact between the governments in four years.

Malaysia reports difficulty in implementing its reform efforts designed to force consolidation in its banking industry.

China announces its intent to help Indonesia by bartering some goods and reiterates its commitment not to devalue its currency.

On April 10, **Indonesia** signs its third IMF Letter of Intent since the onset of the crisis. The compromise agreement will allow Jakarta to maintain certain subsidies for foods, medicines, fuel, other commodities, and interest rates for small companies and cooperatives. In return, it commits to dismantling monopolies and unfair practices. The new accord includes a government-backed plan to restructure U.S. $68 billion in foreign corporate debt, a provision which was not included in the first two IMF agreements. Indonesia also pledges to expedite the pace of banking reform and to maintain high interest rates to stabilize the *rupiah*.

Indonesia announces that 95% of the country's 200 banks will require new capital. The government closes 7 of the banks and brings an additional 7 under official supervision, bringing the total number of banks under supervision of the Indonesian Bank Restructuring Agency to 54.

The Future . . .

In mid-1998, it was difficult to predict what would develop next in the region. Although most analysts agreed that the currency component of the crisis was passing, the broader implications of the crisis on future global investment and trade were uncertain. In addition, the crisis had affected the real economies of each country very differently, and each country would require its own unique recovery program.

Most observers were optimistic about the prospects of the majority of affected countries. Thailand, Malaysia, and South Korea seemed to be making important steps to encourage economic recovery. Even Indonesia—despite its history of political and social instability and inability to meet IMF requirements—appeared to be preparing for a credible economic recovery with its latest IMF agreement. In a 1998 report on the crisis, Goldman Sachs economists emphasized their optimism: "Total returns on a basket of Asian economies may well exceed returns on holdings of U.S. dollars by a substantial margin over the next 12 months. . . . The time may soon be right to invest in a basket of Asian currencies, to take advantage of greater stability in nominal exchange rates," while acknowledging "there is no quick-fix available for the Asian crisis, as there was for Mexico in 1995."[24]

Optimistic forecasts assumed that necessary policy reforms in affected countries could withstand political instability and civil unrest. Furthermore, forecasts relied on China not devaluing its currency. If either of these assumptions were to fail, it was feared that the crisis would intensify and spread beyond the region. Only time would tell whether April 1998 represented the start of Asia's recovery or just the eye of the storm.

Exhibit 1 Selected Asian Economies: Basic Economic Data

	1975–1982	1983–1989	1990	1991	1992	1993	1994	1995	1996	1997[a]
China										
Real sector										
Real GDP growth[b]	6.0	10.7	3.8	9.2	14.2	13.5	12.6	10.5	9.6	8.8
Inflation[b,c]	2.1	9.0	2.1	2.7	5.4	13.0	21.7	14.8	6.1	1.5
Domestic saving	39.3	35.2	38.1	38.3	37.7	40.6	42.6	41.0	42.9	40.8
Fixed capital formation	21.3	29.5	25.5	27.5	31.2	37.5	36.0	34.7	35.6	35.8
Public sector										
General government balance	-1.0	-1.7	-2.0	-2.2	-2.3	-2.0	-1.6	-1.7	-1.5	-1.5
Public sector balance	...	...	...	...	...	-5.5	-3.6	-3.9	-3.6	-3.4
Monetary sector										
M2 growth (end of year)[b]	22.3	26.1	28.9	26.7	30.8	42.8	35.1	29.5	25.3	...
Domestic credit growth (end of year)[b]	18.8	17.0	23.6	20.0	22.3	42.1	23.8	22.9	25.3	...
Foreign liabilities of banks[d]	3.4	3.3	3.5	4.6	4.0	5.4	7.1	6.4	5.6	...
External sector										
Current account balance	0.7	-1.0	3.4	3.5	1.5	-2.7	1.4	0.2	0.9	2.5
External sector service	0.4	1.0	1.7	1.7	2.3	2.3	2.4	2.2	2.0	1.9
Hong Kong SAR										
Real sector										
Real GDP growth[b]	9.3	7.2	3.4	5.1	6.3	6.1	5.4	3.9	4.9	5.3
Inflation[b,c]	8.6	6.7	9.7	11.6	9.3	8.5	8.1	8.7	6.0	6.5
Domestic saving	29.7	33.6	35.8	33.8	33.8	34.6	33.1	30.4	30.6	30.8
Fixed capital formation	27.8	23.6	26.4	26.6	27.4	27.3	29.8	30.5	31.3	32.0
Public sector										
General government balance	1.5	1.6	0.7	3.2	2.5	2.3	1.3	-0.3	2.2	4.2
Public sector balance	...	...	...	...	...	...	...	...	...	...
Monetary sector										
M2 growth (end of year)[b]	...	...	...	...	8.5	14.5`	11.7	10.6	12.5	...
Domestic credit growth (end of year)[b]	...	...	...	...	9.6	21.0	25.0	8.6	18.0	...
Foreign liabilities of banks[d]	...	...	...	73.5	71.6	69.2	70.6	70.4	66.4	...
External sector										
Current account balance	1.9	8.3	8.9	7.1	5.7	7.4	1.6	-3.9	-1.3	-1.5
External sector service	...	...	...	...	...	...	...	...	...	...
Indonesia										
Real sector										
Real GDP growth[b]	6.2	5.5	9.0	8.9	7.2	7.3	7.5	8.2	8.0	5.0
Inflation[b,c]	15.0	8.1	7.8	9.4	7.5	9.7	8.5	9.4	7.9	8.3
Domestic saving	19.3	23.2	27.9	28.7	27.3	31.4	29.2	29.0	28.8	27.3
Fixed capital formation	19.8	24.3	28.3	27.0	25.8	26.3	27.6	28.4	28.1	26.5
Public sector										
General government balance	...	-1.3	1.3	--	-1.2	-0.7	--	0.8	1.4	2.0
Public sector balance	...	...	...	...	...	...	...	...	...	...
Monetary sector	...									
M2 growth (end of year)[b]	29.3	27.0	44.6	17.5	19.8	20.2	20.0	27.2	27.2	...
Domestic credit growth (end of year)[b]	42.1	48.3	58.3	18.9	14.1	21.0	22.9	21.7	22.7	...
Foreign liabilities of banks[d]	2.2	4.2	11.0	8.6	10.3	10.9	10.9	9.6	8.5	...
External sector										
Current account balance	-1.2	-3.5	-2.8	-3.4	-2.2	-1.5	-1.7	-3.3	-3.3	-2.9
External sector service	3.5	6.8	8.3	8.4	8.7	8.4	8.6	8.5	9.0	10.5

Exhibit 1   (Continued)

	1975–1982	1983–1989	1990	1991	1992	1993	1994	1995	1996	1997[a]
Japan										
Real sector										
Real GDP growth[b]	3.9	4.1	5.1	3.8	1.0	0.3	0.6	1.5	3.9	1.0
Inflation[b,c]	6.6	1.4	3.1	3.3	1.7	1.2	0.7	-0.1	0.1	1.7
Domestic saving	31.9	31.9	33.5	34.2	33.8	32.8	31.4	30.7	31.3	30.8
Fixed capital formation	30.9	28.4	31.7	31.4	30.5	29.5	28.6	28.5	29.7	28.4
Public sector										
General government balance	-4.0	-0.4	2.9	2.9	1.5	-1.6	-2.3	-3.7	-4.1	-2.9
Public sector balance	…	…	…	…	…	…	…	…	…	…
Monetary sector										
M2 growth (end of year)[b]	10.7	9.2	8.2	2.5	-0.1	2.2	3.1	2.8	2.3	…
Domestic credit growth (end of year)[b]	10.6	11.4	9.2	2.9	2.9	0.8	-0.4	1.8	1.4	…
Foreign liabilities of banks[d]	17.2	18.3	19.4	15.3	12.4	11.0	9.7	10.0	10.6	…
External sector										
Current account balance	0.4	3.0	1.5	2.0	3.0	3.1	2.8	2.2	1.4	2.2
External sector service	…	…	…	…	…	…	…	…	…	…
Korea										
Real sector										
Real GDP growth[b]	7.0	9.6	9.5	9.1	5.1	5.8	8.6	8.9	7.1	6.0
Inflation[b,c]	17.6	3.8	8.6	9.3	6.2	4.8	6.3	4.5	4.9	4.3
Domestic saving	25.7	32.7	36.1	35.9	35.1	35.2	34.6	35.1	33.3	32.9
Fixed capital formation	29.4	29.4	37.1	38.4	36.6	36.0	35.7	36.6	36.8	36.6
Public sector										
General government balance	-2.7	-0.3	-0.6	-1.6	-2.6	-1.0	1.0	--	--	--
Public sector balance	…	…	…	…	…	…	…	…	…	…
Monetary sector										
M2 growth (end of year)[b]	30.0	16.6	17.2	21.9	14.9	16.6	18.7	15.6	15.8	…
Domestic credit growth (end of year)[b]	11.6	22.8	24.8	22.4	11.7	12.7	18.4	14.7	19.4	…
Foreign liabilities of banks[d]	9.4	7.3	6.5	7.7	7.6	6.9	8.0	10.1	12.8	…
External sector										
Current account balance	-4.6	2.5	-0.9	-3.0	-1.5	0.1	-1.2	-2.0	-4.9	-2.9
External sector service	…	…	…	…	…	…	…	…	…	…
Malaysia										
Real sector										
Real GDP growth[b]	7.1	5.4	9.6	8.6	7.8	8.3	9.2	9.5	8.6	7.0
Inflation[b,c]	5.3	2.0	2.8	2.6	4.7	3.5	3.7	3.4	3.5	3.7
Domestic saving	21.6	29.4	29.1	28.4	31.3	33.0	32.7	33.5	36.7	37.0
Fixed capital formation	29.4	28.5	32.4	36.4	36.0	38.3	40.1	43.0	42.2	42.7
Public sector										
General government balance	…	-4.0	-2.2	0.2	-3.5	-2.6	2.5	3.8	4.2	1.6
Public sector balance	…	…	…	…	-3.5	-2.6	2.5	3.2	1.6	1.8
Monetary sector										
M2 growth (end of year)[b]	20.2	9.2	10.6	16.9	29.2	26.6	12.7	20.0	…	…
Domestic credit growth (end of year)[b]	5.3	19.9	18.0	18.5	16.6	12.3	14.8	29.5	…	…
Foreign liabilities of banks[d]	6.3	6.7	7.3	9.0	13.0	19.5	8.8	6.5	…	…
External sector										
Current account balance	-2.0	-0.7	-2.1	-8.8	-3.8	-4.8	-7.8	-10.0	-4.9	-5.8
External sector service	3.8	9.0	6.9	5.9	5.6	6.1	5.2	6.6	5.4	8.4

Exhibit 1   (Continued)

	1975–1982	1983–1989	1990	1991	1992	1993	1994	1995	1996	1997[a]
Philippines										
Real sector										
Real GDP growth[b]	5.6	1.1	3.0	-0.6	0.3	2.1	4.4	4.8	5.7	4.3
Inflation[b,c]	11.0	15.4	12.7	18.7	8.9	7.6	9.0	8.1	8.4	5.2
Domestic saving	19.9	18.1	18.7	18.0	19.5	18.4	19.4	17.8	19.7	21.0
Fixed capital formation	26.7	20.7	24.0	20.0	20.9	23.8	23.6	22.2	23.2	25.1
Public sector										
General government balance	-2.0	-2.8	-3.5	-2.1	-1.2	-1.6	-1.6	-1.4	-0.4	-0.9
Public sector balance	...	...	...	...	...	-2.0	-0.6	-0.1	0.1	0.3
Monetary sector										
M2 growth (end of year)[b]	20.5	21.4	22.5	17.3	13.6	27.1	24.4	24.2	23.2	...
Domestic credit growth (end of year)[b]	6.2	21.5	30.7	-2.6	17.6	131.2	19.0	31.3	40.3	...
Foreign liabilities of banks[d]	16.0	12.9	14.9	11.5	12.9	10.9	12.3	13.9	21.9	...
External sector										
Current account balance	-6.5	-0.3	-6.1	-2.3	-1.6	-5.l5	-4.6	-4.4	-4.7	-4.5
External sector service	5.5	8.5	8.1	9.0	7.2	7.8	7.2	6.5	7.3	6.0
Singapore										
Real sector										
Real GDP growth[b]	8.0	6.9	9.0	7.3	6.2	10.4	10.5	8.8	7.0	7.2
Inflation[b,c]	4.2	1.0	3.5	3.4	2.3	2.3	3.1	1.7	1.4	2.1
Domestic saving	33.4	42.0	44.1	45.4	47.3	44.9	49.8	50.0	50.1	50.0
Fixed capital formation	38.2	38.1	31.8	33.3	35.6	35.0	33.6	33.3	36.5	35.4
Public sector										
General government balance	0.6	4.8	11.4	10.3	11.3	14.3	13.7	12.0	8.4	8.3
Public sector balance	...	...	11.4	10.3	11.3	14.3	13.7	12.0	8.4	8.3
Monetary sector										
M2 growth (end of year)[b]	16.2	12.5	20.0	12.4	8.9	8.5	14.4	8.5	9.8	...
Domestic credit growth (end of year)[b]	4.3	5.2	12.3	13.9	5.5	12.0	12.8	17.4	17.3	...
Foreign liabilities of banks[d]	40.4	42.0	39.0	33.6	35.3	34.8	35.6	35.2	36.4	...
External sector										
Current account balance	-8.8	1.8	8.3	11.2	11.3	7.4	17.1	16.9	15.0	14.0
External sector service	...	...	...	...	...	...	...	...	...	...
Taiwan Province of China										
Real sector										
Real GDP growth[b]	8.5	9.2	5.4	7.6	6.8	6.3	6.5	6.0	5.7	6.7
Inflation[b,c]	8.6	1.2	4.1	3.6	4.5	2.9	4.1	3.7	3.1	2.0
Domestic saving	30.2	35.0	29.3	29.5	27.8	27.7	27.1	28.0	28.0	27.9
Fixed capital formation	27.8	20.4	22.4	22.2	23.2	23.7	22.9	22.9	21.0	21.0
Public sector										
General government balance	--	1.3	0.8	0.5	0.3	0.6	0.2	0.4	0.2	0.2
Public sector balance	...	...	...	...	...	...	...	...	...	...
Monetary sector										
M2 growth (end of year)[b]	22.3	24.4	10.5	19.7	19.6	15.5	15.2	9.6	4.7	...
Domestic credit growth (end of year)[b]	36.4	29.9	17.0	26.3	28.5	19.8	16.5	10.6	10.1	...
Foreign liabilities of banks[d]	8.6	5.8	4.8	5.2	4.2	3.9	4.1	4.1	3.3	...
External sector										
Current account balance	1.6	12.9	6.7	6.7	3.8	3.0	2.6	1.9	5.2	4.2
External sector service	...	...	...	...	...	...	...	...	...	...

Exhibit 1   (Continued)

	1975–1982	1983–1989	1990	1991	1992	1993	1994	1995	1996	1997[a]
Thailand										
Real sector										
Real GDP growth[b]	7.0	8.1	11.6	8.1	8.2	8.5	8.9	8.7	6.4	0.6
Inflation[b,c]	9.0	3.1	6.0	5.7	4.1	3.4	5.1	5.8	5.9	6.0
Domestic saving	19.6	25.4	32.6	35.2	34.3	34.9	34.9	34.3	33.1	31.8
Fixed capital formation	23.6	27.7	40.2	41.6	39.2	39.4	39.9	41.8	40.8	35.8
Public sector										
General government balance	-5.8	-3.0	4.4	4.2	2.6	2.1	2.0	2.6	1.6	-0.4
Public sector balance	…	…	…	4.0	1.6	0.9	1.8	2.5	2.2	1.9
Monetary sector										
M2 growth (end of year)[b]	19.3	18.8	26.7	19.8	15.6	18.4	12.9	17.0	16.7	…
Domestic credit growth (end of year)[b]	15.6	19.8	26.8	15.5	18.0	22.7	28.9	23.1	14.0	…
Foreign liabilities of banks[d]	5.8	6.3	6.4	6.0	6.9	11.7	20.3	24.3	23.3	…
External sector										
Current account balance	-5.6	-3.2	-8.3	-7.7	-5.6	-5.0	-5.6	-8.0	-7.9	-3.9
External sector service	3.8	5.8	3.8	4.0	4.3	4.4	4.8	5.0	5.4	7.1

Source: Compiled from International Monetary Fund (IMF), *World Economic Outlook*, December 1997.

Notes: [a]Estimate.

[b]Annual percentage rate.

[c]Consumer price index.

[d]In percent of total liabilities of the banking system.

[e]Includes only goods and nonfactor services.

[f]Excludes prepayments and refinancing and includes staff estimates of short-term interest payments.

Exhibit 2a   General Economic Indicators

Average Korea, Indonesia, Malaysia, Philippines, Thailand

Exhibit 2b   Selected Asian Economies (and U.S.): GDP per capita

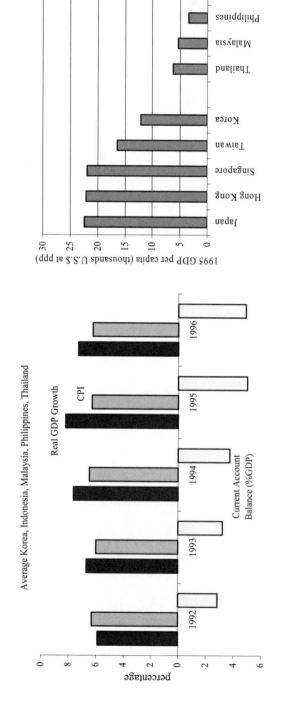

Exhibit 2c   Selected Asian Economies (and U.S.): Real GDP Growth

Exhibit 2d   Selected Asian Economies (and U.S.): Real GDP Growth

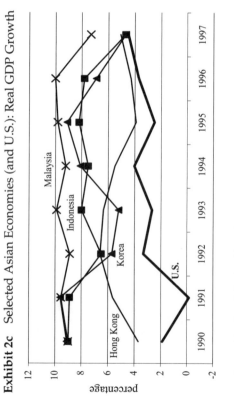

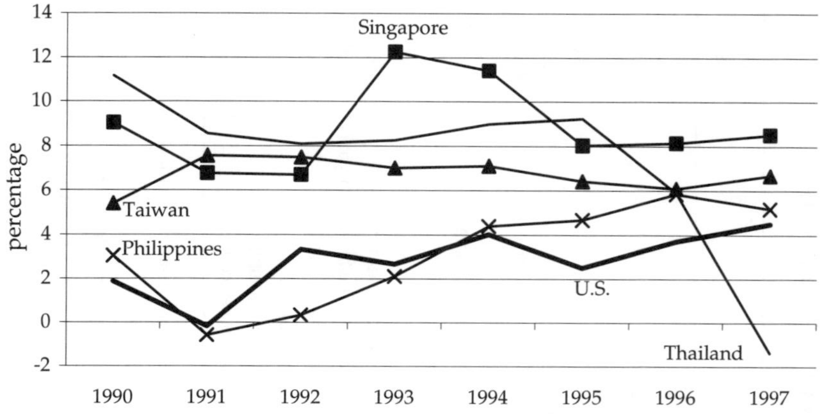

Source (2a–d):   Calculated based on data from EIU Country Data, September 2004.

Exhibit 3a Selected Asian Economies: Manufacturing Wages

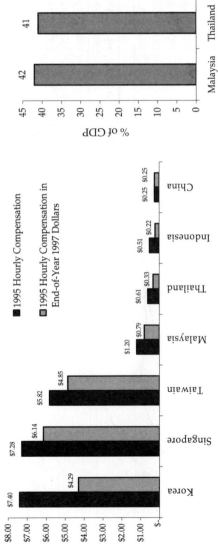

Source: Adapted from Fidelity Investments.

Exhibit 3b Selected Asian Economies: Investment Spending (% GDP, 1996)

Source: Adapted from IMF, *World Economic Outlook*, December 1997.

Exhibit 3c Thailand: Investment, Consumption, and Current Account

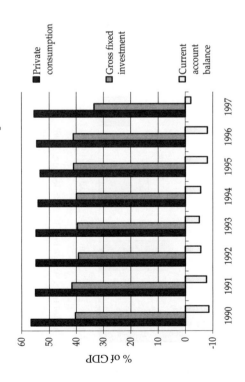

Source: Calculated based on data from EIU Country Data, September 2004.

Exhibit 3d Mexico & Thailand: Priv. Consump and Fixed Inv. (% GDP)

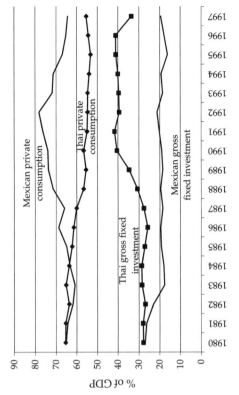

Sources: Adapted from IMF, IFS CD-ROM, February 2004; and EIU Country Data, September 2004.

Exhibit 4b   Selected Asian Economies: Export Market Growth

annual % change, USD basis	1989	1990	1991	1992	1993	1994	1995	1996	1997
China	10.2	17.9	16.2	18.0	8.0	31.9	23.0	1.5	21.0
Indonesia	15.3	15.9	13.5	16.6	8.4	8.8	13.4	9.7	7.3
Korea	2.8	4.2	10.6	6.6	7.3	16.8	30.2	3.8	5.0
Malaysia	18.2	18.3	16.5	18.6	15.6	24.8	25.8	5.8	0.7
Philippines	10.3	4.0	8.7	11.2	13.7	20.0	31.6	16.7	22.9
Thailand	25.8	14.9	23.2	14.2	13.2	23.1	24.7	(1.3)	3.3

Source: Calculated based on data from EIU Country Data, September 2004.

Exhibit 4d   Selected Asian Economies: Exchange Rates

Real effective exchange rate (CPI-based, 1990=100)

	1990	1991	1992	1993	1994	1995	1996	1997
China	100	85	82	87	68	75	83	89
Indonesia	100	99	97	102	102	99	39	35
Korea	100	99	93	89	90	90	120	108
Malaysia	100	98	104	105	102	102	106	105
Philippines	100	100	111	111	116	119	131	130
Thailand	100	102	103	104	107	111	112	97

Nominal exchange rate (end-year against USD, 1990=100)

	1990	1991	1992	1993	1994	1995	1996	1997
China	100	104	110	111	162	159	159	159
Indonesia	100	105	108	111	116	121	125	245
Korea	100	106	110	113	110	108	118	237
Malaysia	100	101	97	100	95	94	94	144
Philippines	100	95	90	99	87	94	94	143
Thailand	100	100	101	101	99	100	101	187

Source: Calculated based on data from EIU Country Data, September 2004.

Exhibit 4a   Selected Asian Economies: Corporate Leverage

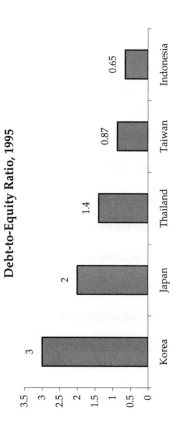

Debt-to-Equity Ratio, 1995

Source: Adapted from André Perold, HBS lecture, 1998.

Exhibit 4c   Selected Economy Long-term Interest Rates

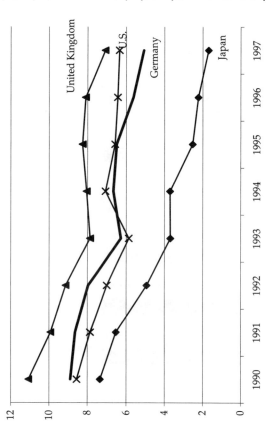

Source: Compiled from IMF, *International Financial Statistics CD-ROM*, February 2004.

Exhibit 5a Local Bank Lending (% GDP)

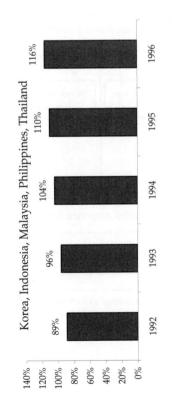

Korea, Indonesia, Malaysia, Philippines, Thailand

Source: Adapted from Radelet and Sachs, "Onset of the East Asian Financial Crisis," 1998.

Exhibit 5b Selected Asian Economies: Financial Institutions Claims on the Private Sector (as % GDP)

	1990	1996
Korea	56.8	65.7
Malaysia	71.4	144.6
Thailand	83.1	141.9
Philippines	19.3	48.4
Indonesia	50.6	55.4
Taiwan	97.0	165.0

Source: Compiled from EIU Country Data, September 2004.

Exhibit 5c Net External Private Capital Flows

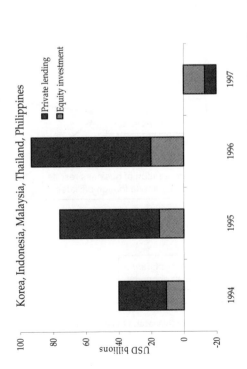

Korea, Indonesia, Malaysia, Thailand, Philippines

Source: Adapted from Institute of International Finance, "Capital Flows to Emerging Market Economies," 1998.

Exhibit 5d Claims Held by Foreign Banks (U.S. $274.4 billion as of June, 1997)

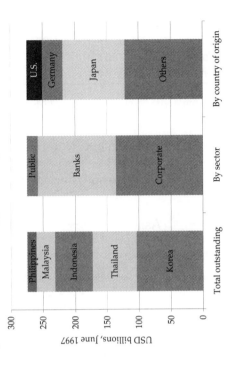

Source: Adapted from Radelet and Sachs, "Onset of the East Asian Financial Crisis," 1998.

Exhibit 6   Selected Asian Economies: Public Equities Markets (*U.S.$ billions*)

	Malaysia	Indonesia	Thailand	Korea	Singapore	Japan	U.S.
Market Value on 12/92	71	11	39	66	194	2,301	3,643
Date of Market Peak	Feb-97	Jan-97	Jan-96	Oct-95	Jul-97	Apr-96	na
Peak Market Value	207	79	112	124	626	3,777	na
Market Value on 12/97	64	21	16	27	421	2,218	8,929

Source: Adapted from André Perold, HBS lecture, 1998.

Exhibit 7   Interdependence on Interaction between Japan and Asia

Transmission Mechanism of the Asia Crisis

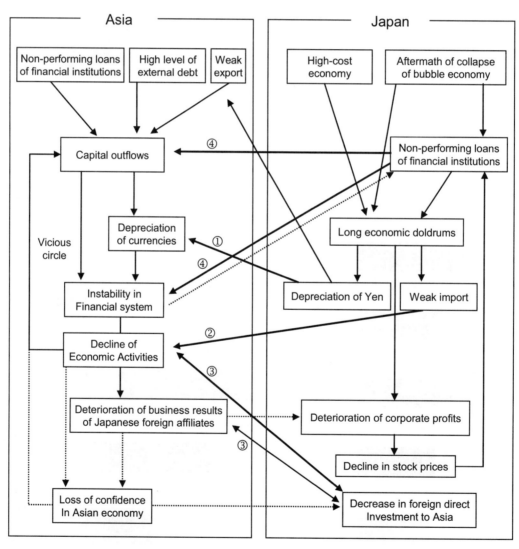

Source: Adapted from the Research Division, the Bank of Tokyo-Mitsubishi Ltd.

Endnotes

1 Martin Wolf, "No More Than a Blip," *The Financial Times*, July 15, 1997.

2 Paul Krugman, "What Happened to Asia?" prepared for a conference in Japan, January 1998, available at <web.mit.edu/krugman/www/DISINTER.htm>, accessed August 12, 2004.

3 For a detailed explanation of this approach to the Mexican devaluation of 1994-95, see Rudiger Dornbusch and Alejandro Werner (1994), "Mexico: Stabilization, Reform and No Growth," *Brookings Papers on Economic Activity*, No. 2.

4 This section was a simplified synopsis of the "first generation" speculative attack model exemplified by Paul Krugman (1979), "Speculative Attacks on Exchange Rate Pegs," *Journal of Money ,Credit and Banking*, No. 12. For a simpler version, see Robert Flood and Peter Garber (1984), "Speculative Attacks: Some Linearized Examples," *Journal of International Economics*, No. 17.

5 From George Lodge and Courtenay Sprague, "Korean Development and Western Economics," HBS Case No. 797-008.

6 Chung Hee Park, *The Country, The Revolution and I* (Seoul: Hollym Co., 1963).

7 From: *Freedom in the World: 1997-1998* (New York: Freedom House, 1998); Country Profile, 1996-1997 (Thailand), (London: The Economist Intelligence Unit Limited, 1996); *The Economist*; *The Asian Wall Street Journal*; *The New York Times* (from July 1997–April 1998).

8 *Thailand - A Country Study* (Department of State, Federal Research Division Library of Congress. Edited by Barbara Leitch LePoer Research Completed September 1987).

9 From Forest Reinhardt, "Malaysia in the 1990s (A)," HBS Case No. 797-074; Tarun Khanna, Michael Yoshino and Danielle Melito Wu (1997), "Sime Darby Berhad, 1995," HBS Case No. 797-017; *Trends in Developing Economies 1996* (Washington, DC: IBRD/The World Bank, 1996).

10 From Neil Gelfand and Mark Hilderbrand (MBAs '96) "Indonesia (A)," HBS Case No. 796-125; EIU Country Profile, 1996-1997 (Indonesia), (London: The Economist Intelligence Unit Limited, 1996).

11 From Nouriel Roubini (1998), "What Caused Asia's Economic and Currency Crisis and Its Global Contagion?" McKinsey & Company; Harvard Institute for International Development; Merrill Lynch; Reuters; *The Economist*; *The Wall Street Journal*; *The Asian Wall Street Journal*; *The New York Times*; *The Financial Times*, Bloomberg (from July 1997–April 1998).

12 Martin Wolf, "No More Than a Blip," *The Financial Times*, July 15, 1997.

13 Paul Krugman, *What Happened to Asia?* 1998.

14 Keith Richburg, "Captive Of a Boom Gone Bust; Will Asia's Economic Tigers Recover From the Crisis?" *The Washington Post*, October 12, 1997.

15 "Malaysia's Pyrotechnic Display," *The Washington Times*, October 5, 1997.

16 Jeffrey Sachs, "The Wrong Medicine for Asia," *The New York Times*, November 21, 1997.

17 In the previous political transition in Indonesia (in 1965-67), more than half a million people died in bloody violence.

18 Knut Engelmann, "IMF says Asia crisis to slow global economic growth," Reuters News, December 20, 1997.

19 Joseph Rajendran, "SE Asia Currencies Lower; Rgt At New Low; Focus On Rupiah," *Capital Markets Report*, January 2, 1998.

20 Interview with Soedradjad Djiwandono, March 4, 1998.

21 "S. Korea President-Elect Warns Of Hardships Under IMF Plan," *Dow Jones International News*, January 18, 1998.

[22]   "Indonesian plan to peg rupiah to the dollar 'premature'," *The Independent - London,* February 14, 1998.

[23]   "IMF agrees to relax Thailand's budget surplus requirement," *Agence France-Presse* , February 12, 1998.

[24]   Gavyn Davies (1998), Causes, Cures and Consequences of the Asian Economic Crisis, (Goldman Sachs).

The Welfare State and its Impact on Business Competitiveness: Sweden Inc. for Sale?

The "Swedish model"—sometimes presented as a "third way" between savage capitalism and unrealistic socialism—was much lauded in the 1960s. It was viewed as a strategy that addressed social concerns while supporting economic growth. However, the financial and currency crisis of the early 1990s threw the model into doubt and prompted much soul searching and reform among Sweden's establishment.

The welfare state introduced in Sweden imposed a high tax burden on individuals and business. By the late 1990s, some concerns were emerging that these costs were acting as a deterrent to doing business in Sweden. In an international market for labor and capital, Sweden was a less attractive home for high-flying MBAs or multinational companies than other countries.

Study Questions

1. Is the Swedish welfare state successful? Along what criteria?
2. Does the welfare state prompt or hinder innovation and business dynamism?
3. If Sweden is concerned with the instabilities and risks of capitalism that arise from the capital market, why does it address these indirectly through the welfare state and labor market regulation rather than directly by intervening more extensively in capital markets?
4. Can the "Swedish model" survive in the context of globalization and European integration?

HUW PILL

The Welfare State and its Impact on Business Competitiveness: Sweden Inc. for Sale?

In principle, there are no contradictions between Sweden's welfare state and economic growth. Today, however, politicians are shying away from reality. This isn't good given today's increasingly competitive business environment. Politicians' most important role is to create a good climate for people and businesses.[1]

— Marcus Wallenberg, president and CEO of Investor AB[a]

In early 2002, after a decade of economic reforms, Sweden had recovered from the deep economic crisis of the early 1990s, when the unemployment rate had soared to 10% and gross domestic product (GDP) had fallen significantly. Over the previous 50 years, Sweden had pursued equality and low unemployment under the "Swedish Model." This model embodied both capitalism and extensive redistribution. Until the early 1990s, many politicians and economists had considered the model a huge success. Unemployment levels had remained at under 2%, and a generous welfare state had taken care of its citizens "from the cradle to the grave." However, the model's success seemed to have come at the expense of economic growth, which had lagged behind the average of the Organization for Economic Cooperation and Development (OECD) countries. In 2001, Sweden faced an important decision: Should it continue to decrease the size of the welfare state, or should the public sector's extent be restored to the level seen before the crisis?

Sweden's policies were having an increasing impact on the private sector. Sweden had been the home of some of the world's most well-known engineering and pharmaceutical companies, including Volvo, Saab, Scania, ABB, Electrolux, AstraZeneca, and Pharmacia. However, since 1992, more than 20% of the 50-largest Swedish multinational corporations had relocated. Several reasons were cited for this trend, including Sweden's high taxes on capital and individual income and the country's resulting difficulty in attracting foreign management talent. In 2001, the Swedish press speculated whether Ericsson—one of the leading global manufacturers of telecommunications equipment and a symbol of Sweden's success in high technology—would become the next to defect. With a growing number of operations based in London, the company appeared to be considering moving its headquarters from Sweden, where only 3% of its sales were generated.

---

[a] At the end of 2001, the Wallenberg family, one of the most powerful industrial dynasties in Europe, controlled more than one-third of the market capitalization of the Stockholm Stock Exchange through a web of family foundations, cross-ownerships, and holding companies. The Wallenbergs were major shareholders in several prominent Swedish companies, such as Ericsson, SEB, AstraZeneca, ABB, and Scania. Investor AB was their main holding company.

Professor Huw Pill, Petter Johnsson (MBA 2002), Ola Nordquist (MBA 2002), and Research Associate Ingrid Vogel prepared this case from published sources. Cases are not intended to serve as endorsements, sources of primary data, or illustrations of effective or ineffective management.

Background

Sweden is located on the eastern part of the Scandinavian peninsula (see **Exhibit 1**). It is the fourth-largest country in Europe, with an area one-tenth larger than California. The landscape features 100,000 lakes and vast forests but few navigable rivers. The capital, Stockholm, is located at the same latitude as the southern tip of Greenland, but the climate is much milder due to the Gulf Stream. The country has a developed transportation network and is rich in iron ore and hydroelectric power.

Demographic and Social Characteristics

In 2002, Sweden had 8.9 million inhabitants. More than 80% of them lived in the southern third of the country.[2] Sweden had one of the world's highest life expectancies and one of the lowest birth rates. While the population historically had been homogeneous, Sweden admitted large numbers of immigrants during the second half of the 20th century. Initially, immigrants were attracted by a labor shortage in the country, but during the past few decades they came mainly for political reasons. In 1999, 11% of residents were foreign born. Roughly half of them had become Swedish citizens.

Although only 4% of Swedes claimed to practice religion actively, evangelical Lutheran values were deeply rooted in society. Sweden had the most broadly educated population in the developed world with regard to primary and secondary levels of schooling but relatively few people with university degrees.[3]

Economic Development

Sweden progressed from one of Western Europe's poorest nations at the beginning of the 20th century to the world's fourth-wealthiest nation, as measured by GDP per capita, in 1970. Initially, commodities such as iron ore, forestry products, and steel constituted the bulk of exports. Over time, engineering products became dominant as Sweden was transformed into an advanced industrial nation. The Swedish innovations underlying this industrial revolution included centrifugal machines, ball bearings, safety matches, and telephone equipment. Access to foreign markets and a series of improvements in transportation and communications technology were crucial in promoting Sweden's economic growth, given the country's small home market (see **Exhibits 2–5** for basic historical macroeconomic data).

Political System

Sweden enjoyed a stable political system throughout the 20th century. The country was a constitutional monarchy, meaning that the monarch only had representational and ceremonial duties. Legislative power lay with the *Riksdag* (the Swedish Parliament), which was elected for four-year terms and consisted of a single chamber. Parliament elected the prime minister, who appointed all other members of the government. The electoral system was proportional, although there was a hurdle rate of 4% of the national vote for a party to be represented in Parliament. Since the 1950s, the Swedish party system had usually been divided into two political blocs, socialists and non-socialists. In 2002, seven parties were represented in Parliament. The country joined the European Union (EU) in 1995 but chose not to adopt the euro, Europe's single currency, in 1999.

Apart from two brief periods of interruption (1976–1982 and 1991–1994), the Social Democratic Party (SDP) had been in parliamentary power since the 1930s, when it began to lay the foundations of the Swedish welfare state. Despite its dominance, the SDP had rarely held an absolute majority in Parliament. The party had instead usually governed with the help of (often silent) support from the political left or center.

Theory behind the Swedish Model

The Swedish welfare state creates a safety net for everyone and motivates people to accept change. Our citizens value living in a country with equal opportunity and solidarity. However, we became victims of our own success and were overly ambitious in the 1970s, when we politicized too many areas of citizens' lives.[4]

— Ingvar Carlsson, prime minister of Sweden, 1986–1991 and 1994–1996

The welfare state that evolved in Sweden during the 1930s and 1940s was the centerpiece of the Swedish Model. To attain the goals of this model—full employment and equality—Sweden combined a market-driven and export-oriented production system with a redistribution policy based on social solidarity.

Full Employment

The Swedish Model sought to establish full employment through the application of two submodels. The models were largely successful, as from 1950–1980, unemployment rarely rose above 2%.

The first submodel, developed by labor union economists Gösta Rehn and Rudolf Meidner, focused on the short- and medium-term conflict between full employment and price stability. It proposed that the government use restrictive fiscal and monetary policies to prevent excess demand for labor in stronger regions and sectors of the economy. The reduction of general demand resulted in "islands of unemployment" in Sweden's weaker sectors and regions, which the government tackled through selective labor-market policies such as retraining and relocation assistance.

The second submodel, known as the EFO Model (or the Scandinavian model of inflation),[5] sought to preserve the long-term competitiveness of Swedish industry and thus national employment. It argued that in export-oriented industries, nominal wage increases should be restricted to inflation-adjusted productivity improvements. This would ensure that cost pressures were contained in a manner that maintained Sweden's international competitiveness with a fixed exchange rate. Wage increases in all other sectors of the economy should increase in line with wage increases in the competitive export-oriented sector. This policy tended to exert upward pressure on prices of non-traded goods and services (see **Exhibit 6**).

Equality

The second pillar of the Swedish Model was equality in income and opportunity. This was achieved through the combination of a solidaristic wage policy and a comprehensive and universal welfare system.

Under the solidaristic wage policy, workers performing similar tasks were to be paid the same wages irrespective of their employer's profitability, size, or location ("equal pay for equal work"). Solidaristic wage policies were also designed to encourage the wages of lower-paid, less-skilled workers to increase more rapidly than the average worker's wages (see **Exhibits 7a–7b**).

Under the Swedish welfare system, citizens had access to extensive public and social services. These included generous transfer payments and a national social insurance system that financed health and social care for all Swedish residents. Contingent transfer benefits (enjoyed by all residents) included unemployment benefits, sickness benefits, pensions, parental benefits, and child allowances. Means-tested transfer benefits (which depended on income levels) included social assistance, housing allowances, child care, maintenance support, and student loans. The welfare system in Sweden was the most extensive in the world.

Key Enablers of the Model

The Swedish Model relied on high taxes in addition to centralized wage bargaining and solidarity between stronger and weaker groups in society.

Limiting nominal wage increases to inflation-adjusted productivity required a strong national confederation of unions and centralized wage bargaining. Thirty affiliated unions jointly constituted the *Landsorganisationen* (LO), the Swedish Confederation of Trade Unions. The LO had responsibility for centralized wage negotiations with the Confederation of Swedish Enterprise, *Svenskt Näringsliv*.[6] Together, these groups set minimum wage increases for entire sectors. Pay packages were negotiated further at the local level.

Within Sweden, there was broad acceptance of the goals of the Swedish Model.[7] Better-off Swedes had historically felt strong solidarity with weaker groups and wanted the state to play a redistributive role in society.[8] At 80% (the highest of any OECD country), the rate of unionization of Swedish workers was high. As such, the interests of society and the unions were similar, which helped make the model successful.[9]

Economic Advantages

The merit of the Swedish Model was the subject of much debate. Proponents believed the model contributed to the health of the Swedish economy. By ensuring social cohesion through low poverty rates and equal access to education and health care, it promoted social—and thereby economic—stability. Many economists considered such stability an important prerequisite for economic growth.

An International Monetary Fund report outlined other ways in which the Swedish Model benefited the economy:

> Dynamic effects arise from coverage against a wide array of risks not insurable in private markets (e.g. the risk of being born to poor or less-educated parents); greater ability to take risks owing to the presence of a strong social safety net; enhanced intergenerational mobility; and greater use of talent resulting from higher female participation rates and the effective incorporation of minorities and immigrants into the labor market.[10]

In addition, advocates of the Swedish welfare state pointed out that wage equality under the solidaristic wage policy was an effective device for exerting pressure on underperforming firms. Combined with programs aimed at retraining workers, wage equality policies forced less efficient firms to rationalize their operations and upgrade the value-add of their goods and services continuously. This improved the overall comparative positioning of Swedish industry.

Economic Disadvantages

On the other hand, critics believed the Swedish Model stifled long-term economic growth through repressing flexibility and adaptability. Economist Per-Martin Meyerson argued that the high levels of taxation required by the model discouraged individuals and companies from risk taking. He also claimed that the solidaristic wage policy coupled with a progressive tax scale decreased employee incentives to work harder or change jobs. Furthermore, he pointed out that government subsidies in industries threatened by international competition had prevented necessary and ultimately inevitable restructuring.

The Swedish Model was thought to disadvantage smaller firms in particular. High corporate taxes made it difficult for all companies, small and large, to fund necessary investment. But accelerated depreciation schemes enabled well-established, high-profit companies to avoid high corporate tax rates while providing limited opportunities for newly started, low-profit firms to do so. In addition, government directives encouraged banks to allocate capital to large companies.[11] Between 1920 and 1946, newly founded companies constituted approximately 4% of the total number of companies. This ratio declined to less than 2% in the 1960s and 1970s and to approximately 1% in the 1980s.[12]

In summary, Meyerson stated that incentives for a profit-oriented and thereby efficient distribution of resources in the Swedish economy were continuously weakened by the welfare state. He argued that in the long run, capitalist allocation of resources could not be reconciled with socialist-inspired redistribution of wealth.[13]

The Swedish Model in Practice

In the beginning of the 1970s the whole world flocked to Stockholm to discover the secrets of the Swedish Model. Foreigners saw Sweden as a land of freedom with no unemployment, clean streets, clean people, trains that ran on time and a welfare state that incorporated the most up-to-date social attitudes and welfare policies. Foreigners flooded into the Venice of the North [Stockholm] seeking the holy grail of economic development and the elixir of everlasting growth.[14]

— William Shepherd, author, *In Praise of the Swedish Model*

Following World War II, Sweden experienced an economic boom. Demand from countries rebuilding their economies after the war created huge export opportunities. Since Sweden had remained neutral, its companies were in a good position to satisfy the needs of countries undertaking post-war reconstruction. Sweden grew rapidly and achieved high levels of employment, while realizing income equality under the already established Swedish Model. Many economists and politicians throughout the world praised the country as a success story.

Cracks in the Model Emerge

In the second half of the 1970s, however, industrial production began to stagnate (see **Exhibit 8**). In the context of a global economic slowdown after the oil price shock of 1973–1974, Sweden's problems were blamed, in part, on two factors.

First, during Sweden's post-war economic boom, established companies tended to dominate the robust export market to the detriment of developing medium-sized enterprises. The formation of new companies actually declined after 1965. Observers questioned whether this had stifled innovation and made Sweden slow to adapt to changes in global export markets.

Second, the slowing economy was blamed on the emergence of influential special interest groups and their role in expanding the welfare state. Starting in the 1970s, special interest groups became an active part of the Swedish Model. While the labor market originally had been regulated through voluntary contracts between the LO and *Svenskt Näringsliv*, in the 1970s the SDP-led government instituted formal legal protections of employees and trade unions.[15] This created a shift in power from employers to unions.[16] As a result, the delicate balance between these two groups was disturbed, resulting in a deterioration in their previously symbiotic relationship.

In one reflection of growing union power, the LO began to exert influence on government economic policy. A large proportion of LO members belonged to the SDP through their local unions, accounting for the majority of total SDP membership. Politicians in power had difficulty countering labor demands, especially when parliamentary power was fragile and terms of office short.

In the mid-1970s, trade union leadership pushed through wage increases in excess of productivity growth (see **Exhibit 9**); the EFO model, which had worked so well in the 1950s and 1960s at keeping wage increases in line with productivity improvements, came under threat. Between 1974 and 1976, industry costs increased nearly 30% more in Sweden than in other European countries as a particularly virulent wage-price spiral took hold.[17] Sweden's share of world exports fell dramatically, and industrial employment plummeted.

Even so, official unemployment remained steady. In supporting the solidaristic model, a rapidly expanding Swedish public sector and government works program picked up those who lost their private-sector industry jobs. National productivity declined as employees moved from the more productive export-oriented industrial sector to the less productive services and government sectors. Göran Johnsson, a union leader, argued: "The labor movement misbehaved, employers did not hold back appropriately, and politicians overexpanded the role of the state and tried to devalue Sweden out of the crisis."[18]

From the mid-1960s to the early 1980s, public expenditures rose from 35% to 60% of GDP. Domestic prices increased markedly, and politicians were forced to raise taxes to finance public sector operations. This, in turn, had an inflationary effect on future wage levels.

The Bubble of the 1980s

Deregulating the credit markets was like opening a floodgate. The banks threw money at people for consumption and real estate speculation. It was impossible for the government to counterbalance the flow of hundreds of billions of krona.[19]

— Ingvar Carlsson, Prime Minister of Sweden, 1986–1991 and 1994–1996

Following the second oil price shock of 1979, economic performance deteriorated further. As growth slowed, the government took a number of steps to try to stimulate the economy. Massive currency devaluations were followed by liberalization of credit and capital controls.

The government implemented a series of currency devaluations (of approximately 26% cumulatively in 1981 and 1982) in an attempt to stimulate the economy. In response, Sweden's export sector boomed. But the devaluations put additional pressure on Sweden's nominal wages. As wages continued to rise significantly faster than growth in productivity, inflation increased. According to Chairman of the Conservative Party Bo Lundgren, the devaluations also prevented necessary restructuring in the private sector.[20] Devaluations were thus seen as a temporary palliative rather than a real solution to Sweden's underlying economic malaise.

In 1982, the SDP returned to power after a six-year period of non-socialist minority government rule in Sweden. It introduced a "free market agenda"[21] involving deregulation of credit and capital markets. At the same time, *Riksbanken*, Sweden's central bank, was given more autonomy to pursue an active monetary policy without direct influence from the government.

With both banks and borrowers unaccustomed and unprepared for managing credit in a free market, the deregulation of the credit and capital markets led to a speculative boom in real estate and construction in the second half of the 1980s.[22] Private consumers were encouraged to borrow, since after-tax real interest rates were often negative and interest on mortgage payments was tax deductible. Tax cuts further encouraged consumption. Household savings dropped to negative 4% of disposable income.[23] The export sector boomed, resulting in increased capacity utilization and labor shortages. By 1990, unemployment dropped to 1.5%.

Public spending increased as public workers demanded a share in Sweden's new prosperity. The SDP recognized the dangers of the overheated economy. But without the ability to restrict credit and capital flows, the government found it difficult to stabilize the economy. The central bank increased interest rates but failed to quiet the boom.

Economic Crisis: 1991–1993

Today it is crystal clear that we should have abandoned the fixed exchange rate much earlier.[24]
— Urban Bäckström, governor of Sweden's central bank

In the early 1990s, Sweden's economic bubble finally burst. Although the crisis came as no surprise to many observers, several factors contributed to exacerbate the severity of Sweden's economic downturn in a way that had not been foreseen.

Recession   Starting in 1991, Europe and the United States faced a severe economic recession. Sweden, with its small, open economy, was heavily exposed to the sudden economic downturn. Between 1991 and 1993, the country experienced a 6% drop in GDP and a 17% fall in industrial output. As inflation fell from over 8% in 1990 to below 2% in 1991, real interest rates increased. This increase, combined with an increase in real estate taxes, caused the collapse of the debt-financed real estate market. Commercial banks faced an increase of bad loans as bankruptcy rates soared. Ultimately, the government had to intervene to protect bank balance sheets.

As confidence in the job market fell, citizens began to save more to protect themselves against possible social benefits reductions. Household savings rates increased by eight percentage points in 1992. At the same time, firms' investment rates fell. With lower investment and saving in the economy, domestic aggregate demand decreased;[25] the gap between potential GDP and actual GDP increased to a level not observed since the Great Depression.[26]

The government's finances deteriorated quickly, moving from a fiscal surplus of 1% of GDP in 1990 to a deficit of 13% in 1993. Subsequently, aggregate government borrowing increased from 43% of GDP in 1990 to 78% in 1994. At the same time, the size of the public sector increased to almost 70% of GDP.[27] By 1993, the goal of full employment could no longer be pursued, and unemployment reached 10% (see **Exhibit 10**).

Currency Peg   On May 17, 1991, Sweden unilaterally pegged its currency within a band to the European Currency Unit (ECU), a basket of currencies of EU member countries.[28] This was seen as the logical next step to the Swedish Parliament's approval of formal application for membership in the EU. The central bank could no longer use devaluations as a tool to stimulate the export industry.

During the summer of 1992, several European currencies relying on the ECU came under attack. As the Swedish economy experienced continued difficulties, international currency speculators began to bet that the central bank would be unable to defend the krona, Sweden's currency. Since the government could no longer protect the currency through foreign exchange control, the central bank was forced to raise the interest rate. In September 1992, the interest rate was set at an unprecedented level of 500%.

The extreme volatility in interest rates was a turning point for politicians and the general public. On November 19, 1992, the central bank capitulated and abandoned the parity of the krona. Under a floating exchange rate the currency rapidly depreciated by over 20% against the ECU.

Urban Bäckström, governor of the *Riksbank,* argued that the fixed exchange rate policy had been a major cause of Sweden's economic crisis. He stated: "If a floating currency had been adopted earlier, the crisis would have been less severe. Experts at the time, however, were stuck in the belief that small open economies needed fixed exchange rates."[29] The depreciation of the krona ended the immediate monetary crisis but created a "dual economy" consisting of a booming export sector and an overall decreasing level of aggregate domestic demand. Sweden dropped to 14th place in global rankings of GDP per capita.[30]

Explanations of Crisis   What were the causes of the crisis, and what had happened to Sweden's economy? Most people pointed to a combination of system failures, changing economic conditions, and distorted incentives. Conservative politicians blamed a too generous welfare state, whereas economists pointed to inconsistent economic policies and fundamental structural problems in the economy.

"The Swedish Model is Sweden's problem,"[31] said Ian Wachtmeister, leader of New Democracy, a small free-market-oriented party that entered the Swedish Parliament in 1991. Carl Bildt, the conservative prime minister elected in 1991, placed much of the blame on disincentives created through excessive benefits put in place by the former SDP governments. In particular, he pointed to absentee rates approaching 25% of the workforce: "When we had the ice hockey world championship on television, for instance, people tended to be very sick."[32]

Sweden had become the "sickest" society in the world, partially due to workers receiving 90% of their salary through health benefits when they were on sick leave. Many companies had to overstaff significantly to manage normal operations. In addition, Finance Minister Anne Wibble claimed that government benefits had taken away people's incentives to save and made them increasingly dependent on subsidies. These benefits were funded by some of the world's highest capital and income taxes, which discouraged many companies and entrepreneurs from staying in Sweden

Meidner, one of the creators of the Rehn/Meidner Model, blamed the crisis on inconsistent government policies and internationalization.[33] He asserted the government made a number of mistakes: It succumbed to pressure from special interest groups, deregulated the financial markets too fast, and failed to do enough in the late 1980s to stop the excessive speculative boom. In addition, he claimed that the Swedish Model worked best in a fairly closed economy where the country faced limited external pressures and the government could make unilateral decisions about distribution and stabilization policies. As Sweden integrated with the rest of the world, it became increasingly difficult for the government to control the economy.

In December 1992, the Swedish government appointed an independent academic commission to analyze the economic crisis and identify potential solutions to Sweden's problems.[34] The commission identified four dimensions of the crisis:

- *Stability problems* resulting from, on the one hand, Sweden's attempt to keep a fixed exchange rate and, on the other hand, an inflationary system of wage formation and expansionary fiscal policies during economic growth periods.

- *Efficiency problems* created through restrictions on competition, mainly shaped by a large government sector and excessive regulation.

- *Problems with growth* in the economy where investment in physical and human capital did not yield desired results. High taxes limited incentives to work and impacted capital allocation negatively.

- *The impact of politics, institutions, and special interest groups,* making it difficult for Sweden to trim benefits. This was due, in part, to short election periods and strong electorate support for a large welfare state.[35] In addition, the central bank enjoyed limited independence compared with other countries. Other institutions had not modernized themselves to face new economic conditions.

Reform of the Welfare State

In September 1991, in the midst of the crisis, Bildt, leader of a minority center-right government, was elected prime minister. The new government was determined to reverse Sweden's poor economic performance. Under Bildt's leadership, an economic austerity program was implemented to bring public finances back under control. In addition, steps were taken to reform the welfare state with an eye on joining the EU by 1995.

Before the SDP-led government had left office, it had simplified the tax code. The maximum marginal personal income tax level was reduced to 50%, and the capital gains tax was set at 30%.[36] The tax reforms broadened the tax base and eliminated several loopholes in the tax code. But, despite these changes, the income distribution was little changed. Bildt's government pushed the tax reform agenda forward by reducing the wealth tax and simplifying rules for small and medium-sized companies. The system of double taxation on corporate dividends, which had particularly penalized small and medium-sized firms that primarily raised equity capital in Sweden, was abolished. Larger firms with access to international capital markets had been able to avoid double taxation. The government began to cut allowances for housing subsidies, child care, pensions, and health and dental care. The central bank was granted more independence and was given a new charter by the government. The new charter shifted the goal of monetary policy from full employment to low inflation, with a target rate of 2%.

The government wanted to push through a more extensive reform agenda but faced resistance from the SDP. In particular, the government had to scale down planned welfare cuts and its privatization program in order to reach an agreement in Parliament. In 1994, the economy started to show signs of recovery.

In September 1994, the SDP returned to office. Many of the reforms that the conservatives had started were continued under SDP Prime Minister Carlsson, who, with the labor unions' backing, had an easier time gaining support for reform.[37] Additional cuts in public employment were made, and the central bank was granted further independence, in line with its European counterparts. However, other reforms were reversed, including Bildt's decreases in the wealth and income tax levels.[38]

Recovery: Mid-1990s to 2000

In the mid-1990s, the Swedish economy rebounded from four consecutive years of recession. The general upswing in the economy helped the SDP toward its goal of balancing public finances through further reductions in government spending. Deregulation of key markets including telecommunications, energy, and banking also contributed to reducing the deficit. In anticipation of its entry into the EU on January 1, 1995, Sweden planned to harmonize a large part of its regulatory framework and market policies with those of the EU. According to economist Joakim Stymne, the reforms made Swedes much more accustomed to and accepting of business demands as many public sector organizations were privatized or encountered competition from privately held entities.[39]

The reforms raised international and domestic confidence in Sweden's economic policy and decreased inflationary expectations. Real GDP grew by 3.3% and 3.7% in 1994 and 1995, respectively, and by an annual average of 2.9% from 1996 to 2000.[40] Driven by rising levels of private consumption and fixed investments (including a boom in residential construction), Sweden's domestic demand increased. However, unemployment remained high as the private sector expanded too slowly to absorb the cutbacks in public sector employment. Not until 1998 did unemployment begin to drop, from 8%–9% to 4%–5%. Although Sweden's macroeconomic recovery was substantial, GDP per capita growth remained lower than the OECD average (but above the EU average). Sweden's overall spending on publicly financed welfare remained the highest in the world (see **Exhibit 11**).

During the 1990s, Sweden developed into a leading nation in information technology, with one of the highest Internet and mobile phone penetration rates in the world. Early deregulation of the telecommunications industry led to intense competition. The presence of domestic telecommunication equipment companies like Ericsson pushed Sweden into the forefront in high-tech inventions and applications.

Entrepreneurship grew rapidly in Sweden, and Stockholm established itself as an IT center. Stymne stated: "The entrepreneurial climate improved dramatically in the 1990s, driven by increased access to venture capital and a change in attitude towards risk taking."[41] Former Prime Minister Carlsson commented that the welfare state encouraged risk taking among the population because the elaborate safety net made the negative consequences of failure less extreme.[42]

By 1999, Sweden's public finances were in the black with a budget surplus of 3% of GDP. However, as national finances improved and confidence rose, special interest groups increased their pressure on the government to increase the size of the welfare state once again.

Looking Ahead

Pressures on the Welfare State

Economic growth slowed significantly during 2001, largely as a result of the economic downturn in the United States and Europe. On the one hand, international observers commented that Sweden would recover, since it was better prepared to cope with economic downturns than previously due to structural changes and trimmed public finances. On the other hand, as a member of the EU, Sweden had given away some of its political and economic independence to Brussels. If Sweden were to participate in the European Monetary Union[a] and adopt the euro, it would surrender additional policy tools to control inflation, interest rates, and the exchange rate to the European Central Bank.

Sweden's new economic policy agenda targeted a government surplus of 2%–3% of GDP over the economic cycle, an annual inflation rate of 2%, and an unemployment rate of less than 4% (with an 80% participation rate of the adult population). But there was concern that the many remaining pressures on the Swedish welfare state would threaten this plan.

First, *internationalization* had increased the mobility of the tax base. Since formal controls on capital, goods, and labor were removed within the EU, individuals, companies, and the financial markets were likely to be sensitive to differential tax levels. Sweden, with exceptionally high income taxes, dual taxation on dividends, a high value-added tax (sales tax), and high taxes on capital, was particularly exposed to "tax arbitrage." According to labor economist Meidner:

> Sweden is too small a country to be able to say that from now on it will pursue an expansionist economic policy and neglect budget problems and even accept some price increases. We know the consequences. The stock market will decline. The value of our currency will fall. As a small country it cannot neglect international reactions to domestic economic policies. …As a small country we cannot pursue an independent economic policy.[43]

Second, *demographic changes* had augmented spending pressures. An aging population added strain to public spending on pensions, health benefits, and other social services.

Third, there was continued *political support for high transfers* based on the deeply rooted Swedish value of solidarity. Many special interest groups proposed increases in public expenditures to maintain income equality and restore the high levels of public services.

Fourth, a *decentralization of the bargaining process* had undermined the measured wage formation process. The historically central negotiations between the LO and *Svenskt Näringsliv* were designed to increase wages at levels supported by productivity gains. Recently, individual trade unions had begun to negotiate independently with companies. There was a risk that this would push the economy into a wage-price spiral, as had happened in the 1970s.

Finally, there were pressures to *boost the growth rate of the economy* through deregulation.[44] There were signs that high tax burdens and limited wage dispersion discouraged people from working more or investing in education. Similarly, housing subsidies and extensive rent control discouraged investment in new capital stock for the rental market. The large size of the Swedish public sector may also have hampered competition and innovation in several key sectors.

The welfare state stood at an important juncture. Following Sweden's recovery from the deep crisis of the early 1990s, the country could move in two directions: Sweden could increase or maintain government spending levels to make up for recent cutbacks, or continue to trim the welfare state and reduce the scale of government intervention.[45] It was questionable whether further reform was possible given the large percentage of the electorate that was dependent on the state for employment and transfer payments. Chairman of the Conservative Party Lundgren stated: "Overcoming this economic dependence of the electorate is my biggest political dilemma."[46]

---

[a] The Swedish government had stated its desire to join the single currency "in principle," provided a set of self-imposed tests were met, but had not yet committed itself to a timetable of joining. Ultimately, of the 15 EU members, only the United Kingdom, Denmark, and Sweden decided not to join the euro.

Pressures on Businesses[47]

Corporations must be managed with a global perspective, but it is bad when they are leaving Sweden for the wrong reasons. We have to have a common national understanding of what the problems with the welfare state are. Today you seem to find the real understanding only in the private sector.[48]

— Marcus Wallenberg, president and CEO of Investor AB

Forty-seven Swedish multinational corporations moved their headquarters from Sweden between 1997 and 2000. Some of these moves resulted from mergers with foreign companies, but many occurred without any change in ownership structure. From 1991 to 2000, foreign ownership on the Stockholm Stock Exchange had increased from 8% to 38% of total market capitalization. Over the same period, Sweden had found it difficult to attract foreign direct investment.

Göran Tunhammar, president of *Svenskt Näringsliv*, pointed to three key reasons for the movement of Swedish companies out of Sweden: capital tax asymmetry (lower taxes on foreign ownership of Swedish companies than on Swedish ownership of Swedish companies); government removal of previous restrictions on sales of corporations to foreign entities;[49] and Sweden's shortage of qualified labor, notably natural scientists.[50]

Consistent with Tunhammar's views, a survey conducted among senior executives in Swedish multinationals identified two primary factors driving the decision to relocate. These were taxes and access to communications and transportation (see **Exhibit 12**).[51] Income taxes impacted both the location decision of Swedish executives and Swedish companies' ability to attract foreign management talent (see **Exhibit 13**). Executive compensation in Sweden was relatively low compared with international standards (see **Exhibit 14**). In addition, stock options were taxed more in Sweden than in countries such as the United States. While Swedish corporate taxes were competitive, the taxes on dividends, capital gains, and wealth were among the highest in the world (see **Exhibit 15**). Proximity to transportation to access customers, suppliers, and investors was the second important factor.

Other corporations, recognizing Sweden's benefits, chose to maintain their headquarters in the country. Many academics pointed to the importance to firms of proximity to industry clusters when deciding where to locate.[52] Sweden had some of the world's most prominent industry clusters within the telecommunications, pharmaceutical, specialty steel, heavy truck, and pulp and paper sectors. Another benefit was that Sweden offered a broadly educated workforce.

Over a 10-year period, however, more than 20% of the 50-largest Swedish multinational corporations had moved their headquarters out of the country. Apparently, Sweden's negative factors were heavily outweighing the positive.

Ericsson's Decision

The Swedish government has not understood that nowadays politics is exposed to international competition. If taxes and the business climate are not good in Sweden, companies will go somewhere else.[53]

— Lars Ramqvist, former CEO and chairman of Ericsson

Ericsson was the leading international manufacturer of advanced systems and products for wired and mobile communications in public and private telecommunications networks. The company was also a significant manufacturer of mobile handsets. Ericsson was Sweden's largest company as measured by market capitalization and had presence in 140 countries. Foreign owners held 48% of

Ericsson's equity capital but controlled only 1.5% of votes. Fewer than half of the company's 85,000 employees worked in Sweden.[54] In 2001, Ericsson had global sales of U.S. $22 billion and enjoyed a global market share of over 30% in mobile wireless systems and 10% in wireless handsets. Only 3% of its revenues came from Sweden (see **Exhibit 16a**).

In the late 1990s, Ericsson was considering moving its headquarters from Sweden. In 1998, the company announced that it had purchased office property in London.[55] Ericsson stated: "The background for the property purchase is that Ericsson sees an increasing need to be represented in London, partly in order to be close to important customers, cooperating partners, financial service centers, and markets."[56] At the same time, the company announced a new organization with corporate offices in London that "will assume a growing role for the corporate management as a whole."[57] By the end of 2001, Kurt Hellström, president and CEO of Ericsson, frequently ran Ericsson's day-to-day operations from the London office. In addition, Sony Ericsson Mobile[a] was headquartered in London. Company officials maintained, however, that Ericsson's headquarters had not officially moved.

Stockholm's prominence as one of the leading telecommunications industry clusters in the world favored keeping Ericsson's headquarters in Sweden. However, Sweden's high taxes and the potential difficulties in attracting foreign management talent seemed to be favoring a decision to relocate (see **Exhibit 16b**).

---

[a] Sony Ericsson Mobile was a mobile handset joint venture between Ericsson and Sony that had the mission of taking away Nokia's dominance in mobile handsets.

Exhibit 1   Map of Sweden

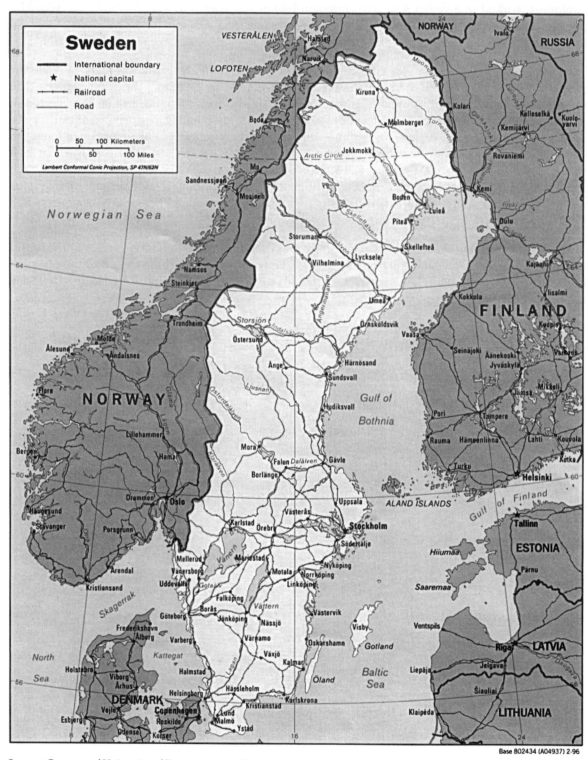

Source: Courtesy of University of Texas at Austin, Perry Castañeda Library Map Collection.

Exhibit 2 Sweden General Economic Indicators

% change over prior year	1970	1980	1985	1990	1992	1994	1996	1998	2000	2001
Real GDP Growth	6.6%	2.0%	2.2%	1.4%	-1.4%	3.3%	1.1%	3.6%	3.6%	1.2%
Real GDP Growth per Capita	5.7%	1.7%	2.0%	0.5%	-2.0%	2.7%	1.0%	3.6%	3.5%	1.7%
Consumer Prices	7.0%	13.7%	7.4%	10.5%	2.3%	2.2%	0.5%	-0.1%	1.0%	2.4%
% GDP										
Investment/GDP	22.1%	20.1%	19.3%	21.5%	17.0%	15.1%	15.7%	16.0%	17.3%	17.5%
Current Account/GDP	-0.8%	-3.6%	-0.9%	-2.7%	-4.3%	0.3%	2.3%	2.0%	3.0%	3.3%
Fiscal Deficit (-) or Surplus/GDP	-1.8%	-8.1%	-7.1%	1.0%	-5.1%	-8.4%	-3.3%	0.4%	6.0%	na
units as shown										
Population (millions)	8.04	8.31	8.36	8.56	8.67	8.78	8.84	8.85	8.87	8.83
Unemployment (%)	1.5	2.0	2.8	1.8	5.6	9.6	9.9	8.4	5.8	5.0
Exchange Rate (krona per U.S. dollar, period end)	5.17	4.37	7.62	5.70	7.04	7.46	6.87	8.06	9.54	10.67
Exchange Rate (krona per euro, period end)	na	5.97	6.37	7.41	7.45	9.30	8.70	8.73	8.56	8.83
Long-term Government Bond Yield (%)	7.4	11.7	13.1	13.1	10.0	9.4	8.0	5.0	5.4	5.1

Sources: Adapted from IMF, *International Financial Statistics CD-ROM*, September 2002; and EIU Country Data, Sweden, October 2002.

Exhibit 3 Sweden National Income Accounts (*billions current kronor*)

	1970	1980	1985	1990	1992	1994	1996	1998	2000	2001
Gross Domestic Product	**172.2**	**528.3**	**866.6**	**1,359.9**	**1,441.7**	**1,596.4**	**1,756.4**	**1,905.4**	**2,098.5**	**2,167.2**
Private Consumption	92.0	273.3	443.7	692.7	777.3	830.9	884.1	956.9	1,060.4	1,079.7
Government Consumption	36.5	153.8	239.2	372.1	402.5	436.9	476.1	509.4	549.0	577.7
Gross Fixed Investment	38.1	106.4	167.0	292.5	244.6	240.5	276.3	304.9	363.3	379.1
Changes in Inventories	5.3	5.9	-0.5	-2.5	-6.7	13.4	2.7	15.0	13.7	3.0
Exports of Goods and Services	41.5	156.5	305.9	406.8	401.6	583.0	685.9	832.6	990.1	1,006.7
Imports of Goods and Services	42.5	166.5	291.2	401.8	377.6	493.7	568.7	713.5	878.0	879.1
GDP at 1995 Prices	*n.a.*	*n.a.*	*n.a.*	*n.a.*	*n.a.*	*1,652.3*	*1,731.8*	*1,831.0*	*1,982.6*	*2,006.5*

Source: Adapted from IMF, *International Financial Statistics CD-ROM*, September 2002.

Note: As reflected in the source, in 1970, 1980, 1985, and 1994 the sum of components of GDP differs from GDP by between one-tenth of 1% and 1%.

Exhibit 4 Sweden Balance of Payments *(millions current U.S. dollars)*

	1970	1980	1985	1990	1992	1994	1996	1998	2000	2001
Current Account	**-253.2**	**-4,331.1**	**-1,010.3**	**-6,338.9**	**-8,827.5**	**742.6**	**5,892.3**	**4,639.4**	**6,616.5**	**6,696.0**
Trade Balance	303.5	-2,198.3	2,384.8	3,402.4	6,720.5	9,557.8	18,636.2	17,631.7	15,215.3	13,831.7
Exports	6,750.2	30,661.5	30,172.9	56,835.0	55,362.8	60,199.0	84,689.6	85,179.0	87,431.0	76,200.0
Imports	6,446.7	32,859.8	27,788.1	53,432.6	48,642.3	50,641.2	66,053.4	67,547.3	72,215.7	62,368.4
Net Services	-423.3	471.3	-560.4	-3,332.2	-2,894.9	-1,015.7	-1,824.9	-3,769.3	-3,188.0	-1,022.7
Net Income	7.7	-1,379.8	-1,977.0	-4,473.2	-10,038.6	-5,919.1	-8,303.0	-5,785.3	-2,063.2	-2,851.6
Net Transfers	-141.1	-1,224.4	-857.6	-1,935.7	-2,614.4	-1,880.3	-2,616.1	-3,437.7	-3,347.6	-3,261.3
Capital Account	**-11.6**	**-73.3**	**-221.4**	**-353.0**	**6.0**	**23.1**	**8.9**	**868.2**	**384.5**	**509.4**
Financial Account	**143.0**	**453.5**	**-2,892.5**	**19,277.5**	**10,214.3**	**6,077.9**	**-10,046.2**	**5,960.7**	**-3,296.6**	**1,824.2**
Net Direct Investment	-104.4	-373.6	-1,412.3	-12,646.6	-424.2	-416.7	380.0	-3,258.4	-17,837.3	6,125.9
Net Short-term Investment	48.3	-266.3	561.9	2,467.5	985.2	-1,738.0	-9,917.8	-16,894.1	-4,068.1	-17,919.4
Net Government	-42.5	-276.8	-5,093.8	-2,775.0	28,230.6	4,784.7	1,514.0	421.5	-577.0	-807.2
Net Other	241.6	1,370.3	3,051.6	32,231.5	-18,577.3	3,447.8	-2,022.3	25,691.8	19,185.8	14,424.9
Net Errors and Omissions	**151.1**	**-1,446.8**	**-526.4**	**-5,034.0**	**5,559.7**	**-4,462.2**	**-2,240.6**	**-8,214.5**	**-3,533.9**	**-10,077.8**
Reserves & Related Items	**-29.3**	**5,397.7**	**4,650.6**	**-7,551.7**	**-6,952.5**	**-2,381.4**	**6,385.6**	**-3,253.8**	**-170.5**	**1,048.2**

Source: Adapted from IMF, *International Financial Statistics CD-ROM*, September 2002.

Exhibit 5 Sweden Fiscal Accounts (*billions current kronor*)

	1970	1980	1985	1990	1992	1994	1996	1998	2000
Deficit (-) or Surplus	**-3.1**	**-43.0**	**-61.5**	**13.6**	**-74.1**	**-133.6**	**-58.0**	**6.8**	**125.8**
Revenue	51.1	185.8	351.8	601.7	610.9	419.1	590.1	696.5	791.0
Grants Received	0.2	1.0	0.0	0.0	0.0	0.0	10.4	9.9	9.0
Expenditure	43.9	208.8	388.3	554.8	666.0	552.7	658.5	699.5	674.2
Lending Minus Repayment	10.5	21.0	25.0	33.2	19.1	na	na	na	na
Financing	**3.1**	**43.0**	**61.5**	**-13.6**	**74.1**	**133.6**	**58.0**	**-6.8**	**-125.8**
Domestic	3.2	25.8	25.4	-9.7	50.3	129.9	27.1	-20.3	8.8
Foreign	-0.1	17.2	36.1	-3.9	23.8	3.8	31.0	13.4	-135.3
Total Debt	**27.9**	**159.6**	**480.5**	**504.1**	**606.3**	**1,098.9**	**1,189.5**	**1,217.6**	**1,008.3**
Domestic	27.9	127.5	341.4	404.3	461.9	586.0	627.9	614.5	598.9
Foreign	0.0	32.1	139.1	99.7	144.4	513.0	561.7	603.1	409.4

Source: Adapted from IMF, *International Financial Statistics CD-ROM*, September 2002.

Exhibit 6   Prices in Sweden Relative to the European Community, 1990

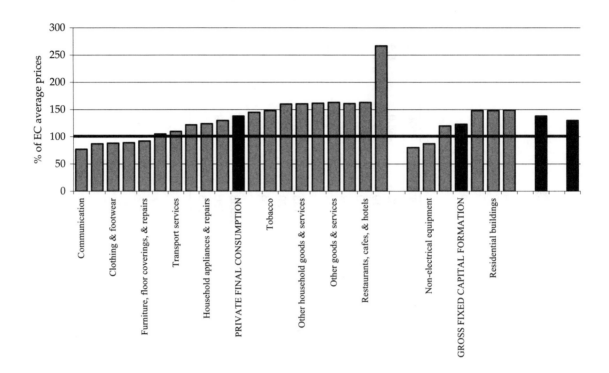

Source: Adapted from Assar Lindbeck, *Turning Sweden Around* (Cambridge, MA: The MIT Press, 1994), p. 80.

Exhibit 7a   Cross-Country Comparison of Income Distribution

	1974/75	1978/79	1980/81	1983	1984/85	1986/87	1988/89	1990/91	1992	1994	1995
Gini Coefficients											
Australia			0.281		0.292		0.304			0.311	
Belgium					0.227		0.232		0.224		
Canada	0.289		0.284			0.283		0.281		0.285	
Denmark						0.254			0.236		0.263
Finland						0.209		0.21			0.226
France		0.293	0.288		0.292		0.287			0.288	
Germany		0.264	0.244	0.26	0.249		0.247			0.261	
Italy						0.306		0.289			0.342
Mexico					0.448		0.467		0.485	0.496	
Netherlands				0.26		0.256		0.266		0.253	
Norway		0.223				0.233		0.231			0.238
Spain			0.318					0.303			
Sweden	**0.215**		**0.197**			**0.218**			**0.229**		**0.221**
U.K.	0.268	0.27				0.303		0.336		0.339	0.344
U.S.	0.318	0.301				0.335		0.336		0.355	

Source: Adapted from Luxembourg Income Study Web site, <http://www.lisproject.org/keyfigures/ineqtable.htm> (accessed October 2002).

Note: Blanks represent missing data.

Exhibit 7b   Income Distribution in Sweden

	Ratio top 10% to bottom 10% income
1975	215.3%
1980	195.5%
1985	197.8%
1990	199.1%
1991	211.2%
1992	210.5%
1993	213.5%
1994	218.6%
1995	220.3%
1996	226.7%
1997	221.6%
1998	223.7%
1999	223.7%
2000	234.6%

Source: Adapted from Statistics Sweden Web site, <www.scb.se/statistik/if0103/if0103tab1eng.asp> (accessed October 2002).

Exhibit 8   Manufacturing Output in Selected Countries, 1950–2001 *(Index 1977=100)*

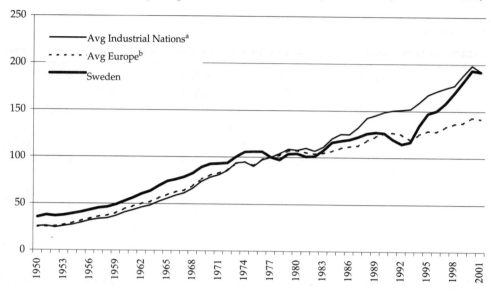

Sources: Adapted from U.S. Department of Labor, Bureau of Labor Statistics, <ftp://ftp.bls.gov/pub/time.series/in/> (accessed September 2002); and IMF, *International Financial Statistics Yearbook CD-ROM*, September 2002.

Notes: Average weighted by GDP.

[a]Industrial Nations include U.S., Canada, Japan, South Korea, Belgium, Denmark, France, Germany, Italy, the Netherlands, Norway, Sweden, U.K.

[b]Europe includes Belgium, Denmark, France, Germany, Italy, the Netherlands, Norway, Sweden, U.K.

Exhibit 9   Growth in Nominal Wages and Productivity in Sweden, 1953–2001

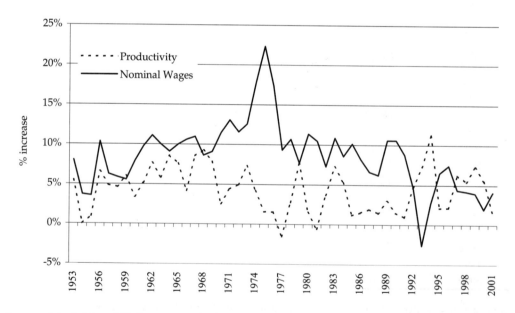

Source: Adapted from U.S. Department of Labor, Bureau of Labor Statistics, <ftp://ftp.bls.gov/pub/time.series/in/> (accessed October 2002).

Exhibit 10   Unemployment in Selected Countries, 1959-2001

Civilian Unemployment *(U.S. Definitions)*

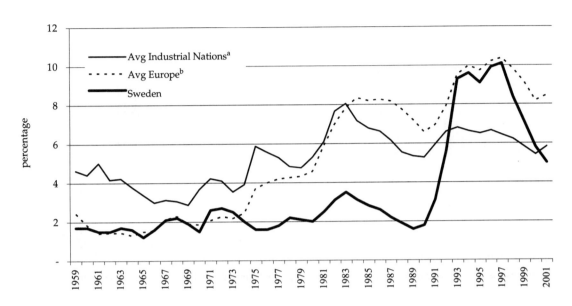

Sources: Adapted from U.S. Department of Labor, Bureau of Labor Statistics, <ftp://ftp.bls.gov/pub/special.requests/
ForeignLabor/flslforc.txt> (accessed September 2002); and IMF, *International Financial Statistics Yearbook CD-ROM*,
September 2002.

Notes: Average weighted by GDP.
[a]Industrial Nations include U.S., Canada, Japan, Australia, France, Germany, Italy, the Netherlands, Sweden, U.K.
[b]Europe includes France, Germany, Italy, the Netherlands, Sweden, U.K.

Exhibit 11   Government Spending Selected Countries as % GDP

	1960	1968	1980	1994	1998
Austria	28.6	33.8	42.8	47.8	47.8
Belgium	28.4	32.9	47.3	54.1	48.4
Germany	28.1	34.0	42.9	46.1	44.8
Italy	26.2	31.0	37.9	51.0	45.7
Japan	13.0	13.9	25.0	27.0	30.0
Netherlands	28.6	37.8	52.0	52.8	43.7
Sweden	26.8	35.9	56.8	66.4	56.7
U.K.	29.7	33.3	41.6	42.3	45.8
U.S.[a]	24.6	28.3	32.4	35.8	33.9

Source: Adapted from OECD Economic Outlook Historical Statistics, 1960–1999.

Notes: Government spending = current exp. on goods and services + current transfers and payments of property income.
[a]Data presented for the U.S. for 1994 and 1998 is taken from 1993 and 1996, respectively.

Exhibit 12   Factors Affecting Management Decision on Headquarters Location, 1999

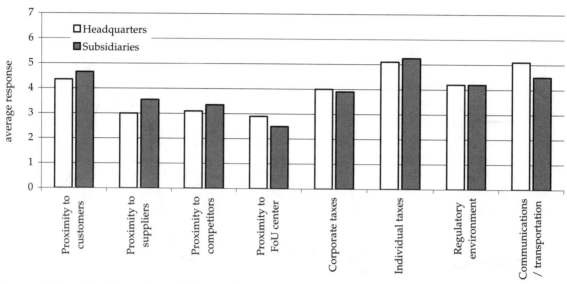

Source: Adapted from Pontus Braunerhjelm, *Huvudkontoren Flyttar Ut* (Stockholm: SNS Forlag, 2001), p. 35.

Note: Scale represents average of company responses, where 0 represents unimportant and 7 represents very important.

Exhibit 13   Tax-wedge for High Income Individuals in Selected Countries, 1998

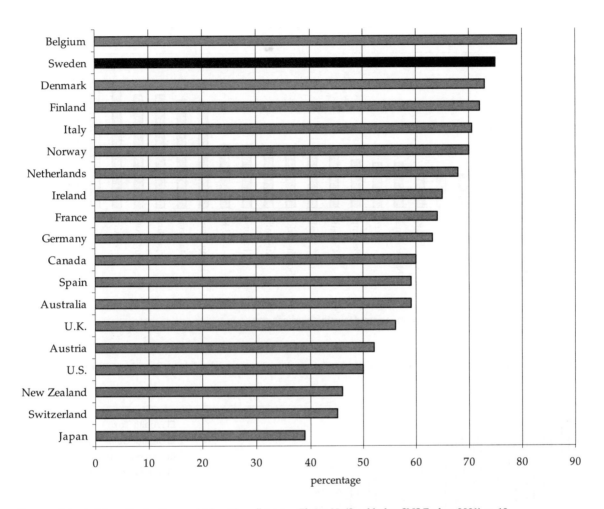

Source: Adapted from Pontus Braunerhjelm, *Huvudkontoren Flyttar Ut* (Stockholm: SNS Forlag, 2001), p. 19.

Note: The tax-wedge measure attempts to incorporate a broad base of individual taxes, including taxes on income, capital gains, consumption, and wealth.

Exhibit 14   CEO Pay as Multiple of Manufacturing Worker Pay, 1999

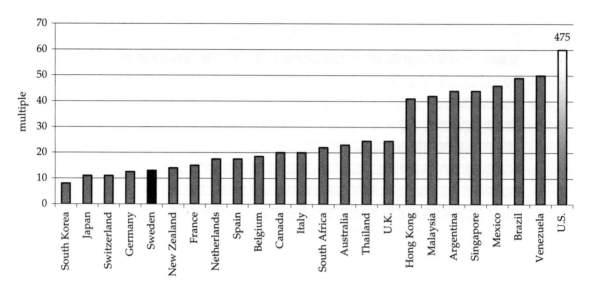

Source: Adapted from "Executive Pay," *The Economist*, September 30, 2000.
Note: U.S. CEO pay is 475 times the average manufacturing worker's pay.

Exhibit 15   Total Ownership Taxes in OECD Countries Compared with in Sweden, 1999

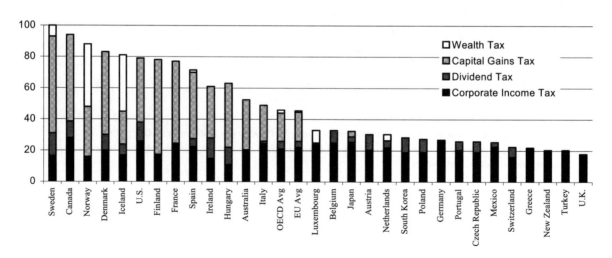

Source: Adapted from Pontus Braunerhjelm, *Huvudkontoren Flyttar Ut* (Stockholm: SNS Forlag, 2001), p. 19.

Exhibit 16a Ericsson's Revenue per Geographic Region, 1999–2001

	1999	2000	2001
Sweden	4%	3%	3%
Other Western Europe	36%	33%	28%
Central and Eastern Europe, Middle East, and Africa	14%	14%	15%
North America	12%	13%	14%
Latin America	14%	16%	15%
Asia Pacific	21%	21%	25%
Total	100%	100%	100%
Total *(SEK, billions)*	215,403	273,569	231,839
Exchange Rate *(krona per U.S. dollar)*	8.5	9.5	10.7
Total *(U.S.$ billions)*	25,342	28,691	21,733

Source: Adapted from Ericsson Annual Report 2001, Financial Statements, p. 22.
Note: Due to rounding, sum of 1999 components does not equal 100%.

Exhibit 16b CEO Compensation for Ericsson and Comparable Companies, 2001
(U.S.$ millions, except employees)

Company	Location	Number Employees	Revenues	Total CEO Compensation	Comments
Ericsson	Sweden	85,200	21,733	1.6	Additional minor option value.
Lucent Technologies	U.S.	77,000	25,132	21.6	
Motorola	U.S.	111,000	30,004	4.0	
Nokia	Finland	54,000	28,150	1.4	Compensation excludes options.
Nortel Networks	Canada	94,500	17,510	45.2	Compensation for 2000.
Vodafone	U.K.	100,000	24,800	19.0	Compensation excludes options.

Sources: Adapted from various issues of Executive PayWatch; company financial statements; Fortune magazine; R.O.B. Report on Business Magazine; and Yahoo Finance.
Note: Companies define compensation differently, meaning that the data does not lend itself to direct comparison. Hence, the table is for illustrative purposes only.

Endnotes

[1]   Marcus Wallenberg, president and CEO of Investor AB, interview with the authors, April 15, 2002.

[2]   "Sweden, Country Profile 2001," The Economist Intelligence Unit, 2001.

[3]   Assar Lindbeck, *Turning Sweden Around* (Cambridge, MA: The MIT Press, 1994).

[4]   Ingvar Carlsson, prime minister of Sweden, 1986–1991 and 1994–1996, interview with the authors, April 15, 2002.

[5]   This model derives its name from the initials of the three chief economists in the early 1960s of the white-collar trade union, the Confederation of Swedish Enterprise, and the Swedish Confederation of Trade Unions. Edgren, Faxen, and Odhner were instrumental in outlining the consensus view on wage bargaining between Swedish employers and workers.

[6]   Previously known as Svenska Arbetsgivareföreningen (SAF).

[7]   Rudolf Meidner, "The Swedish Model in an Era of Mass Unemployment," *Economic and Industrial Democracy*, 1997.

[8]   Bertram Silverman, "The rise and fall of the Swedish model: Interview with Rudolf Meidner," *Challenge*, 1998.

[9]   "Sweden, Country Profile 2001," The Economist Intelligence Unit, 2001.

[10]   "Sweden: Selected Issues – The Role of Government," International Monetary Fund, September 2001.

[11]   Gunilla Bornmalm-Jardelöw, professor of economics at the Gothenburg School of Economics and Commercial Law, interview with the authors, April 12, 2002.

[12]   Assar Lindbeck, *Det Svenska Experimentet* (Stockholm: SNS Förlag, 1998).

[13]   Per-Martin Meyerson, *The Welfare State in Crisis – The Case of Sweden: A Critical Examination of Some Central Problems in the Swedish Economy and Political System* (Stockholm: Federation of Swedish Industries, 1982).

[14]   William Shepherd, *In Praise of the Swedish Model*, 1999, <http://hem.passagen.se/aibpeter/swedishmodel/inpraise.html> (accessed October 2002).

[15]   The Saltsjöbaden Agreement of 1938 was an agreement between labor and capital to avoid any third-party involvement—including the government—in the affairs of the workforce.

[16]   Göran Tunhammar, president of Svenskt Näringsliv, interview with the authors, March 26, 2002.

[17]   Per-Martin Meyerson, *The Welfare State in Crisis – The Case of Sweden: A Critical Examination of Some Central Problems in the Swedish Economy and Political System* (Stockholm: Federation of Swedish Industries, 1982).

[18]   Göran Johnsson, chairman of the Swedish Metalworkers' Union, interview with the authors, March 25, 2002.

[19]   Ingvar Carlsson, prime minister of Sweden, 1986–1991 and 1994–1996, interview with the authors, April 15, 2002.

[20]   Bo Lundgren, chairman of the Conservative Party, interview with the authors, April 12, 2002.

[21]   Timothy Canova, "The Swedish Model Betrayed," *Challenge*, May/June 1994.

[22]   For example, the ceiling on housing loans from banks and financial institutions was removed.

[23]   Assar Lindbeck, "Options for economic and political reform in Sweden," *Economic Policy*, October 1993.

[24]   Urban Bäckström, governor of Sweden's central bank, interview with the authors, April 11, 2002.

[25]   Assar Lindbeck, "Options for economic and political reform in Sweden," *Economic Policy*, October 1993.

[26]   Thorvaldur Gylfason, "The Swedish Model under Stress," *SNS Economic Policy Group Report*, 1997.

[27]   "Sweden Country Profile 2001," The Economist Intelligence Unit, 2001.

[28]   Nils Lundgren and Hans Tson Söderström, "Kronförsvaret Hösten 1992 – Var det Värt Sitt Pris?" *Ekonomisk Politik - En Vänbok till Assar Linbeck*, 1995.

[29]   Urban Bäckström, governor of Sweden's central bank, interview with the authors, April 11, 2002.

30   Assar Lindbeck, "Options for economic and political reform in Sweden," *Economic Policy*, October 1993.

31   Paul Klebnikov, "The Swedish Disease," *Forbes*, May 24, 1993.

32   Paul Klebnikov, "The Swedish Disease," *Forbes*, May 24, 1993.

33   Bertram Silverman, "The rise and fall of the Swedish model: Interview with Rudolf Meidner," *Challenge*, January/February 1998.

34   Led by Assar Lindbeck, professor emeritus at the Institute for International Economic Studies at the Stockholm University.

35   The electoral period for the Swedish Parliament was increased from three to four years in the early 1990s.

36   Referred to as the Tax Reform of 1991.

37   Ingvar Carlsson, prime minister of Sweden, 1986–1991 and 1994–1996, interview with the authors, April 15, 2002.

38   Assar Lindbeck, "Det Svenska Experimentet," *SNS Förlag*, 1998.

39   Joakim Stymne, chief economist of Alfred Berg, interview with the authors, April 11, 2002.

40   "Sweden Country Profile 2001," The Economist Intelligence Unit, 2001.

41   Joakim Stymne, chief economist of Alfred Berg, interview with the authors, April 11, 2002.

42   Ingvar Carlsson, prime minister of Sweden, 1986–1991 and 1994–1996, interview with the authors, April 15, 2002.

43   Bertram Silverman, "The rise and the fall of the Swedish model: Interview with Rudolf Meidner," *Challenge*, January/February 1998.

44   "Sweden—Assessment and Recommendations," *OECD Economic Survey*, March 1, 2001.

45   "Sweden: Selected Issues—The Role of Government," International Monetary Fund, September 2001.

46   Bo Lundgren, chairman of the Conservative Party, interview with the authors, April 12, 2002.

47   Large parts of this section are based on research presented in Pontus Braunerhjelm, *Huvudkontoren flyttar ut* (Stockholm: SNS Förlag, 2001).

48   Marcus Wallenberg, president and CEO of Investor AB, interview with the authors, April 15, 2002.

49   Prior to 1992 government approval was necessary.

50   Göran Tunhammar, president of *Svenskt Näringsliv*, interview with the authors, March 26, 2002.

51   Pontus Braunerhjelm, *Huvudkontoren flyttar ut* (Stockholm: SNS Förlag, 2001).

52   For example, EF, the large Swedish professional education company, moved its headquarters to Boston to be close to the "educational" cluster in the Boston area and to attract top management talent.

53   Björn Carlsson, "Jakten på den låga skatten," *Göteborgs-Posten*, April 5, 2002.

54   "Ericsson 4Q report 2001," January 25, 2002.

55   Ericsson later sold this office property to relocate to smaller office space in line with an ongoing restructuring effort.

56   "Ericsson acquires office property in London," Ericsson press release, August 21, 1998.

57   "Ericsson's new organization," Ericsson press release, September 30, 1998.

Inequality and the "American Model"

The official data suggest inequality has been rising in the United States on various dimensions since 1973. Many causes of such inequality have been postulated: technological change; globalization; demographic factors; and changes in public policy (notably changes in taxation during the Reagan presidency).

Whether rising inequality matters is an open question. Some dimensions of inequality may be of concern, whereas other dimensions may be viewed as less problematic. To the extent that rising inequality is seen as a social problem that needs to be addressed, various policy proposals have been advocated.

Study Questions

1. Which is of greater concern: poverty or inequality? Should we be concerned with rising inequality in the United States?
2. How should business respond to inequality? Does it create business opportunities?
3. What are the causes of inequality in the United States?
4. What policy responses are appropriate? Can the United States learn from the experience of other countries discussed in this course? If so, what lessons should it draw?

RAFAEL DI TELLA
INGRID VOGEL

Inequality and the "American Model"

America before 1930 was a society in which a small number of very rich people controlled a large share of the nation's wealth. We became a middle-class society only after the concentration of income at the top dropped sharply during the New Deal, and especially during World War II . . . . Incomes then stayed fairly equally distributed until the 1970s: the rapid rise in incomes during the first postwar generation was very evenly spread across the population.

Since the 1970s, however, income gaps have been rapidly widening . . . . Claims that we've entered a second Gilded Age aren't exaggerated. In America's middle-class era, the mansion-building, yacht-owning classes had pretty much disappeared . . . . in 1970 the top 0.01 percent of taxpayers had 0.7 percent of total income, that is, they earned "only" 70 times as much as the average, not enough to buy or maintain a mega-residence. But in 1998 the top 0.01 percent received more than 3 percent of all income. That meant that the 13,000 richest families in America had almost as much income as the 20 million poorest households; those 13,000 families had incomes 300 times that of average families.

You might think that 1987, the year Tom Wolfe published his novel "The Bonfire of the Vanities" and Oliver Stone released his movie "Wall Street," marked the high tide of America's new money culture. But in 1987 the top 0.01 percent earned only about 40 percent of what they do today, and top executives less than a fifth as much. The America of "Wall Street" and "The Bonfire of the Vanities" was positively egalitarian compared with the country we live in today.[1]

—Economist Paul Krugman

As we consider the causes and consequences of inequality, we should also be mindful that, over time, the relationship of economic growth, increases in standards of living, and the distribution of wealth has evolved differently in various political and institutional settings . . . . We need to ask . . . whether we should be concerned with the degree of income inequality if all groups are experiencing relatively rapid gains in their real incomes, though those rates of gain may differ. And, we cannot ignore what is happening to the level of average income while looking at trends in the distribution . . . .[2]

— Chairman of the Federal Reserve Alan Greenspan

Since the late 1970s, there has been enormous change in the distribution of income and wealth in the United States. Despite growing levels of GDP per capita and low rates of unemployment, the United States faced both higher levels of, and faster increases in, economic inequality than other developed nations (see **Exhibit 1**).[3] From 1947 to 1979, in what became known as the "Great Compression,"[4] family incomes increased by 120% for the lowest-income quintile and 94% for the top-income quintile.[5] In stark contrast, from the late 1970s to the late 1990s, America's lowest-income families experienced real income decreases exceeding 6%, while families in the top quintile saw incomes increase more than 30% in real terms.[6] Most dramatically, the famous "Krugman calculation" showed that between 1977 and 1989, 70% of the rise in average family incomes went to the top 1% of families.[7]

Increasingly concentrated income distribution was reflected in a fractal-like pattern among the nation's wealthiest households. Most of the increase in incomes for the top quintile could be attributed to gains of the top decile (households with incomes starting at $80,000 in 1998), which grew in large part due to gains of the top 1% (starting at $230,000). In turn, most of the increase in the top 1% could be attributed to gains of the top 0.1% (starting at $790,000), which grew in large part as a result of gains of the top 0.01% (starting at $3.6 million). [8]

Vigorous debate surrounded the degree of inequality in the United States, the sources of that inequality, and what could be done to reduce inequality. Indeed, many skeptics questioned whether anything *should* be done to address inequality. They argued that as long as the poor had the opportunity to move up the income scale, "unequal outcomes" were really just a matter of personal choice. A 2002 *Business Week* segment entitled "The Rich Get Richer, and That's O.K." argued: ". . . as long as growth is strong and poverty is low, a little inequality is a small price to pay."[9]

Some evidence, however, pointed to a high price of inequality. Many political economists suggested, for example, that a very unequal income distribution could induce social unrest, which in turn might discourage productive investments. Alternatively, in a majoritarian democracy, large income gaps could indirectly slow growth by encouraging voters to favor excessive taxes on productive activities.[10]

Several studies linked inequality more directly with lower standards of living—not just for the less well off, but for all members of society. For example, studies relating income inequality to poor health found (as summarized by an economist at the Brookings Institution): "Countries and communities with above-average inequality have higher mortality rates than countries or communities with comparable incomes and poverty rates but lower inequality."[11] Similarly, other studies linked high inequality to high crime rates and to the enormous prison population in the United States.[a]

Another emerging body of research focused on happiness, as measured by surveys,[b] as an indicator of overall welfare. In studies with data from the Organization for Economic Cooperation and Development (OECD), economists, controlling for respondents' level of income, found that people tended to report lower happiness levels when income inequality was high. Interestingly, the Europeans appeared to be more concerned with inequality than the Americans. Furthermore, those most bothered by income inequality appeared to be the poor in Europe and the rich in the United States.[12]

---

[a] The U.S. rate of incarceration in prison and jail at year-end 2001 was 686 inmates per 100,000 U.S. residents (U.S. Department of Justice, Bureau of Justice Statistics Bulletin, <http://www.ojp.usdoj.gov/bjs/pub/pdf/p01.pdf>, accessed November 14, 2002). Rates in Canada, Australia, and most of Western Europe were between 55 and 125.

[b] The data used in one such study (Alesina, Di Tella, and MacCulloch, 2002) was based on 123,668 answers to a survey on happiness. In the United States, respondents were asked: "Taken all together, how would you say things are these days—would you say that you are very happy, pretty happy, or not too happy?"

Measuring Inequality

Disagreement exists about how inequality should be measured. Although most studies focus on income, wages, and wealth, many analysts argue that other metrics, such as standards of living, are more relevant. Others argue that relative measures are irrelevant and that the key issue is the absolute number of people living in poverty. Still others view inequality as tolerable as long as there is opportunity for lower-income households to move up the income scale.

Measures of Inequality

Income   Most studies of inequality focus on income distribution using annual data from the U.S. Bureau of the Census, the Congressional Budget Office, or income statistics published by the Internal Revenue Service. Census Bureau pretax-income data for 2001 indicated that the share of total household income was 3.5% for the bottom quintile, 14.6% for the middle quintile, and 50.1% for the top quintile of the income distribution. From 1979 on, the data demonstrated a clear trend toward increasing income inequality (see **Exhibit 2**).[13]

Wages and Wealth   The two primary components of income were wages and returns on assets. In 1999, wages accounted for approximately 71% of income, down from 74% in 1979, while returns on assets—including interest, dividends, capital gains, and rental income—increased from 16% to approximately 22% of income. Government transfers and other items accounted for the balance (see **Exhibit 3**).[14] As with income, the pattern of wage levels and returns from wealth across the population over time demonstrated growing inequality. In fact, inequality measured by levels of wealth was more extreme than inequality measured by either wages or returns from wealth (compare **Exhibits 3 and 4**).   In 1995, the wealthiest 10% of the U.S. population held approximately 90% of stocks and mutual funds, financial securities, trusts, and business equity.[a][15]   In 1999, more than 64% of all capital gains income was realized by families in the top 5% of the income distribution.

Living Standards   Critics argued that studies of income inequality were faulty in that they ignored taxes and noncash welfare payments. Some suggested an adjustment to account for the fact that households at the bottom of the distribution tended to work fewer hours than those at the top: In 1998, married-couple families with children in the lowest quintile worked 2,612 hours on average, whereas those in the top quintile averaged 4,271 (not accounting for the number of workers per family).[16] Adjusting for these and other factors, the Heritage Foundation, a conservative think tank based in Washington, D.C., found less income discrepancy, with 12% of income going to the bottom quintile and 37% to the top in 1997.[17] Those concerned with inequality, however, showed that regardless of what assumptions were made and how extreme or mild inequality appeared in a single year, income inequality was still increasing over time (see **Exhibit 5**).[18]

While data on incomes, wages, and wealth clearly showed growing inequality, data on living standards painted a somewhat different picture. Economists found evidence that while income inequality was on the rise, happiness inequality in the United States, as measured through surveys, appeared to remain relatively stable (see **Exhibit 6**).[19] One possible explanation was that many people at the top of the income distribution worked significantly longer hours than those at the bottom or middle. The happiness loss from the extra hours canceled out the happiness gain from extra income.

---

[a] The 90% datum is a gross number and therefore different from data presented in **Exhibit 4**, which shows net wealth (assets minus liabilities).

Data on consumption presented a similar picture. At a symposium on inequality in 1998, Alan Greenspan remarked: "Ultimately, we are interested in the question of relative standards of living and economic well-being. Thus, . . . we will also want to consider the distribution of consumption, which likely has the advantage of smoothing through transitory shocks affecting particular individuals or households for just a year or two."[20] He pointed out that inequality measured by consumption was less severe than inequality in income and that, in contrast to income inequality, consumption inequality did not increase during the 1990s (see **Exhibit 7**). In addition, he presented data on ownership of consumer durables that demonstrated almost perfect equality in many cases (such as with microwave ovens, freezers, cars, and washing machines).

Indeed, Greenspan was not the first to make this observation. In 1990, Robert Rector, a policy analyst at the Heritage Foundation, relied on consumption data to challenge how "poor" America's poor really were. He noted that: " 'Poor' Americans today are better housed, better fed, and own more property than did the average U.S. citizen throughout most of the 20th century."[21] In 1998, he pointed out that 41% of households living below the official poverty line owned a home, 70% owned a car, 27% owned two or more cars, and 67% had air conditioning.[22]

Poverty

It is common, among the nonpoor, to think of poverty as a sustainable condition—austere, perhaps, but they get by somehow, don't they? They are "always with us." What is harder for the nonpoor to see is poverty as acute distress: The lunch that consists of Doritos or hot dog rolls, leading to faintness before the end of the shift. The "home" that is also a car or a van. The illness or injury that must be "worked through," with gritted teeth, because there's no sick pay or health insurance and the loss of one day's pay will mean no groceries for the next. These experiences are not part of a sustainable lifestyle, even a lifestyle of chronic deprivation and relentless low-level punishment. They are, by almost any standard of subsistence, emergency situations. And that is how we should see the poverty of so many millions of low-wage Americans—as a state of emergency.[23]

> —Essayist and cultural critic Barbara Ehrenreich, who chose to experience life as a member of the "working poor" and wrote about it in her widely read book *Nickel and Dimed*

Many participants in the debate argued that relative levels of income, wealth, or living standards were irrelevant: The important issue to analyze was the absolute number of families living in poverty. However, agreeing on a standard definition for poverty proved challenging. According to the 1999 official federal poverty line, a family of four in the United States with an income level below $16,895 would be considered poor.[24] According to this figure, 11.8% of the population was living in poverty in 1999, an improvement over the 22.4% poverty rate in 1959[25] (see **Exhibit 8**).

Critics believed this formula for measuring poverty belied the true state of America's poor.[26] It was originally calculated in the 1960s as three times the price of the minimum food basket a family required. Since then, it was adjusted only for inflation according to the consumer price index. As such, it did not account for the increasing relative costs of housing, health care, and transportation. By the late 1990s, average family expenditure on food was just one-fifth of income, down from one-third in the 1960s. Other problems with the federal poverty line included its use of uniform costs of living across all regions in the country and its disregard of the effects of income taxes and welfare benefits. In 2000, correcting for these and other assumptions, policy experts in Massachusetts created a new standard to define poverty. They found that 27% of the state's families were living in poverty under this theoretical threshold, as opposed to 9% as measured under federal poverty standards.[27]

Arguing that poverty was sometimes a choice, still others discounted the issue altogether. In 1999, Martin Feldstein, head of the Council of Economic Advisers during the Reagan administration, stated:

> Not all poverty can be attributed to involuntary unemployment or to the lack of earning ability. Individual choices, rational or irrational, can lead to poverty. Some individuals who are in poverty may be making considered choices. For example, some individuals may choose leisure (not working or working very little) over cash income even though this leaves them poorer than they otherwise would be. Choosing not to work may be an increasingly important source of poverty. Over time, the standard of living that is possible without working has increased for some segments of the population as a result of the rise in the real value of cash and in-kind welfare benefits.[28]

Opportunity

. . . Most Americans believe that their society provides opportunity to advance for those who are willing to work hard . . . The emphasis that our country has historically placed on equality of opportunity and the strides that we as a nation have made . . . sustain support for a standard of equal opportunity but not for a standard of equal outcomes.

Americans are not inclined to a politics of envy. They are inclined to the idea that opportunity is present to those who avail themselves of it.[29]

—Political scientists Everett Carll Ladd and Karlyn H. Bowman

The United States has its historical foundations in providing a unique "land of opportunity" where, at least in theory, anyone, even from the most modest backgrounds, can become successful. Entrepreneurs such as Mary Kay and Ross Perot, who propelled themselves from the lower or middle echelons of society to become fabulously wealthy and famous, seemed to confirm this legend. The majority of Americans (60%) believed the poor were lazy whereas this was the case with only 26% of Europeans (see **Exhibit 11a**). Indeed, polling data throughout the 1990s demonstrated that, despite growing economic inequality, most Americans still believed in the "American Dream" (see **Exhibit 9a**). As a consequence, even those with low incomes largely agreed that the government should not seek to redistribute income through taxes or assistance (see **Exhibit 9b**).

Many economists confirmed this view. Michael Cox, senior vice president and chief economist at the Federal Reserve Bank of Dallas, was a vocal proponent of the mobility argument. In popular newspaper articles and books, he drew on a number of studies to argue that mobility in the United States was fluid (see **Exhibit 10a**). He stated: "When income mobility is examined for individuals over a long period of time, there's strong evidence to contradict notions of a society settled into stagnant income classes."[30]

Other economists, however, challenged such findings and claimed that mobility in the United States was in fact low. Specifically, they claimed Cox's analysis was faulty since it failed to account for age by comparing incomes of the study group to the overall population over time rather than just to itself. They also found flaw with the fact that the study tracked individual rather than family income.[31] Cox's challengers adjusted the analysis to address the first concern and showed that in the early 1990s, 75% of individuals who started in the bottom quintile ended up in the same quintile one year later.[32] Adjusting for both concerns, researchers found that between 1969 and 1994, 41% of those in the bottom quintile had remained in the bottom quintile, and 25% had only moved to the next quintile of income distribution (see **Exhibit 10b**).[33]

In contrast to Americans, Europeans largely considered class (a proxy for their position in the income distribution) as fixed and saw little hope for economic mobility (see **Exhibit 11a**).[34] Ironically, the latest mobility research indicated substantially more mobility in European countries than in the United States (see **Exhibit 11b**).[35]

Origins of Inequality

Yet another debate surrounded identifying the sources of economic inequality in the United States. Many blamed globalization and an influx of immigrants, while others held the rapid pace of technological change and trickle-down economic policies enacted by conservative governments as responsible. Still others blamed deunionization and a fundamental shift in corporate culture from modesty to avarice.

Globalization

In political debate, globalization was attacked equally from the left, such as by consumer-rights advocate Ralph Nader, and from the right, such as by conservative Republican Pat Buchanan, as the culprit of rising inequality within the United States. Most infamously, in the 1992 U.S. presidential debates, Reform Party candidate Ross Perot predicted that the North American Free Trade Agreement would create a "giant sucking sound of jobs being pulled out of this country."

Indeed, many academic studies attributed at least a portion of income inequality to immigration and trade.[36] Immigration was blamed for putting downward pressure on wages by widening the labor pool.[37] International competition and increased imports from low-wage countries were blamed for reducing manufacturing wages and employment in the United States, particularly for less-skilled workers. Furthermore, as U.S. manufacturing operations moved overseas or were forced to close down, more workers entered the service sector. The service sector offered significantly lower wages for entry-level workers and more rapidly increasing wage inequality.[38]

Other studies argued that globalization did not contribute to inequality.[39] They countered the argument that foreign trade was to blame with data indicating that industries unaffected by trade reduced their use of low-skill workers just as much, and in many cases even faster, than trade-affected industries.[40] Other studies questioned the role of immigration in wage inequality by pointing out that legal immigrant workers were just as likely to have college degrees as native workers.[41] On average, legal immigrant workers had just one year less education than the native worker.[42] In addition, it was often argued that illegal immigrants tended to fill positions that U.S. workers rejected.

Technology

There was a divisive split between those who blamed globalization and those who blamed technology for growing inequality. Many economists argued that technology and computerization benefited skilled, highly educated labor while reducing demand for and wages of less-skilled labor.[43] They pointed to the income premium of young college-educated men over high school-educated men with similar experience, which increased from 30% in 1979 to 74% in 1989. This premium rose at the same time as the supply of college-educated workers rose, leading many economists to argue that nonsupply factors—such as rapid technological change—were responsible for the increase.[44]

This increase in wage premiums of college-educated workers, however, slowed in the 1990s, when the pace of technological change was most rapid.[45] If technology were indeed to blame for rising inequality, it might be expected that the rates of change of technology and inequality would be similar. Furthermore, many researchers argued that technological change also often benefited less-skilled workers through automatization of more complex tasks. More sophisticated technology provided an interface for less-skilled workers to operate more productively in the economy.

Government Policy

America in the 1920s wasn't a feudal society. But it was a nation in which vast privilege—often inherited privilege—stood in contrast to vast misery. It was also a nation in which the government, more often than not, served the interests of the privileged and ignored the aspirations of ordinary people.

Those days are past—or are they? Income inequality in America has now returned to the levels of the 1920s. Inherited wealth doesn't yet play a big part in our society, but given time—and the repeal of the estate tax—we will grow ourselves a hereditary elite . . . set apart from the concerns of ordinary Americans . . . . And the new elite, like the old, will have enormous political power.[46]

—Paul Krugman

Another important element in the inequality debate was the role of government policy, especially with regards to the decline in the real value of the minimum wage and changes in tax policy that predominately benefited the wealthy.

Minimum Wage   Between 1979 and 1989, the real value of the minimum wage dropped from $6.53 to $4.50 (in 1999 dollars). In 1999, despite four increases in the 1990s, the real value of the minimum wage was still 21% below its 1979 value.[47] A particularly large effect of the lower minimum wage during the 1980s on inequality took place through an increase in the dispersion of wages of women at the low end of the income distribution.[48]

Taxes   In stark contrast to President Jimmy Carter's administration, President Ronald Reagan's administration favored changes in taxes that disproportionately benefited the rich. Reagan passed an across-the-board tax cut of 5% in 1981, 10% in 1982, and 10% again in 1983 (which favored the better off, whose initial tax rates were highest); his Tax Reform Act of 1986 reduced the number of individual income tax brackets to two and resulted in a decrease in the top marginal tax rate from 50% to 28%. According to the theory of trickle-down economics popular with Reagan's administration, decreasing taxes to the investor class would lead to an increase in spending, which would in turn stimulate the economy and improve the economic well-being of all citizens.

Under President Bill Clinton in the 1990s, taxes became somewhat more progressive (see **Exhibit 12**). This was partially reversed in 2001 by President George W. Bush with the repeal of the estate tax.

Decreased Strength of Unions

The declining strength of unions also contributed to inequality. In 1979, unions represented 24% of the labor force. By 2001, only 13.5% of workers were unionized.[49] Not only were fewer workers receiving (the typically) higher union wages, but nonunion employers no longer felt compelled to raise wages as a response to the threat of unionism.[50] Furthermore, decreased union power allowed within-firm wage inequality to increase in favor of managerial and professional positions. The AFL-CIO, a federation of unions in the United States representing 13 million workers, estimated that up to

40% of the increase in income inequality between 1980 and 1997 could be attributed to the decline in union density.[51]

Corporate Avarice

Other economists emphasized the role of a shift in corporate culture in explaining rising income inequality, particularly at the very top of the income distribution. As Krugman pointed out, "in the 1960s, America's great corporations behaved more like socialist republics than like cutthroat capitalist enterprises . . . . For a generation after World War II, fear of outrage kept executive salaries in check. Now the outrage is gone."[52] Between 1989 and 1999, median executive pay (including salaries, bonuses, incentive awards, stock options exercised, and stock granted) increased in real terms by 90.6%, while median hourly wages for all workers increased by 2.4%.[53] In 2000, the *Economist* reported that CEO pay in the United States was 475 times as high as the average manufacturing worker's pay.[54] The average compensation of the top 100 CEOs was $37.5 million, equivalent to more than 1,000 times the pay of the average worker.[55] For example, in 2002, Chairman of the Board and CEO of Dell Computer Corporation Michael Dell received $15.9 million in total compensation (including stock option grants), exercised $81.0 million in stock options from previous years, and held an additional $122.6 million in unexercised stock options. In 2000, Chairman of the Board of Enron Corporation Ken Lay received $33.5 million in total compensation (including stock option grants), exercised $123.4 million in stock options from previous years, and held an additional $361.6 million in unexercised stock options.[56]

Krugman suggested a number of explanations for the explosion in executive pay: questionable corporate governance methods, the new "superstar" status of top executives, and a push in academic literature, popularized in the press and incorporated into consultant recommendations, toward aligning management interests with those of stockholders through grants of stock and options.[57]

Critics of the "corporate avarice" argument claimed that executive pay was justified and coincided with huge gains for stockholders. They also pointed out the increased complexity of executive positions and argued that a business landscape of intensified competition and rapidly changing technology supported the premium awarded to strong, capable, and proven leadership.

Reducing Inequality

Some observers suggested that inequality was just an inevitable side effect of economic growth and that, therefore, no action should be taken to reduce inequality (see **Exhibit 13**). Others suggested that the government bear responsibility for reducing inequality among its citizens, as European governments tended to do (see **Exhibit 14**). Still others wanted corporations to play an active role in improving conditions for workers and local communities.

One option for the government often emphasized in public debate was to focus on improving the prospects of upward mobility for low-income families rather than attempting to redistribute income directly. Education reform and job training were considered areas that might yield significant results. However, there was no consensus on either issue. With regards to education, some experts recommended devolving increasing responsibility to local areas, while others argued for more national standards. With regards to training, many argued that a market-based system, under which private-sector training would pay for itself, was the only workable solution. Others argued that companies would be loath to train low-skilled, low-wage workers—who would benefit most from training programs—given the likelihood such trainees would eventually defect to other companies.

Regardless, education reform and government-led job training would require significant funding, and the commitment of taxpayers appeared questionable.

Others argued for more direct government intervention in reducing inequality. Examples of possible steps included improving welfare benefits, raising the minimum wage, and introducing more progressive taxes. All of these, however, were highly controversial.

Welfare Benefits

In 1996, welfare was substantially reformed in the United States with the Personal Responsibility and Work Opportunity Reconciliation Act. The reform made welfare benefits conditional; recipients would be expected to "earn" aid by engaging in constructive behavior such as job searching, training, or community service. In contrast, individuals in need had previously been "entitled" to aid, to a large extent irrespective of their behavior.

Many observers heralded the program as a great success. By 2001, the number of people on welfare had decreased by 60% nationally.[58] The largest component of welfare recipients, single mothers, experienced dramatic improvement in employment. In addition, child poverty rates were down significantly.

The recession of 2002, however, began to take its toll as the number of welfare recipients rose, putting the new welfare model under stress for the first time. In 2002, the welfare program was due to be reauthorized by Congress; not surprisingly, left-leaning and right-leaning members vigorously debated whether to shift the welfare program back toward an entitlement system, which many argued would reintroduce a "poverty trap,"[a] or whether to boost work requirements, which critics argued would be unworkable in a slowly growing economy.[59]

Minimum Wage

Increasing the minimum wage was another option considered. Some economists argued that raising the minimum wage would primarily benefit teenagers and would increase unemployment. Those in favor of raising the minimum wage pointed to data that showed minimum wage earners contributed 54% of their family's weekly earnings, indicating that many had significant family responsibilities and would benefit greatly from an increase.[60] There was no conclusive study on whether a higher minimum wage increased unemployment. However, some influential small-scale industry studies based on statewide minimum wage increases indicated that employment was not threatened by increases in the cost of labor.[61]

Taxes

Although most researchers agreed that pretax income was the most important component of income inequality, many people argued for a more progressive tax system. Tax policies that rewarded additional work, such as the earned income tax credit (EITC), were considered most promising. The EITC is a refundable tax credit designed to supplement the earnings of low-income workers and is available only to those families with a working taxpayer. It was argued that the EITC

---

[a] A "poverty trap" occurs when the combination of losing state-benefit entitlements and paying taxes makes poor families worse off in work than under welfare.

contributed more to the increases in the employment of single mothers and reductions in child poverty than other programs, including the 1996 welfare reform act.[62]

The thresholds and credits of the EITC were designed to ensure that a person working full time on minimum wages would live above the poverty line. In 2001, the qualifying income thresholds were less than $28,281 for a family with one child, $32,121 for a family with more than one child, and $10,710 for a family with no children.[63] The credits were up to $2,428, $4,008, and $364, respectively.[64]

Many proponents of the EITC suggested that the thresholds and credits be modified to account for families with three children. They also suggested that the implicit marriage penalty be addressed.[65] Others argued that the EITC was already too high, and that the credits combined with welfare benefits pushed many recipients well above the poverty line.[66]

Tax modifications for America's wealthiest members were also proposed. Most controversially, in his book *Top Heavy: A Study of the Increasing Inequality of Wealth in America*, Edward N. Wolff argued that a wealth tax should be levied in the United States,[67] as it was in several European countries, including the Netherlands, Norway, Iceland, and Sweden. In 1996, Wolff recommended a tax of 0.05% on assets from $100,000 to $199,999, up to 0.3% on assets of $1 million and above (excluding houses, pensions, and a maximum amount on cars). He stated: "Such an extension may not only promote greater equity in our society—particularly, by taxing those more able to pay taxes—but may also benefit the economy by providing households with an incentive for switching from less productive to more productive forms of assets."[68]

Corporate Responsibility

Others argued that private companies should take an active role in reducing income inequality by including employees and the local community in important company decisions. They pointed to the lower levels of inequality in most of continental Europe and argued that not only did the government contribute to equity among citizens, but corporations also played a significant role. They attributed this largely to the reliance of much of continental Europe on a stakeholder model of corporate governance. The expectation that company directors consider the interests of employees, bankers, suppliers, customers, and the community at large, in addition to the interests of shareholders, provided an important check on management power. Decisions to downsize, grant executive compensation packages far in excess of those of employees, or accept takeover offers would have to be approved by a larger constituency. They also hypothesized that the ability of European companies to take a longer-term view of profits allowed them to consider investing more in training and development and other programs beneficial to equality with longer payback periods.

Skeptics argued that encouraging corporate responsibility for improving equality would be difficult under the U.S. shareholder-dominated system of corporate governance. Only in relatively rare instances where improved equality could be spun as value enhancing, for example as a public relations or marketing tool, would beneficial programs be adopted. Given the active market for corporate control in the United States, public companies that pursued social objectives at the expense of shareholder value would leave themselves vulnerable to hostile takeovers.

Exhibit 1   Earnings Inequality Growth Across Countries

Ratio of the earnings of the 90th-percentile worker to the 10th-percentile worker

Country	Early 1980s	Late 1980s	Mid-1990s
United States	3.65	4.14	4.43
Japan	3.01	3.16	3.02
Western Germany	2.69	2.46	2.32
France	3.24	3.28	3.06
Italy	2.94	2.16	2.80
United Kingdom	2.79	3.28	3.37
Canada	4.01	4.40	4.20
Australia	2.74	2.87	2.92
Austria	3.45	3.51	3.66
Denmark	2.14	2.18	--
Finland	2.46	2.57	2.34
Netherlands	--	2.61	2.59
New Zealand	--	2.92	3.40
Norway	2.06	1.98	--
Portugal	--	3.49	4.05
Sweden	2.04	2.12	2.21
Switzerland	--	2.70	2.75

Source: Adapted from Mishel, Bernstein, and Schmitt, *The State of Working America 2000/2001*, p. 384 (based on OECD data).

Exhibit 2   U.S. Real Family Income, by Income Group, 1947–2001 (*upper limit of groups in 2001 dollars, except 95th percentile, which shows lower limit*) and Share of Aggregate Income Received, by Income Group, 1947–2001

Year	Lowest Quintile	Second Quintile	Middle Quintile	Fourth Quintile	95th Percentile [a]
1947	$ 10,662	$ 17,205	$ 23,330	$ 33,103	$ 54,333
% share of total	5.0%	11.9%	17.0%	23.1%	17.5%
1967	$ 18,455	$ 30,294	$ 40,624	$ 55,692	$ 89,484
% share of total	5.4%	12.2%	17.5%	23.5%	16.4%
1973	$ 20,986	$ 34,629	$ 48,316	$ 66,445	$ 103,586
% share of total	5.5%	11.9%	17.5%	24.0%	15.5%
1979	$ 22,280	$ 36,637	$ 51,903	$ 71,470	$ 114,657
% share of total	5.4%	11.6%	17.5%	24.1%	15.3%
1989	$ 22,062	$ 38,601	$ 56,247	$ 82,096	$ 136,431
% share of total	4.6%	10.6%	16.5%	23.7%	17.9%
1995	$ 21,997	$ 38,047	$ 56,503	$ 83,350	$ 142,633
% share of total	4.4%	10.1%	15.8%	23.2%	20.0%
1999	$ 24,246	$ 42,064	$ 63,096	$ 93,562	$ 164,686
% share of total	4.3%	9.9%	15.6%	23.0%	20.3%
2001	$ 24,000	$ 41,127	$ 62,500	$ 94,150	$ 164,104
% share of total	4.2%	9.7%	15.4%	22.9%	21.0%

Source: Adapted from U.S. Census Bureau, Historical Income Tables—Families, <http://www.census.gov/ftp/pub/hhes/income/histinc/f02.html> and <...f01.html> (accessed April 1, 2003).

Note: [a]95th percentile real family income numbers refer to lower limits.

Exhibit 3   U.S. Sources of Household Income by Income Type, 1999

Income Group	Share of Each Group's Income (i.e., wages and salaries account for 56.6% of the income of the bottom fifth of households)				Share of Income Type by Group (i.e., the bottom fifth of households earn 2.7% of all U.S. wages and salaries)			
	Wage and Salary	Returns on Assets	Government Transfers and Other	Total	Wage and Salary	Returns on Assets	Government Transfers and Other	Total
Top fifth	67.50%	30.50%	2.10%	100.00%	54.30%	80.90%	16.70%	57.60%
Top 1%	41.6	58.2	0.2	100.0	10.4	47.8	0.4	17.8
96–99%	73.6	24.8	1.6	100.0	14.7	16.3	3.2	14.3
91–95%	81.9	15.5	2.6	100.0	12.0	7.5	3.9	10.5
81–90%	82.2	13.5	4.3	100.0	17.2	9.3	9.2	15.0
Bottom four-fifths	76.50%	10.00%	13.50%	100.00%	45.70%	19.70%	83.60%	42.50%
Fourth fifth	81.8	11.0	7.2	100.0	22.7	10.0	20.6	19.8
Middle fifth	76.1	10.9	13.0	100.0	12.9	6.1	23.0	12.1
Second fifth	71.7	8.0	20.3	100.0	7.4	2.7	21.7	7.3
Bottom fifth	56.6	5.6	37.8	100.0	2.7	0.9	18.3	3.3
All	71.40%	21.70%	6.90%	100.00%	100.00%	100.00%	100.00%	100.00%

Source: Adapted from Mishel, Bernstein, and Schmitt, *The State of Working America 2000/2001*, p. 85.
Note: Returns on assets include interest income, dividends, realized capital gains, and rental income.

Exhibit 4   U.S. Average Wealth by Wealth Class, 1962–1998 (*thousands of 1998 dollars*)

Wealth Class	1962	1983	1989	1992	1995	1998
Top fifth	$587.40	$864.50	$1,017.10	$991.90	$917.80	$1,126.70
% total wealth	*81.0*	*81.3*	*83.5*	*83.8*	*83.9*	*83.4*
Top 1%	$4,851.80	$7,175.10	$9,101.70	$8,796.40	$8,422.50	$10,203.70
96–99%	768.10	1,186.80	1,313.40	1,351.40	1,192.90	1,441.20
91–95%	359.10	516.20	565.50	559.30	504.50	623.50
81–90%	202.90	278.70	315.90	283.90	263.90	344.90
Bottom four-fifths	$34.60	$49.60	$50.20	$48.00	$44.00	$56.10
% total wealth	*19.1*	*18.7*	*16.5*	*16.2*	*16.1*	*16.6*
Fourth fifth	$ 97.20	$ 133.60	$ 150.00	$ 135.70	$ 124.90	$ 161.30
Middle fifth	39.40	55.50	58.80	51.90	49.10	61.00
Second fifth	6.90	12.50	10.20	10.50	9.60	11.10
Bottom fifth	-5.30	-3.20	-18.40	-6.00	-7.60	-8.90

Source: Adapted from Mishel, Bernstein, and Schmitt, *The State of Working America 2000/2001*, p. 260.
Note: Wealth is defined as net wealth (household assets minus debt).

Exhibit 5 U.S. Growth of Household Income Inequality Using Various Income Definitions

Inequality measure and income definition	Inequality value		
Gini coefficients	1979	1989	1999
Census money income *(excludes noncash government assistance, taxation, and capital gains)*	.403	.429	.446
Pretax market income *(subtracts government cash transfers and adds realized capital gains and employer-provided health insurance)*	.460	.492	.509
After-tax market income *(adjusts pretax market income for income taxes)*	.429	.465	.484
Comprehensive income *(includes cash and noncash government transfers and adjusts for taxes)*	.359	.389	.405

Source: Adapted from Jared Bernstein, Lawrence Mishel, and Chauna Brocht, "Any Way You Cut It: Income Inequality on the Rise Regardless of How it's Measured," Briefing Paper of the Economic Policy Institute, 2000, p. 4.

Note: Refer to **Exhibit 13** for an explanation of the Gini coefficient.

Exhibit 6   U.S. Happiness Inequality and Income Inequality, 1975–1997

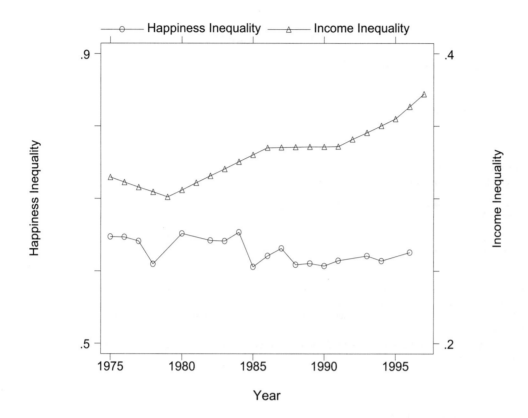

Source: Adapted from Di Tella and MacCulloch, "Income, Happiness and Inequality as Measures of Welfare," August 22, 2002, p. 45.

Notes: "Income Inequality" is measured as the Gini coefficient of after-tax household disposable income, as reported in the Luxembourg Income Study.

"Happiness Inequality" is the standard deviation of the three categorical responses, for each year, to the question "Taken all together, how would you say things are these days—would you say that you are very happy, pretty happy, or not too happy?", derived assuming a cardinal scale with equal distance between the three categories.

Exhibit 7   U.S. Household Income and Expenditure Inequality

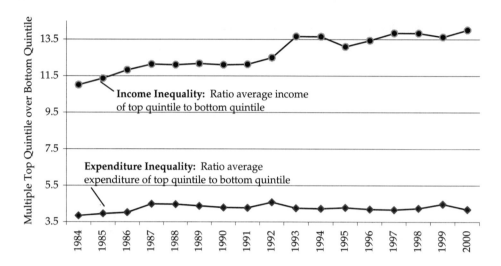

Sources: Calculated by casewriter based on data from (for income) the U.S. Bureau of the Census, average household income, <www.census.gov/ftp/pub/hhes/income/histinc/h03.html> (accessed November 7, 2002); and (for expenditure) the U.S. Bureau of Labor Statistics Consumer Expenditure Survey, <www.bls.gov/cex/home.htm> (accessed November 7, 2002).

Note: Average expenditure includes items such as food, household, entertainment, and so on, as well as pension and insurance contributions.

Exhibit 8   U.S. Poverty Rate, 1959–2001 *(as % population)*

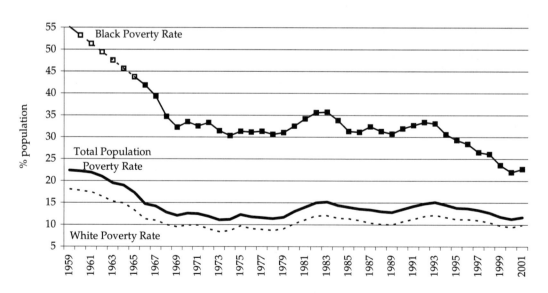

Source: Adapted from U.S. Bureau of the Census, <http://www.census.gov/prod/2002pubs/p60-219.pdf> (accessed December 10, 2002).

Note: Data for black poverty rate from 1960–1965 is estimated based on interpolating 1959 and 1966 data.

Exhibit 9a   Attitudes Toward the American Dream in the United States

Question: I'd like to talk with you now about a term with which you are probably familiar—the American Dream. Do you personally feel that the American Dream is very much alive today, somewhat alive, or not really alive?

Percentage of respondents answering:

	Very Much Alive	Somewhat Alive	Not Really Alive
1986	32	55	11
1990	23	50	20
1992	16	52	26
1993	20	50	22
1995	22	52	21

Source: Adapted from Ladd and Bowman, *Attitudes Toward Economic Inequality*, 1998, p. 74, referring to Roper Starch Worldwide surveys.

Exhibit 9b   Attitudes Toward Government Redistribution in the United States

Question: Some people think that the government in Washington ought to reduce the income differences between the rich and the poor, perhaps by raising the taxes of wealthy families or by giving income assistance to the poor. Others think that the government should not concern itself with reducing this income difference between the rich and poor. Here is a card with a scale from 1 to 7. Think of a score of 1 meaning that the government ought to reduce the income differences between the rich and poor, and a score of 7 meaning that the government should not concern itself with reducing income differences. What score between 1 and 7 comes closest to the way you feel?

Percentage of respondents answering that the government ought to reduce income differences (scores 1–2):

	1978	1984	1994	1996
Income				
<$20,000	32	35	27	32
$20,000–29,999	8	25	24	28
$30,000–49,999	6	19	16	20
$50,000+	28	27	20	20
Education				
<H.S. grad.	33	42	37	38
H.S. grad.	31	33	23	26
Some college	17	27	22	29
College grad.	21	19	16	21
Gender				
Male	28	31	19	26
Female	33	34	27	29

Source: Adapted from Ladd and Bowman, *Attitudes Toward Economic Inequality*, 1998, p. 112, referring to National Opinion Research Center surveys.

Exhibit 10a Income Mobility in the United States—Not Controlling for Age

1975 income group	% in each quintile in 1991				
	Lowest	2nd	Middle	4th	Top
Lowest fifth	**5.1**	14.6	21.0	30.3	29.0
Second fifth	4.2	**23.5**	20.3	25.2	26.8
Middle fifth	3.3	19.3	**28.3**	30.1	19.0
Fourth fifth	1.9	9.3	18.8	**32.6**	37.4
Top fifth	0.9	2.8	10.2	23.6	**62.5**

Source: Adapted from Cox and Alm, "By Our Own Bootstraps," 1995, p. 8, which presents an analysis of data from the University of Michigan's Panel Study of Income Dynamics (PSID).

Note: The PSID tracks individuals' income over time. This table represents 3,725 individuals from 1975 to 1991.

Exhibit 10b Income Mobility in the United States—Controlling for Age

1969 income group	% in each quintile in 1994				
	Lowest	2nd	Middle	4th	Top
Lowest fifth	**41.0**	24.9	16.2	12.1	5.8
Second fifth	22.4	**24.7**	23.9	16.1	13.0
Middle fifth	16.9	21.0	**23.5**	22.8	15.9
Fourth fifth	11.3	18.5	19.7	**24.2**	26.3
Top fifth	9.5	10.6	16.6	24.5	**38.8**

Source: Adapted from Mishel, Bernstein, and Schmitt, *The State of Working America 2000/2001*, p. 77, which presents unpublished tabulations of Peter Gottschalk based on the PSID.

Note: Unlike the table in **Exhibit 10a**, this table controls for age by comparing the income of the sample only to itself as it ages, not to the larger population. It also tracks family income rather than individual income. This avoids the problem of attributing mobility to, for example, a teenager from a well off family who takes a minimum wage job during high school before joining the workforce in a more determined way after college.

Exhibit 11a   Beliefs about the Poor in Europe and the United States

	European Union	United States
	% total population who:	*% total population who:*
Believe poor are trapped in poverty	60	29
Believe luck determines income	54	30
Believe the poor are lazy	26	60

Source: Adapted from Alesina, Glaeser, Sacerdote, "Why Doesn't the U.S. Have a European-Style Welfare State?" 2001, p. 57.

Exhibit 11b   Income Mobility in Selected Countries

1991 Earnings Status of 1986 Bottom-Quintile Workers

	No Longer Employed Full Time	Still Bottom Fifth	Moved to Second Fifth	Moved Above Second Fifth
U.S.	41%	31%	17%	11%
Western Germany	39%	27%	17%	17%
France	23%	36%	24%	18%
Italy	8%	44%	25%	23%
U.K.	13%	36%	28%	24%
Denmark	27%	32%	21%	21%
Finland	26%	29%	20%	25%
Sweden	28%	36%	18%	18%

Source: Adapted from Mishel, Bernstein, and Schmitt, *The State of Working America 2000/2001*, p. 386.

Notes: Because of rounding, horizontal components do not add exactly to 100%.
Data is based on surveys conducted by the OECD. In 1986, workers whose earnings placed them in the bottom quintile were surveyed. The same workers were surveyed again in 1991.

Exhibit 12   Average Effective Federal Tax Rates in the United States, 1977–1999

Income Group	1977	1989	1995	1999
Bottom fifth	8.4%	8.8%	6.0%	4.6%
Second fifth	14.9%	15.3%	14.6%	13.7%
Middle fifth	19.2%	18.9%	19.7%	18.9%
Fourth fifth	22.1%	21.5%	22.5%	22.2%
Top fifth	28.5%	25.9%	29.6%	29.1%
Top 10%	30.5%	26.8%	31.3%	30.6%
Top 5%	32.6%	27.4%	33.0%	31.8%
Top 1%	37.3%	28.1%	36.5%	34.4%
Ratio of Tax Rates				
Top fifth/bottom fifth	3.4	2.9	4.9	6.3
Top fifth/middle fifth	1.5	1.4	1.5	1.5
Top 5%/bottom fifth	3.9	3.1	5.5	6.9

Source: Adapted from Jared Bernstein, Lawrence Mishel, and Chauna Brocht, "Any Way You Cut It: Income Inequality on the Rise Regardless of How it's Measured," Briefing Paper of the Economic Policy Institute, 2000, p. 7.

Exhibit 13 Relationship between U.S. Inequality and Growth

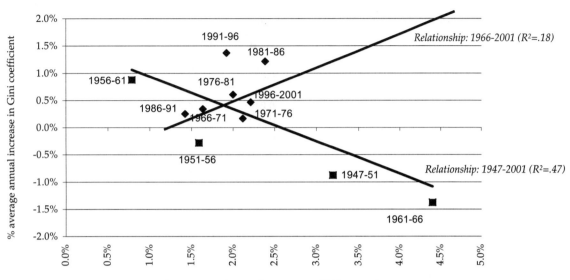

% average real annual increase in GDP per capita

Sources: Adapted from (for Gini coefficients) U.S. Census Bureau, <http://www.census.gov/ftp/pub/hhes/income/histinc/f04.html> (accessed November 14, 2002); and (for GDP per capita) U.S. Bureau of Economic Analysis <http://www.bea.gov/bea/dn/nipaweb/TableViewFixed.asp#Mid> (accessed November 14, 2002).

Notes: Over the entire period 1947–2001, more growth appears to be associated with more equality. This divides into two distinct periods. Between 1947 and 1966, more growth appears to be strongly correlated with more equality (R^2=.91). Between 1966 and 2001, more growth is associated with less equality, but the relationship is weak (R^2=.18).

The *Gini coefficient* of income is measured by sorting each person's income from least to greatest and then plotting on a Lorenz curve the cumulative share of income against the cumulative % of the population represented (see diagram at right). The coefficient = **A** / (**A+B**).

The coefficient ranges from zero to one, with zero indicating perfect equality (all income distributed equally to all households) and one indicating perfect inequality (all income accruing to one household).

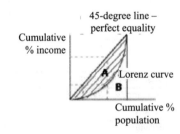

Exhibit 14 Government Expenditure on Social Programs, 1995

% GDP	Total	Old age, disability, and survivor benefits	Family benefits	Unemployment and labor market programs	Health benefits	Other
U.S.	15.8	7.3	0.6	0.6	6.3	1.0
European Union	25.4	12.4	2.1	3.2	5.9	1.8
France	30.1	14.1	2.6	3.1	8.0	2.3
Germany	28.0	12.5	2.0	3.7	8.1	1.6
Sweden	33.0	14.8	3.9	4.7	5.9	3.8
U.K.	22.5	10.6	2.4	1.3	5.7	2.5

Source: Adapted from Alesina, Glaeser, Sacerdote, "Why Doesn't the U.S. Have a European-Style Welfare State?" 2001, pp. 5–6.

Data Appendix

Table A   Distribution of Income or Consumption *(sorted by Gini coefficient)*

	Year	Income (i) or Consumption (c)	Gini	Bottom 10%	Bottom 20%	Top 20%	Top 10%
Austria	1987	i	0.231	4.4	10.4	33.3	19.3
Denmark	1992	i	0.247	3.6	9.6	34.5	20.5
Japan	1993	i	0.249	4.8	10.6	35.7	21.7
Belgium	1992	i	0.250	3.7	9.5	34.5	20.2
Sweden	1992	i	0.250	3.7	9.6	34.5	20.1
Finland	1991	i	0.256	4.2	10.0	35.8	21.6
Norway	1995	i	0.258	4.1	9.7	35.8	21.8
Italy	1995	i	0.273	3.5	8.7	36.3	21.8
Germany	1994	i	0.300	3.3	8.2	38.5	23.7
Pakistan	1996-97	c	0.312	4.1	9.5	41.1	27.6
Canada	1994	i	0.315	2.8	7.5	39.3	23.8
Spain	1990	i	0.325	2.8	7.5	40.3	25.2
Netherlands	1994	i	0.326	2.8	7.3	40.1	25.1
France	1995	i	0.327	2.8	7.2	40.2	25.1
Greece	1993	i	0.327	3.0	7.5	40.3	25.3
Poland	1996	i	0.329	3.0	7.7	40.9	26.3
Switzerland	1992	i	0.331	2.6	6.9	40.3	25.2
Australia	1994	i	0.352	2.0	5.9	41.3	25.4
Israel	1992	i	0.355	2.8	6.9	42.5	26.9
Portugal	1994-95	i	0.356	3.1	7.3	43.4	28.4
Ireland	1987	i	0.359	2.5	6.7	42.9	27.4
U.K.	1991	i	0.361	2.6	6.6	43.0	27.3
Indonesia	1996	i	0.365	3.6	8.0	44.9	30.3
India	1997	c	0.378	3.5	8.1	46.1	33.5
Uganda	1992-93	c	0.392	2.6	6.6	46.1	31.2
China	1998	i	0.403	2.4	5.9	46.6	30.4
U.S.	**1997**	**i**	**0.408**	**1.8**	**5.2**	**46.4**	**30.5**
Thailand	1998	c	0.414	2.8	6.4	48.4	32.4
Turkey	1994	c	0.415	2.3	5.8	47.7	32.3
Bolivia	1990	i	0.420	2.3	5.6	48.2	31.7
New Zealand	1991	i	0.439	0.3	2.7	46.9	29.8
Kenya	1994	c	0.445	1.8	5.0	50.2	34.9
Peru	1996	i	0.462	1.6	4.4	51.2	35.4
Philippines	1997	c	0.462	2.3	5.4	52.3	36.6
Malaysia	1995	i	0.485	1.8	4.5	53.8	37.9
Russian Federation	1998	c	0.487	1.7	4.4	53.7	38.7
Venezuela	1996	i	0.488	1.3	3.7	53.1	37.0
Nigeria	1996-97	c	0.506	1.6	4.4	55.7	40.8
Mexico	1995	i	0.537	1.4	3.6	58.2	42.8
Chile	1994	i	0.565	1.4	3.5	61.0	46.1
Zimbabwe	1990-91	c	0.568	1.8	4.0	62.3	46.9
South Africa	1993-94	c	0.593	1.1	2.9	64.8	45.9
Brazil	1996	i	0.600	0.9	2.5	63.8	47.6

Source: Adapted from World Bank, *World Development Report 2000/2001*, pp. 282–283.

Note: For high-income economies, including the U.S., this table uses data from the Luxembourg Income Study database. Therefore, the data for the U.S. are different from other case data, which relies heavily on Census Bureau data.

Endnotes

1   Paul Krugman, "For Richer," *The New York Times*, October 20, 2002, available on The Unofficial Paul Krugman Archive Web site, <http://www.pkarchive.org/> (accessed November 5, 2002).

2   Alan Greenspan, "Income Inequality: Issues and Policy Options," remarks at a symposium sponsored by the Federal Reserve Bank in Kansas City, Jackson Hole, Wyoming, August 28, 1998, <http://www.federalreserve.gov/ boarddocs/speeches/1998/19980828.htm> (accessed October 25, 2002).

3   See Peter Gottschalk and Timothy M. Smeeding, "Empirical Evidence on Income Inequality in Industrialized Countries," Luxembourg Income Study Working Paper No. 154, for further information.

4   Krugman, "For Richer," October 20, 2002.

5   Jared Bernstein, Elizabeth C. McNichol, Lawrence Mishel, and Robert Zahradnik, *Pulling Apart: A State-by-State Analysis of Income Trends* (Washington, D.C.: Economic Policy Institute, January 2000).

6   Ibid.

7   Paul Krugman, "The Rich, the Right, and the Facts," *The American Prospect* vol. 3 no. 11, September 1, 1992.

8   Krugman, "For Richer," October 20, 2002.

9   Michael J. Mandel, "25 Ideas For a Changing World —6. The Rich Get Richer, and That's O.K.," *Business Week*, August 26, 2002. This article is cited in Krugman, "For Richer," October 20, 2002.

10 Timothy M. Smeeding, "American Income Inequality in a Cross-National Perspective: Why are We so Different?" Luxembourg Income Study Working Paper No. 157, May 1997.

11 Gary Burtless, "Growing Income Inequality: Sources and Remedies" in Henry J. Aaron and Robert D. Reischauer, eds., *Setting National Priorities, The 2000 Election and Beyond* (Washington, D.C.: Brookings Institution Press, 1999).

12 Alberto Alesina, Rafael Di Tella, Robert MacCulloch, "Inequality and Happiness: Are Europeans and Americans Different?" unpublished draft, June 2002.

13 U.S. Census Bureau, Historical Income Tables – Households, <http://www.census.gov/ftp/pub/hhes/income/histinc/ h02.html> (accessed October 18, 2002).

14 Bernstein, McNichol, Mishel, and Zahradnik, *Pulling Apart: A State-by-State Analysis of Income Trends*, January 2000, p. 38.

15 Bernstein, McNichol, Mishel, and Zahradnik, *Pulling Apart: A State-by-State Analysis of Income Trends*, January 2000, p. 38, footnote 11, citing Edward Wolff, "Recent Trends in Wealth Ownership," April 20, 1999.

16 Larry Mishel, Jared Bernstein, and John Schmitt, *The State of Working America 2000/2001* (Ithaca, New York: Cornell University Press, 2001), p. 98.

17 Robert Rector and Rea S. Hederman, "Income Inequality: How Census Data Misrepresent Income Distribution," A Report of the Heritage Center for Data Analysis, September 29, 1999, <http://www.heritage.org/Research/Labor/loader.cfm?url=/commonspot/security/getfile.cfm&PageID= 14713> (accessed November 5, 2002).

18 Jared Bernstein, Larry Mishel, Chauna Brocht, "Any Way You Cut It: Income Inequality on the Rise Regardless of How It's Measured," Economic Policy Institute Briefing Paper, p. 4.

19 Rafael Di Tella, Robert MacCulloch, and Richard Layard, "Income, Happiness and Inequality as Measures of Welfare," October 29, 2002, unpublished draft, p. 10.

20 Alan Greenspan, "Income Inequality: Issues and Policy Options," August 28, 1998.

21 Robert Rector, "How 'Poor' are America's Poor?" The Heritage Foundation Policy Research and Analysis, September 1990, <http://www.heritage.org/Research/Welfare/BG791.cfm> (accessed November 5, 2002).

22 Rector, Robert, "America Has the World's Richest Poor People," *The Wall Street Journal*, September 24, 1998.

23 Barbara Ehrenreich, *Nickel and Dimed* (New York, New York: Henry Holt and Company LLC, 2001), p. 214, as cited in Heather Boushey, Chauna Brocht, Bethney Gundersen, Jared Bernstein, *Hardships in America: The Real Story of Working Families* (Washington, D.C.: Economic Policy Institute, 2001), <http://www.epinet.org/books/hardships.pdf> (accessed November 6, 2002), p. 51.

[24]   Mishel, Bernstein, and Schmitt, *The State of Working America 2000/2001*, p. 285.

[25]   Ibid, p. 289.

[26]   Constance F. Citro and Robert T., eds., *Measuring Poverty: A New Approach* (Washington, D.C.: National Academy Press, 1995), as cited in Boushey, Brocht, Gundersen, Bernstein, *Hardships in America: The Real Story of Working Families*, 2001.

[27]   "The Self Sufficiency Standard: Where Massachusetts Families Stand," Women's Educational and Industrial Union, Boston, MA, 2000.

[28]   "Reducing Poverty, Not Inequality," *The Public Interest,* Fall 1999.

[29]   Everett Carll Ladd and Karlyn H. Bowman, *Attitudes Toward Economic Inequality* (Washington, D.C.: The AEI Press, Publisher for the American Enterprise Institute for Public Policy Research, 1998), pp. 114–115.

[30]   W. Michael Cox and Richard Alm, "By Our Own Bootstraps: Economic Opportunity and the Dynamics of Income Distribution," *Annual Report of the Federal Reserve Bank of Dallas*, 1995, p. 10, <http://www.dallasfed.org/htm/pubs/pdfs/anreport/arpt95.pdf> (November 5, 2002).

[31]   Bernstein, Mishel, and Brocht, "Any Way You Cut It: Income Inequality on the Rise," p. 10.

[32]   Peter Gottschalk, "Family Income Mobility: How Much is There, and Has it Changed?" In James A. Auerback and Richard S. Belous, eds., *The Inequality Paradox: Growth of Income Disparity* (Washington, D.C.: National Policy Association, 1998). As cited in Bernstein, McNichol, Mishel, and Zahradnik, *Pulling Apart: A State-by-State Analysis of Income Trends*, January 2000, p. 36, footnote a.

[33]   Unpublished tabulations of Panel Study of Income Dynamics data by Peter Gottschalk, as cited in Bernstein, McNichol, Mishel, and Zahradnik, *Pulling Apart: A State-by-State Analysis of Income Trends*, January 2000, p. 36.

[34]   Adapted from Alberto Alesina, Edward Glaeser, Bruce Sacerdote, "Why Doesn't the U.S. Have a European-Style Welfare State?" *Brookings Papers on Economic Activity*, 2:2001, p. 57.

[35]   Mishel, Bernstein, and Schmitt, *The State of Working America 2000/2001*, p. 386.

[36]   For a survey of studies, see John O'Loughlin, "Economic Globalization and Income Inequality in the United States," in Lynn Staeheli, Janet Kodras, and Colin Flint (eds.), *State Devolution in America: Implications for a Diverse Society* (Thousand Oaks, CA: Sage Publications, 1997), pp. 21–40, <http://www.colorado.edu/IBS/PEC/johno/pub/inequality.pdf> (accessed November 5, 2002).

[37]   Mishel, Bernstein, and Schmitt, *The State of Working America 2000/2001*, p. 176.

[38]   O'Loughlin, "Economic Globalization and Income Inequality in the United States," 1997.

[39]   See, for example, Timothy Smeeding, "Globalization, Inequality and the Rich Countries of the G-20: Evidence From the Luxembourg Income Study (LIS)," Luxembourg Income Study Working Paper No. 320, July 2002.

[40]   Gary Burtless, "Worsening American Income Inequality: Is world trade to blame?" *Brookings Review* vol. 14 no. 2, Spring 1996, <http://www.brook.edu/dybdocroot/press/review/burtsp96.htm> (accessed November 6, 2002).

[41]   Mishel, Bernstein, and Schmitt, *The State of Working America 2000/2001*, p. 180.

[42]   O'Loughlin, "Economic Globalization and Income Inequality in the United States," 1997.

[43]   Edward N. Wolff, see <http://www.levy.org/research/bios/wolff.html>.

[44]   Mishel, Bernstein, and Schmitt, *The State of Working America 2000/2001*, p. 195.

[45]   Ibid, p. 197.

[46]   Krugman, "For Richer," October 20, 2002.

[47]   Mishel, Bernstein, and Schmitt, *The State of Working America 2000/2001*, p. 186.

[48]   David Lee, "Wage Inequality During the 1980s: Rising Dispersion or Falling Minimum Wage?" *The Quarterly Journal of Economics*, Volume 114 Issue 3, August 1999, pp. 941–1025.

[49]   Bernstein, McNichol, Mishel, and Zahradnik, *Pulling Apart: A State-by-State Analysis of Income Trends*, January 2000, p. 35.

[50]   Mishel, Bernstein, and Schmitt, *The State of Working America 2000/2001*, p. 180.

51 Thomas I. Palley, "Accounting for Income Inequality in the U.S.: The Role of Unions, the Minimum Wage, Unemployment, Family Structure, and International Trade" *E031, AFL-CIO Economic Policy Papers*, 1999, p. 1, <http://www.aflcio.org/economicpolicy/E031.pdf> (accessed November 6, 2002).

52 Krugman, "For Richer," October 20, 2002.

53 Mishel, Bernstein, and Schmitt, *The State of Working America 2000/2001*, p. 208.

54 "Executive Pay," *The Economist*, September 30, 2000.

55 Krugman, "For Richer," October 20, 2002.

56 Executive compensation from AFL-CIO Web site, <http://www.aflcio.org/cgi-bin/aflcio.pl>.

57 Krugman, "For Richer," October 20, 2002.

58 "Welfare Reform Redux," The NewsHour with Jim Lehrer, Transcript #7330, May 14, 2002.

59 This section draws on Robert Rector, "The Baucus 'Work' Act of 2002: Repealing Welfare Reform," *Heritage Foundation Reports*, September 3, 2002.

60 Adapted from Mishel, Bernstein, and Schmitt, *The State of Working America 2000/2001*, p. 187.

61 David Card and Alan Krueger, "Minimum Wages and Employment: A Case Study of the Fast-Food Industry in New Jersey and Pennsylvania," *American Economic Review*, 84, September 1995, pp. 772-793. This study found that a minimum wage increase in New Jersey, which affected 50% of fast-food workers, caused a 15% rise in labor costs but only led to a 2.2% increase in prices. It did not increase unemployment.

62 "Good News for Low-Income Families: Expansions in the Earned Income Tax Credit and the Minimum Wage," Council of Economic Advisers, December 1998.

63 IRS Web site, <http://www.irs.gov/individuals/article/0,,id=96406,00.html> (accessed November 6, 2002).

64 Pamela Friedman, "The Earned Income Tax Credit, Welfare Information Issue Notes," April 2000, <http://www.welfareinfo.org/friedmanapril.htm> (accessed November 5, 2002).

65 Senator Kay Bailey Hutchison, Senate Floor Speech, March 7, 2001 -- Page: S1923, Congressional Record, Proceedings and Debates of the 107th Congress, First Session, Tax Relief, <http://www.senate.gov/~hutchison/speec153.htm>.

66 Brian M. Riedl and Robert E. Rector, "Myths and Facts: Why Successful Welfare Reform Must Strengthen Work Requirements," The Heritage Foundation, Research: Welfare, July 12, 2002, <http://www.heritage.org/Research/Welfare/BG1568.cfm> (accessed November 5, 2002).

67 Edward N. Wolff, *Top Heavy: A Study of the Increasing Inequality of Wealth in America* (Washington, D.C.: The Brookings Institution, 1994).

68 Edward N. Wolff, "Time for a Wealth Tax?" *Boston Review*, February/March 1996, <http://bostonreview.mit.edu/BR21.1/wolff.html> (accessed November 5, 2002).